C000044302

Crime and Immigration

International Library of Criminology, Criminal Justice and Penology – Second Series
Series Editors: Gerald Mars and David Nelken

Titles in the Series:

Crime and Immigration

Edited by

Joshua D. Freilich

John Jay College of Criminal Justice, The City University of New York, USA

and

Graeme R. Newman

University at Albany, USA

ASHGATE

© Joshua D. Freilich and Graeme R. Newman 2007. For copyright of individual articles please refer to the Acknowledgements.

All rights reserved. No part of this publication may be reproduced, stored in a retrieval system or transmitted in any form or by any means, electronic, mechanical, photocopying, recording or otherwise without the prior permission of the publisher.

Published by
Ashgate Publishing Limited
Gower House
Croft Road
Aldershot
Hampshire GU11 3HR
England

Ashgate Publishing Company
Suite 420
101 Cherry Street
Burlington, VT 05401-4405
USA

Ashgate website: http://www.ashgate.com

British Library Cataloguing in Publication Data
Crime and immigration. – (International library of
    criminology, criminal justice and penology. Second series)
    1. Crime – Social aspects 2. Emigration and immigration –
    Social aspects
    I. Freilich, Joshua D. II. Newman, Graeme R.
    364.3'086

Library of Congress Cataloging-in-Publication Data
Crime and immigration / edited by Joshua D. Freilich and Graeme R. Newman.
        p. cm.– (International library of criminology, criminal justice and penology; 2nd series)
    ISBN-13: 978-0-7546-2449-3 (alk. paper)
    1. Crime. 2. Emigration and immigration. 3 Alien criminals. I. Freilich, Joshua D. II.
    Newman, Graeme R.

    HV6030.C714 2007
    364.3086'912–dc22   2006043036

ISBN 13: 978-0-7546-2449-3

Printed and bound in Great Britain by TJ International Ltd, Padstow, Cornwall

Contents

PART III TRANSNATIONAL CRIME AND ILLEGAL IMMIGRATION

PART IV IMMIGRANTS AS VICTIMS

Acknowledgements

The editors and publishers wish to thank the following for permission to use copyright material.

American Sociological Association for the essay: M. Craig Brown and Barbara D. Warner (1992), 'Immigrants, Urban Politics, and Policing in 1900', *American Sociological Review*, **57**, pp. 293–305.

Blackwell Publishing for the essays: Hans-Jörg Albrecht (1987), 'Foreign Minorities and the Criminal Justice System in the Federal Republic of Germany', *Howard Journal of Criminal Justice*, **26**, pp. 272–86; Matthew T. Lee, Ramiro Martinez Jr and Richard Rosenfeld (2001), 'Does Immigration Increase Homicide? Negative Evidence from Three Border Cities', *Sociological Quarterly*, **42**, pp. 559–80; Copyright © 2001 Midwest Sociological Society; John Salt (2000), 'Trafficking and Human Smuggling: A European Perspective', *International Migration*, **38**, pp. 31–56. Copyright © 2001 IOM.

International Journal of Comparative and Applied Criminal Justice for the essays: Graeme Newman, Joshua D. Freilich and Gregory J. Howard (2002), 'Exporting and Importing Criminality: Incarceration of the Foreign Born', *International Journal of Comparative and Applied Criminal Justice*, **26**, pp. 143–63; Minoru Yokoyama (1999), 'Analysis of the Crimes by Foreigners in Japan', *International Journal of Comparative and Applied Criminal Justice*, **23**, pp. 181–213.

International Review of Victimology for the essay: Peter L. Martens (2001), 'Immigrants as Victims of Crime', *International Review of Victimology*, **8**, pp. 199–216. Copyright © AB Academic Publishers.

Northwestern University School of Law for the essay: Shlomo Shoham (1962), 'The Application of the "Culture-Conflict" Hypothesis to the Criminality of Immigrants in Israel', *Journal of Criminal Law and Criminology*, **53**, pp. 207–14. Reprinted by special permission of Northwestern University School of Law.

Pacific Sociological Association for the essay: Daniel P. Mears (2001), 'The Immigration-Crime Nexus: Toward an Analytic Framework for Assessing and Guiding Theory, Research, and Policy', *Sociological Perspectives*, **44**, pp. 1–19. Copyright © 2001 Pacific Sociological Association.

Sage Publications, Inc for the essays: Marlyn J. Jones (2002), 'Policy Paradox: Implications of U.S. Drug Control Policy for Jamaica', *Annals of the American Academy of Political and Social Science*, **582**, pp. 117–33; Meredith W. Watts (2001), 'Aggressive Youth Cultures and Hate Crime: Skinheads and Xenophobic Youth in Germany', *American Behavioral Scientist*, **45**, pp. 600–15; John Z. Wang (2001), 'Illegal Chinese Immigration Into the United States:

A Preliminary Factor Analysis', *International Journal of Offender Therapy: Comparative Criminology*, **45**, pp. 345–55; Dina Siegel and Frank Bovenkerk (2000), 'Crime and Manipulation of Identity Among Russian-Speaking Immigrants in the Netherlands', *Journal of Contemporary Criminal Justice*, **16**, pp. 424–44; Alexander T. Vazsonyi and Martin Killias (2001), 'Immigration and Crime Among Youth in Switzerland', *Criminal Justice and Behavior*, **28**, pp. 329–66; Robert C. Davis and Nicole J. Henderson (2003), 'Willingness to Report Crimes: The Role of Ethnic Group Membership and Community Efficacy', *Crime and Delinquency*, **49**, pp. 564–80; Yaw Ackah (2000), 'Fear of Crime Among an Immigrant Population in the Washington, DC Metropolitan Area', *Journal of Black Studies*, **30**, pp. 553–73.

Springer for the essays: Joanna Goodey (2000), 'Non-EU Citizens' Experiences of Offending and Victimisation: The Case for Comparative European Research', *European Journal of Crime, Criminal Law and Criminal Justice*, **8**, pp. 13–34; Marianne Junger and Wim Polder (1992), 'Some Explanations of Crime Among Four Ethnic Groups in the Netherlands', *Journal of Quantitative Criminology*, **8**, pp. 51–78; Sandra Wachholz and Baukje Miedema (2000), 'Risk, Fear, Harm: Immigrant Women's Perception of the "Policing Solution" to Woman Abuse', *Crime, Law and Social Change*, **34**, pp. 301–17. Copyright © 2000 Kluwer Academic Publishers.

Every effort has been made to trace all the copyright holders, but if any have been inadvertently overlooked the publishers will be pleased to make the necessary arrangement at the first opportunity.

Preface to the Second Series

The first series of the International Library of Criminology, Criminal Justice and Penology has established itself as a major research resource by bringing together the most significant journal essays in contemporary criminology, criminal justice and penology. The series made available to researchers, teachers and students an extensive range of essays which are indispensable for obtaining an overview of the latest theories and findings in this fast changing subject. Indeed the rapid growth of interesting scholarly work in the field has created a demand for a second series which like the first consists of volumes dealing with criminological schools and theories as well as with approaches to particular areas of crime criminal justice and penology. Each volume is edited by a recognised authority who has selected twenty or so of the best journal articles in the field of their special competence and provided an informative introduction giving a summary of the field and the relevance of the articles chosen. The original pagination is retained for ease of reference.

The difficulties of keeping on top of the steadily growing literature in criminology are complicated by the many disciplines from which its theories and findings are drawn (sociology, law, sociology of law, psychology, psychiatry, philosophy and economics are the most obvious). The development of new specialisms with their own journals (policing, victimology, mediation) as well as the debates between rival schools of thought (feminist criminology, left realism, critical criminology, abolitionism etc.) make necessary overviews that offer syntheses of the state of the art.

GERALD MARS
Honorary Professor of Anthropology, University College, London, UK

DAVID NELKEN
Distinguished Professor of Sociology, University of Macerata, Italy;
Distinguished Research Professor of Law, University of Cardiff, Wales;
Honorary Visiting Professor of Law, LSE, London, UK

Introduction

The push and pull of migration has been with us for eons. Individuals, groups and entire nations have been expelled by their enemies, while others have fled the terrible conditions of their place of birth. Peoples, tribes and families have left their homes in search of a better place. They have been enticed by promises of work and a better quality of life; they have been exploited by their new-found hosts for their cheap labour; they have demanded rights equal to those of their hosts; and they have borne the hardship of leaving their loved ones at home. Men have been separated from women, husbands from wives, parents from children. In some places they have taken advantage of the opportunities offered them and have risen to high levels of government and commerce. In other places they have been denied opportunities, and in some locations they have spurned opportunities afforded them and have never risen above a menial level.

Their hosts have always been ambivalent about them. They know that migrants enrich their countries culturally and economically, but they resent their dependence upon them for the menial services that they provide and take any opportunity to blame them for the ills of society. It is alleged that certain groups migrate to specific nations to take advantage of their generous welfare provisions. Under this view, migrants are responsible for the increased taxes that are necessary to fund such programmes. It is also argued that migrants are more deviant than non-migrants and are responsible for environmental harm (through increased population density), disease, unemployment, crime and even terrorism in the destination countries. This perspective maintains that certain countries sometimes intentionally export their dangerous classes abroad.

A related claim is that some nations and groups deliberately plant their members abroad – akin to the 'Trojan Horse' – as sleeper cells to eventually undermine and destroy the host country from within. The participants in the 9/11 and 3/11 attacks in the United States and Spain are often cited as examples to bolster this argument. Still others claim that the goal of certain migrant groups is to 'conquer' and rule the destination nations.

Conversely, others contend that migrants provide needed services and enrich their host countries. Indeed, the noted sociologist Robert J. Sampson recently speculated on the Op-Ed page of the *New York Times* that increased migration to the United States might be the 'hidden' explanation for the recent large drop in crime. Proponents of migration argue that whatever illegal behaviour migrants participate in is the result of either the blocked structural opportunities or the entrenched racism that they must endure. The solution therefore is not to punish the migrants, but to provide better living conditions and opportunities to the foreign-born and to eliminate biased policies and practices.

The essays collected in this volume unavoidably reflect this ambivalence. In fact, events of the twenty-first century appear to be intensifying the problem of migration. People are on the move as never before; forced migration is rampant on the African continent; voluntary migration, fuelled by globalization is rapidly transforming the traditional societies of Europe, Asia-Pacific and North America. We are aware that few, if any, of the very difficult problems inherent in migration and crime are anywhere near a solution. We have therefore chosen essays that provide an objective account of the many theoretical, policy and scientific issues surrounding the problem of migration and crime.

This book provides a broad overview of the migration–crime nexus and includes essays from different disciplines (for example, criminal justice, psychology, political science and sociology), employing different methodologies (both quantitative and qualitative), on a multitude of important topics (for example, conceptual and empirical pieces, offending and victimization issues, policing, incarceration, and deportation policies, hate crimes, organized and transnational crimes, trafficking and illegal migration, gangs, and fear of crime and reporting issues), on both the micro and macro levels in different countries and locations (for example, Canada, Europe as a whole, Germany, Great Britain, Israel, Jamaica, Japan, Switzerland and the United States).

Theory and Policy

The essays on the theory and policy of migration and crime examine these larger issues in different ways. Shlomo Shoham (Chapter 1) opens Part I by focusing on migration, culture conflict and crime. While the relationship between culture conflict and migration is reciprocal and cultural conflict may encourage migration, there is little doubt that conflicts of culture also occur as a result of immigration. The forms that these conflicts take are varied. Shoham's classic study focuses on culture conflict as a cause of crime – in this case, in Israel. Certainly the disproportionate criminality of immigrants is not a foregone conclusion, as Hung-en Sun and Jack Reed (Chapter 6) conclude in their review of research conducted in Europe. Yet, as Daniel Mears observes in Chapter 2 in some settings, especially where there is a high crime rate, such as in Washington DC, people fear immigrants. This occurs even though in such settings it is common that, far from committing more crime than other groups, immigrants are in fact more often victims of crime. Then again, Graeme Newman, Joshua Freilich and Gregory Howard (Chapter 3) report that the foreign born are incarcerated at a much higher rate than the host populations. Their study found, in fact, that in a few cases the number of migrants incarcerated abroad was almost 50 per cent of the number of prisoners housed in their country of origin.

Inadequency or perhaps even absence, of policy in regard to immigrants who commit crime may contribute to these confusing findings. Marlyn Jones (Chapter 4) argues that the practice of deporting illegal immigrants convicted of drug dealing simply displaces the crime to places least able to deal with it, thus fuelling the illegal drug trade rather than controlling it. Relatedly, it is alleged by some that a number of these deportees – 'corrupted' by the conditions they faced in their host countries – bring back to their countries of origin certain practices – such as violent gang initiations and practices – that were before this time unknown. Joanna Goodey (Chapter 5) points to probably the most significant reason why immigration policy is often driven by stereotypes of various ethnic minorities: lack of research. Indeed, Newman, Freilich and Howard had great difficulty in finding data on the foreign-born in prison. Many authorities simply did not bother to record such information.

Offending

The notion that culture conflict is the cause of higher criminality in immigrants is dismissed by Hans-Jörg Albrecht (Chapter 7) in his careful study of minorities in the criminal justice system of the Federal Republic of Germany. Marianne Junger and Wim Polder (Chapter 8) follow this finding with a convincing study of both recorded and self-reported delinquency that compare Moslem youths with matched samples of young Dutch boys in Holland. The rates of crime for the Dutch boys are significantly higher than those of the immigrants; the hypothesized causes of criminality support control theory and appear to operate similarly for both groups. Matthew Lee, Ramiro Martinez and Richard Rosenfeld (Chapter 14), also demonstrate convincingly that immigration did not contribute to the increased homicide rates of Latinos and Native Americans in three border towns in the USA. Finally, James Lynch and Rita Simon (Chapter 13) in their cross-national study, found that nations with liberal immigration policies generally had immigrant populations whose crime rates were lower than those of their hosts.

On the other hand, in Chapter 9, Arye Rattner finds that immigrant Russians to Israel do commit crime at a higher rate than Israelis. In addition, Dina Siegel and Frank Bovenkerk (Chapter 12) found that when they focused on organized crime, Russians were overrepresented in this crime in the Netherlands and that this had also fuelled a particular 'cultural identity' of immigrant Russians. Minoru Yokoyama (Chapter 10) also found that, during the economic depression of the 1990s, foreigners committed more crime than their Japanese hosts, and they were also blamed more often for the increase in crime. By contrast, unravelling the complexity of immigrant crime, Alexander Vazsonyi and Martin Killias (Chapter 11) found that, although there was little difference between Swiss youth crime rates and those of first-generation immigrants, rates for second-generation immigrants were considerably higher. It seems likely, therefore, that if culture conflict is operating, it plays itself out as conflict between second-generation children and their immigrant parents.

Further complicating matters is the fascinating account by M. Craig Brown and Barbara Warner (Chapter 15) who studied the relationship between ethnic groups, including immigrants (the foreign born), and policing in 1900. They found that where ethnic minorities had established themselves through community groups that had standing with political bosses, particularly in US cities, deals could be made for services and special attention from the urban police. In this way the 'threat' of the presence of foreigners or ethnic minorities was assuaged or mitigated by 'sensitive' police action.

Overall, the mixed findings from these studies highlight the importance of context in terms of location, the specific migrant group, and the time period under consideration. This is especially important today when many look upon all migrants as a threat to their national identity, heritage, livelihood and public safety. In other words, rather than arguing that all migrants are more likely to offend, or that all migrants are more law-abiding or hapless victims of racism and/or blocked opportunities, it is necessary to specify which migrant group in which country in which time period is at issue.

Transnational Crime and Ilegal Immigration

Transnational crime and illegal immigration have increased in visibility and severity, probably in concert with globalization and particularly as a result of the demand for women and children in the international sex trade. There has also been an increase in the smuggling of individuals into countries where there is a demand for cheap labour but whose immigration policies make it difficult for workers to gain entry into the country. In some cases, the increased illegal migration, while supported or tolerated by the parts of the private sector that benefit from it, has also produced a backlash among segments of the general population. The recent highly publicized emergence of the paramilitary 'Minutemen' – and offshoots – in the United States that has promised to 'patrol' the border with Mexico to effect citizen arrests against drug smugglers and illegal migrants is just one example of the intensity demonstrating the debate.

In Chapter 16 John Salt shows how complex the issues concerning illegal immigration and human trafficking are. This is especially the case when a symbiosis between trafficker and trafficked arises (in this instance in European countries) where there is a demand for illegal immigrants for cheap labour and the sex trade, and at the same time a willingness of migrants to allow themselves to be trafficked to gain entry into these countries with the hope of improving their quality of life.

Further, many feeder countries, especially for the sex trade, encourage their citizens to migrate on the assumption (and sometimes requirement) that they will remit valuable currency back to their home country. John Wang (Chapter 17) catalogues the extent of global smuggling of humans from China and identifies the transnational criminal groups that have sprung up to exploit the opportunities of the 'demand and supply' of cheap labour in the global marketplace. One of these transnational criminal groups, the Jamaican Posse, is described by Jones (Chapter 4), who shows how this group emerged out of the economic and political chaos of Jamaica in the 1990s to establish a far-reaching criminal organization that specialized in human trafficking, gun running, drug smuggling and money laundering.

Contributing to the 'symbiosis' between traffickers and trafficked identified by Salt, the sanctuary movement in the US provides aid and sustenance for illegal immigrants as described by Gregory Wiltfang and John Cochran (Chapter 18).

Immigrants and Victims

The view of immigrants as victims naturally arises. While many, if not most, seek new opportunities in their new country, many are also victimized along the way as they are trafficked; alternatively, after they reach their destinations they are victimized by hate groups and even by government policies and practices. Peter Martens (Chapter 19), has found that immigrants in Sweden, especially those whose physical appearance makes them stand out, are more often victimized by personal crimes, though not by property crimes. In Chapter 20 MeredithWatts shows how the anti-foreigner violence of the 1980s in Germany was transformed into severe violence by skinheads and hate groups after unification. More disturbing, though, was the finding that at least one-third of the violence against minorities came from youths who were not affiliated with those groups. Xenophobia and fear of crime among immigrant populations fuels this victimization as Yaw Ackah (Chapter 21) reports in his study of a Washington, DC, locality.

This negative view of immigrants has spawned the view that they would be unwilling or reticent to report their own victimization to the authorities, but at least one study, including that by Robert Davis and Nicole Henderson (Chapter 22), has demonstrated that this is not the case in New York City. Finally, Sandra Wacholz and Baukje Miedema (Chapter 23) draw our attention to the plight of immigrant women who are particularly vulnerable to economic deprivation and domestic violence. Their study of a small group of immigrant women in Canada uncovered a number of fears harboured by women about police intervention in domestic situations.

Conclusion

The conflicting findings displayed by this collection of studies echoes the almost chaotic state of immigration no matter where in the world one looks. Far more research is needed on every aspect of migration as it relates to crime and justice. A sensible start would be for countries to begin systematically to collect information on immigrants so that research into the many problems relating to immigrant crime and victimization could be addressed. Alas, many countries, if not most, have no idea how many illegal immigrants reside in their countries or even who they are. One is forced to conclude that many of these host countries do not want to face up to the social and political problems brought about by both legal and illegal immigration. Without research based on valid and reliable data, government policies are destined to remain deeply political and divisive. In fact, such policies become part of the problem rather than its solution.

Part I
Theory and Policy

[1]

THE APPLICATION OF THE "CULTURE-CONFLICT" HYPOTHESIS TO THE CRIMINALITY OF IMMIGRANTS IN ISRAEL

SHLOMO SHOHAM

The author is Head of the Department of Criminology in Bar-Ilan University, Ramat-Gan, Israel. A former member of the Faculty of Law of the Hebrew University in Jerusalem, Dr. Shoham studied criminal law and criminology at both the Hebrew University and the Institute of Criminology in Cambridge, England.

The United States, with its periods of mass immigrations, has been a logical focus of the study of culture-conflict and its effect upon the criminality of immigrants. In the following article, Dr. Shoham points out that Israel, with its more recent experience of mass immigrations, has also become a fruitful source for such study. Dr. Shoham first sketches some of the findings of the American research and then, against that background, presents his own findings with respect to the crime rates of immigrants who have come to Israel since 1948; the crime rates of immigrants from the various continents; the types of offences committed by immigrants from different regions; and the "second generation" problem, concerning delinquency rates of juveniles with immigrant parents. The differences between the Jews of oriental and European origin are among the special demographic features of the Jewish community in Israel which Dr. Shoham describes as unique sources for future study.—EDITOR.

It has been recognized that a basic distinction should be made between the etiology of crime as a social phenomenon inherent in a given society and the process (i.e., the "recruiting") by which a certain individual becomes a criminal or commits a criminal act. The latter is studied from the point of view of the individual, whereas the former is regarded from the point of view of the group, community, or nation and is expressed in crime *rates*.[1] It should be mentioned that most efforts in criminology from the "positive school" on were directed at the explanation of crime on the personal level. But with the development of modern sociology and especially the so-called "formal school of sociology," which was mostly concerned with forms of human interaction,[2] more attention was given to the phenomenon of crime on the social level. The concept of conflict, which is one form of interaction,[3] was thus utilized by some American sociologists to explain the differential crime rates in given communities.[4]

One of the most lucid adaptations of the idea of conflict to crime causation was carried out by Sellin in his monograph *On Culture Conflict and Crime*.[5] Sellin pointed out that the conflict relevant for criminological research is the clash between conduct norms brought about "as by-products of a cultural growth process—the growth of civilization—as the result of the migration of conduct norms from one culture complex or area to another. However produced, they are sometimes studied as mental conflicts[6] and sometimes as the clash of cultural codes."[7]

It should be pointed out that the concept of culture-conflict as expounded by Sellin is intrinsically different from the concept of conflict as used by the formal school of sociology. Shaw and Mckay, for instance, used the concept of culture conflict to explain social "disorganization" which ensues from *group* conflict.[8] The same meaning was apparently given to culture-conflict (on the social level) by Sutherland when he spoke about

[1] See SUTHERLAND, THE SUTHERLAND PAPERS 11 (Cohen, Lindesmith & Schuessler ed. 1956).

[2] See PARK & BURGESS, INTRODUCTION TO THE SCIENCE OF SOCIOLOGY (1942).

[3] See Simmel, *The Sociology of Conflict*, 9 AM. J. SOCIOLOGY 490 (1903–1904).

[4] See Sutherland, *Crime and the Conflict Process*, 13 J. JUVENILE RESEARCH 38 (1929); 2 THOMAS & ZNANIECKI, THE POLISH PEASANT IN EUROPE AND AMERICA 1753–55 (Knoph ed. 1927); Kobrin, *The Conflict of Values in Delinquency Areas*, 16 AM. SOCIOLOGICAL REV. 653 (1951).

[5] SELLIN, ON CULTURE CONFLICT AND CRIME (Social Science Research Council 1938).

[6] It seems that the idea of culture conflict as mental conflict has influenced Sutherland in formulating his differential association theory, which presumably explains criminal behavior on the personal level. This idea seems inherent in his statement that "a person becomes delinquent because of an excess of definitions favorable to violation of law over definitions unfavorable to violation of law." SUTHERLAND, *op. cit. supra* note 1, at 20. See also *id.* at 9.

[7] SELLIN, *op. cit. supra* note 5, at 58.

[8] SHAW & MCKAY, JUVENILE DELINQUENCY AND URBAN AREAS (1942).

"differential group organization," brought about when "several criminals perfect an organization and with organization their crimes increase in frequency and seriousness; in the course of time this arouses a narrower or a broader group which organizes itself against crime, and this tends to reduce crimes. *The crime rate at a particular time is a resultant of these opposed organizations*".[9]

But here apparently something is amiss, because obviously the *whole* volume of crimes in a given community cannot be explained by "differential group organization." It explains no doubt the rate of *organized* or professional crime, but surely it does not account for the rates of crimes of passion and isolated crimes in a given community. In contrast, Sellin's exposition of culture-conflict as a conflict of *conduct norms*, not only among different groups but also within the group itself and between the individual and his group, may account for the sum total of crimes in a given community.[10] In other words the higher the volume of clashes among the legal norms, folkways, and values in a given community, the higher the crime rate. It should be stressed however that this hypothesis has not yet been fully tested.

CULTURE-CONFLICT, IMMIGRATION, AND CRIME IN THE U.S.A.

The phenomenon of culture-conflict on the social level may be observed no doubt in the general growth of civilization and especially in the clashes of norms and values resulting from industrialization and urbanization of various communities. But the study of the conflict process in these instances is highly problematic from the methodological point of view, and the sheer length of time involved makes the possibility of comprehensive research highly remote. Most of the research on culture-conflict and crime has therefore dealt with the clashes among divergent cultural codes and especially the conflict between the conduct norms of immigrant groups and the norms prevailing in the receiving country.[11] It is only natural that much of the research in this field has been carried out in the U.S.A., which was until recently a country experiencing mass immigration.[12]

The results of the research on the problem of immigration and crime carried out in the U.S.A. have been more often contradictory than consistant. This of course may be partly attributed to the heterogeneity of methodology employed by the various investigators. It is possible nonetheless to summarize some of the more conspicuous findings of this research as follows:

A. The crime rate of the immigrants taken as a group was at first believed to be lower than the crime rate of the native group.[13] But then it was realized that foreign-born criminal groups are, on the average, older than native-born criminal groups with native parentage,[14] and a study by Van Vechten[15] indeed revealed that, when compared on the basis of age, the criminality of immigrants exceeded the criminality of native-born whites by a ratio of ten to nine.

B. There is a wide difference in the extent and nature of the criminality of immigrants from different countries of origin and different ethnic groups.[16]

C. Immigrants presumably have a higher crime rate in the U.S.A. than in their countries of origin.[17] It should be stressed however that there is no conclusive evidence to this effect due to the differences between the definitions of "crime" and "offence" in the countries of origin and in the United States.

D. There is a marked consensus among the various investigators that the crime rate of native-born (or those who immigrated very young) of foreign-born parents is considerably higher than the rates of either the foreign-born or the relevant age groups of native-born of native parentage.[18]

Origins Law of 1924. From then onwards the restrictive legislation became tighter, and after passage of the McCarran-Walter Act of 1952, immigration to the United States became quantitatively insignificant.

[13] NAT'L COM'N ON LAW OBSERVANCE AND ENFORCEMENT, REPORT ON CRIME AND THE FOREIGN-BORN (1931).

[14] STOFFLET, A STUDY OF NATIONAL AND CULTURAL DIFFERENCE IN CRIMINAL TENDENCY (No. 185 Archives of Psychology 1935).

[15] Van Vechten, *Criminality of the Foreign Born*, PROCEEDINGS OF THE SEVENTIETH ANNUAL CONGRESS OF CORRECTION OF THE AM. PRISON ASS'N 505 (1940).

[16] NAT'L COM'N ON LAW OBSERVANCE AND ENFORCEMENT, *op. cit. supra* note 13, at 109; DEPT. OF COMMERCE, BUREAU OF THE CENSUS, PRISONERS IN STATE AND FEDERAL PRISONS AND REFORMATORIES 28 (1934); Wood, *Minority Group Criminality and Cultural Integration*, 37 J. CRIM. L. & C. 498 (1947).

[17] THOMAS & ZNANIECKI, *op. cit. supra* note 4; YOUNG, THE PILGRIMS OF RUSSIAN TOWN (1932).

[18] YOUNG, *op. cit. supra* note 17, at 209–10; Van Vechten, *supra* note 15; Ross, *Crime and the Native-*

---

[9] SUTHERLAND, *op. cit. supra* note 1, at 21.
[10] SELLIN, *op. cit. supra* note 5, at 66 *et seq.*
[11] *Id.* at 70. As to the possible impact of immigration on deviant behaviour, see EISENSTADT, THE ABSORPTION OF IMMIGRANTS 20 *et seq.* (London 1954).
[12] The first law that restricted the flow of mass immigration to the United States was the National

However a very important exception, relevant to the culture-conflict hypothesis, should be noted. The delinquency rate of juveniles with immigrant parentage is considerably lower in immigrant communities which display a strong primary-group control of their members, have inner cohesion, and practice flexible but not weak home control over the young.[19] Taft, while commenting on these findings, says:

"Some immigrants have been protected against crime by life in the ghettos of our cities and in homogeneous immigrant colonies in rural areas. There they have established fairly effective institutions and primary relations.... Immigrants who only gradually give over their old world patterns of behaviour are in general seldom seen in our criminal courts. [The immigrant thus] becomes assimilated more slowly possibly, but much more effectively. Not nonassimilation but overrapid Americanization spells crime."[20]

In other words the danger of culture-conflict is most imminent when the original norms and values of the immigrant have disintegrated rapidly, and a cultural vacuum or chaos is created. The immigrant group is not yet ready, or time is insufficient, for an orderly absorption of the norms and values of the receiving group. The younger generation is therefore more susceptible to the criminogenic "street-culture." In contrast, a slow and gradual absorption of the culture of the receiving group, accompanied by a gradual replacement of the original norms and values, causes not a clash or conflict but a synthesis which enhances the observance of the acquired norms rather than their breach.

IMMIGRATION AND CRIME IN ISRAEL

The study of the relation between immigration and crime in Israel is complicated by the fact that Israel is quite unique from the demographic point of view. The flow of Jewish immigration to the country has been almost continuous (with marked fluctuations of course) from the beginning of the century to this present day. After the creation of the State of Israel in 1948, the flow of mass immi-

gration greatly increased, but even before 1948 the Jewish community in Palestine was basically immigrant. Eisenstadt thus says:

"The Yishuv (i.e., the Jewish community in Palestine) was not merely an immigrant-absorbing community. More probably, than any other modern absorbing country ... it was also a community which immigrants had created. The time-span between the establishment of its first institutional outlines and the influx of waves of immigrants was very short, sometimes almost non-existant, and its institutional structure was in continuous formation and development while these various waves were entering."[21]

The most conspicuous fact about Jewish immigration to Israel is that at the establishment of the state, on the 14th of May 1948, there were 649,633 Jews in the country. Within nine years (i.e. until the end of 1957) 896,355[22] new immigrants had arrived and had to be absorbed by the former, who were clearly a minority from the quantitive point of view. The flow of immigration after May 1948 may be divided into three periods:

1948-1951—period of mass immigration.

1952-1954—period of a relative decline in immigration.

1955-1957—renewal of immigration (especially from Europe and North Africa).

A rough idea of the great variety of ethnic groups among the immigrants, the differences in their cultural backgrounds, and the extent of conflict among the various conduct-norms liable to ensue may be surmised from Table I. This table shows the distribution of Jewish immigrants·by country of birth. The right column shows the origin of "old" immigrants (arrival before May 1948); the middle column shows the origin of "new" immigrants (arrival after May 1948); and the left column shows the distribution of the latter in percentages.

It is necessary to point out a demographic fact concerning the Jewish community both in Palestine and in the State of Israel which will be highly relevant in our later analysis of data concerning the criminality of immigrants. This is the apparent dichotomy of oriental and so-called Sephardic Jews, and the Jews, mostly of European descent, known as Ashkenazi Jews. The Sephardic Jews trace their origin to the Jewish community expelled from Spain in 1492. These were probably a small

---

Born Sons of European Immigrants, 28 J. CRIM. L. & C. 208 (1937); W. C. SMITH, AMERICANS IN PROCESS 8 (1937).

[19] Lind, *The Ghetto and the Slum*, 9 SOCIAL FORCES 206 (1930); W. C. SMITH, *op. cit. supra* note 18, at 214; Hayner, *Delinquency Areas in the Puget Sound Region*, 39 AM. J. SOCIOLOGY 319 (1933).

[20] TAFT, CRIMINOLOGY 159-60 (3d ed. 1956).

[21] EISENSTADT, *op. cit. supra* note 11, at 46.

[22] STATISTICAL ABSTRACT OF ISRAEL 1957-58, table 2, at 7, table 5, at 59.

TABLE I

DISTRIBUTION OF JEWISH·IMMIGRANTS BY COUNTRY OF BIRTH[22]

Country of Birth	Percentage of Immigrants After 1948	No. of Immigrants After 1948	No. of Immigrants Before 1948
All Countries............	100.0	896,655	452,158
Asia.....................	*29.6*	*259,648*	*40,776*
Turkey..................	4.4	38,071	8,277
Iran....................	14.2	125,413	7,995
Iraq....................	3.3	29,528	3,536
Yemen..................	6.2	45,781	14,566
Aden....................	0.4	3,448	1,272
India...................	0.7	6,069	72
Other countries..........	1.4	11,338	5,058
Africa..................	*25.2*	*221,500*	*4,033*
Tunisia, Algeria, Morocco & Tangier............	17.6	154,905	904
Liberya..................	3.7	32,849	873
Union of South Africa....	0.1	982	259
Other Countries.........	3.8	32,764	1,907
Europe..................	*44.3*	*388,458*	*377,487*
U.S.S.R.................	1.4	11,994	52,350
Poland..................	15.8	136,620	170,127
Rumania................	14.0	123,562	41,105
Bulgaria................	4.4	38,559	7,057
Yugloslavia..............	0.9	7,842	1,944
Greece..................	0.3	2,579	8,767
Germany................	1.0	8,908	52,951
Austria.................	0.3	2,906	7,748
Czeckoslovakia..........	2.2	19,161	16,794
Hungary......:.......	2.6	23,263	10,342
U.K....................	0.3	2,500	1,574
Netherlands.............	0.2	1,434	1,208
France..................	.0.5	3,769	1,637
Italy...................	0.2	1,510	1,554
Other Countries.........	0.4	3,611	2,329
America & Oceana.....:..	*0.9*	*7,330*	*7,579*
U.S.....................	0.3	1,987	6,635
Canada.................	0.0	363	316
Argentina..............	0.3	2,766	238
Other Countries in America..............	0.3	2,039	318
Australia & New Zealand	0.0	175	72
Not stated..............	—	19,419	22,283

[22] *Id.*, table 6, at 60.

TABLE II

PERCENTAGE OF ADULT IMMIGRANT OFFENDERS AMONG TOTAL OFFENDER POPULATION FOR THE YEARS 1951–1957

Year	1951	1952	1953	1954	1955	1956	1957
Percentage of Immigrant Offenders	60.7	65.7	67.1	65.8	66.2	68.9	66.7

nucleus of the Jews who lived in Palestine before the beginning of immigration at the end of the 19th century and whose origin cannot be clearly ascertained.[24] The oriental Jews are those who immigrated to Palestine and to Israel from eastern countries and especially from the regions formerly included in the Ottoman Empire.[25] The economic and educational standard of the oriental Jews is as a rule lower than the standard of Jews of European origin.

The Criminality of Adult "New" Immigrants

Our definition of "new" immigrants as those Jews who entered the country after the establishment of the state in May 1948 may seem quite arbitrary, and indeed from many aspects it is. It may be justified, nevertheless, for our purposes if we bear in mind that the rate of Jewish immigration to Palestine during the Second World War and the last years of the British mandate is quite low when compared with the mass immigration during the first years of the state. There are also grounds to believe that absorption of the "old" immigrants by the receiving community was much more effective,[25] and their integration quicker, than that of the "new" immigrants.

Table II shows the percentage of immigrant adult offenders (15 years of age and above) among the total population of offenders convicted of "serious"[27] offences.

The average percentage of "new" immigrants among the total population for the years 1953–1957 was approximately 60%, whereas the average percentage of adult immigrant offenders among the total population of immigrants for the same years was 67.2%, i.e., an excess of more than 7%.

[24] See POLIAK, THE JEWS OF PALESTINE AT THE WAR'S END 12 *et seq.* (Palestine 1945) (in Hebrew).
[25] See EISENSTADT, *op. cit. supra* note 11, at 90.
[25] *Id.* at 58 *et seq.*
[27] Minor offences, i.e., assaults, brawls, and offences against police regulations (contravention), were not included.

When we compare the ratio of these percentages with the ratio between the criminality of the native-born (including the pre-1948 immigrants) and their percentage of the total population, we observe that the criminality of adult "new" immigrants in Israel exceeds the criminality of the native-born (and the "old" immigrants) at the rate of 4 to 3 (or 10 to 7.5).[28] We may conclude that this rate is quite high if we bear in mind Van Vechten's findings concerning the relevant rate in the United States, which was 10 to 9.[29]

An interesting comparison may be made among the rates of serious offences committed by immigrants from the various continents. The rates were computed from data collected in 1957, which were the best data available. These rates were, for serious offences per 1000 immigrants from Africa, 13; Asia, 10; and from Europe and America, 5.

It should be mentioned that the overwhelming majority of immigrants from Africa have come from North Africa.[30] They belong to the "Moghrebite" community, and they have as a rule an ethnic and cultural background quite distinct from that of the rest of the oriental Jews. The Asian Jews belong mostly to the category of "oriental" Jews, whereas the relatively few American immigrants are mostly of European origin or parentage. The clue to these differential crime rates may quite possibly be found in the culture-conflict hypothesis, because as we have already mentioned the general cultural, economic, and educational standards of the North African and Asian immigrants are relatively low. It may be that the clash between the cultural codes, norms, and values of these immigrants and those of the receiving community causes a relative increase in the crime rate of these immigrants.[31] Note the

[28] The rates have been computed from "raw" data received from the Central Bureau of Statistics, Israel.
[29] Van Vechten, *supra* note 15, at 505–16. The shortcomings of this comparison are obvious, because Van Vechten compared the criminality of *all* the foreign born with that of the native born. If we had done the same, and based our comparison on the corresponding age groups, the criminality of our foreign born would have been much higher than that of the native born, but for our present purposes the rate as computed above is adequate because our main concern is with the criminality of immigrants who entered the country after 1948.
[30] See Table I.
[31] Eisenstadt has said, "The . . . disorganization of the immigrant group, instability of social relations, and of various types of norm-breaking, juvenile delinquency, crime etc. is strongest among those groups whose cultural and educational standards are much lower than those of the absorbing society." *Op. cit. supra* note 11, at 260–61.

TABLE III

DISTRIBUTION OF ADULT IMMIGRANT OFFENDERS ACCORDING TO TYPE OF OFFENCE (IN PERCENTAGES)

	Europe & America	Africa	Asia
Offences Against Public Public Order	18	16	16
Offences Against the Person	26	30	27
Offences Against Morality	2	2	2
Offences Against Property	25	27	26
Burglary	*2*	*2*	*1*
Arson & Damage to Property	*6*	*10*	*9*
Forgery & Embezzlement	2	1	1
Miscellaneous	19	12	18
Total	100%	100%	100%

relatively low rate of criminality of the European and American immigrants, whose general cultural and educational standards were similar or nearer to the standard of the receiving community.

Another aspect of the culture-conflict hypothesis may be studied by analyzing the types of offences committed by the various immigrant groups.[32]

The first impression one receives from Table III is the relative preponderance of the more serious offences among the African immigrants, because the item "Miscellaneous" usually refers to the less serious offences, and this item is quite low among the Africans. Another is the high percentage among the Africans of offences against the person. It is permissible to add to this type the offences of arson and damage to property, inasmuch as the latter are committed as a rule out of violence and aggression and not for the sake of pecuniary gain. The resulting sum is 40% for the Africans, but only 32% for the Europeans. These figures may indicate the existance of a cultural tradition among the African immigrants of settling disputes by violence, a method of "self-help" which may have been more or less accepted conduct in their countries of origin. It should be stressed however that these comparisons provide only a suggestion for further research to determine whether the excess of violence among the North African offenders is embedded in the mores of their countries of origin, or whether some special

[32] This has been done in many researches carried out in the United States in order to determine what offences are characteristic to the criminals in the various immigrant groups. See TAFT, CRIMINOLOGY 154 *et seq.* (3d ed. 1956).

attributes of their communities of origin or the receiving community hindered the process of integration, thereby causing real or illusory feelings of discrimination and increased violence. Whatever the case, our rough and to be sure quite superficial analysis of the data indicates that further research into the problem of culture-conflict-as related to immigration and crime in Israel may bear fruitful implications concerning the etiology of crime.

Juvenile Delinquents of Immigrant Parentage

It has already been mentioned that the main problem of culture-conflict with respect to crime and immigration arises with the second generation. The native-born of immigrant parentage, or those who came very young, are the most prone to suffer from the effects of their parents' immigration.

The conduct norms of their parents diverge as a rule from the prevailing norms in the receiving country. The process of integration may also injure and sometimes shatter the social and economic status of the head of the family. This and other effects of the process of integration may weaken the cohesion of the family unit and thus hamper the family control over the young. The oriental Jewish father, however poor he may be, is always the omnipotent pater-familias. But when he comes to-Israel, the different social set-up may prevent him from fully exercising his former status, he may be given a job not to his liking, and the different living conditions may shatter his previous convictions and leave him in a state of confusion in which he cannot exercise proper control over his family. The youngster may also realize that his father is not the omnipotent patriarch he was supposed to be, and sometimes when he comes home from school he may see his father signing a document with his ink stained thumb.

All these factors presumably increase the susceptibility of the children of immigrant parents to absorb the so-called "street-culture" and to become juvenile delinquents.[33]

Table IV shows the rates of Jewish juvenile

TABLE IV
RATES OF JUVENILE DELINQUENCY IN ISRAEL FOR THE YEARS 1949–1959[34]

Year	Absolute Numbers	Rate per 100,000 of the Population	Percentage in the Age Groups
1949	1000	99	0.68
1950	1147	95	0.67
1951	1300	93	0.66
1952	1500	103	0.74
1953	1541	103	0.75
1954	2072	136	0.96
1955	2471	155	1.06
1956	2623	157	1.06
1957	·2933	166	1.03
1958	3407	188	1.08
1959	4089	220	1.32

delinquency.[35] The middle column shows the rates per 100,000 inhabitants, and the right column shows the percentage of delinquents in their age group. It is obvious that the rate of juvenile delinquency in Israel has been rising constantly.

We may ask whether this increase is linked with immigration, or more precisely, what is the relative role of immigrant delinquents?[36] In the last two years for which data is available, the rates of immigrant delinquents per 100,000 new immigrants were 311 in 1958 and 282 in 1957, whereas the rates for the total population were 188 and 166 respectively. The ratio for both years is .10 "new" immigrant delinquents for 6 of the total population. It should be mentioned that immigrant families as a rule have more children than the older population, but this fact cannot decrease the significance of the unusually high rate of immigrant delinquency or of the possible application of the culture-conflict hypothesis.

Some relevant conclusions may also be drawn from the reports of the regional probation officers for the years 1957–58[37]. These reports, although

[33] As to the possible impact of these factors on juvenile delinquency see SHAW & McKAY, REPORT ON SOCIAL FACTORS IN JUVENILE DELINQUENCY (Report No. 13, 2 Report on the Causes of Crime, National Commission on Law Observance and Enforcement 1937); DRUCKER & HEXTER, CHILDREN ASTRAY (1923); 1 THOMAS & ZNANIECKI, *op. cit. supra* note 4, at 711; Abrahamson, *Family Tension Basic Cause of Criminal Behavior*, 40 J. CRIM. L. & C. 330 (1949); Kobrin, *The Conflict of Values in Delinquency Areas*, 16 AM. SOC. REV. 653 (1951).

[34] Source: The Juvenile Probation Service, The Ministry of Social Welfare, Israel.
[35] The relevant age groups are 9–16 for boys and 9–18 for girls. Children below 9 are not criminally responsible, whereas boys above 16 and girls above 18 are considered adults.
[36] The rates for *native*-born delinquents of immigrant parentage could not be determined. The necessary data are not yet fully available, inasmuch as criminal responsibility begins at the age of 9, and "new" immigrants are those who entered the country after 1948.
[37] MINISTRY OF SOCIAL WELFARE, JUVENILE PROBATION SERVICE REPORT (1958).

not based on refined statistical analysis, contain valuable observations based on daily contact with the population of the region and its delinquents. For example, the regional probation officer for the Tel-Aviv area reports that there are nine main centres of delinquency in his area, seven of which are wholly or mainly inhabited by "new" immigrants. The probation officer of Haifa reports that the greatest delinquency rate in his area is in Tira, which is a large settlement near Haifa wholly inhabited by "new" immigrants. The highest rate of delinquency in the whole country was recorded in the rural region of the Jerusalem area. The population of this region is composed entirely of "new" immigrants. The rates per 100,000 inhabitants in that region were 455 in 1957 and 355 in 1958, whereas the corresponding rates for the town of Jerusalem were only 189 and 279 respectively.

Recent data as to the ethnic origin differentiation of delinquency are not available as yet. The latest findings in this context are the data examined by the Agranat Committee on Juvenile Delinquency in Israel.[33] This committee examined the delinquency rates for the years 1951–1953 and found a great preponderance of delinquency among the oriental Jews over the delinquency among the European Jews. This conclusion applied not only to new immigrants but also to "old" immigrants and native-born. The committee concluded:

"The process of the social and cultural integration of the oriental immigrant boy is seemingly accompanied by internal and external conflicts which result inter-alia in delinquency. The delinquency proneness of these boys is augmenting the more the receiving community refrains from guiding and helping them to find their place in the new society. In that case a boy may develop a feeling that he is being discriminated against; the delinquency proneness therefore increases with the accumulation of real or illusory discrimination and failure experiences with the result that the rate of delinquency of the oriental boy increases the longer his stay in the country. The European boy on the other hand shows a better capacity of adaptation to the environment irrespective of the fact whether the receiving community is fully prepared to assist him in the process of integration or not, the latter is therefore less prone to seek anti-

social substitutes of satisfaction and consequently the longer he stays in the country the less his susceptibility of turning delinquent."[39]

The committee states however that due to insufficient statistical data this conclusion should be regarded as a working hypothesis only to be confirmed or refuted by further research. It states however that, "prima-facie the cultural differences (i.e., oriental-European) have a greater causal significance than the sheer fact of immigration."[40]

It may be worthwhile to point out that according to the basic premises of the culture-conflict hypothesis, immigration and different ethnic origin are actually two aspects of the same thing. A clash of conduct norms with a resultant increase in crime may result from the conflict of norms and values among individuals and groups, within a given community, who have different cultural definitions due to different cultural traditions and backgrounds. But the same clash may result when members of one cultural group migrate to a community having a different culture.[41] The chances are that when a vast array of groups of different cultural traditions meet—not in a mutual country of origin, but through migration to a new country—the degree of culture-conflict, with the resultant crime and delinquency rates, will be higher among the new groups than among members of the receiving community, even though the receiving community is composed of divergent ethnic and cultural groups. This point, of primary importance for our present purposes, was partly confirmed by the data presented in this paper. The relative causal significance of immigration and different ethnic origins to the etiology of culture-conflict—important as it is—is really not relevant for our present purposes. The committee has pointed out that a comparison between the relevant data of two years (i.e., 1951 and 1953) was not sufficient for conclusive results. We may add that the time span between 1948–49 (the beginning of new immigration) and 1951 or 1953 was not long enough for the process of culture-conflict to crystalize its effects on the nature and rates of delinquency among the immigrants; moreover there was not yet any native-born second generation to be studied, and we have seen that one of the major points in the culture-conflict hypothesis

---

[33] JUVENILE DELINQUENCY IN ISRAEL (Ministry of Justice 1956).

[39] *Id.* at 19.
[40] *Ibid.*
[41] See SELLIN, *op. cit. supra* note 5, at 63.

concerns the second generation. A wide and thorough research into the problem of the impact of immigration on crime and delinquency in Israel, if undertaken now, will have at its disposal the relevant data from the last decade, including the 9–15 age group of the native-born second generation.

CONCLUSION

The purpose of this paper is to state the problem of culture-conflict and crime in relation to the criminality of immigrants in Israel. The criminality and delinquency of "new" immigrants tends to be considerably higher then the criminality and delinquency of the native-born and "old" immigrants. Differential crime and delinquency rates are also apparent between the European and the oriental Jews, the rates of the latter tending to be higher. We may state therefore that these primary findings call for further research into the nature and extent of culture-conflict and crime in Israel in relation to the "new" immigrants. The vast array of ethnic groups among the immigrants, the diversity of their cultural traditions, and the special social structure of the receiving community afford a unique opportunity to test one of the basic issues of the etiology of crime on the social level.[42]

[42] A research project on the criminality of immigrants in Israel is scheduled to be completed in 1962.

[2]

THE IMMIGRATION-CRIME NEXUS: TOWARD AN ANALYTIC FRAMEWORK FOR ASSESSING AND GUIDING THEORY, RESEARCH, AND POLICY

DANIEL P. MEARS*

ABSTRACT: *If media accounts are to be believed, immigration to the United States is a primary cause of increased crime rates. Review of recent anticrime policies targeting immigrants would lead one to the same conclusion. Yet most empirical research suggests precisely the opposite conclusion: many immigrant groups consistently demonstrate significantly lower crime rates than do native populations. Moreover, despite early sociological research focusing on the relationship between immigration and crime, relatively little attention has been given to a range of critical theoretical and methodological issues bearing on this relationship. Taking these observations as a point of departure, several critical theoretical and methodological issues are outlined to develop an analytic framework for more systematically guiding and assessing research on the immigration-crime nexus. It is concluded that such a framework is needed for developing improved theories and facts as well as more efficient and effective policies.*

Perhaps more than any other social phenomena, immigration and crime—and especially the nexus between the two—inspire fear and confusion. It should not be surprising, therefore, that much attention has been given to policy formation aimed at controlling immigration-related crime (Bean and Fix 1992; Brimelow 1995; Butcher and Piehl 1998; Hagan and Palloni 1998; Martinez 2000; Simon and Lynch 1999; Tanton and Lutton 1993; Teitelbaum and Weiner 1995; Tonry 1997b; Waters 1999; Yeager 1997). Unfortunately, research to date has relied primarily on limited data and theorizing. This research in turn has provided a questionable foundation for enhancing our understanding of the relationship between immigration and crime and for informing efficient and effective policy creation. For example, as Butcher and Piehl (1998) have emphasized, both research and media accounts frequently fail to distinguish between legal and illegal immigrants, or, perhaps more important, between crime committed by immigrants and crime not

2   SOCIOLOGICAL PERSPECTIVES   Volume 44, Number 1, 2001

committed by immigrants but that nonetheless is the direct or indirect result of immigration processes. Similarly, it is rarely noted that crime associated with immigration may be the result of higher rates of immigrant victimization rather than of offending (McDonald 1997). The situation is such as to lead one recent study to conclude that "the link between immigration and crime is misleading, to the extent of constituting a mythology" (Hagan and Palloni 1999:630).

Taking these observations as a point of departure, this article outlines an analytic framework for assessing and guiding theory, research, and policy on the relationship between immigration and crime. This framework consists of several dimensions, including clarifying the units of analysis used in research and that are the focus of policies; developing a clearer understanding of the types of crime data and facts and rates that exist or that can be created; applying, testing, and modifying contemporary individual and ecological-level sociological theories of crime, with attention to immigration-specific considerations; and identifying particular policy goals and feasible and effective strategies for achieving these goals. The central argument is that these dimensions should be implicitly or explicitly articulated in theoretical and empirical research on, as well as policies that address, the relationship between immigration and crime. A further argument is that the failure to do so will result in potentially inaccurate and misleading understandings of this relationship and, by extension, in the development of inefficient and ineffective policies. It is, for example, by clearly addressing such dimensions that researchers may be better able to assess whether, how, and to what extent immigration and criminal justice policies can "bias and distort public perceptions of immigration and crime," as Hagan and Palloni (1999:617) have observed about seemingly neutral policies targeting Hispanic immigrants. Before describing the outlines of this framework, a brief review of current theoretical and empirical research is provided, along with discussion of media accounts and recent crime-fighting policies targeting immigrants.

BACKGROUND

Concern about the immigration-crime nexus has a long-standing history in the United States that dates back to colonial times, with considerable policy and research attention given to it since the turn of the twentieth century (Hagan and Palloni 1998; McDonald 1997; Yeager 1997). This concern appears to have been motivated in part by anti-immigrant, xenophobic sentiments (Butcher and Piehl 1998:458; Teitelbaum and Weiner 1995), a phenomenon not unique to the United States (Chapin 1997; Ferracuti 1968; Yeager 1997). These sentiments have been premised on the assumption that immigrants engage in more criminal activity (e.g., violent or property crime) than non-immigrants,[1] and, more generally, that they cause a host of other social problems, such as depleting welfare resources, increasing native-born unemployment and housing shortages, overwhelming school and health systems, and undermining the existing social order (Butcher and Piehl 1998; Chapin 1997; Hawkins 1995; McDonald 1997; Sachs 1996; Schuck 1996; Tonry 1997b; Yeager 1997).[2] Yet this assumption, in part fueled by the historical fact that the British not infrequently shipped convicts to America (Erkirch

1987), almost as consistently has been contradicted by the empirical record, including, notably, government-sponsored commissions such as the 1911 U.S. Immigration Commission and the 1931 Wickersham Commission (McDonald 1997; Tonry 1997a; Waters 1999). As Yeager (1997:162) has noted: "The reality is that ... immigrants generally have lower propensities for crime than their native-born counterparts, except where a group's cultural traditions legitimize certain illegal acts" (see also Butcher and Piehl 1998; Chapin 1997; Ferracuti 1968; Hagan and Palloni 1998, 1999; Tonry 1997b). This assessment requires qualification—it does not, for example, consider the ecological-level impacts of immigration processes—but it nonetheless highlights the consistent disjuncture between public sentiment and policy and what is known about immigration-related crime.

Theoretical research on the relationship between immigration and crime has been nominal. Perhaps the most prominent sociological theory to address it is Shaw and McKay's (1942) recently revisited theory of social disorganization (Sampson and Raudenbush 1999; Waters 1999). Their theory suggests that crime is more likely in "socially disorganized" areas marked by high levels of poverty, ethnic heterogeneity, and residential mobility. It further suggests that immigrant youths should be more likely to engage in criminal activity because of the difficulty of becoming integrated into urban American life. This difficulty, Shaw and McKay (1942) argued, stems both from residing in socially disorganized areas and from several immigrant-specific experiences, including potentially conflicting value orientations, greater allegiance among U.S.-born immigrant youths to their peers rather than to their parents, confusion about traversing a wide variety of cultures in ethnically heterogeneous neighborhoods, disinvestment in the inner city and investment in moving to the suburbs, and a general lack of social capital in meeting the challenges of contemporary American life (Waters 1999:23). In addition to social disorganization theory, at least two other prominent theories have been used to examine the immigration-crime nexus. The first, strain theory, involves a focus on blocked socioeconomic opportunities as contributing to crime and delinquency; the second, cultural deviance theory, derived primarily from Sutherland's (1934) pioneering work on acculturation, centers on the idea that certain groups have or develop distinctive cultural traditions that either promote or are accepting of criminal behavior (see, generally, Akers 1999; Empey, Stafford, and Hay 1999; Tonry 1997a).[3]

With rare exception (Martinez 2000; Tonry 1997b; Waters 1999), none of these theories or their variants has, in recent years, been systematically applied or assessed in relation to immigration-related crime, much less used appropriate or higher-quality data sources that can be aggregated and disaggregated to different units of analysis or that can be used for computing different types of crime rates (see, however, Butcher and Piehl 1998; Hagan and Palloni 1999). Moreover, the little research that exists either does not generally support these theories or suggests a much more complicated picture than what each theory alone provides or can accommodate. As noted above, research dating back to the turn of the century indicates that on the whole immigrants—typically conceptualized as the "foreign born" versus the "native born"—are less, not more, prone to criminal activity than nonimmigrants (Butcher and Piehl 1998; Chapin 1997; Hagan and

Palloni 1998; Schuck 1996; Tonry 1997b; Waters 1999; Yeager 1997). There are exceptions, however, including the relatively consistent finding that children and grandchildren of first-generation immigrants, especially young and poorly educated males, are more likely than their parents to be involved in crime (Tonry 1997a; Waters 1999; Yeager 1997; see, however, Butcher and Piehl 1998). There also are notable complexities that existing theories are unable to address. For example, some immigrant groups have higher crime and imprisonment rates than nonimmigrants, while others have considerably lower rates, even when age and gender compositional differences are taken into account (Hagan and Palloni 1999; Tonry 1997b; Waters 1999);[4] different immigrant groups in similar socioeconomic structural contexts frequently evidence different crime patterns (Tonry 1997a:22–23; Waters 1999:25–27); and, although cities with high immigration rates tend to have higher crime rates, there appears to be little or no relationship between changes in immigration and changes in crime, whether controlling for compositional factors such as age and gender or not (Butcher and Piehl 1998; cf. Waters 1999).

Although sociological criminology consistently refutes the simplistic image of immigrants as being more "criminal" than native-born residents, concern about both legal and illegal immigration emerged as a prominent policy issue in the United States during the 1990s (Butcher and Piehl 1998; McDonald 1997).[5] This concern resulted in the passage of laws aimed at controlling immigration, especially illegal immigration, and related crime (Brimelow 1995; Sachs 1996; Schuck 1996; Tanton and Lutton 1993; Yeager 1997). The 1994 Violent Crime Control and Law Enforcement Act, for example, "created unprecedented levels of Federal resources . . . to control illegal immigration and the crimes committed by and against illegal immigrants, [authorizing] $1.2 billion for specialized enforcement provisions, including border control, criminal alien deportation, asylum reform, and a criminal alien tracking system" (McDonald 1997:6).[6] These more restrictive, "get tough" immigration policies also have involved extensive partnering efforts among local, state, and federal immigration and crime control agencies (Butcher and Piehl 1998; McDonald 1997). Unfortunately, not only are these policies grounded on data of limited accuracy, but they appear to have been driven by media case study accounts of gangs, drug traffickers, and organized crime, as well as research based on law enforcement (e.g., arrest) and prison data (see Hagan and Palloni 1999; Kleinknecht 1996; McDonald 1997; Sachs 1996; Sanoff 1996; Tanton and Lutton 1993; Thom 1997), which provide a limited basis for generalizing about immigration-related crime. Moreover, the policies to date have been largely reactive; recent efforts, for example, have been aimed primarily at providing greater incarceration resources and enhancing the efficiency of law enforcement responsiveness to immigrant crime as well as apprehending and deporting illegal immigrants (Brimelow 1995; Butcher and Piehl 1998; McDonald 1997; Schuck 1996).

TOWARD AN ANALYTIC FRAMEWORK

Critical issues in the immigration–crime nexus that remain largely unaddressed include systematic attention to computation of crime rates and estimates for different units of analysis (e.g., individuals, cities, states, countries); the limited accuracy and utility of existing data; application and tests of contemporary criminological theory, as well as modification or elaboration of criminological theory in ways that can accommodate immigration-specific factors; and, finally, policy interventions that are based on theoretically informed research rather than primarily on media and case study accounts of gangs, drug trafficking, and organized crime, or on data of questionable validity and generalizability. It is to these types of issues that the following discussion turns, with the goal of developing an analytic framework for guiding and assessing theory, research, and policy on the immigration-crime nexus.

Before proceeding, however, two points bear emphasizing. First, there is no claim here to presenting a definitive conceptual framework, or even to identifying new or original issues and problems, although several of the specific points discussed below have not been addressed to date. Rather, the overriding goal is to highlight some of the most prominent analytic issues—frequently overlooked in existing research in media accounts, and in recent local, state, and federal legislation—that confront researchers and policy makers as they strive to understand and affect immigration-related crime. Second, the strategy adopted here is to provide as comprehensive a listing of issues and illustrations as possible rather than to provide an empirical analysis from which a smaller set of points might be drawn. Although the latter are needed, a basic contention of this article is that in the absence of greater attention to the broader set of analytic issues raised here, further empirical research likely will have less of an impact on cumulative knowledge or on policy formation than it otherwise might, or, conversely, its impact may well reflect unwarranted assumptions about the utility of certain data or the precise extent to which findings from specific studies are generalizable (see, generally, Blalock 1989; Butcher and Piehl 1999; Freese 1972; Hagan and Palloni 1998, 1999; Merton 1968; Wagner 1985).

Units of Analysis

The importance of distinguishing between different spatiotemporal units of analysis (e.g., individuals, groups, cities, states, countries, etc., measured across space and/or over time) increasingly is being recognized in fields such as psychology, public health, epidemiology, and sociology (Gibbs 1997; Monahan and Steadman 1983; Mrazek and Haggerty 1994). A correlation between individual-level offending and individual-level socioeconomic status need not, for example, imply a correlation between crime rates and aggregate-level socioeconomic measures (e.g., poverty); and the same is true, of course, in reverse (i.e., aggregate-level analyses need not imply specific individual-level relationships). Similarly, the results from a cross-sectional analysis of states at one point in time need not parallel results from other cross-sectional analyses at other points in time; nor need they necessarily parallel those from a time-series analysis of each state over a specified period, or even from all states combined over the same period (Butcher and Piehl 1998; Firebaugh 1978, 1980; Land, Cantor, and Russell 1995).

Although this observation may appear obvious, it bears emphasizing that researchers, journalists, and policy makers frequently generalize results from one unit of analysis to another. Indeed, it is not uncommon to find reviews of gang and prison research that generalize to entire populations. One recent review, for example, which examined research on immigrant gangs and the prevalence of illegal immigrants among prison inmates, concluded that "under current immigration laws and procedures, frighteningly large numbers of newcomers see crime as their avenue to the American dream" (Tanton and Lutton 1993:217). Although this assertion may be true, it does not necessarily follow from analysis of gang (or prison data), just as an increase in youth gangs in the United States does not necessarily mean that youths in general have become more prone to criminal behavior (Snyder and Sickmund 1999). This issue pertains not simply to misgeneralizing from individuals to aggregate ecological units, or vice versa, but to comparisons involving cross-sectional versus longitudinal analyses. For example, and as noted earlier, areas with relatively higher immigration rates appear also to have relatively higher crime rates, yet changes in immigration rates appear to have little or no association with changes in crime rates (Butcher and Piehl 1998). From both a theoretical and a policy perspective, it remains unclear exactly how to interpret these findings or to what extent they accurately reflect patterns of actual immigration-related crime (Hagan and Palloni 1999). It is clear, however, that without reference to findings from different units of analysis, there is a risk of misgeneralizing results, with the potential in turn of drawing unwarranted theoretical or policy inferences (Gibbs 1997).

This situation contrasts markedly with research in criminology, immigration, and sociology generally, in which multiple sources of data are used to delimit the generalizability of findings within a given unit of analysis, as well as to other units and to spatiotemporal comparisons (Orum, Feagin, and Sjoberg 1991). In the field of criminology, for example, there is a rich tradition of using self-report offending and victimization survey data, which provide a markedly different and generally better source of information than do arrest and prison data in terms of estimating individual- and aggregate-level crime counts and of identifying the causes of crime (Empey, Stafford, and Hay 1999). By contrast, research on the immigration-crime nexus is restricted almost invariably to aggregate-level, official statistics based on arrest or prison data, or, again, on case studies of gangs. One consequence is that although research and policy inferences frequently are drawn from these kinds of data, in reality we know little about the relevance to immigration-related crime of a wide range of individual- and aggregate-level factors suggested by criminological research (e.g., previous criminal behavior, peer associations, family functioning, education, employment, community-level informal social control; Akers 1999) or by immigration research (e.g., motivation for immigrating, intended length of stay, proficiency in English, educational and job skills, differential age, gender, and fertility rates among immigration groups; Tonry 1997b).

The limitations of currently available data are discussed in greater detail below, but analytically, and focusing here on units of analysis, they have profound theoretical and policy implications for understanding and addressing the immigration-crime nexus. Suppose, for example, that there has been an increase over a five-year period in immigrant violent crime along the Texas-Mexico border but a decrease during this same period along the California-Mexico border. There is, first, the need to determine whether such changes are "true" changes; but then the issue arises, what are the causes of these changes, and does an understanding of these causes provide an understanding of differences in immigrant crime rates across states or immigrant youth gang activity nationally? Until these comparisons are explicitly addressed, we risk not only misgeneralizing the theoretical and policy implications of our research but also missing opportunities to identify how immigration and crime are potentially linked to broader sociological phenomena (Hagan and Palloni 1999; Sampson and Lauritsen 1997; Sutherland 1934; Tonry 1997b).

Crime Data and Types of Crime Facts and Rates

Although data limitations are endemic to research on immigration and crime, respectively, these limitations are at once both more serious and compounded in research on immigrant crime and immigration-related crime. Much research focuses, for example, primarily on case studies of particular ethnic gangs or on analyses of illegal immigrants (e.g., Tanton and Lutton 1993), even though illegal immigrants comprise but a small proportion of all immigrants to the United States (Butcher and Piehl 1998:458). More generally, relatively little data exist that provide systematic individual- or aggregate-level information about immigrants, immigration processes, or community-level factors bearing on immigration-related crime (Waters 1999:45–48; see also Butcher and Piehl 1998; Chapin 1997; Hagan and Palloni 1998, 1999; Martinez 2000).

Available data consist primarily of official arrest and incarceration statistics, which frequently do not reflect true overall or specific crime rates (Sampson and Lauritsen 1997; Sutherland 1934), much less crime rates for immigrant populations (Hagan and Palloni 1998; Tonry 1997b).[7] For example, increased arrest rates of immigrants may result as much from increased hostility toward immigrants or surveillance by law enforcement, or from a lack of knowledge among immigrants about how to traverse the legal system, as from any actual increase in criminal activity among immigrants (Butcher and Piehl 1998; Hagan and Palloni 1999; Sampson and Lauritsen 1997; Tonry 1997b; Yeager 1997). Also, insofar as illegal as opposed to legal, immigrants, are disproportionally represented in the criminal justice system, this may reflect more on the social capital of legal immigrants or on the areas in which they reside than any actual differences in rates of offending (see McDonald 1997:3). Moreover, these kinds of data generally do not capture the crimes associated with immigration that involve aiding and abetting illegal immigration or immigrant victimization (Martens 1998; Martinez 1997). As one researcher has observed:

> A wide range of predators victimize illegal immigrants. Guides and organized gangsters have robbed, raped, and killed them; abandoned them in the desert; tossed them overboard at sea or out of speeding cars under hot pursuit; or forced them to work in sweatshops or prostitution rings to pay off the cost of the trip. Bandits prey upon them during their journeys. Xenophobes and hate-mongers terrorize them. Some employers cheat them of their earnings. The fact that illegal immigration is a crime makes the immigrants particularly vulnera-

ble because they are unlikely to seek the protection of the law. (McDonald 1997:4)

One way to highlight both the limitations of current data sources and the types of analyses that have been conducted to date, as well as to identify the advantages of alternative types of data, is to identify several key dimensions along which crime facts/rates can be created. One key distinction is between actual (i.e., true/accurate) and known (i.e., official) data sources. This distinction allows one to put into context what is known about a particular phenomenon from what can be known.[8] In the present context, for example, the relevant distinctions pertain to actual and known immigration rates, actual and known crime rates, and actual and known immigrant crime rates. Another key distinction is between offending and victimization; this distinction is important not only because offending and victimization reflect different, albeit related, phenomena but also because the causes of one are not necessarily or even probably the same as those of the other. A third distinction is between the prevalence and incidence of offending and/or victimization. When offenders are the focus of analysis, the term "prevalence" is used (i.e., the number of offenders in a given population), and when offenses are the focus of analysis, the term "incidence" is used (i.e., the number of offenses in a given population).[9] The relevance of this distinction should be evident: prevalence rates and incidence rates can vary independently. For example, consider a city of 100,000 in which 100 offenders commit one crime apiece compared with a city of 100,000 in which 100 offenders commit 10 crimes apiece. Although the prevalence rates will be similar (100 per 100,000), the incidence rates will not be (100 per 100,000 and 1,000 per 100,000, respectively).[10]

Combining these three dimensions gives rise to the grid presented in Table 1, which identifies various types of crime rates that can be generated for any given crime or category of crime (e.g., violent, property, drug). The main point to draw from this table is that while "a" through "d" represent the ideal sources of data needed for obtaining accurate estimates of the prevalence and incidence of immigrant offending and victimization, "e" through "h" represent the least useful or accurate sources. Unfortunately, almost invariably it is these latter sources of data—the most misleading and the least generalizable—that are relied on in discussions of immigrant crime.[11] Indeed, the situation is aggravated by the lack of consistently collected or accurate data on other relevant dimensions, including immigrant-on-immigrant, immigrant-on-nonimmigrant, and nonimmigrant-on-immigrant crime; legal versus illegal immigrant crime rates; trajectories of offending among different types of offenders and immigrant populations; and sociodemographic immigrant data (age, gender, country of origin, duration of stay, education, occupation, etc.), much less individual-level data on the types of criminogenic factors discussed above (previous criminal history, peer association, family functioning, etc.). As discussed below, it is not economically feasible to obtain all relevant data, but it is possible to begin making forays and to use such attempts to highlight the limited utility of the data that to date have provided the basis for understanding the links between immigration and crime (Tonry 1997b).

TABLE 1
Immigrant Crime Rates: Prevalence and Incidence of Offending and Victimization Using Actual and Known Counts

		Prevalence			Incidence			
		Immigrant Offending (O)		Immigrant Victimization (V)		Immigrant Offending (O)		Immigrant Victimization (V)	
		Actual	Known	Actual	Known	Actual	Known	Actual	Known
		a		b		c		d	
	Actual	$PO\dfrac{A_O}{A_P}$	$PO\dfrac{K_O}{A_P}$	$PV\dfrac{A_V}{A_P}$	$PV\dfrac{K_V}{A_P}$	$IO\dfrac{A_O}{A_P}$	$IO\dfrac{K_O}{A_P}$	$IV\dfrac{A_V}{A_P}$	$IV\dfrac{K_V}{A_P}$
Immigrant Pop. (P)		e		f		g		h	
	Known	$PO\dfrac{A_O}{K_P}$	$PO\dfrac{K_O}{K_P}$	$PV\dfrac{A_V}{K_P}$	$PV\dfrac{K_V}{K_P}$	$IO\dfrac{A_O}{K_P}$	$IO\dfrac{K_O}{K_P}$	$IV\dfrac{A_V}{K_P}$	$IV\dfrac{K_V}{K_P}$

[a] Actual prevalence of immigrant offending: actual number of immigrant offenders divided by actual number of immigrants.
[b] Actual prevalence of immigrant victimization: actual number of immigrant victims divided by actual number of immigrants.
[c] Actual incidence of immigrant offending: actual number of offenses committed by immigrants divided by actual number of immigrants.
[d] Actual incidence of immigrant victimization: actual number of immigrant victimizations divided by actual number of immigrants.
[e] Known prevalence of immigrant offending: known number of immigrant offenders divided by known number of immigrants.
[f] Known prevalence of immigrant victimization: known number of immigrant victims divided by known number of immigrants.
[g] Known incidence of immigrant offending: known number of offenses committed by immigrants divided by known number of immigrants.
[h] Known incidence of immigrant victimization: known number of immigrant victimizations divided by known number of immigrants.

Individual- and Ecological-Level Theories of the Immigration-Crime Relationship

In a recent review of research on the criminality of the children of immigrants in European countries, Yeager (1997:163) concluded that "the precursors to [their] behavior look very much like the classic causes of delinquency: poverty, racism, school failure, unemployment, family disorganization, drug addiction, and the like." Unfortunately, as applied to the United States, such statements must remain speculation until more systematic, comprehensive, and accurate data are compiled that can be used to test contemporary criminological theories. However, future research efforts aimed at collecting such data clearly can be informed by current theories of immigration and crime. In this section, several of the more prominent theoretical issues that have yet to be adequately addressed are outlined.

First, dependent variables are needed that reflect both standard criminological concerns (e.g., crime among individuals and specific age, gender, and racial/ethnic populations, crime rates across cities and states; Empey, Stafford, and Hay 1999; Hagan and Palloni 1999; Yeager 1997) and more recent ones (e.g., identifying differential life-course offending and victimization trajectories; Sampson and Laub 1993; Tonry 1997b; Toussaint and Hummer 1999).

Second, research is needed on whether, to what extent, and how traditional and more recent sociological criminology theories apply to individual- and aggregate-level immigration-related crime patterns (see, e.g., Hagan and Palloni 1999). At the individual level, this means closer scrutiny of the link, if any, between such factors as age, gender, peer association, family dynamics, education and employment, and access to guns and criminal behavior and victimization among immigrants. At the aggregate level, it means closer scrutiny of how poverty, social and economic inequality, racial/ethnic composition and differentiation, drug and gun markets, collective efficacy, and the like, are related, if at all, to various immigrant crime rates (see Akers 1999; Butcher and Piehl 1998; Empey, Stafford, and Hay 1999; Hagan and Palloni 1998; Hawkins 1995; Martinez 2000; Sampson and Lauritsen 1997b; Tonry 1997b; Waters 1999; Yeager 1997).

Third, greater attention should be given to the relevance of immigration-specific factors to individual- and aggregate-level crime patterns. For example, do the reasons that immigrants leave their countries, or that entire waves of immigration occur, have any bearing on crime (Tonry 1997a:24)? Although existing evidence is suggestive (Tonry 1997b), we lack any systematic or coherent basis for identifying linkages between when, why, and how immigration occurs and its relation to changes in crime. Consider, for example, the following factors linked to migration flows and their potential relevance for understanding the immigration-crime nexus: historical context (e.g., changes in citizenship, assimilation, and border enforcement laws); cultural dissimilarities between sending and receiving countries; intended durations of stay; assimilation processes; nativism/xenophobia; international markets; migrant networks; domestic economies; and economic and political policies in sending and host countries.[12]

Fourth, a wide range of specific issues that have been touched on in research on the immigration-crime nexus remain underresearched. Among immigrant populations that engage in disproportionately more crime, is a criminal culture "imported" or "assimilated" from the host country, in this case the United States (Rattner 1997)? Are there in fact distinctive cultures among different immigrant populations or subpopulations that affect their greater or lesser involvement in crime (Sutherland 1934)? Do transitions into the United States have differential impacts on certain immigrant populations that in turn render them more prone to criminal offending or victimization (Butcher and Piehl 1998)? How do immigrants' previous criminal histories change, if at all, on arrival to the United States (Toussaint and Hummer 1999; Waters 1999)? Given empirical evidence to the contrary, is the considerable attention given to drug and gun markets, as well as to the age composition of immigrant groups and their U.S.-born descendants, warranted (Bilchik 2000; Hagan and Palloni 1999)? What, if any, are the impacts on crime rates of different fertility rates among immigrant groups (Hagan and

Palloni 1999; Waters 1999)? What accounts for differences in offending and victimization among first-generation immigrants and their U.S.-born children, and for different generational crime patterns among diverse immigrant groups (Martinez 2000; Tonry 1997a; Waters 1999)? To what extent do programs and policies aimed at facilitating assimilation affect immigrant crime (Waters 1999)? And, finally, what is the impact of immigration on local communities, and how does it affect offending and victimization rates of both immigrant and nonimmigrant populations (Butcher and Piehl 1998)?

Developing Better Conceptualized and Targeted Policies

The foregoing dimensions have direct bearing on informing public policy: better data are needed for ascertaining whether, to what extent, and why there may be an immigration-crime nexus, and better sociological theories are needed to explain this nexus and its precise contours. Theories in particular are critical for efficient and effective policy formation; without them policies risk being either too broad or overly, perhaps inaccurately, narrow. (Whether improved theories would in fact have an impact on policy formation is, of course, another matter; Calavita 1992.) As Butcher and Piehl (1998:467) have noted: "Fully understanding the routes through which immigration may affect crime is important for a targeted policy response." Unfortunately, to date policies have tended toward the two extremes, either focusing too broadly on halting legal as well as illegal immigration or focusing too narrowly on particular reactive interventions, such as increased enforcement of deportation initiatives (McDonald 1997; Schuck 1996; Teitelbaum and Weiner 1995). In the first instance, these policies frequently have suffered from considerable ambiguity about their precise goals; in the latter, they have tended to be too narrow to achieve a broader goal, such as substantially reducing overall crime rates (Butcher and Piehl 1998:486).

A more efficient and effective alternative is (a) to identify target populations most at risk of involvement in serious and/or violent criminal activity or of disrupting community-level dynamics and social order and then (b) to determine the most feasible and effective interventions for targeting these populations. In assessing the latter, it is likely that a dual focus on risk and protective factors will yield considerably more efficient and effective initiatives than a focus only on the most at-risk populations (see, e.g., Howell and Hawkins 1998). Risk factors are individual or sociological conditions that directly, indirectly, or in conjunction with other conditions give rise to crime, whereas protective factors are those that help reduce it.[13] For example, research to date suggests that young male, U.S.-born descendants of immigrants, particularly the poorly educated, are more likely than other populations to be involved in crime. It thus is reasonable to suspect that policies targeting this population may be more likely to result in a larger reduction in immigration-related crime than those targeting other populations (Butcher and Piehl 1998; Tonry 1997a; Yeager 1997). In a study of immigration and crime in Sweden, for instance, Martens (1998) found evidence to suggest that the social welfare system there, which targets the less well-to-do and their families and children, contributed to lower levels of offending among children of immigrants. However, even with knowledge about the most at-risk populations, the precise types of policies that may be most effective can vary dramatically. Policy initiatives can, for example, focus solely on risk factors (e.g., limiting the admission of younger, male immigrants), or they can target at-risk populations and then attempt to enhance protective factors aimed at reducing their involvement in criminal activity (e.g., provision of educational and vocational training).

It is important, however, to emphasize that a "one size fits all" approach is unlikely to be effective, much less efficient (Tonry 1997b). For instance, the programs that have the most impact on young males likely may not necessarily have the desired impact on young females or other immigrant populations. Perhaps more important, it merits emphasizing that there may be community-level initiatives that yield much greater crime-reduction benefits than initiatives that focus on youths specifically (Howell and Hawkins 1998), including programs oriented toward facilitating the transition of entire immigrant populations, drawing on the informal social controls that immigrant groups bring with them, and assimilating immigrant and nonimmigrant populations to their respective social and cultural traditions (Hagan and Palloni 1999; Waters 1999). Of no small consequence in each of these instances is the possibility that such approaches may have an impact on offending and victimization among not only immigrant populations but non-immigrant ones as well.

DISCUSSION AND CONCLUSION

Perhaps few other areas of research and policy are as in need of a guiding framework for organizing and assessing theory, research, and policy than the focus on the relationship between immigration and crime. Assumptions about this relationship abound, yet few have any basis in empirical fact. Theory development aimed at explaining either individual- or ecological-level variation in immigration and crime patterns is nominal, and, among existing theories, none enjoys any consistent support. Moreover, severe limitations constrain the usefulness of existing data for generating valid estimates of immigration, crime, or immigration-related crime, much less their usefulness for testing theory. Such limitations assume particular importance in a social and political context of consistently anti-immigrant sentiment (Butcher and Piehl 1998; Hagan and Palloni 1998; McDonald 1997; Simon and Lynch 1999; Yeager 1997). Indeed, as Hagan and Palloni (1999:629) observed: "It is of particular concern, in the political and economic context of cost shifting, that the same correctional departments that collect crime statistics may have a direct financial interest in the size of their immigrant inmate populations and in seeing these numbers reported and well publicized."

The theoretical and methodological limitations identified here are far from academic but rather strike directly at the heart of effective policy making: if we are to develop better policies, then better sociological theories and facts are needed. Since development of a general theory of the immigration-crime nexus likely is premature,[14] the goal of this article has been to develop an analytic framework that can provide a more explicit and systematic basis for assessing and guiding theory and research and, ultimately, for developing more effective policies. This framework involves attention to the following dimensions: units of analysis; crime rates, including types of crime rates and the usefulness of different sources of data; individual- and ecological-level theories of the immigration-crime relationship; and development of more carefully conceptualized and targeted interventions and policies.

By using these dimensions to guide theory, research, and policy efforts, we have a basis by which to situate their broader relevance for understanding and, where it is deemed appropriate, influencing immigration-crime patterns. The framework provides a starting point for highlighting key issues and questions that remain unaddressed. For example, although sociologists have devoted considerable attention to understanding crime patterns at different units of analysis, such attention generally has not carried over to the study of the immigration-crime nexus. Thus one frequently finds discussions about individual-level offending that elide into ecological-level implications, and vice versa, with little or no theoretical, logical, or empirical grounds for doing so. Such discussions become especially problematic in the absence of systematic research at multiple units of analysis (Butcher and Piehl 1998; Hagan and Palloni 1999). At present, for instance, there is a conspicuous absence of research on community-level factors that may bear on any putative link between immigration and crime (Sampson and Lauritsen 1997). This oversight is unfortunate, if only because any potential large-scale crime impacts of immigration likely may result not from increasing proportions of immigrant criminals but from structural conditions that affect immigrant populations, or, conversely, from immigration processes that affect structural conditions and that in turn have direct or indirect effects on both immigrant and nonimmigrant populations (Butcher and Piehl 1998; McDonald 1997; Sampson and Raudenbush 1999; Yeager 1997).[15] In short, researchers and policy makers currently face the critical challenge of clearly identifying individual- versus aggregate-level predictors of the impact of immigration on individual- and aggregate-level patterns of crime among immigrants and nonimmigrants.

Second, most studies and policies have relied on the least accurate and least useful sources of data for understanding the link between immigration and crime. Indeed, we currently lack the kind of data required for systematically and comprehensively assessing the precise nature of "the" relationship between immigration and crime (Hagan and Palloni 1998, 1999; Yeager 1997:162). We need, for instance, accurate pre- and postimmigration prevalence and incidence rates for offending and victimization, as well as estimation of these rates by types of crimes, with breakdowns for specific immigrant populations. In developing such estimates, we need data that can provide accurate estimates of inter/intraimmigrant and nonimmigrant offending and victimization, much as has been done in research focusing on inter/intraracial variation in crime (Parker and McCall 1999; Sampson and Lauritsen 1997). It bears stating explicitly that the issue of race/ethnicity and crime is, of course, inextricably linked both to criminal justice processing and to immigration (Gabor 1994; Hagan and Palloni 1999; Sampson and Lauritsen 1997; Tonry 1997b). Thus insight into the immigration-crime nexus has direct implications for understanding the relationship between race/ethnicity and crime, and vice versa. In addition, further research is needed on identifying and explaining over-time trajectories of offending and victimization among immigrants after their arrival to the United States (Butcher and Piehl 1998; Toussaint and Hummer 1999). Although collection of data necessary to address some of these questions is not likely to be forthcoming in the near future, primarily because of the associated costs, significant advances can be made through employment of multiple and more diverse methodologies, including the use of self-report offending and victimization surveys in select areas and for select populations and the use of comparative case studies of immigrant transitions from one area into another (Tonry 1997b).

Third, and tied to data concerns, more textured theoretical accounts of individual- and ecological-level immigration impacts on crime are needed. Many of the types of factors suggested by contemporary crime theories (peer associations, strain, social bonds, family structure, poverty, social control, etc.) have yet to be evaluated on a systematic basis with immigrant populations or areas in which large populations of immigrants reside. Although relatively more research has focused on immigration-specific factors (the effect of being a first-generation immigrant versus a U.S.-born descendant of immigrants, the motivation for immigrating, etc.), such research still remains rare and generally is far from comprehensive (e.g., Butcher and Piehl 1998; Hagan and Palloni 1999; Martinez 2000; Tonry 1997b; Waters 1999; Yeager 1997). This is unfortunate not only because developing informed theoretical accounts of the immigration-crime nexus is important in its own right (e.g., to dispel certain myths about immigration-crime links; see Hagan and Palloni 1999) but also because such accounts provide an opportunity to modify, expand, and ultimately improve criminological and immigration theory. In turn, they can provide a more defensible foundation for policies aimed at controlling immigration-related crime. Indeed, a central benefit of improved theory is the ability to identify potential immigration-related crime increases or decreases that we might otherwise fail to recognize.

The dimensions examined here—units of analysis, immigration/crime data and crime rates, individual- and ecological-level theoretical accounts of the relationship between immigration and crime, targeted policy formation—are interrelated, with direct implications for sociological criminology and for policy formation. For example, establishing accurate facts about the prevalence of offending among different immigrant populations in different areas is a necessary precursor to providing explanations about the immigration-crime nexus. At the same time, contemporary crime and immigration theory indicates the need for disaggregating crime rates along certain dimensions (e.g., age and gender, foreign-born vs. U.S.-born, country of origin, motivation for immigrating) as well as for collecting additional data on various potential criminogenic factors (e.g., peer associations, family structure, community socioeconomic context) for specific immigrant groups. The collection of better facts and the development of more refined theories together can contribute directly to identifying the conditions under which immigration increases or decreases crime among immigrants, nonimmigrant populations, and ecological areas (e.g., communities, cities). This knowledge can be used to determine whether the disproportionate presence of immigrants in arrest and incarceration statistics is due to actual offending or to racial/ethnic disparities in processing (Hagan and Palloni 1999; Tonry 1997b). Ultimately, such facts and theories are necessary for helping to avoid the errors and injustices that can emerge when policies are based on untested assumptions and biases; they may even contribute to the development of more efficient, effective, and equitable crime-reduction policies. To be sure, past experience in the United States (Calavita 1992) and elsewhere suggests that greater understanding will not necessarily or even probably lead to improved policy making (Tonry 1997b), but clearly it is a step in the right direction.

Acknowledgments: I am grateful to Ronald Angel, Frank Bean, Eliza Evans, Charles Haynes, Emily Leventhal, Mark Stafford, Danielle Toussaint, and the anonymous reviewers for *Sociological Perspectives* for their many helpful comments and suggestions throughout the development of this article.

NOTES

1. Throughout this article, "crime" refers to conventional crime categories (e.g., violent and property offending/victimization) and not, unless so specified, to illegal immigration.

2. Such concerns rarely find a strong or consistent basis in empirical fact. For example, studies of the economic effects of immigration reveal considerable dissensus, with some research showing positive impacts, other research showing no impacts, and still other research showing negative impacts (see, e.g., Bean and Fix 1992; Borjas 1990; Brimelow 1995; Fix and Passel 1994; Massey 1988; Portes 1995b; Schuck 1996).

3. It should be emphasized that each of these theories in fact embodies quite large and diverse bodies of conceptualization and theorizing (Akers 1999; Empey, Stafford, and Hay 1999).

4. Focusing on illegal immigrants, McDonald (1997:3–4) has noted: "Without adjustments for the age and gender of the immigrant population, [many estimates] probably overstate the relative criminality of the illegal population because a disproportionate number of the illegal immigrants were likely to have been single males in their crime-prone years."

5. Although there are considerably more legal than illegal immigrants in the United States, the public consistently believes otherwise (Butcher and Piehl 1998:458).

6. The general toughening of U.S. immigration policies has involved extensive revisions to criminal laws pertaining to deportation and illegal entry, including tougher criminal penalties for reentry after deportation and creation of numerous restrictions on immigration (McDonald 1997).

7. Setting aside the issue of obtaining an accurate count of illegal immigrants who commit crime, estimating illegal immigration is exceedingly difficult (McDonald 1997:3). Current estimates suggest that of the total U.S. population, five million (2%) are illegal immigrants, most of whom did not cross over from Mexico and many of whom (close to 41%) entered legally and then overstayed their visas (McDonald 1997:3).

8. In the same vein, Monahan and Steadman (1983:147) have noted: "The true/treated distinction [in epidemiological research] is particularly apposite to analyzing the relationship between crime and mental disorder because it helps disentangle the legal and policy issues involved."

9. I do not use "prevalence" and "incidence" here in the epidemiological sense (Monahan and Steadman 1983; Mrazek and Haggerty 1994).

10. A related distinction involves reference to the frequency of offending per offender, what is sometimes referred to as "lambda."

11. For a similar observation regarding research on the relationship between crime and mental disorder, see Monahan and Steadman 1983.

12. The relevant literature is vast, but some useful starting points are: Alba and Nee 1997; Bach 1992; Bean and Fix 1992; Calavita 1992; Dinnerstein and Reimers 1986; Edmonston and Passel 1994; Fischer 1989; Fix and Passel 1994; Granovetter 1995; Gordon 1964; Grasmuck and Pessar 1991; Gurak and Caces 1992; Higham 1958; Martinez 2000; Massey 1988; Massey et al. 1993, 1994; Portes 1995a, 1995b; Portes and Bach 1985; Reimers 1992; Roberts 1995; Sassen 1988, 1995; Teitelbaum and Weiner 1995; Tonry 1997b; Toussaint and Hummer 1999; Waters 1999; Yeager 1997; Zolberg 1995.

13. The terms "risk" and "protective" derive from epidemiology and encompass a broad range of biological, psychological, and community-level factors (Mrazek and Haggerty 1994).

14. Portes (1997a) has echoed a similar view in writing about the intersection of theoretical and empirical literatures on immigration and economics.

15. Observing that the precursors to youth crime among descendants of immigrants appear to be similar to those identified in the criminological literature (e.g., poverty, school failure, family disorganization), Yeager (1997:163) has commented that "perhaps this [similarity] is more a comment on the host country than on immigration per se."

REFERENCES

Akers, Ronald. 1999. *Criminological Theories: Introduction and Evaluation.* 4th ed. Los Angeles, CA: Roxbury.

Alba, Richard and Victor Nee. 1997. "Rethinking Assimilation Theory for a New Era of Immigration." *International Migration Review* 31:826–74.

Bach, Robert. 1992. "Settlement Policies in the United States." Pp. 145–64 in *Nation of Immigrants*, edited by G. Freeman and J. Jupp. New York: Oxford University Press.

Bean, Frank D. and Michael Fix. 1992. "The Significance of Recent Immigration Policy Reforms in the United States." Pp. 41–55 in *Nation of Immigrants*, edited by G. Freeman and J. Jupp. New York: Oxford University Press.

Bilchik, Shay. 2000. *1999 National Report Series Juvenile Justice Bulletin: Challenging the Myths.* Washington, DC: U.S. Department of Justice, Office of Juvenile Justice and Delinquency Prevention.

Blalock, Hubert M., Jr. 1989. "Toward Cumulative Knowledge: Theoretical and Methodological Issues." Pp. 15–37 in *Crossroads of Social Science: The ICPSR 25th Anniversary Volume.* New York: Agathon Press.

Borjas, George J. 1990. *Friends or Strangers: The Impact of Immigrants on the U.S. Economy.* New York: Basic Books.

Brimelow, Peter. 1995. *Alien Nation: Common Sense about America's Immigration Disaster.* New York: Random House.

Butcher, Kristin F. and Anne M. Piehl. 1998. "Cross-City Evidence on the Relationship between Immigration and Crime." *Journal of Policy Analysis and Management* 17:457–93.

Calavita, Kitty. 1992. *Inside the State.* New York: Routledge.

Chapin, Wesley D. 1997. "Ausländer raus? The Empirical Relationship between Immigration and Crime in Germany." *Social Science Quarterly* 78:543–58.

Dinnerstein, Leonard and David Reimers. 1986. "Strangers in the Land: Then and Now." *American Jewish History* 76:107–16.

Edmonston, Barry and Jeffrey S. Passel, eds. 1994. *Immigration and Ethnicity: The Integration of America's Newest Arrivals*. Washington, DC: Urban Institute Press.

Empey, LaMar T., Mark C. Stafford, and Carter H. Hay. 1999. *American Delinquency: Its Meaning and Construction*. 4th ed. Belmont, CA: Wadsworth.

Erkirch, Roger A. 1987. *Bound for America: The Transportation of British Convicts to the Colonies, 1718–1775*. New York: Oxford University Press.

Ferracuti, Franco. 1968. "European Migration and Crime." *Collected Studies in Criminological Research* 3:9–76.

Firebaugh, Glenn. 1978. "A Rule for Inferring Individual-level Relationships from Aggregate Data." *American Sociological Review* 43:557–72.

———. 1980. "Cross-National versus Historical Regression Models: Conditions of Equivalence in Comparative Analysis." *Comparative Social Research* 3:333–44.

Fischer, David H. 1989. *Albion's Seed: Four British Folkways in America*. New York: Oxford University Press.

Fix, Michael and Jeffrey S. Passel. 1994. *Immigration and Immigrants: Setting the Record Straight*. Washington, DC: Urban Institute Press.

Freese, Lee. 1972. "Cumulative Sociological Knowledge." *American Sociological Review* 37:472–82.

Gabor, Thomas. 1994. "The Suppression of Crime Statistics on Race and Ethnicity: The Price of Political Correctness." *Canadian Journal of Criminology* 36:153–63.

Gibbs, Jack P. 1997. "Seven Dimensions of the Predictive Power of Sociological Theories." *National Journal of Sociology* 11:1–28.

Gordon, Milton M. 1964. *Assimilation in American Life*. New York: Oxford University Press.

Granovetter, Mark. 1995. "The Economic Sociology of Firms and Entrepreneurs." Pp. 128–65 in *The Economic Sociology of Immigration*, edited by A. Portes. New York: Russell Sage Foundation.

Grasmuck, Sherri and Patricia R. Pessar. 1991. *Between Two Islands*. Berkeley: University of California Press.

Gurak, Douglas T. and Fe Caces. 1992. "Migration Networks and the Shaping of Migration Systems." Pp. 156–76 in *International Migration Systems: A Global Approach*, edited by M. Kritz, L. L. Kim, and H. Zlotnik. Oxford: Clarendon Press.

Hagan, John and Alberto Palloni. 1998. "Immigration and Crime in the United States." Pp. 367–87 in *The Immigration Debate: Studies on the Economic, Demographic, and Fiscal Effects of Immigration*, edited by J. P. Smith and B. Edmonston. Washington, DC: National Academy Press.

———. 1999. "Sociological Criminology and the Mythology of Hispanic Immigration and Crime." *Social Problems* 46:617–32.

Hawkins, Darnell F. 1995. "Ethnicity, Race and Crime: A Review of Selected Studies." Pp. 11–45 in *Ethnicity, Race, and Crime*, edited by D. F. Hawkins. Albany: State University of New York Press.

Higham, John. 1958. "Another Look at Nativism." *Catholic Historical Review* 44:147–58.

Howell, James C. and J. David Hawkins. 1998. "Prevention of Youth Violence." Pp. 263–315 in *Youth Violence: Crime and Justice: A Review of Research*, vol. 24, edited by M. Tonry and M. H. Moore. Chicago: University of Chicago Press.

Kleinknecht, William. 1996. *The New Ethnic Mobs: The Changing Face of Organized Crime in America*. New York: Free Press.

Land, Kenneth C., David Cantor, and Stephen T. Russell. 1995. "Unemployment and Crime
     Rate Fluctuations in the Post–World War II United States: Statistical Time-Series
     Properties and Alternative Models." Pp. 55–79 in *Crime and Inequality,* edited by
     J. Hagan and R. D. Peterson. Stanford, CA: Stanford University Press.
Martens, Peter L. 1998. "Immigrants, Crime, and Criminal Justice in Sweden." Pp. 183–255
     in *Ethnicity, Crime, and Immigration: Comparative and Cross-National Perspectives. Crime
     and Justice: A Review of Research,* vol. 21, edited by M. Tonry. Chicago: University of
     Chicago Press.
Martinez, Ramiro, Jr. 1997. "Homicide among the 1980 Mariel Refugees in Miami: Victims
     and Offenders." *Hispanic Journal of Behavioral Sciences* 19:107–22.
———. 2000. "Immigration and Urban Violence: The Link between Immigrant Latinos and
     Types of Homicide." *Social Science Quarterly* 81:363–74.
Massey, Douglas S. 1988. "Economic Development and International Migration in Compar-
     ative Perspective." *Population and Development Review* 14:383–414.
Massey, Douglas S., Joaquin Arango, Graeme Hugo, Ali Kouaouci, Adela Pellegrino,
     and J. Edward Taylor. 1993. "Theories of International Migration: A Review and
     Appraisal." *Population and Development Review* 19:431–66.
———. 1994. "An Evaluation of International Migration Theory: The North American
     Case." *Population and Development Review* 20:699–753.
McDonald, William F. 1997. "Crime and Illegal Immigration: Emerging Local, State, and
     Federal Partnerships." *National Institute of Justice Journal* 232:2–10. Washington, DC:
     U.S. Department of Justice, National Institute of Justice.
Merton, Robert K. 1968. *Social Theory and Social Structure.* New York: Free Press.
Monahan, John, and Henry J. Steadman. 1983. "Crime and Mental Disorder: An Epidemio-
     logical Approach." Pp. 145–89 in *Crime and Justice: An Annual Review of Research,* vol.
     4, edited by M. Tonry and N. Morris. Chicago: University of Chicago Press.
Mrazek, Patricia J. and Robert J. Haggerty, eds. 1994. *Reducing Risks for Mental Disorders:
     Frontiers for Preventive Intervention Research.* Washington, DC: National Academy
     Press.
Orum, Anthony M., J. R. Feagin, and G. Sjoberg. 1991. "The Nature of the Case Study." Pp.
     1–26 in *A Case for the Case Study,* edited by J. R. Feagin, Anthony M. Orum, and
     G. Sjoberg. Chapel Hill: University of North Carolina Press.
Parker, Karen F. and Patricia L. McCall. 1999. "Structural Conditions and Racial Homicide
     Patterns: A Look at the Multiple Disadvantages in Urban Areas." *Criminology* 37:447–
     77.
Portes, Alejandro. 1995a. "Economic Sociology and the Sociology of Immigration: A Con-
     ceptual Overview." Pp. 1–41 in *The Economic Sociology of Immigration,* edited by A.
     Portes. New York: Russell Sage Foundation.
———, ed. 1995b. *The Economic Sociology of Immigration.* New York: Russell Sage Foundation.
Portes, Alejandro and Robert L. Bach. 1985. *Latin Journey.* Berkeley: University of California
     Press.
Rattner, Arye. 1997. "Crime and Russian Immigration: Socialization or Importation? The
     Israeli Case." *International Journal of Comparative Sociology* 38:235–48.
Reimers, David. 1992. *Still the Golden Door: The Third World Comes to America.* 2d ed. New
     York: Columbia University Press.
Roberts, Bryan R. 1995. "Socially Expected Durations and the Economic Adjustment of
     Immigrants." Pp. 42–86 in *The Economic Sociology of Immigration,* edited by A. Portes.
     New York: Russell Sage Foundation.
Sachs, Lowell. 1996. "Treacherous Waters in Turbulent Times: Navigating the Recent Sea
     Change in U.S. Immigration Policy and Attitudes." *Social Justice* 23:125–36.

Sampson, Robert J. and John H. Laub. 1993. *Crime in the Making: Pathways and Turning Points Through Life.* Cambridge, MA: Harvard University Press.

Sampson, Robert J. and Janet L. Lauritsen. 1997. "Racial and Ethnic Disparities in Crime and Criminal Justice in the United States." Pp. 311–74 in *Ethnicity, Crime, and Immigration: Comparative and Cross-National Perspectives.* Crime and Justice: A Review of Research, vol. 21, edited by M. Tonry. Chicago: University of Chicago Press.

Sampson, Robert J. and Stephen W. Raudenbush. 1999. "Systematic Social Observation of Public Places: A New Look at Disorder in Urban Neighborhoods." *American Journal of Sociology* 105:603–51.

Sanoff, Alvin P. 1996. "The Hottest Import: Crime." *U.S. News & World Report,* September 30, p. 49.

Sassen, Saskia. 1988. *The Mobility of Labor and Capital.* New York: Oxford University Press.

———. 1995. "Immigration and Local Labor Markets." Pp. 87–127 in *The Economic Sociology of Immigration,* edited by A. Portes. New York: Russell Sage Foundation.

Schuck, Peter H. 1996. "Alien Rumination." *Yale Law Journal* 105:1963–2012.

Shaw, Clifford R. and Henry D. McKay. 1942. *Juvenile Delinquency and Urban Areas: A Study of Rates of Delinquents in Relation to Differential Characteristics of Local Communities in American Cities.* Chicago: University of Chicago Press.

Simon, Rita J. and James P. Lynch. 1999. "A Competitive Assessment of Public Opinion Toward Immigrants and Immigration Policies." *International Migration Review* 33:455–67.

Snyder, Howard N. and Melissa Sickmund. 1999. *Juvenile Offenders and Victims: 1999 National Report.* Washington, DC: U.S. Department of Justice, Office of Juvenile Justice and Delinquency Prevention.

Sutherland, Edwin H. 1934. *Principles of Criminology.* Chicago: Lippincott.

Tanton, John and Wayne Lutton. 1993. "Immigration and Criminality in the U.S.A." *Journal of Social, Political and Economic Studies* 18:217–34.

Teitelbaum, Michael S. and Myron Weiner. 1995. "Threatened Peoples, Threatened Borders: Migration and U.S. Foreign Policy." Pp. 13–38 in *Threatened Peoples, Threatened Borders: World Migration and U.S. Policy,* edited by M. S. Teitelbaum and M. Weiner. New York: Norton.

Thom, Linda H. 1997. "Immigration's Impact on Teen Pregnancy and Juvenile Crime." *Population and Environment* 18:473–82.

Tonry, Michael. 1997a. "Ethnicity, Crime, and Immigration." Pp. 1–29 in *Ethnicity, Crime, and Immigration: Comparative and Cross-National Perspectives.* Crime and Justice: A Review of Research. vol. 21, edited by M. Tonry. Chicago: University of Chicago Press.

———, ed. 1997b. *Ethnicity, Crime, and Immigration: Comparative and Cross-National Perspectives.* Chicago: University of Chicago Press.

Tonry, Michael and Mark H. Moore, eds. 1998. *Youth Violence.* Crime and Justice: A Review of Research, vol. 24. Chicago: University of Chicago Press.

Toussaint, Danielle W. and Robert A. Hummer. 1999. "Differential Mortality Risks from Violent Causes for Foreign- and Native-Born Residents of the USA." *Population Research and Policy Review* 18:607–20.

Wagner, David G. 1985. *The Growth of Sociological Theories.* Beverly Hills, CA: Sage.

Waters, Tony. 1999. *Crime and Immigrant Youth.* Thousand Oaks, CA: Sage.

Yeager, Matthew G. 1997. "Immigrants and Criminality: A Cross-National Review." *Criminal Justice Abstracts* 29:143–71.

Zolberg, Aristide R. 1995. "From Invitation to Interdiction: U.S. Foreign Policy and Immigration Since 1945." Pp. 117–59 in *Threatened Peoples, Threatened Borders: World Migration and U.S. Policy,* edited by M. S. Teitelbaum and M. Weiner. New York: Norton.

[3]

Exporting and Importing Criminality: Incarceration of the Foreign Born

GRAEME NEWMAN[1]
State University of New York at Albany

JOSHUA D. FREILICH[2]
John Jay College of Criminal Justice

GREGORY J. HOWARD[3]
Western Michigan University

Since previous studies have found that crime rates vary by immigrant group there is a need to dis-aggregate immigrants by country of birth in order to obtain a more accurate representation of the relationship between migrants and crime. This study examines data from six countries (Australia, Canada, France, Italy, the Netherlands, and the U.S.A.) on the country of birth of their inmate populations. The following observations are reasonable conclusions from the data available. First, the percentages of each home country's inmate population that is foreign-born varies remarkably. Second, in general foreign-born inmates tend to come from regions outside the region within which the host country was located, though in most cases from regions that were proximate. Third, given the small number of countries reporting, it is intriguing that just a small number of countries and regions can account for such a high proportion of a home country's inmate population if one includes the numbers of a country's citizens who are housed in foreign prisons as part of that original country's inmate population. The paper concludes with a discussion of a number of policy implications that flow from these findings.

Introduction

While some people perceive migrants in a benign or positive light, others are more hostile in their views. In some cases, foreigners have been regarded as less fortunate souls who fled terrible conditions (e.g., discrimination, oppression, warfare, or poverty) in their country of birth in an attempt to make a better life for themselves elsewhere. Similarly, foreigners have also been conceived as productive individuals who, by providing needed services, contribute to the economic well-being of the destination country. Many native-born citizens, however, view immigrants much more critically. Migrants are often looked upon as unwelcome additions to the destination country who weaken society by both taking unfair advantage of generous welfare programs and committing large numbers of crimes. It should not come as a surprise, therefore, that for generations criminologists have focused on the relationship between migration and crime.

144   *NEWMAN, FREILICH, AND HOWARD*

The issue of immigration and crime is not only multifaceted and complex, but it also encompasses a wide range of subissues. For the most part, criminologists have examined whether immigrants commit more crime than the native-born population, studied the crime rates of second and third generation immigrants, sought to explain why some immigrants turn toward the path of crime, analyzed victimization rates of immigrants, and suggested policies to lower the crime and victimization rates of immigrants (see for example, Freilich, Newman, Shoham, and Addad 2002; Tonry 1997). For example, although the public in many locations views immigrants as crime prone, research findings have usually indicated that first generation immigrants have a lower crime rate than the native-born population. The literature also suggests, though, that the crime rate increases among second generation immigrants (see for example, Killian 2002; Lynch and Simon 2002; Sun and Reed 1995; Yeager 1996). Sun and Reed (1995), like many other scholars, have hypothesized that cultural and structural factors may account for this phenomenon. In general, even though many immigrants live in poverty they are, nevertheless, grateful for the refuge granted to them by the host country. Their children, conversely, who also grow up amidst deprived surroundings do not embrace "the ideology of resignation and contentment that kept their forebears satisfied" (245). Instead these individuals "seek the same chances and yearn for the same living standards as their hosts" (245) and when they find their opportunities blocked they may very well turn to crime as a solution. Likewise, third generation immigrants have also been found to have higher rates of criminality than their ancestors (see Yeager 1996).

What has been discussed less is the exchange of criminals between and among nations. Do not countries exchange consumer goods, military weapons, and all sorts of luxuries? All countries, in short, both import and export various items. We propose to examine the migrant crime connection on the international level in terms of specific nations importing and exporting criminals. The literature, after all, has also found that crime rates vary by immigrant group. Killian (2002) summarizes the research by stating, "Thus, the findings on immigration and crime point to two consistent factors: children of immigrants commit more crime than their parents and different immigrant groups engage in crime at different rates" (122-23; see also Sheu 2002; Sun and Reed 1995; Yeager 1996). This latter conclusion clearly indicates the need to disaggregate immigrants by country of origin in order to obtain a more accurate representation of the relationship between migrants and crime. In other words, it is too simplistic to discuss immigrants and crime; instead we need to specify the immigrant groups to which we refer.

In the pages that follow, we analyze the immigrant and crime relationship under the rubric of an import export model, with particular reference to one aspect of crime control: incarceration. We begin by describing the precise focus of our study and our data and methods. After setting forth our results we conclude by offering some tentative conclusions as well as discussing a number of policy implications.

Focus of the Current Study

It is remarkable, given the widespread interest and concern about immigrant populations and their relationship to crime and criminal justice issues, that so few countries collect or make available data concerning such groups. The current study has managed to obtain data on the country of birth of the inmate populations of just six countries: Australia, Canada (federal prison system only), France, Italy, Netherlands, and the USA (federal plus 15 states[4]), and even these are incomplete. We recognize that country of birth may not be considered by some to be a completely satisfactory indicator of "foreign" status, since it does not take into account how long the individual has resided in the host country. It is possible that some immigrants residing in the host country, at times almost from birth, may very well have become naturalized citizens. Some may question whether these naturalized citizens should be included in an "immigrant" category. Nevertheless, an examination of foreign-born individuals has advantages over other indicators such as "citizenship" which, unless supported by documentation, may not be reliable when it depends on individual self-categorization. Furthermore, and more significantly, in most cases it is simply not feasible to utilize a measure of citizenship since such data are usually not collected.

Previous studies have also used country of birth as a measure of immigrant groups or "foreigners." Lynch and Simon (2002) recently argued that this distinction is a valid one. As they point out, this indicator identifies groups that are part of the "out" group of a society. Individuals who are naturalized citizens are usually differentiated from native citizens by language, accent and culture. An immigrant's country of birth very often remains a signifier of exclusion regardless of whether or not the individual becomes a citizen. We therefore view the category of country of birth as a reasonable identifier of foreign status that most likely underestimates the number of foreigners in the prisons of the six countries studied.

We have used incarceration as the indicator of criminal involvement for a number of reasons. The first obvious reason is that it is the indicator for which more countries appear to collect foreign-born status information. Second, we consider the presence of persons housed in prison populations to be an important indicator not only of their possible involvement in criminality, but also of the official activities of the criminal justice system that processes offenders, and places them in prison. It is the indicator of the most serious cases, both from the point of view of the criminality of the offender, and the sanctions of the criminal justice system. Finally, the difficulties of comparing official criminal justice data across nations are well known (Newman 1999; Newman and Howard 1999). We consider ourselves on safer ground using incarceration statistics, since they are measures of actual persons located in specific places, and are therefore easily countable. Their offender status is comparatively clear: they are either prisoners or they are not. The only shortcoming of prison population data is that they do not give an accurate measure of the movement of individuals in and out of the prison system; this is a feature of prisons that is usually measured by counting the number of admissions, rather than the static population. However, admissions data are particularly difficult to obtain, and in fact are virtually nonexistent in many countries (as reported by the series of UN Surveys of Crime Trends and Criminal Justice Systems 1998; 2000). In sum, while prison populations do not tell the whole story, they reveal much about how many persons are locked up in any particular country at roughly one point in time. Of course, it is important to recognize that by using incarceration data we are studying a special class of offenders, and not examining the whole range of possible criminality. Again, we point out that any error involved in such measurement is likely to be an underestimate of the criminal involvement of foreigners.

The six countries selected for study are those that had data available. Moreover, these six nations have long histories of importing foreigners into their respective countries, for various reasons. They are also conveniently located in the major large geographic regions of the world. This is an important feature since it is the movement of populations from one geographic location to another that is the essential definer of migration. In addition, they have differing policies concerning their legal treatment of immigrants, with some making it less difficult for foreigners to be lawfully admitted into the country, while others have more restrictive entry policies. Lynch and Simon (2002) point out, for example, that "the [admission] policies followed in Australia, Canada and the United States are much more inviting. They allow relatively large numbers of persons in, do not impose excessive screening on those persons... The policies in these nations allow for a variety of reasons for admission including family reunification, economic needs of the nation, and refugee status" (73). The admission policies of France, though, are more restrictive. Lynch and Simon again note that "while France has fairly high rates of admission, it is almost entirely based on family reunification which can be seen as a way of screening and limiting new entries. Without a substantial number of new admissions, the volume of persons that can be admitted for purposes of family reunification must decline... So... it is not a policy that is designed to perpetuate a steady flow of immigrants into the host nation" (73-74).

Similarly, some of these six countries make it easier for legal immigrants to shake off their foreign status to become citizens, while others make it more burdensome. The naturalization policies of Australia, Canada and the United States, not surprisingly, are reasonably lenient (see Lynch and Simon 2002). The Canadian naturalization policy, for instance, states that applicants for naturalized citizenship must pay an application fee, be at least eighteen years of age, be a legal permanent resident, have lived in Canada for at least three out of the past four years from the day they apply, know either the English or French languages, not be charged or convicted of a crime, be familiar with the rights and responsibilities of Canadians and have some knowledge of Canadian history and geography (see Citizenship and Immigration Canada 2001).

The naturalization process in the Netherlands, meanwhile, is much more arduous. In addition to fee, residency (i.e., five years), age (i.e., eighteen and above), language (i.e., Dutch), knowledge, and lack of crime conviction requirements (which are all somewhat similar to the Canadian guidelines), the Netherlands naturalization process, besides being time consuming, also holds that applicants will be denied citizenship if they are a danger to the government or the environment of Holland (Dutch Consulate 2001). This last requirement is obviously a major difference between the Netherlands and the other countries discussed thus far. The exact meaning of what constitutes a "danger" to the government or the environment of Holland is not altogether clear. This rather vague requirement evidently grants much latitude to the naturalization office of the Netherlands.

In sum, although the data collected have some shortcomings, as a first exploration of the patterns of importation and exportation of foreign inmates, the data have revealed some challenging findings that deserve careful consideration, and certainly warrant further investigation. We next discuss our measures and results.

Measuring and Comparing Foreign-born Inmate Populations

Terminology. The first important distinction to be made is that between the *host* prison population and the *home* prison population. By host prison population we mean countries that house inmates who were born in a different country from the one in which they are currently incarcerated. By home prison population we mean the prison population of the inmate's own country of birth. Thus, American-born inmates who are housed in U.S. prisons are part of the home population. Mexican-born inmates who are housed in U.S. prisons are part of the host prison population. Mexican-born inmates who are housed in Mexican prisons are part of the home prison population.

Ideally, it would be preferable to compare foreign-born inmate *rates* between host countries and home countries, using as the base the population of the respective country of birth group. However, the availability of data on foreign-born populations is extremely limited in the countries under study. In fact, even obtaining the number of inmates by country of birth has been a major undertaking. The majority of countries either do not collect such information, or if they do, do not make the information available to the public or researchers.

Results

Eighty-eight percent of a possible 202 countries are represented in the foreign-born prison populations of the six countries reporting data on foreign-born inmates for this study. These are, of course, very incomplete data for the purpose of computing the numbers of foreign-born inmates throughout the world. One could reasonably expect that all countries of the world would be represented in foreign-born prison populations if they all reported such information. Given the impossibility of computing rates, two ways of comparing the raw numbers have been adopted. The first has been to compute the total numbers of foreign-born inmates across each of the six host countries. We consider the grand total of these foreign-born inmates to represent a "sample" of foreign-born inmates of the world. As noted above, the six countries providing data for this study are countries that both have a long historical tradition of immigration into their countries, and represent most major world geographic regions. They provide a reasonable rough guide as to the housing of foreign-born inmates throughout the world. Table 1 displays these totals according to region of place of birth. Percentages of the total sample of foreign-born inmates can then be computed to show the comparative distribution of foreign-born inmates according to region of origin, as seen in Figure 1. We can see from Table 1 and Figure 1 that the main regions of the world from which foreign-born inmates originate are Central America and Northern Africa. These two regions account for 49 percent and 19 percent respectively of all foreign-born inmates held in prisons in the six countries for which we have data. They are followed at some distance by Southern Europe (9%) and South America (7%). Examining each region at a time, we obtain a better picture of the movement of foreign-born inmates from feeder countries to recipient countries (see below).

Table 1: Number of Foreign-born Inmates Reported in Six Countries (USA, Canada, Italy, Australia, Netherlands and France) by Region of Origin

Region	Number of inmates
Central America	103,526
Northern Africa	39,987
Southern Europe	19,419
South America	13,886
Western Africa	5,613
South Eastern Asia	4,706
Eastern Europe	4,410
Western Europe	3,661
Central Africa	3,513
Northern Europe	2,941
European Asia	2,838
Eastern Asia	1,921
Central Asia	1,662
Western Asia	1,598
Oceania	1,433
Eastern Africa	826
North America	780
Southern Africa	489

EXPORTING AND IMPORTING CRIMINALITY 149

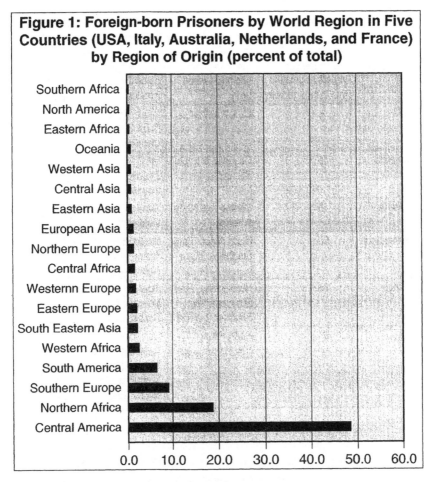

Figure 1: Foreign-born Prisoners by World Region in Five Countries (USA, Italy, Australia, Netherlands, and France) by Region of Origin (percent of total)

The percentages can also be computed to show the percentage of each individual host country's inmate population that is foreign, and from which country. This comparison is demonstrated in Table 2 and Figure 2. We can see there that the foreign-born inmate population in some countries, such as U.S.A., is only a tiny proportion of the country's home prison population, yet the U.S.A. accounts for a very high portion of the total of foreign-born inmates from our "world" sample. In contrast, Italy's home population is composed of more than half foreign-born, and it also accounts for a high proportion of inmates born in other regions. As we will note below, this applies particularly to those born in Albania, who account for a disproportionately high portion of the Italian prison population. In fact, it is possible to examine which countries are the main recipients of foreign-born inmate populations. These are summarized in Table 3.

Table 2: Proportions of Host Inmate Populations that are Foreign-born, and Their Origins

Host Country	Percentage of inmate population that is foreign born	Major regions of origin of foreign born	Top imports percent of total inmates	Number of Countries represented
USA	8	Central America	Mexico (5%), Cuba (1%), Unknown (2%)	170
Australia	16	Oceania, Europe, SE Asia	UK (5%), New Zealand (4%), Vietnam (3%)	9
Canada	5	Central and North America	Jamaica, USA, Vietnam	72
Netherlands	50	North Africa, East European Asia	Morocco (11%), Turkey (7%), Algeria (4%)	90
France	36	North Africa, East European Asia, Southern Europe	Algeria (9%), Morocco (7%), Tunisia (3%)	123
Italy	51	North Africa, Southern Europe	Morocco(11%), Yugoslavia (7%), Albania (6%), Tunisia (6%), Algeria (5%)	96

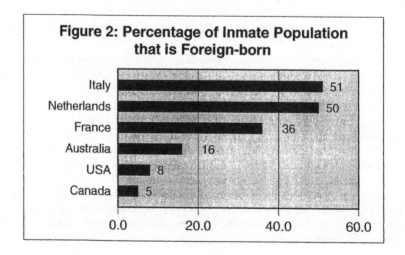

Figure 2: Percentage of Inmate Population that is Foreign-born

EXPORTING AND IMPORTING CRIMINALITY 151

Table 3: Major Recipient Countries of Foreign-born Inmates

Region of Origin	Major Recipient Countries Percent of Regional Emigrants	
	Country	Percent
Central America	USA	99
Northern Africa	Italy	58
	France	34
Southern Europe	Italy	74
	France	12
	USA, Australia, Netherlands	13
South America	USA	70
	Italy	16
	Netherlands, France	13
Western Africa	Italy	56
	France	31
	USA, Netherlands	13
South Eastern Asia	USA	77
	Australia	12
Eastern Europe	Italy	53
	France	22
	USA	19
	Netherlands, Canada	6
Western Europe	USA	60
	Italy	17
	France	15
	Netherlands	7
Central Africa	USA	62
	France	34
Northern Europe	Australia	42
	USA	36
	France	13
	Netherlands, Canada	7
European Asia	France	40
	Netherlands	35
	USA	14
	Italy, Australia, Canada	10
Eastern Asia	USA	72
	Netherlands	10
	France	8
	Italy	7
Central Asia	USA	37
	Italy	30
	Netherlands	15
	France	13
	Canada	5

Table 3 Continued

Western Asia	USA	31
	Italy	27
	France	16
	Australia	16
	Netherlands	9
Oceania	Australia	59
	USA	38
Eastern Africa	France	39
	Italy	36
	Netherlands	15
	USA	10
North America	USA	68
	Canada	11
	Australia	7
	Netherlands, France, Italy	15
Southern Africa	France	64
	Italy	20
	USA, Netherlands	16

Countries as "Importers" and "Exporters" of Foreign-born Inmates

How are the recipient country proportions related to the prison populations of the countries from which the foreign-born originate? While, as noted, we do not have rates with which to compare, we can look at foreign inmate populations as a percentage of the inmate population from whence the foreign-born inmates in the six reporting countries come. These are summarized in Figure 3; it shows the foreign-born inmate populations in host countries expressed as a percentage of the whole inmate population of that particular country. For example, in the case of Albania, the number of prisoners in Albania itself (i.e., the home prison population) in 1997 was 1,077. However, the number of Albanian inmates in foreign countries (i.e., the host countries) was 3,509. Thus, Albania's inmate population abroad is over 3 times higher than its inmate population at home. In addition, Italy carries the burden of the Albanian prison population, with a total of 3,391 Albanian-born prisoners.

Looking at the highly ranked countries that "export" their inmate population to other countries, we see that there is a group of ten countries, Jamaica, Suriname, Tonga, Mexico, Dominica, Virgin Islands (U.S.), Haiti, Guyana, Guam (U.S.), Dominican Republic, close to half of whose inmate populations are in foreign prisons. This group is followed by a second, larger group of countries who export a smaller number of inmates. The countries comprising this group are: American Samoa (U.S.), El Salvador, Cuba, Morocco, Algeria, Tunisia, Liechtenstein, Senegal, Antigua and Barbuda, St. Lucia, Bahamas,

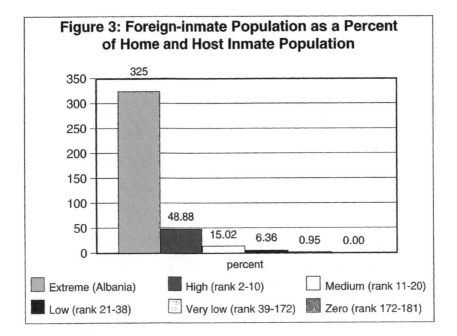

Figure 3: Foreign-inmate Population as a Percent of Home and Host Inmate Population

Cape Verde, Guernsey (U.K.), Barbados, Grenada, Colombia, Puerto Rico (U.S.), Trinidad and Tobago, Guatemala, New Zealand, and Western Samoa. The remaining countries have negligible numbers of inmates represented in foreign or host countries.

The home and host inmate populations have an interesting relationship. Some key factors contributing to high foreign-born inmate populations in a given country are both the proximity and number of immigrants in the host country. We see in Table 3, for example, that the U.S.A., being the closest geographically to Central America, is the major recipient of individuals who are born in that region. A closer look at movement from regions to particular host countries reveals the following:

From Central America: If we look at the individual countries, we see that Mexico exports its inmates to the U.S.A. In 1997, the inmate population of Mexico was 103,262. In that same year, there were over 50,000 Mexicans in U.S. prisons. Thus, if these inmates were housed in their own country, the number of inmates in Mexican prisons would increase by 50 percent. Major contributing nations to the U.S.A. foreign-born population were Cuba, Dominican Republic, Jamaica, El Salvador, Puerto Rico (U.S.), Haiti, Honduras, and Guatemala, followed in fewer numbers by most countries of Central America and the Caribbean.

From North America: The major contributor to the U.S.A. inmate population was Canada. Over 60 percent of foreign-born North Americans resided in

U.S. prisons, although the rest was mostly made up in even amounts across Australia, Netherlands, France, and Italy.

From South America: Over 70 percent of South American-born were housed in U.S. prisons. Major contributing countries were Peru, Guyana, Ecuador, Venezuela, Argentina, Brazil, and Chile.

Perhaps the most significant pattern of foreign-born inmate populations in terms of regions is the movement of populations from parts of the African Continent to European nations. If we take France, Italy and the Netherlands as representing West European nations, we see a clear pattern of high African-born representation in their inmate populations. Following from Table 3, these may be summarized, as follows:

From Central Africa: Thirty-four percent of Central African-born inmates were incarcerated in France. However, 62 percent of Central African inmates were also incarcerated in the U.S.A. The major African countries exporting criminality were Congo to the U.S.A. and the Democratic Republic of Congo to France.

From East Africa: France and Italy housed over 30 percent each of East African inmates. Somalia, Tanzania and Kenya were the main exporters to Italy, and Somalia, Madagascar and Mauritius were the main exporting countries to France.

From North Africa: The major recipients were Italy with over 50 percent of the North African inmates exported, and France receiving over 34 percent. The major exporting countries were Morocco, Algeria, and Tunisia to both countries.

From Southern Africa: The major recipients were France (64%) and Italy (20%), with France receiving the bulk of inmates from Angola, and Italy mainly from South Africa.

From Western Africa: The major recipients were again Italy (56%) and France (31%). For Italy the bulk of inmates were born in Nigeria, Senegal, Ghana, Ivory Coast and Mali. Major countries contributing to the French prison population were those listed for Italy, and in addition Cape Verde and Guinea.

From Central Asia: The major countries receiving inmates born in Central Asia are U.S.A. (37%), Italy (30%), Netherlands (15%) and France (13%). The major contributing countries were India, Iran, Pakistan and Afghanistan to the U.S. prison populations, and the same countries plus Iraq and Sri Lanka to Italy.

From Eastern Asia: The U.S.A. houses 72 percent of inmates born in Eastern Asia, inmates mainly come from China, the Republic of Korea, Japan, Hong Kong, and Taiwan.

From South East Asia: The U.S.A. and Australia, both Pacific nations, are recipients of the majority of South East Asian inmates, with 77 percent and 12 percent respectively. Major contributing nations were Vietnam (by far the largest contributor), Philippines, Laos, Cambodia, and Thailand. Vietnam, in fact, contributed a noticeable number of inmates to all countries surveyed.

From Western Asia: The U.S.A. (31%) and Italy (27%) were the main recipients of inmates born in Western Asia. The major feeder countries were Israel, Lebanon, Syria, and Jordan to the U.S.A., and the same countries except Lebanon to Italy.

From European Asia: France and the Netherlands accounted for over 70 percent of inmates from this area, with France receiving 40 percent and Netherlands 35 percent. The major contributing country of the region was Turkey.

From Eastern Europe: Italy, France, and the U.S.A. were the main recipients of inmates born in this region, with 53 percent, 22 percent, and 19 percent respectively. The major contributing countries were Rumania, Poland and Bulgaria to Italy, Rumania and Poland to France, and Poland, Hungary, Moldova and Rumania to the U.S.A.

From Northern Europe: We have mentioned two contributing factors to inmate foreign-born populations: the actual numbers of immigrants of the respective country, and the geographical proximity between the host and home country. Another factor clearly in play in regard to this region of the world as a source of foreign-born inmate population is historical proximity. The major recipients of inmates born in Northern Europe are the U.S.A. (36%) and Australia (42%). While the U.S.A. is comparatively close to Northern Europe, Australia is as far away as a country could be. The explanation must be tied to Australia's historical relationship with Europe, particularly its close relationship with the United Kingdom. The major contributing countries of Northern Europe to the foreign-born inmate populations in the U.S.A. and Australia were England and Wales, Ireland, and Scotland.

From Southern Europe: Italy was the major recipient of foreign-born inmates (excluding Italians of course) from this region, housing 74 percent of foreign-born inmates from this region, followed by France with 12 percent. The major contributing countries were Albania, Yugoslavia, and Croatia.

From Western Europe: The U.S.A. accounted for over 60 percent of the inmates born in Western Europe, followed at a distance by Italy and France with around 15 percent each. The main feeder countries were Germany, Netherlands and France.

From Oceania: Supporting the proximity hypothesis, the major receiving countries were Australia (59%) and the U.S.A. (38%). The major contributing countries were New Zealand to Australia and Guam to the U.S.A.

Overall trends suggest that most movements of foreign-born to other countries have been from region to region. Only in two instances has the movement been from or among countries within the region: these were Oceania, in which the major portion of foreign-born inmates in Australia were New Zealanders, and the portion of inmates in Italy from other countries of Southern Europe.

Are countries with high prison rates likely to export their "excess" criminality to other countries? Durkheim famously argued, after all, that crime is not only inevitable, but that it is also "a factor in public health, an integral part of all healthy societies... once this... surprise has been overcome, however, it is not difficult to find reasons explaining this normality and at the same time conforming it" (1962: 67). In particular, Durkheim maintains that crime provides three benefits to society. Besides reinforcing the social solidarity of society, crime and punishment also educate members of society as to the moral boundaries of that society as well as allow for innovation and progress to occur. Durkheim cautions, however, that the normality of crime only exists "provided that it attains and does not exceed, for each social type, a certain level" (1962: 66). Applying Durkheim's paradigm to the global level, a society that has too much or too little crime would be abnormal and in need of correction.

We can give some rough answers to this question from the data presented so far. One might expect, for example, that the U.S.A., with one of the highest inmate populations in the world, would be a major exporter of its product to other countries. This prediction is not only based upon Durkheim's thesis, but is also consistent with simple economics: countries that are high producers of products are the higher exporters, and those that produce very low amounts of a particular product should be high importers. At the opposite end of the spectrum, Albania, being a very low producer of home prison population, should be a high importer of inmates. This is clearly not the case, as we have seen above. However, among the countries that are high importers, such as Italy, France, and Netherlands, we can see that the hypothesis is borne out: they have relatively low incarceration rates compared to the rest of the world, especially the western world, so they import a higher number of foreign-born inmates. An import export model consistent with Durkheim's thesis seems worthy of further investigation for the high import countries, even though overall, the model is not supported by the data. If we examine the home prison populations of countries and compare them to the foreign-born prison populations of the home country, there is no correlation between the two sets of data (Pearson r = .03). Examining the patterns of foreign-born in individual countries helps clarify the picture. We have, of course, strained the meaning of the terms "import" and "export" but they do serve the purpose of highlighting the considerable discrepancies in the real economic burdens shouldered by host countries, in contrast to feeder countries.

Discussion

Only tentative conclusions can be made given the very limited amount of data available. However, some of the findings are sufficiently clear as to warrant further in-depth study of this topic and the collection of more data. The following observations are reasonable conclusions from the data available:

1. Given the small number of countries reporting, it is intriguing that, if one includes the numbers of a country's citizens who are housed in foreign prisons as part of that original country's inmate population, only a small number of countries and regions account for a high proportion of that home country's

inmate population. The most striking example is Albania, where there are twice as many Albanian-born inmates residing in foreign prisons (and most of them in Italy) than there are in Albania itself. Similarly, close to half of Mexico's inmates are actually housed in North American prisons, mostly in the U.S.A. And one should add as far as the U.S.A. is concerned, this is a gross underestimate, since more than two-thirds of the United States (including California and Texas which both incarcerate large numbers of Mexican-born inmates) do not report inmate data by country of birth.

2. With the possible exception of Italy, foreign-born inmates tended to come from regions outside the region within which the host country was located, though in most cases from regions that were proximate. For example, Central America was a feeder for the U.S.A., North Africa for Southern and Western Europe, and Southern Europe for Western Europe. The only clear exceptions were Africa to the U.S.A., and Europe to Australia. Historical rather than geographical factors obviously play a part in this pattern.

3. The percentages of each home country's inmate populations that are foreign-born vary remarkably, as can be seen in Figure 2. Why is this? For the U.S.A. the simple answer is that the U.S. prison population is so high compared to the rest of the world that the number of foreign-born inmates is comparatively minuscule. Yet, we have seen that the portion of foreign-born inmates of the "world" of foreign-born inmates is accounted for to a substantial degree by the U.S.A. If we adopt the hypothesis that it is the size of the home prison population that affects the comparative portion of foreign-born prison population, we may look at the opposite end of the spectrum, that of Albania. This country has a very low home prison population, as we noted earlier. Yet, it exports a very high number of inmates to other countries, particularly Italy. Perhaps the reason for this is that the low prison population in Albania is a function of informal sanctions that occur in that country, particularly in regard to violent crimes which may often be dealt with through feuding subcultures and vendettas (Marongiu and Newman 1987). In other words, serious violent crime is not dealt with by the authorities, and since violent crime is usually the main crime for which the serious punishment of prison is used, we would expect Albania to have a low prison rate. We would also expect that the subcultural ethos of vendetta would be exported to other countries, and there result in more crime. Hence, the Albanians are found in higher proportions in foreign prisons.

Policy Implications

The high portions of foreign-born prisoners found in Italy, France, and the Netherlands, compared to Canada, Australia, and the U.S.A. raises a number of important issues. Since the subcultural explanation does not hold for at least France and the Netherlands, in terms of their having low prison populations, other explanations are required. On the surface, one is inclined to ask whether foreign-born populations are being selected at a higher rate than native populations. Is this a function of there simply being more persons of foreign birth in these countries than in other host countries? This is not likely, since the U.S.A. has a very high foreign-born population compared to France, Italy, and Netherlands. There appear to be only three explanations, all of which implicate a number of policy concerns.

1. Convict Prone: One possibility is that the foreign-born populations in these host countries are disposed for whatever reason to committing the kinds of crimes that get them sent to prison. Accepting the conclusion that foreign populations are "convict prone" (not unusual, since many visa or entry applications to countries require individuals to answer a question concerning their past criminal convictions), could very well lead to more restrictive immigration laws and policies. For instance, in a number of countries, extreme nationalists, and in some cases racists, have proposed to prohibit all immigration in order to prevent crime. The French writer Jean Raspail, in fact, wrote a highly controversial, characterized by many as racist, novel entitled *Camp of the Saints*, in the early 1970s. Raspail's work takes the immigrant as criminal allegation one step further. Rather than just painting immigrants as garden-variety criminals, Raspail sketches a picture where immigrants are used as soldiers to overthrow destination governments from within. His book describes a situation where nations of the third world encourage many of their citizens to migrate to France in order overwhelm it. Raspail writes in the introduction to the 1985 French edition that: "*Camp of the Saints* is a novel that anticipates a situation which seems plausible today and foresees a threat that no longer seems unbelievable to anyone: it describes the peaceful invasion of France, and then of the West, by a third world burgeoned into multitudes" (xiii). Opponents of immigration frequently rely upon this book in formulating their arguments in favor of banning immigration.

Another related suggestion, expounded by some ultranationalists and racists, is a form of "national profiling." This policy seeks to import immigrants from "good" countries (i.e., countries whose émigrés commit few crimes), while severely limiting, if not barring altogether, immigrants from "bad" countries who are characterized as unneeded criminals. The national and global ramifications of such a policy promise to be both dramatic and controversial as is evident in the debate on racial profiling which has recently convulsed the American political scene. Another proposal considers the role of subterfuge. At times countries have allowed entry to criminal immigrants under false pretenses, mistakenly assuming that they were law abiding. Once again, one way to confront this would be for countries to design and imple-. ment better screening and enforcement mechanisms at their national borders. To be most effective, such a policy would require the cooperation of both home and host countries.

Finally, if the conclusion is drawn that certain segments of the foreign-born population are crime prone, then it might be argued that home countries should be held responsible for their actions. Accordingly, home countries would be financially liable for the costs associated with the incarceration of their crimi-

EXPORTING AND IMPORTING CRIMINALITY 159

nal émigrés in the host country. The consequences of such a policy could be quite important for both the home and host countries. Besides possibly disrupting foreign relations which were close or less than friendly, such a policy could significantly affect the financial condition of both the home and host countries. Assuming for the moment that home countries like Mexico or Albania would agree to pay the incarceration costs of their citizens being held abroad (in the United States and Italy respectively), their budgets for incarceration would double or triple. Conversely, such a policy would greatly benefit those host countries that house large percentages of foreign-born individuals in their prisons. In the case of Italy and the Netherlands, for example, such a policy would reduce expenditures devoted to incarceration by fifty percent.

2. *Social Conditions*: A second scenario concludes that elements of the social and political arrangements in the host country are conducive to immigrant crime. Immigrants, after all, not only often face steep challenges in their daily lives, but are frequently treated as standing outside mainstream society (see for example, Australian Department of Immigration and Multicultural Affairs 2001: 5; Encyclopedia Americana: Citizenship 2001; Lynch and Simon 2002). Sun and Reed (1995) explain that: "Migrant workers are likely to inhabit the worst housing in the poorest areas of inner cities... segmentation of the labor market in host countries impedes foreigner's upward mobility... That immigrants must struggle with many social maladies found in run down urban areas has furnished the perception that they rank high in crime and delinquency, and that this phenomenon is directly related to their status as immigrants" (233). Furthermore, immigrants are often accused of taking scarce jobs and housing away from more deserving native-born citizens, and may also endure racism and hate crimes. In many cases, the fact that one is foreign-born may be all that is necessary to engender hostile emotions in the native-born population. That an immigrant is a naturalized citizen may only increase the antipathy felt by many towards him or her. For some social movements and groups (especially right-wing ones), citizenship may be viewed as a matter of blood as opposed to the American concept of citizenship based on culture and values. From this perspective, naturalized citizens may be considered by many to be "inferior foreigners."

Thus, rather than viewing the host country as an unwitting victim of the crimes committed by the undesirables of other countries, this perspective draws the opposite conclusion. Law-abiding migrants are "transformed," in some host countries, into criminals due to the terrible conditions that they must endure. Furthermore, some observers have pointed to cases where deported migrant criminals have created criminal organizations and unleashed crimes which were heretofore unknown to the home country. Some Central American immigrants to the United States, for example, who were convicted of felonies, completed their sentences, and were repatriated to their native lands, have created criminal gangs that had never before existed in their home countries. For this reason, some contend that the host country should be held financially responsible for the damage caused to the home country. Following the argument raised in the "Crime Prone Section," host countries would be required to assume the incarceration costs of these émigrés in the home countries. Once again, the same foreign policy and financial concerns would apply.

Another solution might be for host governments to eliminate the terrible conditions facing migrants. Social programs could be designed which enhanced opportunities for foreigners. More specifically, programs to increase the educational and job prospects available to foreigners could be devised. In addition, exposing the native-born population to a multicultural perspective, could lead to a decrease in antiforeign sentiment. Finally, crime preventive policies, such as those outlined by Clarke (2002), could also be developed.

3. Official Practices: A final related possibility is that there is bias operating in the host countries' administrative, legal, or criminal justice systems. Such discrimination could either result in higher portions of persons originating from foreign countries being selected, processed and sent to prison by the criminal justice system, or create (and perhaps reinforce) the social conditions conducive to crime commission. Those countries in which foreign inmates account for nearly half their inmate populations would seem to have a lot to answer for. The very high rates of foreign-born incarceration raise questions. Clearly more research is needed to determine whether foreign-born populations commit crimes at such a high rate. The answer to this question brings with it serious policy implications. If discrimination within the criminal justice system is a factor, then policies to remove such practices are the obvious solution.

Besides possible systematic discrimination against foreigners in the criminal justice system, is the prospect that the wide variety of legal restrictions imposed upon foreigners by many host governments creates a cruel environment in which crime is more likely to flourish. As a result, some argue that much of the current "legal discrimination" directed against foreigners which reinforces their outsider status should be repealed. Such a solution would again have major consequences since currently there are a myriad of distinctions made by most governments between citizens and foreigners.

The hurdles faced by noncitizens are, perhaps, most vividly illustrated at international airports around the globe. Individuals who are not citizens of the destination country, and who lack the necessary entry papers, are usually denied entry and deported while all other individuals are admitted. Citizens of the destination country normally go to a special line for passport inspections, while tourists and noncitizens generally have to wait in a different, more time consuming line. The Australian office in charge of naturalization, in fact, clearly states on its web site that one benefit of Australian citizenship is that "you hold an Australian passport, which can make it easier to re-enter the country if you leave to travel overseas" (Australian Department of Immigration and Multicultural Affairs 2001: 5). The burdens placed on foreigners only increase upon their entry into the destination country.

In most countries around the world, tourists or legal immigrants whose visas expire may be subject to deportation. In the U.S.A. not only can illegal

EXPORTING AND IMPORTING CRIMINALITY 161

aliens be deported, but, as we just noted, even legal immigrants, who are not citizens, may be deported if they commit a felony. In many countries, moreover, noncitizens are denied the right to vote, run for office, serve in that nation's armed forces, or work in certain public service occupations (see for example, Australian Department of Immigration and Multicultural Affairs 2001: 5). Perhaps more fundamentally, legal immigrants, unlike native-born citizens, are not automatically granted citizenship. Instead, legal immigrants must meet a number of clearly defined requirements before obtaining citizenship. For instance, in Germany, until recently, an individual who was born of Turkish parents in Germany was still legally classified as a foreigner.

In a number of countries, immigrants are subject to internal regulations that are not applicable to the native-born population. Lynch and Simon (2002) write that "In Germany... guest workers must apply for residence and work permits. These permits must be renewed upon change of employment or residence... These episodic checks give immigration authorities the chance to intrude into the lives of immigrants. Although the likelihood of interference may be small, there is the chance that the required permits may not be renewed and the foreign national will be required to leave. This uncertainty reinforces the perception that foreigners are outsiders" (75-76). While the United States does not have such internal procedures in place, it does have other regulations that at times severely hamper the lives of immigrants. During the Mariel Boat lift, the American government classified the Cuban émigrés as parolees which is a "temporary admission status granted to aliens who appear to be inadmissible" (Clark 1991: 5). Most of the arriving Cubans, after processing procedures, were released into the community. However, "the U.S. Immigration and Naturalization Service refused to admit approximately two-thousand Mariels, deeming them unfit due to mental illness or criminal records" (Clark 1991: 5). These Cuban detainees, although officially detained under civil law, were actually under preventive detention and many of them were ultimately "incarcerated for at least six years" (Clark 1991: 7) even though they had not been convicted of committing any crime on American soil. Clark explains that this policy received strong support from the American public. It would be hard to imagine a similar policy being successfully implemented against native-born Americans.

Many Western European countries, due to economic factors, imported foreign workers in the Post World War Two era. Sun and Reed (1995) describe the "harsh" restrictions placed upon these migrants. Switzerland, for instance, forbade these workers from switching occupations, bringing over family members, or staying long term in the country. All of this was done in an effort "to block permanent settlement" of these migrants in Switzerland (Sun and Reed 1995: 231). Similarly, a number of countries, have actually encouraged immigrants to leave their country. Both the Netherlands and France, for example, have in the past encouraged certain categories of immigrants, to leave the country and not return (see Lynch and Simon 2002; Reed and Sun 1995).

162   *NEWMAN, FREILICH, AND HOWARD*

Distinctions are not only made between legal immigrants and citizens, at times even naturalized citizens are treated differently from native-born citizens. In the United States, for instance, a naturalized citizen is ineligible to be President or Vice President; only native-born citizens may hold these offices. In addition, in the United States naturalized citizens, unlike native citizens, may have their citizenship revoked for certain activities: "Naturalized citizens who subsequently are believed to have been members of allegedly subversive organizations sometimes have been charged with falsifying their original applications for citizenship; in these cases they have been subjected to possible revocation of citizenship and deportation. ... The purpose of these provisions is to deny U.S. citizenship to the Alien who does not transfer his permanent allegiance to the United States in good faith. In practice, however, they impose restrictions on the naturalized citizen that do not apply to the native-born" (Encyclopedia Americana: Citizenship 2001: 6).

Clearly the situations of migrants are very complex, and vary widely from country to country. The interrelationship between official and unofficial policies of governments with the daily circumstances of immigrants obviously needs much closer examination. Many countries already complain of the burden of unwanted immigrants knocking at their doors. These same countries also, however, benefit in significant ways from the exploitation of cheap immigrant labor. We have also seen that while some cast blame on home countries for dumping their criminals elsewhere, others castigate host countries for converting law-abiding migrants into criminals. The data of this study, as limited as they are, nevertheless add to the growing concern of all countries of the world regarding the effects of uncontrolled migration on host populations. For example, the spread of diseases, such as tuberculosis through migration, threatens to bring back nearly eradicated diseases. The present data suggest that criminality may spread in the same way, and like tuberculosis, its rise or fall in the host country will depend on the country's official and unofficial policies in dealing with immigrant populations.

NOTES

1. Contact information: Graeme Newman, School of Criminal Justice, Draper Hall, State University of New York at Albany, 135 Western Avenue, Albany, NY 12222. Phone: 518-442-5223. Email: harrowhest@aol.com

2. Contact information: Joshua D. Freilich, Room 520T, Department of Sociology, John Jay College of Criminal Justice, 899 10th Avenue, New York, NY 10019. Phone: 212-237-8668. Email: jfreilich@jjay.cuny.edu

3. Gregory J. Howard, Department of Sociology, Sangren Hall, Western Michigan University, Kalamazoo, MI 49008. Phone: 616-387-3595. Email: gregory.howard@wmich.edu

4. Wisconsin, Missouri, New Jersey, New York, North Carolina, Maine, Maryland, Kansas, Oklahoma, Georgia, Connecticut, Oregon, Nevada, New Mexico, Ohio, aliens only.

REFERENCES

Australian Department of Immigration and Multicultural Affairs. 2001. *How to apply for Australian citizenship.* [Online] http://www.citizenship.gov.au/how.htm. (Accessed September 10).

Citizenship and Immigration Canada. 2001. *How to become a Canadian citizen.* [Online] http://www.cic.gc.ca/english/citizen/howto-e.html. (Accessed September 10).

Clark, D. 1991. *The Mariel Cuban problem.* Albany, NY: New York State Department of Correctional Services.

Clarke, R.V. 2002. "Protecting immigrants from victimization: The scope for situational crime prevention." Pp. 103-120 in J.D. Freilich, G. Newman, S.G. Shoham, and M. Addad. (Eds). 2002. *Migration, culture conflict and crime.* Brookfield: Ashgate.

Durkheim, E. 1962. (Eighth Edition). *The rules of sociological method.* Chicago: University of Chicago.

Dutch Consulate. 2001. *Personal Correspondence.* September 10.

Encyclopedia Americana. 2001. Citizenship. [Online] http://gi.grolier.com/presidents/ea/side/citizen/html. (Accessed September 10).

Freilich, J.D., G. Newman, S.G. Shoham, and M. Addad. (Eds). 2002. *Migration, culture conflict and crime.* Brookfield: Ashgate.

Killian, C. 2002. "Bicultural competence: A means to crime reduction among the children of immigrants?" Pp. 121-130 in J.D. Freilich, G. Newman, S.G. Shoham, and M. Addad. (Eds). 2002. *Migration, culture conflict and crime.* Brookfield: Ashgate.

Lynch, J.P., and R. Simon. 2002. "A comparative assessment of criminal involvement among nations and natives across seven nations." Pp. 69-88 in J.D. Freilich, G. Newman, S.G. Shoham, and M. Addad. (Eds). 2002. *Migration, culture conflict and crime.* Brookfield: Ashgate.

Marongiu, P., and G. Newman. 1987. *Vengeance: The fight against injustice.* New Jersey: Littlefield Adams.

Newman, G. (Ed). 1999. *Global report on crime and justice.* New York: Oxford University Press.

Newman, G., and G.J. Howard. 1999. "Introduction: Data sources and their use." In G. Newman, (Ed). 1999. *Global report on crime and justice* (pp. 1-23). New York: Oxford University Press.

Raspail, J. 1985. *The camp of the saints.* Petoskey, MI: The Social Contract Press.

Sheu, C.J. 2002. "Confucianism as a control theory explanation of crime among overseas Chinese in southeast Asia." Pp. 297-322 in J.D. Freilich, G. Newman, S.G. Shoham, and M. Addad. (Eds). 2002. *Migration, culture conflict and crime.* Brookfield: Ashgate.

Sun, H., and J. Reed. 1995. "Migration and crime in Europe." *Social Pathology,* 1(3): 228-248.

Yeager, M.G. 1996. *Immigrants and criminality: A meta survey.* Ottowa, Canada: Ministry of Citizenship and Immigration, Government of Canada.

[4]

Policy Paradox:
Implications of U.S. Drug
Control Policy for Jamaica

By MARLYN J. JONES

ABSTRACT: U.S. drug control policies impose supply reduction targets on source and transit nations without regard for their social, economic, or political environments. Simultaneously, immigration policies deport drug felons to these countries. This article advances the argument that these policies have displaced responsibility for U.S. crime problems. As a result, there is displacement of criminal activities to areas of least resistance, with drug transit nations being disproportionately affected. The article addresses, in part, the paucity of drug policy literature on the Caribbean drug transit region. It discusses the nexus between U.S. drug and immigration policies and the resulting consequences for Jamaica, a drug transit country. Jamaica is of special interest because of its long-standing presence on the U.S. drug policy agenda and its stereotyping in journalistic discussions.

Marlyn J. Jones is a criminologist at California State University, Sacramento, where she serves as assistant professor in the Division of Criminal Justice. Her research interests include Caribbean criminology, policy analysis, and issues of race and gender.

THE perception that ethnics and foreigners are primarily responsible for America's drug problems creates a nexus between drug and immigration policies. This nexus materializes as a dominant policy issue between the United States and its western hemispheric neighbors. This happens because the U.S. government considers illicit drugs and illegal immigration terrorist enterprises that undermine its national security.

Deportation has emerged as the panacea for drug and crime problems. Consequently, individuals, many of whom were convicted on drug-related offences, are being deported to drug-producing and/or transit nations that must be constantly cognizant of U.S.-imposed drug policy targets. The issue for U.S. policy consideration is how to manage tradeoffs between these goals. Instead of asking why the United States should keep deportable felons, I suggest that this question should be revised. Rather, one should ask whether the United States is achieving its articulated goals. And even if the goals are being achieved, are the consequences of the policy unjustifiable? Herein I argue that the supply reduction goals are not being achieved and the underlying premises of the supply reduction policy are unrealistic and unrealizable. A primary result is the displacement of drug-related crime and violence into, and the exacerbation of economic problems in, areas of least resistance.

U.S. DRUG POLICY

A basic objective of U.S. counternarcotics policy is to bolster political will in the key source and transit countries. The intent is to prevent drug interests from becoming entrenched. As stated in the 2000 *International Narcotics Control Strategy Report* (INCSR) (http://www.state.gov/g/inl/rls/nrcrpt/2000/index.cfm?docid=886),

In those nations where political leaders have had the courage to sacrifice short-term economic and political considerations in favor of the long-term national interest, we have seen the drug trade falter. And where political will has wavered, we have seen the drug syndicates flourish and corruption set in.

Consequently, supply reduction at the source has become the cornerstone of a U.S. drug policy that also advocates the creation of a drug-free America by 2007. This mandate was reenforced by the United Nations General Assembly Special Session on Drugs in its 1998 declaration for a drug-free world by 2008.

Two of the four primary assumptions of the drug policy about supply reduction at the source are the following:

1. Production and distribution of illicit-drugs in the source zone can be controlled and reduced by appropriate crop control, economic development, legal and institutional reforms, international cooperation, and demand reduction activities.

2. Political, economic and social instability in the countries of the source and transit zones will not prevent host governments from pursuing effective drug control efforts. (Performance Management Evaluation 2000, Appendix E-109)

U.S. DRUG CONTROL POLICY AND JAMAICA 119

FIGURE 1
FIVE-POINT GROWER-TO-USER CONTINUUM

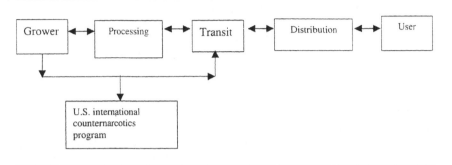

The INCSR also states that supply reduction initiatives focus on critical points along a five-point grower-to-user chain linking the consumer in the United States to the grower in a source country (see Figure 1).

A primary supply reduction goal is to prevent drugs from entering the United States. While this is a noble and worthwhile gesture, because the international counternarcotics program emphasizes the first three links, success in curtailing the entry of drugs into the United States will have a disproportionate effect at the terminating or transit point. Yet despite a plethora of drug policy literature focusing on source countries, little if any information currently exists on drug policy consequences at transit points. It becomes important therefore to assess the feasibility of U.S. drug policy assumptions and evaluate the imposition of antidrug targets at transit zones.

Failure to achieve U.S. drug control targets has a range of consequences, such as decertification. Certification is the U.S. government's annual assessment of whether governments of major drug-producing countries and transit zones have cooperated fully with the United States. The certification process also assesses whether countries have taken adequate steps on their own to meet the goals and objectives of the 1988 United Nations drug convention. Noncomplying countries may be decertified. Decertification involves the withdrawal of all but humanitarian and antinarcotic aid and the withholding of U.S. vote from international funding agencies such as the International Monetary Fund. Decertification has economic consequences; however, supply reduction targets are implemented without regard for the social, political, and economic environment in which these societies operate. The supply reduction assumptions also incorporate the supposition that the United Nations will not change the schedule for drugs. Cumulatively, the impositions and suppositions lead one to question whether they impose undue hardship on the targeted countries.

The 2000 INCSR states that in Colombia, which produces the bulk of illicit narcotics entering the United States, coca cultivation has expanded, efficiency in extracting cocaine from the coca leaf has increased, and narco-political alliances have been strengthened. The Clinton administration allocated $1.3 billion in assistance[1] to Colombia's antidrug efforts. The Bush administration renamed it the Andean Initiative (White House 2000). Fiscal year 2002 budget now requests $882 million for the Andean region, with half earmarked for Colombia (Bureau of Western Hemispheric Fact Sheet 2001). Will these initiatives in Colombia lead to displacement and thereby exacerbate problems in neighboring countries?

DISPLACEMENT

Displacement refers to an empirical phenomenon that implies that efforts to suppress criminality result in compensating behavior. Accordingly, changes occur when there is increased law enforcement directed at one area. Gabor (1981) suggested that crime displacement, or adjustments to circumvent preventive measures, can occur along three dimensions—spatial, temporal, or qualitative. These involve a mass shift in criminal activity from one type of crime to another or from one geographical area to another.

The drug control arena exhibits a high degree of displacement, such as shifts in the method of operation, changes in geographical areas of operation, or criminal movement away from drug-related activities. Flexibility in trafficking and distribution routes contributes to

geographical displacement. Smith (1992, 13) noted that during the 1980s, increased risk of apprehension in the Caribbean led the Colombian cartels to move transit routes from Florida to Mexico. The *National Drug Control Strategy* (Executive Office of the President 1997, 1998, 1999, 2000, 2001) also acknowledges this flexibility, stating that traffickers often switch routes and modes of transportation. What, if any, will be the current displacement consequences?

Arganaras (1997) identified three main harmful effects of previous U.S. counternarcotics policy in Bolivia, a source country. These included the institutionalization of a permanent army of unwaged laborers, the militarization of law enforcement, and the devaluation of political goods in the formal democracy. Craig (1987), in an assessment of drug-producing states, also found social, economic, and political consequences of illicit narcotics control for the source countries. These include violence within the country, corruption at all levels, and economic effects that had penetrated many aspects of the society. Political consequences were most evident in the government's inability to control outlying areas and loss of legitimacy for failure to control such trafficking or to enforce the rule of law within the country (Craig 1987, 2).

JAMAICA AS A U.S. FOREIGN (DRUG) POLICY CONCERN

Early drug policy literature identified Jamaica as one of three primary sources of marijuana entering the United States. By 1986, Jamaica, with Belize, Mexico, and Colombia, was listed among the four Caribbean Basin territories that supplied 90 percent of all the marijuana imported into the United States (Maingot 1989, 1994; McDonald 1988; Executive Office of the President 1998; Stone 1991). The INCSR currently designates Jamaica as a major transit point for cocaine entering the United States from South America. U.S. customs also notes that Jamaica is the embarkation point of the largest number of passengers arrested with drugs at U.S. airports. In addition, the Immigration and Naturalization Service and the Drug Enforcement Administration (n.d.) allege that Jamaican drug gangs (termed *posses*) are involved in criminal activities within the United States. Immigration and Naturalization Service statistics indicate that the island is one of the top ten countries for illegal immigrants and fifth for aliens deported from the United States. Consequently, Jamaica, the largest English-speaking Caribbean island, is an excellent case for examining the feasibility of U.S. drug policy assumptions about achieving antidrug targets.

JAMAICA'S SOCIAL, ECONOMIC, AND POLITICAL ENVIRONMENT

Crime trends can be seen as reflectors of social problems within a society. Crime and violence in Jamaica have become of increasing concern both internally and externally. The perception of Jamaica as violent is evident in media reports while the internal reality is reflected in the island's homicides, violent crime rates, and gun-related incidents. These, along with fear of crime, are escalating, and social unrest is occurring more frequently. The consequences for the island have been, and continue to be, devastating, with tourism, the primary foreign exchange earner, being most vulnerable.[2] Because this industry is vulnerable to crime and U.S. State Department travel advisories, violence has significant repercussions on Jamaica's social, economic, and political environments.

LAW ENFORCEMENT AND POLITICAL EXPLANATIONS FOR JAMAICA'S CRIME RATE

The growth of violence is considered the most dramatic manifestation of a decline in Jamaica's social environment. Over the years, a number of Jamaican commissions, councils, task forces, and reports have had the country's crime and violence as their focus.

The Wolfe Report (Wolfe 1993) emerged from public concern over violent upsurges throughout Jamaica between 1991 and 1992. It was constituted to advise on appropriate strategies consistent with the pursuit of justice in the maintenance of law and order (p. 99). The Wolfe Report identified fifteen factors classifiable as social, economic, political, psychological, and administrative that contribute to Jamaica's crime situation. These include problems with the security forces, intolerable and inhumane prison conditions, and a high percentage of foreign female prisoners convicted of drug felonies.

The Wolfe Report recommended implementing recommendations from previous task forces to ameliorate the causes of crime.

CRIME IN JAMAICA

No single factor can adequately account for increased violence in Jamaica. Harriott (1996) noted that Jamaica has become a highly criminogenic society characterized by, among other factors, pervasive criminality that manifests as "disregard for law across all social classes and a developed well-integrated underground economy" (p. 79). Although the violence has changed qualitatively, it has become central, institutionalized, and embedded in different aspects of the national life (Harriott 1996, 80). In the past, political violence and social and economic arrangements were often profiled as possible causes.[3] Violence in Jamaica was of two basic types: geographical and political (Gay and Marquart 1993). The first existed between residents of communities of the corporate areas of Kingston and St. Andrew that differed politically. The second centered on election or other political-party–related concerns.

POLITICAL ENVIRONMENT

Academics and journalists have long documented an intricate connection between politics and violence in Jamaica. Allegedly, politicians imported and distributed guns into poverty-stricken garrison communities to intimidate and coerce community members into party alliance. Several incidents reinforce this belief. These include poignant examples of Jamaican politicians who over the years have attended events such as funerals of individuals of questionable character. These events have generated much controversy within the Jamaican society.

The National Committee on Political Tribalism (Ministry of National Security and Justice 1997) was established "to consider and recommend practical steps to reduce Jamaica's political tensions and violence" (p. 2). *Political tribalism,* as defined by Blackman (1992), refers to adherence to a political party based on emotional commitment and irrespective of any policy-related or ideological considerations. A manifestation of political tribalism is the use of violence in political activities. The Tribalism Report reiterated the findings of the Wolfe Report and also noted that the high inflow of guns from the United States contributes to Jamaica's crime problems.

In the past, political tribalism and the culture of violence were used to explain increases in Jamaica's crime and violence. Several sources now posit that trade in guns and hard drugs have replaced political tribalism as primary causes of Jamaica's crime (Gunst 1988; Small 1995; Stone 1991). Political and law enforcement personnel attribute current resurgence in Jamaica's violent crime to two main phenomena: deportations from America and "new levels of criminality spurred by international dimensions . . . dedicated to overwhelm our security forces and any institutions which stand in their way" (Crime the target 2001).

DEPORTATION

In 1998, the first full year after implementation of legislation to effect expedited deportation, more than 170,000 individuals were deported from the United States—up from 69,226 in 1996 and 1,000 in 1986. Of the 171,154 deportations in 1998, 56,011 had criminal convictions, with 47 percent having drug convictions (U.S. Department of Justice n.d.-a, n.d.-b). Most countries to which individuals are deported evince underdevelopment, deteriorating economy, and high levels of unemployment.

In 1998, U.S. deportations increased 85 percent over the 1994 totals, but the total proportion of criminals dropped from 66 percent in 1994 to 32.5 percent in 1998. Between 1990 and 1998, more than 12,000 persons were deported to Jamaica, with 71 percent or 8,626 arriving from the United States. Of this number, only 11 percent or 989 were illegal residents. Although criminals comprised only 32.5 percent of persons deported from the United States in 1998, approximately 77 percent of the 1,483 Jamaicans deported from the United States had criminal convictions. Only 16 percent (239 persons) were categorized as illegal aliens; the remainder had criminal convictions, with 49 percent (724 persons) convicted for possession of illegal drugs and 7 percent (116 persons) for illegal possession of firearms. Other categories of offences include robbery, wounding and assault, murder/manslaughter, rape and indecent assault, kidnapping, and money laundering.

Reports consistently cite deportees' contribution to violent crimes in Jamaica. Official sources note that these individuals return with a bag of tricks learned in the United States. Justification for attributing increasing violence to deportees is that current incidents such as carjacking, extortions, dismemberment, and drive-by shootings are not typical of earlier activities. Instead, these acts are part of U.S. drug-related activities and the emergence of American-style violent crime gangs.

A correlation between Jamaican crime trends and deportations indicates that major crimes, especially homicides, rapes, carnal abuse, robberies, and gun-related incidents, have increased concurrently with the commencement of mass deportations to Jamaica (Jamaica Constabulary Force 1996, 1997, 1998a, 1998b, 1999, 2000). Reports of deportee involvement in the Jamaican crime scene published by the *Jamaica Gleaner Online* for 21 June 1999 (Nation at risk 1999) and repeated on 29 June 1999 (Monitoring deportees 1999) assert that from June 1997 to January 1999, deportees were implicated in 600 murders, 1,700 armed robberies, 900 rapes, 150 shootouts with the police, 200 cases of extortion, 3 cases of murdering witnesses, and 10 cases of arson. It is important to note, however, that without empirical studies, the language used says that deportees are "implicated" rather than "responsible for" these crimes.

GUNS

The international world was recently privy to scenes of gunmen engaging Jamaican police in gun-fire.[4] The entry of guns into Jamaican society is a primary factor in the increase in violence. Between 1995 and 1999, guns were used in approximately 65 percent of all homicides, 50 percent of all robberies, and 22 percent of rape/carnal abuse. Customs and the police have seized many caches of guns, with semiautomatic and submachine weapons now replacing revolvers (Edwards 1999). Of the confiscations by the Contraband Enforcement Team, all but one piece was loaded in a United States port (Edwards 1999, 30).

The Jamaican police are concerned with the number of illegal guns because many have strong drug links. Thus, guns entering the region from the United States have been a contentious issue between Caribbean countries and the United States. However, the Bush administration reiterated its opposition to the 2001 United Nations draft accord on the international sale of small arms, warning that it might constrain the legitimate weapons trade and infringe on the right of American citizens to bear arms (Lynch 2001). Drug felons transported to a smaller geographical area, with their gun and drug gang rivalries, have consequences for the social, economic, and political environment. The result is a diversion of resources from areas such as health and education as they make demands on criminal justice resources. The number of riots that have occurred within Jamaica during the past three years suggests that this phenomenon has become the Jamaican response to many situations. Upheavals have historically been associated with the urban poor and disaffected, but recent disturbances have permeated the entire island. Stone (1986) and Harriott (1996) have noted that when massive behavior changes occur in a society during a short time period, there is usually a convergence of factors causing the change, not just one factor.

CHANGES IN THE JAMAICAN DRUG SCENE

The above discussion indicates that the underlying assumptions about the domestic conditions at drug source or in transit zones are incorrect. Of significance, however, is that increased violence, corruption, and gun crimes are currently being observed in the Caribbean region. The Jamaican drug scene exhibits changes consistent with the displacement hypothesis. Jamaica Constabulary Force statistics for the period from 1990 to 1999 show an increase in the volume of drugs transiting the island. These changes include resurgence in the growth of ganja, a shift from marijuana to cocaine, an increase in the volume of cocaine, the spread of drug activities throughout the island, and increased involvement of Colombians in the Jamaican drug scene.

RESURGENCE IN GROWTH OF GANJA

Newspaper reports and analyses of narcotics statistics indicate that the amount of ganja seized continues to be high, with 55,869.59 kilograms seized in 2000. In 1998, 22,924.98

kilograms were seized, down from 24,728.74 kilograms in 1997 and a high of 41,262.7 in 1996 (Anderson 2000). On Thursday, 8 February 2001, compressed ganja weighing 2,727.27 kilograms, or 5,999 pounds, was seized in containers at Kingston Wharves. Three days later, law enforcement interdicted another shipment weighing 18,312 pounds. Methods of concealment are diverse. These include agricultural products such as nutmeg and manufactured goods such as textiles.

The 1999 INCSR reiterates that the United States has provided funding for the Jamaican government's counternarcotics efforts continuously since 1987 and "has provided more counter-narcotics assistance to Jamaica than to any other Caribbean country" (http://www.state.gov/www/global/narcotics_law/1999_narc_report/carib99_part3.html). Citing marijuana shipments leaving Jamaican ports for the United States in commercial cargo, the INCSR was critical of security at Jamaican ports. However, the United States has reduced eradication funding to the island. The U.S. government is reducing its funding of Jamaica's marijuana eradication program in the hope that the Jamaican government will take up the slack (Williams 2000b). In 1999, the Jamaican government agreed to begin paying half of the marijuana cutters' salaries beginning in June 2000 and their full salaries beginning in June 2001. The preferred mode of eradication for the United States is aerial spraying of herbicide. Citing environmental concerns, Jamaica refuses to use this method. Instead, police and military

personnel manually eradicate crops. The military have recently been redeployed to the prisons because of labor problems with the prison officers, leaving the responsibility to the police who lack resources and are generally overwhelmed by other domestic crime concerns. With Jamaica's lack of resources to police the harbors and ports (Poor parish with a marvelous serenity 2000), the island becomes an attractive arena in which to conduct illicit narcotic activities. There is now an increase in the quantity of cocaine transiting the island, along with the observed presence and heightened activities of Colombians in Jamaica.

INCREASE IN VOLUME OF COCAINE

The 2000 INCSR, released in March 2001, reveals that the amount of cocaine transiting Jamaica to the United States has quadrupled compared to the same period in 1999, making Jamaica the leading transshipment point in the Caribbean (Ja holds cocaine ranking 1999). The Port Security Corp. acknowledges that attempts to smuggle cocaine through the ports have increased. This is confirmed by Jamaica Constabulary Force statistics on narcotic drugs seized and destroyed that reveal that cocaine seizures tripled between 1996 and 1998. Information is that 1,143.91 kilograms of cocaine were seized in 1998. By comparison, 2,444.46 kilograms were seized between January and 9 December 1999, an increase of 1,300.55 kilograms. In 2000, 1,624.4 kilograms were seized, and 517.99 kilograms were seized up to 30 June 2001.[5]

Factors facilitating this change include lack of resources to police the coastline and drug traffickers' use of technology. Other reasons are that shipment of ganja involves more skill, and cocaine is an easier drug to transship because it has less weight and more value. Law enforcement officials attribute these changes to the dynamism of the trade wherein larger quantities of cocaine are easier to move using body carriers (Jones 1999; INCSR 1999) who are primarily women. Women's involvement in the drug trade and the resulting consequences reinforce the label *feminization of the drug trade* and the reality that the war on drugs has become a war against women. For example, a 14 May 2001 article in the *Jamaica Gleaner Online* (Roxborough 2001) reports that Jamaican women are increasingly being arrested in other jurisdictions for drug-related offences. The number of Jamaican women in British prisons increased from 100 to more than 400 in three years, and between April 1999 and March 2000, 65 percent of the 450 people arrested at British airports for trafficking cocaine came off flights from Jamaica.

Another noticeable change in the Jamaican drug scene is the concentration of cocaine activities in eastern parishes such as the coasts of Portland and St. Thomas. However, lack of resources poses a grave danger as smugglers being pursued by the U.S. Coast Guard under the Shiprider Agreement often unload their cargo. While reports indicate increasing victimization of individuals who have allegedly found this unloaded cargo, very little cooperation is given to the police in their efforts to address the issue (Williams 2000c).

INCREASED PRESENCE OF COLOMBIANS

During the past few years, local and U.S. drug enforcement agents have established that Jamaica is being used as a transshipment point for narcotics and that there is a direct drug link among Jamaicans, Bahamians, and Colombians for this purpose (see the 1999 INCSR). Some Jamaican narcotics officers refer to these forged linkages as the JBC[6] connection wherein Jamaicans provide the routes previously established to traffic ganja, the Bahamians provide navigational services, and the Colombians provide the drugs.

Media reports (Williams 2000a), as well as the INCSR, now indicate increased activities and the presence of Colombians operating in Jamaica. A recent article by the Caribbean News Agency, published in the *Jamaica Gleaner Online* (Sinclair 1999b), cites U.S. State Department sources saying that Colombian drug traffickers have infiltrated many of the Eastern Caribbean nations and have established the services of regional organizations to move drugs in the region. A three-year investigation dubbed White Seas, an initiative of the United States, Canada, Jamaica, and the Bahamas, provided additional evidence of Colombian activities in the region. This investigation revealed that drugs were transported via speedboats from Jamaica and the Bahamas into Miami for distribution in American and Canadian cities (U.S., Canada, Jamaica, Bahamas smash drug ring 2001).

An insider assessment of the cocaine subculture titled "Cocaine Threatening the Nation," published in the *Jamaica Gleaner Online* on 23 January 2000, reiterates the growing importance of Jamaica as a strategic transshipment point in the Colombian cocaine trade and suggests that it is more than a question of geography. Instead, factors include the relative ease with which the traffickers are able to carry out their activities.

The report further explains that heightened surveillance by the U.S. drug enforcement authorities and the local police appears to have had little impact on the trafficking. Colombians gain entry to the island in numerous ways (Sinclair 1999a); consequently, more Colombian nationals may be operating in Jamaica than official estimates indicate.

Colombians are also implicated in increases in gang/turf war, corruption,[7] gun crimes, and stockpiling of cocaine. According to Williams (2000a), increases in gang/turf war in the inner city of Kingston are the result of Colombians operating in Jamaica who want to reduce the number of individuals with whom they deal. Similarly, Professor Don Robotham (2001), in a commentary about the July 2001 West Kingston Affair, noted that the event should not be viewed solely through a domestic political lens. He asserted

that no politician or political party is in the position of providing the caliber of guns and ammunitions evident in West Kingston. Consequently, current political instabilities are different from earlier ideological ones. Robotham asserted that sections of West Kingston have become an axis for the international drug trade between Colombia and the rest of the hemisphere. Jamaican media increasingly report activities and influences of Colombians on the Jamaican drug scene.[8] Consequently, though couched in diplomatic terms, the prime minister's statement (Crime the target 2001) on the announcement of the West Kingston Inquiry about "new levels of criminality spurred by international dimensions" is very informative.

Another consequence attributed to the presence of Colombians is the stockpiling of cocaine. According to Jamaican intelligence sources, Colombian drug traffickers bring cocaine to Jamaica to be stockpiled. The cocaine arrives in bulk and leaves in smaller shipments for other places, such as the Bahamas (Jamaica holds cocaine ranking 1999). Colombians are also linked with cruise shipping, especially in tourist areas (Robotham 1999a, 1999b), the potential economic repercussions of which are significant because tourism is vulnerable to U.S. State Department activities and advisories.

Jamaica's involvement in the drug trade has created a dual effect. On one hand, the creation of armed gangs fosters insecurity within the country. On the other hand, these participants become the heroes of the dispossessed youth in their communities. At a minimum, the drug situation has consequences for the policy environment and especially for law enforcement (Thwaites 1999).

An analysis of Colombia's drug situation and the operation of cartels indicates that the operation of Colombians in Jamaica could have consequences for law enforcement and policy implementation (Thwaites 2000). Thachuk (1997) described the activities of Colombian drug traffickers in Colombia as *plomo o' plata*. The English translation of this phrase, "silver or the bullet," gives an indication of the dangers of Colombian drug traffickers to Jamaican society. These include increased drug usage with an attendant rise in addiction and a growth in the incidence of irrational, violent crime that has the potential to undermine and corrupt the government. Recent allegations are that some members of the police force have succumbed to corruption.[9]

While acknowledging that "Jamaica's counter narcotics efforts have taken place against a backdrop of severe resource constraints caused by a continuing recession," the 2000 INCSR derides Jamaica, noting that increased trafficking "indicates the need for the GOJ to intensify and focus its law enforcement efforts and to enhance its international co-operation." Clearly, the United States sees the increased volume of drug trafficking to be a shortcoming of Jamaican initiatives rather than the result of its drug policy. Intensification of law enforcement could prove a problem. The island's law enforcement practices are currently under international scrutiny. Amnesty International (2001) issued a scathing report of law enforcement in Jamaica titled *Jamaica: Killings and Violence by Police. How Many More Victims?* that documents gross abuses by law enforcement personnel.

SUMMARY/ CONCLUSION

U.S.-funded antidrug initiatives in Colombia result in compensating behavior such as displacement activities. Observed changes in Jamaica include an increase in crime and violence, a worsening of the formal economy, increased presence of Colombian nationals, and an increase in the amount of drugs transiting the island. These are contrary to the drug policy assumptions respecting source countries' capabilities and domestic conditions. Consequently, the premises underlying the supply reduction policy are incorrect. More important, attempts at conforming to U.S.-imposed targets lead to undue costs for these societies. Many cannot afford to expend the level of resources required to sustain antidrug initiatives.

While domestic concerns necessitate a focus on wealth creation or poverty alleviation, a disproportionate antidrug budget diverts resources from said programs, thereby increasing the likelihood of negative economic growth. A depressed or stagnant economy increases the likelihood that the mass of unemployed and underemployed population will engage in illegal drug trade. Moreover, large-scale legal and illegal immigration are the most prominent symptoms of economic instability in the Caribbean. These thwart the goals of reducing illegal immigration or severing drugs at the source.

Policy impositions are having consequences for the entire Caribbean region. Problems are displaced into areas where the resources for addressing drug issues are minimal, with some countries being disproportionately affected. Jamaica, already lacking in resources, is in for a rough time.[10] For example, recent newspaper headlines such as "Jamaica Tops Region in Cocaine Transshipment" (Associated Press 2001) and "This Is Bigger than Us: Cops Helpless as Drug Planes Land at Airport" (http://www.jamaica-gleaner.com/gleaner/20010325/lead/lead1.html) indicate some of the consequences for Jamaica. Simultaneously, it appears that the Colombian crackdown has accelerated the dispersion of drug trafficking activities throughout the Caribbean region. Its major consequence, however, may be the transformation of Jamaica's political tribalism into a narco-political tribalism. Cumulatively, both immigration and drug policies allow deported persons to continue their drug- and gun-related activities. Since these changes were observed before full implementation of Plan Colombia, it is reasonable to conclude that further displacement will occur. Similarly, displacement of U.S. antidrug initiatives may be exacerbated by the refusal to implement more restrictive gun policies.

Not only have the U.S. policies failed to achieve their goals; they have had adverse consequences for some countries. Yet fear of repercussions such as decertification limits governmental responses to domestic drug control initiatives. Consequently, Caribbean countries are not at liberty to implement best practices from other jurisdictions or implement policies that are not endorsed by the United States. This indicates that the conceptualization of drug war casualties needs to be broadened.

Notes

1. The Colombian government has developed a comprehensive, integrated strategy called Plan Colombia to address Colombia's drug and interrelated social and economic troubles. Plan Colombia focuses on five strategic issues: (1) the peace process, (2) the Colombian economy, (3) the counterdrug strategy, (4) the reform of the justice system and the protection of human rights, and (5) democratization and social development (Executive Office of the President 2001, 14). The program is expected to cost $7.5 billion, with $1.6 billion proposed U.S. support over the fiscal years 2000 and 2001. This represents an increase of $1.3 billion from the previous $330 million (Strategy FY 2001 Budget, 14-22). As stated therein,

> Since there is no single solution to Colombia's difficulty . . . it is in the national interest of the United States to stem the flow of illegal drugs and to promote stability and strengthen democracy in Colombia and the Andean region. (P. 16)

Thus, the U.S. contribution to Plan Colombia has five components centered on reducing the supply of Colombian drugs to the United States.

2. For example, after the April 1999 incident, visitor arrivals decreased, requiring an infusion of U.S.$1.8 million to help bolster Jamaica's international image (Virtue 1999). The same effects were noticed after the recent West Kingston events of 7-10 July 2001.

3. Chuck (1999) suggested that the decline in the economy accounts for the cycle of brutality that has overtaken the society. He suggests that the worsening economy has affected the quality of life and promoted the decline of civility and decency. In fact, nowhere is it more dramatically displayed than in the inner cities. The rising tension, gang warfare, protection money, lack of opportunities and deteriorating conditions can all be traced to an economy derailed and heading for disaster.

4. This was the perception of Father Howard Rochester, then at St. Richard's Catholic Church, Red Hills, who also became a casualty of this siege when he was found murdered in October 2000. Examples of this siege include the Tivoli Gardens incident of May 1997, so named because the Jamaican security forces and residents of Tivoli Gardens in West Kingston engaged in what the press labeled a "battle." Between 19 and 21 April 1999, the island was again under siege as Jamaicans engaged in mass demonstrations or as both the local and international press labeled it, "rioted" in response to a 30 percent increase in the price of petrol. Again in June of 1999, Kingston experienced a spate of killings with approximately sixty-six people killed in seventeen days. The Mountain View incident, so named because residents of the area, in solidarity with the gunmen, declared the area off limits to police, happened in April 2000. Gunmen engaged the police in continual gun battle, often forcing them into retreat. Criminal justice statistics for 2000 reveal that seventy people were murdered in the first twenty-five days of April 2000, fifty-six of them in the Kingston Metropolitan region. In the latest incident, twenty-five people were killed during the period of 7-10 July 2001.

5. See Jamaica holds cocaine ranking (1999) regarding information on the seizure of a Colombian boat with 700 kilograms of cocaine. This amount increases the seizures to 1,217.99 kilograms for this period.

6. JBC is also the acronym for the now defunct Jamaica Broadcasting Corporation.

7. For example, the *Jamaica Daily Gleaner* of 27 October 2000 reported that prison warders and police officers were being questioned to ascertain who aided and abetted two Colombians who were released from the correctional facility where they were being held.

8. A poignant story from the *Jamaica Gleaner Online* for Thursday, 19 July 2001 titled "Mystery Surrounds Theft of Drug Boat from Police Custody" (2001) reports that

> Colombian drug traffickers have been using a seized boat they stole from police custody last month to continue their trade in Jamaican territorial waters.... But local law enforcers are unable to catch up with the drug smugglers [because] their marine vehicles are no match for the twin-engine boats used by the traffickers.

The boat was seized in April with twenty-four cocaine packets weighing approximately 700 kilograms (1,540 pounds) with a Jamaican street value of $195 million.

9. In January 1998, Police Commissioner Francis Forbes transferred 56 of the 127 police personnel from Portland because some were suspected to have been involved in cocaine trafficking in the parish.

10. This is confirmed by activities during 7-10 July 2001, now referred to as the West Kingston Affairs, when media coverage showed gunmen engaging the Jamaican police in three days of cross fire.

References

Amnesty International. 2001. Jamaica: Killings and violence by police. How many more victims? *Jamaica Gleaner Online*, 4 October. Available from http://www.jamaica-gleaner.com/pages/amnesty/full/index.html.

Anderson, Omar. 2000. Less ganja, more cocaine in Jamaica. *Jamaica Gleaner Online*, 5 March. Retrieved from http://www.jamaica-gleaner.com/gleaner/20000305/index.html.

Arganaras, Fernando Garcia. 1997. Harm reduction at the supply side of the drug war: The case of Bolivia. In *Harm reduction: A new direction for drug policies and programs*, edited by Patricia G. Erickson, Diane M. Riley, Yuet W. Cheung, and Patrick A. O'Hare. Toronto, Canada: University of Toronto Press.

Associated Press. 2001. Jamaica tops region in cocaine transshipment. *Jamaica Gleaner Online*, 12 March. Retrieved from http://www.jamaica-gleaner.com/gleaner/20010312/news/news3.html.

Blackman, Kenneth. 1992. Jamaica: Drugs, politics and poverty blamed for wave of violence. *Interpress Service*, 6 March.

Bureau of Western Hemispheric Fact Sheet, Andean Regional Initiative. 2001. Retrieved 16 May from http://www.state.gov/e/rls/index.cfm?docid=2980 [2001-09-18].

Chuck, Delroy. 1999. Vortex of decline. *Jamaica Gleaner Online*, 30 June. Retrieved from http://www.go-jamaica.com/gleaner/19990630/.

Cocaine threatening the nation. 2000. *Jamaica Gleaner Online*, 23 January. Available from http://www.go-jamaica.com.

Craig, Richard B. 1987. Illicit drug traffic: Implications for South American source countries. *Journal of Intra-American Studies and World Affairs* 29 (2): 1-34.

Crime the target—PM announces West Kingston inquiry. 2001. *Jamaica Gleaner Online*, 16 July. Retrieved from http://www.jamaica-gleaner.com/gleaner/20010716/lead/lead2.html.

Drug Enforcement Administration. n.d. *The Jamaican posse*. Intelligence bulletin 90 (2). New York: New York Field Division, Unified Intelligence Division.

Edwards, D. T. 1999. The prevalence of firearm related offenses in Jamaica and implications for national security. M.Sc. diss., Royal Military College of Science, Department of Defense, Management and Security Analysis, Cranfield Security Centre, Shrivenham, UK.

Executive Office of the President, United States, Office of National Drug Control Policy. 1997. *National drug control strategy*. Retrieved from http://www.whitehousedrugpolicy.gov/publications/policy/ndcs01/index.html.

———. 1998. *National drug control strategy*. Retrieved from http://www.whitehousedrugpolicy.gov/publications/policy/ndcs01/index.html.

———. 1999. *National drug control strategy*. Retrieved from http://www.whitehousedrugpolicy.gov/publications/policy/ndcs01/index.html.

———. 2000. *National drug control strategy*. Retrieved from http://www.whitehousedrugpolicy.gov/publications/policy/ndcs01/index.html.

———. 2001. *National drug control strategy*. Retrieved from http://www.whitehousedrugpolicy.gov/publications/policy/ndcs01/index.html.

Gabor, Thomas. 1981. The crime displacement hypothesis: An empirical examination. *Crime & Delinquency* 27:390-404.

Gay, Bruce W., and James M. Marquart. 1993. Jamaican posses: A new form of organized crime. *Journal of Crime and Justice* 16 (2): 139-70.

Gunst, Laurie. 1988. *Born fi dead*. New York: Holt.

Harriott, Anthony. 1996. The changing social organization of crime and criminals in Jamaica. *Caribbean Quarterly* 42 (2/3): 61-81.

Ja holds cocaine ranking. 1999. *Jamaica Gleaner Online*, 19 October. Retrieved from http://www.jamaica-gleaner.com/gleaner/19991019/f2.html.

Jamaica Constabulary Force. 1996. *Annual report*. Kingston, Jamaica: Government Printing Office.

———. 1997. *Annual report*. Kingston, Jamaica: Government Printing Office.

———. 1998a. *Annual report*. Kingston, Jamaica: Government Printing Office.

———. 1998b. [Crime statistics]. Unpublished raw data.

———. 1999. [Crime statistics]. Unpublished raw data.

————. 2000. [Crime statistics]. Unpublished raw data.

Jamaica holds cocaine ranking. 1999. *Jamaica Gleaner Online*, 19 October. Retrieved from http://www.jamaica-gleaner.com/gleaner/19991019/index.html.

Jones, Karen. 1999. Narcotic strategy yields result. *Jamaica Gleaner Online*, 15 June. Retrieved from http://www.jamaica-gleaner.com/gleaner/19990615/index.html.

Lynch, Colum. 2001. U.S. fights UN accord to fight small arms. *Washington Post*, 10 July, A01. Retrieved from http://www.washingtonpost.com/wp-dyn/world/A38049-2001Jul9.html.

Maingot, Anthony. 1989. The drug menace to the Caribbean. *The World and I* (July): 128-35.

————. 1994. *The United States and the Caribbean*. Boulder, CO: Westview.

McDonald, Scott B. 1988. *Dancing on a volcano: The Latin American drug trade*. New York: Praeger.

Ministry of National Security and Justice. 1997. *Report of the National Committee on Political Tribalism*. Kingston, Jamaica: Government Printing Office.

Monitoring deportees. 1999. *Jamaica Gleaner Online*, 29 June. Retrieved from http//:www.jamaica-gleaner.com/19990629.

Mystery surrounds theft of drug boat from police custody. 2001. *Jamaica Gleaner Online*, 19 July. Retrieved from http://www.jamaica-gleaner.com/gleaner/20010719/lead/lead4.html.

Nation at risk. 1999. *Jamaica Gleaner Online*, 21 June. Retrieved from http//:www.jamaica-gleaner.com/19990621.

Office of National Drug Control Policy. 1998. *Performance measures of effectiveness*. Washington, DC: Executive Office of the President, Office of National Drug Control Policy.

————. 2000. *Performance measures of effectiveness*. Washington, DC: Executive Office of the President, Office of National Drug Control Policy.

Performance Management Evaluation. 2000. Washington, DC: Executive Office of the President, Office of National Drug Control Policy.

Poor parish with a marvelous serenity. 2000. *Jamaica Gleaner Online*, 23 March. Retrieved from http://www.jamaica-gleaner.com/gleaner/20000323/index.html.

Robotham, Don. 1999a. Crime and public policy in Jamaica (part 2). *Jamaica Gleaner Online*, 17 August. Retrieved from http://www.jamaica-gleaner.com/gleaner/19990817/cleisure/index.html.

————. 1999b. Roots of crime (2). *Jamaica Gleaner Online*, 19 August. Retrieved from http://www.jamaica-gleaner.com/gleaner/19990819/cleisure/index.html.

————. 2001. The cocaine connection. *Jamaica Gleaner Online*, 17 July. Retrieved from http://www.jamaica-gleaner.com/gleaner/20010717/cleisure/cleisure2.html.

Roxborough, Pat. 2001. J'cans crowd UK prisons—British team coming to probe reasons local women smuggle drugs. Jamaica Gleaner Online, 14 May. Retrieved from http://www.jamaica-gleaner.com/gleaner/20010514/lead/lead2.html.

Sinclair, Glenroy. 1999a. Colombians held in hotel. *Jamaica Daily Gleaner*, 16 July.

————. 1999b. U.S. finds most drugs on passengers from Jamaica. *Jamaica Gleaner Online*, 21 September. Retrieved from http://www.jamaica-gleaner.com/gleaner/19990921/f2.html.

Small, Geoff. 1995. *Ruthless: The global rise of the yardies*. London: Warner Books.

Smith, Peter. 1992. The political economy of drugs: Conceptual issues and policy options. In *Drug policy in the Americas*, edited by Peter Smith. Boulder, CO: Westview.

Stone, Carl. 1986. *Class, state and democracy in Jamaica*. New York: Praeger.

———. 1991. Hard drug use in a black island society. *Caribbean Affairs* 4 (2): 142-61.

Thachuk, K. 1997. Plomo o plata: Politics, corruption and drug policy in Colombia. Ph.D. thesis, Simon Fraser University, Burnaby, British Colombia, Canada.

Thwaites, Daniel. 1999. The usual suspect. *Jamaica Gleaner Online*, 16 July. Retrieved from http://www.jamaica-gleaner.com/gleaner/19990716/index.html.

———. 2000. How low can we go? *Jamaica Gleaner Online*, 20 October. Retrieved from http://www.jamaica-gleaner.com/gleaner/20001020/cleisure/cleisure4.html.

U.S., Canada, Jamaica, Bahamas smash drug ring. 2001. Retrieved from http://www.wjin.net/html/news/7197.htm/2/5/01.

U.S. Department of Justice, Immigration and Naturalization Services. n.d.-a. *Detention and removal fact sheet and statistics*. Retrieved from http://www. ins.usdoj.gov/graphics/publicaffairs/factsheets/Deten.pdf 2000-12-13.

———. n.d.-b. *Statistics*. Retrieved from http://www.ins.usdoj.gov/graphics/aboutins/statistics/Illegals.htm 2001-08-01.

Virtue, Erica. 1999. Gas riots leave long-term damage. *Jamaica Gleaner Online*, 14 November. Retrieved from http://www.go-jamaica.com/gleaner/19991114/f1.html.

White House, Office of the Press Secretary. 2000. Press release on Colombia assistance package. Grand Canyon, AZ: Office of the Press Spokesman.

Williams, Lloyd. 2000a. Colombians take control of local cocaine trade. *Jamaica Gleaner Online*, 23 January. Retrieved from http://www.jamaica-gleaner.com/gleaner/20000123/index.html.

———. 2000b. US$ ganja cut-back. *Jamaica Gleaner Online*, 13 March. Available from http://www.jamaica-gleaner.com.

———. 2000c. Washed up cocaine, gunman and violence. *Jamaica Gleaner Online*, 24 January. Retrieved from http://www.jamaica-gleaner.com/gleaner/20000124/index.html.

Wolfe, L. 1993. *Report of the National Task Force on Crime*. Kingston, Jamaica: Government Printing Office.

[5]

Non-EU Citizens' Experiences of Offending and Victimisation: The Case for Comparative European Research

Joanna Goodey[1]

1. INTRODUCING THE RESEARCH 'GAP'

This paper aims to address crime, as everyday *petty* offending and victimisation, by non-EU citizens in the EU. While the media, and some academics and NGOs, have tended to focus on the more extreme or headline grabbing criminal activities of some migrant groups – for example: illegal trafficking in human beings;[2] drugs and weapons smuggling[3] – this paper examines the neglected and mundane nature of much of migrant crime which is experienced as both offending and victimisation.

Specifically, the British focus on 'ethnic minorities and crime' and the German focus on 'foreigners and crime' will be re-appraised in consideration of a more wide-ranging debate that lies with ethnicity, nationality and citizenship in a European setting. While, in the case of Britain, it can be argued that the absence of focused research on non-British citizens and crime is simply a reflection of the relative insignificance of these groups in Britain's crime statistics, this does not address the connections that have been made in Britain between immigration, social problems and crime. There is comparative research, at a European level, that has yet to be undertaken on the public and political stereotyping of migrants as 'undesirables' or as potentially criminal, which needs placing alongside the reality of their criminal activities.

While Europe is progressively closing its doors to uncontrolled immigration, the factors which 'push' and 'pull' people to migrate to Europe will not go away. Economic

---

1. Lecturer in Criminology at the Centre for Criminal Justice Studies, The University of Leeds, UK. Currently on a two-year sabbatical, as a Marie Curie Research Fellow, at the Centre for International Crime Prevention at the United Nations in Vienna.
2. *See* the website of the International Organisation for Migration, based in Geneva, which references its work on trafficking in women: http://www.iom.ch; also the United Nations (1999) *Global Programme Against Trafficking in Human Beings*, published by the UN Office for Drug Control and Crime Prevention in Vienna.
3. R. Lewis, 'Drugs, War and Crime in the Post-Soviet Balkans', in V. Ruggiero, N. South and I. Taylor, eds, *The New European Criminology: Crime and Social Order in Europe* (London 1998) pp. 216–229; B. Tupman, 'Keeping an Eye on Eastern Europe', 11(4) *Policing* (1995) pp. 249–260.

migrants, asylum seekers and refugees will continue to knock at Europe's doors and will enter by legal or illegal means. European governments are increasingly responding to non-EU citizens, who want to gain entry to the Union, in a negative way. The presence of the 'other', as non-EU citizen, has primarily been problematised with regard to limited European resources and the threat posed to each country's national security. Immigration is now explicitly and implicitly associated with a host of social problems faced by each member State which, in turn, are attributed as causal factors towards crime. Through this process of association, migrants, in general, are criminalised.

The populist criminalisation of migrants is largely based on the negative stereotyping of certain groups which is not wholly grounded in 'fact'. There is an absence of information from criminal justice sources, both within individual EU countries and between countries, which can be utilised in the attempt not only to answer questions in consideration of non-EU citizens' engagement with and experiences of crime but, also, to gauge their experiences of victimisation and criminal justice. What does exist are partial accounts of different groups' experiences at various stages of the criminal justice system. While this paper cannot provide a picture of the extent and nature of crime by and victimisation against non-EU citizens in the EU, it does set out to define the 'problem' in question and suggest means by which it might be more thoughtfully addressed.

Dedicated research is needed to expose the reality of non-EU citizens' experiences of offending and victimisation, as a reflection of their marginalised social position, while resident in the EU. This paper will address this aim with respect to: first, 'who' and 'what' is being discussed in relation to stereotypes and political reaction to the 'problem' of immigration; second, evidence from Germany and Britain in consideration of the question of non-EU citizens and 'crime'; third, a brief introduction to the author's current work, as co-ordinator of a six country team, which is undertaking developmental research on non-EU citizens and 'crime'.

2. PROBLEMATISING IMMIGRATION AND MIGRANTS

2.1. Defining 'non-EU citizens'

Before commenting on the stereotypes that surround 'migrants', 'foreigners' or 'minorities' in Europe (as non-EU citizens are variously labelled), the paper needs to clarify 'who' it is referring to; namely, non-EU citizens, be they economic migrants, asylum seekers or refugees.[4] The groups in question can come from anywhere outside the EU but are variously represented in different EU countries by, for example: long established groups of migrant workers from Turkey, Greece and Italy; recent influxes of people following the break-up of the USSR; refugees from war in the Balkans; migrants from north Africa; and past and present movements of various groups from the Indian sub-continent. The intricacies of 'who' is being considered, under the

---

4.　In this paper reference is generally made to 'non-EU citizens' or, at times, 'migrants' as a collective term for these groups.

Non-EU Citizens' Experiences of Offending and Victimisation

catch-all phrase 'non-EU citizens', will be discussed in more detail in the second part of the paper, suffice to say that criminal justice authorities, the press and the public are all guilty, at times, of negatively labeling these various groups as *one* social 'problem'.

Non-citizenship status is extremely important as a basis for classification with regard to minority rights in Europe. While the European Convention on Human Rights protects not only the citizens of a state but also other people affected by the actions of the state, the bulk of European legislation on minority rights focuses its attention on the category of 'national' minorities which, by implication, suggests that citizenship or nationality status is all important.[5] As Miall comments: 'One can identify as weaknesses in the current legal regime, first, the lack of a satisfactory definition of minorities and the uncertainty over whether minority rights are restricted to nationals of the states in which they dwell.'[6]

There exists a citizenship hierarchy with, in first place, the nationals of individual states in which they reside, followed by other EU nationals with, in third place, non-EU nationals. In addition to this there is a hierarchy of non-EU nationals which, one might argue, is implicitly based on colour more than the generalising category of 'nationality' which, of course, can include any number of races/ethnicities.[7] The hierarchical interplay of nationality and ethnicity/race with gender, class and age, differentially impacts on individual and collective experiences of citizenship and non-citizenship.[8] However, regardless of individual experiences of citizenship, citizenship itself does provide people with a recourse to rights; rights which have implications for treatment at the hands of the criminal justice system. Non-citizenship status places an individual in a particularly vulnerable situation should something go wrong with respect to their stay in a host country; for example, if they commit a crime or are victimised.

Non-EU citizens experience differential treatment in the EU according to their status as economic migrants, asylum seekers or refugees. While economic migrants have been nominally accepted in Europe over the last few decades, this 'acceptance' is waning as a reflection of Europe's fluctuating economies and the development of 'fortress Europe'. However, economic migrants, if legally present in the EU, enjoy an enhanced status and more freedoms (such as the ability to work) than asylum seekers whose very title describes their marginal status. Asylum seekers are increasingly perceived as being motivated by the same concerns as economic migrants;[9] that is, wanting a 'better life' through enhanced employment opportunities. As the 'push' factors behind

---

5. P. Keller, 'Re-thinking Ethnic and Cultural Rights in Europe', 18(1) *Oxford Journal of Legal Studies* (1998) pp. 29–59; M. Mitic, 'Protection of National Minorities in Europe', XLIX *Review of International Affairs* (1998) pp. 1070–1071, Belgrade; F. Webber, 'Governing Racism: The Corruption of the Executive', 39(1) *Race and Class* (1997) pp. 19–35.
6. H. Miall, ed., *Minority Rights in Europe: The Scope for a Transnational Regime* (London 1994) p. 114.
7. The same 'colour' hierarchy also exists for nationals of EU countries. However, for the purposes of this paper, the focus is on non-EU citizens.
8. R. Lister, *Citizenship: Feminist Perspectives* (London 1997).
9. D. Joly, *Temporary Protection within the Framework of a New European Asylum Regime*, paper written for conference 'Refugees from the Former Yugoslavia in the European Union', Vienna (May 1998).

Non-EU Citizens' Experiences of Offending and Victimisation

asylum seekers' emigration to the EU are questioned, so public and politicians are less sympathetic to their situation.

However, once again, one can speculate that the significance of colour, with regard to both asylum seekers and refugees, is perhaps more important in the public and political consciousness than the 'refugee' label; as Cook notes: 'The essentially racialised nature of the panic surrounding refugees and asylum seekers is highlighted by the contrasting political responses to (predominantly white) refugees caught up in the civil war in the former Yugoslavia [in comparison with 'black' refugees/asylum seekers].'[10] Writing this paper after Cook, in the late 1990s when EU repatriation of refugees from Bosnia is well underway, one is able to question the general application of Cook's assertion. European Union policy concerning refugees and asylum seekers is, at times, more complex than a reductionist focus on 'race' or 'colour' would have us think. Also, as Melossi[11] notes, Europe's problematisation of immigration reflects the internal problems of EU countries and the complex development of EU citizens' own identities.

A migrant's status in the EU can be simplistically but usefully interpreted with regard to his or her relative state of legality or illegality with respect to the individual's recourse to rights. In particular, an immigrant's illegal status has huge implications with regard to the 'dark figure of crime' which represents their unrecorded experiences of offending and victimisation. Illegal migrants' marginal status on the fringes of society (more than legal non-citizens such as refugees) makes them extremely vulnerable to 'crime' as offenders and victims. Their 'non-status' in the eyes of the law impacts on their willingness to interact with criminal justice agencies. The individual migrant's actions as offender or victim are likely to be pre-judged by criminal justice agencies according to the legal status of the migrant in question. The receiving country's assignment of a label (economic migrant; asylum seeker; refugee) is important with regard to the rights it affords the receiver. While it can be argued that the public perception of migrant categories is merging, the discretionary and sometimes inaccurate labelling of migrants, by a host country's institutions, continues to have a significant impact on the stereotypes which follow the individual or the group during their residence in the EU. With this in mind, the following section will refer to the stereotyping of and the political response to non-EU citizens as a 'group'.

2.2. Stereotyping 'migrants'

Describing the work of the department of ethnic broadcasting at the Süddeutscher Rundfunk (German radio station), and its attempt to educate people to the reality of Germany's immigrant population, Meier-Braun comments: 'There is a severe lack of

---

10. D. Cook, 'Racism, Citizenship and Exclusion', in D. Cook and B. Hudson, eds, *Racism and Criminology* (London 1993), p. 152.
11. D. Melossi, 'Remarks on Social Control, State Sovereignty and Citizenship in the New Europe', in V. Ruggiero, N. South and I. Taylor, eds, *The New European Criminology: Crime and Social Order in Europe* (London 1998) pp. 52–63.

Non-EU Citizens' Experiences of Offending and Victimisation

information about current trends of migration and the world refugee problem.'[12] In general, public opinion about immigration to Europe is not informed by widely available and accurate information from reliable sources. Instead, much of what the public thinks about migrants and the subject of immigraton is based on inadequate media reporting which may include the occasional piece on government policy. The mere hint that migration to Europe will continue (and perhaps increase) is not generally viewed sympathetically by the press which informs the public which, in turn, is reflected in the political rhetoric of governments. As Schilling notes: 'refugee and migration movements – seen from an international perspective – have to be considered mainly as a phenomenon in the Third World and of the Third World';[13] a fact which is rarely highlighted in discussions of the immigration demands placed on the EU.

There are a host of stereotypes that are conjured up in the popular imagination when reference is made to 'refugees', 'asylum seekers' and immigration in general. Many stereotypes concentrate on negative images such as competition for jobs and scarce welfare resources, cultural conflict and the threat of crime. Commenting on 'Race in the British News' in the run up to the 1997 general election, Law[14] notes the persistent link between race, violence, dangerousness and crime, alongside the message that migrants are a welfare burden and prone to deception which, therefore, demands their racialised control. While Law's research shows that anti-racist news treats migrants in a sympathetic and humanitarian fashion, the tabloid press (with the widest readership in Britain) continues to carry items hostile to migrants; for example, Law refers to the following *News of the World* headlines: 'We catch 350 migrants in wedding con scandal' (18/1/97); 'Cheating migrants grave fiddle' (30/3/97); 'Dole fraudsters ferry hop to a fortune' (11/5/97). Similarly for Germany, Albrecht (in reference to work by Kubink[15]) notes: 'Content analysis of print media in Germany reveal that two-fifths of articles related to foreigners highlight the topic of 'crimes committed by foreign minorities' ... Drug trafficking and organized crime were the subjects of approximately 60 per cent of mentions, outweighing other types of crimes.'[16] So, the stereotype of 'foreigner' as criminal 'other' is doubly reinforced by the German media's focus on the most serious crimes that *some* members of foreign groups are involved in.

Writing this paper in the summer of 1999, the most recent arrival in the EU of Kosovar Albanian refugees mirrors, to some extent, the reception of Bosnians in the early 1990s and presents a temporary reprieve in the negative stereotyping of 'migrants'. To date, the general response of press, politicians and public to the plight of Kosovar Albanians has been sympathetic. The 'victim' label has been assigned to this group. However, even in the case of Kosovar refugees their image is muddied as associa-

12. K.H. Meier-Braun, 'Migration, Asylum and Foreigners in the German Media', in F. Heckmann and W. Bosswick, eds, *Migration Policies: A Comparative Perspective* (Stuttgart 1995) p. 342.
13. R.S. Schilling, 'Refugees and Immigration in Europe and the Third World', in F. Heckmann and W. Bosswick, eds, *Migration Policies: A Comparative Perspective* (Stuttgart 1995) p. 263.
14. I. Law, *'Race' in the British News* (The University of Leeds, UK: 1997).
15. M. Kubink, *Verständnis und Bedeutung von Ausländerkriminalität*: Eine Analyse der Konstitution Sozialer Probleme (Pfaffenweiler 1993).
16. H.-J. Albrecht, 'Ethnic Minorities, Crime and Criminal Justice in Germany', in M. Tonry, ed., *Ethnicity, Crime and Immigration* (Chicago 1997) p. 46.

Non-EU Citizens' Experiences of Offending and Victimisation

tions are made between the refugees and, in particular, Albanians' reputation for law-lessness; as Lewis notes: 'While Kosovo, Albania and Macedonia have been particularly associated with heroin production and transport in recent years, smuggling, black marketeering and gangsterism have been evident in all disputed territories.'[17]

The collapse of Albania's pyramid selling schemes in 1997 and the country's rapid demise into anarchy, alongside the question marks that are placed over the KLA's (Kosovan Liberation Army) sources of revenue, serve to enhance the 'criminal' label of Albanians and, by association, Kosovar Albanians. As reported by *The Daily Telegraph* (12/4/99), a conservative British broadsheet, in an article titled 'Gangsters "smuggling refugees to the West"', 'Fears are growing that Kosovar and Albanian gangsters could try to exploit the refugee crisis in the Balkans. The racketeers known to be involved in illegal immigration and drug running are worrying police forces across Europe.' While the *Telegraph* article is an atypical example of press coverage of the Kosovan crisis, it illustrates the extent to which negative and criminal connections are readily made – and in some cases justified – between refugees, illegal immigration and crime as a problem facing western Europe.

When the media is not reporting on the negative impact of uncontrolled migration to the EU, reference is occasionally made to the victimisation of migrants in the EU. Germany witnessed a number of racist arson attacks against migrants which were extensively reported by the press in the early 1990s.[18] However, in the same breath in which the press might condemn the actions of racist 'thugs' there is also negative news coverage of the 'threat' posed by immigration. An article in *The Observer* (4/10/98), a left-leaning British newspaper, about refugees from the former Yugoslavia in the small British seaside town of Margate, notes that local newspapers have 'fanned the flames' of racism through unsubstantiated reports on the numbers and negative impact of refugees. It appears that any links that are to be made between refugees' former victimisation and their current residence in the EU might soon be forgotten or readily ignored by disgruntled locals if refugees outstay their welcome. While the occasional horrific case of racism against migrants is reported by the press, the obvious connections between negative reports on immigration as a social 'problem' and the popular expression of racism against migrants (whether they be refugees, asylum seekers or migrants looking for economic betterment) are not, generally, alluded to by the press.

Meier-Braun[19] notes how the German tabloids, mirroring their British equivalents, have enhanced negative images of asylum seekers and refugees. Having said this, Meier-Braun goes on to suggest that the media could play a positive role in a campaign of anti-racist education. Sarah Spencer[20] reinforces the point that Meier-Braun makes by stressing the need for accurate and positive information to be passed on to the public with regard to the 'real' social and economic impact of immigration. However, in

---

17. R. Lewis, *loc. cit.*, p. 219.
18. A. Das, 'Frankfurt', in A. Dummett, ed., *Racially Motivated Crime* (London 1997) pp. 31–61; R. Witte, *Racist Violence and the State* (London 1996).
19. K.H. Meier-Braun, *loc. cit.*, pp. 337–342.
20. S. Spencer, ed., *Strangers and Citizens: A Positive Approach to Migrants and Refugees* (Institute for Public Policy Research 1994) pp. 1–17.

Non-EU Citizens' Experiences of Offending and Victimisation

contrast to Meier-Braun and Spencer, Albrecht is somewhat sceptical with regard to the potential impact that positive educational policies, aimed at counteracting racism against migrants, can have; as he comments: 'The effects of dissemination of such information on public views and attitudes, however, may be marginal.'[21] Albrecht discusses the relationship between the public's fear of crime and the question of immigration and concludes that there is little evidence, to date, that accurate information about the minimal risks to the social fabric from immigration results in a corresponding reduction in the public's fear of crime. Without engaging in the fear of crime debate in this paper, one could suggest that any fears the public expresses, regarding crime by migrants, are also deeply connected with questions of 'race' and racism which centre on the threat of cultural conflict. Colin Webster's[22] research with British Pakistanis and white racists notes the rejection of the 'victim' stereotype by young male Pakistanis, and their corresponding adoption of a 'defensive aggressive' stance, which results in former white aggressors perceiving themselves as the new 'victims' of Asian crime. Perhaps the same reversal in 'victimhood' can be generally witnessed with respect to indigenous European communities who perceive the threat of crime in relation to immigration and the cultural 'other'. However, having said this, one cannot deny the fact that some members of migrant communities are engaged in crime and, even, racism.[23]

One can heed the comments of Launer and Palenski in reference to the similar 'crisis' of immigration in the United States: 'American criminal justice policymakers are repeatedly pressed to respond to the new immigrant crime problem. Yet, public policy suffers from both a lack of fact and theory when it comes to new immigrant crime.'[24] In the same vein as the American warning, a 1992 Council of Europe publication on new migration flows in Europe, in reference to Germany and Austria, notes: 'Judging from the given information, immigration from Eastern Europe has clearly been increasing in both Germany and Austria ... It has, however, not even nearly reached the volume one would expect when listening to public debates.'[25] Negative stereotypes about migrants abound and the connections are regularly made between immigration, social problems and crime; connections which, even if correct, are not always based on solid information. Just as the press and the public are ill-informed, there is an absence of comprehensive information available to governments about the subject of 'migrants and crime'.[26] No single European state currently collects extensive information about migrants' offending *and* victimisation, and the data that is collected is not transferable between states. The absence of accurate information is particularly worrying when one considers the extent to which the populist claims and demands of the new right in Europe (note the recent success of Jörg Haider's right wing

---

21. H.-J. Albrecht, *loc. cit.*, p. 42.
22. C. Webster, 'The Construction of British "Asian" Criminality', 25(1) *International Journal of the Sociology of Law*, (1997) pp. 65–86.
23. J. Goodey, 'Examining the White Racist/Black Victim Stereotype', 5 *International Review of Victimology* (1998) pp. 235–256.
24. H.M. Launer and J.E. Palenski, eds, *Crime and the New Immigrants* (Springfield, USA 1989) p. ix.
25. E. Hönekopp, 'The Cases of Germany and Austria', in *People on the Move: New Migration Flows in Europe* (Strasbourg 1992) pp. 132.
26. M. Tonry, ed., Ethnicity, *Crime and Immigration* (Chicago 1997) pp. 1–29.

Non-EU Citizens' Experiences of Offending and Victimisation

Freedom Party in Austria) are encroaching on moderate centrist politics. The next pages will comment on the official response of politicians, at international and national level, to the question of immigration and crime.

2.3. The official response to the 'problem' of immigration

Commenting on immigration policy in Britain, David Coleman states: 'Case histories of many claimants make it clear that asylum claiming is often illegal immigration pursued by other means.'[27] Coleman adds that the British government, along with other member states of the EU, appears to believe that almost all new refugee pressure is conventional betterment migration and, therefore, illegitimate and illegal; as the Office for National Statistics states with regard to its over view of Britain in 1998: 'In recent years there has been a significant change in both the numbers and the motivation of those seeking asylum in Britain, with many asylum seekers apparently motivated by economic rather than political factors.'[28] Coleman's claims and the statement by the Office for National Statistics would appear to support the anti-immigration stance of the populist press with the implication that asylum claimants are simply economic 'scroungers'. However, turning to a United Nations publication on international migration and development, one can note the following in contradiction to Coleman: 'the notion that poverty produces refugee flows is inconsistent with the fact that extreme economic deprivation usually does not generate sizeable numbers of asylum seekers or refugees. Sustained economic deprivation is more likely to produce powerlessness than migration ... individuals are more likely to flee from situations that seriously threaten their lives and well-being than from those that curtail their political and economic rights.'[29] In other words, economic betterment is not, always, the first reason why people decide to leave their home country, their way of life and, often, their family to take up residence in another country (witness the mass exodus of refugees from Kosovo in 1999).

Beyond the question of 'legitimacy', with respect to the historical and narrow grounds for refugee status which excludes economic 'push/pull' factors, there lies the question of the ambiguous interpretation of 'rights' (as already referred to) with regard to non-EU citizens who gain entry to the EU. A matter of concern in this paper is the extent to which non-EU citizens (be they legal economic migrants, refugees, asylum seekers or illegal migrants) experience 'crime' in Europe and, with particular regard to 'rights', criminal justice intervention when they are victimised or are charged with having committed crimes. However, it is extremely difficult to determine the nature of criminal justice treatment received by non-EU citizens and, in particular, illegal migrants, when adequate information is unavailable from government and criminal justice sources with which to review the situation in and between EU countries.

The inadequacy of information with regard to the crime and criminal justice

---

27. D. Coleman, 'Immigration Policy in Great Britain', in F. Heckmann and W. Bosswick, eds, *Migration Policies: A Comparative Perspective* (Stuttgart: Enke 1992) p. 122.
28. Office for National Statistics, *Britain 1998: An Official Handbook* (London: HMSO 1998) p. 37.
29. United Nations, *International Migration and Development* (New York 1997) p. 52.

Non-EU Citizens' Experiences of Offending and Victimisation

experiences of non-EU citizens is partly a reflection of the recent re-emergence and recognition of the 'problem' of refugee movements in the world and, more specifically, in Europe. Refugees were not the 'issue' in recent decades that they became in the 1990s; this is particularly the case when one considers the unknown numbers of illegal migration movements in the world today. The UN notes: 'The demographic impact of international migration is particularly important in Europe, where almost 88 per cent of the population growth during the period 1990–1995 came from international migration'.[30] However, the UN proceeds to note: 'in the traditional market economy countries of Europe they [migrants] constituted over 6 per cent of the population.'[31] In real terms, numbers of migrants in Europe may not be as dramatic as the first percentage indicates when one considers the actual numbers involved alongside the different rules for granting citizenship in EU member states.[32] However, with the UN noting that illegal migration is 'one of the fastest growing forms of migration in the world today',[33] one begins to contemplate the extent of the problem of human trafficking and the profits that are made from this by organised crime networks. Likewise, the marginal status of illegal migrants in the EU, if they do not claim asylum status, places people in a highly vulnerable setting with respect to crime (as potential offenders and victims).

If one traces the evolution of European migration policies from the 1970s,[34] the trend is towards a negative response to immigration. Whereas migrants were generally regarded as necessary for economic development up until the 1970s, the dramatic escalation in asylum claims to Europe in the 1980s and 1990s reflects people's reliance on other means for entry into Europe following the closure of a more open immigration policy and, alongside this, the increased pressures on Europe from those fleeing civil war and conflict. European Union agreements, such as Schengen's (1985 and 1990) internally 'open' border controls and the Dublin Convention on Asylum (1990) (with its aim to standardise the management of asylum claims throughout the EU; as yet a theoretical proposition rather than practice), have not been able to cope with the fluctuating demands of immigration. It would appear to be the case that decisions at national level continue to take precedence over decisions at an EU wide level. This would seem to reflect the very immediate and practical demands of immigration that various countries have faced over the last few years. Germany, responding to the lion's share of migration movements in the EU in the 1990s, has had to cope with large scale immigration from former communist countries in the east with additional pressures from significant numbers of refugees and asylum seekers fleeing the war in the former Yugoslavia. Britain, on the other hand, has not experienced these particular pressures to the extent that Germany has.

---

30. United Nations, *op. cit.*, p. 12.
31. United Nations, *op. cit.*, p. 13.
32. One can note here the relative ease with which one can become a naturalised French citizen in comparison with the stringent application procedures in Germany that refer back to German ancestry residing with grandparents.
33. United Nations, *op. cit.*, p. 27.
34. J. Salt, 'Current and Future International Migration Trends Affecting Europe', in *People on the Move: New Migration Flows in Europe* (Strasbourg 1992) pp. 41–81.

Non-EU Citizens' Experiences of Offending and Victimisation

Regardless of whether responses to immigration are led by individual member states of the EU or the EU as a whole, the collective message is that migrants are not wanted in the EU and are increasingly perceived as a social and criminal threat. Nowhere is this anti-migrant stance better illustrated than with regard to the adoption of 'temporary protection' (TP) status, during the period 1992–93, in the asylum regime of the EU. The crisis in the former Yugoslavia resulted in the development and wholesale adoption of TP by the European Union with support from the United Nation's High Commissioner for Refugees (UNHCR); a procedure which was applied again, in 1999, in response to the reception of Kosovan refugees in the EU. TP cleverly circumnavigates the demands of the Geneva Convention which, upon the award of refugee status, effectively grants the receiver permanent residence and the possibility of integration in the country of settlement. Instead TP, as its name suggests, determines to send refugees home once it is deemed safe for them to return. Commenting on TP policy in the EU, Danièle Joly notes: 'These people [from the former Yugoslavia] in no way would come to stay … In other words if one cannot keep refugees out the next best solution seems to be to receive them for a limited period and send them home as soon as possible … This TP proposition enabled governments to satisfy the strands of public opinion which advocated a humanitarian policy vis-à-vis the refugees and those who spoke against immigration.'[35] While burden sharing between countries was supposed to be part of the TP measure, the numbers accepted, in reality, varied widely between countries, with Germany receiving around 300,000 and the UK receiving less than 10,000.[36] The application of TP has meant, in general, that the level of social rights for TP persons is not as good in the EU in comparison with people awarded refugee status under the Geneva Convention; however, as Joly notes: 'On the whole TP persons enjoyed slightly better rights than asylum-seekers although not in every respect.'[37] While UNHCR called for improved standards of treatment for TP persons in line with refugees, the EU has, so far, proved unwilling to encourage the settlement and integration of TP persons with the aim of returning them home. Since the end of 1996, when UNHCR ended TP status for refugees from the former Yugoslavia, voluntary and forced repatriation of TP persons to their 'home' countries has been in operation. Perhaps the war in the former Yugoslavia and the ensuing crisis in Kosovo, which has seen the reinstatement of a TP related programme for Kosovar Albanians, could have been better forewarned to meet the mass influx of people that the EU was, and is, so ill-prepared for. Better management and accurate information concerning immigrant groups can only serve to control if not allay fears with respect to the presence of the 'other' in Europe.

As the above illustrates, the greatest challenge to a comprehensive and coherent scheme for managing immigration demands in the EU lies with the shifting nature of migrant movements and populations. Each EU country receives varying numbers of immigrants from different countries and with different motives for trying to obtain access to the EU. Traditionally, Britain's pattern of immigration from the Caribbean and Indian subcontinent (in the second half of the twentieth century) has reflected

---

35. D. Joly, *op. cit.*, p. 3.
36. D. Joly, L. Kelly and C. Nettleton *Refugees in Europe: The Hostile New Agenda* (London 1997).
37. D. Joly, *op. cit.*, p. 17.

Non-EU Citizens' Experiences of Offending and Victimisation

its colonial past, while Germany's pattern of immigration (from the 1960s through to the 1980s) reflected its deliberate policy of 'guest worker' recruitment during this period. The overthrow of communism in the former USSR, the subsequent unification of Germany, on-going war in the Balkans and continued pressures to migrate from north Africa and other parts of the developing world, have all placed pressure on Europe to receive new migrants. At the same time, Europe is experiencing its own internal problems in relation to unemployment and strains on its (formally generous) state benefits. How then should the reality of continued immigration to Europe be treated with respect to the above negative stereotypes; in other words, isn't it time for the EU to consider the production of more accurate information with regard to the specific question of migrant groups' relationship to 'crime' as offending, victimisation and criminal justice response?

3. DEVELOPING ACCURATE INFORMATION ON NON-EU CITIZENS AND 'CRIME'

3.1. Existing evidence from Germany and Britain

Within the EU, Germany and Britain have some of the most extensive official and independent research data on 'minorities and crime'. However, the definition of 'minorities' differs dramatically between the two countries with respect to its meaning. In Britain, the focus is on British citizens as 'ethnic minorities'. In Germany, the focus is on 'foreigners' as 'minorities'. And, having presented Britain and Germany as possessing some of the best EU data on 'minorities and crime', the following paragraphs should make it abundantly clear that this data is inadequate as a basis from which to undertake comparative research on non-EU citizens as offenders and victims of crime in the EU.

3.2. Germany

Germany has perhaps the richest statistical data on the subject of 'foreigners and crime' using the categorisation of people according to 'foreign citizenship'. While the variable 'citizenship' (or 'nationality') has been excluded from federal court statistics since 1984, it has remained with police statistics. Having recorded 'foreign citizenship', the police proceed to divide foreign suspects into three categories: 'illegals', 'guest workers' and 'tourists'. Alongside the police data, the prisons simply record 'foreign citizenship' on the basis of a 'Yes/No' category and do not proceed to provide an additional breakdown according to nationality.

While German criminal justice data can provide a wealth of information concerning the subject of non-EU citizens and 'crime', information is not recorded with respect to the ethnicity of suspects and offenders. 'Ethnicity' is absent from Germany's crime statistics, by law, as a reflection of the country's Nazi past; to gather information on ethnicity carries with it sinister implications in Germany. Having said this, although the German police are not supposed to note the origin of particular ethnic groups, they circumnavigated this 'problem' with respect to Roma or 'gypsies' with use of the classification, in relation to suspects, 'numerous changes of the place of residence';[38] hence, a common European 'folk devil', throughout the centuries, is recorded 'unofficially' in the official criminal justice statistics. In contrast, Germany's largest immigrant group, 'ethnic Germans',[39] with over two million re-naturalised in Germany during the period 1968–1992, do not show up in the crime statistics as a special 'ethnic' group; however, as Albrecht notes: 'Recently, the Organization of German Police suggested that the increase in the crime rate among the German population, especially among German youth during the last few years, was due to the heavy immigration of ethnic Germans from eastern Europe'.[40]

What we are able to gauge from the German statistics is the wide variation in suspect and offender rates between nationalities and according to which German state is being surveyed. This points to a number of factors, not least of which is the role of statistical accuracy and discretionary police work, that contribute towards an explanation of national differences in offending. As Albrecht notes with respect to general patterns in Germany: 'Offender rates of police recorded crime among some minorities are two to four times that observed in society at large ... Some minorities have below average offender rates, for example, Spanish and Portuguese';[41] and: 'The proportions of Turkish, Italian, and Greek suspects, for example, have decreased dramatically over the last ten years, while the proportions from former Yugoslavia, Romania, Poland, the former Soviet Union, and some African countries increased considerably ... These shifts point to a significant shift in immigration patterns.'[42] Numerous variables, besides longitudinal immigration patterns, must be considered with regard to variations in apparent rates of offending between nationalities; for example: the unemployment rate for certain migrant groups, particularly for young men; the demographics of different migrant groups, again emphasising numbers of young men; and the area of residence of a particular group with respect to localised conflicts. Similarly, broad references to different nationalities' offending characteristics must not neglect to consider the type of crimes committed by different groups or within different groups.

Research in Germany has indicated that illegal migrants, tourists and asylum seekers tend to commit petty offences such as shoplifting[43] or offences related to immigration. In comparison, Germany's foreign resident population tend to commit more serious offences. Explanations for this may lie with the long-term residence of Germany's

---

38. W. Feuerhelm, 'Die fortgesetzte "Bekämpfung des Landfahrerunwesens"', 71 *Monatsschrift für Kriminologie und Strafrechtsreform* (1988) p. 306.

39. Germans who emigrated to the east and whose descendants can claim at least one German grandparent.

40. H.-J. Albrecht, 'Minorities, Crime and Criminal Justice in the Federal Republic of Germany', in I.H. Marshall, ed, *Minorities, Migrants and Crime* (London 1997) p. 88. *See also* M. Rebmann, *Ausländerkriminalitat in der Bundesrepublik Deutschland* (Freiburg 1998).

41. H.-J. Albrecht, 'Ethnic Minorities, Crime and Criminal Justice in Germany', in M. Tonry, ed, *Ethnicity, Crime and Immigration* (Chicago 1997) p. 50.

42. H.-J. Albrecht, *l*, p. 57.

43. E.H. Ahlf, 'Ausländerkriminalität in der Bundesrepublik Deutschland nach Öffnung der Grenzen', 3 *Zeitschrift für Ausländerrecht* (1993) pp. 132–138; as quoted in Albrecht, *loc. cit.*, p. 59.

Non-EU Citizens' Experiences of Offending and Victimisation

foreign resident population and the likelihood that second and third generation migrants are more involved in serious crime. In comparison, illegals, tourists and asylum seekers' more recent and marginal status in Germany does not encourage their involvement in serious offending. Particularly in the case of illegal migrants, their marginal social and economic status encourages their involvement in petty offending as a survival strategy. However, this is not to deny the fact, and the concerns of many governments and NGOs, that some migrant groups are involved in serious offending, such as drug/weapon smuggling and people trafficking, which victimises other migrants and EU citizens and can pose a threat to national security. But, as Karydis notes: 'Migrants do commit crimes and we must examine the extent, the structure, the qualities and the reasons for this criminality. Moreover, as we will discover, the degree of the involvement of the different ethnic groups with criminal activities is significantly different, and this calls for close examination of the facts and the social reality of crime.'[44] Here, one can note the damaging effect of the media's blanket references to the 'Russian mafia', as a problem related to immigration, which has an impact on other migrant groups. Negative stereotyping of a certain migrant group can transfer to other migrants who are not involved in serious crime. As Rawlinson comments, with regard to western Europe's insecurities about the criminal 'other' which are played on by the media's portrayal of the mafia threat: 'the media offers an equally prejudiced and simplistic interpretation of the Russian 'mafia' and threatens to obfuscate and consequently exacerbate the actual dangers presented by its proliferation.'[45] Stereotyping migrants as 'one' group hides the reality of inter-nationality crime rates and, also, intra-nationality crime with respect to differences within groups.

Reflecting criminological research on national populations and crime, researchers can expect to find that female or older non-German citizens are less likely than the men in their group and, in particular, the younger men, to commit crime. Also, in consideration of diversity within nationality groups, one is reminded of the other side of offending which is, of course, victimisation. What is often forgotten in consideration of the question of 'minorities and crime' is that many migrants, because of their marginal status, are victims of crime. Young men are in the highest risk group for offending and victimisation in any society and women are at highest risk of victimisation from crimes that take place in the home. Migrant women's doubly marginal status in society, as women and as minorities, places them in a particularly vulnerable position with regard to victimisation from their own community and from members of the host society. While German police statistics are a valuable source of data on suspects and offenders according to nationality, the same cannot be said with respect to victims. German researchers have undertaken a number of extensive victim surveys over the past few years but,[46] unlike the British Crime Surveys or the pioneering work of the Islington Crime Survey in London,[47] there has been no systematic data gathered on

---

44. V. Karydis, 'Criminality and Criminalisation of Migrants in Greece', in V. Ruggiero, N. South and I. Taylor, eds, *The New European Criminology* (London 1998) p. 356.
45. P. Rawlinson, 'Mafia, Media and Myth: Representations of Russian Organised Crime', 37(4) *The Howard Journal of Criminal Justice* (1998) p. 346.
46. K. Boers, *Sozialer Umbruch und Kriminalität in Deutschland* (Opladen 1997).
47. T. Jones, B. Maclean and J. Young, *The Islington Crime Survey* (Aldershot 1989); A. Crawford, T. Jones, T. Woodhouse and J. Young, *The Second Islington Crime Survey* (Enfield 1990).

Non-EU Citizens' Experiences of Offending and Victimisation

the victimisation experiences of minorities in Germany. Alongside the debate of whether ethnicity ought to be recorded by the German police in order to identify police bias, perhaps the greatest omission in German research to date on 'minorities and crime' lies with the absence of comprehensive data on non-German citizens' experiences of victimisation alongside their experiences of offending.

3.3. Britain

In Britain the subject of 'minorities and crime' has tended to focus on one or two areas; that is, offending by and victimisation against Britain's ethnic minorities and the actions of the criminal justice system with respect to these groups.[48] 'Minorities' has implicitly come to mean ethnic minorities who are British citizens. There are a few exceptions in which researchers have specifically investigated the experiences of minority non-British citizens in the criminal justice system (for example, Penny Green's edited collection looks at foreign drug couriers[49]); however, examination of minority/majority differences in rates of offending, victimisation and criminal justice response have centred around colour as the variable for comparison, rather than nationality, as British research has been framed under the heading of 'race relations' and the subjects in question tend to be British citizens. So, the concept of 'minority' as 'other' is largely limited in Britain to an internal examination of minority British citizens in the 'race and crime' debate. While British criminology is taking an increased interest in 'European' criminology and, in particular, organised crime and policing in mainland Europe,[50] the same degree of attention is not being paid to the everyday experiences of offending and victimisation for minority groups, as non-EU citizens, in the EU. British criminology's concept of the 'minority', of the 'other', and crime, remains limited and internalised.

One must turn to the prison statistics as the only national source of information in Britain on 'minorities and crime' which dates back to the mid 1980s. However, while the prison statistics provide a breakdown of prisoners' ethnicity from this period, nationality has only been statistically presented since 1993. Turning to the prison statistics for 1997[51] one can note that 8 per cent of the 'prison population'[52] were foreign nationals (a proportion which has remained the same since 1993), while 6 per cent of the *sentenced male* prisoner population were foreign nationals. The prison statistics for 1997 note that 'Over a third (36 per cent) of male foreign nationals were of European

---

48. M. Fitzgerald, (1993) *Ethnic Minorities and the Criminal Justice System* (London 1993); D. Smith, 'Race, Crime and Criminal Justice', in M. Maguire, R. Morgan and R. Reiner, eds, *The Oxford Handbook of Criminology* (Oxford 1994) pp. 1041–1117.
49. P. Green, ed, *Drug Couriers: A New Perspective* (London 1996).
50. V. Ruggiero, N. South and I. Taylor, *The New European Criminology* (London 1998); J. Sheptycki, 'Policing, Postmodernism and Transnationalism', 38(3) *British Journal of Criminology* (1998) pp. 485–503.
51. Home Office *Prison Statistics: England and Wales 1997* (London 1998).
52. The prison statistics simply refer to 'the prison population' at points wherein one can assume that reference is being made to the combined figures for the sentenced and remand prison populations and the male and female prison populations.

Non-EU Citizens' Experiences of Offending and Victimisation

nationalities, with another 20 per cent being nationals of Asian countries, 19 per cent being African and 16 per cent West Indian.'[53] The prison statistics' comprehensive list of foreign nationals has to be worked through in detail to determine whether the category 'European' is referring to EU or Non-EU citizens; the four highest figures in the 'Total Europe' category, male and female, are: The Irish Republic with 734 imprisoned;[54] Turkey and the Netherlands jointly with 155; and Cyprus at 77.[55] The prison statistics also provide information concerning 'population in prison by ethnic group, type of prisoner, sex and nationality' and 'population in prison under sentence by ethnic group, nationality, offence and sex'. A staggering 89 per cent of non-criminal prisoners, in 1997, were foreign nationals with 90 per cent of these held under immigration offences. In comparison, for sentenced criminal offenders, 32 per cent of foreign males and 13 per cent of British males were in prison for drug offences (with male foreigners including higher proportions of drug offenders in *all* ethnic groups surveyed), and 69 per cent of foreign females were in prison for drug offences (with, apart from the ethnic group 'South Asian', female foreigners including higher proportions of drug offenders in *all* ethnic groups surveyed).

The above figures inform us, to an extent, about the nature of offences committed by foreigners who are imprisoned in Britain. However, the figures do not tell us everything and are particularly confusing with regard to prisoners' nationality and ethnicity. Classification of a prisoner according to his or her nationality cannot accurately reflect ethnicity; for example, in the case of an offender from the United States or the former Yugoslavia. Similarly, the ethnic categories which are reduced in the published prison statistics to the four broad groupings of 'White', 'Black', 'South Asian' and 'Chinese and Other'[56] do not tell us anything about nationality beyond reference to British or foreign nationals. Although these ethnic groupings reflect the revised 1992 categories that were adopted for the prison statistics, they remain as broad, generalising categories that are not able to distinguish, for example, between 'White' ethnicities. One could argue that a further useful category of analysis would be 'religion'. Different patterns of imprisonment might emerge if this category is considered alongside the categories of ethnicity (which, in the tradition of British race relations research is based on colour) and nationality.

Having begun to find fault with British prison statistics as a basis for interpreting foreigners' involvement with 'crime' one only has to turn to the remainder of criminal

---

53. Home Office, *op. cit.*, p. 105.
54. The Irish are one of the most under-researched and 'forgotten' groups in British social and criminal statistics. Coleman's (*op. cit.*, p. 126) comments, with regard to British immigration policy, reflect this: 'there has never been any gathering of statistics on movements from the Irish Republic or (until 1962) of movements from any Commonwealth country'.
55. Home Office, *op. cit.*, p. 115.
56. In 1992 ethnic classification and how it is measured was changed in the production of prison statistics. Before 1992 the categories were 'White', 'West Indian, Guyanese, African', 'Indian, Pakistani, Bangladeshi', 'Chinese, Arab, Mixed Origin' and 'Other' and a prisoner's ethnic group was noted by the prison officer upon entering prison (Home Office prison statistics 1985). From 1992 the categories were self-selected by prisoners and are 'White', 'Black' (with further breakdown into Black-African, Black-Caribbean, Black-Other), 'South Asian' (with further breakdown into Asian-Bangladeshi, Asian-Indian, Asian-Pakistani) and 'Chinese and Other Asian' (with further breakdown into Asian-Other and Chinese) (Home Office prison statistics 1993).

Non-EU Citizens' Experiences of Offending and Victimisation

justice statistics for England and Wales to find a complete absence of data with regard to non-British citizens. As already stated, the focus of British research is on British ethnic minorities, as offenders and victims of crime, with extensive research undertaken on subjects such as police 'stop and search' practices,[57] sentencing in court[58] and racial harassment and victimisation.[59] One has to turn to the work of organisations such as 'Human Rights Watch' to find rare qualitative evidence of racist victimisation in Britain against particularly vulnerable non-EU citizens.[60]

Marian Fitzgerald, representing the British Home Office's official position on 'minorities and crime', has raised some noteworthy points which are of particular interest with regard to this paper; for example, she states: 'both the debate on offending and that on victimisation have been conducted in highly "ethnicised" terms. Moreover, the failure of criminologists to make any connections between the two debates clashes with their increasing recognition that victims and offenders are not discrete categories. Rather, they overlap in ways that have not only conceptual implications but that raise important questions for criminal justice practitioners.'[61] Fitzgerald makes the important observation that offender and victim populations are often one and the same; that is, namely, the urban poor. Breaking down the category of the 'poor', one generally finds experiences of both offending and victimisation over-represented amongst certain ethnic minority groups who tend to be the most disadvantaged in society. However, having said this, one has to emphasise the point that 'minority' groups are not a homogeneous whole. Between and within the umbrella term 'minority group' one finds a wide variety of experiences of offending and victimisation which are a reflection of the intersection of many variables working on the individuals who make up the group, which include (besides ethnicity): gender, age, religion and area of residence. One of the main concerns of research which attempts to document the 'crime'

---

57. C. Norris, N. Fielding, C. Kemp and J. Fielding, 'Black and Blue: An Analysis of the Influence of Race on Being Stopped by the Police', 43 *British Journal of Sociology* (1992) pp. 207–224; D. Smith, *Police and People in London: I, A Survey of Londoners* (London 1983). From April 1983 HMIC (Her Majesty's Inspectorate of Constabulary) has required all police forces to record the ethnic origin of all members of the public who are stopped and searched by the police; before this date this procedure was carried out on a voluntary basis by some police forces. The 1991 Criminal Justice Act (s. 95) was a particular landmark in ethnic monitoring because it required the Home Secretary to publish 'information' to assist those responsible for criminal justice to avoid discrimination. Similarly, a letter was also sent to all Chief Constables from the Home Office indicating that from April 1996 all police forces would be 'required' to introduce a system of ethnic monitoring of suspects and offenders; however, there are a number of problems with this monitoring process that have not made it fully operational (Home Office, 1997 'Ethnic Monitoring in Police Forces: A Beginning').
58. R. Hood, *Race and Sentencing* (Oxford 1992); M. Walker, 'The Court Disposal and Remands of White, Afro-Caribbean and Asian Men (London) 1983', 29(4) *British Journal of Criminology* (1989) pp. 353–367.
59. B. Bowling, *Violent Racism* (Oxford 1998); A. Sampson.and C. Phillips, *Multiple Victimisation: Racial Attacks on an East London Estate* (London: Police Research Group, Crime Prevention Unit Series No. 36, HMSO 1992).
60. Human Rights Watch, *Racist Violence in the United Kingdom* (New York: Human Rights Watch Publications 04 1997); for example, this edition refers to racial harassment of Somalian refugees in Sheffield.
61. M. Fitzgerald, 'Minorities, Crime and Criminal Justice in Britain', in I.H. Marshall, ed, *Minorities, Migrants and Crime* (London 1997) p. 36.

28

Non-EU Citizens' Experiences of Offending and Victimisation

experiences of Europe's 'other' minorities must be to break down generalising categories into more accurate reflections of these groups' (and groups within groups) experiences.

There are two points that need to be taken from Fitzgerald and considered with regard to this paper; first, the parallel experiences of offending and victimisation for many minority groups and, second, the over-representation of minorities as offenders and victims. However, having noted these two points, one can proceed to comment on Fitzgerald's omission of any in-depth commentary regarding non-British citizens as offenders and victims, let alone any discussion on the more specific categorisation of non-EU citizens. As with most British research examining 'minorities and crime', reference to immigration, migrants and nationality is usually limited to the historical migration of former Commonwealth and British citizens from the Caribbean, east Africa and the Indian sub-continent to Britain.[62] Here, one can add a third point for consideration to those raised by Fitzgerald – the need to examine 'other' minorities beyond reference to minority citizens.

4. DEVELOPING NEW RESEARCH

Michael Tonry's edited book 'Ethnicity, Crime and Immigration'[63] presents international chapters on 'minorities and crime' and 'immigration and crime' and goes some way towards an integrated discussion of minorities as citizens/non-citizens with regard to race/ethnicity. Tonry refers to the study of minorities and immigration as: 'two subjects that are seldom brought together which, once brought together, can teach more than either alone.'[64] However, because the chapters in Tonry's collection are internal reviews of individual countries, the interpretation of 'minorities and crime' is necessarily limited in the cases of countries, such as Britain, to a discussion of 'minorities' that is quite specific and frequently tied to the traditional interpretation of these groups either through the lens of immigration *or* 'race and crime' research. Like Tonry's book, Marshall's edited collection 'Minorities, Migrants and Crime'[65] also presents within country analyses and, therefore, suffers from the same bounded interpretation of 'minorities'. Similarly, both books are restricted in their scope because their approach to the subject of 'crime' is to focus on offending by rather than victimisation against minorities.

The greatest challenge to researchers interested in cross-national perspectives on 'minorities and crime' is to develop comparative research. As the brief introduction to research in Germany and Britain illustrates, this is no easy task. A number of barriers stand in the way of comparative research across criminal justice jurisdictions and different cultures; namely, different laws, different criminal justice practices, different systems for classifying 'minorities' and different research cultures and practices.[66]

---

62. M. Phillips and T. Phillips, *Windrush: The Irresistible Rise of Multi-Racial Britain* (London 1998).
63. M. Tonry, *op. cit.*
64. M. Tonry, *op. cit.*, p. 3.
65. I.H. Marshall, ed, *Minorities, Migrants and Crime* (London 1997).
66. L. Hantrais and S. Mangen, eds, *Cross-National Research Methods* (London 1996).

Non-EU Citizens' Experiences of Offending and Victimisation

So, while Germany has ample police data on differential offending patterns between nationality groups, Britain has good data on the nationality and ethnicity of prison inmates. However, the two sets of data are not comparable with regard to 'what' and 'who' is being researched. In particular, with reference to 'who' is being researched, one has to note that Germany and Britain have different populations of 'minorities' both between and within (depending on where research is undertaken) the two countries. Attempting to start with some common basis for research, this paper has steered the discussion towards an interpretation of non-EU citizens' involvement in 'crime', as offending and victimisation, in the EU. This provides a starting point from which to narrow the discussion of 'minorities and crime' but it does not overcome the problems of trying to compare very different populations and different criminal justice data.

New dedicated fieldwork is called for if cross-national research on minority experiences of 'crime' is to progress beyond the current limitations imposed by reliance on non-comparative secondary sources. In 1994 the European Journal on Criminal Policy and Research reported on a forthcoming research initiative by Michael Tonry and Roger Hood to examine 'race, ethnicity and criminal justice' in Europe and North America. The project description stated: 'Ultimately the ideal would be to initiate a number of empirical comparative studies, using a common model and common standardized instruments.'[67] To date, Tonry and Hood's initiative has resulted in the 1997 publication 'Ethnicity, Crime and Immigration', edited by Tonry, and empirical research in a couple of fieldwork sites.[68]

There remains a research 'gap' with respect to a large, cross-national study employing the same standardised research instruments. To this end, the author began a research project in January 1999. Funded by the European Science Foundation (ESF), the project, much like Tonry and Hood's 1994 initiative, ultimately aims to conduct empirical fieldwork with non-EU citizens in, potentially, six EU countries: Austria, Germany, Italy, The Netherlands, Spain and the United Kingdom.[69] However, it is easier to articulate than actualise cross-national, comparative fieldwork on non-EU citizens and 'crime'. Funding, time and the dynamics of an international research team are on-going challenges to successful research. The primary purpose of the ESF grant is to facilitate the development of research networks and research ideas which might, at a later stage, be operationalised. At the time of writing this paper, the author's ESF team is in the process of developing a viable research plan for comparative research between the six countries. As yet, the sample populations and the methodological and theoretical underpinnings of the research have to be finalised.

Standardised questionnaires are on obvious research tool for cross-national application. While questionnaire response rates can be disappointing and are, of themselves,

---

67. *European Journal on Criminal Policy and Research*, 2(3) edition on 'Ethnic Prejudice and Violence' (1994) p. 109.
68. Personal communication with Michael Tonry.
69. The research has been funded by the Standing Committee for the Social Sciences of the European Science Foundation and runs for 18 months from 1st January 1999. The opinions of the author, while writing as the project leader, do not necessarily reflect the opinions of the other members of the research team.

Non-EU Citizens' Experiences of Offending and Victimisation

problematic with regard to the representativeness of the population surveyed and the accuracy of responses, they are a means by which research can be standardised and applied across countries. The International Crime Victimisation Survey (ICVS) is an example of a research questionnaire which has been successfully applied in different countries in the attempt to more accurately gauge people's experiences of victimisation.[70] The ICVS obtained sufficient numbers of respondents in the countries and cities it surveyed but, as the authors of the survey themselves note, can be negatively critiqued with respect to aspects of its methodology (such as the use of phone based questioning) and the transferability of its ideas and questions across different world cultures (such as questions on violence in the home). Regardless of the many criticisms that can be levelled at the ICVS, the survey is an important milestone in the development of new comparative research between countries. Although the research under discussion here is restricted to EU countries, it is no less challenging than the ICVS because it endeavours to survey the myriad experiences of non-EU citizens from various countries. Likewise, the cultural diversity between and within European countries overlays the interpretation of these marginalised groups' experiences of crime. The multiple layers and hierarchies, as noted earlier, which operate on the individual's experiences of crime and victimisation in the EU, as 'non-citizen', demand a sophisticated level of survey research which is able to account for nationality, ethnicity/race, legal status, gender, age and religion (to name but a few variables).

Questionnaires remain the most convenient method for sampling large numbers of people quickly and for providing a wealth of data for interpretation. However, the challenge for research which is attempting to more accurately understand non-EU citizens' experiences of 'crime' might be more readily met through qualitative research which can unearth individual migrants' biographies of offending and victimisation as part of a continuum. From qualitative biographical accounts, connections can be made to collective experiences of 'crime' between different categories of non-EU citizens in different countries. It should also be remembered that these groups share a number of characteristics that deems it important they are researched through standardised methods in order to highlight any shared features of their offending and victimisation. The social, economic, political and cultural marginalisation of the most vulnerable populations in the EU demands that their present scapegoating as 'problem' and, in particular, criminal problem, be more accurately interpreted to reflect the 'realities' of their criminal experiences.

4.1. The ethics of research

German criminal justice statistics do not record 'ethnicity' for fear that such data will be utilised by those who want to 'prove' (as attempted by early scientific criminology and incorporated into Nazi ideology) that certain minorities are disproportionately inclined to offend. It could be suggested that the monitoring of minority

---

70. J.J.M. van Dijk, P. Mayhew and M. Killias, *Experiences of Crime Across the World: Key Findings of the 1989 International Crime Survey* (The Netherlands 1990); J.J.M. van Dijk and P. Mayhew, *Crime Victimization in the Industrialized World* (The Netherlands 1992).

Non-EU Citizens' Experiences of Offending and Victimisation

groups' criminality simply promotes negative constructions of these groups; the logical conclusion of this argument being that no monitoring should take place. In comparison, British criminal justice has been heavily influenced by the 'race relations' debate in Britain which supports the use of ethnic monitoring as a means to check and counteract discrimination by criminal justice agencies against minority groups; as Ann Dummett notes in the opening chapter of her edited book which describes a comparative study of anti-racism initiatives in Frankfurt, Lyons and Rome: 'ethnic monitoring is used in Britain as a means of trying to identify discrimination and promote racial equality'.[71] Ethnic monitoring, if undertaken with due care, can cast a more accurate light on who is being victimised, who is victimising, and the response of criminal justice agencies to these problems. If the German system records nationality then, one could ask, why not record ethnicity as both measures can be used for positive *and* negative purposes in the process of labelling particular groups' behaviour.

Any research looking at 'migrants and crime' should be cautious with regard to data control and interpretation. The aim of the author's ESF research is not to 'prove' or 'disprove' that the EU is under threat from the criminal 'other' in the form of the non-citizen. Perhaps the Union should examine its own internal problems of crime, stemming from its indigenous population, before it points a finger at 'outsiders'; and, as noted earlier, the most marginalised and, arguably, the least integrated of non-EU citizens are more likely to be involved in petty criminality rather than serious offending that can be constructed as a threat against national security. Also, any research on 'migrants and crime' should reveal the true extent of intra and inter-group crime and victimisation between similarly disadvantaged people. This returns research to the age old question of whether 'class' is a greater predictor of criminality and the likelihood of victimisation than either race, ethnicity or minority status. However, the juxtaposition of 'class' with 'race/ethnicity' presents something of a tautology as asylum seekers, refugees and some migrants tend to be the poorest groups in any EU country. While Albrecht states that 'the research questions which in the 1960s and 1970s highlighted social class, will in the decades to come be replaced by ethnicity',[72] Fitzgerald (earlier in the same book) says 'Ethnicity, however, is not the place to start [when analysing offending and victimisation]'.[73] Instead, Fitzgerald points to the importance of socio-economic status, geography and demographics when attempting to understand the complex questions surrounding 'ethnicities and crime' while noting, at the same time, that the collective experience of offending and/or victimisation may be ethnic in its impact. Hence the need to understand the intersection between offending and victimisation with ethnicity and socio-economic status in research which is attempting to address the general question of 'migrants and crime'.

The primary consideration here, with regard to the ESF project, is the nature of 'everyday' offending by and victimisation against non-EU citizens in the EU. Much like the drive behind victimisation and self-report surveys on national populations, a central aim of the author's research is to discover the 'normality' of the crime expe-

---

71. A. Dummett, ed., *Racially Motivated Crime* (London: Commission for Racial Equality 1997) p. 16.
72. H.-J. Albrecht, 'Minorities, Crime and Criminal Justice in the Federal Republic of Germany', in I.H. Marshall, ed, *Minorities, Migrants and Crime* (London 1997) p. 103.
73. M. Fitzgerald, *op. cit.*, p. 53.

rience for many non-citizens which may reflect more correctly some of these groups' strategies for survival rather than any innate tendency towards criminality amongst particular groups. Having said this, this is not to idealise the motivation behind some groups' criminality but, more correctly, to expect a diverse range of offending and victimisation experiences within and between the various groups surveyed. Concerns about the threat posed by organised crime to the EU is, in itself, another research topic.

Research might unearth 'problem' groups with regard to their propensity to offend or be victimised. With respect to the former, extreme caution has to be used in the interpretation of this information. New Right politicians may utilise such information for a populist appeal against immigration and, more worryingly, against specific groups of migrants currently in Europe; and, as commented on earlier, negative stereotypes are unlikely to be contained to a single group. Any information on aspects of particular groups' criminality must shift from the analysis of a 'problem group' to an analysis of the 'group's problems' which will need to be met with targeted work that endeavours to combat the root causes of particular groups' offending; such as projects aimed at combating youth crime and unemployment, alongside measures for integration which, in light of non-integrationist developments such as Temporary Protection, are likely to be extremely unpopular amongst politicians. An international survey might also highlight the non-criminal tendencies of certain migrants in comparison with other minorities who share similar cultural, social and economic characteristics; here, the history of the group in question and the context in which they now live become important in the explanation of differences in offending by (and victimisation of) similarly placed groups.

The particular configurations of the local context and the interaction of the indigenous population with migrant groups will have a significant impact on migrants' experiences of offending and victimisation. And, with particular regard to refugees and asylum seekers who have suffered physical and emotional trauma in their home countries, interpretation of these groups' offending and victimisation must also take account of the context from which they have fled. The factors which 'push' people to leave their home countries are often overlooked in research which stresses the 'pull' factors of host countries. The reasons for and the circumstances in which people leave their homes do not stop to influence people at international borders. Future research which is attempting a comprehensive understanding of migrants, asylum seekers and refugees' experiences of offending and victimisation might do well to consider events that occurred prior to residence in the host country. In other words, the social, economic and cultural position in which migrant minority groups find themselves in the EU are not, in themselves, causal explanations of their current experiences of 'crime'.

5. CONCLUDING COMMENTS

Michael Tonry is worth quoting at some length here with regard to his rallying call for comparative research on ethnicity, crime and immigration: 'What needs to be done now is to move beyond single-country analyses to work that integrates those analyses: comprehensive efforts to combine learning on different countries, compre-

Non-EU Citizens' Experiences of Offending and Victimisation

hensive efforts to establish what data are needed and available on each country to answer the questions that should be asked, development of a comprehensive research agenda that can begin to provide policy makers with the information they need to anticipate and work to prevent or ameliorate the kinds of problems that particular kinds of migrant groups are likely to experience.'[74]

In response to Tonry's call, it is hoped that the ESF funded research will be a first step towards the development of truly comparable data on the extent and experiences of non-EU citizens as offenders and victims of crime in the EU. More accurate and comparable data may confirm but, more importantly, may also challenge the criminal stereotypes that surround immigration into the European Union.

---

74. M. Tonry, *op. cit.*, p. 26.

Part II
Offending

[6]

Migration and Crime in Europe

HUNG-EN SUN and JACK REED
School of Criminal Justice, The University at Albany

Since the time of Abraham, migration has been a widely shared experience that evokes the pain and excitement of the human struggle for survival. Year after year, hundreds of thousands of people uproot themselves to embark on this uncertain journey for safety, freedom, and prosperity. The International Organization of Migration estimated that there were approximately 80 million international migrants in 1990, and projected that the number would exceed 100 million by 1992 (IOM, 1990). Encompassed in these figures are countless dreams that may either come true or become nightmares. The movement of people across countries, however, not only affects the lives of migrants themselves — it also succeeds in transforming the social fabric as well as the economic milieu of both sending and receiving countries.

Tangled among the promise and difficulty created by increased migration, crime stands as one of the most urgent and sensitive predicaments to be solved. The end of the Cold War forced numerous states to address internal issues concerning socioeconomic revitalization in their attempts to adjust to demands of the new world order. In this context, migration and crime, a complex problem in which law enforcement, social, and foreign policy considerations are intertwined, will surely become central issues of the international agenda in late 1990s.

Throughout history, voluntary and forced migration has caused the ethnic composition of the European continent to go through countless changes, some of them of significant magnitude. The flow of migration is increasing steadily; there is deceleration in sight. European migration reached the point that, in 1985, France, Germany, and the Benelux countries agreed to refine their policy regarding entrants from Third World countries. The accord included the tightening of border controls and the introduction of tougher entry requirements for migrants (Callovi, 1992). Increased migration also led to the European Convention on Security and Cooperation in Europe, signed in June of 1991. This accord creates a haven where fundamental human rights and basic living standards are respected so that permanent asylum applicants can be accommodated (Castles and Miller, 1993). This severely prohibitive proposal and several other restrictive measures were either implemented or recommended to curb the flow of legal as well as illegal migrants to industrialized nations and ease the tension generated by high levels of migration.

As the proportion of foreign residents in a nation increases, prejudice and suspicion surface between local citizens and immigrants. In some instances, open hostilities result in violent incidents in which foreign nationals are victimized, producing material damages, injuries, and deaths. It is not only extremist Neo-Nazi groups that launch physical attacks against new members of the population; other organized right-wing political forces exploit the xenophobic feelings of the public and capitalize on resentment toward less powerful outsiders. For example, many Italians cast their votes for the anti-immigrant Leagues in regional elections to punish the government for squandering funds in Southern Italy on migrants (Miller, 1991; Perotti and Thepaut, 1990). The

ESSAYS   229

Freedom party in Austria (Castle and Miller, 1993) and the FN in France (Weil, 1991) gained important advancement in municipal, regional, and national races based on explicit anti-immigrant platforms.

Many beliefs nourish this popular discontent with recent immigrants. Perceived competition over constrained labor and housing opportunities are often cited as a predisposing factor of ethnic discord, especially during periods of economic decline (Hollifield, 1992). First formulated in America, the "scapegoat theory" links inhospitable attitudes toward individuals of dissimilar reference groups to frustration (Dollard, 1939). For instance, newly established ethnic minorities have frequently been blamed for the adversity that disturbs the quality of life in the host society. Alleged high criminality is a focal point that has captivated public concern, academic interest, and official control.

At the beginning of this century, for example, the massive arrival of European immigrants to the United States attracted an invaluable amount of research effort toward the analysis of the criminality of urban immigrants. In spite of the research outcomes, however, isolationists succeeded in planting fear in the public mind, as well as in enacting restrictive legislation to keep out unwelcome aliens (Ferracuti, 1968; Shelley, 1981). Seventy years later, this same uneasiness mushrooms silently on the other shore of the Atlantic. Indeed, opinions about the criminal tendencies of immigrants in Europe are generally dim; an official Dutch publication even labeled the children of migrant workers settled in the Netherlands a "social time bomb" (Bovenkerk, 1993).

This pervasive view of foreign minorities as dangerous and crime prone, reinforced by the preoccupation with migrant deviance displayed in the reports of the mass media, aids the institutional marginalization of ethnic minorities in some of the contemporary European countries (Albrecht, 1987). Is the perception of an increased involvement in crime and delinquency an unfair stigma attached to the migrants in Europe? Or is it one more curse that this flock of paradise-seekers cannot escape? Also, what correlates and dynamics precipitate the occurrence of criminal acts in migrants?

In the present paper we examine extant literature that bears on the relationship between international migration, integration, and criminal deviance in Western Europe. The analysis begins with a concise historical account of postwar migration trends. The purpose of providing this information is twofold. First, it will help us to situate distinct pieces of relevant information against an appropriate chronological background. Hopefully, this contextual reading of pertinent materials will shed more light on the problem of migration and crime. In addition, given that the nature and consequences of migration changed in the area over the second half of this century, this temporal framework allows us to track the evolution of the research and theorizing on migration and crime and its correspondence with the unfolding of critical events.

The second part of this review examines relevant empirical studies and theoretical elaborations. Since migration is, by definition, an international phenomenon, it will be tackled from a regional perspective. We concentrate on developed Western European countries (e.g. France, Germany, England, Netherlands and Switzerland) that have traditionally received and accommodated international immigrants, accumulated meaningful records regarding the management of foreign residents, and produced important discussions on the topic. Pursuant to this analytical approach, our interpretative endeavor will transcend the country-specific depiction of migration, conflict, adaptation, and crime that characterizes the majority of the available sources. Findings about unique

230 ESSAYS

features of migration and particular mechanisms of social control of different societies need, and certainly will be integrated into a total picture in which interrelated politico-economic aspects as well as socio-demographic processes are identified.

Our exploration of crucial dimensions of migrant criminality will answer the following general questions:

(i) Does the criminality of immigrants differ significantly from that of the native population in terms of amount and form?

(ii) What causal factors have been identified to explain the criminality of migrants? Are these variables qualitatively different from those producing crime and delinquency among the native population?

The elucidation of these fundamental points will tell us whether the high criminality of international immigrants in Europe is a xenophobic myth (Ferracuti, 1968) or a prediction come true (Bovenkerk, 1993), and whether ethnicity and migration experiences are conducive to or preventive of criminal behavior. If simplistic 'yes'-'no' answers do not apply, what exogenous elements have intervened in the shaping of migrants' criminality? Finally, the role of governmental policy will be assessed and discussed with the hope of constructing a three-dimensional explanation that takes migrants, host countries and global context into consideration.

Migration in Europe

The history of modern European migration can be traced to the rise of colonialism. Driven by imperialist ambitions and economic necessities, European powers steadily expanded their overseas control between the 15th and 19th centuries by conquering and colonizing vast territories in Africa, Asia, the Americas, and Oceania. This inter-continental migration pattern predominated for four centuries.

A new pattern of population movement emerged in the 1800s. The Industrial Revolution, which brought powerful mechanical technology into the production process, set the stage for large-scale labor migration in Europe. Irish and Jewish workers flooded British industrial centers, while France and Germany received migrant workers from Poland, Italy, Belgium, Switzerland, and later from Spain and Portugal. This era of mass migration ended when the First World War broke out. Many migrants responded to the calling of their countries and went back to serve in the armed forces and munitions production (Castles and Miller, 1993). After 1918, a prolonged economic depression, coupled with the prevailing xenophobia, severely curtailed migratory movements. This migratory stagnation lasted until after WWII.

1945-1973

The resurgence of migration, particularly among non-European immigrants, in postwar Western Europe began with economic reconstruction and official attempts to regulate the labor supply through the import of foreign workers (Hollifield, 1992). WWII had profoundly damaged the economic infrastructure of the continent, obligating governments to focus on the rehabilitation of productive apparatus as well as the growth of commercial trade as their acute priorities. During the immediate postwar period, Italy supplied a large part of the foreign labor force in France, Switzerland and Belgium. This trend persisted until the early 1960's when Italy's own economic prosperity dried up its reservoir of labor (Maillat, 1987). The former colonies of Britain, France, and the Netherlands also contributed needed (migrant) labor to their respective work-forces.

The Office of National Immigration was created in Paris to facilitate recruiting and placing of foreign workers in needy sectors of the economy. In conjunction with strengthening the labor force, the employment of migrant workers also served as a safeguard against the pitfalls of rapid economic development. The presence of abundant workers in the market kept wages relatively low and stable, which in turn stimulated investment (Hollifield, 1992). By 1970 France had already accommodated 600,000 Algerians, as well as 140,000 Moroccans and Tunisians. In Britain, the government recruited 90,000 workers from refugee camps and from Italy through the European Voluntary Worker (EVW) program. Harsh conditions were imposed on these laborers: They had no right to sign contracts with private employers, could not bring family with them, and could be deported for undisciplined behavior. While the Swiss government did not devise any centrally planned immigration program, the private sector took the initiative and imported a huge number of seasonal workers and cross-frontier commuters. By the early 1970s these workers formed nearly one third of the total labor force. In order to block permanent settlement, job changing, long-term residency, and family reunion were all restricted in Switzerland (Castles and Miller, 1993).

Despite its flourishing economy and high level of industrial demands, West Germany did not face any serious labor shortages following the end of WWII. Some twelve million ethnic Germans from the communist countries of Central and Eastern Europe, and East Germany provided an immediate injection of labor with the swift and smooth integration of these newcomers into society (Hollifield, 1992). In the late 1950's, when immigration from East Germany subsided, the German government established recruitment offices in Italy, Greece, Turkey, Morocco, Portugal, Tunisia, and Yugoslavia where workers were selected, tested, and contracted, and sent to Germany in groups. By 1973, 250,000 migrants from Turkey and 153,000 from Yugoslavia were admitted, comprising almost half of all immigrants of European origin (Wander, 1990).

The Dutch situation was quite comparable to Germany's in that foreign immigrants did not arrive until 1961. More than 250,000 Dutch "repatriates" entered the Netherlands from Indonesia after its independence in 1949. In response to concerns about overpopulation and meager resourses, the government undertook a bold experiment of orderly emigration to solve the avowed crisis. Potential emigrants received official grants to subsidize their departure to Canada, Australia, or New Zealand (Heeren, 1990). Foreign workers appeared in 1961, when numerous large business organizations started to hire unskilled workers in Yugoslavia, Turkey, and Morocco. These active searches stopped abruptly due to the expiration of hiring contracts with the governments of these countries; but the spontaneous migration continued. After 1965, increasing numbers of black workers from the Caribbean territory of Surinam arrived, and by the late 1970s, some 160,000 Surinamese lived in the Netherlands (Castles and Miller, 1993).

In sum, the majority of international immigrants during both the periods of postwar rebuilding and sustained economic expansion was composed of two clusters of individuals: Colonial workers and migrant workers. Because of this influx, the number of foreign residents in the four traditional receiving countries of continental Europe (France, Germany, Netherlands, and Switzerland) increased from 2.7 million to 6.9 million between 1950 and 1970 (Maillat, 1987). Relying on the flexibility generated by the immigrants, host countries were able to manage the perils of bottlenecks in production and inflationary tendencies that could have stifled economic growth. Nevertheless,

232   ESSAYS

the price workers had to pay to obtain higher wages was excessive.

In the 1960s, there was a rapid expansion of the service sector in Western Europe. Jobs in this sector required higher qualifications, better training and offered greater rewards and more attractive working conditions than industrial employment. Migrants, mostly unskilled manual workers, provided replacements for native workers, who were able to obtain more highly-skilled jobs in this progression toward a post-industrial economy (Heijke, 1987). Within this stratification and ethnic division of labor markets, migrant workers tended to be marginalized and more vulnerable to exploitation than better organized labor segments.

1974-Present

The unexpected oil crisis of 1973-74 struck a severe blow to the economies of Western Europe. Prosperity and full employment became tendencies of the past. Abrupt changes in migration policies signaled the end of an era of active migration. For instance, Germany closed its borders in November of 1973, France in July 1974, and Belgium in August of the same year. Switzerland also had its own policy to correct the problem of *Uberfrendung* (overforeignization). The implementation of a series of maneuvers sought to accomplish two principal goals: (1) The elimination of competition between foreign and local workers for limited jobs by encouraging the return of migrant workers to their countries of origin and by suspending further immigration of new laborers, and (2) The reduction of general xenophobic moods and the assimilation of foreign residents who would not return to host societies (Tapinos, 1993; Hollifield, 1992).

There were two demographic factors that aggravated the surplus of labor. The first contingent of baby boomers poured into the market, which eliminated the shortage of native labor that had given employment opportunities to foreigners. Then, the female labor force swelled gradually. By the mid 1970s, more women participated in production and remained in active service longer. This global economic crisis revealed that jobs held by foreigners were much less secure than those filled by nationals, and unemployment among migrant workers remained higher than among nationals (Hollifield, 1992; Maillat, 1987; Tapinos 1993). In France, as in Germany, foreigners were disproportionately affected by job losses in those sectors which suffered least from growth slowdown (e.g. metallurgic industries, aviation, woodworking, etc.), and in branches where local employment has increased, foreign employment has fallen (OECD, 1994). An estimated 15 percent of the Turkish labor force was unemployed in Germany, compared to 6 per cent of the total labor force. In the Netherlands, at least 33 per cent of Turkish labor force was unemployed when the national unemployment rate was only 12.5 per cent. Among Moroccans in the Netherlands, unemployment reached a peak of 37 percent (Heijke, 1987).

Despite the closure of frontiers to new applicants and financial inducements offered for repatriation, the majority of migrant workers stayed. For example, roughly 60 percent of migrant laborers working in West Germany had done so for more than 10 years (Albrecht, 1991). Immigration populations actually increased during the rest of the decade, as immediate family members joined those who had entered as guest workers. Contrary to the original intent of the European guest worker programs, the nature of immigration turned into an irresistible permanent settlement of ethnic minorities[1].

Family migration changed the social characteristics of immigrants. The proportion of economically active persons, which corresponded with a shift in sex ratios in immigrant population, dropped from about 80 percent in the 1960s to below 50 percent in by the early 1980s. An almost constant influx of females reversed the initial numerical superiority of male migrants (UN, 1980). One of the most striking consequences of family reunification is the emergence of second-generation immigrants, which includes offspring who have either been born in the host country or have come to join their parent(s). In Germany, the Netherlands, and Switzerland, the number of youngsters under the age of 15 increased from 217,000 in 1960 to 1,459,000 by 1981 (UN, 1980; Maillat, 1987). The problems associated with a youthful population such as schooling, integration, career placement, and delinquency, also translated into soaring unemployment among foreign workers in the mid to late 1980s. These second-generation immigrants were now attempting to enter tight labor markets in large numbers.

A global refugee crisis began to develop in the mid-1970s with a mass exodus from Southeast Asia. Between 1983 and 1989 an additional 1.3 million asylum-seekers came to Europe, most of them driven by political crises and armed conflicts in Africa, Asia, and the Middle East. Following the collapse of several major communist regimes in 1989, another 1.3 million people left Eastern Europe and the Soviet Union for the West. During 1992, tens of thousands of displaced people from the former Yugoslavia constituted the largest group of refugees applying for political asylum in Western Europe (Loescher, 1993). These recent waves of forced migrants have enriched the ethnic spectrum of Western Europe as well as engendered new exigencies for local governments.

The settlement of former guest workers and their families coupled with an incoming flood of refugees forged the solidification of ethnic communities, although this self-empowerment has not done very much to improve living conditions. As a group, ethnic minorities still occupy a subordinate position in relation to majority citizens. Migrant workers are likely to inhabit the worst housing in the poorest areas of inner cities (Tomasevski, 1994), while segmentation of the labor market in host societies impedes foreigners' upward mobility (Maillat, 1987). That immigrants must struggle with many social maladies found in rundown urban areas has furnished the perception that they rank high in crime and delinquency, and that this phenomenon is directly related to their status as immigrants. In following sections we will look at some arguments and evidence on the issue of migration and crime.

The Quantitative and Qualitative Aspects of Migrant Criminality

The birth of modern criminology in America was partly stirred by the perceived pernicious dominance of foreigners in urban areas. The first research efforts, and subsequent formulation of causal explanations, scrutinized the relationship between immigrants and crime (e.g. Shaw and McKay, 1942, Sellin, 1938). In the public's mind, the term "immigrant" is often connected with high unemployment, low income, low educational level, high crime rates, and other infirmities that arouse fear and disgust. This collective stereotype is not exclusive to the United States; it can be found in almost every society that experiences immigration (Francis, 1981; Junger, 1989).

Given these perceptions, it seems logical to ask, "Do migrants have higher involvement in crime?" The answer entails making a decision about comparison groups. The criminality of immigrants can be judged against the amount of crime in their home or host countries. In general, only comparisons with host crime rates has been conduct-

234   ESSAYS

ed and reported (these data seem more relevant to the advancement of criminological science as well as to the making of public policy), while comparisons with home crime rates may lack immediate pragmatic value.

In the next section, we survey available data to answer the question about the relative criminality of foreign residents. Special emphasis will be placed on historical and regional facets of the problem. The interpretation of crime trends should not assume a socio-cultural vacuum; instead it must take into account the political and economic dynamics that might have an effect in the production of this specific social fact. In order to fully grasp the scope and implications of this problem, the review of single country statistics will contain contextual information.

One important obstacle to our task is the diversity of languages (e.g. German, French, and Dutch) in which many European studies are published. However, this obstacle granted us a chance to empathically sense the distressful frustration that most migrants must encounter. Two outstanding works by Franco Ferracuti (1968) and Martin Killias (1989) made an important portion of non-English literature accessible and greatly alleviated our pain.

Migration and Crime Literature, 1945-1973

The first postwar evaluations of migrant crime came to light in the 1960s when migratory movements started to gain momentum and receive public attention. Concern over this problem spread across the main receiving countries and resulted in an ever-growing array of research.

West Germany: Using police data, Wenzky (1965) found that foreigners from Mediterranean and African countries working in the industrial area of North Rhine Westfalia were heavily involved in crimes of violence. Migrant workers were responsible for 20 percent of murders committed in 1962-63. Interestingly, this found that many foreigners had a criminal history in their homeland for similar offenses. This situation parallels the Mariel Cuban problem that afflicted the United States in the 1980s, when the government authorized the admission of a group of Cuban prisoners, ex-prisoners, and mental patients as refugees, many of whom later became clients of the American penal system (Clark, 1991). A longitudinal follow-up of crime trends in Dusseldorf discovered that the number of migrant crimes increased somewhat over time (Wehner, 1966). A closer examination of the types of crimes committed indicated the real problem hidden beneath the gross figures: A significant proportion of migrants' offenses pertained to the category of illegal migration. And when Wehner corrected the ratio, the criminality of foreign workers dropped to less than half that of the native population. The participation of migrants in street crimes seemed very rare in this part of Germany.

A rigorous research design by Zimmermann (1966) compared four immigrant groups: Italians, Greeks, Spaniards and Turks. After carefully screening out tourists, foreign military, and international criminals, the author calculated the proportion of crimes committed by host citizens and foreign workers for the year 1965. Generally speaking, the crime rates of native Germans were higher than those of migrant laborers. Among foreigners, Turkish and Greek migrants appeared to be the most deviant, while the Mediterraneans (Italians and Spaniards) were accountable for fewer offenses. Zimmermann also observed an inclination toward violent crime among foreign workers; most of these incidents took place within the boundaries of their ethnic circles.

Based on court files of Stuttgart, Stuttgart-Bad and Esslingen, 110 Italian migrants,

ESSAYS   235

primarily from southern Italy, were compared with 173 native counterparts (Nann, 1967). In this analysis more Germans were convicted of property offenses, while Italians had 4 to 5 times more violent crime convictions between 1960 and 1962.

Switzerland: The comprehensive work of Neumann disputed the general view that Italian workers who populated the area of Zurich Canton were highly crime prone. Police and court records revealed that Italian migrants committed fewer, and less serious, criminal offenses than Swiss citizens (Neumann, 1963). Although Italians had higher rates for assault and larceny, their participation in murder and forcible rape was minimal. Statutory rape comprised three-fourths of sex offenses attributed to Italians and a large percentage of thefts were for shoplifting. Despite empirical evidence contradicting the unfounded anxiety over the dangerousness of Italian migrants, the print media kept propagating xenophobic rumors about the possibility of an imminent breakdown in public safety if the unrestricted import of Mediterranean workers persisted. In 1964, foreign workers reached a record high of 720,901, of which 68 percent were Italians. An analysis of official data on known criminals among in 1965 showed that the crime rate for the Swiss was 441 per 100,000 while only 315 per 100,00 for foreign workers (Graven, 1965). Among migrant workers, Italians, Arabs, Turks, and French citizens were less likely than Austrians and Germans to have contact with the criminal justice system. These results were subsequently replicated by Pradervand and Cardia (1966) in a study that included experimental and control groups. Controlling for social characteristics, the criminality of foreign workers in Geneva ranked in the following way: Fribourgois, Valaisans, Genevois and Italians. The criminal statistics for 1965 also supported the conclusion that foreigners were involved in less criminal activity than natives (Gilloz, 1967).

France: The criminality of foreigners reflected in French official statistics looked more pessimistic. Although the proportion of foreign inmates in the correctional system decreased consistently from 1964 to 1965, they still represented 16.8 percent of the total prison population (Morice, 1967). The inmate population ratio was 1 to 1800 for French nationals and 1 to 550 for immigrants. The situation of Algerians was even more staggering, with an incarceration rate of 1 per 190 Algerians (Radzinowicz and King, 1977). The overrepresentation of Algerians among official criminals was corroborated in a comparison between foreign groups. The analysis of criminal records of 153 immigrants living in Nantes between 1970 and 1973 found that the crime rate within the Algerian group was 1.5 times higher than that of the general French population (Desdevises, 1976). The difference remained even when control variables were introduced. There was, however, less crime among immigrants of European origin. The unusually high crime rate was confined to non-European populations. No evidence of crime-specific specialization along ethnic lines was detected, and the criminality of foreigners and local citizens did not differ qualitatively.

Britain: McClintock and Gibson (1961) showed that Eire-born residents had higher robbery rates than the native population. In an analysis of court data on shoplifting published in 1962, 29 percent of offenders were of foreign origin (Gibbens and Prince, 1962). Among them, females and Europeans formed the largest groups. These ethnic- and offense-specific results, however, cannot be generalized to other minorities and crimes. Five year later, Bottoms inquired into the delinquency among Commonwealth immigrants from the West Indies, India, Pakistan, and West Africa and concluded that the level of deviant behavior was low in most categories, except for violent domestic disputes where rates were approximately twice that of the native population (Bottoms, 1967).

Belgium and the Netherlands: There were few studies available during this early period. Young adult Italians showed no higher participation in criminal activity in research conducted in the Belgian province of Liege (Liben, 1963). Buikhuisen and Timmerman analyzed court data from the province of Groningen for 440 Ambonese migrants and a Dutch control group. The results suggested that although there was more delinquency among second generation boys, first generation Ambonese and second generation girls had low crime rates (1971).

Overview: 1945-1973

Recognizing the existence of idiosyncrasies in each country, the body of literature summarized above demonstrates that immigrants of the pre-closure period did not cause disruption of the social order in host societies. Although a few specific ethnic groups did cause some visible trouble in certain places (e.g. Algerians in France), migrant workers in general respected local legislation and behaved accordingly, frequently better than host citizens. When these results are placed in the context of the social background and working conditions discussed earlier, we wonder how these individuals could withstand the pressure of so many forces conducive to deviance in other populations.

The majority of the migrants were young men away from the close control of their families. They were disconnected from their churches, lived in crowded housing and worked at the most humble jobs with high risks of unemployment. In terms of many theories of crime, these immigrants were among the best criminal candidates, yet they did not fulfill the prophesy of many crime theories. From these data, then, it appears that the right question to ask is not "Why do migrant workers commit crime?" but rather, "Why did they commit so little crime?"

In some countries, foreigners displayed discernible patterns of criminal behavior and engaged in certain types of crime with higher frequencies. Basically, offenses against persons (Lieben, 1963; Wenzky, 1965; Nann, 1967; Bottoms, 1967; Gillioz, 1967) and sexual misbehavior (Neumann, 1963; Handel, 1966) among immigrants was more easily discovered and punished by host authorities. This inclination toward expressive crime rather than instrumental crime does not imply that migrants *always* committed them with greater frequency than the general population, but that in relation to other categories, violent and sexual offenses seemed to be favored (or discovered, or prosecuted) among foreign criminals. The incidence of property offenses varied inconsistently across nations; in some regions, the rates raised above the average, in others, below.

In the next section, we examine whether these same trends are found during the period 1974 through the present.

Migration and Crime Literature, 1974-Present

By the mid-1970s, it became apparent that little reliable information about migrants' criminality was available. The Council of Europe decided to take up this question, and in 1975, a sub-committee on migrant workers and crime appointed by the European Committee on Crime Problems released a report in which recommendations were made to member states (Council of Europe, 1975). The sub-committee urged governments to obtain the data necessary for effective policy making and not to circumscribe the research to the criminality of migrant workers, but instead to study more general social relations and conditions. This proposition exhibited a certain concern for the transformations in the composition of migrant communities taking place as a consequence of changes in European migration policy after 1973.

The gradual feminization of migrant communities, a decrease in employment, the growth of a young generation, and a shift to low-level tertiary sector activities distinguished the recent migration population. A concomitant change in the direction of the criminality of immigrants might be expected. What actually occurred?

Germany: There was only one paper published at the beginning of the period that agreed with earlier research findings and suggested that crime rates among foreign workers was low (Kaiser, 1974). The remaining evaluations, relying primarily on police statistics, testified to an overwhelming increase in migrant criminal activities. Albrecht and Pfeiffer first reported this new trend (1979). Their study of Hamburg, Hanover, Frankfurt, Stuttgart, and Munich between 1973 and 1977 found that crime levels were much higher for immigrant adolescents and young adults than for native Germans of the corresponding age groups, although lower for immigrant children than Germans of the same age. Foreigners also showed a greater likelihood to commit offenses involving sex and "crude behavior" than local citizens. Professional crime such as grand theft, blackmail, and stolen goods dealing was extremely rare among migrants.

A similar picture emerged in West Berlin (Autorengruppe Auslanderforschung, 1981). While the young children of foreign parents appeared law-abiding, immigrant youths over age 14 demonstrated a higher propensity for police contacts. For example, while 5 percent of the general West German population were crime suspects, the percentage of Turks, Greeks, Italians, and Yugoslavs was 15 (Funcke, 1982). In contrast with their remarkable underrepresentation in drug offenses, young Turks and Yugoslavians had a high prevalence in robbery.

Three research pieces of national scope disclosed greater delinquent involvement of immigrant youth, regardless of age (Gebauer, 1981; Chaidou, 1985, Traulsen, 1988). Moreover, the crimes committed by foreigners were no longer an intra-ethnic phenomenon; two thirds of the victims of immigrant youths were Germans (Chaidou, 1985). Overall, crimes committed by immigrant youths were less serious in cases of theft but graver in cases involving violence (Traulsen, 1988). Foreigners accounted for 15 to 29 percent of rapes, murders, bodily injuries, and robberies (Kaiser, 1980).

When comparing court data with police statistics, the higher criminality of Turkish and Italian adolescents found in police data disappeared in court statistics (Mansel, 1986). Evidence suggests that foreigners' children had a lesser chance of being convicted (or, possibly, were changed more often in cases where less evidence was avaiable). In a survey of self-reported delinquency among juveniles in Bremen, immigrant teenagers admitted fewer delinquent offenses than Germans (Schumann et. al., 1987). But since the validity of the measures was not assessed (e.g. through official record check), no conclusive assertions can be made. The reliability of similar self-report instruments have been found to be inferior for ethnic minority youths in the United States (Hindelang et. al., 1981).

In Northrhine-Westphalia the number of convictions per 100,000 population was 2080 for foreigners but only 1163 for German citizens in 1987. Six major ethnic groups showed substantial differences in conviction rates: Portuguese, Spanish, and Greeks rated below, while Italians, Yugoslavs and Turks rated above German natives (Rogers, 1993).

Switzerland: There have been two relevant studies devoted to the problem of immigrants and crime that have yielded conflicting results. The contradiction may be ex-

238   ESSAYS

plained by the difference in samples used. Killias examined records of both the Zurich police and the Geneva juvenile court and found that immigrant male adolescents between ages 15-17 had higher crime rates than Swiss natives, but that younger immigrant boys did not (Killias, 1977). In contrast, Queloz's (1986) analysis of 7,800 court files of the Canton of Neuchatel between 1974 and 1982 showed higher delinquency rates among immigrant boys between 7-14, but not among older adolescents between 15 and 17. Overall, the difference in criminality between immigrants and natives is small in this country.

France: The information pertaining to French ethnic minorities comes substantially from court and prison data. Malewska *et. al.* (1982) documented that 30 percent of the residents of the 66 correctional centers for juvenile delinquents were of foreign origin. Are these figures exaggerated? Two analyses of court files established that second generation immigrants did actually have a disproportionately high number of prosecutions and convictions. Over a 2-month period in Paris, 35 percent of juveniles prosecuted were members of ethnic minorities, 22 percent of which were Maghreb youth (De Carvalho and Lahalle; 1976). In another appraisal of 386 court records, Lahalle estimated that the non-delinquent/delinquent ratios for both minority and French youths were 4 to 1 and 8 to 1 respectively. Although the author may have exaggerated the difference by miscalculating the denominator (Killias, 1989), the trend is unequivocal. The interpretation of conviction statistics by Aubusson de Cavarlay reveals that, holding social class constant, foreigners were convicted for offenses against the public order and for violent crimes more often than the native population (1984). But the variations between French nationals was less important than those between social classes.

Britain: A series of research efforts by Batta and colleagues on minority juveniles in Bradford in the second half of the 1970s concluded that Asian youths seldom had brushes with the law and that very few known offenses could be attributed to this ethnic group (Batta et. al., 1975; Batta, 1978; Mawby et. al.; 1979). These results were even more significant in light of the fact that Asians dwelled in older and poorer accommodations, and contained a higher proportion of male than female teenagers. The low criminality of Asian immigrants was later corroborated by subsequent studies (Rees et. al. 1979) and official investigations (Home Office, 1984).

African ethnic groups experienced severe criminality. Blacks had high official crime rates and suffered more arrests than the white majority in all offense categories (Stevens and Willis, 1979; Home Office, 1984). Coupled with this, respondents of victimization surveys reported more victimizations from black offenders (Tuck and Southgate, 1981; Home Office, 1984). The victims interviewed identified the offender as black about twice as often as the proportion of black residents among the total population would suggest.

Belgium and the Netherlands: In Schaerbeek, Brussels, where many foreigners resided, both native Belgians and immigrants had their own shares of high criminality. The Maghrebs committed more thefts of all kinds while the Belgians dominated car thefts and drug-related offenses (Lahalle, 1981).

In 1981, Junger-Tas collected self-report data on 1,042 native and 58 immigratnt youth living in the area of the Hague (Junger-Tas, 1983). Two years later, another investigation on crime and second generation immigrants took place in Rotterdam and Eindhoven (Junger-Tas, 1985). Police files revealed that Surinamese, West Indians, Moroccans, and Turks committed a disproportionate amount of common thefts and robberies compared to their Dutch counterparts. This conclusion does not extend to violent crimes, however, where few minority adolescents took part.

In a recent study that included 790 subjects aged 12-17 as the sample, Moroccans had the highest arrest rates (34%), followed by, Surinamese (23%), Turks (22%), and Dutch (15%). This clearly indicated a plain overrepresentation of migrant children in police statistics (Junger and Polder, 1992). A similar distribution of delinquency was found in the small town of Gouda (Terlouw and Suzanne, 1989).

Overview, 1974-Present

The Council of Europe reached the conclusion that an increase in the number of foreign inmates in European correctional systems is one of the main features of the prison population of member nations. From 1983 to 1991, for example, France and the Netherlands recorded an increase in prison population of 50 and 87 percent respectively (Tomasevski, 1994). Numerous researchers have questioned the validity and reliability of using official statistics (police, court, and prison records) to measure levels of migrant criminality in a continent where xenophobia has such a long and dreadful history. The noted discrepancies between native and foreign criminality might be due, at least partly, to the discriminatory exercise of discretion by criminal justice officials (Killias, 1989; Tomasevski, 1994; Bovenkerk, 1993; Carr-Hill, 1988). This is especially important when some law enforcement forces, or members of them, have had intimate links with right-wing or nationalist organizations (Junger, 1989; Carr-Hill, 1987). Nevertheless, there is no proof of rampant discrimination that can completely tarnish the utility of official data in estimating the characteristics of criminal offenders (Junger, 1989; Albrecht, 1991).

No one can dispute that the reunion of the family that solidified the strength and stability of ethnic communities had an impact on the societal security of host countries and raised new challenges for European criminal justice systems. The profound reconfiguration of migrant communities in the late 1970s and throughout the 1980s dramatically changed the crime trends among foreigners. The advent of second and third generation immigrants announced the end of "the good old days." Although their presence did not have a homogeneous and invariable influence on the amounts and types of migrants' criminality across provinces or countries, minority youth did create a considerable delinquency problem in Western Europe. There are, of course, exceptions to this general trend, and we still encounter exemplary youth (e.g. Asians) that have successfully resisted the temptation of crime. The exceptions are few however. The rule is that the criminality of migrants has become qualitatively more diverse and quantitatively more abundant in spite of the fact that the tendency of juvenile and young adult crime in the general population has been declining during the same time period (Albrecht, 1987).

The relative ease with which we narrate the history of migrants' criminality in Europe disguises the complexity of the issue. Experts in the field unanimously agree about what happened in the last four decades. There is, nevertheless, a good deal of debate about why and how it occurred the way it did.

Determinants of the Criminality of Migrants: Structure or Culture?

Causality, according to Hume, is not given in the "facts" but imputed to them. Criminologists that have grappled with the problem of migration and crime in European countries have amassed a sizable collection of information and it is time for us to blend this conglomeration of data into a meaningful scheme.

240   ESSAYS

It is said that each generation has the measure and variety of crime that it deserves (Lynch and Groves 1989:7). Aside from the question of merit or blame, this maxim reminds us that crime, a human predicament *par excellence*, must be discerned in its historical context. History develops culture and social structure as well as unfolds *in* culture and social structure. From the criminological perspective, these two pillars form the major sources of crime and delinquency (Kornhauser, 1978).

Culture refers to the shared understandings that engender varying degrees of commitment among members of a social group. Social structure denotes the relatively stable relations among parts of a society that differentiate and define their positions. Most causal hypotheses of migrants' criminality either focus on the values and norms that migrants hold or emphasize their standing in the structural stratification of host societies. The division of the history of contemporary European migration into two periods entails certain elements of arbitrariness, but it does provide an extremely useful framework. The two periods mark two utterly different generations of immigrants, each with its own story.

1945-1973: Determinants of the Criminality of Migrant Workers

In spite of the prejudice arrayed against them, the hordes of migrant workers drawn by expanding economies in Western Europe, practiced a surprising display of self-control and propriety. Counter to all predictions, the comparably low criminality of these immigrants, shown statistically, bestowed an unexpected blessing on the host countries. It should also be noted that certain patterns of deviance stood out as peculiar expressions of foreigners' criminality. Neither the prevalent low criminality of most immigrants nor the salience of violence among Italian workers in some places has eluded the inquiry of experts. The numerical scarcity of crimes poses a puzzling question: What caused immigrants to evidence low criminal participation across ethnic groups, throughout the region, and over so many years?

Deprivation of economic and educational opportunities, population density, residential mobility, community deterioration, and poverty that stems from the uneven distribution of social resources has consistently been linked to the decline of public safety in both industrialized and developing societies (Clinard and Abbott, 1973; Shelley, 1981). A great many theories have been proposed to extricate the structural components and mechanisms that lead to a proclivity for deviant activities among the lowest social strata. This seemingly universal truism has popularized "kind of social space" and "kind of geographic area" theories of crime in which class membership or residential environment are thought of as catalysts of criminal behavior. But migrant workers, as a heterogeneous collectivity, exhibit an inexplicable immunity against the criminogenic conditions that surround them, as compared to citizens of the same classes in the native population.

The asymmetric sex ratio and skewed age structure described by Neumann among Italian workers in Switzerland typified the migrant demographic structure of the region (Neumann, 1963). For example, the female/male disparity in the foreign population was 45:100 for Germany and 77:100 for Switzerland in 1960; most males were aged 20-29 and lived in cities (Maillat, 1987). Foreign workers entered Western European occupational markets as cheap semi-skilled or unskilled laborers. As street crime has long been seen as the business of young urban males, the assumption was that this structurally constrained population would someday become a formidable army of deviants. This did not happen.

If social structure fails to explain the low criminality of foreign workers, can cul-

ESSAYS   241

ture give a more persuasive argument? Did they hold some internalized moral values or behavioral norms that protected them from the constant push of their disadvantages as well as the pull of the availability of deviant opportunities? Many believe that Asian immigrants normally adhere to the legal requirements of their host countries because of the influence of collectivist ideals that permeated their normative systems for centuries (Hayner, 1933; MacGill, 1938; Batta et.al., 1978; Brown, 1990). The steadfast loyalty of Asians to their cultural mandates, even when living in an alien world, greatly reduced the number of clashes with local authorities and earned them a reputation as "model minorities." A similar hypothesis was proffered for migrant laborers in Europe.

The detailed investigation of social background and working conditions of Italian migrants between ages 16 and 25 in Liege suggested that the presence of a growing, vibrant, and receptive Italian community decreased the intensity of new migrants' inter-action with local Belgians (Liben, 1963). This social segregation, partly determined by discrimination, had two decisive effects: (1) It decreased incidents of culture conflicts that may have attracted a more fervent interference from law enforcement agencies; and (2) Helped to preserve the integrity of the home culture. To Liben, the resilience of Italian family bonds paired with rigid paternal authority, served as safeguards that pre-vented their children from succumbing to crime. The weakness of this explication is the assumption that these culturally determined law-abiding migrants came from a country of emigration with a low incidence of crime (Council of Europe, 1975). In other words, there might be certain binding symbols and controls among all Italians that minimize their level of deviance, including that of Italian emigrants. Available cross-national data do not support the hypothesis that Italians foster a conformist culture; crime rates for Italy have traditionally been higher than those for Belgium. Any attempt to locate caus-es of high or low crime rates for particular groups of migrants in their inherent cultural character will have to pass the same test.

If the "nothing but culture" approach cannot forge a compelling argument, a "cul-ture and structure" thesis that considers the goals and attitudes migrants hold for them-selves as well as their location in the social stratification makes a better case. Hoff-mann-Nowotny maintained that a sort of contentment subculture took form among Ital-ian workers in Switzerland from the passive acceptance of their neo-feudalistic subordi-nation to the Swiss majority (Hoffman-Nowotny, 1973). They learned to be complacent with the tough living and working conditions in which they were submerged, and to realistically adjust their aspirations. After all, even though their marginal status had remained unchanged in structural terms, the individual financial situation of immigrants had improved markedly.

A social psychological analysis of group structure and culture conflict of Italians in Germany postulated a parallel hypothesis (Kurz, 1965). According to Kurz, conflicts of allegiance arose among guest workers as they belonged simultaneously to two social groups: The family in Italy and the working group in Germany. The former enjoined them to return to their homeland as soon as possible, while the latter demanded dili-gence in pursuing economic goals. The incomplete incorporation of new life-goals from the host community and strong identification with the family-oriented values of Italian culture emphasized the priority of returning home over the ambition of financial suc-cess. This typical resolution of conflict had protective effects against crime. Both Hoff-mann-Nowotny and Kurz pointed to the abandonment of aggressive financial aspira-

242   ESSAYS

tions as the primary cause of migrants' low criminality. In the classical formulation of strain theory, the combination of cultural imbalance, cultural universalism, and a rigidly stratified opportunity system produces criminal motivation at the individual level. All three elements must converge; none of them by itself causes crime (Merton, 1938; Kornhauser, 1978). The segmentation of the labor market not only gave rise to an underclass composed of foreigners, but also differentiated a less achievement-oriented subculture among them that directly eliminated the cultural universalism required for the criminogenic strain to work. The cultural fragmentation mitigated the latent volatility of structural arrangements in these societies. Hoffmann-Nowotny commented that foreigners' readiness to accept better monetary compensation and higher living standards of the Swiss as being legitimate and distinct from their own brought about their disinterest in property offenses. Since low property crime rates among foreign migrants were not exclusive to Switzerland, this theoretical speculation may well apply to other areas such as Germany.

A very appealing line of discussion is geared toward the influence of governmental immigration policies on the variation of migrants' criminality. The essential purpose of regulating the capital and labor markets to attain sustained economic growth rather than social or demographic concerns drove the politics of immigration during this period. The increasing foreign labor supplies in France and Switzerland in the 1950s and in Germany in the 1960s provided greater flexibility in the labor market (Hollifield, 1992). The use and regulation of foreign workers as fuel in times of intense economic activity and as a shock absorber in times of decline determined that some states would pursue a policy of repatriation to alleviate unemployment when deemed necessary. Immigration controls, length of stay, and the regulation of return migration in Western Europe have been hypothesized to have influenced individual level decision-making and the variation in crime rates at the aggregate level.

To cope with the labor demand, Germany and Switzerland favored a high turnover in migrant workers. All European countries issued work permits for a fixed time period, and without automatic renewal. If the decision to commit a crime is made on the basis of an analysis of the costs and benefits of the action, then the threat of being arrested, punished, and subsequently deported by the justice system would become an intimidating risk that migrants must consider. Given the eager desire to stay in the host society that most alien laborers showed, the prospect of the termination of legal residence may have exerted a powerful deterrent effect against illegal conduct despite the adverse circumstances encountered in their new residential environment (Shelley, 1981). In support of this assumption, Neumann (1963) found that many thefts by migrant workers were committed just prior to their final departure for home, that is, when the dreadful consequences of official reaction started to lose weight (1963).

In addition to their dependence on temporary work permits, migrant workers avoided contact with police and immigration officials because of their unfamiliarity with the host countries' laws, customs and languages. This had the effect of making them almost "overtly submissive to authority" (Clinard, 1978). The strict immigration control and regulation that resulted in the tenuous legal status of the migrant workers imposed an extra restraint on their behavioral choices that native citizens did not have to worry about. From a rational choice point of view, the differential risks and costs of crime commission induced by governmental policy can partially explain the general disparity of crime rates between foreign and native populations.

ESSAYS   243

The scrupulous management of the flow of immigrants to regulate labor and economic markets can alter the social and demographic organization of the receiving country and consequently affect crime trends. The magnitude of this relationship varied, of course, according to the relative size of the foreign population in the country; the significance of the input from immigrants increases as their number swells. In the Netherlands for example, foreign residents, who represented less than 2 percent of the total population, played a very limited role in the area of crime and justice. The effect of migrants' criminality was an important concern in Switzerland, however, where over 75 percent of its unskilled labor force was foreign. It is precisely in Switzerland that public policies in spheres other than criminal justice were influential in shaping the crime problem, or lack of it.

The working class in Switzerland consisted primarily of uneducated migrant workers who gained the right to be admitted due to the desirability of their productive power. These "buffers against market trends" were also buffers against high crime rates (Balvig, 1988). Treated as part of the labor force but not of the population, foreigners at the lowest echelon of the hierarchy were sent out and repatriated when there were no adequate jobs for them, or when they were not adequately qualified for employment. For instance, during the economic crisis of 1974-76, 340,000 jobs were lost while the number of unemployed Swiss rose by only 13,000. Balvig saw this disposal of a high risk population as the root of low Swiss crime rates in general, and of low criminality among migrant workers in particular.

Would foreigners have become more criminal if they were allowed to stay? We may never know. The reality is that the exportation of several hundred thousand social liabilities to other countries not only solved the problem of a labor surplus but also succeeded in maintaining law and order. The broad administrative powers to deport non-citizens that extended to the court and the Alien Police had the effect of reducing criminal recidivism among the 15 percent of the population whose ethnicity or nationality had led them to settle quietly at the bottom of a rich society. Although Switzerland constitutes an exceptional case, it illustrates the way in which protectionist immigration policies can sometimes be transformed into instruments of social engineering, particularly in small immigrant countries.

Along with overall low rates of criminal involvement, the eminence of expressive offenses defined the criminality of migrant workers. Higher incidence of violent and, to a lesser extent, sex crimes were reported in various localities. An examination of the circumstances and characteristics of these offenses found that cultural rather than structural dynamics were associated with this expression of deviant conduct.

With regard to crimes against persons by foreigners, experts pointed to the central importance of cultural norms and differences in its causation and criminalization (Liben, 1965; Wenzky, 1965; Zimmermann, 1966; Sveri, 1966; Nann, 1967; Ferracuti, 1968; Radzinowicz and King, 1977; Shelley, 1981). Ethnic minorities that had been known as more inclined to commit this specific type of offense included Italians (Liben, 1965; Wenzky, 1965; Nann, 1967) and a few Africans (Wenzky, 1965; Radzinowicz and King, 1977). Sellin's culture conflict theory (1938) and Wolfgang and Ferracuti's subcultural theory of violence (1967) composed the theoretical underpinnings of this explanation of migrants' violence. Some immigrants came from cultures with some sort of code which prescribed violent conduct and which was passed on through word and deed

244   ESSAYS

from one generation to the next.

The occurrence of intra-group violence among southern Italians registered in Germany and Switzerland (Nann, 1967; Neumann, 1963) can be better illuminated with a series of comparative analyses of deviance and law. In regions of Southern Italy, particularly Sardinia, inhabitants were indoctrinated into the *barbacino* code which inculcated them with motives, attitudes, and perceptions to resort to violence, especially vendetta homicide, in their interpersonal conflicts (Wolfgang and Ferracuti, 1967; Newman, 1978). Customs and norms embodied in the migrants no doubt had traveled to and settled in their ethnic enclaves as well. Algerian youths in France and Hungarians and Yugoslavs in Sweden also tended to use physical force as a problem-solving tool, a cultural practice that could not escape criminalization in their host societies. Virtues at home such as toughness, masculine dominance and pride could become deviant values in other countries (Radzinowicz and King, 1977; Sveri, 1966).

Both structural and normative factors have been cited as precipitating variables of sex crimes including rape, statutory rape and prostitution. Witschi offered a justification of prostitution that stressed gender imbalance within migrant populations. The decriminalization of prostitution would relieve the sexual tension among alien workers and reduce sexual victimization of Swiss women by these males separated from their families (Witschi, 1966). The high rates of statutory rape by Italian workers in Switzerland resulted from the gap between the two legal cultures. The legal age of adulthood was 14 in Italy, and the resolution to marry the underage female involved could absolve the offender from guilt, whereas in Switzerland a lady could not be legally married before 18 (Neumann, 1963). The cultural component was so obvious in this kind of offense that many guest workers charged with statutory rape used cultural difference as their defense in German courts (Handel, 1966). The sexual misconduct of migrant workers processed by the European justice system should be understood in the light of their unique experience as outsiders in urban societies.

The application of exclusionary policies that included discouragement of family entry, limitation of immigrants' political rights and widespread use of deportation powers socially segregated migrant workers from their hosts. The lack of integration into the local community life obliged migrant workers to find social support among fellow workers and normative guidance in their home culture while striving for a better life in an alien environment. This uncertain existence conditioned migrants to orient their behavior, both social and anti-social, to the normative expectations they were familiar with rather than to the structural exigencies of the residential surroundings.

Thus far we have suggested several explanations of migrant crime relevant to the 1945-1973 time period. Given the changes that occurred in migrant crime trends during the second period (1974-present), we undertake a separate discussion of possible theoretical explanations for these behaviors.

1974-Present: Determinants of the Criminality of Second Generation Immigrants

By the 1980s about 7 million young foreign descendants were growing up, attending school, and looking for jobs in the lands where their parents had first come to work temporarily. The rapid upsurge of these second generation immigrants recast the physiognomy of the criminal population. This generation replaced the low overall rate of criminality of the former generation with an increasing and multiform criminality. In most countries, foreign youths have higher crime rates than native juveniles, and have expanded the assortment of activities to include crimes against property as well as crimes against persons (Killias, 1989). Why have these youngsters drifted away from the paths and wishes of their parents?

Unlike the experience of earlier immigrants and contrary to the prediction of Sellin, an evident dissatisfaction with culture conflict theory has spread among researchers as culture differences have not validly explained both the growth and versatility of young immigrants' criminality. On methodological grounds, there is a complaint about the vague concept of culture conflict which can hardly be operationalized and measured (Kaiser, 1974). And when proper designs were done to test the variable, culture conflict could account for neither the aggregate rates of crime nor the individual frequencies of delinquency (Albrecht and Pfeiffer, 1979; Junger and Polder, 1992). Only some exotic cases of ritual sacrifice, blood feuds, and unconventional religious ceremonies that make up a small portion of the rising foreign crime rate could have been caused by the friction of norms and values. Consequently, most common crimes by young immigrants were left without an explanation.

Likewise, comparative research suggests that despite the variance in the technicalities of law and social control across cultures, the rejection of conventional offenses (like those committed by foreign youths in Europe) is functionally universal (Newman, 1976). Since fundamental values incarnated in the criminal law of receiving countries do not conflict with those of sending countries (Albrecht, 1987), answers should stem from variables other than culture conflict.

After the immigration stoppages of the early 1970s, the integration of ethnic minorities has become a basic social policy goal of host societies. Second-generation immigrants work within institutional frameworks that differ significantly from those operating on their progenitors, and they went through a very singular process of socialization. Children of migrant workers fostered their own distinctive identities and political views. Their more stable and assimilated permanence has slowly eroded the ideology of resignation and contentment that kept their forebears satisfied and in place. With higher expectations, these minority members seek the same chances and yearn for the same living standards as their hosts (Brown, 1990). Criminologists regard this change in life aspirations as an incipient precipitant of the current pattern of migrants' criminality. Attitudes such as consciousness of deprivation and socio-economic inequality (Albrecht, 1991), longing for prestigious consumer goods (Killias, 1989; Brown, 1990), and disillusionment with the country of residence (Shelley, 1981) separate the ideological texture of this generation from that of their predecessors.

Although dissimilar sentiments and ambitions set migrant generations apart, they are very similar in terms of the structural conditions each faces. Deficient schooling and fierce competition among second generation immigrants in declining sectors of occupational markets have kept them at the bottom rung of the social ladder. In Germany, Belgium, and Britain data indicate that some in the second generation have not been able to maintain the social standing of their parents (Wilpert, 1989).

With few exceptions (e.g. Junger and Polder, 1992), most research attests to the strong relationship between socio-economic characteristics of minority residents and crime (Albrecht and Pfeiffer, 1979; Aubusson de Cavarlay, 1984; Rees et. al., 1979; Thanou, 1982; Junger-Tas, 1985; Junger, 1989). However, when basic structural variables were held constant, differences in delinquency rates between minorities and the host majority dwindle considerably or simply vanish (Albrecht, 1987; Mansel, 1986; Junger-Tas, 1985; Aubusson de Cavarlay, 1984; van der Hoeven, 1986). Apparently, disadvantageous living conditions, stigmatization and disapproval have institutionally marginalized foreigners in urban slums and hence increased the likelihood of involvement in illegal activities on the part of immigrants (Albrecht, 1987, 1991). Such deprivation and marginalization also denies them access to wealth and prestige through white-collar crime; the involvement of immigrants in professional, environmental and corporate crime is practically nonexistent (Albrecht and Pfeiffer, 1979; Aubusson de Cavarlay, 1984; Bovenkerk, 1993).

Once again we confront the question of culture or structure. The accumulated information hints at an amalgamation of both, although this time with an emphasis on the unfavorable structural net in which migrants are trapped. The adoption of expectations and goals pertaining to their native counterparts by second generation immigrants has instilled the cultural universalism lacking in the past. As the general level of aspiration has started to soar with no visible improvement in available opportunities, grievances and strain blossom (Killias, 1989). Following this reasoning, Bovenkerk insightfully contends that past underrepresentation of migrant workers among the criminal population was a sign as well as a result of their failure to integrate into society. True, integration and equality will require immigrants to take their full quota of crime just as women's emancipation would produce higher female crime rates (Bovenkerk, 1993). However, cultural segregation or preservation of traditional values may sometimes act as brakes against the propagation of criminal behaviors (Kurz, 1965; Albrecht and Pfeiffer, 1979; Brown, 1990) — although some studies suggest the opposite (e.g. Aronowitz, 1988). Ultimately, it is the perception of a fair possibility of achievement in the educational and occupational systems that determines the preventive or criminogenic function of subcultural values (Killias, 1989).

While some advocate the hastening of assimilation measures to forestall the development of hostile subcultures (Funcke, 1982), Bovenkerk warns against such a naive and simplistic faith in the preventive effect of immigrant integration. Assimilation of second generation immigrants without appropriate improvement of their socio-economic conditions may backfire by aggravating their frustration and discontent. The more young foreigners assimilate the norms and attitudes of the host culture, the more they become susceptible to the same structural constraints that cause native crime.

Influential empirical investigations in post-1974 Western Europe concluded that the factors which best explained crime in general also serve as the best predictors of crime among ethnic minorities (Albrecht and Pfeiffer, 1979; Albrecht, 1991; Junger, 1992). The gradual cultural assimilation and political integration of younger immigrants offset cultural neutralizers and political deterrents that had shielded them from structural pressure and contributed to abnormally low rate of criminality of earlier alien workers. For first generation immigrants, fear of expulsion to their country of origin was a strong deterrent. Second generation immigrants are no longer affected by this condition (Junger and Polder, 1992). This is especially true when many have become citizens in countries with lenient naturalization policies such as the Netherlands and France. The heavy participation of minorities in property offenses across member nations of the Council of Europe (Albrecht, 1991) may well be due to this subcultural transition that liberated the criminogenic influence of unemployment, poor housing, and structural subordination.

ESSAYS   247

   Based on his review of related literature, Albrecht stresses the onerous frailty of internal cohesion that deteriorates the supporting capacity of minority families. Consciousness of deprivation among youngsters and the broadening gap between traditional beliefs of parents and values of the host society undermine the effectiveness of family controls (Albrecht, 1991). In accordance with this observation, robust bonds to family and school, as well as firm commitment to traditional values and activities proved to be essential in keeping Islamic and Surinamese adolescents and young adults from delinquency in the Netherlands (Junger and Polder, 1992), and among Turkish adolescents in Germany (Aronowitz, 1988). The dual socialization that forces a plurality of models and multiple group allegiances upon offspring of immigrants diminishes. Nevertheless, attachment to ethnic symbols and primary groups has moved from imperative to option, from a developmental necessity to a matter of choice. If the crisis of allegiance has loosened the binding strengths of their own ethnic identity and family, marginal economic opportunity precludes the establishment of solid adhesion to institutional beliefs and goals (Albrecht, 1987; Aronowitz, 1988; Liebkind, 1989). Apathy and estrangement flourish because of restrictive legislation that hampers full political participation and limits involvement in civic activities, while lack of material comfort feeds resentment and demoralization. Minority membership is not only a source of strain but also a cause of weak identification with conventional others. At the micro-level, the breakdown of informal control mechanisms constitutes a proximal cause of delinquency by minority juveniles (Albrecht, 1987; Junger and Polder, 1992; Schuler-Springorum, 1983).

   The rise of second generation immigrants compelled governments to substitute exclusionary policies with integration policies to cope with the latent risk of social conflicts. Although the process of adaptation and assimilation has encountered strong resistance and will take many generations to complete, it has already caused a subcultural rupture between different generations of immigrants. Younger foreigners aspire to move from the peripheries where their parents found solace to the center, and to become more active participants in their own lives. As their value orientation resembles more and more that of the native youths, so does their criminality. If poor education, unemployment, inadequate housing and alienation trigger the eruption of criminal behavior in any other social group, the criminality of second generation immigrants should also be examined in the light of the long-term link between ethnic origin and structural disadvantages.

   A comprehensive criminal justice policy package aimed at this issue would require the inclusion of provisions to combat institutional discrimination as well as measures to enhance chances of upward mobility. Someday the issue of the criminality of third or fourth generation immigrants will become theoretically meaningless and politically irrelevant because it will become absolutely indistinguishable from the criminality of majority groups. Thus, it is up to governments to decide whether to adopt a focal approach that emphasizes the control and treatment of criminal immigrants or to embrace the strategic ideal of remolding their countries into more tolerant, fair and just societies.

Conclusion

   Our examination of the empirical literature on migration and crime suggests two things. First, changes in migrant characteristics and immigration policy explain shifts in migration and crime research. Second, differences in the situation of migrants themselves explain the diverse findings of the two periods reviewed. Criminality results from a complex interaction of the motivational and occupational disposition of immigrants and the socio-political dynamics of host societies; it cannot be reduced to the ethnicity of the guests, nor to the structural organization of the hosts.

As the nature of immigration progresses from temporary stay to permanent settlement, and the goal of immigration policy switches from management of foreign labor to integration of ethnic communities, the criminality of immigrants in Western Europe evolves from admirable conformity to alarming rebellion (of second generation minority youth). None of these variables operates in isolation; instead, migrants and receiving countries offer each other both strenuous exigencies and desired benefits in the context of global politics. Variations in the qualitative and quantitative aspects of migrants' criminality respond to diverse immigration, foreign, and social policy moves of European governments, and vice versa. And this intriguing interaction seems to continue.

In recent years, different socio-political events have roused further waves of migratory movements. The disintegration of the Communist bloc, the ethnic carnage in the Balkan Peninsula, global economic warfare, and the removal of border controls have all accelerated the regional influx of asylum seekers and the arrival of permanent immigrants and highly qualified professionals from Third World countries. Although the significance of these demographic changes to public safety is still to be seen, old strains and new opportunities are likely to give birth to innovative forms of criminality among immigrants. Reported crimes committed by Russians and Eastern Europeans ranging from the trafficking of refugees to nuclear material, and more traditional Mafia-style crime such as prostitution and smuggling have increased rapidly in Western Europe (Lemaitre, Gerner, and Hansen, 1993). The import and distribution of illegal workers, prostitutes, and drugs from Eastern Europe, Northern Africa, South America, and Asia are facilitated by the connection between international organizations and local ethnic groups with geographically extended family structures (Bovenkerk, 1993; van Duyne, 1993).

Current trends of organized crime within minority communities should not surprise us. Hagan (1994) holds that residential segregation, ethnic-based inequality, and concentrations of poverty that have evacuated conventional forms of social capital from minority communities often propel subcultural adaptations of recapitalization. Ethnic vice industries providing illicit services to the majority group clientele bring back financial capital and serve a redistributive function for the minority community (Hagan, 1994). How can the problem of ethnic organized crime be solved when it is fulfilling a vital social function regulated by the principles of a market economy? There will be no reduction in the social costs of crime without a broadened partnership of immigrants in the administration of political resources and economic wealth. The exposition of history may end, but history goes on. New international crises and racial conflicts keep pounding the old continent, carving the emergence of a multi-ethnic Europe. Amid the anguish of weeding out deep-rooted fear and misunderstandings, a common motif knits all parties together: The hope for a brighter tomorrow. May this shared dream come true, for the guests and the hosts alike.

Endnotes

1. Family reunification takes two forms. The usual way is the entry of inactive members of the family to join the migrant worker. The alternative, better known in Germany and France, consists of the immigration of economically active married females who accompany or join their husbands.

ESSAYS   249

References

Aubusson De Cavarlay, B. 1984. Condamnations et Condamnes. *Donnes Sociales*. Paris: Institut National de le Statistique et Etudes Economique.

Albrecht, Hans-Jorg. 1987. Foreign Minorities and the Criminal Justice System in the Federal Republic of Germany. *The Howard Journal of Criminal Justice* Vol. 26:272-286.

Albrecht, P. and C. Pfeiffer. 1979. Culture Conflict or Social Deprivation - Attempts to Explain the Crime Rate in the Foreign Population of the Federal Republic of Germany. *Bewaehrungshilfe* V 26: 105-118.

Aronowitz, A. 1989. *Assimilation, Acculturation and Juvenile Delinquency Among Second Generation Turkish Youth in Berlin, West Germany*. Unpublished doctoral dissertation. Albany, NY: State University of New York.

Autorengruppe Auslanderforschung 1981. *Zwischen Ghetto und Knast. Jugendliche Auslander in der Bundersrepublik. Ein Handbuch*. Hamburg:Reinbek.

Balvig, Flemming 1988. *The Snow-White Image: The Hidden Reality of Crime in Switzerland*. Oslo: Norwegian University Press.

Batta, I. D., R. I. Mawby and J. W. McCulloch 1978. Crime, social problems and Asian Immigration: The Bradford Experience. *International Journal of Contemporary Sociology* Vol. 18: 135-168.

Batta, I. D., J. W. McCulloch and N. J. Smith 1975. A Study of Juvenile Delinquency among Asian and half-Asians. *British Journal of Criminology* Vol. 15: 32-42.

Bottoms, A. E. 1967. Delinquency among Immigrants, *Race* Vol. 8:357-383.

Bovenkerk, F. 1993. Crime and the Multi-Ethnic Society: A View from Europe. *Crime, Law and Social Change* V.19: 271-280.

Brown, John 1990. *Insecure Societies*. London: MacMillan.

Callovi, G. 1992. Regulation of European Immigration in 1993. Pieces of the European Community Jig-Saw Puzzle. *International Migration Review*. Vol. 26:2.

Castles, S. and M. J. Miller 1993. *The Age of Migration: International Population Movements in the Modern World*. Basingstoke: Mcmillan.

Chaidou, A. 1984. *Junge Auslander aus Gastarbeiterfamilien in der Bundersrepublik Deutschland: Ihre Kriminalistat nach Offizieller Registrierung und Nach Ihrer Selbstdarstellung*. Frankfurt: Frankfurt am Main.

Clark, David D. 1991. *The Mariel Cuban Problem*. New York State Department of Correctional Services: Albany, NY.

Clinard, Marshall B. and Daniel J. Abbott 1973. *Crime in Developing Countries: A Comparative Perspective*. NY: John Wiley & Sons.

Clinard, Marshal B. 1978. *Cities with Little Crime: The Case of Switzerland*. Cambridge: Cambridge University Press.

Council Of Europe ed. 1975. *Aspects of Criminality among Migrant Workers*. European Committee on Crime Problems, Strasbourg.

De Carvalho-Lahalle, A. 1976. La Deviance chez les Mineurs Fils d'Immigrants. *Reeducation* Vol. 4: 281-183.

Desdevises, M. C. 1976. *La Delinquance des etrangers*. Unpublished thesis. University of Rennes.

Dollar, John et. al. 1939. *Frustration and Aggression*. Yale University Press, New Haven.

Ferracuti, Franco 1968. European Migration and Crime, in *Collected Studies in Criminological Research*. Vol. III. Strasbourg; European Committee on Crime Problems.

Francis, Ronald D. 1981. *Migrant Crime in Australia*, St. Lucia, Australia: University of Queensland Press.

Funcke, L. 1982. Integrationsprobleme de Auslaender in der Bundesrepublik Deutschland und Ihre Auswirkungen auf die Polizei - Aus der Sicht der Beauftragten der Bundesregierung fuer Aus-

250   ESSAYS

laenderfragen, From *Bestandanfnahme und Pespektiven der Verbrechensbekaempfung* pp 59-66.

Gebauer, M. 1981. Kriminalitat der Gastarbeiterkinder, *Kriminalistik* Vol35: 83-86.

Gibbens, T. C. and J. Prince 1962. *Shoplifting.* London: The Institute for the Study and Treatment of Delinquency.

Gilloz, E. 1967. La Criminalite des Strangers en Suisse,*Revue Penale Suisse* Vol. 2: 178-191.

Graven, J. 1965. Le Problem des Travailleurs Etrangers Delinquants en Suisse, *Revue Internationale de Criminologie et de Police Technique* Vol. 19: 265-290.

Hagan, John 1994. *Crime and Disrepute.* Thousand Oaks, CA: Pine Forge Press.

Handel, K. 1966. Verteidigungsvorbringen Italinischer Gastarbeiter, *Kriminalistik* Vol. 20:360-362.

Hayner, Norman S. 1933. Delinquency Areas in the Puget Sound Region, *American Journal of Sociology* Vol. 39: 314-328.

Heeren, Henk J. 1990. The Netherlands, in William J. Serow et. al., ed. *Handbook on International Migration.* NY: Greenwood Press.

Heijke, Hans 1987. The Labor Market Position of Migrants in Selected European Receiving Countries, in OCDE ed. *The Future of Migration.* Paris: OCDE.

Hindelang, Michael J., T. Hirschi and J. G. Weis 1981. *Mesuring Delinquency.* Beverly Hills: Sage.

Hoffmann-Mowotny, Hans Joachin 1973. *Soziologie des Fremdarbeiterproblem.* Stuttgart: Enke.

Hollifield, J. F 1992. *Immigrants, Markets, and States: The Political Economy of Postwar Europe.* Harvard University Press: Cambridge, Massachusetts.

Home Office 1984. *Crime Statistics for the Metropolitan Police District Analysed by Ethnic Group.* London: HMSO.

Huebner, K. 1982. Integration Problems of Foreigners in the Federal Republic of Germany and Their Implications for the Police. from *Bestandsaufnahme und perspectiven der Verbrechensbekaempfung.* Pp. 67-83. Wiesbaden, Germany: Bundeskriminalamt.

International Organization For Migration 1990. *'Background Document'* presented at IOM Seminar on Migration: Geneva.

Junger, Marianne 1989. Ethnic Minorities, Crime and Public Policy, in Roger Hood ed. *Crime and Criminal Policy in Europe.* Oxford: Center for Criminological Research.

Junger, Marianne and Wim Polder 1992. Some Explanations of Crimes among Four Ethnic Groups in Netherlands, *Journal of Quantitative Criminology,* Vol.8, No 1, 1992.

Junger-Tas, Josine 1983. *Minority Juveniles and the Dutch Police.* The Hague: Research and Documentation Center, Ministry of Justice.

Junger-Tas, Josine 1985. Jeunes Allochtones aux Pays-Bas et Leurs Contacts avec la Police. The Hague: Research and Documentation Center, Ministry of Justice.

Kaiser, G. 1974. Delinquency of Foreign Workers and Its Explanation as a Cultural Conflict. *from Foreign Workers in Society and Law.* Munich, Gemany: Verlagsbuchhadlung.

Kaiser, G. 1980. Zur Kriminologie der Gewaltdelikte. *Schriftenreihe der Polizei-Fuehrsungsakademie* N2:129-147.

Killias, M. 1977. Kriminelle Fremdarbeiterkinder? Strukturelle Determinanten der Delinquenz bei Fredarbeitern unter Besonderer Berucksichtigung der Zweiten Generation. *Schweizerische Zeitschrift fur Soziologie* Vol. 3: 3-33.

Killias, M. 1989. Criminality among Second Generation Immigrants in Western Europe: A Review of the Evidence. *Criminal Justice Review* V 14: 13-42.

Kornhauser, Ruth R. 1978. *Social Sources of Delinquency: An Appraisal of Analytical Models.* Chicago: University of Chicago Press.

Kurz, U 1965. Partielle Anpassung und Kulturkonflikt. Gruppenstruktur und Anpassungsdispositionen in Einem Italienischen Gastarbeiter-Lager, *Kolner Z. Soziol. Sozial. Psychol.* 17/4:

ESSAYS   251

814-832.

Lahalle, A. 1981. *La Delinquance des Mineurs Etrangers a Schaerbeek.* Vaucresson: CFRES.

Lemaitre, Pierre, Kristian Gerner and Torben Hansen 1993. The Crisis of Societal Security in the Former Soviet Union, in Ole Waever et. al. ed. *Identity, Migration and the New Security Agenda in Europe.* New York: San Martin's Press.

Liben, G. 1963. Un Reflet de la Criminalite Italienne dans la Region de Liege. *Revue de Droit Penal et de Criminologie* Vol. 44: 205-245.

Liebkind, Karmela 1989. Concluding Remarks, in Karmela Liebkind ed. *New Identities in Europe.* Hants, England: Gower.

Loescher, Gil 1993. *Beyond Charity: International Cooperation and the Global Refugee Crisis.* Oxford: Oxford University Press.

Macgill, Helen G. 1938. The Oriental Delinquent in the Vancouver Juvenile Court, *Sociology and Social Research* Vol. 22: 428-438.

Maillat, Dennis 1987. Long-Term Aspects of International Migration Flows: The Experience of European Receiving Countries. in OCDE ed. *The Future of Migration.* Paris, OCDE.

Malewska-Peyre, H., I. Taboada-Leonetti, M. Zaleska, A. Lahalle, J. Bonerandi, C. Basdevant, A. Eysat and M. Nery 1982. *Crise d'Identite et Deviance chez les Jeunes Immigres.* Paris: La Documentation Francaise.

Mansel, J. 1986. Unterschiedliche Selection von Jungen Deutschen, Turken und Italienern. *Monatsschrift fur Kriminologie und Strafrechtsreform* Vol. 69:309-325.

Mawby, R. I., J. W. McCulloch and I. D. Batta 1979. Crime among Asian Juveniles in Bradford. *International Journal of Sociology of Law* Vol. 7: 297-306.

Mcclinstock, F. H. and E. Ginson 1961. *Robbery in London.* London: McMillan.

Merton, Robert K. 1938. Social Structure and Anomie, *American Sociological Review* Vol. 3: 672-682.

Miller, M. J. 1991. Egyptians now replace other arabs in Saudi jobs. *New York Times,* 4 February.

Morice, E. 1967. *Report Presente a Monsieur le Garde des Sceaux, Ministre de la Justice, 1966.* Paris: Conseil Superieur de l'Administration Penitentiare.

Nann, E. 1967. Die Kriminalistat der Italienischen Gastarbeiter im Spiegel der Auslander Kriminalistat, *Kriminologische Schriftenreihe aus der Deutschen Kriminologischen Gesellschaft* Vol 28. Hamburg: Kriminalistik Verlag.

Neumann, K. 1963. *Die Kriminalitat der Italienischen Arbeitskrafte im Kanton Zurich.* Zurich: Juris Verlag.

Newman, Graeme 1976. *Comparative Deviance.* New York: Elsevier,

Perotti, A. and F. Thepaut 1990. Les Caracteristiques du Debat Sur L'immigration dans le Contexte Italien. *Migration Societe* Vol.2:11.

Pradervand, P. and L. Cardia 1966. Quelques Aspects de la Delinquance Italianne a Geneve, *Revue Internationale de Criminologie et Police Technique* Vol. 20: 43-58.

Queloz, N. 1986. *La Reaction Institutionnelle a la Delinquance Juvenile.* Neuchatel:EDES.

Rees, T., P. Stevens and C. F. Willis 1979. Race, Crime and Arrest - Great Britain. *Home Office Research Bulletin* Vol. 8: 7-13.

Rogers, Rosemarie 1993. Wester European Responses to Migration, in Myron Weiner ed. *International Migration and Security.* Boulder, CO: Westview Press.

Roy, A. Carr-Hill 1987. 'O Bring me Your Poor': Immigrants in the French System of Criminal Justice System. *The Howard Journal of Criminal Justice* Vol 26: 287-302.

Schuler-Springorum, H. 1983. Auslanderkriminalitat: uraschen, umfang und entwicklung, *Neu Zeitschrift fur Strafrecht* Vol. 3: 529-536.

Sellin, Thorsten 1938. *Culture Conflict and Crime.* NY: Social Science Research Council.

Serow, William J., C. B. Nam, D. F. Fly, and R. H. Weller 1990. *Handbook on International Migration.* New York: Greenwood Press.

Shaw, Clifford R. and Henry D. McKay 1942. *Juvenile Delinquency in Urban Areas.* Chicago: Chicago University Press.

Shelley, Louise I. 1981. *Crime and Modernization: The Impact of Industrialization and Urbanization on Crime.* Carbondale, IL: Southern Illinois University press.

Schuler-Springorum, H. 1983. Auslanderkriminalitat: Ursachen, Umfang und Entwicklung, *Neu Zeitschrift fur Strafrecht* Vol. 3:529-536.

Schumann, K.F., C. Berlitz, H. W. Guth, and R. Kaulitzki 1987. *Jugendkriminalitat und die Grenzen der Generalpravention.* Neuwied/Darmstadt.

Stevens, P. and C. F. Williams 1979. Race, Crime and Arrests. *Home Office Research Study No. 58.* London: HMSO.

Sveri, K. 1966. Culture Conflict and Crime, in David Scharz ed. *Svenska Minoriteter.* Stockholm: Aldus.

Tapinos, G. 1973. International Migration in Western Europe, in *Migration-Report of the Research Conference on Migration, Ethnic Minority Status and Social Adaptation* ed. by Otto Klineberg and George DeVos. Rome: U.N. Social Defense Research Institute.

Tapinos, G. 1993. The Dynamics of International Migration in Post-War Europe, in *Migration Policies in Europe and the United States,* ed. by Giacomo Luciani. Dordrecht, the Netherlands: Kluwer Academic Publishers.

Terlouw, G. J. and G. Suzanne 1989. *Een Preventieproject in Gouda, Eerste Resolution van een Project voor Marokkaanse Jongeren.* Den Haag: WODC, Ministry of Justice.

Thanou, G. 1982. Children of Migrant Workers - Factors in Deviance and Integration of Young Immigrants. *Revue Internationale de Criminologie et de Police Technique.* V 35: 391-404.

Tomasevski, Katarina 1994. *Foreigners in Prison.* Helsinki: European Institute for Crime Prevention and Control.

Trauslen, M. 1988. Die Kriminalistat der JungenAuslander nach der Polizeilichen Kriminalstatistik. *Monatsschrift fur Kriminologie und Strafrechtsreform* Vol. 71: 28-41.

Tuck, M. and P. Southgate 1981. *Ethnic Minorities, Crime and Policing: A Survey of Experiences of West Indians and Whites.* London: HMSO.

United Nations 1980. *Trends and Characteristics of International Migration since 1950.* NY: United Nations.

Van Der Hoeven 1986. *De Jeugdpolitie: een Observatie-Onderzoek.* Den Haag.CWOK.

Van Duyne, Petrus 1993. Implications of Cross-Border Crime Risks in an Open Europe. *Crime, Law and Social Change* Vol. 20: 99-111.

Wander, Hilde 1990. Federal Republic of Germany, in W.J. (e)d. *Handbook on International Migration.* NY:Greenwood Press.

Wehner, B. 1966. Gastarbeiter Krimitat - auch ein Schlagwort?, *Kriminalistik* Vol. 20: 175-176.

Weil, P. 1991. Immigration and the Rise of Racism in France:The Contradictions of Miterrand's Policies. *French Society and Politics* Vol. 9: 3-4.

Wenzky, O. 1965. Analyse zur Auslander Kriminalitat. *Kriminalistik* Vol. 19: 1-5.

Wilpert, Czarina 1989. Ethnic and Cultural Identity: Ethnicity and the Second Generation in the Context of European Migration, in Karmela Liebkind ed. *New Identities in Europe: Immigrant Ancestry and the Ethnic Identity of Youth.* Hants, England: Gower.

Witschi, Hans 1966. Probleme der Prostitution, *Kriminalistik* Vol.20: 500-503.

Zimmermann, H. G. 1966. Die Kriminalistat der Auslandischern Arbeiter, *Kriminalistik* Vol. 20:623-625.

[7]

Foreign Minorities and the Criminal Justice System in The Federal Republic of Germany

HANS-JÖRG ALBRECHT

Research Assistant, Max-Planck-Institut für ausländisches und internationales Strafrecht, Freiburg

Abstract: The article addresses problems of ethnic and foreign minorities in the criminal justice system in the Federal Republic of Germany. Analysis of police and court data suggests at first glance that members of foreign minorities commit far more crimes than are committed by the population's majority. But controlling for differences in those variables which make considerable differences between foreign minorities and the population's majority, especially socio-economic status, differences in crime rates fade away. It is argued that cultural conflict theory does not provide an adequate framework for explaining crime occurring within foreign minorities. Available evidence suggests that deprivation and control theories are more powerful in explaining criminal behaviour within ethnic and foreign minorities, they seem also to be more useful in guiding criminal policy dealing with foreign offenders. Although crime problems have been of paramount importance in criminological studies dealing with ethnic and foreign minorities, problems of criminal victimisation should be taken into account, too. Furthermore, problems of processing members of ethnic minorities through the criminal justice system are touched on in the article with special emphasis on those points in the process which are hypothesised to embody great potential for discriminatory decision-making.

Today's deep concern for problems of foreign minorities or 'Gastarbeiter' in the context of criminal justice can be traced back to the end of the sixties and the beginning of the seventies, when the number of migrant workers seeking employment in the Federal Republic of Germany grew considerably. At the beginning of the eighties a peak in the number of foreigners in the Federal Republic of Germany was reached representing an overall proportion of the population approximating 8%. Since 1982 the figure has been gradually declining (1984): ca. 7%), a process which reflects the growing political concern for providing incentives for 'Gastarbeiter' to encourage them to re-emigrate to their home countries, as well as the effects of a declining economy at the end of the seventies and structural changes in employment opportunities in the eighties (see Chaidou 1984, p. 8; Kaiser 1980, p. 362).

Although most foreigners permanently residing in the Federal Republic of Germany come from European countries including Turkey with southern nationalities outweighing central European and northern European countries, the number of immigrants originating from Asian or

African countries doubled between 1974 and 1984 (Statistische Bundesamt 1986), most of them applying for asylum because restrictive immigration laws are limiting the opportunities for regular permits of residence and employment (except for citizens of member countries of the E.E.C.). Nevertheless, African and Asian nationalities play but a minor role in the make-up of the foreign sub-population in the Federal Republic of Germany with a proportion of approximately 10%. Actually two-fifths of the total number of foreigners residing officially in the Federal Republic of Germany (not including tourists, members of military forces and illegal immigrants) may be labelled migrant workers (Gastarbeiter) (see Albrecht 1984). Approximately 80% have been living in the Federal Republic of Germany for more than four years and more than half of them for more than ten years. This distribution of the length of the stay of foreigners indicates that assumptions concerning re-emigration behaviour of migrant workers concluding that they will return to their home countries after limited periods of employment did not receive empirical support. In the long run there will probably remain a substantial subgroup of the population represented mainly by citizens from the south-east of Europe and Turkey.

Marginalisation of Aliens

Crime and crime control have been and remain predominant themes in discussions about social problems associated with ethnic and foreign minorities. Although analysis of crime statistics results in *prima facie* evidence of a stronger involvement in crime on the part of foreign minorities, there is no doubt that public attention paid to criminal activities among foreign minorities is fed by other sources as well. The status of most immigrants is characterised by marginality, which is partially reinforced by the statutes defining the legal status of a foreigner in the Federal Republic of Germany. But the social basis of marginalisation of foreign minorities can be found in stigmatisation and rejection by the population's majority which perceives aliens as endangering safety and stability or by attributing negative characteristics whereby the ascription of proneness to crime is but one, although an essential prejudice among others (Villmow 1983). Obviously rejection of foreign or ethnic minorities is strongest in those segments of society where everyday contacts between members of the host society and members of minority groups are common, with competition and conflicts among the groups in the fields of employment, housing and education serving as reinforcers of negative, sometimes hostile reactions towards foreign minorities.

Theoretical approaches to the problem of marginalisation of foreign minorities and the exaggeration of problems such as crime and deviance can be divided into four groups:

(i) *Anthropological theories* which explain marginalisation by a deeply rooted xenophobia;
(ii) *theories of racism* which stress ideological roots of ethno-centred attitudinal patterns;

(iii) *crisis theories* which hypothesise a relationship between economic crises and the degree of marginalisation of minorities by the population's majority;

(iv) *theories of prejudice* which conceive treatment of ethnic minorities as a special case of society's general reactions toward all minority groups (Even 1984, p. 155).

These social bases of marginalisation of foreign minorities might be relevant also in explaining their skewed representation in mass media reports as well as in criminological studies displaying a preoccupation with the criminal behaviour of members of foreign minorities, while reports and studies on victimisation risks and problems associated with criminal justice processing of foreign offenders are rarely found.

Marginalisation of foreign minorities has *objective* and *perceptual dimensions*. We may define as objective dimensions those properties and characteristics of foreign minorities which in fact make them differ from the majority, such as race, colour, religion and language, as well as those consequences of the minority status which may be labelled as discrimination, such as disadvantages in the labour market, in the education system and in the justice system, which are caused by biased decision making. But aliens and migrant workers in the Federal Republic of Germany should be classified by variables other than nationality. There are subgroups among them which, although differing from the majority in terms of nationality or language such as French, Austrians, Dutch, Englishmen or Americans, do not show up with a marked marginal status. On the other hand there are large groups of Yugoslavs, Greeks, Turks and a smaller number of people from Arab, Asian or African countries displaying larger differences in terms of religious beliefs, cultural values or general behaviour patterns as well as in terms of colour and race, differences which are likely to have stronger effects on the majority's perception. As far as those perceptual dimensions are concerned, members of the host society may perceive members of foreign minorities as dangerous or as crime prone. Correspondingly, members of ethnic minorities may believe that they are treated unfairly by criminal justice authorities. As it is the case with other social issues, problems of foreign minorities may have an objective or just a subjective basis. There may be serious disadvantages which are not perceived as discrimination; on the other hand there may be feelings of discrimination or perceived negative attributes of ethnic minorities without an objective basis. Nevertheless, criminal policy dealing with ethnic minorities must cope with both objective and subjective dimensions.

Crime and Foreign Minorities

Despite the well-known shortcomings of official crime statistics, criminological analysis of crime rates within foreign minorities relies almost exclusively on police statistics (including suspects) and court statistics (including convictions). Taking as a point of departure police based crime statistics it can be observed that a *substantial number* of foreign offenders is suspected of having committed an offence against statutes governing the status of foreigners in the Federal Republic of Germany (Ausländergesetz: for example. illegal immigration). Approximately *one-fifth* of all foreign offenders is charged with such an offence. Leaving aside these offences which are related to the specific status of an alien and turning to those offences which allow comparison with contribution to the crime load by the majority population we may put forward the following questions:

(i)   Do crime rates observed within ethnic minorities differ from those observed in the population's majority?
(ii) Are there differences in the distribution of crime types?

Tables 1a and *1b* display crime rates in different age and gender groups broken down by nationality. It can be shown that in the younger age groups of foreign minorities (children and juveniles) theft is the prevailing crime type. The dominance of theft is especially marked among female foreign child and juvenile offenders as well as male foreign child offenders while in the group of male foreign juvenile offenders grand theft and burglary play a significant role. The same is true for male foreign adolescents (aged 18 to 20 years) and male foreign young adults while in the groups of adult male foreign offenders and in virtually all age groups of female foreign offenders grand theft and burglary are of less importance. Besides minor deviations with male foreign offenders displaying a somewhat higher ratio of violent crimes and female German offenders showing up with a higher ratio of drug crimes, at least in some age groups, the distribution of main crime types is basically the same in foreign minorities and within the German population (*Table 2*). But with respect to relative crime figures rather significant differences became visible. Turning to violent offences (homicide, robbery, assault and rape) it can be shown that rates of violent crimes within the different age groups of males belonging to foreign minorities are considerably higher than those computed for their German counterparts. Although serious crimes such as murder, robbery and assault can still be defined as rare events if taking into account the overall figure of crimes committed by aliens, it is obvious that in every age group considerable differences between foreign minorities and the German population exist. Substantial differences can be observed in the occurrence of rape where foreign minorities show up with offender rates four to five times higher than those in the German population. Considerable differences exist in the case of homicide where offender rates within foreign minorities are two to four times higher than those observable in the German population. Similar differences occur with respect to robbery and assault. But in the context of violent offences two observations derived from criminological studies have to be taken into account. The first observation concerns the fact that almost two-thirds of homicides committed by foreign offenders occur with members of the ethnic minority as victims (Sessar 1981). The second observation refers to violent offences against policemen, where foreign offenders are contributing much less than could be expected by deriving estimates from their overall involvement in violent crimes (Sessar, *et al.* 1980).

275

TABLE 1a

Offender Rates in Different Age Groups Broken Down by Nationality 1982

	suspects																
	children 8–13 years old				juveniles 14–17 years old				adolescents 18–20 years old				young adults 21–25 years old			
	foreign nationality		German nationality		foreign nationality		German nationality		foreign nationality		German nationality		foreign nationality		German nationality	
	male	female	male	female	male	female	male	female	male	female	male	female	male	female	male	female
homicide (incl. attempted homicide, §§ 211) rel.*	1.2	–	0.4	–	16.7	0.8	6.0	0.4	58.6	5.1	16.2	2.0	73.3	2.9	20.0	2.7
robbery (§§ 249, 255, 316a) rel.*	98.8	6.4	40.7	3.7	509.9	11.6	176.3	15.8	639.1	17.2	276.7	16.8	414.2	16.5	182.3	12.7
rape rel.*	5.8	–	0.5	–	56.8	–	15.5	–	189.1	–	36.9	–	176.1	–	38.1	–
aggravated assault rel.*	73.4	14.7	40.5	8.0	742.6	69.8	341.9	41.0	1,646.1	73.7	724.2	45.1	1,462.5	82.7	531.6	43.1
assault rel.*	69.5	8.7	39.5	9.4	588.9	65.1	315.5	47.7	1,146.9	48.5	660.7	51.7	1,283.5	90.6	644.2	53.8
theft rel.*	3,267.6	564.7	1,383.3	549.4	6,074.1	2,097.3	3,185.7	1,285.5	3,739.1	1,518.2	2,500.2	778.3	2,964.8	1,433.9	1,568.4	580.5
grand larceny/burglary rel.*	1,277.6	140.8	516.2	38.4	4,674.4	216.3	2,743.3	107.7	3,818.0	86.9	3,064.5	120.6	1,613.6	56.8	1,495.5	74.9
drug offences rel.*	2.3	0.9	1.5	1.4	190.7	42.6	166.4	85.1	1,706.3	145.5	702.3	199.5	2,030.1	164.7	725.5	180.4
Total rel.*	5,301.2	1,225.2	2,344.9	677.4	15,995.1	3,919.4	8,347.4	1,942.2	20,307.8	3,768.7	11,074.1	1,968.2	19,646.6	3,785.6	8,319.5	1,731.9

Notes: *Suspects/100,000 of the respective population group

(*Source:* Federal Bureau of Investigation (1983); Statistisches Bundesamt (1983, 1984))

TABLE 1b

Offender Rates and Conviction Rates* in Different Age Groups Broken Down by Nationality 1982

		suspects (adults ≥ 25 years old)				suspects total				suspects total		convictions*** (total) 1983	
		foreign nationality male	foreign nationality female	German nationality male	German nationality female	foreign nationality male	foreign nationality female	German nationality male	German nationality female	foreign nationality**	German nationality	foreign nationality	German nationality
homicide (incl. attempted homicide, §§ 211)	rel.*	28.8	2.2	7.0	0.9	29.8	2.0	7.7	1.0	18.3 (16.1)	4.2	6.1	1.3
robbery (§§ 249, 255, 316a)	rel.*	76.7	8.3	27.1	2.4	162.8	9.5	63.3	4.6	99.4 (84.6)	32.5	26.4	12.0
rape	rel.*	54.4	–	10.1	–	64.7	–	13.1	–	37.9 (30.6)	6.2	7.4	2.2
aggravated assault	rel.*	481.3	86.9	137.6	17.3	588.5	75.4	203.5	21.0	376.3 (339.5)	107.8	59.6	27.2
assault	rel.*	539.9	97.0	264.7	28.1	579.0	–	297.4	31.5	372.6 (339.5)	157.9	49.5	30.9
theft	rel.*	1,063.5	907.1	622.5	382.2	1,919.1	955.9	1,040.1	493.4	1,572.3 (1,372.4)	753.4	179.1	250.3
grand larceny/burglary	rel.*	237.2	23.2	206.9	12.9	939.1	59.6	662.8	29.4	575.4 (520.1)	330.7	112.4	88.7
drug offences	rel.*	270.5	23.1	63.5	10.5	441.3	40.6	145.5	38.4	275.5 (160.2)	86.7	82.4	30.4
Total	rel.*	6,591.7	2,207.4	2,787.5	750.8	8,768.2	2,439.7	3,988.5	936.6	6,148.1 (4,823.7)	2,388.0	1,717.2	851.4

Notes: *Suspects/100,000 of the respective population group
** ( ) = without illegal immigrants, members of foreign military forces and tourists
*** Without convictions related to traffic offences

(*Source:* Federal Bureau of Investigation (1983); Statistisches Bundesamt (1983, 1984))

TABLE 2
Distribution of Selected Crime Types in Foreign and German Offender Groups 1982 (%)

	children 8–13 years old				juveniles 14–17 years old				adolescents 18–20 years old				young adults 21–25 years old				adults › 25 years old			
	foreign nationality		German nationality		foreign nationality		German nationality		foreign nationality		German nationality		foreign nationality		German nationality		foreign nationality		German nationality	
	male	female	male	female	male	female	male	female	male	female	male	female	male	female	male	female	male	female	male	female
homicide	0.02	–	0.02	0.02	0.1	0.02	0.07	0.04	0.3	0.1	0.1	0.1	0.4	0.08	0.2	0.1	0.4	0.1	0.2	0.1
robbery	1.9	0.5	1.7	0.5	3.2	0.3	2.1	0.8	3.1	0.5	2.5	0.9	2.1	0.4	2.2	0.7	1.2	0.4	1.0	0.3
rape	0.1	–	0.02	–	0.4	–	0.2	–	0.9	–	0.3	–	0.9	–	0.5	–	0.8	–	0.4	–
aggravated assault	1.4	1.2	1.7	1.2	4.6	1.8	4.1	2.1	8.1	2.0	6.5	2.3	6.5	2.3	6.4	2.5	7.3	3.9	4.9	2.3
assault	1.3	0.7	1.7	1.4	3.7	1.7	3.8	2.5	5.6	1.3	6.0	2.6	15.1	2.4	7.7	3.1	8.2	4.4	9.5	3.9
theft	61.6	78.7	59.0	81.1	38.0	52.1	38.2	66.2	18.4	40.3	22.6	39.6	15.1	38.1	18.9	33.6	16.1	41.2	22.3	52.9
grand larceny/ burglary	24.1	11.5	22.0	5.7	29.2	5.5	32.9	5.5	18.8	2.3	27.7	6.1	8.2	1.5	18.0	4.3	3.6	1.0	7.4	1.7
drug offences	0.04	0.07	0.06	0.2	1.2	1.1	2.0	4.4	8.4	3.9	6.3	10.1	10.3	4.4	8.7	10.5	4.1	1.0	2.3	1.4

(*Source:* Federal Bureau of Investigation (1983); Statistisches Bundesamt (1983, 1984))

278

As far as adult foreign offenders are concerned we have to take into account that comparison of crime rates based on official crime data and population figures will lead to biased results because the distribution of the age variable differs substantially from the age distribution of the German adult population. The *aged* (60 years and over) who are the least prone to criminality everywhere make up a negligible proportion of foreign minorities and approximately one-fifth of the German population is 60 years old or over. If we exclude those aged 50 years and over when calculating crime rates the differences are diminished. But nevertheless comparing crime rates of foreign groups aged 25 to 50 years and crime rates within the corresponding German population, a substantial difference remains. The same is true if the focus is on the subgroup of foreigners which may be termed 'Gastarbeiter' through exclusion of tourists, members of foreign military forces and illegal immigrants from offender data. Although criminological research in the sixties and seventies revealed that in the group of migrant workers crime rates were lower than those in the German population, at the beginning of the eighties considerable differences are evident with an overall offender rate of 5,022 per 100,000 in the group of 'Gastarbeiter' and an overall offender rate of 3,700 per 100,000 in the German population aged 18 to 50 (1982).

From this we may conclude that on the basis of police crime statistics crime rates within foreign minorities exceed by far those in the population's majority. Of special importance seems to be the development of crime rates within the younger age groups of foreign minorities, the so-called second or third generations revealing increasing figures from the end of the seventies to the beginning of the eighties although the general trend in juvenile and young adult crime is moving in the opposite direction.

Analysis of court statistics (which do not allow differentiation along the age and gender variables) reveals that the differences in conviction rates are less pronounced than those in arrest rates, except for murder and manslaughter (*Table 1*). Shrinkage occurs, although adjustment of conviction rates is not possible because court statistics do not allow elimination of convicted tourists, illegal immigrants and members of foreign military forces. It can be suggested that further shrinkages would occur if such adjustment were possible. These differences between police statistics on the one hand and court statistics on the other hand might be explained by wider use of conditional or unconditional dismissal of cases involving foreign offenders by the public prosecutor. The decision to dismiss a case is based upon the assessment of seriousness of an offence which in turn could be interpreted as indicating lower average seriousness of crimes committed by foreign minorities.

Explaining Crime Within Foreign Minorities

Traditionally theorising on criminal activities among immigrants or ethnic minorities stresses the perspective of cultural conflict. Cultural conflict theory assumes that members of ethnic minorities experience stress because of conflicting norms and values which serves as a trigger for deviance and crime. But theories of cultural conflict did not receive empirical support from studies on deviant behaviour of immigrants in the Federal Republic of Germany. First of all the phenomenon that the first generation of immigrants showed up with a lower crime rate than could be observed within the German majority and the observation that the second, third and subsequent generations are more deeply involved in crime than corresponding German groups contradicts the cultural conflict proposition that conflicts between norms and values of the host society and those of the home country should be most acute in the first generation of immigrants. Attempts to adjust cultural conflict propositions to the observation that crime involvement of members of ethnic minorities in the second or third generation is worsening is based on the argument that immigrants of the first generation are primarily concerned with basic problems of life such as finding employment and housing while limiting their daily life activities to the ethnic group they belong to. Thus, migrant workers of the first generation are experiencing in the first place an improvement of life conditions (Schüler-Springorum 1983). The second generation, however, then should be primarily confronted with conflicts between still validated ethnic group norms and values and those of the host society, conflicts which are furthermore driven by limited chances in the educational and labour system. But although there seems to be some evidence that members of foreign minorities may find themselves in situations of cultural conflict, this should not be considered to be a particular experience of ethnic or foreign minorities. Norm and value conflicts can be observed within the German majority, too, because marginal positions in society in general can be described by differences in norm, value or behaviour patterns. Furthermore, there does not exist evidence supporting the assumption that basic norms and values embodied in the criminal law of the home countries of various ethnic and foreign groups are differing from those in the host society. Although marginal differences can be observed (for example, ritual slaughter of animals prescribed by religious beliefs but forbidden by German Animals Protection Law or differences in sentencing conflict; murder where mitigating circumstances may be evaluated differently), these conflicts are of marginal relevance only for police recorded crime. The bulk of property and violent offences cannot be characterised as displaying serious cultural conflicts (Albrecht and Pfeiffer 1979b).

Dissatisfaction with cultural conflict theory has led in recent years to developments in the explanation of crimes committed by members of foreign minorities which stress the importance of depriving life conditions (see Albrecht and Pfeiffer 1979a; Hamburger, *et al.* 1981). According to this line of reasoning crimes committed by members of ethnic minorities should be explained by the same set of deprivation variables as is applied to criminal behaviour in any other social group. Deprivation in terms of unemployment, lack of adequate housing, poor education and professional training affecting minority groups should be relevant in explaining crime in ethnic minorities according to deprivation theory. The minority position is assigned the status of a mediator variable which may reinforce effects of deprivation variables by perceptual processes.

Furthermore, control theory should be taken into account in attempts to explain crimes committed by members of foreign minorities (see Hirschi 1971; Schüler-Springorum 1983). If crime is a function of the strengths of bonds between individual and society, then theoretical expectations meet with data available from the field. Social bonds as suggested by control theory (belief, attachment to relevant others, involvement and commitment) cannot be expected to develop in marginal groups because of obstacles created by laws restricting opportunities to engage in the political system as well as depriving life conditions which limit engagements in conventional, rewarding activities. Furthermore, problems in raising minority children are likely to occur. These experience conflicts caused by needs to adjust to host society when spending their time with mixed peer groups attending school on the one hand and to comply with conventional family standards on the other hand, and these conflicts are likely to affect the development of emotional ties to the family.

Finally, it has been hypothesised that over-representation of members of foreign minorities in police or court statistics may be explained by concentration of control efforts on marginal groups subjecting members of ethnic minorities to sharper and more intense policing and to biased decision making in public prosecutors' offices and courts resulting in a distorted picture of official crime (Villmow 1985). But hitherto research on this topic does not support the assumption that systematic disadvantages in policing and criminal justice processing are existent. Although treatment by police and public prosecutor sometimes is perceived by members of ethnic minorities to be discriminatory, decision-making as measured by dismissal rates or rates of prison sentences does not seem to be influenced by national or ethnic variables (Villmow 1983, p. 332).

In trying to explain crime observed within ethnic minorities we have to take into account that official crime rates might be overestimated when comparing crime rates of foreign minorities and the population at large. Foreign minorities in the Federal Republic of Germany differ from the population at large not only in terms of race, religion or other attributes but also in terms of socio-economic status, education, professional training etc. Especially the so-called 'Gastarbeiter' do not represent a random sample drawn from their home country's population but display selection biased along socio-economic lines with people from the lower socio-economic strata of society being over-represented. Comparisons between crime rates therefore should take into account the differences in those variables obviously strongly related to the occurrence of crime and deviance. But studies on crime and deviance in foreign and ethnic minority groups hitherto rarely took up the problem of controlling differences in estimates on official crime for differences in relevant variables. A piece of research carried through in the state of Saarland could demonstrate that when controlling for socio-economic status, differences in conviction rates are completely reduced (Staudt 1983). Another study on juvenile and youth crime in foreign and German population segments in a south-west German city covering the period 1981 to 1983, also revealed that differences between foreign minority juveniles and German juveniles are virtually non-existent if crime rates for homogenous groups are computed (Oppermann 1986). Furthermore, there seems to exist some evidence that offenders from ethnic minorities commit fewer crimes and are less likely to recidivate or to become chronic offenders. While foreign minority youth in the above mentioned study make up approximately 7% of all youth offenders known to justice authorities in 1983, they are responsible for only 3.2% of the total number of offences committed by all youth offenders in 1983. Analysis of three cohorts of criminal suspects (birth cohorts of 1958, 1950 and 1940) in Bavaria showed that 51% to 54% of male German suspects, 33% to 45% of female German suspects, 32% to 35% of male foreign suspects and 14% to 25% of female foreign suspects reoffended at least once within a risk period of up to twelve years (Steffen 1983). Although incapacitating effects of expulsion or deportation after sentencing or re-emigration within the risk period might contribute to these differences in recidivism rates, further research is needed to identify other relevant variables.

Foreign Minorities and Victimisation

Criminological research has focussed on problems of policing and controlling ethnic minorities. As can be observed with regard to other variables which are perceived as being triggers of crime such as unemployment and alcohol, the role of the minority status in the process of victimisation remained unexplored (see MacNamara and Karmen 1983).

Preliminary data derived from a piece of victimisation research covering the state of Baden-Württemberg shows that members of foreign minorities are subject to higher victimisation risks than the population at large. While 25% of the foreign respondents reported at least one victimising event in the year preceding the interview, less than 20% of the German respondents reported crime victimisation in the same period of time (Arnold 1983).

Victimisation aspects are also important regarding intra-family violence. Research on shelters for battered women and children indicates that a substantial number of clients stem from foreign minorities (10% of women seeking shelter in a home for battered women in West Berlin between June 1978 and December 1979 were Turks or Yugoslavs). The vulnerability of children and women belonging to ethnic minorities is reinforced by their marginal position in society which is causing far greater difficulties in terms of getting help and protection compared with those faced by their German counterparts, firstly as a consequence of lack of knowledge about existing services and problems of language, secondly as a result of the uncertainty concerning their legal status as aliens after divorce or separation (Hagemann-White 1981).

282

Furthermore non-criminal victimisation has to be considered. It can be shown that abortion rates among foreign minority women are exceeding by far those observed among the German population. Investigation of abortion rates in a middle-sized city in the Federal Republic of Germany revealed that within the population of female migrant workers one abortion per 400 women of childbearing age occurs; the corresponding rate for the German population is 1 per 2,000 (Bärtling, *et al.* 1982). Migrant workers also are more often involved in work place accidents than their German counterparts. Estimations indicate that accident rates among migrant workers are twice those among German workers. Another study recently revealed that children belonging to ethnic minorities, especially Turkish children, are considerably more likely to be involved in accidents than are German children. Additionally, migrant workers are more at risk from exploitative employment conditions, with employers hiring immigrants on a non-contractual basis which allows avoidance of social security payments and other social benefits. Recent studies suggest that illegal immigration with the purpose of providing employers with cheap labour is partially organised on a large scale resulting in enormous economic losses in terms of uncollectable taxes and social security payments (Polizeiführungsakademie 1983).

Foreign Minorities and the Criminal Justice System

As far as the relationships between members of foreign minorities and the criminal justice system are concerned, two aspects have to be differentiated. On the one hand general attitudes towards different criminal justice agencies must be considered and on the other hand problems of processing foreign offenders through the justice system have to be taken into account.

Recent research on the first issue could demonstrate that members of foreign minorities (Greek immigrants) evaluate the police far more positively than does the German population. While almost two-thirds of the immigrants believe that the police do at least a 'good job', only one-third of the German population agrees with this proposition. On the other hand data on attitudes toward the role and function of penal law reveal considerable differences between foreign minorities and the German majority with foreign minorities being more in favour of the death penalty and goals of criminal justice and corrections such as punishment and incapacitation (Pitsela 1987).

Problems of processing foreign offenders through the justice system become visible on various levels. An important potential source of problems must be seen in the fact that control and justice agencies such as the police, public prosecution, courts, corrections and probation services are staffed exclusively with German personnel. Although the question has been put forward whether employment opportunities within the criminal justice system should be made available for members of foreign minorities in order to dispel lack of confidence and to reduce tensions and conflicts which are due to deficits in mutual understanding, the problem that the status of a civil servant is bound to German nationality is preventing such an integration of foreign minorities into the criminal justice system.

Problems furthermore arise out of situations of interrogation where policemen, public prosecutors and judges have to rely on interpreters. This is not only a problem in terms of equal opportunities in legal defence and of the quality of decisions but also in terms of the economic burden.[1]

Although discriminatory treatment of foreign suspects by police sometimes is observable and interview data suggest that foreign offenders feel that they are handled differently compared to German suspects, decision making on the different stages of the process (public prosecutor, court) does not seem to be biased along variables such as nationality or race. This holds true for the public prosecutor's decision to prosecute or to dismiss cases as well as for sentencing decisions.

But there are other important fields in the criminal justice system where the status of an alien may lead to systematic differentiation between foreign and German offenders. These are pre-trial detention, treatment within the prison and treatment after sentencing or release from prison. Pre-trial detention may be ordered if it can be assumed with reasonable cause that an offender will not show up voluntarily for a trial. Since decision making in the field of pre-trial detention is in general based upon the assessment of the stability of bonds between offender and conventional society (family, permanent place of residence, employment), members of foreign minorities are more likely to be subject to pre-trial detention, because of perceived risks of re-emigration to their home country.

In the prison system the law governing the alien's status results in systematic differentiation between foreign and German prisoners. Although the prison law itself does not make an explicit distinction between foreign and German prisoners, ordinances regulating the implementation of the Federal Prison Law require that furloughs, prison leaves, admission to open settings etc. must not be allowed if a foreign prisoner is likely to be deported after release from prison.[2]

Administrative bodies controlling and monitoring aliens in the Federal Republic of Germany have wide discretionary power with respect to expulsion and deportation after a criminal conviction. Criminological research on this issue reveals that there do not exist uniform decision-patterns across the various jurisdictions, but large variations ranging from about 20% to 100% expulsion and deportation orders following prison sentences in the case of foreign offenders. Uncertainty is likely to result out of this administrative practice affecting both foreign offenders and their families. On the other hand it should be noted that newly enacted legislation concerning 'transfer of sentenced persons' (Gesetz über die internationale Rechtschilfe in Strafsachen) provides that foreigners convicted and sentenced in the Federal Republic of Germany may serve a prison sentence in their home country if the offender and the foreign government agree.

284

Conclusions

Based on the above outlined problems we may summarise:

(i)   Although crime data derived from police and court statistics demonstrate that crime rates among foreign groups are exceeding those observable in the German population by far, adjustment of crime rates through controlling other theoretically relevant variables such as socio-economic status and age reduce other differences in crime rates considerably.

(ii) Cultural conflict theory does not seem to provide an adequate framework for explaining crime occurring within foreign minorities. Deprivation theory and control theory seem to be more useful in explaining crime within foreign minorities and in guiding criminal policy dealing with the foreign offender.

(iii) Decision making in the fields of pre-trial detention and imprisonment should be rethought in order to avoid differential and disadvantageous treatment of foreign offenders.

(iv) Aliens' laws should be revised in order to reduce the discretionary power in decision-making processes concerning expulsion and deportation.

(v)   More attention should be paid to problems of criminal victimisation within foreign minorities.

Notes

[1] The Police Department in Cologne had to spend in the year 1978 DM164,000 for interpreters; cost-benefit analysis led to the conclusion that hiring interpreters as employees of police departments would be cheaper than ad hoc appointments (see Gundlach 1979).

[2] Foreign male adult prisoners made up 8.4% of the prison population in 1981 (females and juveniles: 7%).

References

Albrecht, H.-J. (1984) 'Problems of policing ethnic minorities in the Federal Republic of Germany', in: J. Brown (Ed.), *Policing and Social Policy: The Cranfield-Wolfson Colloquium on Multi-Ethnic Areas in Europe*, London: Police Review Publishing Co.

Albrecht, P. -A. and Pfeiffer, Ch. (1979a) *Die Kriminalisierung Junger Ausländer*, München: Juventa Verlag.

Albrecht, P. -A. and Pfeiffer, Ch. (1987b) ' "Kulturkonflikt" oder soziale mängellage? Ansätze zur erklärung der Kriminalitätsbelastung der ausländischen wohnbevölkerung in der Bundesrepublik', *Bewährungshilfe*, 26, 115–18.

Arnold, M. (1983) 'Vorläufige ergebnisse einer viktimologischen untersuchung in Baden-Württemberg', (unpublished manuscript) Freiburg.

Bärtling, Th., Jung, H. and Bärtling, K. (1982) 'Schwangerschaftskonflikt und schwangerschaftsabbruch in ausländischen arbeitnehmerfamilien', in: H. Poettgen (Ed.), *Die Ungewollte Schwangerschaft*, Köln: Deutscher Ärzteverlag.

Chaidou, A. (1984) *Junge Ausländer aus Gastarbeiterländern in der Bundesrepublik Deutschland*, Frankfurt: Peter Lang Verlag.

Even, H. (1984) *Soziologie der Ausländerfeindlichkeit*, Weinheim, Basel: Beltz Verlag.

Federal Bureau of Investigation (Ed.) (1983) *Polizeiliche Kriminalstatistik 1982*, Wiesbaden: Federal Bureau of Investigation.

Gundlach, M. (1979) 'Großstadt-ausländerkriminalität unter kriminologischen, (kriminal-)soziologischen und kriminalistischen aspekten', *Die Polizei*, *70*, 349–53.

Hagemann-White, C. (1981) *Hilfen für Mißhandelte Frauen*, Stuttgart: Verlag W. Kohlhammer.

Hamburger, F., Seus, L. and Wolter, D. (1981) *Zur Delinquenz Ausländischer Jugendlicher*, Wiesbaden: Bundeskriminalamt.

Hirschi, T. (1971) *Causes of Delinquency*, Berkeley: University of California Press.

Kaiser, G. (1980) *Kriminologie: Ein Lehrbuch*, Heidelberg, Karlsruhe: C. F. Müller Verlag.

MacNamara, D. E. J. and Karmen, A. (Eds.) (1983) *Deviance: Victims or Victimizers?*' Beverley Hills: Sage.

Oppermann, A. (1986) *Kriminalität Junger Ausländer – Selektion oder Soziale Mängellage? Eine Untersuchung unter Berücksichtigung von Jugendkriminalitätsdaten der Stadt Freiburg*, Freiburg: Fachhochschule für Sozialarbeit.

Pitsela, A. (1987) *Viktimologische Untersuchungen an Griechischen Gastarbeitern*, Freiburg: Eigenverlag Max-Planck-Institut.

Polizeiführungsakademie (Ed.) (1983) *Einschleusung und Illegale Beschäftigung von Ausländern*, Munster: Polizeiführungsakademie.

Schüler-Springorum, H. (1983) 'Ausländerkriminalität: ursachen, umfang und entwicklung', *Neu Zeitschrift für Strafrecht*, *3*, 529–36.

Sessar, K. (1981) *Rechtliche und Soziale Aspekte einer Definition der Tötungskriminalität*, Freiburg: Eigenverlag Max-Planck-Institut.

Sessar, K.. Baumann, U. and Müller, J. (1980) *Polizeibeamte als Opfer Vorsätzlicher Tötung*, Wiesbaden: Bundeskriminalamt.

Statistisches Bundesamt (Hrsg.) (1983) *Bevölkerung und Erwerbstätigkeit. Reihe 2: Ausländer 1982*, Wiesbaden: Statistisches Bundesamt.

Statistisches Bundesamt (Hrsg.) (1984) *Strafverfolgung 1983*, Wiesbaden: Statistisches Bundesamt.

Statistisches Bundesamt (Ed.) (1986) *Statistisches Jahrbuch 1985 für die Bundesrepublik Deutschland*, Stuttgart: Verlag W. Kohlhammer.

Staudt, G. (1983) 'Kriminelles und konformes verhalten der gastarbeiternachkommen; ergebnisse einer pilot-studie und einer sekundärstatistischen analyse', (unpublished manuscript) Saarbrücken.

Steffen, W. (1983) *Intensität und Perseveranz Krimineller Verhaltensweisen*, München: Bayerisches Landeskriminalamt.

Villmow, B. (1983) 'Kriminalität der jungen ausländer: ausmaß und struktur des abweichenden verhaltens und gesellschaftlicher reaktionen', in: H. –J. Kerner, H. Göppinger and F. Streng (Eds.), *Kriminologie – Psychiatrie – Strafrecht*, Heidelberg: C. F. Müller Verlag.

Villmow, B. (1985) 'Gastarbeiterkriminalität', in: G. Kaiser, H. J. Kerner, F. Sack and H. Schellhoss (Eds.), *Kleines Kriminologisches Wörterbuch*, Heidelberg, Karlsruhe: C. F. Müller Verlag.

[8]

Some Explanations of Crime Among Four Ethnic Groups in the Netherlands

Marianne Junger[1] and Wim Polder[1]

Since 1950 there has been large-scale immigration to Western Europe, mainly from Muslim countries. This paper focuses on the degree of involvement in crime of ethnic minority boys as compared to indigenous boys and on the possible causes of these crime involvements. A random sample from three ethnic minority boys (Moroccans, Turks, Surinamese) was taken. A control group consisted of indigenous boys with a comparable socioeconomic background as the minority respondents. Data were gathered about self-report and recorded delinquency, family and school life, leisure time, traditionalism, migration problems, and socioeconomic status. It appears that the arrest rates among the minority youths are substantially higher than among the comparable Dutch boys. A number of explanations are considered: strain, lack of social control, cultural dissonance, and migration problems. Results show that only social control factors explain criminality within the groups, indicating that the causes of criminality among ethnic minority boys may essentially be the same as those among the indigenous boys.

KEY WORDS: ethnic minorities; social control theory; migration; the Netherlands; crime theories.

1. INTRODUCTION

Since the 1950s and 1960s there has been a large-scale migration of laborers from Muslim countries to Western Europe. Although this type of migration almost stopped after the oil crisis (1973), family reunification brought many women and children to join their husbands and fathers. As a result there are large Muslim minorities in many European countries. For

[1]Ministry of Justice, Research and Documentation Centre, P.O. Box 20301, 2500 EH The Hague, The Netherlands.

example, it is estimated that there are about 350,000 Muslims in The Netherlands, 400,000 in the United Kingdom, 1.7 million in West Germany, 2.8 million in France, and 200,000 in Belgium (for an introduction see Gerholm and Litham, 1988).

It is generally believed that these workers will remain in their host countries, although most of them originally planned to stay only temporarily (Gerholm and Litham, 1988). The presence of the minority communities has led to speculations about future developments. For example, will these communities assimilate, or will they integrate but keep certain distinctive traits? Can we expect growing tensions between different ethnic groups?

All over Europe, Muslim immigrants confront greater social problems than most other immigrant groups (Gerholm and Litham, 1988). In addition, it appears that in many countries several ethnic minority groups are overrepresented in official criminality statistics. This has been established for the United Kingdom, France, the Netherlands, Sweden, Belgium, and Germany and in the United States (see, among others, Gould, 1969; Chambliss and Nagasawa, 1969; Nadjafi Abrandabadi, 1983; Stevens and Willis, 1979; Hindelang *et al.*, 1979; Sampson, 1985; Block, 1985; Jäger, 1984; Craen, 1984; Albrecht, 1984, 1987; van der Hoeven, 1986). In general, blacks are overrepresented in the judicial system but Asians are underrepresented in most countries.

The assessment that ethnic minorities who immigrated to the Netherlands will most probably stay and concern about the growing numbers of ethnic minority youth entering the juvenile justice system have led the Research and Documentation Centre of the Ministry of Justice to start an investigation that focuses on two questions. The first concerns involvement in crime: What is the level of involvement in crime among youths of different ethnic minority groups? And if the involvement in crime among youths of ethnic minorities is higher than among Dutch youths, can this difference be accounted for by the relatively weak socioeconomic position of ethnic minorities in Dutch society? The second question is whether the factors related to crime are similar among ethnic minority youths and Dutch juveniles, or whether factors specific to their culture or their migrant status affect their crime rates.

To answer these questions it was decided to study select samples of youths coming from the three largest ethnic minority groups in the Netherlands: the Turks, the Surinamese, and the Moroccans. They are compared with Dutch youths from a similar socioeconomic background.

This article briefly reviews some of the main results of this study. We proceed as follows: First, the research design is introduced (Section 2). Second, a short introduction to the three ethnic minority groups in the Netherlands is given (Section 3). Third, the main results are presented (Section 4).

2. RESEARCH DESIGN

In this section the main features of the research design are presented. For more information see Junger (1990a) and Junger and Polder (1991).

2.1. The Samples

The results bear on four samples: 182 Moroccans, 196 Turks, 206 Surinamese, and 206 Dutch boys 12–17 years old. The three ethnic minority groups were selected randomly. The Dutch sample has been selected by the interviewer in the same neighborhoods as the ethnic minority boys. It was expected that this method would produce a sample of indigenous boys with a socioeconomic background similar to that of the ethnic minorities. This group of Dutch boys is referred to as the "comparable group."

Analyses show that the ethnic minority groups probably form a representative sample of the population from which they were drawn in terms of age, urbanization, and number of respondents who have contacts with the prosecutor (Junger and Zeilstra, 1989).

As the Dutch boys are coming from the same neighborhoods as the ethnic minority boys, opportunity factors related to the physical environment and to the availability of delinquent friends are also held constant and cannot account for differences in crime.

2.2. The Instrument

Most data were gathered by means of structured interviews, during June/July 1985. Information about delinquent behavior was available from the interviews as well as from data on recorded contacts with the judicial system.

2.3. The Measurement of Delinquency

Delinquent behavior has been defined as "those acts which can be brought to court by the public prosecutor." The self-report delinquency measures were based on 16 questions about delinquent activities asked at the end of the interview (see Appendix). Information on recorded delinquency (ever and last year) came from the police stations. We coded all police contacts for property crimes (petty theft, serious property offenses), aggression against persons, vandalism, and sexual offenses or problematic behavior (running away from home). Status offenses only seldom lead to officially registered police contacts or prosecution, except when circumstances are believed to be unusually serious.

When boys with recorded police contacts mentioned no offenses during the interview, the self-report scores have been corrected for the number of arrests known from the police files. In all further analyses, unless stated otherwise, these corrected measures are used.

2.4. Validity Problems

Analyses show that among Turkish and Moroccan respondents, the tendency to give socially desirable answers is stronger than among Surinamese and Dutch respondents. This appears to be the case for questions on self-reported delinquency data, family, school, and leisure time activities. This validity problem makes comparisons between ethnic groups on the basis of self-report information problematic. For example, it cannot be inferred from the findings whether Moroccan parents exercise more or less supervision than Dutch parents. Rather, we have to conclude that the data from the present study are not suitable for comparisons between ethnic groups.[2]

The restriction of the use of comparisons between ethnic groups does not exclude correlational analyses. Although mean scores are not comparable, the rank order *within* ethnic groups need not be strongly affected by the social desirability bias. Correspondence between self-report and police data indicates that the ordering of respondents within ethnic groups is only partially influenced by the tendency to give socially desirable answers (Junger, 1990a). The above-mentioned correction of the self-report data with police data should further reduce this influence. Consequently, correlational analyses that investigate the relations between variables are possible within each of the ethnic groups separately. For more information see Junger (1989a, 1990a).

2.5. Analysis of the Data

Information has been gathered on the following subjects: family relations, functioning at school, leisure time activities, delinquency of peers, values toward delinquent behavior, traditionalism, and problems related to immigration. Table I presents the main fields and indices on which information has been gathered. For each field of inquiry (e.g., family) principal-component analysis (PCA) was used to form relatively homogeneous groups of variables that correspond with one element of the bond to society. Both self-reported delinquency and arrest data have been used as dependent variables. In general, analyses have been performed for the total group and, also,

---

[2]Other research suggests that this validity bias has affected the results of other studies in the same way as in the present research (see, e.g., Mutsaers and Boendermaker, 1990; Baerveldt, 1990).

Table I. Main Fields Covered by the Study and Indices/Variables[a]

Field	Indices/variables
1. Family	Direct controls, family arguments, emotional bond, importance of school, general evaluation of family life, violence
2. School variables	Conflicts, commitment, school results, being expelled from school
3. Leisure time	Frequency, unconventional activities, orientation outside the family, drinking by the respondent, drinking by his friends
4. Values toward delinquency	Opinions on the seriousness of property crimes and aggression against persons
5. Traditionalism	Religiosity, attitudes toward the position of women
6. Problems related to migration	Knowledge of Dutch, family activities, fear for expulsion, length of stay in the Netherlands, orientation toward the country of origin, contacts with friends/neighbors, nationality of parent's friends, expectations about leaving the Netherlands in the next 5 years
7. Socioeconomic status of father	SES, (un)employment
8. Delinquency	Self-report delinquency, arrests

[a]More information about the indices and variables is given in the Appendix.

for each ethnic group separately. Detailed information about the relations between the indices is reported by Junger (1990a).

3. ETHNIC MINORITIES IN THE NETHERLANDS

The largest ethnic minority groups in the Netherlands are the Turks, the Surinamese, and the Moroccans. In 1989 the number of Turks in the Netherlands was approximately 177,000, the number of Surinamese approximately 210,000, and the number of Moroccans 140,000 (Van der Erf, 1989). These three groups are now introduced briefly.

3.1. The Surinamese

Surinam is a South American country, lying between British and French Guyana, and a former colony of the Netherlands.

The Surinamese do not form a homogeneous group. To start with, Surinamese have diverse ethnic backgrounds: Creoles are the descendants of former slaves brought into Surinam under the early colonial system; Hindustani came originally from India and often entered Surinam as contract laborers after slavery was abolished; there are also people from many other countries such as Indonesia and China (Campfens, 1979).

In the present study 51% of the respondents come from Hindu families, 22% describe themselves as being from Creole origin, and 25% have other ethnic backgrounds.

Coming from a former colony, the Surinamese share some elements of Dutch culture: they often speak Dutch and learned about Dutch history and geography at school, and some of them have the same religious background (Catholic or Protestant). Many of them came at a time when the economic recession made jobs hard to find. Surinamese have, in some respects, a position between that of the Dutch citizens and that of other immigrants. In general, Surinamese speak Dutch rather well, their educational level is relatively high, their housing conditions are better, and their socioeconomic status is high in comparison with other immigrants. However, on many of these factors, they do not attain the Dutch average levels (Junger-Tas, 1985; Penninx, 1988).

3.2. Turks and Moroccans

In the beginning the Turks and Moroccans were recruited as workers by employers at a time of shortages on the labor market. They were recruited to do mainly unskilled (and badly paid) labor at a moment of strong economic growth. Since 1973, with growing unemployment in the Netherlands, almost no workers entered the country. But growing numbers of migrants decided to have their families come over to the Netherlands. This trend is still going on today.

As is the case for the Surinamese, neither the Turks nor the Moroccans form homogeneous groups. Moroccans in the Netherlands come from diverse regions in Morocco that differ in many respects in terms of socioeconomic development, language, and traditions. Berbers in Morocco do not always speak and/or understand Arabic. In Turkey, although 90% speak Turkish, there is also diversity in ethnic background and in cultural tradition.

Overall, Turks and Moroccans occupy, in many respects, an unfavorable position in Dutch society. In Turkish and Moroccan communities unemployment rates are high, the average income is low, the educational level is low, housing conditions are bad in comparison with those of Dutch citizens, and illiteracy rates are sometimes high. The number of men who did not have any school education differs largely within the diverse ethnic groups. Findings from a recent study show that 11% of the Turkish and 37% of the Moroccan heads of households have never been to school (Rooduijn and Latten, 1986).

4. RESULTS

The main results of the study are presented below. First, the sample is described in terms of socioeconomic position. Second, information on the

Table II. Socioeconomic Status of the Father (%)[a,*]

	Moroccans (N=(169)	Turks (N=183)	Surinamese (N=148)	Dutch (N=182)	Dutch population[b]
High/liberal professions	1.8	3.3	12.2	12.1	19
Employee	1.2	1.6	8.1	9.9	20
Lower employee	2.4	5.5	18.2	19.2	16
Skilled working class	20.7	29.5	34.5	35.7	28
Unskilled working class	74.0	60.1	27.0	23.1	6

[a]Independently of the employment status of father, information on the SES was asked for.
[b]Source: Reubsaet *et al.* (1982, p. 139).
*$\chi^2 = 152.48122$; df = 12; $P < 0.0000$.

involvement in crime is described for the four ethnic groups. Third, analyses are presented within several theoretical frameworks.

4.1. Socioeconomic Position of the Samples

Some information on the socioeconomic position of the boys in the four samples is provided. As mentioned above the interviewers selected Dutch boys who were living in the same blocks as the ethnic minority boys in order to match on socioeconomic background. The question is to what extent this procedure was successful. Results show that the procedure for interviewing a comparable Dutch group was successful only in part (see Tables II and III). Overall, the method that was followed succeeded in finding Dutch boys coming from the lower strata of Dutch society. Their socioeconomic position is similar to that of the Surinamese boys. But, as mentioned above, both the Surinamese and the comparable Dutch boys are better off than the Moroccan and the Turkish boys. For example, among the Dutch, 23% of the fathers are (or were) unskilled workers, among the Surinamese this is practically the same (27%), but among the Turks and the Moroccans this is much more (respectively, 60 and 74%). With respect to unemployment the Dutch level (17%) is lower than the unemployment level of the ethnic minorities (32 to 43%). This problem does not affect subsequent analyses. As information on unemployment and socioeconomic status is available, if necessary, controls

Table III. Employment Status of the father (%)*

	Moroccans (N=180)	Turks (N=193)	Surinamese (N=165)	Dutch (N=193)
Employed	57.2	68.4	66.7	82.9
Not employed	42.8	31.6	33.3	17.1

*$\chi^2 = 29.60496$; df = 3; $P < 0.0000$.

can be performed for the influence of these factors on delinquent behavior.

It should be noted that it is probably impossible to attain absolute equivalence between groups since the four ethnic groups differ in so many respects. As mentioned before, illiteracy among Moroccans is relatively high. It seems infeasible to select a Dutch sample in which the illiteracy rate will approximate 40%. Consequently, a perfect correspondence between the various ethnic groups on socioeconomic factors will be almost impossible to achieve.[3]

4.2. Involvement in Crime

As mentioned above, information on delinquent behavior was gathered from two sources: the respondents themselves and police files. Looking first at the self-reported figures (see Table IV), it appears that about one-half of the Moroccan and Turkish boys admitted delinquent behavior (respectively, 51 and 54%). Among the Surinamese and the Dutch the number of boys who admitted an offense is higher (respectively, 61 and 68%). Percentages of self-report figures corrected for police contacts are somewhat higher for each ethnic group, and differences are statistically nonsignificant (between 63 and 70%). However, as mentioned above, self-report data are less reliable as a measure of delinquent behavior across ethnic groups and cannot be used for the purpose of comparison (for more information, see Junger, 1990a).

Consequently, we must turn to the police files to find information to compare ethnic groups in terms of delinquency. Police data can be considered

Table IV. Number of Boys Reporting Delinquent Behavior and Boys with Police Contacts (%)

	Moroccans (N = 182)	Turks (N = 196)	Surinamese (N = 206)	Dutch (N = 204)
Self-reported				
Uncorrected*	51	54	61	68
Corrected	63	64	64	70
Arrests				
Ever*	34	22	23	15
Last year*	20	10	10	6

*Chi-square is significant ($P < 0.01$).

[3]The danger exists that one ends with a circular reasoning. In this case the criterion for similarity in background factors becomes the delinquency rates. One way to look at the ethnic groups and to know whether they really have similar sociodemographic characteristics would be to examine the differences in delinquency. As long as differences in crime rates subsist, the researcher can argue that differences between ethnic groups still exist on some background variable.

a relatively unbiased measure of delinquency across ethnic groups (see Junger, 1988, 1990a, b). First, it should also be noted that, as a consequence of the sampling procedure, the Dutch boys are living in the same neighborhood as the ethnic minorities. This excludes the possibility that differences in police patrol (which might be more intensive in neighborhoods with high proportions of ethnic minorities) will have influenced the findings in such a way as to produce higher arrest rates for ethnic minorities. As a result, arrest data are used to assess the involvement in crime of the four ethnic groups. In addition, up to now, no evidence of discrimination by race has been found at the level of the police registration (Junger, 1988). Therefore it seems warranted to conclude that criminal statistics probably provide an adequate index of crime.

Of all the ethnic minority groups Moroccans have the highest arrest rates (34%), while the arrest rates of Turks and Surinamese are 10% lower (22 and 23%, respectively). Comparable Dutch boys have lower rates than the ethnic minorities (namely, 15%; see Table IV). With respect to the arrests during the preceding year, the rank order of the ethnic groups is similar. No differences have been found among ethnic groups in the type of offense or the frequency of offending (see also Junger, 1990a).

Other Dutch studies also found that ethnic minorities were generally overrepresented in police statistics (van der Hoeven, 1986; Essers and van der Laan, 1988). Recently Terlouw and Suzanne (1989) found similar results in Gouda (a small town in the Netherlands). Among the Moroccan boys (12–21 years old) 33% have been arrested; among Dutch boys, 6%. Usually, however, researchers are reticent to conclude that crime rates are indeed significantly higher because they lack an adequate comparison group. Furthermore, these studies were not based on national samples. On the basis of the present study, it can be concluded that, when a Dutch control group with a similar socioeconomic background is used, the differences in crime rates between ethnic groups do not disappear.

4.2.1. Frequency of Arrests

The majority of the boys with police contacts had only one contact with the police (52%). Among the boys with police contacts, 24% had two contacts, 8% had three contacts, and 17% had four or more contacts (ever, $N = 182$). Approximately half of the boys were arrested during the year preceding the interview. In this group, 63% were arrested only once, 22% were arrested twice, and 14% were arrested three times or more ($N = 90$). No differences were found for the overall number of arrests or the number of arrests during the last year in relation to ethnic group ($P < 0.50$).

4.2.2. Type of Offense

Information from the police records was available on the type of offense. The offenses were classified as petty theft (42%), serious property offenses (8%), aggression against persons (2%), vandalism (7%), sexual offenses (1%), problematic behavior (running away from home) (2%), or combinations (38%; $N = 173$). Among boys having police contacts, no differences among ethnic groups were found in type of offense.

4.2.3. Specialization

On the basis of self-report data (uncorrected measures), indications of specialization were sought.[4] Factor analysis showed that the first dimension explained 21% of the variance, the second 10%, and the third 8%. This suggests a one-dimensional solution. Furthermore, the dimensions that appeared from the analysis could not be interpreted in a meaningful way. This finding corroborates many other studies in which no specialization has been found. For example, Dickes (1989) has tried to find dimensionality using several statistical techniques. He concludes that the best model is to scale delinquency on one single dimension (see also Hindelang *et al.*, 1981). As a result the delinquency scales used in the present study are simply counts of the number of offenses (self-report or recorded).

The question that follows naturally from the figures presented above is how to explain the differences in crime rates. In the following sections three types of explanations are considered. Factors derived from strain theory, from control theory, and from approaches looking at the special problems of the migrants in Dutch society are related to crime among the four ethnic groups.

4.3. Strain

Many researchers in the Netherlands have focused upon strain theory, especially in order to explain the crime rates of ethnic minorities. The fact that 49% of the Moroccan men, 56% of the Turkish men, and 43% of the Surinamese men have a job and the others get some form of allowance/ welfare seems to support the main thesis of strain theory as an explanation of the relatively high crime rates in these groups (see Penninx, 1988).

Strain theory, as formulated by Merton (1967), assumes that everybody has been strongly socialized to pursue material success. But not everybody

---

[4]This was tried with nonlinear factor analysis (HOMALS; see Gifi, 1981) and ordinary factor analysis using several rotations techniques (oblique and orthogonal).

has access to the same means to fulfill these wants. Some people are confronted with insufficient resources: they experience strain. Delinquency is a way out of this strain between socialization to conventional goals and restricted opportunities, because it is an alternative road to success (Merton, 1967, p. 146).

The accessibility to goals is determined by the position in the class structure. As a result the "greatest pressures toward deviation are exerted upon the lower strata" (Merton, 1967, p. 144). As people from the lower strata have limited opportunity to realize prosperity, they will relatively often choose "alternative" roads to success. Consequently, strain theory expects a strong correlation between socioeconomic status and unemployment, on the one hand, and criminal behavior, on the other hand.

To test this expectation, socioeconomic status (SES) and unemployment of the father have been related to four delinquency scales: self-report delinquency (ever and last year) and arrest rates (ever and last year). In opposition with strain theory, the results of the present study show that on the individual level, there are hardly any relations between the socioeconomic situation and delinquency. For the four groups together, the correlations between SES and four delinquency measures vary between 0.11 and -0.06 ($P > 0.05$). The correlations between unemployment and the four delinquency measures[5] are nonsignificant with one exception.[6] The correlations for the four ethnic groups separately are hardly any higher (see also Junger and Zeilstra, 1989; Junger, 1990a). The results are illustrated in Table V, which shows the number of boys having police contacts in the case that the father has a job and in the case that the father has no job. Whether or not the father is employed is unrelated to the occurrence of police contacts among the sons.

There is another line of reasoning within the framework of strain theory. It seems possible that not all youths, especially among the ethnic minority groups, have been equally well socialized to the success values of Dutch society. According to Merton (1967) the major socializing institutions are

Table V. Number of Boys with Police Contacts and Employment of Father (%)*

	Moroccans	Turks	Surinamese	Dutch	Total
Father works	31	21	26	13	22
(N)	(103)	(132)	(110)	(160)	(505)
Father does not work	36	25	15	24	26
(N)	(77)	(61)	(55)	(33)	(226)

*Five chi-square tests have been performed; none are significant ($P > 0.10$).

[5]Self-report delinquency ever and last year, arrests ever and last year.
[6]Arrests last year * unemployment: $r = -0.09$, $P < 0.05$, $N = 749$.

the family, the school, and the workplace. In principle, families do not generate strain. Parents will not produce strain because "family largely transmits that portion of the culture accessible to the social stratum and groups in which the parents find themselves" (Merton, 1967, p. 158). This means that, overall, family influences are not very important as a cause of crime. But "schools are of course the official agency for the passing on of the prevailing values, with a larger proportion of the textbooks used in city schools implying explicitly that education leads to intelligence and consequently to job and money success" (Merton, 1967, p. 137). It could be argued that social position in itself is insufficient to locate those who experience strain. To experience strain it is necessary to combine restricted opportunities *with* successful socialization to the conventional success values of our society. The socialization process to these values takes place mainly at school.

In the present article it is assumed that a strong bond to school is indicative of, and will be associated with, a successful socialization to the success values of our society. Accordingly, the relation SES–delinquency will exist only among the pupils functioning well at school. Children of a low SES and a strong bond to school will be both attached to conventional success goals and handicapped in attaining material success. As a result they will experience strain and are likely to have high delinquency rates. Consequently, among pupils of a low social economic status, a strong bond with school will lead to more delinquent behavior rather than less, as social control behavior predicts. This expectation has been tested using log-linear analysis. In this analysis the relation between delinquency, on the one hand, and unemployment/SES, on the other hand, is studied after controlling for school integration and ethnic groups. The main conclusion is that there is no relation between SES or unemployment and delinquent behavior, after controlling for ethnic groups and the bond to school (see the Appendix, Table AII).

These results are illustrated in Table VI.[7] The relation between the bond to school and delinquency is presented for various levels of SES and unemployment. The data do not support the prediction of strain theory. Among children from families with a low SES or with unemployed fathers, a strong bond to school protects against delinquency instead of promoting it. Analyses with recorded delinquency produce similar results (see Junger, 1990a). The results show that the relation between school integration and delinquent behavior holds within each category of SES and employment

---

[7]In Table VI, due to small numbers, it was not possible to split the figures according to ethnic group. However, the analysis presented in the Appendix (Table AII) does control for ethnic group.

Table VI. Percentage of Respondents who Committed at Least One Offense (Self-Report) in Relation to School Integration According to SES and Employment Status of the Father and Relation with Self-Report Delinquency (γ and r)[a]

| | School integration | | | γ | r |
	High	Average	Low		
SES					
High	44	67	100	76	0.34***
(*N*)	(9)	(58)	(15)		
Lower employees	64	64	100	44	0.19*
(*N*)	(11)	(52)	(9)		
Skilled workers	58	63	95	44	0.18**
(*N*)	(24)	(150)	(21)		
Unskilled workers	29	65	90	65	0.29**
(*N*)	(41)	(229)	(19)		
Employment[b]					
Yes	41	67	94	62	0.28***
(*N*)	(71)	(354)	(51)		
No	50	60	100	40	0.25***
(*N*)	(18)	(163)	(23)		

[a]The index school integration is computed as the weighted sum of the four school indices, resulting from the regression analyses with self-report criminality as the dependent variable.
[b]Not included: retired fathers.
* $P < 0.05$.
** $P < 0.01$.
*** $P < 0.001$.

status. Boys who are functioning well in school are less delinquent than those who function poorly, a result that is in agreement with social control theory, as shown below.

4.4. Social Control

Control theory assumes that people always "want more" and that, in contrast with most other theories of crime causation, no special motivation is necessary to pursue short-term pleasures or to act out of self-interest. In that sense, everybody is motivated to commit crimes, at all levels of the social structure (Gottfredson and Hirschi, 1990).

Consequently, the central question in order to explain delinquency according to Hirschi is not "why do they do it" but "why don't we do it" (Hirschi, 1969, p. 34). The answer is that the quality of the social bond is not equally strong for all people. This bond acts as a control mechanism and as a brake to inhibit our deviant tendencies.

In 1969 Hirschi presented his operationalization of social control theory. Although social control applies to all forms of crimes and all types of criminals, Hirschi's (1969) operationalization focused on juveniles. The bond to society has several components. *Attachment to significant others*: youths usually have strong effective ties with their parents, teachers, and friends. *Commitment to conventional subsystems* such as school and work: this is the "rational component" of the bond—a desire to conform and to invest in the future in a conforming way (Hirschi, 1969, p. 20). *Involvement* in conventional activities: this is the way youths function in their family, at school, or at work. To the extent that ties to conventional others are weak, commitment to society is low, and juveniles function inadequately in diverse social institutions, delinquency will not be restrained. *Beliefs* in conventional values: social control theory claims that there is a single value system, with respect to delinquency, condemning delinquent behavior. But although this value system is shared by people, not everybody feels the same commitment to these values. The lack of beliefs prohibiting delinquent behavior probably has an independent effect on the probability of committing delinquent acts.

   In this study, attachment, involvement, and commitment have been operationalized within the fields in which children function: family (six variables), school (four variables), leisure time activities (five variables), and values toward delinquency (one variable). These variables and indices have been related to delinquent behavior in a multiple regression analysis (the various variables described in Table I). The results show that all correlations are statistically significant. Values are related positively to delinquency for each ethnic group $(0.33 < r < 0.46)$. The six family indices are also related to self-reported delinquent behavior $(0.33 < R < 0.46)$ and the three school variables are related to the occurrence of delinquency $(0.42 < R < 0.51)$. Finally, the five variables and indices measuring leisure time activities are also related relatively strongly to delinquency $(0.38 < R < 0.54)$. The total multiple correlations (of all 16 variables/indices taken together) vary between 0.61 and 0.70 (see Table VII).

   These results corroborate the expectations of social control theory. As hypothesized, youths with strong bonds to their family, to school, and to conventional values, and who do not participate in unconventional activities, are likely to have low delinquency rates. Youths with weak bonds to their family, to school, and to conventional values, and who often participate in unconventional activities are likely to have high delinquency rates. These findings hold for each ethnic group. The results are similar when analyses are repeated with arrests as the dependent variable (see Tables VII and AI).

4.5. Culture, Migration, and Delinquency

   Several approaches suggest that the relative high crime rates among ethnic minority groups are the result of particular problems that originate

Table VII. Social Bond Factors and Self-Reported Delinquency: Correlations and Multiple Correlation Coefficients[a]

Bond factor	Moroccans	Turks	Surinamese	Dutch
Values (1 variable)	0.34*	0.37*	0.33*	0.46*
Family (6 variables)	0.46*	0.33*	0.37*	0.44*
School (4 variables)	0.44*	0.44*	0.42*	0.51*
Leisure time (5 variables)	0.39*	0.38*	0.54*	0.54*
Total *R* (16 variables)	0.67*	0.61*	0.67*	0.70*
Expl. variance (%)	45	37	45	49
N Total	182	196	206	204[b]

[a]See Table I for the variables entered at each step.
[b]*N* varies slightly according to missing values.
*$P < 0.05$.

from the fact that they come from a different cultural background and from the migration experience. At least three approaches can be discerned. In this paper I discuss briefly the cultural dissonance approach, the traditionalism approach, and the view that problems resulting from migration might explain the crime rates among ethnic minority groups.

4.5.1. Traditionalism

It has been suggested that some ethnic minority boys are "modernized" when they come into contact with Dutch culture. As a consequence they will lose the bond to their traditional culture. This leads to conflicts with the parents, who will usually be (and remain) very traditional. The main idea seems to be that the loss of the bond to the traditional culture might lead to deviant behavior. Integration in one culture seems to preclude integration in the other. For example, Werdmölder (1985) mentions that the marginal Moroccan boys he studied want to go out to discotheques, meet (Dutch) girls, and wear clothes of the right brand. In other words, they want to participate in the Dutch modern youth culture. As a consequence, integration in the Dutch society leads to a loss of traditional bonds, which then will lead to higher delinquency rates.

However, alternatively it could also be argued that the less traditional families are, the more easily they will be able to participate in Dutch society. As a result less traditional boys will be less delinquent.

Religiosity and attitudes toward the position of women are two concepts that are often referred to when cultural differences are studied (see, e.g., Van den Berg-Eldering, 1981; Risvanoglu-Bilgin *et al.*, 1986). In the present research four indicators have been chosen to measure the bonding of boys to traditional values: their attitudes toward women, their religiosity, the number of children in the family, and urbanization in the country of origin.

Overall, these variables are unrelated to the occurrence of delinquency.[8] Religion appears to be the only one of these factors related to delinquency. It is a rather weak relation (r varies around -0.20). Higher levels of religiosity are related to relatively low delinquency rates. This relation is found among all ethnic groups except the Turks.

4.5.2. Adjustment Problems Resulting from Migration

Several problems can result from migration when people have to begin a new life in a foreign country. They will eventually miss the support of a social network and live in relative isolation (Ferrier, 1988). Problems can occur because migrants do not speak Dutch sufficiently well to integrate in Dutch society. Finally, problems surrounding the legal position in the Netherlands have been mentioned as an obstacle to a proper integration. The relatively weak legal position of the Moroccans and Turks in the Netherlands can lead to difficulties in the assimilation process into Dutch society.

Many of these problems have been mentioned in the literature in connection to the Turks and Moroccans. In many respects they probably do not concern Surinamese to the same extent (see Section 3).

In our study a number of indices/variables measure the extent to which the respondents and/or their parents might encounter relatively severe difficulties in Dutch society as a result of the fact that they are migrants: knowledge of Dutch, family activities, fear for expulsion, length of stay in the Netherlands, orientation toward the country of origin, contacts with friends/neighbors, the nationality of parent's friends, and expectations about leaving the Netherlands in the next 5 years (see also the Appendix).

Practically none of these indices/variables are related in any systematic way to criminality (self-reported or recorded delinquency). Although it is plausible that people need to adjust to a new country, and migration can lead to problems of adaptation, the present research provides no evidence that these problems are related to criminal behavior.

4.5.3. Cultural Dissonance and Delinquency

Youths of ethnic minorities have been described as "living between two cultures" (Tennekes, 1989). According to Budike (1988) most of them find

---

[8]There are some exceptions: the number of children in families has no relation to delinquency among the ethnic minorities but does relate to crime among Dutch boys. The higher the number of children, the higher the number of recorded police contacts. In addition, there is a relation between urbanization level in the country of origin and delinquency among the Surinamese. This relation was found for self-reported delinquency (last year and ever $= -0.20$) but not for the arrest data. A higher urbanization level is associated with relative more self-reported delinquency.

themselves in a situation of "permanent intercultural conflict." These statements are illustrative of the culture dissonance approach. According to this approach youths who are involved in two cultures can experience problems when these two cultures have—partly—different value systems and/or prescribe different behavior in particular situations. For the person placed in such a position, this can have several effects. In principle, these effects can be positive or negative. Dependent on the perception of the subject, cultural dissonance might lead to "conflicts, conformity, deviance, growth, and change" (see Chau, 1989). The outcome can be positive when the differences are stimulating. But, according to most authors, cultural dissonance is a situation of conflict which is painful and confusing (see Maliepaard, 1985, pp. 66-69). The Scientific Council of Government Policy (WRR, 1979) has described the problems of identity which can occur as a result of cultural dissonance.

> Growing up in two worlds with a different social status in each of them, with different opinions, with little understanding for each other, and even sometimes hostile towards each other but that both demand loyalty, poses for this generation [children from migrants] important identity problems, and engenders a lack of normalcy in consequence. (p. 14)

It is not entirely clear how the process actually works. First, integration in a community might be seen as relatively constant over time and over persons. Moroccans will always be integrated to a large extent in their own community and, to a certain degree, in Dutch society. Consequently, one might assume that every Moroccan and Turkish boy coming from another—Islamic—cultural background would experience cultural dissonance. However, this model cannot explain why some members of ethnic minorities commit crimes and others do not.

Second, if integration in both communities varies, it seems plausible that cultural dissonance is possible only when there is a relatively strong integration in both cultures because otherwise the feelings of dissonance will not occur. Consequently, a strong integration in two different cultures could lead to problems like delinquency.

The conclusion that traditionalism or problems resulting from migration do not affect delinquency does not, in itself, support the cultural dissonance approach. However, proponents of the cultural dissonance approach might argue that this assessment is not a dismissal of their thesis. The approach applies to boys who are strongly influenced by *both* communities, because only in this situation cultural dissonance will occur. Consequently, one should look for an interaction effect among integration in the Dutch society, bonds to traditionalism, and delinquency. If this line of reasoning is correct, it might be expected that boys who are strongly integrated in school (an institution functioning according to Dutch standards and representative of Dutch values) but who, at the same time, have traditional attitudes toward the position of women in society, will experience the highest levels of dissonance. Accordingly they should have higher crime rates than other boys. This hypothesis is tested in Table VIII. The mean delinquency levels are broken down for school integration and attitudes toward the position of women. An analysis of variance is performed for each ethnic group.

The data presented in Table VIII confirm what was mentioned above. School integration is related quite strongly to delinquent behavior. When children are well integrated in school, they commit fewer delinquent acts than less integrated children. This holds for each ethnic group and for each level of traditionalism. At the high level of school integration the mean self-report delinquency level varies between 0.40 and 1.17. At the low level of school integration the mean self-report delinquency varies between 1.33 and 4.67.

The attitudes toward the position of women are unrelated to delinquency. This holds also for the three ethnic groups.

Finally, the interaction terms of the three analyses are statistically non-significant. At each level of the index "position of women," the relation between school integration and delinquency is unaltered. Among the youths

Table VIII. School Integration, Attitudes Toward the Position of Women,[a] and Delinquency: Mean Self-Report Delinquency Scores for Three Ethnic Groups and Statistics

Position of women	School integration		
	High	Average	Low
1. Moroccans			
Traditional	0.40	1.06	1.33
Average	1.05	1.07	1.95
Not traditional	0.82	0.91	2.43
2. Turks			
Traditional	0.88	0.78	2.20
Average	0.68	1.47	2.31
Not traditional	0.50	1.00	3.00
3. Surinamese			
Traditional	0.75	1.17	2.71
Average	1.17	1.56	4.67
Not traditional	0.81	1.65	2.38

Main effect	School	Position of women	Interaction
Moroccans	$F=9.4$; $P=0.00$	$F=0.41$; $P=0.66$	$F=0.7$; $P=0.56$
Turks	$F=16.2$; $P=0.00$	$F=0.25$; $P=0.78$	$F=1.0$; $P=0.39$
Surinamese	$F=15.6$; $P=0.00$	$F=2.26$; $P=0.11$	$F=2.2$; $P=0.07$

[a]Women should stay at home (traditional) or go to school (nontraditional).

most likely to be in a position of cultural dissonance (namely, well integrated in school and with traditional attitudes toward women), the mean delinquency rate is relatively low rather than high. This means that, in contrast with cultural dissonance theory, there is no interaction effect of school and "position of women." These analyses were repeated for recorded delinquency and for religion as a measure for traditionalism. The results are similar.

An alternative possibility is that those who have lost the bond to their own community, but are integrated in Dutch society, will have higher rates of delinquency. No support is found for this suggestion either. At each level of school integration, attitudes toward the position of women are not related to delinquency.

5. SUMMARY AND DISCUSSION

The aim of this study is to answer two questions. The first question concerns the involvement in crime among ethnic minority juveniles. Arrest rates have been used to determine the degree of involvement in crime of the respondents, since criminal records proved to be a reliable indicator of the participation in crime among the four ethnic groups. From the arrest data it appears that ethnic minority youths have higher crime rates than Dutch youths, regardless of whether they are compared with Dutch youths of a similar socioeconomic background or with a random sample of Dutch youths. Of all the ethnic minority groups, Moroccans have the highest arrest rates, namely, 34%. They are followed by the Surinamese, with 23%, and the Turks, with 22%. The comparable Dutch youths have a still lower arrest rate, namely 15%; however, Dutch youths from a random sample have an arrest rate of 10%.

It is noteworthy that the Dutch boys have been selected living in the same block as the ethnic minority boys, so that the opportunities to commit crimes (for example, proximity to shops) are similar for both the Dutch and the ethnic minority boys. In addition, this form of matching also controls for the differences that might exist in police patrolling between neighborhoods. Consequently, the difference between the Dutch and the ethnic minority youths cannot result from either differences in the opportunity to commit crime or differences in police patrolling.

Some authors have argued that differences in delinquency rates between ethnic groups will disappear when socioeconomic conditions are taken into account (Albrecht, 1984, 1987; van der Hoeven, 1986). Apparently, even after controlling for socioeconomic background, differences in involvement in crime between ethnic groups persist.

The differences in crime between ethnic groups are simply differences in the level of participation in crime: no differences have been found among ethnic groups as to type of offense or frequency of offending. This supports the thesis of Gottfredson and Hirschi (1990) that the differences that appear between groups are differences in involvement and not in frequency or type of offense.

The second purpose of the study was to investigate whether the causes of crime are similar among the youths or whether factors specific to the culture or the migrant status of the minority groups affect their crime rates. Several theoretical frameworks have been considered.

5.1. Strain Theory

A central aspect of strain theory is that there is a relation between someone's place in the social structure and delinquent behavior. As a result, strain theory predicts a relation between socioeconomic status and unemployment, on the one hand, and delinquency, on the other hand. This relation has not been found. The results show that there are systematic relations between socioeconomic position and delinquent behavior within the ethnic groups.

Another possibility of assessing which people are strained is to look at the combination of the bond to school and SES. The expectation is, according to strain theory, that children of a low SES (or with fathers without a job) *and* strongly attached to school will be seriously handicapped in attaining conventional success goals. This group should feel strained and, accordingly, have high delinquency rates. Again, this prediction could not be confirmed by the data. Youths having a strong bond to school are less delinquent than those having a weak bond. This holds at each level of SES and for fathers with or without a job.

5.2. Social Control Theory

According to social control theory the strength of the social bond will determine the likelihood of delinquent behavior. In the present study the bond to society has been measured over the various fields in which children develop: family, school, leisure time, and peers. Overall, the findings of the present study support social control theory. As hypothesized, youths with strong bonds to their family, to school, and to conventional values, and who do not participate in unconventional activities, are likely to have relatively low delinquency rates. These findings hold for each ethnic group.

5.2.1. Problems Resulting from Migration

The results of this research show that, although migration places people before problems of adaptation, there is no evidence that it leads to delinquent behavior. Delinquent behavior is unrelated to the number of social contacts of the parents, the knowledge and use of the Dutch language, or the fear of expulsion from the Netherlands.

5.2.2. The Traditionalism Approach

Two possible relations of traditionalism with crime might be considered. The first possibility is that the loss of the bond with traditional values has negative effects for the ethnic minority youths and might result in higher crime rates. The second possibility is that less traditionalism leads to better integration in the Netherlands. This could result in lower crime rates. The data do not support either of these expectations. All the indices/variables referring to traditionalism are unrelated to delinquency.

There is one exception: religiosity has a rather weak relation with delinquent behavior. However, religiosity cannot be considered as a factor with a special relevance for ethnic minorities. The fact that this relation also holds for Dutch youths means that its importance is not restricted to ethnic minorities.

5.2.3. Implications for the Cultural Dissonance

Overall the findings do not provide evidence to support the cultural dissonance approach. The fact that traditionalism is unrelated to delinquency is contrary to cultural dissonance prediction. It has also been investigated whether the experience of conflict among youths having strong bonds with Dutch society (namely, with school) and their own traditional culture will lead to relatively high delinquency rates. The findings do not support this thesis.

It is worth mentioning that several authors found that the marginalization process of the Moroccan youths began in Morocco instead of the Netherlands. The majority of the marginal Moroccan youths (in Holland) were deviant already in their country of origin: they were truants, they used alcohol or drugs, and some had already police contacts. This finding suggests that the same factors that cause delinquent behavior in the Netherlands were already operating in Morocco. This is in contradiction to the expectation of the cultural dissonance approach, since it seems unlikely that cultural dissonance could start in Morocco (Werdmölder, 1986; Kaufman and Verbraek, 1986).

Finally, it is noteworthy that Chinese children do share the problems of migration and culture conflict. However, in most countries they have similar or lower crime rates than natives (see, e.g., Junger, 1989b). In the Netherlands the Chinese children arrived during the seventies as a result of family reunion, just as the Turkish and Moroccan children. Consequently, they should also experience cultural dissonance. However, they seem to function relatively well at school. It has been suggested that the strong family ties among Chinese are responsible for these good results at school.

The findings suggest that the problems resulting from migration and differences in cultural background in relation to criminality have been largely overstated.

It has been argued that social control theory is a typically "middle-class" theory, which is based on middle-class values and was developed by middle-class social scientists (Bruinsma, 1990). Consequently, applying social control theory to Islamic and Surinamese youths who are largely lower class and who come from non-Western countries could provide a strong confirmation of the theory. The findings of the present study show that social control theory passes this test.

APPENDIX

The following indices/variables are used in this article.

Family Variables

Direct Controls. Questions were asked about the amount of surveillance of the parents, the feeling of the boys whether they "could do whatever they liked," and whether the parents checked if they did their homework.

Family Arguments. Questions were asked about the amount of arguments in the family.

Violence. This index measures the amount of violence in the family. Questions were asked whether brothers, sisters, and the respondent were beaten.

Emotional Bond. To measure the emotional bond between parents and children, boys were asked if they spoke about their problems with their parents and if they did get compliments when they did something well.

Importance of School. This index measures the degree to which parents think (according to the boy) that school(success) is important.

General Evaluation of the Family Life. Five questions were asked about the respondent's satisfaction with family life.

School Variables

Conflicts. This index measures the number of conflicts with teachers.

Commitment. This has been measured by asking questions about the enthusiasm of the respondent for school, the importance he attaches to school success, and the significance of the opinion of teachers and of good school results.

School Results. This index is based on two questions about repeating classes and the number of insufficient marks.

Being Expelled from School. One question was asked about expulsion from school.

Leisure Time Variables

Frequency. The frequency index measures the amount of time spent outside the home.

Unconventional Activities. This index counts the number of unconventional activities the boys engage in regularly. These activities are going to bars, discotheques, or youth clubs, going to the center of town, or hanging around.

Orientation. Questions have been asked about their favorite place. Some boys answered that they like to be at home. Others mention that they would rather be with friends. The "orientation" index measures the degree to which children are oriented toward the family or, alternatively, toward going out with friends and activities outside the home.

Drinking. Respondents were asked how much alcohol they would drink, and how much alcohol their friends would drink, when going out.

Culture, Migration, and Delinquency

Religiosity. The index is composed of questions about going to church (or the mosque/temple), praying, and following other rules concerning food or fasting.

Attitudes Toward the Position of Women. This index reflects the attitudes of respondents or the importance of girls going to school and the possibility of their having boyfriends. Questions were also asked about who does the shopping (as traditional Islamic women are not supposed to leave their homes on their own).

Number of Children in the Family, Urbanization in Country of Origin and Knowledge of Dutch. Several questions have been asked about the knowledge of Dutch, the use of the Dutch language at home and at school, and the importance parents attach to the knowledge of Dutch.

Family Activities. Questions were asked about activities of the family with other family members (including members of the extended family).

Fear of Expulsion. The boys were asked whether they feared being sent back to their country of origin by their parents or by the police.

Length of Stay in the Netherlands. The degree of orientation to their own community in the Netherlands or the country of origin was measured by the following questions: nationality of parent's friends, contacts with friends/neighbors, frequency of visits to the country of origin, expectation of leaving the Netherlands, and saving to return.

Bond to Conventional Values

To measure the bond to conventional values questions have been asked about the seriousness of several crimes. These questions concerned property crimes and aggression against persons.

Socioeconomic Status (see Table AII)

Socioeconomic status of the father was divided into five categories (from high to low): high/liberal professions, employee, lower employee, skilled working class, and unskilled working class. In addition, respondents were asked whether or not their father had a job.

Delinquency Variables

1. Did you ever not pay (enough) for public transport?
2. Did you ever steal anything at school?
3. Did you ever steal anything from a car?
4. Did you ever steal a bicycle/motorcycle?
5. Did you ever steal something at home?
6. Did you ever do some "joy-riding"?
7. Did you ever sell drugs?
8. Did you ever buy something which was probably stolen?
9. Did you ever threaten to assault anybody using a knife or a gun?
10. Did you ever actually beat or hit anybody?
11. Do you carry a gun?
12. Did you ever force a girl to have sex?
13. Did you ever destroy something which did not belong to you?

In shops, did you ever ...

14. Steal anything worth 10 guilders (±$5) or less?
15. Steal anything worth between 10 guilders (±$5) and 100 guilders (±$50)?
16. Steal anything worth more than 100 guilders (±$50) guilders?

Table AI. Social Bond Factors and Officially Registered Delinquency (Ever): Correlations and Multiple Correlation Coefficients[a]

Bond factor	Moroccans	Turks	Surinamese	Dutch
Values (1 variable)	0.09	0.12*	0.17*	0.28***
Family (6 variables)	0.31**	0.30***	0.27***	0.44***
School (4 variables)	0.46***	0.30**	0.42***	0.29**
Leisure time (5 variables)	0.34***	0.19	0.41***	0.28**
Total R (16 variables)	0.56***	0.44***	0.51***	0.57***
N total	182	196	206	204[b]

[a]See Table I for the variables entered at each step.
[b]N varies slightly according to missing values.
   * $P<0.05$.
  ** $P<0.01$.
 *** $P<0.001$.

Table AII. The Relation Between Delinquency and Unemployment/SES, Controlling for School Integration and Ethnic Groups: Models and Ratio Chi-Square Statistics of Log-Linear Analysis

Model 1	Model 2
Self-report	
Ethnic group * school integration	Model 1 and delinquency * unemployment
Ethnic group * unemployment	
Ethnic group * delinquency	
Delinquency * school	
(1) $\chi^2=30.5$, df$=26$, $P=0.25$	(2) $\chi^2=30.2$, df$=25$, $P=0.22$
Difference $\chi^2(1)-\chi^2(2)=0.3$, df$=1$, $P=0.80$	
Ethnic group * school integration	Model 1 and delinquency * SES
Ethnic group * SES	
Ethnic group * delinquency	
Delinquency * school	
(1) $\chi^2=71.8$, df$=66$, $P=0.29$	(2) $\chi^2=69.5$, df$=63$, $P=0.27$
Difference $\chi^2(1)-\chi^2(2)=2.3$, df$=3$, $P=0.50$	
Arrests	
Ethnic group * school integration	Model 1 and delinquency * unemployment
Ethnic group * unemployment	
Ethnic group * delinquency	
Delinquency * school	
(1) $\chi^2=28.9$, df$=26$, $P=0.31$	(2) $\chi^2=28.9$, df$=25$, $P=0.27$
Difference $\chi^2(1)-\chi^2(2)=0$, df$=1$, $P=1$	
Ethnic group * school integration	Model 1 and delinquency * SES
Ethnic group * SES	
Ethnic group * delinquency	
Delinquency * school	
(1) $\chi^2=58.3$, df$=66$, $P=0.74$	(2) $\chi^2=54.2$, df$=63$, $P=0.78$
Difference $\chi^2(1)-\chi^2(2)=4.1$, df$=3$, $P=0.20$	

REFERENCES

Albrecht, H. J. (1984). Problems of policing ethnic minorities in the Federal Republic of Germany. In Brown, J. (ed.), *Policing and Social Policy; The Cranfield-Wolfson Colloquium on Multi-ethnic Areas in Europe*, Police Review Publication, London.

Albrecht, H. J. (1987). Foreign minorities and the criminal justice system in the Federal Republic of Germany. *Howard J. Crim. Just.* 6: 272–286.

Baerveldt, C. (1990). *School en Delinquency (School and Delinquency)*, Gouda Quint, Arnhem.

Block, C. R. (1985). Race/ethnicity and patterns of Chicago homicide 1965–1981. *Crime Delinq.* 31: 104–116.

Bruinsma, G. J. N. (1990). De schaduwzijde van de sociale controle theorie (The dark side of social control theory). In Zwanenburg, M. A., and Smit, A. M. G. (eds.), *Kleine criminaliteit en overheidsbeleid*, Gouda Quint bv., Arnhem.

Budike, F. (1988). *Reclassering en de tweede generatie allochtonen (Probation and the Second Generation Immigrants)*, Nederlandss Federatie voor Reclasseringsinstellingen, Den Bosch.

Campfens, H. (1979). *The Integration of Ethno-cultural Minorities: A Pluralist Approach. The Netherlands and Canada: A Comparative Analysis of Policy and Programme*, Ministry of Cultural Affairs, Recreation and Social Welfare, The Hague.

Chambliss, W. J., and Nagasawa, R. H. (1969). On the validity of official statistics: A comparative study of white, black and Japanese high-school boys. *J. Res. Crime Delinq.* 6: 71–83.

Chau, K. L. (1989). Socio-cultural dissonance among ethnic minority populations. *Soc. Casework J. Contemp. Soc. Work* 70: 224–230.

Craen, A. (1984). Policing and social policy in the multi-ethnic area of Genk. In Brown, J. (ed.), *Policing and Social Policy; The Cranfield-Wolfson Colloquium on Multi-ethnic Areas in Europe*, Police Review Publication, London.

Dickes, P. (1989). What kind of homogeneity for self-report delinquency items? In Klein, M. (ed.), *Cross-National Research in Self-Reported Crime and Delinquency*, Kluwer Academic, Dordrecht, pp. 249–267.

Essers, A. A. M., and van der Laan, P. H. (1988). *Jeugd en Justitie (Youth and Justice)*, WODC, Ministerie van Justitie, Den Haag.

Ferrier, J. (1988). Casa Migrantes en Opo Fre Bakka (Casa Migrantes and Opo Fre Bakka). *Tijdschrift Jeugdhulpverlening* 16: 224–231.

Gerholm, T., and Litham, Y. G. (1988). The institutionalisation of Islam in the Netherlands, 1961–1986 (Introduction). In Gerholm, T., and Litham, Y. G. (eds.), *The New Islamic Presence in Western Europe*, Mansell, London.

Gifi, A. (1981). *Non-linear Multi-variate Analysis*, Department of Data Theory, University of Leiden, Leiden.

Gottfredson, M. R., and Hirschi, T. (1990). *A General Theory of Crime*, Stanford University Press, Stanford, Calif.

Gould, L. C. (1969). Who defines delinquency: A comparison of self-reported and officially reported indices of delinquency for three racial groups. *Soc. Problems* 16: 325–336.

Hindelang, M. J., Hirschi, T., and Weis, J. G. (1979). Correlates of delinquency: The illusion of discrepancy between self-report and official measures. *Am. Sociol. Rev.* 44: 999–1014.

Hindelang, M. J., Hirschi, T., and Weis, J. G. (1981). *Measuring Delinquency*, Sage, Beverly Hills, Calif.

Hirschi, T. (1969). *Causes of Delinquency*, University of California Press, Berkeley.

Jäger, J. (1984). Ethnic minorities and the police problems in Germany. In Brown, J. (ed.), *Policing and Social Policy; The Cranfield-Wolfson Colloquium on Multi-ethnic Areas in Europe*, Police Review Publication, London.

Junger, M. (1988). Racial discrimination in the Netherlands. *Sociol. Soc. Res.* 72: 211–216.

Junger, M. (1989a). Discrepancies between police and self-report data for Dutch racial minorities. *Br. J. Criminol.* 29: 273–284.

Junger, M. (1989b). Ethnic minorities, crime and public policy. In Hood, R. (ed.), *Crime and Criminal Policy in Europe*, Proceedings of a European colloquium, Centre for Criminological Research, University of Oxford, Oxford.

Junger, M. (1990a). *Delinquency and Ethnicity. An Investigation on Social Factors Relating to Delinquency Among Moroccan, Turkish, Surinamese and Dutch Boys*, Kluwer Law and Taxation, Deventer.

Junger, M. (1990b). Studying ethnic minorities in relation to crime and police discrimination: Reply to Ben Bowling, *Br. J. Criminol.* 30: 493–502.

Junger, M., and Polder, W. (1991). *Achtergronden van delinquent gedrag onder jongens uit etnische minderheden (Background of Delinquent Behaviour Among Boys from Ethnic Minorities)*, WODC, Gouda Quint bv., Arnhem.

Junger, M., and Zeilstra, M. (1989). *Deviant gedrag en slachtofferschap onder jongens uit etnische minderheden (Deviant Behaviour and Victimization Among Youths from Ethnic Minorities)*. WODC, Gouda Quint bv., Arnhem.

Junger-Tas, J. (1985). Allochtonen in Nederland: een inleiding (Immigrants in the Netherlands: An introduction). *Justitiële Verkenningen*, pp. 1–33.

Kaufman, W. J., and Verbraeck, H. T. (1986). *Marokkaan en verslaafd: een studie naar randgroepvorming, heroïne gebruik en criminalisering (Moroccan and Addicted; A Study of Marginalization, Heroin Use and Crime)*, Afdeling Onderzoek ROVU, Gemeente Utrecht, Utrecht.

Maliepaard, R. (1985). *Achtergronden van deviant gedrag bij allochtone jongeren (Background of Deviant Behaviour Among Immigrant Youth)*, Coordinatiecommissie Wetenschappelijk Onderzoek Kinderbescherming, Den Haag.

Merton, R. K. (1967). *Social Theory and Social Structure*, Collier-Macmillan, New York.

Mutsaers, M., and Boendermaker, L. (1990). *Criminaliteitspreventie in het onderwijs (Crime Prevention at School)*, Ministerie van Justitie, WODC, K9, Den Haag.

Nadjafi Abrandabadi, A. H. (1983). L'évolution de la criminalté des étrangers en France. *Rev. Peniten. Droit Pénal* 2: 147–155.

Penninx, R. (1988). *Minderheidsvorming en emancipatie; balans van kennisverwerving ten aanzien van immigranten en woonwagenbewoners (Minority Formation and Emancipation; An Evaluation of Knowledge with Respect to Immigrants and Caravan Dwellers)*, Samsom, Alphen a/d Rijn.

Reubsaet, T. J. M., Kropman, J. A., and van Mulier, L. M. (1982). *Surinaamse migranten in Nederland, de positie van Surinamers in de Nederlandse samenleving (Surinamese Migrants in the Netherlands; The Position of the Surinamese in Dutch Society)*, Instituut voor Toegepaste Sociologie, Nijmegen.

Risvanoglu-Bilgin, S., Brouwer, L., and Priester, M. (1986). *Verschillend als de vingers van één hand (As Different as the Fingers of One Hand)*, COMT, Rijksuniversiteit van Leiden, Leiden.

Rooduijn, M. J., and Latten, J. J. (1986). *De leefsituatie van Turken en Marokkanen in Nederland (The Situation of Turks and Moroccans in the Netherlands)*, CBS-publikaties, Staatsuitgeverij, Den Haag.

Sampson, R. J. (1985). Race and criminal violence: A demographically disaggregated analysis of urban homicide. *Crime Delinq.* 31: 47–82.

Stevens, P., and Willis, C. F. (1979). *Race, Crime and Arrests*, Home Office Research Study No. 58, HMSO, London.

Tennekes, J. (1989). Buitenlandse jongeren en cultuurconflict (Foreign youths and culture conflict). *Migrantenstudies* 5: 24–40.

Terlouw, G. J., and Suzanne, G. (1989). *Een preventieproject in Gouda, eerste resultaten van een project voor Marokkaanse jongeren (A Prevention Project in Gouda, First Results of a Project for Moroccan Youth)*, WODC, Ministerie van Justitie, Den Haag.

Van den Berg-Eldering, L. (1981). *Marokkaanse gezinnen in Nederland (Moroccan Families in the Netherlands)*, Samson, Alphen a/d Rijn,

Van der Erf, R. F. (1989). Beleidsrelevante migranten groepen demografisch gezien (Policy relevant migrants from a demographical point of view). *Migrantenstudies* 5: 11–24.

van der Hoeven, E. (1986). *De jeugdpolitie: een observatie-onderzoek (The Youth Police: An Observation Study)*, CWOK, Den Haag.

Werdmölder, H. (1985). Randgroepvorming: marginalisering en etnitisering onder Marokkaanse jongeren (Marginal groups: marginalization and ethnic revival among Moroccan boys). *Mens Maatschappij* 60: 142–161.

Werdmölder, H. (1986). *Van vriendenkring tot randgroep: Marokkaanse jongeren in een oude stadswijk* (*From Peer Group to Marginal Group: Moroccan Youths in an Old Neighborhood*), Het Wereldvenster, Amsterdam.

WRR (Scientific Council for Government Policy) (1979). *Etnische minderheden* (*Ethnic Minorities*), WRR No. 17, Staatsuitgeverij, Den Haag.

[9]

Crime and Russian Immigration— Socialization or Importation?

The Israeli Case

ARYE RATTNER*

ABSTRACT

Questions about the possible relationship between ethnicity, immigration and crime have been raised since the days of the early pioneers of criminology. Criminological research conducted in Israel in the last three decades pointed clearly at the existence of correlation between crime and ethnic origin as related also to immigration. The current study examines the involvement of Jewish Russian immigrants in crime. While data on the issue is limited the study attempts to examine whether crime is locally produced in Israel as a result of the crisis of immigration, or perhaps imported from the former USSR. Finding tend to show that part of the crime in which recent Russian immigrants are involved in is indeed a result of the difficulties of absorption into a new culture, however, there are indicators that part of the criminal activity is related to the escalating crime rates in the former USSR and therefore being imported from the Eastern Block and results from a spillover effect.

QUESTIONS ABOUT the possible relationships between ethnicity, immigration and crime have been raised since the days of the early pioneers of criminology. In searching for the causes behind high crime rates in certain areas, several early theorists proposed that the answer lay in the conflict between different cultural groups (Sellin, 1938; Sutherland, 1929). Since central city areas were inhabited largely by immigrants, theorists suggested that immigrants' values and norms might differ from those of the cities' general populations. It soon became clear that it was not the areas themselves that were the source of the high crime rates; instead, causes were identified within the immigrants' patterns of socialization to American culture.

Immigration to a new country is mainly considered a process of sociocultural adaptation, which is complex in itself. In addition, its direction is influenced by several factors. On the one hand, adaptation is influenced by attitudes among the host population towards immigrants, as well as the policies pursued by the government of the receiving country with respect to immigrant integration. On the other hand,

* Department of Sociology, University of Haifa, Haifa, Israel.

236   ARYE RATTNER

the process of adaptation is also affected by the type of immigration involved—whether it is economic migration or refugee flight—and by the immigrants' personal characteristics, including age, skills and educational level.

Another intervening variable is the state of the economy in the host country, which determines the ease with which immigrants and citizens can satisfy their economic goals. In many cases, mass immigration today is characterized by the arrival of unprofessional and sometimes unskilled immigrants in a host society with high unemployment. Since movements of immigration from one country do not always parallel fast economic growth in the receiving countries, immigrants may at best find themselves employed as unskilled manual workers in manufacturing industries or in low-waged domestic services. Such a scenario—which has not been unusual in countries absorbing waves of mass immigration in several periods of the twentieth century—places many immigrants at the lower echelons of a blocked economic-mobility structure.

In such contexts, the criminal involvement of members of various ethnic groups has often been explained by the potential of crime as an alternative means of economic mobility. Several studies have examined the involvement of both Jewish and Italian immigrants to the USA in organized crime during the 1920s (Nelli, 1969; Rockway, 1980). For immigrants of certain ethnic origins, a crime career was the quickest way to achieve material success, as well as both individual and social mobility. Three alternative paths of social and personal mobility were open to people living and growing up in early-twentieth-century American immigrant ghettos: (a) the ladder of legitimate work, holding out a prospect of slow economic mobility; (b) higher education, with opportunities to move on to governmental and managerial positions; and, (c) crime, mainly within the underworld and organized crime (Rockway, 1980). In addition to being, for those who chose it, the quickest way to upward mobility, crime also provided a challenge for men of ability, daring and violence. Amir (1979) described the circumstances under which a Jewish immigrant teenager might make criminal behavior his chosen career: "... [He] perceives that, because of his inadequate education, family status, and deviation from archetypal American norms, he is denied access to the life goals ... and the recognized symbols of success: money, prestige, leisure, power and security." Under these circumstances the immigrant teenager described by Amir is detached from his old culture, but has already absorbed the importance of upward mobility and economic advancement. He turns to "instant affluence by deviant method—delinquency, hoodlum behavior and adult criminality." Similar descriptions have been offered of the arrival and socialization process experienced by some immigrants who came to the USA through New York at the turn of the century. Unable to understand urban life, newcomers with minimal income and their large (and growing) families crowded into the less-desirable sections of New York already vacated by poor American families. The atmosphere of loneliness, insecurity and separation from the familiar culture opened

CRIME AND RUSSIAN IMMIGRATION—SOCIALIZATION OR IMPORTATION? 237

the door for gambling and drinking, and attracted criminals who were dispersed in other areas of the city. Immigrants themselves were rarely law-breakers upon arrival, but their offspring were attentive to opportunities to increase their standards of living. Membership in a gang involved in violence, robbery, theft and the disposal of stolen goods provided a sense of belonging and a base for financial gain.

The serious social problems that accompanied the waves of immigration into the USA during the first decades of the century provoked a series of generalizations about the forces that lead immigrants to crime. It has been suggested that: (a) immigrants come from inferior racial stock, and their degeneracy leads to criminality; (b) immigrants are not trained in the codes and ideals of America and therefore commit crime out of ignorance; (c) immigrants are often poverty-stricken, resulting in frustration that creates personal maladjustment of various kinds, including delinquency and criminality.

While many argued during the years that immigration was at its height that immigration was indeed the chief cause of crime, Sutherland and Cressy (1978) have claimed that when age and sex are controlled for, the general crime rates for immigrants are lower than the general crime rates of the native-born. Based on a series of studies from the United States, Australia and Germany, Sutherland and Cressy indicated that in all cases, crime rates for the native-born were as much as twice as high as the crime rate for immigrants. It was only under certain social conditions and for certain types of crime that immigrants exhibited crime rates comparable to those of the native-born. In his study on European migration and crime, Ferracuty (1967) also succeeded in demonstrating that the crime rates of immigrant groups were lower than those of the native-born. In those instances where rates for certain types of crime were higher among members of an immigrant group, these types of crime were usually characteristic of the home country.

Many studies have examined the relationship between crime and immigration in the context of the mass immigration of the early decades of the century. A series of recent studies have focused both on second-generation immigrant crime and on the criminal activity of immigrants who recently fled social, political, and economic changes in Eastern Europe and in Asian countries such as Korea and China (Pogrebin and Poole, 1989; Carter, 1992; Bovenkerk, 1993; Tanton and Lutton, 1993). Van der Hoeven (1986), in a study examining juvenile delinquency in The Netherlands, showed that both Turkish and Moroccan juveniles have scored high on certain crime measures in several Dutch cities. He indicated that the findings could be accounted for by typical criminogenic factors such as age, gender and social class. Junger (1989) has also examined crime patterns among Moroccan, Turkish, Surinam and Dutch boys. Comparing random samples of these groups, she concluded that Moroccan boys, followed by the Turkish ones, had particularly high scores when property offenses and "aggression towards individual persons" were

238   ARYE RATTNER

considered. Here, differences could not be ascribed to any social category other than ethnic origin.

In discussing crime in multi-ethnic societies from a European perspective, Bovenkerk (1993) examined recent crime patterns in several European countries, with an emphasis on the Netherlands, and concluded that there might be a substantial second-generation crime problem. However, a Swiss criminologist who examined evidence in all Western European countries concluded that the available explanations of this problem are far from adequate (Killias, 1989). Killias cited evidence both for higher crime rates among second-generation immigrants and for discrimination and selective perception by police and other criminal justice agencies. The problem, therefore, would be to determine the relative contribution of the various factors. The Dutch case is indeed an extreme one, as no less than 25% of its prison population is foreign, while the total ethnic minority population does not exceed 7%. It would be hard to imagine such gross overrepresentation without considering other causes as well.

As the flow of immigrants from Southeast Asia (e.g., South Korea, China, Japan) to the United States increased in recent years, so did the rates of criminal activities committed by immigrants. Harmon (1984) compared the current involvement and organization of criminal activity among Chinese in the United States to that of the Italian and Sicilian Mafias when they immigrated to the USA. The Italian groups developed their own criminal organizations but maintained close ties to organized crime groups in Italy. Similarly, Chinese crime groups in New York and San Francisco maintain connections with Hong Kong and other areas in China for their heroin supply.

In a 1993 article, Tanton and Lutton reported that criminal activity committed by immigrant aliens in the USA has escalated significantly. According to data from the US Bureau of Prisons, more than 20% of federal inmates are non-US citizens from over 120 countries, half of them convicted on drug offenses. An increase of 600% has been recorded since 1980 in the proportion of alien inmates. Increasing crime problems among immigrants to the US have been reported among several ethnic groups, including Russian Jews, Israelis, Cubans, Jamaicans and Nigerians (Tanton and Lutton, 1993).

Most studies have suggested that crime among immigrants can be seen as the result of a dual conflict—the diminishing ability of immigrants to satisfy their own needs and aspirations, coupled with their failure to establish or maintain a positive identification with the dominant society. At the same time, the question of whether immigrants become criminal after arriving in their host countries or import criminal behavior from their native countries has not been resolved. Nettler (1984) offered a cultural-transmission explanation, arguing that immigrants tend to be involved in types of crime familiar to them from their respective countries of origin. This theory does not necessarily imply that these immigrants were criminals in their countries of origin, but rather that they will tend to engage in types of criminal activity already somewhat known to them. The issue of crime importation was further explored by Conklin (1986), who asserted that US immigrants' involvement in criminal behavior is a function of patterns of criminal activity prior to their landing in the United States, coupled with the difficulties of socio-cultural adaptation. Wood (1947) identified several critical factors related to differences in crime rates across various immigrant groups. He contended that crime rates among immigrants reflect the strength and consistency of the traditions internalized in their native countries, on the one hand, along with the strength and consistency of the traditions they find in their new country.

Israeli Society

Before and after the 1948 establishment of Israel as an independent state, several waves of mass immigration—from Asia, Africa, Eastern and Western Europe and the American continent—turned the country into a melting pot, an almost natural laboratory for examining the absorption of immigrants and the creation of ethno-cultural cleavages. But statehood brought about a radical change in the size and structure of the population. Until 1948, the existing Jewish population consisted of 600,000 residents, most of them immigrants from Western and Eastern European countries. The first eleven years of independence saw a massive wave of immigration, with close to a million people arriving from more than fifty countries. The year 1951 was a turning point in the demographic and ethnic makeup of the new state. The first wave of immigration numbered about 700,000 people, half of them from European countries, among them survivors of the Holocaust and the Nazi concentration camps. The other half came from several Asian and African countries (mainly North African).

The most obvious differences between the European Jews (Ashkenazi) and the Oriental (Sephardic) Jews related to the general conditions of their societies of origin. European societies varied a great deal from one to another, but they were relatively advanced by comparison with the Oriental societies, which included some that were in the process of emerging into modern life and some that were still pacing the treadmill of tradition. The Sephardic immigrants exhibited, upon their arrival, such differences from Ashkenazi immigrants as larger family sizes, lower education levels and lower skills. In addition, most of them adhered so closely to a traditional religious life that modern Israeli life and culture, with its anti-traditional approach, was alien to them. At the time of immigration, a high rate of illiteracy was also observed among Oriental Jews. As a result of material hardship, combined with high rates of unemployment resulting from the lack of economic infrastructure, the average per capita income of an Oriental family between 1948-1960 was about 48% of the average European family.

240   ARYE RATTNER

The political and cultural establishment in Israel, which was dominated mainly by the Eastern European culture, regarded the new Oriental immigrants as inferior. A distinction between center and periphery developed, both spiritually and physically. A particularly significant manifestation of the gap between the two ethnic communities was the much greater frequency among the Orientals of slum-dwelling and crowded housing, as well as higher rates of school dropout and much higher rates of criminality, juvenile delinquency, and other kids of anti-social behavior.

Criminological research conducted in the last three decades pointed clearly at the existence of a correlation between crime and ethnic origin in Israel (Hassin, 1985; Shoham et al., 1966; Shoham, 1966). While examining the relationship between countries of origin and juvenile delinquency in Israel, Hassin found a significant contribution by Oriental Jews to increasing juvenile crime between 1948-1969, followed by a decline in this pattern among Oriental Jews after 1969. The relative contribution of juveniles from families of Asian-African origin to the juvenile crime rate was at times no less than 80%, according to police reports. The most common explanation for these findings was the cultural shock and crisis of absorption experienced by Oriental immigrants. The passing of time and the bridging of ethnic gaps (especially on the socio-economic dimension) contributed somewhat to healing these wounds, and may explain the significant decrease observed in crime rates among the second generation of Oriental immigrants. Similar findings appeared in a study conducted by Shoham et al. (1966), who found that the highest rates of criminal behavior were among juveniles of Sephardic origin who either immigrated as young children or were born shortly after their Oriental parents arrived in Israel. The age of onset of criminal behavior was much lower among juvenile immigrants compared to children of longtime citizens. Criminal behavior was attributed to negative socialization among the immigrants, as well as to cultural conflict.

Despite the evidence pointing to a relationship between negative socialization, cultural conflict and criminal behavior, other explanations were not excluded. In another study, Shoham (1966) hypothesized that immigrants from North African countries might perceive violent behavior differently than longtime citizens and immigrants of other origins. Shoham speculated that this might result from North Africans' origins in a more traditional culture, contributing to higher rates of criminal behavior in general and violent behavior in particular. Several other studies have not excluded the possibility that aggressive and violent behavior was perceived differently among North African immigrants, and therefore used more frequently (Ailam, 1978; Shoked, 1981).

Beyond some ethnographic and anthropological studies that speculated that crime might have been imported by the earlier Oriental immigrants, no empirical studies have substantiated this hypothesis. It was only later, when another wave of both Russian and Georgian Jews came to Israel during the 1970s, that the issue of crime importation was raised again. Amir (1985) examined the involvement of

Georgian Jews from the USSR in criminal activity in Israel. According to Amir, their criminal behavior was imported from Georgia, where violent behavior and other types of criminal activity were quite frequent. According to Amir, Georgians' involvement in criminal activity and violent behavior—black-marked trade in stolen goods, smuggling, burglary and extortion—was tolerated to a certain degree in the USSR, explaining the "relative speed with which some of the Georgian Jewish immigrants found their way to similar occupational ventures in Israel" (Amir, 1985).

Since 1989, Israel has witnessed another wave of immigration, this time almost entirely from Russia and the former USSR. The extensive socio-economic and political changes initiated by Mikhail Gorbachev under the reform and openness programs of *perestroika* and *glasnost*, which eventually contributed to the dissolution of the Soviet Union, also introduced a great deal of social instability and a breakdown of social order. The fall of communism and the loss of state control also opened the way to increasing anti-Semitism, leading hundreds of thousands of Jews to attempt to leave Russia and other republics of the former USSR and to immigrate to Israel, Europe and North America.

Seeing itself as the homeland for Jewish people from all over the world, Israel became a natural shelter for many of the Russian immigrants. Under the provisions of the Law of Return, every Jew is granted Israeli citizenship almost automatically (upon presentation of sufficient evidence of Jewish identity). However, the influx of Jewish immigrants from the former USSR has caught the State of Israel unprepared for the absorption of hundreds of thousands of immigrants in a relatively short period of time.

Several features have become characteristic of this wave of immigration: First, the housing infrastructure in Israel could not accommodate hundreds of thousands of new immigrants, so a quick decision was made to house Russian immigrants in mobile homes, which were assembled overnight into temporary communities. While the initial intention was not to leave immigrants in these places for more then one or two years, many could not find alternative housing and so remained for several years more in what quickly became deteriorating slums and "greenhouses" for crime and other social problems. Second, already having at this point its own 11% unemployment level, the State of Israel could not absorb all the new immigrants into its labor market. While most of the Russian Jews were educated and highly skilled, no place could be found for so many musicians, mine and electrical engineers or physicians and dentists with diplomas that were not recognized either in Israel or in any other western country. For many of the newly arrived immigrants, the dream of Israel as a "land of milk and honey" has become a nightmare. Unemployment among Russian Jews has reached close to 75% at times, and those lucky enough to be employed have worked as street cleaners, as janitors in both public and private organizations, and in other low-paid services. Frustration, anger and despair has driven many of the new immigrants to alcoholism (which some of them had already experienced back in Russia) as well as crime.

Social unrest and instability, combined with socio-economic and political changes in the former USSR, have been reflected there in an unprecedented increase in crime. Dashkov (1992) reported that from 1979 to 1983 the number of recorded crimes almost doubled. While the situation stabilized somewhat in 1986 and 1987, and a drop in crime rates was even realized, the trend changed again during the following years. A dramatic change was noticed between 1988 and 1990, with a crime increase of 3.8% from 1987 to 1988, 31.8% from 1988 to 1989, and 13.3% from 1989 to 1990.

Recent studies (Saviuk, 1990; Alimov, 1988) have documented the changes in crime trends in the former USSR, both in violent and property crime, since *perestroika* and the fall of communism. While violent crime has remained predominantly domestic, violence in the framework of organized crime has increased as well, characterized by audacity, sophistication and cruelty. Organized crime has established itself in the political and economic structure of the Eastern Block. Its activities include the smuggling of consumer goods, people, raw material and vehicles. Organized crime activity also involves weapons theft, drug production and trafficking, prostitution, fraud, extortion, embezzlement and money laundering. While it is unknown how far organized crime has infiltrated into the political and economic structure of the former USSR, it is clear that it has spread beyond the borders of the Eastern Block, into other European countries such as Germany, the Czech Republic, Slovakia, the Nordic region (Denmark, Norway, Finland) and Holland, as well as Greece, Turkey and Israel (Ulrich, 1994).

The current study attempts to expose, through simple statistics, some of the characteristics of criminal activity committed by Russian immigrants in Israel, and to examine whether any consistent patterns exist within it. In general, Israeli police will not release official statistics about the involvement of Russian immigrants in criminal activity, at least in part to avoid the labeling and stigmatization of the entire community of Russian Jews, still in the early stages of absorption into Israeli society. However, a recent police report (Police, 1995) made public, for the first time, some very general statistics about the criminal activity of Russian immigrants in Israel.

Out of the total 75,789 criminal cases solved by Israeli police in 1994, 7.8% involved an offense committed by a Russian immigrant who migrated to Israel after 1989. This reflected an increase of 18.1% in the involvement of Russian immigrants in crimes that has been solved by Israeli police. Among the Russian immigrants involved in criminal activity in 1994, 23.3% had committed a bodily harm offense, 33.4% a property offense, and 21.1% an offense against public order (Police, 1995).

Data

This study uses an update of a data base that has been retrieved from official police records for the period 1980-1994, for the purpose of a different study. The existance of the variable country of birth and year of immigration has enabled us ot utilize this data base for the purpose of this study as well. The data base includes a sample of 124,000 police records. A random sample of 3673 persons who had their first police contact during each of theses years, was drawn from the police computerized central files. For each person drawn in the sample the entire criminal history has been retrieved, a process that has yielded a total of 124,000 records. For the purpose of this study we selected only those who immigrated to Israel after 1989 from one of the former USSR countries.

Findings

Table 1 indicates the number of immigrants who came to Israel from the former USSR between 1989-1994, a total of 540,616. While the bulk of the immigrants came in 1990, around 65,000 immigrants arrived in each of the following years. We notice from Table 1 that there is an almost linear relation between the decrease in the number of immigrants over the years, and the increase in the number of police arrest records. While 2.7% of the entire police records population related to Russian immigrants in 1991, the percentage of police records related to people of Russian origin is 3.5 times larger in 1994, reaching 9.6% of the record population.

Table 2 exhibits the contribution of Russian immigrants to criminal behavior. While reported crime statistics have been known to be misleading even in the categories of conventional crime, this might be even more of a problem when examining the involvement of Russian immigrants in criminal activity. Concerns have been expressed on several occasions that much of the criminal activity committed by Russians involves extortion, illegal and black-marked trading, smuggling and

Table 1

Contribution of New Immigrants from Former Soviet Countries to Criminal Activity in Israel, Compared with Contribution of Longtime Citizens

Year	No. of immigrants from former USSR	% of records[i] of immigrants	% of records of veteran citizens
1989	12,912	N/A	N/A
1990	185,173	1.1	98.9
1991	144,678	2.7	97.3
1992	65,093	5.5	94.5
1993	68,000	8.1	91.9
1994	64,760	9.6	91.4

244   ARYE RATTNER

Table 2
Distribution of Offenses for New Immigrants and Longtime Citizens[ii]

Offense	Veteran citizens	New immigrants
Public order	26.7	19.9
Human bodily harm[iii]	16.4	18.4
Sex	2.0	2.8
Morals[iv]	0.2	0.4
Drugs	14.0	5.2
Breaking and entering (B&E)	6.8	8.3
Car theft	1.8	1.4
Theft from vehicle	5.3	5.4
Other theft	7.7	17.0
Other property off.	10.6	11.1
Fraud	5.7	7.4
Other	2.8	2.7
Total	100%	100%

prostitution. There is no doubt that a large part of this kind of criminal activity is not reflected in the official police statistics.

The contribution of Russian immigrants to crime in Israel is mainly reflected in four broad categories of offenses: public order offenses (26.7%), human bodily harm offenses (16.4%), property offenses (breaking and entering (B&E), car theft, theft from vehicle, other theft and other property offenses, 32.2%), and fraud (5.7%).

Official crime statistics commonly do not reflect organized crime activity, although drugs, morals and fraud-related crime reports might provide an indication to a certain extent. However, the question of whether criminal acts committed by Russian immigrants mainly involved single individuals or groups of more then one person might be a rough indicator of the degree of collective criminal activity.

The findings from Table 3 exhibit that in at least in three crime categories, police records reflect that criminal actions involving more then one offender occur with significant frequency. Forty-five percent of the records in the category of "moral offense" reflect the activity of two or more persons. Three other categories in which a significant number of records indicate the collaboration of two or more offenders are B&E, fraud and drug offenses. Even in the category of human bodily harm, which typically involves criminal offenses committed by single individuals (such as assaults), 15% of the records involve more then one suspect.

Discussion

Out of the 75,789 criminal cases that were solved in 1994 by Israeli police, 5,947 (7.8%) as reported by police authorities, were cases involving Russian immigrants. According to Israeli police headquarters, this represents an increase of

CRIME AND RUSSIAN IMMIGRATION—SOCIALIZATION OR IMPORTATION? 245

Table 3

Distribution of Crime Committed by Single Individuals and Groups among New Immigrants, 1993-1994

Offense	No. records with 1 offender	%	No. of records with 2 and more offenders	%
Public order	865	88.3	115	11.7
Human bodily harm	642	85	113	15
Sex	270	90	30	10
Morals	137	55	113	45
Drugs	255	75	85	25
Breaking & enter.	780	65	420	35
Fraud	403	74	142	26

18.1% a since 1993. However, it is important to note that Israeli crime statistics have not undergone any dramatic overall changes due to the contribution of Russian immigrants to criminal behavior. More important is the relatively fast entry and socialization of Russian immigrants into the subculture of criminality in Israel.

The 9.6% of police records (as reflected by our data) that involve Russian immigrants just about mirrors Russian immigrants' representation of 9.7% among Israel's 5.5-million person population. However, the rapid increase from 2.7% of records in 1991 to 9.6% in 1994 indicates that as time goes on, some of the immigrants do not settle successfully (financially, socially, etc.) and criminal behavior becomes their alternative way of life. This hypothesis is further supported by the fact that the main immigrant contribution to criminal behavior (as far as reported crime is concerned) falls within the various categories of property offenses.

Over 43% of the crime committed by new immigrants consists of breaking and entering, theft and other property offenses. These criminal activities, especially if conducted in an organized way, yield the fastest profits for the individuals involved, both in the theft and in the trade of stolen goods. The findings from Table 3 indeed indicate that 35% of records of property offenses involve two or more collaborators. Some of these property offenses are staged by groups and are well-organized. Groups of immigrants work together to set up networks, select sites for car thefts, burglaries and break-ins based on "intelligence information," plan escape routes and organize distribution centers for stolen goods. In his study on the involvement of Georgian Jews in crime in Israel, Amir (1985) made a distinction between organized crime and organized criminality, characterizing the latter as mainly ethnically-based operations.

Although less evident in the official statistics, the contribution of Russian immigrants is also noticeable in crime categories such as morals, drugs and fraud. Although only 0.4 of the records belonging to Russian immigrants involve moral offenses (procurement, soliciting for prostitution, etc.), much of this criminal activity

246   ARYE RATTNER

goes unreported. Prostitution, for example, was viewed as socially deviant behavior during the period of the former Soviet Union, but it was not considered a major criminal problem. With the downfall of the old government, organized crime and prostitution became intermingled. Prostitution controlled by organized crime has moved beyond the large Russian cities, and is currently exported to other countries, including Israel. Some of these activities are part of the organized crimes that elude official statistics. While Israeli authorities refuse to deal publicity with the matter or to release any official data, Israeli newspapers provide anecdotal information on young Russian women who are coerced into the "skin trade." Some of these women are kidnapped to Israel with false promises of a better life.

A similar phenomenon may be observed under the category of fraud offenses. Crimes such as fraud, illegal trading, smuggling, extortion, embezzlement and the production of counterfeit currency have become widespread in the former Eastern Bloc countries. The constant flux of Jewish immigrants from the former USSR to Israel, along with the fact that Jews are almost automatically accepted as citizens in Israel, makes the country a fertile ground for such illegal activity. Israeli police authorities confess to their inability to fight the various new techniques used for fraud, money laundering and extortion (Yediot Acharonot, 26 May 1995). This inability to fight financial crime is partially explained by the fact that the ethnically-based criminal organization has its roots in the countries of origin. As one official put it, "We don't know where it begins and where it ends. . ." (Yediot Acharonot, 26 May 1995, p. 13). This is another indication that much of the criminal activity of this kind is undetected and unreported. Blood revenge, kidnapping and extortion have become common among some of the ethnically-based criminal groups as means used to threaten victims and prevent them from reporting crimes to the authorities.

A careful examination of the presence of Russian immigrants in Israeli criminal circles, including the volume and types of criminal behavior, indicates that not all of this activity is locally based. While some immigrants' criminality may result from poor socialization into Israeli society, another part bypasses Israeli custom and border authorities and is illegally imported to the country.

NOTES

[i]   Figures in both columns represent percentages of records from sample population of immigrants and veteran citizens.

[ii] Figures in both columns represent percentages from sample population of records for each group.

[iii] The category of human bodily harm offenses includes the following offenses: causing bodily harm, assaulting a public official, assault, criminal negligence and kidnapping.

[iv] The category of moral offenses includes: procurement, soliciting for prostitution, soliciting to commit acts of prostitution, maintaining a brothel, seducing/soliciting minors, distributing pornographic material and loitering for the purpose of prostitution.

REFERENCES

AILAM, Yitzhak
1978 "Using force among Morrocon and Georgian Immigrants." *Megamot* 24: 169-185. (In Hebrew)

ALIMOV, S.
1988 "The Prevention of Violent Crime: Problems and Results." In: Dashkov, 1992.

AMIR, Menachem
1979 "Organized Crime in Israel and the United States." *Crossroads*, Winter, 1979.

ASHBURY, Herbert
1934 *All Around Town*. New York: Knopf.

ASHBURY, Herbert
1942 *The Golden Flood*. New York: Knopf.

BOVENKERK, Frank
1993 "Crime and the Multi-ethnic Society: A View from Europe." *Crime, Law and Social Change* 19 (3): 271-280.

CARTER, David L.
1992 "A Forecast of Growth in Organized Crime in Europe: New Challenges for Law Enforcement." *Police Studies* 15 (2): 62-74.

CONKLIN, Jonh E.
1986 *Criminology*. MacMillan.

DASHKOV, Gennady V.
1992 "Quantitative and Qualitative Changes in Crime in The USSR." *British Journal of Criminology* 32 (2): 160-166.

FERRACUTI, Franco
1967 "The Subculture of Violence: Towards an Integrated Theory." In: *Criminology*. London: Tavistock.

HANDLIN, Oscar
1951 *The Uprooted*. New York: Grosset & Dunlap.

HARMON, James, Jr.
1984 "Organized Crime of Asian Origin. President's Commission on Organized Crime." United States Government Printing Office.

HASSIN, Yael
1985 "Relationship Between Country of Origin and Juvenile Deliquency in I Israel 1948-1977." *Crime and Social Deviance* 13: 79-99. (In Hebrew)

JUNGER, M.
1989 *Delinquency and Ethnicity*. Deventer/Boston: Kluwer.

KILLIAS, M.
1989 "Criminality among Second-Generation Immigrants in Western Europe: A Review of the Evidence." *Criminal Justice Review* 14 (1): 13-42.

NELLI, S. Humbert
1969 "Italians and Crime in Chicago: The Formative Years, 1890-1920." *American Journal of Sociology* 74 (4): 373-391.

NETTLER, Gwynn
1984 *Explaining Crime*. New York: McGraw-Hill.

POGREBIN, Mark R. and Eric D. POOLE
1989 "South Korean Immigrants and Crime: A Case Study." *The Journal of Ethic Studies* 17 (3): 47-81.

248   ARYE RATTNER

POLICE
  1995 *Collection of Essays and Legislation*, edited by Avi Zelba. Israel Police: Unit of Community
       Policing.
ROCKAWAY, Robert A.
  1980 "The Rise of the Jewish Gangster in America." *Journal of Ethnic Studies* 8 (2): 31-44.
SAVIUK, L.
  1990 "Criminological Studies of Crime." In: Dashkov, 1992.
SELLIN, Thoresten
  1938 "Culture Conflict and Crime." New York: Social Science Research Council, Bulletin 41.
SHOHAM, Shlomo
  1966 "Immigration and Crime in Israel." In: *Crime and Social Deviation*, edited by S. Shoham.
       Chicago, Henry Regency Co.
SHOHAM, Shlomo and Rasak ABED-EI
  1966 "Immigration Ethnicity and Ecology as Related to Juvenile Delinquency in Israel." *British
       Journal of Criminology* 6 (4): 391-409.
SHOKED, Moshe
  1981 "Explaining Paterns of Aggression Among Morrocon Immigrants." *Megamot* 27: 397-411.
SUTHERLAND, Edwin H.
  1929 "Crime and the Conflict Process." *Journal of Juvenile Research* 13: 38-48.
SUTHERLAND, Edwin, H. and Donald R. CRESSY
  1978 *Criminology*. Philadelphia: J.B. Lippincott.
TANTON, John and Wayne LUTTON
  1993 "Immigration and Criminality in the U.S.A." *The Journal of Social, Political and Economic
       Studies* 18 (2): 217-234.
ULRICH, Christopher J.
  1994 "The Proce of Freedom The Criminal Threat in Russia, Eastern Europe and the Baltic
       Region." Research Institute for the Study of Conflict and Terrorism, Stockholm, Sweden.
VAN DER HOEVEN, E.
  1986 *Allochtone Jongeren bij de jeugdpolitie*. The Hague: CWOK
WOOD, Arthur L.
  1947 "Minority Group Criminality and Cultural Integration." *Journal of Criminal Law and Crim-
       inology* 37: 498-510.
Yediot Achronot
  1995 "The Caucasian Mafia Was Here." Pp. 12-14 in: *Israeli Daily News Paper*, May 5.

[10]

Analysis of the Crimes by Foreigners in Japan[1]

MINORU YOKOYAMA

Kokugakuin University, Tokyo

In Japan, the crimes committed by foreigners have not historically been considered a primary social problem prior to the 1980s. In the decade of the 1980s, many foreigners entered Japan in hopes of making a substantial amount of money. With the increase in the total number of new alien entrants, the crimes by foreigners gradually increased. However, all of the publicity focused on the country's economic prosperity and little attention was drawn to crimes by foreigners.

After the summer of 1990, a severe economic depression began. As the depression deepened, the crimes by foreigners increased drastically. The quality of these crimes became aggravated. This paper analyzes such phenomena through a study of empirical data, formal statistics, media resources, and a host of other resources. The paper will conclude that the economic elements played an important role in the development of criminal activity by alien newcomers to Japan.

Crimes by Foreigners as a Social Problem

Before World War II, many Japanese emigrated to Hawaii, Canada, and the west coast of the United States. Meanwhile, Japan did not zestfully accept immigrants. Regardless of this barrier, in the late 19th century, Chinese settled in Japan and established a China town in large harbor cities such as Yokohama, Kobe and Nagasaki. After the Sino-Japanese War in 1895, a number of Chinese youngsters moved to Japan to experience the country's modernization. In addition, Koreans immigrated to Japan after being colonized by Japan in 1910. Although many Chinese and Koreans lived in Japan, their crimes were not noticed as a significant social problem.

Japan ran short of labor forces during the war against China and World War II. At that time, many male Koreans were compulsorily taken to Japan.[2] They were compelled to work hard as veritable slaves in the mining, construction, and manufacturing industries. They were then liberated from slave labor after the end of World War II in 1945. However, many of them remained Japan,[3] while being severely discriminated against by Japanese. Their poor communities resembled slums, in which crime rates, particularly for juvenile crimes, were high.

The standard of life for Chinese and Korean people in Japan eventually improved alongside the high economic growth during the period just prior to the oil shock in 1973. In addition, the discrimination they felt by Japanese waned gradually with the spread of the democratic movement, enhanced education, and the emergence of civil movements in the late 1960s. Today, the crimes by the Chinese and Korean residents do not draw attention as a social problem.

Since 1980 many foreigners have come to Japan mainly for the purpose of making money through the country's economic growth and expansion. In the 1990s their crimes started to become a bona-fide, publicized social problem in Japan. In this paper the writer like to focus on the crimes committed by non-permanently-staying foreigners (refers to temporary, alien residents, excluding both those qualified to stay permanently and those affiliated with U.S. military forces).

Foreigners Coming to Japan after 1980

An increase in the total number of foreigners coming to Japan in the 1980s was evident. The number of legally entering foreigners increased from 1,296,000 in 1980 to 2,260,000 in 1985 and to 3,504,000 in 1990 (Table 1). We can analyze the reasons of this increase from two viewpoints: [1] the domestic factors in Japan and [2] the factors in foreign countries, from which temporary alien residents came. Focusing on these two factors, this paper carries out the analysis from a historical perspective.

Immediately after the defeat of World War II Japanese soldiers and settlers in the occupying Asian countries returned to Japan. Japanese suffered from poverty in the late 1940s. To open up a "brave new world," many Japanese immigrated to foreign countries such as Brazil and Peru.[4] On the other hand, to endure the pressure of the excess population, our national government adopted a policy of the severe regulation of immigration to Japan. After the end of the Vietnam War in 1975 many Vietnamese escaped from their mother country by boat. These boat people sometimes landed in Japan. However, the Japanese government did not grant them permission to settle in Japan as political refugees. This policy was criticized by foreign countries, especially developed countries which did accept boat people. In response to the pressure from foreign countries in 1981, the Immigration Control Law was replaced by the Immigration-Control and Refugee Recognition Law. However, even under this new law Japan did not readily admit the entry of "alien plain laborers."

A multitude of Asian people went to Arabian countries to work as laborers after the oil shock in 1973. However, due to a depression around 1980 Arabian countries began to regulate the entry of alien pain laborers. On the other hand, Japanese currency became highly evaluated because of the strong economy based mainly on the export industry. Japan then became a target for Asian people to work overseas and make money.

In the early 1980s Japan became the consumers' society, in which sexual services were in great demand. Supplying males with sexual services such as prostitution and strip shows was a prosperous business. The industry thus began to make alien females provide Japanese males with sexual services. Therefore, around 1983 many females came to Japan from other Asian countries such as the Philippines, Taiwan and Thailand (Yokoyama, 1995: 57). To

CRIMES BY FOREIGNERS IN JAPAN   183

work illegally, they visited Japan by the visa slated for sightseeing or show business, with which recruiters and racketeers provided them.

First, we saw many females entering Japan in the disguise of dancers and singers by the visa for show business from Philippines and Taiwan.[5] In the 1990s many Thai females entered Japan by the visa for sightseeing or by forged passports through the medium of organizations for slave trafficking.[6] Usually they are not informed of the place of work in advance, when they are recruited in their mother countries. After their arrival at Japan they are informed that they owe a large amount of money for paying costs of their travel and those of the mediation by recruiters and racketeers (Yokoyama, 1993b: 79). To pay the advanced money imposed fraudulently upon them, they are confined and compelled to work as prostitutes by racketeers. They are often put under the supervision of the Boryokudan, the Japanese gangsters' group known as "Yakuza" in foreign countries.

In the 1980s Japan enjoyed an economic boom. Japanese youngsters, above all else, did not want to engage themselves with dangerous, dirty, and unglamorous hard work. Thus, there was a shortage in the labor supply, especially in secondary industries such as manufacturing and construction. At the beginning this shortage was filled by the illegal alien laborers coming to Japan by the visa for sightseeing.

In 1983 the national government established a policy to accept more alien students, advocating the slogan of accepting a total of 100,000 in a year by the beginning of 21st century.[7] Soon afterward, in 1984, it began to allow foreigners to take the visa easily for studying in Japan. Most commonly issued were visas for studying within six months at a professional school for Japanese language or some occupational skill. With such visas in hand, many Chinese and Koreans rushed to Japan.

It was very difficult for Korean youngsters to study abroad before 1985, because of the economic and political conditions in their country. In the late 1980s, the Korean political system was democratized and witnessed high economic growth. Then, in January, 1989, the Korean government abolished the regulation of traveling abroad. Therefore, more Koreans were allowed to enter Japan for the purpose of study.

The Chinese government did not admit people to go abroad for their private purposes. In 1986, however, it mitigated its severe control of going abroad (Mo, 1994: 14). At that point, Chinese, especially those living in the Fujian Province, rushed to Japan by the visa for studying within six months at a professional school. The total number of Chinese entrants by this visa increased drastically from 250 in 1984 to 7,200 in 1987 (Yashiro, 1993: 56). The main purpose of many entrants by this visa was to make money. Without going to a professional school, which had guaranteed their entrance into Japan in order to earn tuition proceeds, they worked illegally day and night. With hard work, some Chinese could earn 600,000 yen (US$5,200) in a month(Mo, 1994: 109). After overstaying illegally for several years they returned to their home with a large sum of money. By this money they built gorgeous houses, at which they wished to live idly for the remainder of their lives.

In November of 1988, The Japanese government decided to check severely the application documents for the visa for studying at a professional school in order to exclude many Chinese entrants whose main purpose was to make money by working illegally in Japan.[8] However, the shortage of labor power was keen. The issue of whether or not to accept alien plain laborers was often discussed. Then, in December of 1989, the Immigration-Control and Refugee Recognition Law was revised (Yokoyama, 1993a: 203). Under this revised law people of Japanese ancestry became qualified to stay in Japan as settlers who can work legally. On the other hand, this law aims to control illegal alien entrants and overstayers more severely. It prescribes punishment on persons who employ foreigners illegally, and on brokers who introduce foreigners illegally to employers.[9]

Prior to the enforcement of the revised Immigration-Control and Refugee Recognition Law on June 1, 1990, many illegal overstayers appeared before the immigration office in fear of rumored severe punishment (Yokoyama, 1993b: 72). Receiving the order of compulsory extradition, they returned to their mother countries at their own expense. However, by the estimation of the Immigration Bureau of the Ministry of Justice a total of 106,000 foreigners remained illegally on July 1, 1990 (Table 1).

To fill the shortage of labor power, the large-sized companies, especially those manufacturing automobiles and electric appliances, recruited many people of Japanese ancestry mainly from Brazil and Peru. By the estimation of the Association of People of Japanese Ancestry in 1992, the people of Japanese ancestry coming from South America totaled to over 200,000, of which Japanese Brazilian and Japanese Peruvian amounted to 160,000 and 28,000 respectively (Asahi Newspaper, October 9, 1992). However, the Japanese economy has plummeted since the summer of 1990. With the deepening of the depression, foreigners staying in Japan confronted a trying situation.[10] To take advantage of this situation, the Boryokudan began to exploit illegal overstayers by employing them at a cheap wages or by dispatching them to work in manufacturing and construction (White Paper on Police in 1991: 195).

Table 1 shows the total number of foreigners entering legally into Japan. There was tremendous growth in this number during the period from 1988 to 1989, as many Chinese and Korean rushed to Japan with the visa for studying at a professional school. Then, for a one year period, there was another large growth spurt of legal entrants, because many people of Japanese ancestry came to Japan from South America. The estimated total number of foreigners staying illegally in Japan increased drastically from 106,000 in 1990 to 299,000 in 1993 (Table 1). In the summer of 1990, the depression began. It may be surmised that even during the period from 1990 to 1993 there was the continuous increase in the number of the illegal entrants, because the Japanese currency remained strong to the foreign one owing to a large amount of trade surplus.

CRIMES BY FOREIGNERS IN JAPAN   185

Table 1. The Total Number of Alien Legal Entrants and the Estimated Total Number of Alien Illegal Stayers

Year	Alien Legal Entrants		Alien Illegal Stayers	
	Number*	Index	EstimatedNumber**	Index
	(Unit: thousand)	(1990 = 100)	(Unit: thousand)	(1990 = 100)
1980	1,296	(37)	-	(-)
1985	2,260	(64)	-	(-)
1986	2,021	(58)	-	(-)
1987	2,161	(62)	-	(-)
1988	2,414	(69)	-	(-)
1989	2,986	(85)	-	(-)
1990	3,504	(100)	106	(100)
1991	3,856	(110)	160	(151)
1992	3,926	(112)	279	(263)
1993	3,747	(107)	299	(282)
1994	3,831	(109)	294	(277)
1995	3,732	(107)	287	(271)

Sources: *White Paper on Police in 1996*, p. 298.
White Paper on Crime in 1996, p. 70.
White Paper on Crime in 1994, p. 236.
Japan's Statistics in 1986, p. 22.

* The number published by the Immigration Control Bureau of the Ministry of Justice.

** The number estimated on the basis of official data by the Immigration Control Bureau of the Ministry of Justice.

Also evident was the temporary bottom of the depression at the end of 1993. However, the rebound from this bottom was slow. Reflecting this economic situation, after 1993 the total number of the illegal stayers remained stable. In 1993 companies were obliged to report annually on their employment of alien laborers at the beginning of June to a chief of the public employment security office. They then became more nervous about being imposed punishment for their illegal employment of foreigners. Therefore, it became difficult for the illegal entrants and overstayers to find a well-paying job. They had to stay illegally for the longer period in order to earn money-- at least enough to pay their travel expenses, which they had borrowed in advance in their mother country. This seems to be another reason why the estimated total number of the illegal stayers remained stable after 1993. In this regard, by the estimate at the beginning of November, 1995, the illegal stayers totaled to

284,744, of which the rate of Korean, Thai, Philippine and Chinese amounted to 17.4%, 15.1%, 14.4% and 13.5% respectively (White Paper on Labor in 1996: 56).

Trend in Crimes by Foreigners during the Decade from 1985

This paper will use official data to grasp the trend in the crimes by foreigners. It would be desirable to show the rate of alien criminals per alien population. However, the writer had access to only official data on the legally entering foreigners and the registering alien stayers. It was not possible to obtain the exact data on alien illegal entrants and overstayers. Therefore, the writer had to use absolute numbers in the analysis.

The numbers of alien criminals on official statistics may reflect not only the real trend in the crimes by foreigners, but also the policy of the law enforcement agencies against them. In Japan this policy does not seem to fluctuate frequently and to change greatly from place to place, as the law enforcement agencies are strictly controlled by the centralized national government.

Japan has had a Penal Code after the example of those in continental countries such as France and Germany. Most crimes prescribed in the Penal Code seem to be "mala in se," that is, wrongs in themselves. Therefore, first of all, this writer would like to analyze the trend in the total number of suspects caught for non-traffic Penal Code offenses[11] (Table 2). In case of all these suspects the total number dropped from 432,250 in 1985 to 293,264 in 1990, reflecting the decrease in the total number of juvenile offenders.[12] In the early 1990s the juvenile offenders continued to decrease. However, the total number of adult offenders arrested by the police increased from 110,936 in 1990 to 144,115 in 1995. Then, the trend in all suspects caught for the Penal Code offenses was stable in the early 1990s (Table 2).

A similar trend was evident in the total number of suspects of alien stayers other than non-permanent residents for the Penal Code offenses during the decade from 1985. The majority of those stayers are Korean qualified to stay permanently in Japan. Today, they enjoy stable lives similar to ones of Japanese residents, without being influenced seriously by the economic depression. Therefore, there were little differences between the trend in the total number of all suspects and that of suspects of other alien stayers during the decade from 1985 (Table 2). To the contrary, in case of the non-permanently-staying foreigners, the total number of suspects arrested for the Penal Code offenses raised drastically during the decade from 1985 (Table 2).

First, there was a drastic increase during the period from 1987 to 1988, during which many Chinese rushed to Japan with the visa for studying at a professional school. Chinese suspects caught for the Penal Code offenses increased from 778 in 1987 to 1,643 in 1988 (Table 4). The total number of the suspects of non-permanent stayers remained stable for the following two years. For these years it was easy for foreigners to find a well-paid job due to the extreme shortage of labor power in the economic prosperity, that is, the

CRIMES BY FOREIGNERS IN JAPAN   187

Table 2. The Total Number and the Index* of Alien Suspects Caught by the Police for Non-traffic Offenses

Year	Total of All Suspects for Penal Code Offenses	Penal Code Offenses			Offenses of Special Laws		
		Total of All Foreigners	Non-permanent Stayers	Other Stayers**	Total of All Foreigners	Non-permanent Stayers	Other Stayers**
1985	432,250 (147)	8,606 (112)	1,370 (46)	7,236 (154)	6,946 (203)	2,449 (137)	4,497 (275)
1986	399,886 (136)	8,384 (109)	1,626 (55)	6,758 (143)	6,647 (194)	2,438 (136)	4,209 (257)
1987	404,762 (138)	8,696 (113)	1,871 (63)	6,825 (145)	5,898 (172)	2,191 (122)	3,707 (227)
1988	398,208 (134)	9,585 (125)	3,020 (101)	6,565 (139)	4,417 (129)	1,566 (87)	2,851 (174)
1989	312,992 (107)	8,245 (107)	2,989 (100)	5,256 (111)	3,525 (103)	1,629 (91)	1,896 (116)
1990	293,264 (100)	7,692 (100)	2,978 (100)	4,714 (100)	3,427 (100)	1,792 (100)	1,635 (100)
1991	296,158 (101)	9,606 (125)	4,813 (162)	4,739 (102)	4,103 (120)	2,457 (137)	1,649 (101)
1992	284,908 (97)	10,807 (140)	5,961 (200)	4,846 (103)	5,067 (148)	3,495 (195)	1,572 (96)
1993	297,725 (102)	12,182 (158)	7,276 (244)	4,906 (104)	6,610 (193)	5,191 (290)	1,419 (87)
1994	307,965 (105)	11,906 (155)	6,989 (235)	4,917 (104)	8,142 (238)	6,587 (368)	1,555 (95)
1995	293,252 (100)	11,234 (146)	6,527 (219)	4,707 (100)	7,098 (207)	5,449 (304)	1,649 (101)

* Index: 100 is equivalent to the total number in 1990.

** Foreigners qualified to stay permanently, those affiliating with the U. S. forces and those without any nationality.

Sources: National Police Agency, *Crimes in 1995*, p. 399, and *that in 1993*, p. 399. *White Paper on Crime in 1996*, p. 403.

"bubble economy" of real-estate speculation and excessive lending. Many foreigners worked hard, albeit illegally, day and night, which was overlooked by the police and the immigration office. As they were satisfied with earning a large sum of money, they suffered less frequently from tension.

In the summer of 1990 the long-term economic depression began. In addition, in June of 1990 the revised Immigration-Control and Refugee Recognition Law was enforced to regulate more severely the alien illegal working, and to punish employers and brokers for their illegal employment and their mediation for foreigners. Therefore, many foreigners, especially illegal entrants and overstayers, were first of all discharged by their employers. It became difficult for them to find new jobs. They were then put under serious stress, which created a myriad of interpersonal troubles. Consequently, they are more inclined to commit acts of crime. The total number of the alien suspects without qualification for permanent staying increased from 2,978 in 1990 to 7,276 in 1993. It then declined a little during the period from 1993 to 1995, which might be parallel to the trend in the estimated total number of the illegal stayers (Table 1).

Table 3 shows the total number of the suspects of non-permanently-staying foreigners by their offense categories.[13] Concerning heinous offenses the total number was low around 1985. However, it double for one year from 1987 to 1988. Again, it increased drastically from 111 in 1990 to 246 in 1993. From a detailed analysis, the homicide committed by non-permanent stayers raised from 31 in 1990 to 72 in 1993, while their robbery increased from 65 to 142. In majority of the homicide cases foreigners killed other foreigners, because they had some trouble in the emotional or economic relation with the latter,[14] or because they intended to deprive the latter of money or some property.[15] With the deepening of the economic depression, robbery committed by foreigners also increased.[16]

Alien criminals use dangerous weapons more frequently than Japanese criminals.[17] Therefore, the visibility of their heinous offenses such as homicide and robbery is high.[18] The mass media is inclined to report their heinous offenses sensationally. For example, for the first half of 1997 they sensationalized several reported cases of kidnapping (Nihon Keizai Newspaper, February 12; Asahi Newspaper, February 19; Kanagawa Newspaper, May 7; Asahi Newspaper, June 10; Asahi Newspaper, June 21)[19] Such sensationalized reporting may perpetuate the image of "dangerous foreigners."

The total number of violent offenses doubled during the decade from 1985. However, the rate of increase is lower than that of other offense categories in Table 3. Usually they commit acts of violence to other foreigners rather than Japanese. Such victims, particularly those staying illegally in Japan, do not want to report to the police.[20] Therefore, the dark number of their violent offenses seems to be large. The total numbers of non-permanently-staying foreigners charged with the theft and the embezzlement of a lost or deserted possession[21] remained stable for two years from 1988. Thereafter, with the deepening of economic depression, they increased. For three years from 1990

CRIMES BY FOREIGNERS IN JAPAN

Table 3. The Total Number and the Index* of Foreign Suspects** Caught by the Police for Non-traffic Penal Code Offenses by Their Offense Categories

Year	Total	Heinous Offenses	Violent Offenses	Theft	Embezzlement of a Lost Thing***	Intellectual Offenses	Offenses against Public Morality	Others
1985	1,370 (46)	28 (25)	125 (80)	906 (55)	181 (23)	39 (28)	59 (83)	32 (56)
1986	1,626 (55)	20 (18)	113 (72)	1,044 (63)	269 (34)	94 (68)	51 (72)	35 (61)
1987	1,871 (63)	38 (34)	121 (77)	1,177 (71)	369 (47)	62 (45)	68 (96)	36 (63)
1988	3,020 (101)	78 (70)	135 (86)	1,816 (110)	796 (101)	86 (62)	63 (89)	46 (81)
1989	2,989 (100)	94 (85)	138 (88)	1,776 (107)	748 (95)	104 (75)	54 (76)	75 (132)
1990	2,978 (100)	111 (100)	157 (100)	1,656 (100)	787 (100)	139 (100)	71 (100)	57 (100)
1991	4,813 (162)	126 (114)	174 (111)	2,493 (151)	1,754 (223)	94 (68)	85 (120)	87 (153)
1992	5,961 (200)	185 (167)	213 (136)	2,944 (178)	1,975 (251)	443 (319)	113 (159)	88 (154)
1993	7,276 (244)	246 (222)	277 (176)	3,995 (241)	2,219 (282)	260 (187)	167 (235)	112 (196)
1994	6,989 (235)	230 (207)	246 (157)	3,937 (238)	2,076 (264)	218 (157)	153 (215)	129 (226)
1995	6,527 (219)	201 (181)	255 (162)	3,900 (236)	1,555 (198)	302 (217)	150 (211)	164 (288)

* Index: 100 is equivalent to the total number in 1990.
** Suspects of non-permanently-staying foreigners
*** Most of cases are the riding of a deserted bicycle.

Heinous offenses: homicide, robbery, arson and rape
Violent offenses: assault, bodily injury, intimidation and extortion
Intellectual offenses: fraud, ordinary embezzlement and forgery
Offenses against public morality: gambling and lottery, and indecent assault

Sources: National Police Agency, *Crimes in 1995, pp. 414-415, and that in 1993, pp. 414-415*

the theft and the embezzlement of a lost or deserted possession increased by 2.4 times and by 2.8 times, respectively. It seems that the non-permanent stayers committed these crimes more frequently, because they fell into poverty during this depression.

In the 1990s the alien theft groups have developed.[22] Although there was multi-nationality in some theft groups,[23] the theft groups are usually composed of persons of same nationality. Especially, Chinese who could not find a well-paid job after the "bubble economy," have founded the well-organized theft group.[24] We saw even a theft group organized by the "stockholders" like a joint-stock corporation.[25] Some theft groups are linked with the international gang groups. Especially, Chinese theft groups have wide channels to the domestic and overseas underground Chinese organizations through their human networks, which have developed from the mutual aid system in their native community.[26] In addition, many professional theft groups visited from Hong Kong[27] and Korea.[28]

Concerning intellectual offenses there was a drastic increase in 1992. Of 443 alien suspects, 369 were caught for forgery. After the enforcement of the revised Immigration-Control and Refugee Recognition Law, the entrance into Japan and the overstaying in Japan were severely checked. Therefore, illegal entrants and overstayers had a great demand for forged documents in order to evade the severe check at the immigration office and the arrest by the police. The forgers provided them with forged documents such as a certification of alien registration as a legal stayer[29] and a document for disguised marriage with Japanese[30] (White paper on Police in 1993: 110).

Foreigners charged with offenses against public morality also increased for the decade from 1985. For three years from 1990 they increased by 2.35 times. Especially, illegal gambling and lottery increased from 48 in 1990 to 126 in 1993. Some foreigners who had lost a well-paid job in the depression, might undertake illegal gambling and lottery to make a fortune in quick fasion.

Trend in the Alien Offenders by their Nationality

Table 4 shows the trend in the alien non-permanently-staying offenders by their nationality for the decade from 1985. In the late 1980s many Chinese rushed to Japan with the visa for studying at a professional school, in order to work illegally. In parallel with this phenomenon Chinese suspects arrested for the non-traffic Penal Code offenses increased drastically from 321 in 1985 to 1,709 in 1989. Immediately after the enactment of the revised Immigration-Control and Refugee Recognition Law, Chinese who saved a large sum of money, returned to their home. However, Chinese continued to come to Japan by fair means or foul with a dream to make a large, quick sums of money. Many of them were not able to find jobs in the economic depression. In such an environment, Chinese offenders increased drastically from 1,288 in 1990 to 2,942 in 1994.

Table 4. The Total Number and the Index* of Alien Suspects** Caught by the Police for Non-traffic Penal Code Offenses by Their Nationality

Year	Total	China	Korea	Iran	Thailand	Philippine	Other Asia	Brazil	U.S.A.	Others
1985	1,370 (46)	321 (25)	401 (77)	41 (41)	26 (48)	108 (71)	125 (32)	8 (15)	97 (76)	243 (·81)
1986	1,626 (55)	505 (39)	407 (79)	37 (37)	25 (46)	131 (87)	194 (50)	10 (19)	99 (78)	218 (72)
1987	1,871 (63)	778 (60)	312 (60)	29 (29)	29 (54)	168 (111)	230 (59)	7 (13)	100 (79)	218 (72)
1988	3,020 (101)	1,643 (128)	398 (77)	37 (37)	41 (76)	148 (98)	295 (76)	17 (32)	107 (84)	334 (111)
1989	2,989 (100)	1,709 (133)	392 (76)	31 (31)	43 (80)	110 (73)	360 (93)	19 (36)	112 (88)	213 (71)
1990	2,978 (100)	1,288 (100)	517 (100)	99 (100)	54 (100)	151 (100)	388 (100)	53 (100)	127 (100)	301 (100)
1991	4,813 (162)	1,732 (134)	728 (141)	561 (567)	119 (220)	214 (142)	527 (136)	134 (253)	191 (150)	607 (202)
1992	5,961 (200)	1,933 (150)	876 (169)	771 (779)	158 (293)	259 (172)	762 (196)	174 (328)	162 (128)	866 (288)
1993	7,276 (244)	2,668 (207)	987 (191)	544 (549)	260 (481)	366 (242)	936 (241)	223 (421)	153 (120)	1,139 (378)
1994	6,989 (235)	2,942 (228)	775 (150)	294 (297)	223 (413)	396 (262)	797 (205)	301 (568)	161 (127)	1,100 (365)
1995	6,527 (219)	2,919 (227)	752 (145)	167 (169)	213 (394)	301 (199)	729 (188)	318 (600)	135 (106)	647 (215)

* Index: 100 is equivalent to the total number in 1990.
** Suspects of non-permanently-staying foreigners

Sources: National Police Agency, *Crime in 1995*, pp. 410-411 and *that in 1993*, pp. 410-411

In the late 1980s many Koreans came to Japan with the visa for studying. However, the rate of newcomers with the expressed purpose of making money by illegal means, was lower than Chinese. The Korean newcomers enjoyed the better life in Japan because of the support of their richer parents and relatives, especially those living in Japan for a long time with the qualification for permanent staying. Therefore, the Penal Code offenses by Korean non-permanent stayers remained stable in the late 1980s. In the economic depression, the total number of Korean offenders increased from 517 in 1990 to 987 in 1993. However, the rate of increase was lower than that in case of other Asian nationality.

Japan concluded a mutual treaty for entering without a visa with Iran in order to secure the import of oil. Therefore, after the end of a war between Iran and Iraq in 1988 many male Iranians came to Japan (Tamaki, 1995: 275). As they had a career of high education, their main purpose was not always to make money by illegal means. However, many Iranian remained in Japan after the expiry of their legal stay. The estimated number of Iranian illegal overstayers raised 764 in July, 1990, to 21,719 in December, 1991 (Immigration Bureau, 1993: 100). Then, in April of 1992, Japan suspended the abovementioned treaty with Iran. In the early 1990s Iranian stayers gathered at the Yoyogi Park and the Ueno Park in Tokyo to exchange information. Therefore, the visibility of their deviant behavior, for example, the sale of forged pre-paid phone cards, became high. Iranians were more severely discriminated as dangerous foreigners by the Japanese. In such a situation the total number of Iranian offenders increased to 771 in 1992. Thereafter, the corresponding number declined on a parallel with the decrease in the total number of Iranian illegal overstayers.

Before 1987 the majority of the illegal laborers were Philippine females. They provided Japanese males with their sexual services. However, such females decreased after 1987. Therefore, in 1987 there was a peak in the total number of Philippine offenders in the late 1980s. In the early 1990s many Thai females entered Japan. To pay the advanced money imposed on them, they were compelled to commit prostitution. In such a hard situation Thai females committed more frequently crimes. For three years from 1990 the total number of Thai criminal suspects increased by 4.8 times. The other Asian people came to Japan mainly to make money by their illegal labor.[31] Therefore, they were also influenced greatly by the economic depression in the early 1990s. For three years from 1990, the total number of other Asian offenders increased by 2.4 times.

After 1990 many people of Japanese ancestry came to Japan with the qualification for legal working. Therefore, during the period from 1990 to 1995 the total number of Brazilian registering for legal stay increased from 56,429 in 1990 to 176,440 in 1995 (Ministry of Justice, 1996: 8). For the same period the total number of Brazilian criminal suspects increased by 6.0 times, which was higher than the increase rate of the number of Brazilian registration. Although Brazilians enjoyed a more stable life than the illegal alien stayers, some of them have been put under stress in the economic depression. During

CRIMES BY FOREIGNERS IN JAPAN   193

the same five years, the total number of the registering Peruvian, most of whom had Japanese ancestry, also increased from 10,279 in 1990 to 36,269 in 1995. The increase in the total number of "others" in Table 4 in the early 1990s was brought mainly by the increase in Peruvian criminal suspects.

During the period from 1985 to 1995, the total number of the legal entrants with the nationality of the United States increased from 487,713 in 1985 to 558,474 in 1995, that is, by 1.1 times. On the other hand, during the same period the total number of American offenders increased by 1.4 times. Because of fewer illegal entrants and overstayers, American stayers seem to enjoy a comfortable life in Japan with less necessity to commit crime.

Crimes by Foreigners at Present

We see some gap between the total number of suspects caught by the police and that of those received by public prosecutors. In 1995 the former and the latter amounted to 293,252 and 242,768, respectively. The difference of both numbers amounted to about 50,000 or 17% of the former, most of which were diverted as minor offenders from the criminal justice system. In 1995 the police arrested 6,527 non-permanently-staying foreigners for the non-traffic Penal Code offenses, while the public prosecutors received 3,997. The difference of both numbers amounted to about 2,500. The diversion rate was 39%. The greater diversion rate was brought by the policy of the police that minor offenders of alien illegal entrants and overstayers should be referred to the immigration office for extradition as early as possible. Next, this paper will analyze the crimes by non-permanently-staying foreigners on the basis of the annual report of statistics on prosecution for 1995 (Table 5).

Of all suspects received by public prosecutors for the non-traffic Penal Code offenses in 1995, only 1.6% were alien non-permanently-staying offenders. Analyzing by crime categories, this rate was greatly exceeded by that of four kinds of crimes; forgery of securities (32.3%), obstruction of traffic by negligence (7.4%), robbery (6.6%) and forgery of documents (4.1%).

Foreigners often forged pre-paid cards for telephone, railway tickets and Pachinko, a kind of pinball game. First, they forged prepaid phone card in order to sell them to acquaintances who wanted to correspond at a cheap price to their family and friends in their mother country. Thus, they became professional forgers to make money. Recently, they made a fortune forging pre-paid cards for Pachinko, a kind of legal gambling. Two leading companies for publishing the pre-paid Pachinko cards estimated that a total loss by the forged cards amounted to 63,000,000,000 yen (US$504,000,000) at their accounts settled in March, 1996 (Nihon Keizai Newspaper, May 22, 1996). The rate of foreigners charged with the forgery of documents is also higher. As was previously mentioned, documents are mainly forged to make some foreigners evade the severe check by the immigration office and the police.

Foreign ships are sometimes stranded on Japan's shore, or collide with another ship in Japan's territorial sea. In such a case a captain and a pilot are

Table 5. Suspects Received by Public Prosecutors for Non-traffic Penal Code Offenses in 1995

	All Suspects	Non-permanently-staying Foreigners	
		Total	Rate
	(A)	(B)	(B/A x 100)
Total	242,768 (100.0)	3,997 (100.0)	1.6
Interference with government officers in the performance of their duties	1,114 (0.5)	22 (0.6)	2.0
Arson	809 (0.3)	7 (0.2)	0.9
Obstruction of traffic by negligence	1,077 (0.4)	80 (2.0)	7.4
Home-breaking	4,440 (1.8)	96 (2.4)	2.2
Forgery of documents	2,302 (0.9)	94 (2.4)	4.1
Forgery of securities	1,128 (0.5)	364 (9.1)	32.3
Obscenity	4,206 (1.7)	68 (1.7)	1.6
Rape	1,412 (0.6)	23 (0.6)	1.6
Gambling and lottery	3,776 (1.6)	87 (2.2)	2.3
Homicide	2,141 (0.9)	44 (1.1)	2.1
Bodily injury	28,526 (11.8)	273 (6.8)	1.0
Injury by negligence	1,296 (0.5)	17 (0.4)	1.3
Arrest and confinement	552 (0.2)	6 (0.2)	1.1
Theft	126,555 (52.1)	2,328 (58.2)	1.8
Robbery	2,575 (1.1)	171 (4.3)	6.6
Fraud	10,361 (4.3)	77 (1.9)	0.7
Extortion	9,297 (3.8)	36 (0.9)	0.4
Embezzlement	30,682 (12.6)	81 (2.0)	0.3
Offenses relating to stolen goods	1,158 (0.5)	28 (0.7)	2.4
Destruction or concealment of goods	2,897 (1.2)	50 (1.3)	1.7
Others	6,464 (2.7)	45 (1.1)	0.7

Source: Ministry of Justice, *Annual Report of Statistics on Prosecution for 1995*

charged with the obstruction of traffic by negligence.[32] The total number of foreigners arrested by the police for robbery increased from 6 in 1985 to 35 in 1990 and 124 in 1993.[33] (Crimes in 1993: 412-413 and that in 1995: 412-413). On the basis of these statistics the police warned the public against the increase in the heinous offenses by the foreigners coming recently to Japan. However, as shown in Table 3, the increase rate of heinous offenses in the early 1990s was not higher than that of total alien suspects. The rate of alien suspects charged with extortion was lower than that of Japanese suspects. If alien extortioners carry or use some weapon, they are usually arrested for robbery instead of extortion.

Table 6 shows the total number of alien non-permanently-staying offenders by their nationality. Concerning theft, there were high rates for Vietnamese (92.4%), Peruvian (74.1%) and Brazilian (68.9%). The Vietnamese entering Japan as a refugee were qualified to settle themselves or stay permanently in Japan. The non-permanently-staying Vietnamese, most of whom are qualified for settlement in Japan, commit scarcely any other crime than theft.[34] As they are guaranteed their settlement, they may be more immune from financial stress, which would induce them to commit heinous or violent offenses.

Most Peruvians and Brazilians living in Japan are qualified to settle themselves as those of Japanese ancestry. Therefore, they do not often suffer serious conflicts, which induce them to commit a crime other than theft. Another reason why foreigners with qualification for settlement in Japan have the high rate of theft, is that they are not diverted by the police for extradition in case that they commit a minor theft.

The Koreans and Americans are richer than foreigners coming from developing countries. Among them fewer people purpose mainly to make stable money as plain laborers in Japan. Non-permanent stayers from Korean and those from the United States commit theft less frequently due to their economic condition. Among Chinese offenders there was a relatively high rate of those charged with the forgery of securities (16.8%). The reason is that around 1995 police succeeded in rounding up some Chinese organized groups to forge pre-paid cards, especially those used for Pachinko.[35]

Korean suspects are charged with various kinds of crimes. There was a high rate in such crime categories as bodily injury (17.3%) and gambling & lottery (12.1%). In Japan many Koreans and their descendants live with the qualification for permanent staying. Therefore, the Korean non-permanent stayers have more complex human networks than those of other nationalities. The conflicts in their human relations may induce them to commit bodily injury more frequently. Some of the permanently-staying Koreans became a member of the Boryokudan in the situation of being discriminated by Japanese (Huang and Vaughn, 1992: 24). One of main income resources of the Boryokudan is the illegal gambling and lottery.[36] Non-permanently-staying Koreans may have more chances to involve themselves in illegal gambling and lottery through their contact with the Boryokudan.

Table 6. The Total Number of Alien Suspects* Received by Public Prosecutors for Non-traffic Penal Code Offenses by Their Nationality in 1995

	Total	China	Korea	Iran	Thailand	Philippine	Vietnam	Brazil	Peru	U.S.A.	Others
Total	3,997 (%)	1,580 (%)	421 (%)	160 (%)	137 (%)	135 (%)	249 (%)	241 (%)	351 (%)	88 (%)	635 (%)
Obstruction of traffic by negligence	80 (2.0)	22 (1.4)	28 (6.7)	0 (0.0)	2 (1.5)	14 (10.4)	0 (0.0)	0 (0.0)	0 (0.0)	1 (1.1)	13 (2.0)
Home-breaking	96 (2.4)	31 (2.0)	16 (3.8)	5 (3.1)	2 (1.5)	0 (0.0)	1 (0.4)	7 (2.9)	6 (1.7)	5 (5.7)	23 (3.6)
Forgery of documents	94 (2.4)	22 (1.4)	23 (5.5)	3 (1.9)	6 (4.4)	4 (3.0)	0 (0.0)	0 (0.0)	31 (8.8)	0 (0.0)	5 (0.8)
Forgery of securities	364 (9.1)	266 (16.8)	11 (2.6)	13 (8.1)	1 (0.7)	9 (6.7)	3 (1.2)	0 (0.0)	9 (2.6)	0 (0.0)	52 (8.2)
Obscenity	68 (1.7)	28 (1.8)	7 (1.7)	2 (1.3)	0 (0.0)	2 (1.5)	0 (0.0)	0 (0.0)	7 (2.0)	1 (1.1)	21 (3.3)
Rape	23 (0.6)	4 (0.3)	4 (1.0)	4 (2.5)	0 (0.0)	0 (0.0)	0 (0.0)	2 (0.8)	2 (0.6)	0 (0.0)	7 (1.1)
Gambling and lottery	87 (2.2)	24 (1.5)	51 (12.1)	1 (0.6)	2 (1.5)	1 (0.7)	0 (0.0)	2 (0.8)	0 (0.0)	1 (1.1)	5 (0.8)
Homicide	44 (1.1)	12 (0.8)	6 (1.4)	2 (1.3)	12 (8.8)	5 (3.7)	0 (0.0)	1 (0.4)	0 (0.0)	0 (0.0)	6 (0.9)
Bodily injury	273 (6.8)	60 (3.8)	73 (17.3)	9 (5.6)	9 (6.6)	14 (10.4)	7 (2.8)	21 (8.7)	5 (1.4)	22 (25.0)	53 (8.3)
Theft	2,328 (58.2)	955 (60.4)	129 (30.6)	65 (40.6)	85 (62.0)	63 (46.7)	230 (92.4)	166 (68.9)	260 (74.1)	35 (39.8)	340 (53.5)
Robbery	171 (4.3)	38 (2.4)	6 (1.4)	36 (22.5)	7 (5.1)	2 (1.5)	1 (0.4)	21 (8.7)	17 (4.8)	10 (11.4)	33 (5.2)
Fraud	77 (1.9)	41 (2.6)	10 (2.4)	0 (0.0)	1 (0.7)	1 (0.7)	0 (0.0)	0 (0.0)	0 (0.0)	1 (1.1)	23 (3.6)
Extortion	36 (0.9)	11 (0.7)	9 (2.1)	1 (0.6)	1 (0.7)	1 (0.7)	2 (0.8)	4 (1.7)	0 (0.0)	0 (0.0)	7 (1.1)
Embezzlement	81 (2.0)	22 (1.4)	15 (3.6)	1 (0.6)	0 (0.0)	9 (6.7)	2 (0.8)	6 (2.5)	3 (0.9)	6 (6.8)	17 (2.7)
Others	175 (4.4)	44 (2.8)	33 (7.8)	18 (11.3)	9 (6.6)	10 (7.4)	3 (1.2)	11 (4.5)	11 (3.1)	6 (6.8)	30 (4.7)

Suspects of non-permanently-staying foreigners

Source: Ministry of Justice, *Criminal Report of Statistics on Prosecution for 1995*, pp. 222-225

Among Iranian offenders was a relatively high rate of those charged with robbery. After 1992 many Iranians who achieved their goal in Japan, returned to their mother country. The others remained in Japan, the majority of whom overstayed illegally without finding well-paid occupations. They were also heavily discriminated against by Japanese residents. Therefore, they would commit robberies more frequently than other foreigners. As many Iranians fought as soldiers in the war between Iran and Iraq, they were prone to use violent means while committing such crimes.

From Thailand and the Philippines many females continue to come to Japan. They are often compelled to work as prostitutes under the control of exploitative employers and racketeers. In the extremely unendurable situation of cruel exploitation they sometimes kill an employer or a racketeer.[37] It is one of reasons why the rate of homicide has been relatively high among Thai and Philippine suspects in 1995. The rate of homicide is highest in case of Thai stayers, as Thai female stayers are more frequently put under cruel exploitation. Philippine stayers tend to organize a group on the basis of their native community and their blood relationship. Troubles in such a group or between such groups sometimes leads to homicide (Kanagawa Newspaper, November 1, 1997).

Trend in Alien Offenders of Special Laws

In Japan many special laws also prescribe criminal punishment. Many of the offenses of these prescriptions must be "mala prohibita," that is, the breach of laws, which enjoin only positive duties without any intermixture of moral guilty. This paper will now analyze the alien offenses of special laws excluding traffic laws.

Table 2 shows the trend in the offenders of special laws for the decade from 1985. The trend in case of non-permanent stayers was different from one in "other stayers," most of whom are qualified to stay permanently in Japan. In the late 1980s there was a drastic decrease in suspects of alien other stayers. This phenomenon was brought mainly by the decrease in offenders of the Alien Registration Law. Under the Alien Registration Law, foreigners who needed the alien registration had their finger prints taken. Around 1985 the opposition to this system surged. Many foreigners, particularly Koreans with qualification for permanent staying, refused to give their finger prints at the time of renewing the registration. They were charged with an offense of the Alien Registration Law, which is typical of "mala prohibita." However, with the improvement of the finger printing system the total number of suspects charged with this offense decreased drastically in the late 1980s.[38]

In the early 1990s the total number of suspects of alien other stayers for offenses of special laws was stable. Their offenses of special laws did not seem to be influenced seriously by the economic depression. To the contrary, the offenses of special laws by non-permanent stayers increased drastically since 1988.

Table 7 shows the total number of the non-permanently-staying offenders of special laws, who were arrested by the police for the decade from 1985. At the economic boom around 1988 there was a low total number of the offenders of main special laws except for the Alien Registration Law. The non-permanent stayers charged for offenses of the Alien Registration Law also decreased after the improvement of the finger printing system.

In case of the offenses of the Firearms and Swords Control Law there was a peak in 1985. In June of 1984, the Yamaguchi-gumi, the largest Boryokudan in Japan, was split into two after the dispute about the succession of presidency (Yokoyama, 1994: 10). They fought each other severely around 1985. The case of shooting at the time of a fight between the Boryokudan members increased from 68 in 1984 to 246 in 1985 (White Paper on Police in 1989: 20). Therefore, around 1985 the Boryokudan members had a strong demand for firearms. In response to this demand, more foreigners seemed to participate with smuggling firearms into Japan. After the enforcement of the Law to Cope with Boryokudan in 1992 the shooting by Boryokudan members declined.[39] Nevertheless, alien suspects were arrested for offenses of the Firearms and Swords Control Law increased even after 1992. In Japan the price of firearms is high, because they are strictly controlled under the law. Therefore, in spite of decreases in the demand after 1992, more foreigners smuggled firearms into Japan to profit in the black market.

Many alien females work as prostitutes under the control by racketeers. They are rarely caught for offenses of the Prostitution Prevention Law, because they are compelled to work at disguised brothels. Furthermore, racketeers are more rarely arrested for the offense of the Prostitution Prevention Law. Therefore, the total number of suspects for this law, as shown in Table 7, is at the tip of the iceberg. Under the Prostitution Prevention Law the main offenders arrested by the police are prostitutes soliciting on the street.

In the early 1990s there was more frequently the alien poor prostitutes soliciting on the street, who were liberated from the control by racketeers after paying up the advance money. This is perhaps one explanation why foreigners caught for offenses of the Prostitution Prevention Law increased in the early 1990s.

In Japan, drug abuse is controlled under several laws. In the late 1980s, especially during a boom around 1988, the offenses of the drug control laws by non-permanently-staying foreigners were not serious. The mass media infrequently reported foreigners bringing marijuana for their personal use, who were arrested by the police for an offense of the Hemp Control Law.[40] To the contrary, in the 1990s more foreigners were charged for offenses of the drug control laws. Many of them were caught for smuggling drugs into Japan to make money.

The total number of alien offenders of the Immigration-Control and Refugee Recognition Law was also low during three years from 1988. During this period the country enjoyed an economic boom in which it witnessed the shortage of labor power. Many small-to-medium-sized enterprises were compelled

CRIMES BY FOREIGNERS IN JAPAN 199

Table 7. The Total Number and the Index* of Alien Suspects** Caught by the Police for Non-traffic Special Laws

Year	Total	1) FSCL	2) LBAPM	3) PPL	4) HCL	5) LCNPS	6) SDCL	7) OL	8) ICRRL	9) ARL	Others
1985	2,449 (137)	48 (192)	37 (76)	51 (33)	98 (120)	17 (52)	105 (59)	0	853 (91)	1,054 (447)	186 (183)
1986	2,438 (136)	23 (92)	29 (59)	42 (27)	84 (102)	9 (27)	97 (54)	0	1,125 (120)	864 (366)	165 (179)
1987	2,191 (122)	32 (128)	46 (94)	53 (34)	101 (123)	13 (39)	115 (64)	0	1,097 (117)	664 (281)	70 (76)
1988	1,566 (87)	24 (96)	40 (81)	86 (55)	74 (90)	29 (88)	36 (20)	0	750 (80)	470 (199)	57 (62)
1989	1,629 (91)	19 (76)	29 (59)	101 (65)	50 (61)	25 (76)	69 (39)	0	908 (97)	359 (152)	69 (75)
1990	1,792 (100)	25 (100)	49 (100)	156 (100)	82 (100)	33 (100)	179 (100)	0	940 (100)	236 (100)	92 (100)
1991	2,457 (137)	45 (180)	83 (169)	287 (184)	85 (104)	59 (179)	142 (79)	0	1,469 (156)	178 (75)	107 (116)
1992	3,495 (195)	87 (348)	43 (88)	362 (232)	153 (187)	114 (345)	276 (154)	13	2,166 (230)	138 (58)	143 (155)
1993	5,191 (290)	75 (300)	65 (133)	423 (271)	247 (299)	142 (430)	288 (161)	62	3,618 (385)	114 (48)	159 (173)
1994	6,587 (368)	76 (304)	106 (216)	367 (235)	258 (315)	130 (394)	338 (189)	78	4,886 (520)	160 (68)	188 (204)
1995	5,449 (304)	85 (340)	80 (163)	238 (153)	178 (217)	110 (333)	485 (271)	48	3,837 (408)	183 (78)	205 (223)

* Index: 100 is equivalent to the total number in 1990.
** Suspects of non-permanently-staying foreigners
1) FSCL: Firearms and Swords Control Law
2) LBAPM: Law on Business Affecting Public Morals
3) PPL: Prostitution Prevention Law
4) HCL: Hemp Control Law
5) LCNPS: Law to Control Narcotic and Psychiatric Substances
6) SDCL: Stimulant Drug Control Law
7) OL: Opium Law
8) ICRRL: Immigration-Control and Refugee Recognition Law
9) ARL: Alien Registration Law
Sources: National Police Agency, *Crimes in 1995*, pp. 420-421 and *that in 1993*, pp. 420-421

to employ alien plain laborers illegally. Therefore, the police and the immigration office were not earnest over catching alien illegal laborers for an offense of the Immigration-Control and Refugee Recognition Law.

In June of 1990, the revised Immigration-Control and Refugee Recognition Law was enforced. Since the summer of 1990 the economic depression began, under which the demand of plain laborers declined. Therefore, the police and the immigration office strengthened the control of illegal alien laborers. On the other hand, there were still many Asian people who wanted to make money by working in Japan. As the legal ways for them to enter Japan were strictly regulated, they smuggled themselves into Japan by the medium of the organizations for human trafficking. In addition, in the deepening of depression more foreigners overstayed illegally to make money. Therefore, the total number of alien suspects charged for offenses of the Immigration-Control and Refugee Recognition Law increased drastically in the early 1990s. The human resources and the facilities to enforce this law are not enough.[41]

Offenses of Special Laws by Foreigners at Present

In 1995 the offenders of special laws of the non-permanent stayers received by public prosecutors totaled to 8,533 (Table 8). It was larger than the corresponding number of those caught by the police (Table 7), because the public prosecutors received suspects not only from the police but also other investigation agencies such as the immigration office, the maritime security agency, and the narcotic agent.

The rate of alien suspects per all those for offenses of special laws was 8.9% in 1995 (Table 8); this was higher than 1.6% in case of the non-traffic Penal Code offenses (Table 5). There were extremely high rates in the case of both the Immigration-Control and Refugee Recognition Law and the Alien Registration Law, followed by the Opium Law, and by the Law to Control Narcotic and Psychiatric Substances.

In the early 1990s more foreigners participated in smuggling hard drugs into Japan (Table 7). However, Japanese have scarcely abused drugs except for a stimulant drug composed of methamphetamine (Yokoyama, 1991). Therefore, we witnessed the relatively high rates of alien suspects in case of the drug control laws except for the Stimulant Drug Control Law. The black market for a stimulant drug is almost completely controlled by the Boryokudan (Tamura, 1992: 99). Therefore, the rate of alien suspects charged with offenses of the Stimulant Drug Control Law was only 3.0%, although the absolute number of these suspects amounted to 731.

The rate of alien suspects charged with offenses of the Prostitution Prevention Law amounted to 21.7%. With the development of the crafty call-girl system since 1975 the police could not easily crack down on Japanese prostitutes (Yokoyama, 1995: 56). On the other hand, in the 1990s the police arrested more frequently alien prostitutes soliciting on the street. This could explain why the aforementioned rate was relatively high.

Table 8. Suspects Received by Public Prosecutors for Offenses of Non-traffic Special Laws in 1995

	All Suspects	Non-permanently-staying Foreigners	
		Total	Rate
	(A)	(B)	(B/A x 100)
Total	95,486 (100.0)	8,533 (100.0)	8.9
Firearms and Swords Control Law	4,135 (4.3)	103 (1.2)	2.5
Law on Business Affecting Public Morals	1,991 (2.1)	48 (0.6)	2.4
Prostitution Prevention Law	1,172 (1.2)	254 (3.0)	21.7
Hemp Control Law	1,804 (1.9)	215 (2.5)	11.9
Law to Control Narcotic and Psychiatric Substances	425 (0.4)	170 (2.0)	40.0
Stimulant Drug Control Law	24,110 (25.2)	731 (8.6)	3.0
Opium Law	134 (0.1)	60 (0.7)	44.8
Immigration-Control and Refugee Recognition Law	6,834 (7.2)	6,281 (73.6)	91.9
Alien Registration Law	212 (0.2)	188 (2.2)	88.7
Others	54,669 (57.3)	483 (5.7.)	0.9

Source: Ministry of Justice, *Annual Report of Statistics on Prosecution for 1995*

Table 9 shows the total number of alien suspects charged with offenses of special laws by their nationality. The highest rate was for Chinese suspects that is, 22.1%, although this was lower than the 44.7% in case of Chinese caught by the police for non-traffic Penal Code offenses (Table 4). Among alien offenders of the Firearms and Swords Control Law, Chinese had the highest rate of 33.0%. After the enforcement of the Law to Cope with Boryo-kudan in 1992, the police strengthened the regulation of firearms. Therefore, the total number of firearms forfeited by the police increased from 948 in 1991 to 1,702 in 1995 (White Paper on Police in 1996: 144). In 1995 the rate of the forfeited firearms made in the United States, in China and in the Philip-pines amounted to 34.7%, 17.9% and 9.9%, respectively. Previously, the firearms were mainly smuggled by Japanese, especially by those affiliating

Table 9. The Total Number of Alien Suspects* Received by Public Prosecutors for Offenses of Non-traffic Special Laws by Their Nationality in 1995

	Total	1) FSCL	2) LBAPM	3) PPL	4) HCL	5) LCNPS	6) SDCL	7) OL	8) ICRRL	9) ARL	Others
Total	8,533 (100.0)	103 (100.0)	48 (100.0)	254 (100.0)	215 (100.0)	170 (100.0)	731 (100.0)	60	6,281 (100.0)	188 (100.0)	483 (100.0)
China	1,886 (22.1)	34 (33.0)	11 (22.9)	39 (15.4)	3 (1.4)	1 (0.6)	14 (1.9)	0	1,680 (26.7)	44 (23.4)	60 (12.4)
Korea	755 (8.8)	9 (8.7)	19 (39.6)	3 (1.2)	3 (1.4)	0 (0.0)	48 (6.6)	0	478 (7.6)	44 (23.4)	151 (31.3)
Iran	1,424 (16.7)	9 (8.7)	0 (0.0)	0 (0.0)	82 (38.1)	41 (24.1)	165 (22.6)	53	1,005 (16.0)	27 (14.4)	42 (8.7)
Thailand	1,070 (12.5)	3 (2.9)	11 (22.9)	157 (61.8)	7 (3.3)	18 (10.6)	4 (0.5)	1	826 (13.2)	19 (10.1)	24 (5.0)
Philippine	1,138 (13.3)	9 (8.7)	6 (12.5)	0 (0.0)	9 (4.2)	2 (1.2)	436 (59.6)	0	624 (9.9)	32 (17.0)	20 (4.1)
Vietnam	109 (1.3)	0 (0.0)	0 (0.0)	0 (0.0)	0 (0.0)	42 (24.7)	5 (0.7)	0	56 (0.9)	1 (0.5)	5 (1.0)
Brazil	46 (0.5)	4 (3.9)	0 (0.0)	0 (0.0)	6 (2.8)	4 (2.4)	9 (1.2)	0	12 (0.2)	2 (1.1)	9 (1.9)
Peru	276 (3.2)	1 (1.0)	0 (0.0)	2 (0.8)	1 (0.5)	6 (3.5)	4 (0.5)	0	258 (4.1)	1 (0.5)	3 (0.6)
U.S.A.	66 (0.8)	4 (3.9)	0 (0.0)	0 (0.0)	22 (10.2)	1 (0.6)	17 (2.3)	0	5 (0.1)	0 (0.0)	17 (3.5)
Others	1,763 (20.7)	30 (29.1)	1 (2.1)	53 (20.9)	82 (38.1)	55 (32.4)	29 (4.0)	6	1,337 (21.3)	18 (9.6)	152 (31.5)

* Suspects of non-permanently-staying foreigners
1) FSCL: Firearms and Swords Control Law
2) LBAPM: Law on Business Affecting Public Morals
3) PPL: Prostitution Prevention Law
4) HCL: Hemp Control Law
5) LCNPS: Law to Control Narcotic and Psychiatric Substances
6) SDCL: Stimulant Drug Control Law
7) OL: Opium Law
8) ICRRL: Immigration-Control and Refugee Recognition Law
9) ARL: Alien Registration Law
Sources: Ministry of Justice, *Crime Report of Statistics on Prosecution for 1995*, pp. 222-225

with the Boryokudan, from the United States and from the Philippines. In the early 1990s more Chinese became engaged with the firearms smuggling.

Regarding offenses of the Law on Business Affecting Public Morals, the purpose of which is the regulation of the business such as a bar and a cabaret, we saw the high rates in Koreans, Chinese and Thai. Many Koreans with qualification for permanent staying have worked at the tertiary industry since the end of World War II. Therefore, Korean non-permanent stayers have more chances to work as a manager or an employer at the business affecting public morals. They committed more frequently such offenses to this law as the illegal business at the prohibited zone and that without permission by the prefectural public safety commission.

As was described earlier, in the early 1990s many Thai females were compelled to work as prostitutes. Therefore, 61.8% of alien offenders of the Prostitute Prevention Law were Thai. Correspondingly, Thai females who became bar managers, that is, managers of disguised brothels after paying up the advanced money, might commit some offenses of the Law on Business Affecting Public Morals. Recently, the mass media sometimes reported Colombian females fraudulently taken to Japan and compelled to work as prostitutes by the imposition of a large sum of advanced money, that is, about 5,000,000 yen (US$40,000) under the supervision of the Boryokudan. The route of this trafficking seems to be maintained by the connection between the Boryokudan and the Colombian organization for human trafficking (Asahi Newspaper, March 29, 1998). The latter may be a sub-organization of Colombian drug cartels, which aim to develop the network for smuggling and distributing cocaine in Japan. If the cartels would succeed in establishing this network, they might use Colombian prostitutes as cocaine sellers at the bottom of the network like is done in the United States (Savona, 1992: 120).

After the enforcement of the revised Immigration-Control and Refugee Recognition Law in June of 1990, many Iranians returned to their mother country for fear of criminal punishment imposed for their illegal overstay in Japan. However, Iranians who did not yet achieve their purpose, especially that of making money, remained in Japan. With the deepening of the depression some of them became distributors of stimulant drugs at the bottom of a pyramid system of the Boryokudan.[42] Therefore, Iranians were more frequently arrested for offenses of the Stimulant Drug Control Law.

Iranians who believe in gaining good opportunities in Japan to make money, repeatedly come to Japan in an illegal way; specifically, they often smuggle drugs.[43] The mountain area in Iran is a part of the Golden Crescent, at which people grow the opium poppy and the hemp. Therefore, it is easier for Iranians to get drugs such as opium and heroin in their mother country. Therefore, Iranians showed the high rate of the offenses of the Hemp Control Law (38.1%), the Law to Control Narcotic and Psychiatric Substances (24.1%) and the Opium Law (88.3%).

Concerning offenses of the Law to Control Narcotic and Psychiatric Substances Vietnamese and Thai also showed the high rates of 24.7% and 10.6%,

respectively. They more easily get morphine and heroin, as their mother countries are located near the Golden Triangle. Interestingly, there has recently
been a documented increase in the smuggling of psychiatric substances from
Thailand[44] (Asahi Newspaper, December 9, 1996).

Since the police succeeded in eradicating the production of stimulant drug
around 1954 after its first spread (Yokoyama, 1991: 6-7), there has been no
underground factory in Japan to produce stimulants. Since 1970, the beginning
of the second spread of stimulants, the Boryokudan has established the network for smuggling and distributing stimulant drugs. The bases, from which a
stimulant drug was smuggled into Japan, were Korea from 1975 to 1981,
Taiwan from 1984 to 1991 and China after 1995[45] (Kanagawa Newspaper,
January 7, 1997). These main routes for smuggling have been strictly controlled by the Boryokudan. Table 9 shows that the Philippine had the high rate
of offenses of the Stimulant Drug Control Law. Many of them seemed to
commit these offenses under the control of the Boryokudan.[46] As illegal drugs
are more frequently traded in secret through a portable telephone and an internet, it becomes more difficult for the law enforcement agencies to eradicate
them.

In case of offenses of the Immigration-Control and Refugee Recognition
Law Chinese had the highest rate (26.7%), followed by Iranian (16.0%) and
Thai (13.2%). After 1995 there was an increase in the total number of Chinese
who smuggled themselves in a group into Japan mainly by sea by the medium
of the Chinese organizations for human trafficking known as "Snake
Head."[47] In 1997 the police and the maritime security agency arrested a total
of 1,360 foreigners for smuggling themselves in a group, of which 1,209 or
88.9% were Chinese (Asahi Newspaper, April 4, 1998). The way of human
trafficking has become crafty.[48] The "Snake Head" has established the
connection with the Boryokudan in order to succeed in the human
trafficking.[49]

After making money foreigners often send portions of it back to their
homes. Many foreigners use the underground bank organized by those of the
same nationality. Recently, the police cracked down on the organizers of the
underground bank for offenses of the Bank Law. For the first time the underground bank for Chinese was exposed (Asahi Newspaper, June 3, 1997). The
underground banks for Korean (Asahi Newspaper, October 28, 1997), for
Nepalese (Asahi Newspaper, November 6, 1997), and for Iranian (Asahi
Newspaper, May 2, 1998) were also raided.

Conclusions

This paper has analyzed the crimes by foreigners from a historical perspective. By this calculus, the writer has traced the development of the crimes by
non-permanent stayers, who have increased since 1980. In the process of this
development the economic elements seem to play an important role, although
foreigners of the different nationality commit the different kind of crimes

owing to their indigenous cultural and social background, and owing to their situation in Japan.

First, economic elements were used to induce foreigners, especially those living in Asian countries, to come to Japan. In the 1980s Japan enjoyed great economic prosperity. To supply Japanese males with sexual services, many Asian females were taken to Japan as prostitutes. Then, in the process of the shortage of labor power many Asian males began to come to Japan in order to make money by working illegally. As their purposes were achieved in the economic prosperity, they committed crimes only infrequently.

There was a serious economic depression in Japan after the summer of 1990. In the deepening of this depression employers discharged alien laborers, especially those of illegal entrants and overstayers. On the other hand, the police and immigration office strengthened the arrest of alien illegal laborers. Nevertheless, Asian people, particularly the Chinese, continued to smuggle themselves into Japan in hopes of making money. Due to the loss of available jobs, many alien stayers had to resort to illegal methods to earn their living. Therefore, the crimes by foreigners increased drastically in the early 1990s.

In addition, the quality of alien crimes became aggravated. Like Iranian sellers of stimulant drugs, some foreigners began to commit crime under the control of the Boryokudan. Others committed crimes in conjunction with the Boryokudan, as was seen in the case of Chinese human trafficking. Like the members of a theft group some became hardened, professional criminals. Professional criminals such as Korean pickpockets also visited Japan to pursue their profitable activities. Without coping with these serious crimes, Japanese will not continue enjoy the security that they currently possess.

Japan is quickly becoming an aging society.[50] Therefore, without alien labor power it will not be able to maintain its present system. Therefore, the country needs to establish policies that allow it to live in harmony with foreigners. Under this fundamental policy, Japanese residents would have to think about the measures to cope with the crimes by foreigners. The traditional measures, which have been developed in the Japanese climate, will need to be adjusted to alien offenders with their own cultural and social background. In addition, to suppress the international crimes like the trafficking of drugs and firearms, Japanese investigation agencies need to cooperate with the corresponding agencies in foreign countries, and with the international agencies like the Interpol.

Next, this paper will consider the experience of the crimes by foreigners from the viewpoint of an international comparison. Michael Tonry (1997: 22-25) deduces several hypotheses from the results of the European researches on immigration and crime, although he points out that many categories of immigrants do not fall within any generalization. The first hypothesis is that self-selected economic migrants from many Asian cultures have lower crime rates than the resident population in the first and in subsequent generations. In Japan many alien non-permanent stayers came from Asian countries. However, it is difficult to prove that they have a lower crime rate due to sharing their own

Asian culture. Coincidentally, the estimated percentage of the non-permanent-ly-staying foreigners among all population of 14 and over 14 years old in 1995 amounted to about 0.9%, while that of alien non-permanently-staying suspects among all of those caught for the Penal Code offenses by the police was 2.2% (White Paper on Police in 1996: 297). The alien non-permanent stayers, most of whom share an Asian heritage, seem to commit crimes more frequently than the resident population.

The second hypothesis is that cultural differences between structurally similarly situated immigrants can result in sharply different crime patterns. In Japan we see the sharply different offense patterns among alien non-perma-nently-staying offenders by their nationality (Table 6 and Table 9). However, the offense patterns between Brazilian and Peruvian are rather similar. As most of them are people of Japanese ancestry, they may be not only structural-ly similarly situated in Japan, but also share the similar culture, which is composed of Latin-American and Japanese influences.

According to Michael Tonry there are grounds for hypothesizing that, all else being equal, some countries' policies for aiding immigrants' assimilation, can reduce crime rates, including those of their second- and third-generation descendants. After World War II, Koreans were discriminated against and perpetually insulted by Japanese. They lived in poor communities with high crime rate. However, their situation has been improved by several factors, one of which is the change in policies of Japan's government for them. Then, even during the economic depression in the early 1990s their crime trend became stable like the Japanese (Table 2).

The last hypothesis is that the reasons groups migrate powerfully shape criminality and other indications of successful adaptation. There are two main reasons why many foreigners have come to Japan recently; to study and to make money. It appears that foreigners coming to Japan for the purpose of making money are more prone to commit crimes, because most of them must work illegally. This may be true especially during the economic depression.

During the period from 1955 to 1990 Japan continued to enjoy economic prosperity, although it sometimes experienced a short-term recession. At last, during the "bubble economy" in the late 1980s, Japanese lived in an affluent society, at which the residents believed that the economic factors were not so important in causing a crime, as Marxists pointed out. In the early 1990s, the country plunged into an economic crisis. The drastic change in the economic conditions influenced more seriously on the alien illegal labors, especially those with the purpose of making money, as they were treated as temporary labors in the labor market. Surely, they did not fall in an absolute poverty. However, they were more prone to committing crimes. Although the poverty is not a single motive for committing crime, one should not neglect the im-portant role of economic elements in causing criminal activity.

NOTES

1. The previous version of this paper was presented at the 49th Annual Meeting of the American Society of Criminology held on November 19-22, 1997, in San Diego.

2. Many female Korean were compulsorily taken to battlefields to serve as a prostitute for Japanese soldiers. The compensation for them did not draw attention until the early 1990s.

3. Immediately after the Pease Treaty in 1951 Korean and Chinese taken compulsorily during the war were specially qualified to stay permanently. At the end of 1995 the total number of Korean stayers and their descendants with this qualification amounted to 557,921, while the corresponding Chinese and their descendants numbered 4,685 (Statistics on Staying Foreigners in 1996: 6-7). In addition, there were 22,201 Korean and 23,568 Chinese with the qualification to stay permanently in Japan, most of whom are the comer to Japan prior to 1940 and their descendants.

4. Before the World War II we saw Japanese emigrants. Most of them settled down at the places in the United States and Canada along the Pacific Ocean.

5. In 1994 the total number of foreigners coming by the visa for show business amounted to 90,562, of which 53,000 were Philippine females with certification of their position as dancers or singers issued by the Philippine government. As the results of the roundups the immigration office found that only 20% of them worked for the show business (Asahi Newspaper, July 22, 1995). Others seemed to work to provide Japanese males with the sexual services.

6. According to the Asahi Newspaper, March 16, 1993, a Thai broker sold a Thai female to a Japanese broker at 1,500,000 yen (US$12,000)or 2,000,000 yen (US$16,000). The Japanese broker in conjunction with the Boryokudan, the Japanese gangsters' group, gained the margin of 1,000,000 yen (US$8,000). Finally, the Thai female owed 3,500,000 yen (US$28,000) or 4,000,000 yen (US$32,000) to her employer, that is, an owner of the disguised brothel.

7. In the fiscal 1983 the number of alien students totaled only to 10,428 (Murata, 1990: 308).

8. Thereafter, the total number of alien entrants with the visa for studying at a professional school decreased from 35,107 in 1988 to 18,183 in 1989 (White Paper on Labor in 1996: 53). By the way, in 1995 the total number of those with the visa for studying at a professional school and those with the visa for studying at a university amounted to 9,928 and 10,155 respectively.

9. Immediately after the enforcement of the revised Immigration-Control and Refugee Recognition Law of 1990 the police did not actively catch people for the promotion of illegal employment of foreigners. However, as the labor shortage was mitigated by the legal alien laborers of Japanese ancestry with the deepening of the economic depression, the police began to round up the offenders more earnestly. The total number of suspects charged with the promotion of illegal employment of foreigners increased from 306 in 1991 to 777 in 1993, and dropped to 432 in 1995 (White Paper on Police in 1996: 306).

10. In October, 1990, the Ministry of Health and Welfare issued the direction not to apply the welfare aid to foreigners neither with the visa for settlement nor with the qualification for permanent staying (Kanagawa Center of Human Rights, 1996: 54). In March, 1992, it prohibited admitting alien illegal laborers to the health insurance. Since then, illegally-staying foreigners have not been guaranteed even the minimum standard of life, which Article 25 of the Constitution prescribes.

11. With the motorization many persons who kill or injure another by an traffic accident on the road are charged with the professional negligence causing death or bodily injury, a crime prescribed in the Penal Code (Yokoyama, 1990: 68). The term of "non-traffic Penal Code offenses" is composed of all Penal Code offenses excluding the above-mentioned offense. In 1995 the police caught 970,179 suspects for some Penal Code offense, of which 676,927 were charged with the professional negligence causing death or bodily injury by traffic accidents (White Paper on Crime in 1996: 404).

12. In the early 1980s the second baby boomers became adolescent. In 1983 we saw a peak in the total number of juvenile offenders brought mainly by the net-widening of guidance activities of the police (Yokoyama, 1989). As the baby boomers became adult, the total number of juvenile

offenders caught by the police decreased from 261,634 in 1983 to 250,132 in 1985, to 182,328 in 1990 and to 149,137 in 1995 (White Paper on Crime in 1996: 422).

13. In Japan the offense categories such as the heinous offenses, violent offenses, intellectual offenses and offenses against public morality have been commonly used in the official statistics on crimes.

14. Many foreigners who want to make money, come to Japan, separating from their family. They sometimes have some emotional troubles with a person of the same nationality such as falling in love, which may cause a homicide. For example, Asahi Newspaper, May 2, 1996, reported us that a Chinese male killed a Chinese female who had lost her love to him.

15. In 1993 the police arrested 72 foreigners for a homicide, of which 44, 9 and 19 killed persons with the same nationality, those with other nationality, and Japanese respectively (White Paper on Crime in 1994: 247). On the other hand, the police arrested 142 alien robbers, of which 31, 15 and 96 victimized persons with the same nationality, those with other nationality, and Japanese respectively. By the way, in 1995 the Tokyo District Court imposed the death penalty on two Chinese robbers for stabbing two Japanese persons to death (Nihon Keizai Newspaper, December 15, 1995). Prior to this case any non-permanently-staying foreigner was not sentenced to the death penalty after the World War II.

16. We began to see even an alien group for robbery. In 1996 the police rounded up a group of four Chinese for robbing another Chinese repeatedly(Kanagawa Newspaper, February 8, 1996).

17. The police arrested an American male for shooting a guard by a pistol at his attempted robbery (Asahi Newspaper, August 4, 1997). It was a sensational news, because Japanese rarely use firearms at the time of committing a crime. Even professional housebreakers invade a house for a theft without carrying a weapon in fear of being arrested for robbery, for which they may be sentenced to the long-term imprisonment.

18. We were surprised by a robbery at a bar in Ginza, the most prosperous area in Tokyo. In this case six Chinese males threatened about thirty customers and employees at the bar by knives and imitative guns, and robbed them of money and valuable things equivalent to 17,000,000 yen (US$136,000)(Asahi Newspaper, March 1, 1996). They committed this robbery because of their poverty after the loss of a job. By the way, one of suspects was a former police officer in Shanghai (Nihon Keizai Newspaper, May 10, 1996).

19. In the former three cases all of both kidnappers and victims were Chinese, while in the latter two cases a Japanese was kidnapped by a group of kidnappers composed mainly of Chinese. Chinese commit a kidnapping more frequently owing to the conflicts over the money, above all, the advanced money, which the illegal entrants promise to pay.

20. To the contrary, in case that an alien criminal victimizes Japanese, the reportability to the police may be higher. For example, a company managing many supermarkets all over the country adopts the policy of referring all alien shoplifters to the police.

21. With the decrease in serious offenses since the 1970s, the police have earnestly caught even such a person as those riding a bicycle temporarily without the permission of its owner. Therefore, most of the embezzlement of a lost or deserted thing are the riding of a deserted bicycle. If a foreigner would ride a deserted bicycle or use any deserted valuable thing as recycling, he might be charged with the embezzlement of a lost or deserted thing.

22. The total number of the theft committed in a group of over ten foreigners, which the police cleared, increased from 1 in 1993 to 935 in 1997 (Asahi Newspaper, March 8, 1998). The police estimate that there are over thirty Chinese theft groups in Japan (Asahi Newspaper, March 18, 1998). According to Toshihide Aikawa (1997: 12) Iranian organize two or three theft groups in the Tokyo metropolitan area, who use violent means while breaking into a building and stealing in it.

23. The police exposed a car theft group of fifteen members with multi-nationality; three Japanese, seven Sri Lankan, one Pakistani and three Burmese (Asahi Newspaper, January 21, 1998). They divided a role. Sri Lankan stole about 370 vehicles valued at 1,500,000,000 yen (US$12,000,000), which Japanese and Pakistani transported to a harbor. Then, Sri Lankan smuggled them mainly to Myanmar and Malaysia.

24. Asahi Newspaper, September 30, 1996, reported that the police raided a group of nine Chinese for stealing clothes valued at a total of 170,000,000 yen (US$1,360,000). Many of them became a member of this theft group after the loss of their job in the depression. Even receiving a

reward for stealing, some lived precariously from day to day owing to their obligation to pay the advance money and their indulgence in gambling. In addition, some Chinese theft groups organized a market to sell the stolen goods (Asahi Newspaper, March 18, 1998).

25. In 1997 the police revealed an illegal enterprise for stealing at the Pachinko parlor (Asahi Newspaper, March 8, 1998). Each of thirteen Chinese invested 300,000 yen (US$2,400) as "a stockholder" to this enterprise. Their main job was to steal balls by using ROM, a part of the computerized Pachinko machine, in order to exchange these balls into cash. Every time the accumulated illegal profits reached to 6,500,000 yen (US$52,000), they were distributed equally among "stockholders." If "a stockholder" would be arrested by the police, he would be paid 2,000,000 yen (US$16,000) as a compensation. The enterprise as an organization for organized crime had rules to control "stockholders." For example, if "a stockholder" would leak some secret in the enterprise, he would be discharged. If he would delay his arrival at a Pachinko parlor, a place for stealing, for over ten minutes, he would be fined 10,000 yen (US$80).

26. The Chinese theft group for stealing luxury cars produced by Mercedes-Benz had a route to smuggle the stolen cars into China via Hong Kong (Asahi Newspaper, February 8, 1997). Foreigners of other nationality also organize a group to steal cars and to smuggle them into overseas. Kanagawa Newspaper, February 8, 1997, reported such a group of Sri Lankan. On the other hand, Japanese professional thieves scarcely commit a car theft, because the domestic market of stolen cars is not attractive to them. As Japan becomes affluent with goods, the main objects of their stealing are cash and treasures (Yokoyama, 1985: 195).

27. The police rounded up a group of three professional thieves coming from Hong Kong for a burglary at a clothing store (Nihon Keizai Newspaper, February 10, 1997). By the visa for a short stay they visited Japan several times for stealing by the violent means. The police estimated that they stole goods valued at a total of 130,000,000 yen (US$1,040,000).

28. The police arrested one of three Korean professional pickpockets in a team for picking cash and credit cards from a shoulder bag of a lady standing on the platform at the railway station (Asahi Newspaper, April 11, 1997). Three pickpockets used a tear spray and brandished a kitchen knife to escape from the arrest. An arrested Korean of these three had come to Japan by the legal visa six times at the interval of two weeks for previous five months. The police estimated that this pickpocket group was composed of about twenty, who came in a team to Japan from Seoul (Kanagawa Newspaper, April 11, 1997). In addition, professional thieves of several groups coming from Korea by the visa for a short stay sneaked into houses to steal cash, precious metals and jewels. The police estimated that during one year since April, 1996, they committed about 120 thefts, by which we were damaged at a total of 200,000,000 yen (US$1,600,000) (Nihon Keizai Newspaper, May 13, 1997). One suspect for sneak-thieving could come to Japan 33 times since 1991 with a visa given easily at the Japanese embassy, because he got the qualification of a Christian priest in 1993 (Nihon Keizai Newspaper, July 28, 1997). By the way, Japanese professional pickpockets have almost disappeared with the high growth of economy (Yokoyama, 1985: 197).

29. The price of a forged certification of alien registration is between 20,000 yen (US$160) and 50,000 yen (US$400) at the black market (Asahi Newspaper, August 5, 1997). To prevent forgery, the form of a certification of alien registration was changed in April, 1997.

30. The police arrested a Taiwanese broker for filling falsely in the attestation in order to certify the disguised marriage of a Chinese female, a client, with a Japanese male as the legal one (Nihon Keizai Newspaper, February 19, 1997). The broker received a total of about 500,00,000 yen (US$4,000,000) from twenty five alien clients. By the way, if a foreigner would marry a Japanese, he/she could obtain the qualification for settling down in Japan.

31. Japan had a mutual treaty with Pakistan and Bangladesh for entering without a visa. In the economic boom many people came from both countries for illegal working. Then, the above-mentioned treaty was suspended in January, 1989. Reflecting this process, the total number of Pakistani caught for illegal working increased from 196 in 1986 to 3,886 in 1990, and declined to 793 in 1991 (Immigration Bureau, 1993: 106). The corresponding number of Bangladeshi raised from 58 in 1986 to 5,925 in 1990, and dropped drastically to 293 in 1991.

32. In case of collision with another ship on June 24, 1996, a Korean captain was charged with the obstruction of traffic by professional negligence, although a Japanese pilot steered the ship at the time of collision (Asahi Newspaper, September 29, 1996).

33. Thereafter, the corresponding number dropped to 104 in 1995 (Crimes in 1995: 413).

34. It is difficult for the settled Vietnamese to work hard for long hours together like Japanese employees owing to their different life style (Aikawa, 1997:153). Giving up working in the Japanese way, many of them become independent traders of the used things such as cars and motorcycles. To get their "goods" easily, they sometimes organize a theft group. For example, the police raided a group of ten Vietnamese and five Japanese (Nihon Keizai Newspaper, September 21, 1997). They were charged with stealing about 4,000 motorcycles and smuggling them to Vietnam and Hong Kong. The total price of stolen motorcycles amounted to 500,000,000 yen (US$4,000,000).

35. In 1995 the police arrested a Chinese suspect for using the forged pre-paid card for the Pachinko game (Asahi Newspaper, February 9, 1996). By their searching at his apartment, a total of 15,000 forged Pachinko cards valued at 60,000,000 yen (US$480,000) were forfeited. Asahi Newspaper, July 11, 1996, reported that the police cracked down on a group of twelve Chinese for forging and using the phone cards and the pre-paid cards for the Pachinko game in order to make money. By the way, the machine for forging the pre-paid Pachinko cards is sold at about 8,000,000 yen (US$64,000) at the underground market controlled by foreigners and the Boryokudan (Asahi Newspaper, May 4, 1996).

36. The police conducted a research to estimate the annual income of all Boryokudan groups. By their estimation the total of their income amounted to 1,301,900,000,000 yen (US$10,415,200,000), of which 16.9% were gained from the illegal gambling and bookmaking (White Paper on Police in 1989: 46). By the way, 34.8% were from the illegal sale of a stimulant drug.

37. Most of killed persons were alien female bosses or managers of the disguised brothel, who had been promoted from the exploited position of a prostitute after paying up the advanced money. In 1991 three Thai females in Shimodate City killed their Thai female boss, a manager of a bar owned by a Japanese, because they were too severely exploited by her (Association for Supporting Three Thai Females in Shimodate Case, 1995). Asahi Newspaper, March 16, 1993, reported us that in 1992 six Thai females killed a Taiwanese female boss of their bar in Tokyo, and five Thai females working at a bar in Mobara City killed their female manager coming from Singapore.

38. In 1985 public prosecutors received 3,320 alien suspects for offenses of the Alien Registration Law, of which 2,669 or 80.4% were Korean (Annual Report of Statistics on Prosecution for 1985: 200-201). On the other hand, in 1990 they received only 485, of which 273 or 56.3% were Korean (Annual Report of Statistics on Prosecution for 1990: 194-195).

39. The total number of the shooting at the time of fight between Boryokudan members dropped to 29 in 1992 (White Paper on Police in 1989: 20).

40. Many of American suspects for offenses of the Hemp Control Law seemed to be charged with possessing marijuana for their personal use (Table 9).

41. Especially, the human resources under the Immigration Bureau is not enough. The total number of the immigration officers amounted to 2,458, of which 915 were an immigration guard in charge of raiding the illegal entrants and overstayers (Asahi Newspaper, July 10, 1996). Only fifty immigration guards covered the area of Tokyo and eight prefectures in the Kanto Koshin-etsu district. In addition, we have only a few houses to detain illegal entrants and overstayers before the extradition to their mother country or another country. Therefore, it is said that the police discharge foreigners overstaying within three years in case of catching only for overstaying, if the latter are guaranteed by some Japanese.

42. The sale of a stimulant drug is one of main income resources for the Boryokudan, as I mentioned at the Note 36). After the enforcement of the Law to Cope with Boryokudan in 1992 the police controlled more severely the illegal activities of the Boryokudan. Therefore, to maintain the network to sell a stimulant drug, they employed some Iranian as a seller. First, we saw the Iranian seller at Shinjuku in Tokyo around 1992. The territory of Iranian sellers have spread to the satellite cities of Tokyo (Nihon Keizai Newspaper, March 30, 1998). Japanese sellers have had the moral not to sell a stimulant drug to the high-school students. However, Iranian sellers do not share such a moral. After soliciting the high-school students around large railway stations, the Iranian sell a two or three doses of stimulant drug to them at the lower price. Teenagers, especially female ones, who admire the western culture, become customers easily from curiosity (Kanagawa Newspaper, May

15, 1996). Recently, we witness more teenagers indulging in a stimulant drug without noticing it. They enjoy sniffing its smoke in place of injecting it in the usual way.

43. Some Iranian with the career of being extradited from Japan to Iran after a guilty sentence, come repeatedly to Japan for the drug smuggling with a forged passport of the different nationality such as Greek and Hollander. Since the beginning of 1996 the Tokyo Metropolitan Police Agency arrested a total of eleven disguised Iranian for offenses of the drug control laws (Asahi Newspaper, October 4, 1997).

44. The police arrested two Thai males for smuggling psychiatric substances into Japan (Kanagawa Newspaper, March 19, 1997). They bought a set of the substances at 3,200 yen (US$26) in Thailand, and sold this set as the drug for diet at 15,000 yen (US$120) to Thai females working as a prostitute in Japan.

45. By the international cooperation the Japanese police succeeded in eradicating the smuggling route from Korea and Taiwan. However, in the late 1990s many underground factories to produce a stimulant drug moved from Taiwan to Fujian Province in China (Asahi Newspaper, May 3, 1998).

46. In November, 1994, some Philippine females were caught for selling a stimulant drug under the control of the Boryokudan (White Paper on Police in 1995: 140). By the way, the Boryokudan members often inject prostitutes with a stimulant drug to exploit them as a pimp (Yokoyama, 1995: 140).

47. The "Snake Head" is a general name to call many Chinese organizations for human trafficking, jobs of which are divided into three kinds. The first organizations in China bear the part of recruiting illegal emigrants to foreign countries such as Japan and the United States, and receiving a deposit from them. The members of the second organizations guide them from the meeting place to the destination, that is, some landing place in a foreign country. Those of the third ones wait for them at the destination, transport them to some large city, and give a shelter until they find a job. The big bosses of the "Snake Head" seem to be entrepreneurs in Hong Kong and in Taiwan who provide a fund for the "Snake Head" (Asahi Newspaper, February 26, 1997).

48. For example, the route of human trafficking has become complicated. In February, 1997, four Chinese who tried to fly to Japan, were arrested at the airport in Shanghai (Asahi Newspaper, March 19, 1997). First, they went by land to Thailand through Myanmar. After buying a forged passport at about 3,000,000 yen (US$24,000) in Thailand, they returned to China. Then, they failed to smuggle themselves into Japan from Shanghai.

49. After the enforcement of the Law to Cope with Boryokudan in 1992 the Boryokudan began to help the human trafficking organized by the "Snake Head" (Kanagawa Newspaper, January 27, 1997). In December, 1996, the Tokyo Metropolitan Police Agency arrested three Chinese affiliating with "Snake Head" and nine Japanese including a Boryokudan executive for the assistance of human trafficking. In this case several Boryokudan members under the direction of their executive transported a group of Chinese illegal entrants from the landing seashore to Tokyo, and provided them with a shelter. The "Snake Head" got 700,000 yen (US$5,600) from each of these entrants as a trafficking fee. Then, they paid a total 28,000,000 yen (US$224,000) to the Boryokudan for their assistance, and a total of 3,000,000 yen (US$24,000) to a Japanese fisherman who provided a boat for illegal entrants to land from a Chinese ship. When the illegal entrants leave their homeland, they pay about 10% of the trafficking fee as a deposit, and promise either to pay the remainder of the trafficking fee by working in Japan, or to make their family pay the remainder after their success in landing Japan. In the former case the remainder is severely exacted by the member of the "Snake Head" in conjunction with the Boryokudan (Kanagawa Newspaper, February 12, 1997). In February, 1997, seven Chinese were arrested for kidnapping four Chinese to get a ransom from their rich families in China. Three of seven suspects confessed that they joined this kidnapping, because they had failed to find a well-paid job to pay the remainder of trafficking fee (Asahi Newspaper, February 22, 1997). By the way, the trafficking fee increased ten times for this decade (Kanagawa Newspaper, February 22, 1997).

50. The percentage of the age group under 15 years old among all population in Japan decreased from 35.4% in 1950 to 15.2% in 1998, while the corresponding percentage of that of 65 and over 65 increased from 4.5% to 16.0% (Asahi Newspaper, May 5, 1998).

REFERENCES

Aikawa, T. 1997. *A Broker for Illegal Entrants — Life of a Scoundrel* (written in Japanese). Tokyo: Soshi-sha.

Association for Supporting Three Thai Females in Shimodate Case. 1995. *Letter from Thai Females to Japan, a Society for Prostitution* (written in Japanese). Tokyo: Akashi-shoten.

Huang, F.F.Y., and M.S. Vaughn. 1992. "A Descriptive Analysis of Japanese Organized Crime." *International Criminal Justice Review*, 2: 19-57.

Immigration Bureau, Ministry of Justice. 1993. *Control of Entry into and Departure from Japan in 1992* (written in Japanese). Tokyo: Printing Bureau of the Ministry of Finance.

Kanagawa Center of Human Rights. 1996. *Introduction to Human rights at the Age of Internationalization* (written in Japanese). Tokyo: Akashi-shoten.

Ministry of Justice. 1996. *Statistics on Staying Foreigners in 1995*. Tokyo: Ministry of Justice.

Mo, B. 1994. *Snake Head* (written in Japanese). Tokyo: Soshi-sha.

Murata, Y. 1990. "Charm and Problem of Studying in Japan from the Viewpoint of Alien Students" (written in Japanese). In: A. Sawada and K. Kadowaki, eds. *Internationalization of Japanese*: 308-325. Tokyo: Nihon Keizai Newspaper.

Savona, E.U. 1992. "The Organized Crime/Drug Connection." In: H.H. Traver, and M.S. Gaylord, eds. *Drugs, Law and the State*: 99-117. Hong Kong: Hong Kong University Press.

Tamaki, M. 1995. "Trend in Asian People Staying in Japan" (written in Japanese). In: H. Komai, ed., *Foreigners Toward Settlement*: 255-289. Tokyo: Akashi-shoten.

Tamura, M. 1992. "The Yakuza and Amphetamine Abuse in Japan." In: H.H. Traver, and M.S. Gaylord, eds. *Drugs, Law and the State*: 99-117. Hong Kong: Hong Kong University Press.

Tonry, M. 1997. *Ethnicity, Crime, and Immigration*. Chicago and London: The University of Chicago Press.

Yashiro, A. 1993. "Situation of Working of Legal Entrants" (written in Japanese). In: T. Hanami, and Y. Kuwahara, eds., *Your Neighbors — Alien Laborers*: 37-73. Tokyo: Toyo Keizai Shinpo-sha.

Yokoyama, M. 1985. "Criminal Policy against Thieves in Japan." *Kangweon Law Review*, 1: 191-217. Chun Chon, Korea.

_____. 1989. "Net-Widening of the Juvenile Justice System in Japan." *Criminal Justice Review*, 14(1): 43-53.

_____. 1990. "Criminalization against Traffic Offenders in Japan." International Journal of Comparative and Applied Criminal Justice, 14(1 & 2): 65-71.

_____. 1991. "Development of Japanese Drug Control Laws toward Criminalization." *Kokugakuin Journal of Law and Politics*, 28(3): 1-21. Tokyo: Kokugakuin University.

_____. 1993a. "Problems on Internationalization" (written in Japanese). *Kokuga-kuin Journal of Law and Politics*, 30(4): 167-206. Tokyo: Kokugakuin University.

_____. 1993b. "Social Pathology in Internationalization" (written in Japanese). In: M. Yajima and S. Yonekawa, eds., *Pathology in Mature Society*: 63-86. Tokyo: Gakubun-sha.

_____. 1994. "Change in Japanese Organized Crime and the Enactment of the Law to Cope with Boryokudan in 1991." Paper presented at the 13th World Congress of Sociological Association held in 1994, in Bielefeld, Germany.

_____. 1995. "Analysis of Prostitution in Japan." *International Journal of Comparative and Applied Criminal Justice*, 19(1): 47-60.

[11]

IMMIGRATION AND CRIME AMONG YOUTH IN SWITZERLAND

ALEXANDER T. VAZSONYI

Auburn University

MARTIN KILLIAS

University of Lausanne

The current investigation examined rates and predictors of deviance in a sample of Swiss youth. Data were collected from 3,136 youth; 800 cases were identified as first-generation (35%) or second-generation (65%) immigrant youth. We found that second-generation immigrant male youth were more deviant than Swiss adolescents, second-generation immigrant male youth were also more deviant than first-generation immigrants. Few important differences were found on measures of self-control and measures of perceived sanctions (get caught, shame/guilt, loss of respect) by immigrant status, and the predictive model employed explained between 23% and 51% of the variance in total deviance. Implications for crime and deviance in Switzerland are discussed.

Unlike the United States, Europe continues to wait for a decline in crime rates. So far, the evidence shows that crime rates across Europe are increasing or are stable at a relatively high level. These trends are derived from the international crime victimization surveys of 1989, 1992, and 1997 for a number of European countries (Mayhew &

AUTHORS' NOTE: *We would like to thank all Swiss schools, administrators, and students for their cooperation in this monumental undertaking. Thank you also to Lloyd Pickering and Lara Belliston at Auburn University for their assistance with data collection as well as to countless undergraduates in the Department of Human Development and Family Studies. This research was supported in part by a grant to the first author from the Competitive Research Grant-In-Aid Program, Office of the Vice President for Research, Auburn University, Auburn, AL. Please address all correspondence to the first author at the Department of Human Development and Family Studies, Auburn University, 284 Spidle Hall, Auburn, AL 36849; e-mail: vazsonyi@auburn.edu.*

van Dijk, 1997). England and Wales, according to police and British Crime Survey data, show a steadily increasing trend over the past 20 years (Langan & Farrington, 1998), with only 1997 showing a moderate decrease (Mirrlees-Black, Budd, Partridge, & Mayhew, 1998). For many years, Switzerland in particular was known as a low-crime country, an image largely reflected in Clinard's (1978) research. Although contested by later writers (Balvig, 1988), Clinard's conclusions were well supported by the results of the first international crime victimization survey of 1989, which showed this country to be at the low end among the 14 participating Western nations (van Dijk, Mayhew, & Killias, 1990). A recent comparison of police data and four surveys conducted in Switzerland between 1984 and 1998 showed quite consistent overall trends (Killias, Clerici, & Berruex, 1998). Rates of burglary and assault were about twice as high in 1996-1997 than a decade before, whereas theft of cars, motorcycles, and bikes showed stable or decreasing trends. Given the increase in most European countries during the same period, Switzerland continues to show rather moderate levels of serious crime such as burglary and violent crimes (Mayhew & van Dijk, 1997), although it is no longer among the countries with the lowest crime rates. In homicides, Switzerland even ranks at the European average, a position probably due to the wide availability of guns in private households; this is so despite the low levels of violence in general (Killias, 1995). With the exception of the United Kingdom (Langan & Farrington, 1998) and probably the Netherlands, crime in Europe continues to be substantially lower than in the United States; this is particularly true for homicides.

The first cross-national study of self-reported juvenile delinquency in Western countries (Junger-Tas, Terlouw, & Klein, 1994) allowed an assessment of Switzerland's position in detail. The Swiss sample, which consisted of a nationally representative random sample of 970 juveniles ages 14 to 20, showed relatively high levels of minor property offenses (particularly shoplifting) among Swiss youth (Killias, Villetaz, & Rabasa, 1994), as well as relatively widespread use of illicit soft and hard drugs (Killias & Ribeaud, 1999). However, violence was relatively rare, particularly if more serious forms of assault were considered—a finding that is consistent not only with comparisons based on victimization surveys, but also with a variety of police and other data collected in 10 European countries under the auspices of the Council of Europe (Council of Europe, 1995).

More recent evidence on violence in Switzerland suggests, however, that the picture seems to have changed. For example, in his analysis of police data, Eisner (1997, 1998) found substantially increasing crime trends, particularly among youth of immigrant background. This is consistent with national police statistics that show, particularly for the last few years, substantial increases in crimes committed by foreign nationals (adults of whom many are without residence in the country) and juveniles residing in Switzerland (Polizeiliche Kriminalstatistik, 1998). After a continuous increase over more than a decade, the proportion of foreign nationals among offenders known to the police has increased, from about 30% in 1983 to just over 50% in 1997. Regional statistics show quite similar recent trends (e.g., Fehr, 1998). For example, data suggest increases in crimes overall between 1996 and 1997 of almost 10%. Furthermore, data also suggest important increases in crimes perpetrated by youth between the ages of 18 and 20 years; also, 52% of all crimes were perpetrated by foreigners. These numbers are remarkable in light of 1990 data by the Council of Europe (1995) that show that Switzerland had by far the highest proportion of foreign nationals among offenders known to the police (or processed by the criminal justice system).

Switzerland's recent problems with crime, especially with violence, thus seem to be related to increasing offending rates among juveniles in general and young immigrants in particular. Therefore, the first goal of the present investigation is to identify and compare rates of deviance among native Swiss youth, second-generation immigrant youth, and young immigrants of the first generation. The second goal is to explain variability in deviance in all three groups by employing a predictive model that includes self-control and three types of perceived sanctions for norm-violating conduct. These variables are based on a control theory perspective as formulated by Gottfredson and Hirschi (1990) in their general theory of crime. Given the general nature of this theory and its independence of any particular cultural conditions, it requires multiple tests in as many cultural settings as possible. In the present research, our interest will be to see whether the same explanations, as derived from the theory, will hold not only for Swiss youth, but also for first- and second-generation immigrant youth residing in Switzerland.

IMMIGRATION AS A FACTOR IN SWISS CRIME

Over the last century, immigration to Switzerland has reached higher proportions than in any other European country. It started massively during the early 1950s, long before it became significant elsewhere in Europe. Therefore, it is an interesting context to study crime in relation to immigration, because there is not only a substantial number of foreign nationals of very different backgrounds, but also a significant second generation. Before 1980, several studies (summarized in Killias, 1997) consistently reached the conclusion that first-generation immigrants had crime rates lower than Swiss nationals of comparable backgrounds, and that the picture was somewhat less clear for juveniles belonging to the so-called second generation. During the 1980s, the picture seems to have changed in the sense that foreign nationals younger than age 30 became more frequently involved in offenses known to the police. Careful scrutiny allowed ruling out discrimination as an important source of this discrepancy (Killias, 1997). In addition, illegal immigration and abuse of asylum seekers' status became much more frequent in recent years, particularly after the beginning of the war in former Yugoslavia. Thus, an increasing proportion of foreign nationals registered as offenders in Swiss data are indeed not immigrants in the classic sense, but often come to the country with the prevailing project of committing certain criminal offenses (Killias, 1997). This increasing role of transnational crime may indeed offer a possible explanation of the absence of major decreases in crime in Switzerland and in Western Europe in general over the last few years.

The recent waves of massive immigration from former Yugoslavia and other countries of that region led to a major shift in the composition of Switzerland's population.[1] In 1984, three out of five immigrants originated from Switzerland's neighboring countries (Italy, France, Germany, and Austria; Killias, 1997), whereas in 1997, the proportion of these countries fell to 38%, with an increase in immigrants from former Yugoslavia to 23% (Swiss Federal Statistical

Office, 1999). These persons brought a considerable number of children and teenagers to the country. These youth encountered substantial problems at school and on the labor market, mostly due to language problems. Thus, the traditional second generation that was raised in the country no longer constitutes the only group of immigrant youth. There are also substantial numbers of first-generation immigrant youth. The very different life history and experiences to which these youth (summarized in Killias, 1997) were exposed is likely to be related to behavioral problems like deviance, drugs use, and delinquency.

The current investigation was conducted to study the significance of these experiences and to assess the role of control variables across the three groups. This is the only way to gather significant data on the personal situation and migration history of these youth. The present research will allow an assessment of the role of different migration experiences and cultural backgrounds on deviance for the first time. This is not to say that self-reported delinquency surveys comparing immigrants and Swiss nationals have not been conducted in Switzerland. Indeed, the Swiss sample of the international self-reported delinquency study (Junger-Tas, Terlouw, & Klein, 1994) addressed this particular issue. Findings suggested that foreign nationals had consistently lower delinquency rates than Swiss juveniles of the same age (Killias, Villetaz, & Rabasa, 1994). Methodological research conducted in the Netherlands (Junger, 1990) and, on a far larger scale, in the United States (Sampson & Lauritsen, 1997) allows consideration that self-reported delinquency rates among minorities may be systematically underestimated in comparison with rates from majority youth. A few other studies on drug abuse (summarized in Killias, 1997) in which the written interview method was used may have been less vulnerable to underestimates of deviance among minority youth—the differences between Swiss and foreign youth were more in line with official data. In other words, minority youth were overrepresented in drug offenses in comparison with majority adolescents. Despite these problems of differential validity of self-reported measures of delinquency in samples of majority and minority youth, the present research is important in the sense that it allows a comparison of rates of self-reported deviance in representative samples of immigrant (first and second generation) and Swiss youth; the current study includes data on more than 800 immigrant adolescents. It also allows an assessment of whether the same factors, derived from a control theory framework, are associated with deviance observed among first-generation immigrant youth, second-generation immigrants, and Swiss youth.

In the current section, a prediction model will be developed based on previous work from two primary areas of the research part of control theory. Prediction in this case is used in the sense of association or correlation because the current data are cross-sectional. The two areas of work were chosen because of their parsimony and generality or universality. These research areas and associated variables were included because we hypothesized that they should operate in a similar manner in different groups examined, independent of immigrant status.

A GENERAL THEORY OF CRIME: SELF-CONTROL

Gottfredson and Hirschi (1990) have proposed a testable theory of juvenile delinquency and later crime, namely self-control theory, which links the family context via proximal personality constructs to delinquency. The authors have suggested that early childhood socialization experiences in the family context are critical in establishing an individual's level of self-control. This is consistent with other research on children during early and middle childhood. Individual differences at these ages are highly predictive of later adolescent misconduct (e.g., Pulkkinen & Pitkänen, 1993). Pulkkinen (1982) has suggested that

> prosocial, or positive social, behavior can be understood as an expression of strong self-control in a constructive rather than a submissive way . . . Children are likely to be prosocial if they have nurturant and attentive parents who are good models of prosocial behavior, use reasoning in discipline, maintain high standards, reward cooperative behavior, and encourage their children to accept responsibility for others. (p. 70)

Gottfredson and Hirschi maintain that individual differences in levels of self-control explain the propensity to engage in norm-violating conduct. They also suggest that human beings are neither innately good nor bad, so individuals are not predisposed in any way to commit delinquent acts. Rather, given the right circumstances and opportunity, a large number of individuals would engage in less serious forms of delinquent behaviors. What makes individuals conform?

In their theory, Gottfredson and Hirschi (1990) have suggested that an individual who is consistently monitored by parents is more likely to develop internalized norms of conformity and higher levels of self-control; therefore, he or she is also less likely to engage in delinquent behaviors. This is also consistent with case studies done in the 1960s and 1970s that suggested that child-rearing practices contribute to the development of self-control personality patterns (e.g., Rawlings, 1973). Alternatively, someone who was left to his or her own devices and did not learn to delay gratification and plan for tomorrow, will be more likely to behave with little or no regard for fellow human beings and society at large. This person will be more likely to deviate given the right opportunity. According to the theory and research on personality development (e.g., Pulkkinen & Pitkanen, 1993), subsequent to early socialization experiences that occur primarily in the family context, the behavioral dimension of self-control becomes trait-like or stable and is highly predictive of later delinquent behaviors. Pulkkinen (1982) has found a continuity of 50% in levels of self-control over a period of 12 years. About half of her sample remained in high, average, and low groups over this period. She concluded that "the use of a large number of behavioral indicators in the analysis of individual differences revealed enduring individual tendencies in coping with impulses" (p. 101). Furthermore, she suggested that low self-control was associated with a selfish, parent-centered treatment of children, whereas average to high levels of self-control were related to child-centered guidance. Based on such work, Gottfredson and Hirschi suggest that an 11-year-old with low levels of self-control will be at greater risk of engaging in later delinquent behaviors, independent of current levels of aggression or involvement in delinquent behaviors. They also hypothesize that the self-control to delinquency relationship should be largely invariant across different populations.

A number of cross-sectional studies in the criminology literature have provided empirical evidence that self-control is negatively associated with self-reported and official delinquency (e.g., Arneklev, Grasmick, Tittle, & Bursick, 1993; Brownfield & Sorenson, 1993; Grasmick, Tittle, Bursick, & Arneklev, 1993; Longshore, Turner, & Stein, 1996; Piquero & Rosay, 1998; Vazsonyi, Pickering, Junger, &

Hessing, 2001). Conceptually, this means that an individual's level of self-control is highly correlated with delinquency and may be predictive of later delinquent conduct. Therefore, the current investigation includes a measure of self-control in the predictive model and examines whether self-control is predictive of different types of deviant behaviors for native Swiss youth, second-generation immigrant youth, and first-generation immigrant adolescents residing in Switzerland.

PERCEIVED SANCTIONS: CAPTURE,
GUILT/SHAME, AND EMBARRASSMENT

Gottfredson and Hirschi (1990) suggest that individuals who have been adequately socialized develop self-control. This trait-like quality effectively protects individuals from engaging in norm-violating conduct or deviance. When individuals have good self-control, they have internalized what is acceptable and unacceptable behavior in society, what is consistent with norms and what is not. It follows then that these individuals may have also developed a conscience that monitors their conduct. In effect, this conscience may regulate an individual's behavior, and furthermore, may evoke feelings of guilt or shame—personally, vis-á-vis parents or family members, or vis-á-vis others, such as close friends—if internal standards of appropriate conduct and behaviors are violated. Although this is not something Gottfredson and Hirschi explicitly discuss, this line of reasoning appears reasonable and consistent with their argument.

Perhaps the oldest method of preventing crimes and norm-violating conduct in a community is ostracism. Zippelius (1986) traces practices of community exclusion, shunning, and expulsion throughout history, from early Greek history, *atimia*, or "denying the outcast the protection of goods and life and leaving him with no alternative but flight abroad" (p. 161) to revocation of citizenship in more modern legal systems following a severe crime against the community. In a number of recent studies, Grasmick and colleagues (Grasmick, Blackwell, & Bursick, 1993; Grasmick, Blackwell, Bursick, & Mitchell, 1993; Grasmick & Bryjak, 1980; Grasmick & Bursick, 1990; Grasmick, Bursick, & Arneklev, 1993) tested the deterrent effects of perceived sanctions on norm-violating conduct, including interpersonal violence, drunk driving, theft, and tax evasion. In an attempt to overcome shortcomings of early work on the threat effects of legal sanctions on norm-violating conduct, which largely showed a very small effect, Grasmick and Bursick (1990) developed a broader strategy to assess the effects of sanctions.

Grasmick and Bursick (1990) hypothesized that both a person's conscience (internalized norms) and attachment to significant others (family members or friends) may also operate in deterring a person from engaging in norm-violating conduct. They suggest that "both conscience and significant others potentially influence criminality by decreasing the expected utility of crime" (p. 839). Thus, Grasmick and Bursik suggested that perceived shame or guilt following a norm-violating act could be considered "a form of self-imposed, or reflective punishment" (p. 840). Similarly, they suggest that perceived embarrassment by an actor vis-á-vis family members or friends may decrease the expected utility of crime. The implication of this informal social control mechanism is that a person may evaluate whether the loss of respect and the potential loss of friendship, support, and a relationship outweigh the benefits of committing a specific norm-violating act. In conclusion, Grasmick and Bursick suggested that three distinct costs may factor into the rational decision an actor may engage in when evaluating whether to comply with the law or social norms or not: state-imposed physical or material deprivation, self-imposed shame, and socially imposed embarrassment.

The goals of the current investigation are as follows: First, the study seeks to identify and compare rates of deviance among native Swiss youth, second-generation immigrant youth, and young immigrants of the first generation. Second, the study seeks to explain variability in deviance in all three groups by employing a predictive model that includes self-control and three types of perceived sanctions for norm-violating conduct.

METHOD

PARTICIPANTS

Data were collected from 4,018 Swiss adolescents who attended schools in a mid-sized city in eastern Switzerland, as part of the International Study of Adolescent Development (ISAD) (Vazsonyi & Pickering, 2000; Vazsonyi et al., 2001). Because the present study surveyed a student population and given that compulsory education ends at about age 15, those not attending school were not included in the population studied. According to 1990 census data, about 12% of juveniles ages 15 to 19 living in the region studied (Canton of St. Gallen) are not pursuing school beyond that age (Swiss Federal Statistical Office, 1997); for those ages 16 to 19, this figure is 14%. Although the resulting limitations must be kept in mind when interpreting the findings, especially because those not pursuing any form of education after age 16 are disproportionately female and of recent immigrant background, former research has also documented great difficulties in reaching this group by other methods, such as personal interviews (Killias et al., 1994).

About two thirds of the sample were apprentices, whereas one third were Gymnasium students or teacher's college students. This approximates the population composition by educational track (Swiss Federal Statistical Office, 1997). Of all 4,018 respondents, no parental birth information was available for 178 Swiss-born youth and 18 foreign-born youth. Neither personal nor parental information was available for an additional 222 participants. All participants with missing data on personal birth or parental birth history were excluded from the current study. The current investigation included all students who were 15 ($n = 150$), 16 ($n = 667$), 17 ($n = 854$), 18 ($n = 852$), and 19 ($n = 613$) years old, resulting in a final study sample of 3,136 (mean age = 17.86 years, $SD = 1.1$). Based on two items assessing the participant's birth country and parents' birth country, participants were categorized as native Swiss youth ($n = 2,338$, mean age = 17.84, $SD = 1.1$), second-generation immigrant youth ($n = 521$, mean age = 17.85, $SD = 1.1$; parents born abroad and respondent born in Switzerland), and first-generation immigrant youth ($n = 277$, mean age = 17.99, SD = 1.2; parents and participant born abroad).[2]

Of the 798 immigrant youth, the largest proportion indicated that their parents originated from a southern European country, such as Italy, Spain, or Portugal (39.5%), followed by a central European country (24.3%; e.g., Germany or Austria), an eastern European country (16.4%; e.g., Hungary, Poland, or former Yugoslavia), northern European countries (4.1%), the Far East (3.3%), the Middle East (2.9%), Africa or America (each 1.6%). A little more than 6% of the immigrant sample indicated that their parents were born in an "other" country. The final sample composition of native, second-, and first-generation youth slightly oversampled foreign youth (25%); recent national estimates suggest that about 15% of inhabitants of Switzerland are immigrants (Swiss Federal Statistical Office, 1997). Nevertheless, because group comparisons were the focus of the current study, no changes were made to the sample composition.

MEASURES

Immigrant Status

Immigrant status was determined by two single items: (a) "In which country were you born?" and (b) "In which country were your parents born?" Both items had the same 10 response categories: (a) Switzerland, (b) central Europe (e.g., Germany), (c) southern Europe (e.g., Italy, Spain, Portugal, Greece, etc.), (d) eastern Europe (e.g., Hungary, Rumania, Bulgaria, Poland, etc.), (e) northern and western Europe and Scandinavian countries (e.g., the Netherlands, Belgium, Norway, etc.), (f) America (e.g., North America, Canada, central America, and South America), (g) Africa, (h) Middle East (e.g., Syria, Israel, Iran, etc.), (i) Far East (e.g., India, Japan, China, etc.), and (j) other country. Three mutually exclusive categories were formed on the basis of these two items: Swiss (both respondent and parents were born in Switzerland), second-generation immigrants (parents born abroad and respondent born in Switzerland), and first-generation immigrant (parents and respondent born abroad).

Demographic Variables

A series of demographic questions assessed participants' backgrounds, including "Which of the following categories best applies to you?" Participants rated one of seven mutually exclusive categories: 1 = biological parents, 2 = biological mother only, 3 = biological father only, 4 = biological mother and stepfather, 5 = biological father and stepmother, 6 = biological parent and partner, and 7 = other persons. They also rated parental education for each parent individually: "What type of education does your father/stepfather/or male provider have?" Responses included 1 = does not apply, 2 = compulsory education, 3 = *Sekundarschule* (compulsory education), 4 = Sekundarschule and an apprenticeship, 5 = business diploma or additional education past the apprenticeship, 6 = *Gymnasium* or teacher's college, and 7 = college/university.

Participants also answered whether their parent(s) were employed: "Does your mother/stepmother/or female provider work?" Responses included "does not apply," "retired," "unemployed," "looking for work," "part-time work," "full-time work," and "multiple jobs." Finally, participants also rated an overall family income: "From the following options, please select an estimated annual income (*Bruttoeinkommen* = gross pay) of your family." There were five responses to choose from in Swiss Francs: 1 = 30,000 or less, 2 = 30,000k to 60,000, 3 = 60,000 to 90,000, 4 = 90,000 to 120,000, and 5 = 120,000+.

Deviance

Lifetime deviance was measured by the 55-item Normative Deviance Scale (NDS) newly developed for the ISAD project (Vazsonyi et al., 2001). The scale was developed to measure deviance in the general adolescent population, and therefore did not examine only status and index offenses. Rather in addition to those offenses, it also measured less serious forms of norm-violating conduct in the school context or simply while spending time with friends. This conceptualization of deviance is consistent with results from nationally representative data sets (e.g., the National Youth Survey; Huizinga, Menard, & Elliott, 1989) that show that more than 90% of sampled men and women indicate having committed at least one delinquent act. In addition, deviance was assessed employing a multiple-item, scalar approach. Very few such self-reported deviance scales with psychometric properties exist because most self-report instruments in criminology use single-item crime measures. The current investigation examined all seven subscales of the NDS (vandalism, alcohol, drugs, school misconduct, general deviance, theft, and assault). The appendix includes the items and subscales of the NDS. An overall deviance score was also computed by averaging all 55 items. Responses for all items on the NDS were given on a 5-point Likert-type scale and identified lifetime frequency of specific behaviors (1 = *never*, 2 = *one time*, 3 = *2-3 times*, 4 = *4-6 times*, and 5 = *more than 6 times*). Reliability coefficients on the different subscales for the entire sample ranged from $\alpha = .76$ to $\alpha = .90$. The total deviance score scale, which consisted of 55 items, was also very reliable ($\alpha = .96$).

Self-Control

Participants rated a 6-factor, 24-item measure assessing self-control (Grasmick et al., 1993). This measure is unique because it measures self-control independent of antisocial, aggressive, or delinquent behaviors. Items include "I often act out of the spur of the moment without stopping to think" or "Excitement and adventure are more important to me than security." Respondents rated each statement by selecting one of the following five ratings: 1 = *strongly disagree*, 2 = *disagree somewhat*, 3 = *neutral*, 4 = *agree somewhat*, and 5 = *strongly agree*. A self-control score was computed by taking the average of all 24 items. The self-control scale was reliable ($\alpha = .82$).

Perceived Sanctions

Perceived sanctions were assessed by a series of 24 items developed for the current investigation based on previous conceptual and measurement work by Grasmick and Bursick (1990). Three sets of eight items measured the likelihood of getting caught, perceived guilt/shame, and potential loss of respect by people who mattered/are close on a series of descriptions of deviant behaviors. Deviant behaviors ranged from acts of vandalism ("smashing bottles on the street or damaging a street sign") to assault ("using a weapon, e.g., a knife, gun, blunt object, or stick, to hit someone or to injure them"). Specific questions were as follows: "Do you think someone would find out if you . . . ," "Would you feel guilty, shameful, or would you regret if you . . . ," and "Would most people, whose opinion is important to you, lose respect if you . . . ?" The following responses format was employed: 1 = *absolutely not*, 2 = *probably would not*, 3 = *probably would*, and 4 = *definitely would*. Three scale scores were computed by taking the average of all eight items in the section. Reliability estimates suggested that each scale was internally consistent (α range = .83 for "finding out" to α = .89 for "loss of respect").

PROCEDURE

A standard data collection protocol was followed at all study locations. The protocol was approved by a university institutional review board and consisted of a self-report data collection instrument, which included instructions on how to complete the survey, a description of the ISAD project, and assurances of anonymity and confidentiality. Much attention was given to the development of the ISAD survey instrument, particularly by developing new or employing existing measures that could be used cross-culturally without losing nuances or changing meanings. The survey was translated and back-translated by a bilingual translator whose native language was German. Surveys were examined by additional bilingual translators and when translation was difficult or ambiguous, consensus was used to produce the final translation.

The questionnaires were administered to all participants during a 1- to 2-hour period. All students were invited to participate in the study. A small number of questionnaires that were less than 50% complete were not used for further evaluation and were excluded from the study. Participation rates were 76% at the Swiss apprenticeship training school (Gewerbliche Berufsschule) and 89% at the Swiss Gymnasium and teacher's college. Participation was comparatively low in the apprenticeship training school because individuals who completed schooling in the evenings were not invited by the school administration to complete a survey. Also, some apprentices were simply not available during the 2-week data-collection period or did not take classes at the time of the data collection. Finally, because the apprenticeship training school had instruction for predominantly male professions, the sample collected at this study site was disproportionately male (70%).

Design and Analysis

In a first set of analyses, background and demographic variables were compared by immigrant status (Swiss, second-generation immigrants, and first-generation immigrants). Next, representative items assessing adolescent deviance were compared by immigrant status and gender; more specifically, rates of participation were compared (i.e., what number of adolescents in each group indicated some participation). Third, mean deviance scores (vandalism, alcohol, drugs, school misconduct, general deviance, theft, assault, and total deviance measure) were compared by immigrant status and gender using one-way ANOVA with post hoc Scheffé contrasts. The same analytical approach was then used to compare differences in levels of self-control and perceived sanctions (likelihood of getting caught, perceived guilt, and loss of respect by people who mattered) by immigrant status and gender. Finally, different types of deviant conduct were predicted in a series of set hierarchical regression analyses. For these analyses, the described predictive model was employed and compared by immigrant status and gender in an attempt to establish whether the efficiency of the predictive model differed as a function of immigration status. Because of the trait-like quality of the self-control construct, it was entered first in regressions; all three measures of perceived sanctions were entered second in a set.

RESULTS

Table 1 includes the results of initial frequency comparisons on the home situation, parental educational level, parental employment, and family income by immigrant status. A very similar number of adolescents reported two biological parent homes in all three groups (84%, 83%, and 81% for Swiss youth, second generation, and first generation, respectively). Significant differences were found for parental educational attainment. In particular, whereas 40% of Swiss mothers completed an apprenticeship and 22.4% completed additional educa-tion beyond that, only 24% of second-generation and 11% of first-generation immigrants completed an apprenticeship, and 22.5% and 26.7% of first-generation immigrants) completed "additional" educa-tion. More than 9% of first-generation immigrant mothers completed some university study, as compared to 5.7% in second-generation immigrant and only 3.2% of Swiss mothers. A similar pattern emerged on paternal education, although differences were less pro-nounced. Almost an equal percentage of fathers completed university study in all three groups. Slightly more Swiss mothers worked in this sample, especially as compared with first-generation immigrants. Twice as many Swiss mothers than second-generation immigrants reported multiple jobs; there were three times as many Swiss mothers working multiple jobs as compared with first-generation immigrants. Substantial differences also emerged in overall family income. About one seventh (14.1%) of Swiss families enjoyed an income of 120,000 Swiss Francs or more as compared with 11% of second-generation immigrants and 9% of first-generation immigrants. Although 22.3% of Swiss families reported an income of 60,000 or fewer Swiss Francs per year, 33.8% second-generation immigrants and 47.7% of first-generation immigrants did the same. To further examine these differ-ences, one-way ANOVA with Scheffé post hoc contrasts were com-pleted for maternal and paternal education as well as family income by immigrant status; these analyses were completed separately for men and for women. For men, a significant mean level difference was found between Swiss youth ($M = 3.37$; $SD = 1.36$) and first-genera-tion immigrants ($M = 3.04$; $SD = 1.49$). A significant mean level dif-ference was also found for maternal education, although no contrasts reached statistical significance. Finally, all three groups significantly differed from each other on the measure of family income (Swiss, $M = 3.35$, $SD = 1.06$; second-generation immigrants, $M = 2.96$, $SD = 1.12$; and first-generation immigrants, $M = 2.62$, $SD = 1.08$). In con-trast, female groups did not differ on any of the three measures of social status.

In a next step, responses in individual deviance items were com-pared by immigrant status and gender. Table 2 includes frequencies of

TABLE 1: Descriptive Statistics of Demographic Variables by Immigrant Status and Gender (in percentages)

	Immigrant Status		
Demographic Variable	Swiss (n = 2,321)	Second Generation (n = 517)	First Generation (n = 274)
Home situation			
Two biological parents	84.1	83.1	80.7
One biological parent (only)	8.1	9.8	7.3
One stepparent	3.1	3.7	4.4
Other (e.g., biological parent & significant other, etc.)	4.7	3.4	7.6
Parental education			
Mother			
Realschule/sekundarschule (9-year compulsory education)	35.7	45.0	55.9
Lehre (3- or 4- year apprenticeship training)	40.0	24.0	10.7
Handelsdiplom/weiterbildung (business degree/postsecondary education)	7.5	7.7	10.7
Gymnasium/lehrerseminar (university prep./teacher's college)	11.7	9.1	6.7
Universität (college/university)	3.2	5.7	9.3
Father			
Realschule/sekundarschule (9-year compulsory education)	28.9	34.3	45.5
Lehre (3- or 4- year apprenticeship training)	30.8	24.2	14.5
Handelsdiplom/weiterbildung (business degree/postsecondary education)	15.6	10.8	5.8
Gymnasium/Lehrerseminar (university prep./teacher's college)	6.6	3.5	4.0
Universität (college/university)	14.9	16.7	16.4
Parental employment			
Mother			
Not working (retired, currently looking for work)	23.4	21.8	35.7
Part-time work	50.4	43.7	22.0
Full-time work	19.2	30.0	38.6
Multiple jobs	6.0	3.1	2.2
Father			
Not working (retired, currently looking for work)	2.6	8.6	10.4
Part-time work	1.5	2.3	5.1
Full-time work	85.6	80.0	74.0
Multiple jobs	7.1	4.4	3.6

(continued)

TABLE 1 Continued

	Immigrant Status		
Demographic Variable	Swiss (n = 2,321)	Second Generation (n = 517)	First Generation (n = 274)
Family income (Swiss francs)			
30,000 or less	3.0	6.5	13.0
30,000 to 60,000	19.3	27.3	34.7
60,000 to 90,000	33.3	33.8	27.4
90,000 to 120,000	21.7	15.4	12.6
120,000 or more	14.1	10.9	9.0

NOTE: Percentages are based on those who answered because the question applied to them. Participants were given the option to answer "Does not apply" for parental education and employment; these figures are not included in the table and make up the difference between the sum of all categories and 100%.

total students who admitted to committing a behavior at least once and a p level from the chi-square test. Analyses were completed separately for men and for women. Very few important differences emerged in female comparisons. In fact, only two chi-square statistics reached significance in 10 comparisons. Second-generation female youth were more likely to have beat up a person who subsequently required medical attention and were more likely to have used a weapon in a fight. In male comparisons, all chi-square values reached statistical significance with the exceptions of major theft, hitting another person, and frequency of drinking hard liquor. A similar pattern emerged for male youth in items assessing greatest interpersonal violence, namely that second-generation immigrants indicated the greatest frequency of serious violence (beating up a person or using a weapon in a fight), closely followed by first-generation adolescents. For hard drug use, first-generation immigrant youth reported the highest level, followed by second-generation immigrant youth. Swiss youth reported the greatest consumption of alcohol and were very similar to second-generation immigrants on minor theft. This was also the case with soft drug use, hard liquor consumption, and vandalism; however, in all four cases, second-generation immigrants scored slightly higher than Swiss youth, who in turn scored higher than first-generation immigrants.

TABLE 2: Chi-Square Tests of Percentage of Adolescents Reporting Participation in Select Deviant Behavior Items by Immigrant Status (in percentages)

Deviant Behavior	Male (n = 1,916)				Female (n = 1,151)			
	Swiss (n = 1,412)	Second Generation (n = 337)	First Generation (n = 212)	p	Swiss (n = 909)	Second Generation (n = 180)	First Generation (n = 62)	p
Smash bottles	68.5	73.0	62.7	.050	33.6	37.2	33.7	ns
Drink hard liquor	70.4	73.2	62.9	ns	57.2	60.7	51.6	ns
Drink alcohol	82.7	80.8	69.5	.001	72.7	74.2	65.1	ns
Use soft drugs	52.6	56.2	45.9	.000	38.9	47.5	37.1	ns
Use hard drugs	12.0	15.0	20.6	.018	5.3	6.1	1.6	ns
Steal (minor)	62.7	66.4	49.0	.004	42.4	52.2	38.7	ns
Steal (major)	17.5	23.6	20.9	ns	3.3	5.6	.0	ns
Hit another person	68.5	68.9	65.9	ns	45.1	45.6	33.9	ns
Beat up person (medical attention)	18.5	31.4	30.7	.000	3.2	7.8	1.6	.001
Use a weapon (for a fight)	18.6	24.8	21.6	.028	2.5	5.0	3.2	.011

NOTE: Numbers in this table represent the percentage of students in each group who answered that they have participated in this activity.

347

Subsequent one way ANOVA on the deviance measure subscales and the total deviance scale further substantiated initial frequency comparisons. Because of observed differences by gender in the frequency comparisons, all subsequent analyses were completed separately for male and female youth. Table 3 includes the results of one way ANOVA with post hoc Scheffé contrasts by immigrant status. In only one case were female immigrants significantly more deviant than Swiss youth, namely school misconduct. Second-generation youth were more deviant than Swiss youth and first-generation immigrants. Two more significant mean level differences were found employing post hoc Scheffé contrasts: second-generation immigrants were more deviant on the "general" and on the "vandalism" measure. Only 7 of 24 significant mean level contrasts were found for male youth. Second-generation immigrants were more likely to commit acts of vandalism, more likely to misbehave in school, more likely to engage in general deviance, and more deviant overall (total deviance measure) than Swiss youth. Second-generation immigrant youth were also more likely to use drugs, engage in general deviance, and overall, were more deviant on the total deviance measure than first-generation immigrants.

In the last series of one-way ANOVA, elements from the predictive model, self-control, get caught, shame/guilt, and loss of respect, were compared by immigrant status for male and for female youth. Table 4 includes the results of these analyses. No statistically significant mean level differences were found for men; two were found for women. In comparison with second-generation immigrant youth, Swiss women indicated that they would perceive more guilt/ shame if committing a deviant act. Also, Swiss youth indicated a greater likelihood that they would get caught than did their first-generation immigrant peers.

Finally, in a series of set hierarchical regression analyses, each type of deviance—vandalism, alcohol use, drug use, school misconduct, general deviance, theft, and assault—and a total deviance score were predicted by a model that included three measures of social status, namely maternal and paternal education, family income, and self-control, and three measures of perceived sanctions. In a first step, the three measures of social status were entered; in the second step, self-control was entered; and in the final step, the three measures of perceived sanctions were entered. The predictive strength by each set of vari-

TABLE 3: One-Way ANOVA of Deviance Scales and Total Deviance by Immigrant Status

Deviance Measure	Males (n = 1,916)								Females (n = 1,151)							
	Swiss (n = 1,412)		Second Generation (n = 337)		First Generation (n = 212)				Swiss (n = 909)		Second Generation (n = 180)		First Generation (n = 62)			
	M	SD	M	SD	M	SD	F	p	M	SD	M	SD	M	SD	F	p
Vandalism	1.81	0.77	1.95	0.83	1.83	0.86	4.01	.02[a]	1.32	0.42	1.39	0.52	1.23	0.30	3.83	.02[c]
Alcohol	2.33	0.95	2.37	0.98	2.19	1.00	2.28	.10	1.86	0.81	1.91	0.80	1.84	0.83	0.31	.73
Drug use	2.28	1.13	2.38	1.20	2.08	1.14	4.56	.01[b*, c]	1.87	0.81	1.79	0.94	1.89	0.99	1.20	.30
School misconduct	2.10	0.77	2.24	0.81	2.13	0.90	4.16	.02[a]	2.01	0.66	2.19	0.74	1.87	0.70	7.50	.00[a, c]
General deviance	2.10	0.75	2.23	0.81	2.06	0.81	4.48	.01[a, c]	1.69	0.50	1.73	0.58	1.55	0.45	3.10	.05[c]
Theft	1.67	0.80	1.79	0.92	1.61	0.89	3.55	.03[c*]	1.30	0.45	1.39	0.54	1.25	0.42	3.40	.04[a*]
Assault	1.77	0.73	1.86	0.80	1.79	0.86	2.11	.12	1.32	0.43	1.38	0.55	1.23	0.38	2.70	.07[c*]
Total deviance	2.06	0.72	2.17	0.77	2.00	0.80	4.39	.01[a, c]	1.67	0.51	1.76	0.56	1.58	0.46	3.40	.03[c*]

NOTE: Superscripts represent statistically significant Scheffé post hoc comparisons.
a. Swiss versus second-generation immigrants.
b. Swiss versus first-generation immigrants.
c. Second- vs. first-generation immigrants.
*$p < .01$.

TABLE 4: One-Way ANOVA of Self-Control and Perceived Sanctions by Immigrant Status

	Male (n = 1,916)								Female (n = 1,151)							
	Swiss (n = 1,412)		Second Generation (n = 337)		First Generation (n = 212)		F	p	Swiss (n = 909)		Second Generation (n = 180)		First Generation (n = 62)		F	p
	M	SD	M	SD	M	SD			M	SD	M	SD	M	SD		
Self-control	3.51	0.41	3.50	0.43	3.49	0.44	0.24	.79	3.60	0.34	3.60	0.38	3.53	0.49	1.13	.32
Get caught	2.40	0.61	2.41	0.65	2.33	0.78	1.32	.27	2.63	0.56	2.54	0.53	2.43	0.80	5.01	.01[b]
Shame/guilt	2.73	0.78	2.62	0.81	2.68	0.91	2.22	.11	3.14	0.65	2.99	0.69	3.17	0.77	4.05	.02[a]
Loss of respect	2.75	0.79	2.75	0.80	2.76	0.90	0.02	.98	2.96	0.68	2.91	0.71	2.92	0.92	0.60	.55

NOTE: Superscripts represent statistically significant Scheffé post hoc comparisons.
a. Swiss versus second-generation immigrants.
b. Swiss versus first-generation immigrants.

ables was evaluated by computing an R^2 change score with an associated F change score and p values. Table 5 includes the results of this analysis for male youth, and Table 6 includes the results of analyses on female youth.

Social status was found predictive of deviance primarily for male youth, although these variables never reached significance for first-generation male immigrant youth. Social status accounted for 1% to 2% of the variance in deviance for Swiss youth; for second-generation immigrants, the three variables accounted for between 4% and 10%. Social status was not statistically significant for female youth, with the exception of school misconduct; therefore, again, social status was not statistically significant for first-generation immigrants.

Both measures of self-control and measures of perceived sanctions for deviant behaviors were highly predictive of all deviance subscales and total deviance. Self-control accounted for 13.2% of Swiss men (12.2%, Swiss women) of the variance explained in total deviance , whereas perceived sanctions explained 20.7% for Swiss men (23.5%, Swiss women). For second-generation immigrants, the variables accounted for 22.1% (27.7%) and 17.8% (23.1%). For first-generation immigrants, self-control accounted for 11.9% (16.3%) of the variance and perceived sanctions accounted for 11.0% (7.1%). The final model including all three sets of variables accounted for a substantial amount of variance in the total deviance score. For Swiss male youth, it accounted for 36% of variability; for second-generation immigrants, the model accounted for 48%, whereas for first-generation immigrants, it accounted for 23%. Similar findings emerged for the amount of variance explained in female total deviance: 36% for Swiss, 51% for second-generation immigrants, and 16% for first-generation immigrants.

For male youth (female youth), the model accounted for the least amount of total variance predicting assault, namely 18% (5%), 28% (12%), and 12% (not significant) respectively. None of the steps of the model reached significance for first-generation female immigrants. It is also noteworthy that most regression models for first-generation immigrants did not reach statistical significance, perhaps largely due to small sample size and low statistical power. Furthermore, variability in the predictors did not seem to account for as much variability in

(text continues on p. 356)

TABLE 5: Set Hierarchical Regression Analyses Predicting Male Deviance With Self-Control and Perceived Sanctions by Immigrant Status

	Swiss (n = 1,412)			Second Generation (n = 337)			First Generation (n = 212)		
	R^2	F	p	R^2	F	p	R^2	F	p
Vandalism									
Step 1	.012	5.020	.002	.057	4.820	.003	.004	0.180	.907
Step 2	.107	145.550	.000	.260	91.370	.000	.121	19.990	.000
Step 3	.165	91.540	.000	.090	11.980	.000	.092	5.510	.001
Total R^2	.284			.407			.213		
Alcohol									
Step 1	.023	9.390	.000	.095	8.460	.000	.033	1.670	.177
Step 2	.084	112.240	.000	.103	30.710	.000	.062	9.890	.002
Step 3	.117	59.940	.000	.098	11.030	.000	.125	7.550	.000
Total R^2	.224			.296			.187		
Drug use									
Step 1	.010	3.890	.009	.063	5.360	.001	.039	1.980	.119
Step 2	.081	105.660	.000	.108	31.170	.000	.057	9.110	.003
Step 3	.162	86.170	.000	.188	23.200	.000	.078	4.440	.005
Total R^2	.253			.359			.135		
School misconduct									
Step 1	.024	9.900	.000	.044	3.680	.013	.018	0.890	.446
Step 2	.082	109.920	.000	.173	53.150	.000	.077	12.280	.001
Step 3	.110	55.860	.000	.078	8.710	.000	.054	3.010	.032
Total R^2	.216			.295			.131		

General Deviance

Step 1	.014	5.760	.001	.097	8.600	.000	.011	0.520	.672
Step 2	.110	149.230	.000	.190	63.980	.000	.139	23.510	.000
Step 3	.142	76.470	.000	.124	16.590	.000	.082	5.020	.002
Total R^2	.266			.411			.221		

Theft

Step 1	.007	2.950	.032	.035	2.900	.036	.019	0.910	.437
Step 2	.087	115.210	.000	.141	40.980	.000	.081	13.000	.000
Step 3	.176	95.680	.000	.180	22.070	.000	.078	4.460	.005
Total R^2	.270			.356			.156		

Assault

Step 1	.015	5.990	.000	.065	5.570	.001	.006	0.310	.816
Step 2	.086	114.120	.000	.099	28.530	.000	.041	6.210	.014
Step 3	.076	36.440	.000	.114	12.470	.000	.083	4.500	.005
Total R^2	.177			.278			.124		

Total Deviance

Step 1	.017	7.040	.000	.085	7.480	.000	.024	1.210	.308
Step 2	.132	185.200	.000	.221	76.530	.000	.119	19.950	.000
Step 3	.207	127.410	.000	.178	27.310	.000	.110	6.930	.000
Total R^2	.356			.484			.229		

NOTE: Step 1 in the regression equation included maternal education, paternal education, and family income; Step 2 included self-control; and Step 3 included the three perceived sanctions scales. Nonsignificant R^2 values at $p < .05$ were not included in the total R^2 value.

TABLE 6: Set Hierarchical Regression Analyses Predicting Female Deviance With Self-Control and Perceived Sanctions by Immigrant Status

	Swiss (n = 909)			Second Generation (n = 180)			First Generation (n = 62)		
	R^2	F	p	R^2	F	p	R^2	F	p
Vandalism									
Step 1	.000	0.110	.953	.002	0.080	.970	.060	0.930	.435
Step 2	.093	76.680	.000	.227	40.590	.000	.016	0.720	.400
Step 3	.125	39.910	.000	.092	6.130	.001	.075	1.180	.328
Total R^2	.218			.319					
Alcohol									
Step 1	.001	0.140	.935	.039	1.870	.138	.038	0.580	.633
Step 2	.086	70.720	.000	.225	42.060	.000	.193	10.800	.002
Step 3	.167	55.740	.000	.118	8.610	.000	.077	1.490	.232
Total R^2	.253			.343			.193		
Drug Use									
Step 1	.002	0.600	.613	.035	1.680	.173	.111	1.840	.154
Step 2	.085	69.470	.000	.151	25.520	.000	.074	3.920	.054
Step 3	.201	70.070	.000	.273	22.660	.000	.079	1.440	.247
Total R^2	.286			.424			.074		
School Misconduct									
Step 1	.079	21.530	.000	.087	4.400	.005	.229	4.350	.009
Step 2	.060	52.260	.000	.148	26.700	.000	.025	1.450	.235
Step 3	.089	28.730	.000	.171	12.980	.000	.046	0.870	.465
Total R^2	.228			.406			.229		

	ΔR²	F	p	ΔR²	F	p	ΔR²	F	p
General Deviance									
Step 1	.002	0.410	.744	.015	0.730	.537	.053	0.820	.491
Step 2	.089	73.150	.000	.245	45.780	.000	.202	11.670	.001
Step 3	.173	58.400	.000	.142	10.680	.000	.077	1.540	.219
Total R^2	.262			.387			.202		
Theft									
Step 1	.009	2.290	.078	.007	0.330	.802	.035	0.540	.661
Step 2	.062	50.090	.000	.112	17.630	.000	.185	10.230	.003
Step 3	.139	43.730	.000	.077	4.330	.006	.062	1.150	.341
Total R^2	.201			.189			.185		
Assault									
Step 1	.003	0.750	.521	.041	2.000	.117	.063	0.990	.407
Step 2	.029	22.480	.000	.116	18.960	.000	.005	0.230	.632
Step 3	.020	5.250	.001	.033	1.850	.141	.156	2.690	.059
Total R^2	.049			.116					
Total Deviance									
Step 1	.007	1.810	.144	.031	1.470	.227	.108	1.780	.164
Step 2	.122	105.460	.000	.277	55.170	.000	.163	9.590	.003
Step 3	.235	92.070	.000	.231	22.540	.000	.071	1.450	.244
Total R^2	.357			.508			.163		

NOTE: Step 1 in the regression equation included maternal education, paternal education, and family income; Step 2 included self-control; and Step 3 included the three perceived sanctions scales. Nonsignificant R^2 values at $p < .05$ were not included in the total R^2 value.

356   CRIMINAL JUSTICE AND BEHAVIOR

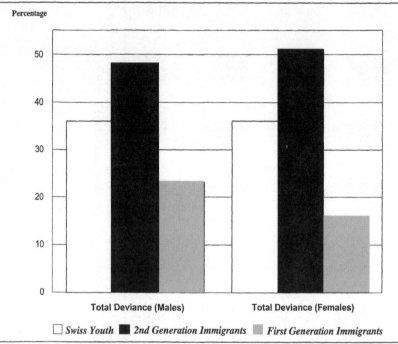

Figure 1:   Amount of Total Variance Explained in Male and Female Total Deviance by Immigrant Status.

deviance of first-generation immigrant youth as compared with Swiss or second-generation immigrant youth. Figure 1 summarizes the total amount of variance explained in male and female total deviance by immigrant status.

DISCUSSION

DEVIANT CONDUCT BY IMMIGRANT STATUS

A number of important findings emerged from the current investigation. First, second-generation immigrant youth residing in Switzerland consistently reported the highest levels of deviant conduct for both male and female adolescents. Even on variables for which no statistically significant differences were found, the same trend or pattern of mean deviance levels was observed. This finding is consistent with recent figures comparing rates of crime and convictions in the native Swiss population versus the immigrant population (Bundesamt für Statistik, 2000). In particular, we found significantly greater male vandalism, male and female school misconduct, male general deviance, and male total deviance in comparison with Swiss youth. Second-generation immigrant male youth were also significantly higher on total deviance scores than first-generation male immigrants. Finally, second-generation female immigrants were significantly higher on measures of vandalism, school misconduct, and general deviance than first-generation female adolescents. This suggests that male and female immigrant youth who were born in Switzerland and presumably enjoyed most of their socialization there, were more deviant than Swiss adolescents and that they were more deviant than foreign-born youth. All observed differences were found on less serious forms of deviance, such as vandalism and school misconduct as opposed to theft and assault behaviors. It is also noteworthy that most differences were rather small in magnitude and therefore limited from a functional standpoint. Nevertheless, these findings are consistent with some previous work in Europe based on official records (reviewed in Killias, 1989) but inconsistent with most studies based on self-reported delinquency, including a previous study on this subject in Switzerland (Killias et al., 1994). It may be that the cultural response bias, as assessed by Junger (1990) using the reverse-record check method in a study comparing Dutch, Surinamese, Turkish, and Moroccan juveniles in the Netherlands, affects delinquency and deviance measures less in a written interview situation than in the case of personal interviews. Alternatively, it is also plausible that second-generation immigrant youth in this study were simply overreporting their rates of deviance in comparison with the other two groups. It is interesting that these individuals reported slightly lower levels of internalized sanctions of shame and guilt in comparison with Swiss youth and even first-generation immigrant youth, which might mean lower levels of socialization. Unfortunately, we did not have official data to further test some of these ideas. Furthermore, the current investigation did not examine whether mean level differences in predictors used in the model could account for mean level differences in observed deviance. Subsequent efforts will likely further examine this issue.

Second, the absence of differences between first-generation immigrant and Swiss youths, particularly with respect to more serious acts, is unexpected in light of previous work based on official crime data, which showed rapidly increasing violence rates among immigrant youth during the 1990s and comparatively stable (and much lower) rates for Swiss adolescents (Eisner, 1998). Preliminary findings from the 1998 Swiss Crime Victimization Survey (Killias & Berruex, 1999) and from previous crime surveys (summarized in Killias, 1997) suggest that the disproportionate crime rates among immigrants in police statistics are probably real and not a matter of differential reporting. How can these conflicting pictures be reconciled? In projecting future trends, Killias (1997) concluded,

> There may be little basis for concern for the future of the second generation as long as Switzerland's public schools are able successfully to integrate immigrant children, that is, to equip them adequately for the Swiss labor market and as long as jobs will be available in sufficient number and quality. (p. 400)

He further noted that the major concerns should lie with immigrants who illegally enter the country. In the present study, however, only youths who attended noncompulsory schools were included, most of whom implied that they had to fulfill some basic intellectual and disciplinary requirements. This means that the present study covered those who succeeded at least to some extent at school and might successfully enter the Swiss labor market in a few years. Thus, those who came recently to the country—often after the age of compulsory schooling—and who lack any chance to enter existing educational tracks or the labor market, have not been included. It may be this more marginal and problematic group that disproportionately contributes to increasing trends in serious crime among immigrant youths. Based on a study evaluating youth who participated in a nationwide health risks survey in Switzerland, Michaud, Ferron, and Narring (1996) concluded that absentee students—those who did not attend school regularly or at all (about 5% in their study)—"were much more prone to risk-taking behavior than their peers" (p. 378). Although we have no data to indicate the exact size of this group in the current study, this issue is a limitation and qualifies the findings presented here.

Acculturation and Strain Effects

Previous explanations and findings have led to the belief that immigrant youth who have resided longer in a host country were more likely to conform with the host nation's norms and mores. Based on Dutch, British, and Swiss data that suggest that minority youth are less delinquent than indigenous youth, Junger-Tas (1997) hypothesized that immigrant youth who have acculturated and integrated into their host culture would be approximately equally likely to engage in norm-violating conduct as adolescents from the host country. This is a very plausible explanation; however, it is not supported by the findings in the current investigation. In fact, youth of immigrant parents, who had been born in Switzerland and enjoyed most or all of their education and socialization in Switzerland, were more deviant than Swiss youth. These adolescents were also consistently more deviant than unacculturated, first-generation immigrant youth who only recently arrived in the country.

Based on the current data, one alternative explanation is that youth who arrive in Switzerland are largely similar in their rates of deviance. Subsequently, due to differences in economic opportunities and success, second-generation immigrants are at greater risk of engaging in norm-violating conduct than both first-generation immigrants and Swiss natives. Based on ideas by Merton, these youth develop the greatest motivation to resort to illegitimate means to achieve cultural goals of success. Empirical tests of Merton's strain theory have produced mixed support (Kornhauser, 1978; Wilson & Herrnstein, 1985). Considering the plausibility of the strain idea in the current study, we find in the current study that the highest proportion of university-educated fathers were found in second-generation immigrant families, although only very small differences existed among all three (Swiss, 14.9%; second-generation, 16.7%; and first-generation, 16.4%). It is interesting that in this representative study, fathers of immigrants appear to be more educated in both immigrant groups in comparison with Swiss fathers. Similar findings can be observed for mothers, although the difference of a higher education was much more dramatic, once again favoring immigrant youth (Swiss, 3.2%; second-generation, 5.7%; and first-generation, 9.3%). Although significant mean level differences were found between Swiss youth and first-generation immigrants on parental education as well as differences on self-reported family income, where Swiss youth reported the highest level followed by second-generation youth and first-generation youth, social status accounted for the greatest amount of variability in deviance for second-generation immigrant youth. Part of the problem in the current study was the relatively small number of first-generation immigrant youth: a larger number would have allowed a more complete assessment of the impact of social status on deviance. This latter finding suggests that differences within the second-generation immigrant youth group on measures of social status accounted for a substantial amount of variability despite the fact that social status explained very little variability in Swiss youth.

It is quite possible that some immigrants acculturate in their new country and become successful in Switzerland more quickly than others, especially those who arrive in Switzerland with only menial labor skills. This might be illustrated in the current study by slightly greater variability in measures of social status as well as sanctions for second-generation immigration youth. For this latter group, it would be very difficult to acculturate and be successful—at least at the high level that the Swiss are generally accustomed to. Therefore, this might partially account for the large explanatory power of social status for second-generation immigrants. We need to point out that the explanatory power is greatest despite some nonsignificant mean level differences on the predictor variables, as mean level differences and the rank ordering of data are independent. Also, the current study did not conclude the importance of social status across groups and whether differences between groups accounted for differences in behavioral outcomes—it simply examined the predictive power of social status within each group.

Observed similarities in rates of deviance among the three groups should not come as a great surprise. Given the relative similarity of the three groups in social status and educational attainment, second- and even first-generation immigrants included in this study are typically those who have, to some extent at least, successfully been socialized into Swiss social life. Because most crime theories developed in the United States, including community-level explanations as formulated by Sampson and Lauritsen (1997), suggest explanations for groups who differ very markedly on a number of important independent variables, the absence of much difference in deviance and delinquency in the three groups in this study is, ultimately, not inconsistent with these theories. Rather, our findings suggest that delinquency, and serious acts in particular, can be relatively successfully prevented if minority youths get a fair chance to integrate into the general society through adequate educational and job opportunities. Nevertheless, because of the large-scale, population-based, epidemiological approach of this study to adolescent deviance, very seriously deviant individuals—those not attending school—were not closely investigated. Although the current approach lends itself to valid and important generalizations about different groups within a study, it does not allow an emphasis on and conclusions about the outliers in the deviancy distribution. Thus, it is quite possible that small numbers of more seriously criminal and deviant individuals reside in the first-generation immigrant youth group, for example. However, this was not the goal or emphasis of the current investigation.

Control Theory Model

Some interesting similarities and differences emerged from the predictive model by immigrant status. As hypothesized, all three sets of variables—social status, self-control, and perceived sanctions—accounted for variability in adolescent deviant conduct, although social status was largely unimportant in women and in first-generation immigrants. The predictive model generally worked in a similar manner in all three groups, although it accounted for the least amount of variance in both male and female first-generation immigrants. The model accounted for the highest level of variance in less serious forms of deviance and the least level in the most serious forms of deviancy (e.g., assault). Given that few important mean level differences were observed in levels of self-control or in levels of perceived sanctions among the three groups, other unmeasured or untested variables seem to have played an important part in explaining adolescent deviance, especially in first-generation immigrant youth. For example, it is possible that because first-generation immigrant youth reported the lowest levels of deviance, in effect, the least amount of variability could be explained. Again, another issue about first-generation immigrants in the current study is the relatively small sample size, especially for women.

In conclusion, the current investigation contributes to our understanding of immigration and crime in Switzerland in two important ways. First, few differences on measures of deviance emerged between Swiss youth, second-generation immigrant youth, and first-generation immigrants in this study, although second-generation immigrants reported greater involvement in deviant behavior than both first-generation immigrant youth and Swiss youth. Related to this, it appears that youth who are pursuing some form of education during middle and late adolescence are quite conforming, which suggests that social integration may have been partially achieved through integration at school. Second, control theory as tested appears to be tenable across the adolescent groups in the current investigation. This suggests that the theory and related explanatory constructs are generalizable across different countries as well as across different adolescent populations within a country.

APPENDIX
The Normative Deviance Scale (NDS)

Vandalism: Have you ever . . .
    Smashed bottles on the street, school grounds, or other areas?
    Intentionally damaged or destroyed property belonging to your parents or other family members (e.g., brothers or sisters)?
    Intentionally damaged or destroyed property belonging to a school, college, or university?
    Intentionally damaged or destroyed other property (e.g., signs, windows, mailboxes, parking meter, etc.) that did not belong to you?
    Intentionally damaged or destroyed property belonging to your employer or at your workplace?
    Slashed or in any way damaged seats on a bus, in a movie theater, or something at another public place?
    Written graffiti on a bus, on school walls, on rest room walls, or on anything else in a public place?
    Committed acts of vandalism when coming or going to a football game or other sports event?
Alcohol use: Have you ever . . .
    Consumed hard liquor (e.g., tequila, whiskey, vodka, or gin) before you were 16?
    Consumed alcoholic beverages (e.g., beer, wine, or wine coolers) before you were 16?
    Got drunk (intentionally) just for the fun of it (at any age)?

Got drunk just to fit in and be part of the crowd (at any age)?
Lied about your age to buy alcohol before you turned 16?
Had an older brother/sister or friend buy alcohol for you?
Bought alcohol for a brother/sister or friend?

Drug use: Have you ever . . .
Used tobacco products regularly (e.g., cigarettes, chew, snuff, etc.)?
Used "soft" drugs such as marijuana (grass, pot)?
Used "hard" drugs such as crack, cocaine, or heroin?
Gone to school when you were drunk or high on drugs?
Gone to work when you were drunk or high on drugs?
Gone to a concert when you were drunk or high on drugs?
Gone to a club/dance/party when you were drunk or high on drugs?
Gone to a club/dance/party to get drunk or high on drugs?
Sold any drugs such as marijuana (grass, pot), cocaine, or heroin?

School misconduct: Have you ever . . .
Cheated on school tests (e.g., cheat sheet, copy from neighbor, etc.)?
Been sent out of a classroom because of "bad" behavior (e.g., inappropriate behaviors, cheating, etc.)?
Been suspended or expelled from school?
Stayed away from school/classes when your parent(s) thought you were there?
Intentionally missed classes more than a number of days for "no reason," just for fun (e.g., there was no family emergency)?
Been in trouble at school so that your parents received a phone call about it?
Skipped school/work (pretending you were ill)?

General deviance: Have you ever . . .
Intentionally disobeyed a stop sign or a red traffic light while driving a vehicle?
Been on someone else's property when you knew you were not supposed to be there?
Failed to return extra change that you knew a cashier gave you by mistake?
Tried to deceive a cashier to your advantage (e.g., flash a larger bill and give a smaller one)?
Let the air out of the tires of a car or bike?
Lied about your age to get into a nightclub/bar?
Made nuisance/obscene telephone calls?
Avoided paying for something (e.g., movies, bus or subway rides, food, etc.)?
Used fake money or other things in a candy, coke, or stamp machine?
Shaken/hit a parked car just to turn on the car's alarm?
Stayed out all night without informing your parents about your whereabouts?

Theft: Have you ever . . .
Stolen, taken, or tried to take something from a family member or relative (e.g., personal items, money, etc.)?
Stolen, taken, or tried to take something worth 20 Swiss francs or less (e.g., newspaper, pack of gum, mail, money, etc.)?
Stolen, taken, or tried to take something worth between 20-150 Swiss francs (e.g., shirt, watch, cologne, video game cartridge, shoes, money)?
Stolen, taken, or tried to take something worth more than 150 Swiss francs (e.g., leather jacket, car stereo, bike, money, etc.)?
Stolen, taken, or tried to take something that belonged to "the public" (e.g., street signs, construction signs, etc.)?

Stolen or tried to steal a motor vehicle (e.g., car or motorcycle)?
Bought, sold, or held stolen goods or tried to do any of these things?
Assault: Have you ever . . .
    Hit or threatened to hit a person?
    Hit or threatened to hit your parent(s)?
    Hit or threatened to hit other students/peers or people?
    Used force or threatened to beat someone up if they didn't give you money or
        something else you wanted?
    Been involved in gang fights or other gang activities?
    Beaten someone up so badly they required medical attention?

NOTES

1. Along with Germany, Switzerland absorbed the bulk of refugees from these countries
coming to Western Europe. According to estimates, about 40% of all Albanian refugees from the
Serbian province of Kosovo are currently staying in Switzerland.

2. Participants were instructed to mark a non-Swiss country for parental birthplace even if
only one parent satisfied this condition.

REFERENCES

Arneklev, B. J., Grasmick, H. G., Tittle, C. R., & Bursick, R. J. (1993). Low self-control and
    imprudent behavior. *Journal of Quantitative Criminology, 9*, 225-245.
Balvig, F. (1988). *The snow-white image: The hidden reality of crime in Switzerland*. Oslo, Nor-
    way: Norwegian University Press.
Brownfield, D., & Sorenson, A. M. (1993). Self-control and juvenile delinquency: Theoretical
    issues and an empirical assessment of selected elements of a general theory of crime. *Deviant
    Behavior, 14*, 243-264.
Bundesamt für Statistik. (2000). *Pressemitteilung: Kriminalität von Asylsuchenden: Analyse
    einer kleinen Gruppe von Verurteilten*. Neuchatel, Switzerland: Bundesamt für Statistik.
Clinard, M. (1978). *Cities with little crime: The case of Switzerland*, Cambridge, UK: Cam-
    bridge University Press.
Council of Europe. (1995). *European sourcebook of crime and criminal justice statistics*.
    Strasbourg: Council of Europe.
Eisner, M. (1997). *Das Ende der zivilisierten Stadt? Die Auswirkungen von Modernisierung und
    urbaner Krise auf Gewaltsdelinquenz*. Frankfurt, Germany: Campus Verlag.
Eisner, M. (1998). Jugendkriminalität und immigrierte Minderheiten im Kanton Zürich. In
    S. Bauhofer, P. H Bolle, N. Queloz, (Eds.), *Jugend und Strafrecht* (pp. 103-138). Zürich:
    Rüegger.
Fehr, B. (1998, February 2). Kantonspolizei St. Gallen (press conference).
Gottfredson, M. R., & Hirschi, T. (1990). *A general theory of crime*. Stanford, CA: Stanford Uni-
    versity Press.
Grasmick, H. G., Blackwell, B. S., & Bursick, R. J. (1993). Changes in the sex patterning of per-
    ceived threats of sanctions. *Law and Society Review, 27*, 679-704.

Grasmick, H. G., & Bryjak, G. J. (1980). The deterrent effect of perceived severity of punishment. *Social Forces, 59,* 471-491.

Grasmick, H. G., & Bursick, R. J. (1990). Conscience, significant other, and rational choice: Extending the deterrence model. *Law and Society, 23,* 837-861.

Grasmick, H. G., Bursick, R. J., & Arneklev, B. J. (1993). Reduction in drunk driving as a response to decreased threats of shame, embarrassment, and legal sanctions. *Criminology, 31,* 410-467.

Grasmick, H. G., Blackwell, B. S., Bursick, R. J., & Mitchell, S. (1993). Changes in perceived threats of shame, embarrassment, and legal sanctions for interpersonal violence, 1982-1992. *Violence and Victims, 8,* 313-325.

Grasmick, H.G., Tittle, C. R., Bursick, R. J., & Arneklev, B. J. (1993). Testing the core empirical implications of Gottfredson and Hirschi's General Theory of Crime. *Journal of Research in Crime and Delinquency, 30,* 5-29.

Huizinga, D., Menard, S., & Elliott, D. (1989). Delinquency and drug use: Temporal and developmental patterns. *Justice Quarterly, 6,* 419-455.

Junger, M. (1990). *Delinquency and ethnicity.* Boston: Kluwer.

Junger-Tas, J. (1997). Ethnic minorities and criminal justice in the Netherlands. In M. Tonry (Ed.), *Ethnicity, crime, and immigration: Comparative and cross-national perspectives* (pp. 257-310). Chicago: University of Chicago Press.

Junger-Tas, J., Terlouw, G.-J., & Klein, M. (1994). *Delinquent behavior among young people in the western world: First results of the International Self-Report Delinquency Study.* Amsterdam: Kugler.

Killias, M. (1989). Criminality among second-generation immigrants in Western Europe: A review of evidence. *Criminal Justice Review, 14,* 13-42.

Killias, M. (1995). La criminalisation de la vie quotidienne et politisation du droit penal. *Revue de droit suisse, 114,* 365-458.

Killias, M. (1997). Immigrants, crime, and criminal justice in Switzerland. In M. Tonry (Ed.), *Ethnicity, crime, and immigration: Comparative and cross-national perspectives* (pp. 375-406). Chicago:University of Chicago Press.

Killias, M., & Berruex, T. (1999) Strafanzeige: Keine Frage des Zufalls, *Crimiscope, 3.* Lausanne: Institut de Police Scientifique et de Criminologie–Université de Lausanne.

Killias, M., Clerici, C., & Berruex, T. (1998). L'Evolution de la criminalite en Suisse depuis les annees 80: Stagnation, recul ou augmentation? Les sondages de victimisation confrontes aux statistiques de police. *Bulletin de Criminologie, 24,* 57-80.

Killias, M., & Ribeaud, D. (1999). Drug use and crime among juveniles: An international perspective. *Studies on Crime and Crime Prevention, 8,* 189-209.

Killias, M., Villetaz, P., & Rabasa, J. (1994). Self-reported juvenile delinquency in Switzerland. In J. Junger-Tas, G.-J. Terlouw, & M. Klein (Eds.), *Delinquent behavior among young people in the western world: First results of the International Self-Report Delinquency Study* (pp. 186-211). Amsterdam: Kugler.

Kornhauser, R. (1978). *Social sources of delinquency: An appraisal of analytic models.* Chicago: University of Chicago Press.

Langan, P. A., & Farrington, D. P. (1998). *Crime and justice in the United States and in England and Wales, 1981-96* (NCJ 169284). Washington, DC: Bureau of Justice Statistics

Longshore, D., Turner, S., & Stein, J. A. (1996). Self-control in a criminal sample: An examination of construct validity. *Criminology, 34,* 209-228.

Mayhew, P., & van Dijk, J.J.M. (1997). *Criminal victimisation in eleven industrialised countries: Key findings from the 1996 International Crime Victims Survey.* Leyden, The Netherlands: Wetenschappelijk Onderzoek-en Documentatiecentrum.

Michaud, P. A., Ferron, C., & Narring, F. (1996). Immigrant status and risk behaviors. *Journal of Adolescent Health, 19,* 378-380.

Mirrlees-Black, C., Budd, T., Partridge, S., & Mayhew, P. (1998). The 1998 British crime survey: England and Wales. *Home Office Statistical Bulletin, 21.*

Piquero, A. R., & Rosay, A. B. (1998). The reliability and validity of Grasmick et al.'s self-control scale: A comment on Longshore et al. *Criminology, 36,* 157-173

Polizeiliche Kriminalstatistik 1997. (1998, March 27). (Press Conference).

Pulkkinen, L. (1982). Self-control and continuity from childhood to late adolescence. *Lifespan Development and Behavior, 4,*63-105.

Pulkkinen, L., & Pitkänen, T. (1993). Continuities in aggressive behavior from childhood to adulthood. *Aggressive Behavior, 19,* 249-263.

Rawlings, M. L. (1973). Self-control and interpersonal violence: A study of Scottish adolescent male severe offenders. *Criminology,* 11, 23-48.

Sampson, R. J., & Lauritsen, J. L. (1997). Racial and ethnic disparities in crime and criminal justice in the United States. In M. Tonry (Ed.), *Ethnicity, crime, and immigration: Comparative and cross-national perspectives* (pp. 311-374). Chicago: University of Chicago Press.

Swiss Federal Statistical Office. (1997). *Statistical data on Switzerland 1997.* Bern, Switzerland: Swiss Federal Statistical Office.

Swiss Federal Statistical Office. (1999). *Annual Population Statistics.* Neuchatel, Switzerland: Swiss Federal Statistical Office.

van Dijk, J.J.M., Mayhew, P., & Killias, M. (1990). *Experiences with crime across the world.* Boston: Kluwer.

Vazsonyi, A. T., & Pickering, L. E. (2000). Family processes and deviance: A comparison of apprentices and non-apprentices. *Journal of Adolescent Research, 15,* 368-391.

Vazsonyi, A. T., Pickering, L. E., Junger, M., & Hessing, D. (2001). An empirical test of a general theory of crime: A four-nation comparative study of self-control and the prediction of deviance. *Journal of Research in Crime and Delinquency, 38,* 91-131.

Wilson, J. Q., & Herrnstein, R. J. (1985). *Crime and human nature.* New York: Simon & Schuster.

Zippelius, R. (1986). Exclusion and shunning as legal and social sanctions. *Ethology and Sociobiology, 7,* 159-166.

[12]

Crime and Manipulation of Identity Among Russian-Speaking Immigrants in the Netherlands

DINA SIEGEL
FRANK BOVENKERK
Willem Pompe Institute for Criminal Law and Criminology, the Netherlands

This article reports on an ethnographic study of Russian-speaking immigrants in the Netherlands. Using interviews and media accounts, explanations are found for Russian immigrants' choice of the Netherlands as a place to conduct organized crime operations, why criminal proceeds are invested inside the Netherlands, and why there is a prevailing view of consensual organized crime activity as being nonserious. The negative public identity of Russian immigrants and how they have chosen to manipulate their criminal image, rather than contest it, are examined. It has become part of a social process in which a new Russian ethnic identity is constructed.

A COMMUNITY STUDY ON RUSSIAN ORGANIZED CRIME

Immigrants and ethnic minorities are often documented as being well represented in organized crime, and this presents the challenge of explaining it. To what extent are immigrant populations involved in serious criminal activity, and what has been the nature of their involvement? If we take the two parts of this question to refer to concrete, limited entities, three links can be drawn: (a) Criminal emigration has reproduced a community of criminals in another country, (b) crime has emerged from the second generation of the immigrant community, or (c) organized crime and the immigrant community coexist on the basis of mutual dependence. The third option can refer to either a parasitic or a symbiotic interrelationship.

According to the criminal export model, the Mafia disperses its members across the globe for the purpose of establishing criminal trade posts. The first emigrants are vanguards for the organization and can serve as brokers in establishing contact with the local business world and the underworld. This is how the Sicilian Mafia is thought to have built up branches all over the world from Palermo, and the Triads did the same from Hong Kong, as did the Colombian cartels from Medellin and Cali. This export model has been seriously criticized as being a product of racial and ethnic prejudice, and present-day American textbooks on organized crime (cf. Albanese, 1996; Lyman & Potter, 1997) go to great lengths to demonstrate numerous errors and misconceptions in what has been denounced as the "alien conspiracy model." Recently, the model has been implicitly confirmed by the discovery of transnational criminal organizations (Williams, 1995). The globalization of industry and trade has produced the concurrent expansion of the illegal economy. Following the logic of the model, only a few enterprising members of the organization need to travel, and they can engage in their activities irrespective of the existence of an immigrant community of their fellow countrymen. Nigerian con men and drug traders operate this way in Western Europe, for example, where apart from the community in Great Britain, there is almost no Nigerian presence. No immigrant community is needed for this type of criminal enterprise.

The second model approaches organized crime as something that has been created by immigrants who have secured a niche in the underworld of the country where they have settled. Criminologists such as Albini (1971), Block (1985), and Haller (1971) point out that the immigrant racketeering businesses in the United States constitute a local initiative responding to the economic demands or political contradictions in the receiving society, rather than something that has been masterminded from some distant criminal capital overseas. Prohibition in the United States in the 1920s, prostitution, and gambling have all provided wonderful opportunities for a second generation of socially disadvantaged immigrants with poor prospects for legitimate upward social mobility. This second model, which could be labeled *second generation social mobility crime*, presupposes the presence of a sizeable immigrant community and ample young males who are eager to get rich illegally. Organized crime then emerges from the immigrant community, and the rackets are an integral part of the local, ethnic minority economy.

According to the model of mutual dependence, transnational criminal organizations follow the emigration pattern and exploit their fellow countrymen and the social infrastructure they have built. Martens (1986) includes two interrelationships between criminal organizations and ethnic communities: parasitic and symbiotic. In parasitic interrelationships, the immigrant community may be victimized by extortionists, as in the case of Chinese shopkeepers or Russian businessmen, or forced to assist in the transnational criminal enterprise by giving shelter to fugitive contract killers, for example, as in the case of the Italian Mafia in southern Germany. The pressure on the immigrant community might manifest itself as a threat to harm relatives who have

426 Journal of Contemporary Criminal Justice / November 2000

stayed behind. In a symbiotic interrelationship, immigrants may also be lured into the criminal project by the offer of opportunities that are hard to refuse. Turkish Mafia *Baba* in Western Europe seems to have very few problems recruiting personnel for the heroin trade among the second generation (Bovenkerk & Yesilgoz, 1998). The initiative may also be taken the other way around, as gangsters from the immigrant community exploit opportunities based on their national background. They can turn into smugglers of people or human organs from their native country or importers of drugs or women for prostitution. Their international links provide opportunities for laundering money (underground banking) and investing the proceeds of their activities without much risk.

These three options seem to exhaust the logical possibilities, and this typology enables us to classify concrete cases of ethnic minority–organized crime. However, its theoretical power is limited because it fails to explain the development of the interrelationship mechanisms involved. In our fieldwork among Russian speakers in the Netherlands, typologies of this kind did little to help us understand the dynamics of the criminalization process that newcomers go through.

One underlying problem is that the two key concepts, organized crime and ethnicity (or the ethnic community), are taken for granted. Of course, the concept of organized crime and the Mafia as a generic category has been the subject of extensive discussion. Mafia organizations are usually described as concrete structures or networks in time and space, with a fixed number of individuals moving about in an underworld of their own, according to certain rules, codes, and values. However, the Mafia has also been conceived as merely an image or a myth that is socially constructed by the authorities or the media (Smith, 1990). The concepts of ethnicity or the ethnic community are equally problematic. Do ethnic groups really consist of people who share a common past or whose way of life is guided by the same set of cultural rules, or are they merely a collective illusion or a recent invention for reasons of political mobilization? Does a tangible community consist of people actively engaged in maintaining social boundaries, or are communities nothing more than a fiction devised by their members or governmental creations for the management of social problems? The answers to these questions depend on what theoretical point of view is taken. Are we reasoning from an essentialist or a constructivist point of departure?

New cultural anthropology (Baumann, 1999) cautions us against notions such as ethnicity, community, and culture, and we can expand this list to include concepts like organized crime and underworld. Instead of being an abstract notion employed for analytical purposes, these concepts assume a real quality. They are reifying notions, and these qualities seem to govern the movements of people independently of their own will. For example, essentialist reasoning postulates that Sicilian society brings forth the Mafia. This may mean that being born in Sicily implies being socialized into a culture that produces the Mafia. However, individuals are not passive carriers of a particular ethnicity or a criminal subculture (Gambetta, 1993, p. 10). Instead, they are active agents engaged in the creation of their own realities. According to a constructivist notion of culture, ethnicity and community are concepts that should not be taken as the explanation but as subjects that need to be explained. This also applies to crime.

In constructing their culture, people do not have a total freedom of choice. Their range of choices is restricted to a limited set of influences and experiences to which they are exposed. Migrants and ethnic minority populations in particular go through an extensive set of cultural orientations from which, to a certain extent, they can choose their own combinations. The wide range they choose from include the cultural orientations toward the country of origin (at the time of departure and at the present time) and cultural orientations in the new country such as specific subcultures of peer groups, of social class, of groups in urban and rural environments, and so on. These various influences should include the ideas and images about them that are held by others. Migrants do not move into a cultural void. Adopting an interactionist approach means that perceptions and judgments about them that are formed within the receiving society have to be taken into account. Creating their own culture implies a process of adaptation to the new country that includes an ongoing process of decisions to accept these preconceived ideas about themselves, which eventually can become a self-fulfilling prophecy, or to fight them, for example, by organizing an antidefamation group. Eriksen (1993) stated that "they can sometimes function as self-fulfilling prophecies" (p. 24).

Ethnic identities created by people who consider themselves to be similar are situated in a constantly changing social context, and their identity at the moment is therefore flexible and multiple. Ethnicity may originate from a shared illusion on the part of the participants, but it becomes a real device that can be strategically used to mobilize power. It also lends itself for manipulation to promote specific interests. Immigrants may find themselves pictured as criminals, and those among them who actually engage in deviant behavior may find that their crimes are stereotyped as ethnic crimes. They learn to comprehend the reactions on the part of law enforcement officials toward their behavior as resulting from specific cultural knowledge about the ethnic group to which they are considered to belong. Some immigrants may choose a criminal lifestyle or a career in the rackets, and they have to decide how to respond to perceptions of their ethnicity and learn how to use it to their own advantage. The cultural defense claim in the courtroom that we find in countries with a multicultural political ideology is a case in point. Self-defined ethnic criminals may choose their line of criminal activity in accordance with

428   Journal of Contemporary Criminal Justice / November 2000

the constellation of cultural orientations and the anticipated responses to their ethnic behavior. Ethnicity may then become a useful asset when engaging in criminal activity.

This type of constructivist approach steers criminology a long way from the questions it traditionally seeks to answer. Instead of explaining variations in crime based on the ethnicity factor, we now wonder how minorities construct their own ethnic identities to manipulate the situation to their own advantage. In terms of the given typology, there is obviously a symbiotic interdependence between the immigrant community and organized crime. However, the relationship is not between concrete entities with clear membership and boundaries, but it is between mere images of ethnic and criminal groups. To understand ethnic organized crime, we need to go beyond the study of concrete criminal groups and take the entire ethnic group formation process and the crime that this group produces into account.

Emigration from the former Soviet Union and the creation of an expatriate Red Mafia provide a magnificent opportunity to study the process of ethnic organized crime. The emigration itself constitutes a recent and ongoing movement of people, many of whom have not decided to settle. The two main waves of emigration from the former Soviet Union took place between 1968 and 1983 (with several breaks) and in the period since 1988, when Gorbachev introduced his reforms, including the right of free movement. The most important Russian-speaking communities were established in the United States, Israel, Germany, Canada, and South Africa. Although the majority of the emigrants were Jews, there were also Germans, Ukrainians, and Armenians. Some of these communities have been studied in detail by social scientists, but not much is known about the relationship between organized crime and these ethnic communities.

The emigrant population contains people from a wide range of countries, regions, and ethnic and religious groups. It is not very specific in terms of occupations and educational levels; in fact, the variety of professions and skills is striking when compared to other emigrations. Yet, they are generally perceived as the Russian emigrants who settle as the Russian community. There have been constant rumors about crime among the immigrants and a fear that the Red Mafia is ubiquitous. At the same time, it is still far from clear exactly what the Russian Mafia means—a centrally directed syndicate or a loose configuration of regional crime traditions? The public and law enforcement officials both find it hard to specify exactly what groups have been active in which sectors of organized crime. To a certain extent, the immigrant groups as a whole are suspected of taking part in Russian organized crime. To what degree does the immigrant population live up to the expectations?

RESEARCH METHODS

Up to now, criminological research into organized crime has been almost completely dependent on police sources and legal documents. Information can also be gleaned from interviews with established and prestigious godfathers in the world of crime, who are flattered to have their life histories written. All these sources provide the kind of information that focuses on the internal workings of the criminal organization. The ethnic minority, the organization, and its leaders belong only in the picture as a provider of manpower. In these descriptions, the contours of the local community remain vague.

How much can we learn about organized crime by focusing on the immigrant community? Anthropological fieldwork methods have scarcely been used in criminology as a whole. The participant observation method is not used in criminological research for the following reasons. First, the researcher has to fluently speak the language of the ethnic group he is studying, or even better, he has to be one of them. In the Russian community, it may be extremely difficult because anyone who does not speak Russian is a foreigner who is not to be trusted. Fortunately, the Russian background of one of the authors is an advantage in this regard. Second, it is important to introduce the subject of study in a way that the community understands. Based on very special perceptions developed among Russians on crime and illegality, telling Russian speakers that we are studying the Russian business community in the Netherlands makes it clear to one and all that the real subject is the Mafia. Third, some criminologists also have ethical objections to field research among criminals (Sutherland & Cressey, 1960, p. 69). To us, however, trying to get closer to respondents does not necessarily mean identifying with them.

Some of the best studies on organized crime have been successful because they entail participant observation of a whole community. This provides a wide range of interesting information. Ianni (1972) demonstrated the value of field research: "My training and subsequent field experience have convinced me that direct observation of human action is better than the collection of verbal statements about that action if one would understand how a social system functions" (p. 182). Polsky (1971) interviewed hustlers and described their lives after years of participant observation:

> Experience with adult, unreformed, "serious" criminals in their natural environment . . . has convinced me that if we are to make a major advance in our scientific understanding of criminal lifestyles, criminal sub-cultures, and their relation to the larger society, we must undertake genuine field research on these people. (p. 115)

430 Journal of Contemporary Criminal Justice / November 2000

Similarly, Chambliss (1975) wrote that although field research is difficult, it is not impossible:

> It is possible to find out what is going on "out there." We are not permanently stuck with government reports and college students' responses. The data on organized crime as other presumably difficult-to-study events are much more available than we usually think. All we really have to do is to get out of our offices and onto the streets. The data are there; the problem is that too often sociologists are not. (p. 39)

We have studied the images and perceptions of crime and criminals through participant observation inside the Russian-speaking community in one country, the Netherlands, especially in Amsterdam (with numerous immigrants from Moscow) and Rotterdam (where those from St. Petersburg migrated). Surprisingly enough, it was not so difficult to find respondents. In fact, no topic of conversation seems to be as popular among Russian speakers as Russian organized crime.

EMIGRATION FROM THE FORMER SOVIET UNION TO BELGIUM AND THE NETHERLANDS

The total number of Russian immigrants to Belgium and the Netherlands is not anywhere near the numbers that were anticipated when the Soviet Union came to its end in 1990 and 1991. In Belgium and the Netherlands, the total number of residents from the former Soviet Union states does not exceed 10,000. Most of them are Jews who either arrived directly from the former Soviet Union or first spent some time in Israel. Many allegedly arrived with forged documents, which they feel was one of the reasons that the Dutch Jewish Social Work Agency (*Joods Maatschappelijk Werk*) stopped helping Russian Jews apply for Dutch citizenship. Even if we include the numerous undocumented migrants, their total would still be no more than twice this number. But in fact, Russian speakers are no more than a tiny fraction of the Dutch and Belgium populations. They are perceived as constituting a monolithic block, but in reality, the group is heterogeneous. We have observed a wide variety of professions: scientists, businessmen, housewives, street musicians, prostitutes, doctors, and sportsmen. The generalized perception among the host society (it is hard to correct these views because there are so few opportunities to get acquainted with individual Russians) contributes to further stereotypes.

In the Low Countries (the Netherlands, Belgium, Luxembourg, and the northwest of France), the Russian immigrants live up to their reputation, just as they have in the United States and Israel. Between 1992 and 1997, six cases of homicide shocked the Dutch. The victims were businessmen, and one was a highly qualified technician. Vadim Rozenbaum, who was murdered in 1997, is the best known victim. Questions were posed in the Dutch Parliament because Mr. Rozenbaum was killed after giving information to the Dutch police about a Mafia group. In a rather small and peaceful country like the Netherlands, six murder cases in an annual total of about 35 underworld killings are too large a share for the Russian speakers. It was especially frightening because all the killings were carried out so professionally that no suspects could be arrested in the Netherlands (although suspects in the Rozenbaum case have been arrested in Israel).

THE NEGATIVE IDENTITY OF
RUSSIAN-SPEAKING IMMIGRANTS

The key to understanding the Russian immigrants' perception of crime in the Netherlands is clearly the negative image that preceded their arrival in Belgium and the Netherlands. Authors writing about Russian émigrés in other countries have observed the same sequence of events. Rosner (1995) studied Russian immigrants in the Brighton Beach area of Brooklyn in the 1970s and noted that the criminal stereotype was waiting for them when they arrived. There had been newspaper reports about merciless Russian gangsters, and the Russian mob had been romanticized in novels and films. The American public found it "sexy to read about immigrants from the former Soviet Union who were involved in criminal activities on a grand scale" (Rosner, 1995, p. 29). It was not long before the Russian-speaking immigrants in the United States confirmed the stereotype. To be sure, many immigrants considered their behavior normal. Crime had been a survival strategy under Communist rule, and the immigrants had learned to cope with the bureaucratic system in ways that Americans regarded as graft and as involving illicit goods and services. Their skills at beating the system proved equally functional in the new city, where the urban conditions did not basically differ from those of Odessa.

Amir (1996) has demonstrated the same mechanism in the case of Georgian Jews coming to Israel in the mid-1970s. From the onset of their immigration, the Israeli media painted a frightening picture of special types of Georgian criminals who committed very serious offenses (p. 28). In Israel, some immigrants similarly lived up to the expectations, and the entire group of Georgian Jews was stigmatized as a result.

A similar development took place in Europe. From the moment when the Russians broke loose after the Iron Curtain was lifted in 1990 to move to Western Europe, the media focused nonstop on Russian prostitution, document forgery, drug trafficking, brand-name swindling, and protection rackets. Once the political barriers ceased to exist and Russia became connected to the modern mass transport network, Russian criminal organizations tried to expand internationally and look for new markets.

How did the media know? The first sources of information were the U.S. police investigations and criminological reports (cf. Finckenauer & Waring, 1997) referring to large networks of Russian émigré criminals. Germany, Austria, and Switzerland were next: The Russian Mafia was coming! Then the news hit the press that Russians were buying the must luxurious property on the French Côte d'Azur. In France, Germany, and Belgium, popular scientific books on the Russian Mafia contained fantastic stories on deviant Russian criminal behavior. The criminal network seemed to follow the path of emigration. Nodal points became Tel Aviv, Berlin, Vienna, and Antwerp, which seems to prove the first criminal export model pertaining to how the Mafia establishes criminal posts around the world.

The first alarming account of the Red Mafia in the Netherlands came in 1994 when the annual report of the Dutch Secret Service seriously cautioned Dutch businessmen venturing into Russia and predicted the Mafia's imminent arrival on Dutch soil. Nothing was known with any certainty at the time. East Europeans had been trading in stolen secondhand Dutch cars, and there were rumors about Russian prostitution rings. The most frightening story came from The Hague, where the local underworld had emerged victorious over the Russian-speaking mob in the red light district. The Russians left the scene with the message, "We'll be back!"

Russian criminologist Gurov (1995) thinks that more than anything else, the Netherlands serves as a place for the international mob to meet. Russian criminologists claim to have identified no fewer than 110 Russian gangs that operate internationally, and Dunn (1997) reports the presence of the Podolskaya gang, the Tambovskaya gang, and one of the Chechen gangs in the Netherlands, and the Solntsevskaya and Tsentralnaya gangs in Belgium. According to Dunn, the main activity of the Podolskaya gang is the production of counterfeit food products and liquor for sale back in Russia (p. 69). The Moscow-based Pushkinskaya gang also produces counterfeit Stolichnaya vodka in the Netherlands for resale in Russia (p. 84).

Official reports from the former Soviet Union have also contributed to the growing fear that the Russians are coming to the West. Almost all the academic literature in Russia, and numerous popular crime magazines and other publications, often in conjunction with Western authors, inform the European readers that the former Soviet Union is too small a territory for the activities of the Russian criminal organizations (Gurov, 1995; Konstantinov &

Dikselius, 1997). According to Russian sources, the Russian Mafia is continuously searching for new markets and fields of activity in the West.

Organized crime has been discovered in the Netherlands ever since the second half of the 1980s, and special police task forces (IRT) have been formed
to find out more about specific aspects of it. The target of the task force in
northeast Netherlands includes Eastern Europe. In 1995, the kidnapping of
Boris Fastovsky, a Russian Jewish businessman from St. Petersburg, confirmed the suspicion that the Mafia was now there. The Amsterdam police
launched an extensive search for the corpse but proved unable to retrieve it.
The police unit started the systematic investigation (which basically means
collecting the cases and criminal information from all over the Netherlands in
one database) on extortion, fraud, and Russian involvement in prostitution. A
parliamentary fact-finding commission (Van Traa) submitted a report in 1996
that gave a group of university professors the opportunity to scrutinize the
criminal material. They arrived at a similar conclusion: The first signs of
Russian-speaking organized crime are in evidence.

Academic researchers have posed the relevant questions. First, because the
Russian mob obviously has not stopped at the Dutch borders, why have these
gangsters selected the Netherlands? Belgium and the Netherlands are both
well placed on the transport map. Antwerp and Rotterdam are among the
largest ports in the world, and the Amsterdam Schiphol airport and the
Zaventem airport in Brussels are part of the gateway to Europe. Antwerp has
the leading diamond and gold industries. The closed traders' world provides
a perfect opportunity for smuggling. In addition, there is the legal system.
The Dutch tradition of tolerance (or indifference as some may claim) toward
deviant behavior (pornography, prostitution, drugs) and the ensuing relaxed
criminal law system—with relatively short sentences and humane prison
conditions—make for an attractive environment to do business without risks.

The second relevant criminological question pertaining to any sort of organized crime is where does the money go? The Dutch authorities first had to
understand that Russian speakers brought money into the country rather than
take it out as other international criminal groups do when they send the proceeds of their criminal activities back home. The Netherlands is an attractive
place to invest money. It has a solid banking system and a hard currency.
There is evidence (e.g., in the vicinity of Eindhoven) that Russians are investing in Dutch real estate. The Dutch banks are now on the alert; if the money
they keep in Russian accounts later proves to have been obtained by criminal
enterprise, they may have to give it back. The evidence of Russian financial
interests in the Netherlands has led the Dutch authorities to launch a new
large-scale police operation by the IRT special task force, which was meant
to remain secret but was leaked to the press.

434   Journal of Contemporary Criminal Justice / November 2000

IMPLOSION OF A BAD REPUTATION
WITHIN THE IMMIGRANT GROUP

The prevailing image of the Russians who have recently left their homeland is negative. This has directly influenced all the Russian immigrant communities and has seriously hampered the individual life chances of all Russians, who are now viewed as potential members of the Mafia or at least as being connected to it. They are confronted with discrimination in the labor market: Russian diplomas and other documents are not accepted because they are suspected of being forgeries, and Russian women are often treated as harlots. Falcon Square in Antwerp is considered Russian territory and a place for ordinary Belgian citizens to stay away from because it is a place to hire killers and thugs.

If a group is large enough to generate power and includes an elite group to provide leadership, an immigrant community can organize to protest. In the United States and in Israel (cf. Zionist Forum), the Russian antidefamation movement has successfully campaigned for respect. However, if the immigrant group is small and fragmented and almost powerless, as in the Low Countries, the negative image is hard to combat. There is a chance of it coming to pertain to the group as a whole. Our first impression has been that all the Russian speakers in the Netherlands tend to be very suspicious toward each other. Although many Russians love to meet their compatriots, many refuse to patronize the only Russian club in Amsterdam because it is a mob hangout. Unsolicited encounters between Russians who are not acquainted with each other often lead to an aloof stance. The unspoken question is always there: Is the other person engaged in illegal activities in the Netherlands, the former Soviet Union, or both? Immigrants do not tend to integrate easily and have shielded themselves from Dutch society at large. They do not follow the news. They may only privately oppose the bad image, and they regard the Dutch public and especially the police as being naive and childish.

According to the immigrants, the Dutch authorities are predominantly focused on petty crime and traditional activities such as prostitution, trafficking in women, and the drug trade. In their view, more serious criminals engaged in transferring and laundering money or investing in real estate and other legitimate businesses (such as jewelry shops in Antwerp and restaurants and grocery stores in Amsterdam) go almost unnoticed by the Dutch police and the media. To the Russian speakers, the real Mafia engages in murder, kidnapping, extortion, and other acts of serious violence that accompany serious crime. They view the Russian Mafia, however, as a distant threat, rather than as an everyday reality or threat to their lives. In this context, their own perception of crime and criminality is important. Most illegal activities are not considered to be Mafia or even criminal activities, and they may engage

in these activities themselves. What is wrong with forging documents or bribing officials? As one respondent explained, "Bribing is a form of saying
'Thank you!'"

Immigrants exhibit three identity layers: "We are harmless immigrants";
"Maybe we do have criminal habits, but that is an acceptable deviance"; and
"We can manipulate the image." They are aware that in the Benelux, the dominant opinion about the connection between Russian-speaking immigrants
and criminal organizations is different. They also know that Russians have a
deeply rooted negative image in the Netherlands. Russian speakers have
three options: They can accept, protest, or take advantage of it. Many have
chosen the last option, constructing new sociocultural patterns while emphasizing and using familiar concepts and stereotypes.

MANIPULATION OF IDENTITY

Upon their arrival in the West, it did not take the Russian speakers long to
realize that their interests could be served by claiming their ethnic rights.
They understood the power of their ethnic identity, their Russianness. They
clearly defined their aims, and their ethnicity played an instrumental role.
Various studies have described the manipulation of identity by ethnic groups,
including the strategies used by Russian Jewish politicians in Israel to mobilize Russian voters during the preelection campaign (Siegel, 1998).

In *Krasnaya Mafia*, Gurov (1995) cited a typical anecdote. Militia General
V. Ignatov was walking one night to his hotel in Rome with two female translators. It was hot, and he took off his shirt. Suddenly, they were surrounded by
youngsters who tried to approach the women. "The General did not call the
police. He came to the youngsters and said 'I am *russo mafiosi*,' after which
the racketeers disappeared" (pp. 309-310).

The Red Mafia has a name in Germany, but its horrible reputation is known
all over the world. Like elsewhere, most Russian speakers in the Netherlands
were horrified by the Red Mafia images. Very soon, however, immigrants discovered that a criminal image could be turned to their advantage. It has since
become a manipulation asset. We will illustrate this theoretical point with
several examples we came across during our fieldwork.

Russian Call Girls

Natasha and Lena (all the names have been changed) had been dreaming of
working in the West for some time to earn enough money to "build a normal
life" in their hometown. They got their chance when Lena met Eric, a Dutch
tourist, and asked him about the possibility of moving to the Netherlands.
After a few months and some red tape, she and her friend Natasha came to the

436 Journal of Contemporary Criminal Justice / November 2000

Netherlands as tourists. Lena was officially registered as living together (common law marriage) with Eric in one of the small Dutch cities. However, Eric lived somewhere else with his real girl friend. Natasha and Lena were paying him a small sum (around NLG 600) to stay at his house.

The girls told me that they did not intend to work as call girls in the beginning. Natasha even worked in a Dutch family as a baby-sitter for a few months. They soon came in contact with other Russians in the Netherlands and made a lot of new friends, who they spent their time with going on picnics (usually during the mushroom season with bottles of vodka and self-prepared mushroom dishes) and to concerts and clubs.

Once the money was almost gone, they worked for some time cleaning houses. After a few months, they met Svetlana, who worked for one of the Dutch escort services. They would not work for the official escort company because they did not have work permits, but they liked the idea of "starting their own business." According to them, they quickly had a circle of regular clients, almost all of them were Russian businessmen who came to the Netherlands for business (mostly *shopniks*, Russians who came to the Netherlands to buy merchandise and cars for resale in Russia). One of the girls told us the following:

> Actually I would prefer Dutch or other Europeans as clients, Russians are so coarse and do not pay much. Sometimes I meet Dutch men, we talk about literature and music, they know a lot about Russia and Russians, they usually work with Russians.

They worked for some time at home or sometimes "out," and then they went to Russia for summer vacation and to renew their visa and came back.

Lena recounted,

> I had just returned from Russia when we were called by a man who spoke English. He told us he would like to talk to us. Natasha stayed at home to unpack, and I went to meet him. He was not Dutch, maybe Turkish or something, he spoke with an accent. The man was a local pimp who had somehow heard about us.

She told him that they "already have Russian Mafia protection in the Netherlands and if he wants to meet the guys she will arrange the meeting." The pimp never bothered them again. They were approached by other pimps two more times, and they used the same story. Once they hear about Russian protection, the men disappear. The girls used the imaginary Mafia threat to chase away any local pimps who bullied them. This was only possible because the image of violent and criminal Russians was widespread and accepted in Dutch society. Anyone who knew what Russian Mafia means preferred not to become involved.

After the economic crisis in Russia in 1998, the girls lost many of their clients and stopped working. In addition to the issue of identity manipulation, there is another myth in this case, the inevitable link between Russian prostitutes and criminal organizations. The image was constructed with reference to all Russian prostitutes, who are allegedly forced by Russian criminal organizations to work against their will in Western Europe. Almost all media accounts contain heartbreaking stories about girls who were promised jobs as models, dancers, or waitresses in Western clubs and offices but instead landed in brothels and massage parlors without any money, passports, or ways to protest or complain. Of course in many cases, these stories are based on real facts and evidence. However, much less is known about voluntary prostitution and the financial situation of Russian women who have opted for it themselves. This variant of prostitution seems to be perceived by Russian women as temporary work, an economic necessity, or even simply as an adventure in a foreign country. According to one of the girls, "in the Netherlands, the norms are much healthier and more normal than in Russia."

Russian Musician

The story appeared in *De Volkskrant* (August 17, 1999), a leading Dutch daily newspaper. Victor, a young musician from a Russian provincial town, came to the Netherlands to work temporarily at De Efteling, a popular theme park for children. After some time, another Russian immigrant by the name of Alexander invited him to work and play at his restaurant. During his time off, Victor and a group of other Russian musicians played on the streets of Amsterdam. Alexander did not like this, and the relationship between the two became further strained when Victor got a Dutch girlfriend. According to the newspaper account, Alexander was jealous and spread bad stories about Victor, one of which even appeared in the press, claiming that the Russian Mafia was taking over the Russian Cultural Center (RCC). Victor was also accused of threatening to kill Alexander and take over his restaurant. Victor was described as an illegal alien who was connected to the Moscow Mafia. The police were called in, but they believed Victor and not his boss.

The story was probably meant for the Dutch public because very few Russians knew about it or attached much importance to it. Some Russian-speaking respondents who did know the story referred to Victor's dubious background but "would not venture to say [it] was right." They also said that the journalist did not know what she was talking about because Alexander was German and not Russian, but according to some Russian respondents, he tried to "play Russian," dressed in national costumes, and created a Russian ethnic atmo-

438 Journal of Contemporary Criminal Justice / November 2000

sphere at his "elitist and very expensive private club." Based on the media coverage, some points can be made. First, Victor's story is an example of identity manipulation in which another Russian immigrant is portrayed using the prevailing ethnic stereotype in describing his personal relationship with an ex-compatriot. He transmits the negative image of Victor to a wide public. The criminal context played an instrumental role here in attracting the public attention to a trivial personal conflict. The image of Victor, as a representative of the Mafia, and the emphasis on his Russianness by another immigrant can also be viewed as protest against the generalization and stigmatization by the whole community. Using the dominant stereotypes, Alexander presented a positive image of himself. He had joined the Dutch society and adopted Dutch views toward minorities. He himself was a good immigrant who was well integrated in the Netherlands. He also reinforced the potential fear of the Russian Mafia, revealing the Russian criminal in the Netherlands and demonstrating how Russian immigrants help to discover and combat crime.

Second, Alexander probably based his accusations on his previous knowledge about Victor. An article about the Russian Mafia in the Netherlands in *Penthouse* (December 1998) magazine was mentioned by some of our respondents. The article referred to Victor as a "poor Russian musician" without any connection to Alexander. Alexander was "adopted by the former director of the RCC," the Russian Cultural Center in Amsterdam, who later discovered that Victor was working for a Moscow-based Mafia gang and selling information to former KGB officials.

If Alexander knew about Victor's criminal activities, it still did not keep him from employing somebody with that kind of background at his restaurant. He simply ignored this knowledge, but he later manipulated it when the situation changed. He publicized Victor's negative image, using precisely the facts that he hid and ignored before.

Mushroom Picnic

Autumn is mushroom season in Russia. After the first mushroom showers, families and friends spend their weekends in nearby forests. For some of them, picking mushrooms means preparing for long Russian winters. They load their cars and trailers with orange- or brown-cap mushrooms, which they dry or pickle later at home. However, for most of them, picking mushrooms is a social event, an opportunity to meet friends and relatives and to spend time drinking, eating, and singing together.

Upon their arrival in the Netherlands, the Russian speakers found out that some of the familiar sorts of mushrooms are growing in Dutch forests. Although there is no longer a need to pick them in preparation for winter, it is still an attractive social event. However, they found out that, in the Netherlands, picking mushrooms is forbidden because of environmental considerations. This prohibition does not stop them. At one mushroom picnic, I joined a group of around 20 Russian speakers, who gathered to drive *po grybi* (for mushrooms). The plan was to go to the forest; pick mushrooms; have a picnic with homemade food, vodka, and guitar music; and then drive back to someone's home, cook the mushrooms, and have a garden party.

Four cars arrived at the woods near Amersfoort with straw baskets, kitchen knives, and rucksacks. Before they scattered in the woods, one of them gave a short speech:

> Remember, picking mushrooms is illegal in the Netherlands. [Another man expressed his dismay at how stupid this was!] They can arrest you or give you a fine. So the only thing to do is give them the impression you do not understand what they are saying. Convince them that in Russia everybody does it, and for many villagers, it is the only way to get through the winter. Tell them whatever nonsense they want to hear. Tell them you are Russians and you never heard that picking mushrooms is illegal.

Next, everyone dispersed in small groups of two or three. Later, Natasha told me that she and her husband came across a Dutch couple. Although they looked as if they were peacefully out for a stroll, they forgot to cover their basket. The Dutch man became angry, shouting, "Why do you pick mushrooms, don't you know it is forbidden? Do I have to call a forest guard? It is against the law!" Although her Dutch was fluent, Natasha answered him in poor English that they did not know it was illegal, that they were Russians, and that they always picked mushrooms in Russia. The Dutch man turned out to be a biologist. When he heard Natasha's story, he started patiently explaining about the ecological significance of mushrooms. Natasha's husband was an ecologist at Moscow University, and he disagreed. They had a long argument. Finally, the Dutchman became angry again and called the police on his cell phone. Natasha threw away all the mushrooms and they left.

The others had not had any problems, and that evening, deep plates of mushroom soup and other dishes were served. When discussing Natasha's story, one man said, "If there is no logic to a law, it is not logical to obey it. Laws should be written for people and not for squirrels." He also said that for his first few months in the Netherlands, he lived by illegally fishing and illegally picking mushrooms. Everyone laughed and decided to gather again the next Sunday for another mushroom picnic. Natasha and her husband agreed to come again.

440 Journal of Contemporary Criminal Justice / November 2000

The Case of One Jewish Organization

The first group of Russian Jews arrived in the Netherlands in 1990. The first address for most of them was the headquarters of Joods Maatschappelijk Werk, the Jewish Social Work Agency on De Lairessestraat in Amsterdam. Some of them came there directly from Amsterdam's Schiphol airport. Those who first came in contact with the foreign police were placed in centers for asylum seekers, where they announced that they were Jewish and made contact with the Jewish Social Work Agency. To become a client and get assistance there, the Russian Jews had to prove that they were Jewish. One of the coordinators at the agency made the following statement to the local Jewish newspaper in 1994:

> If it is at all possible, we need to see the original birth certificates, passports and sometimes the *ketuba* (religious marriage contract) of their parents and grandparents. If there is any hesitation we do not accept them as clients. Two or three years ago we did. But it slowly became known how advantageous it is to be Jewish, and there developed a black market in documents in the former Soviet Union. (NIW, February 18, 1994, p. 16)

According to another social worker, if in the beginning people would produce *spravka* (reference) from the Jewish community in the former Soviet Union that confirmed that they were Jewish, it would enable them to become clients of the Jewish Social Work Agency. However, the translator (herself a Russian Jew) helped attract attention to certain details that were "not totally clear." The officials at the agency started to ask for other papers or for more documents. They now paid attention to many details, such as the color of the ink, yellow spots, and dampness.

As suspicion grew, the Dutch agency consulted the German Jewish Social Work Agency in Frankfurt. In 1994, one of the social workers from the German Jewish Social Service came to the Netherlands to share her experience and teach the Dutch social workers how to deal with suspicious documents. According to the director of the German organization, the social worker who was sent to the Netherlands told people to deal with these documents based on their own personal experience and intuition. Only if a case was very unclear did she suggest that they send the potential client to the police to have the documents examined by an expert. Neither the German nor the Dutch social workers at the Jewish Social Work Agencies had any professional education or training in identifying false documents. No experts from any professional organizations were ever consulted. No papers were sent to the police or to any other officials for professional control. One of my respondents told me that she personally asked an official at the agency to submit her papers to a professional expert if he did not believe her. The official refused.

In 1994, the Jewish Social Work Agency decided to stop assisting Russian Jews in the application procedure for Dutch citizenship. There were headlines about the Russian Mafia at the time. There were also reports from other European countries, the United States, and Israel. According to the Jewish Social Work Agency, it was a well-known fact that Georgians were coming into the country with forged documents. The decision to stop helping the immigrants was needed if the Jewish Social Work Agency was to keep from giving the impression that it was aiding and abetting Russian criminals. The agency worked in close conjunction with other official agencies and was dependent on them. It did not want to lose the financial and moral help it was getting from the Dutch authorities.

In this case, the bureaucratic organization was manipulating and exploiting the dominant stereotypes and image of Russian-speaking immigrants. First, it welcomed every Russian Jew without going into the details of his or her official documents, whereas later, it refused to help any of the potential clients and generalized them into one negative category without differentiating between individuals and life stories. Actually, the Jewish Social Work Agency may have stopped assisting Russian-speaking clients because it simply lost interest. According to some of its former clients, Russian Jewish immigrants enabled the agency to obtain a great deal of money from the Dutch government to assist in its efforts. The agency made expensive repairs to the building on De Lairessestraat and purchased new furniture and modern equipment. Some of the Russian Jews accused the agency officials of using the money reserved for the facilitation of the emigration process and integration of the immigrants in the Netherlands for their own purposes. "When we told the social workers that there were mice at our house [the shelter for asylum seekers], they told us we better buy a cat. They did not send us any help," the former resident of the shelter in Amsterdam told us. Another respondent told us she had only one broken chair in her room. When she asked for help, the agency official told her that there was no money left. At the same time, there was suddenly new furniture at the administrative offices. There are also numerous complaints about the agency's assistance in obtaining housing. According to another respondent, the officials were corrupt and received gifts from their clients. "They based their help on nonobjective criteria, on personal benefit, or sympathy," another respondent told us. She was refused a room at the shelter in Amsterdam in favor of another immigrant who, according to her, had better personal connections. "The real help we got from volunteers, ordinary people who really cared about us, many of them orthodox Jews," she revealed.

442 Journal of Contemporary Criminal Justice / November 2000

When the residents at the shelter for asylum seekers in Amsterdam felt that the agency was not paying adequate attention at all to their interests, they wrote an angry open letter demanding that the agency help them solve the housing problem. According to some of the Russian Jews who signed this letter, the Jewish Social Work Agency was angry with "these ungrateful Russians" and that this was one of the reasons it no longer wanted to promote their interests. Another explanation is that as long as the Dutch authorities financed the Jewish Social Work Agency, Russian Jewish immigration became an important and urgent issue. However, as soon as the funding stopped, the agency looked for a reason to stop the project. That is when it was alleged that the officials there started to stigmatize the whole community of Russian Jews as criminal and thus "remained loyal to the Dutch interest," formulating new plans and projects. As the director of the Jewish Social Work Agency told us, "We represent the interests of the whole Jewish community in the Netherlands and have other clients besides the Russians. Anyway, the Dutch Jewish opinion about the Russians is very poor."

CONCLUSION

Our first impressions of organized crime among Russian speakers in the Low Countries seem to corroborate the findings of Finckenauer and Waring (1997) in that there is no evidence of a tangible well-organized Red Mafia outside the former Soviet Union, and perhaps not even in Russia. However, this does not mean that the image of a strong international organization does not have very real consequences! The criminal image of Russian immigrants is widespread in Europe, and the Russian-speaking immigration is recent enough to allow us to follow the development of this image in the media and through interviews. This situation can be seen as supporting the social constructionist approach in criminology, which focuses on how individuals come to be defined through their public image. Interestingly, it appears that many Russian immigrants themselves believe in the criminal import model in which some of their fellow countrymen are considered to be potentially part of an alien conspiracy.

If we shift from the traditional approach, which studies criminal groups and the influence of race and ethnic background on patterns of crime, to the study of immigration and the development and invention of ethnicity, a new and fruitful field of study presents itself. It starts by acknowledging that immigrants have to deal with the negative identity that is already there when they arrive. This holds true for the image of Russians in the United States, Germany, and other countries in Europe (Rosner, 1995). Anthropological fieldwork has shown that Russian speakers in the Netherlands have chosen to manipulate and exploit their criminal image rather than contest it. The result of this interaction is a self-fulfilling prophecy. The image of organized crime sets a behavior pattern for some immigrants, and privately or collectively, they have learned to manipulate it to further their economic and political interests. Russianness is created and socially implemented. It provides a neutralization technique for people who get caught: How could they, as Russians, know that their customs would be illegal in another country? Real or played connections with the Russian mob serve to scare away economic competitors. In personal conflicts, it can be advantageous to use the criminal stereotype against the opponent. The criminal reputation of Russian immigrants can even be used to stop further immigration, as in the case of the Dutch Jewish community that does not want its good name tarnished by newcomers. The Russian-speaking immigrants and the criminals among them are not the passive objects of prejudice and stereotypes; they are actively engaged in a process of constructing and exploiting their own image. Taken to its logical consequence, one might say that the criminalization of a group or a category of people is one aspect of the formation of ethnicity.

REFERENCES

Albanese, J. (1996). *Organized crime in America* (3rd ed.). Cincinnati, OH: Anderson.

Albini, J. L. (1971). *The American Mafia: Genesis of a legend.* New York: Irvington.

Amir, M. (1996). Organized crime in Israel. *Transnational Organized Crime, 2*(4).

Baumann, G. (1999). *The multicultural riddle: Rethinking national, ethnic, and religious identities.* New York: Routledge.

Block, A. A. (1985). *East side-West side, organizing crime in New York, 1930-1950.* New Brunswick, NJ: Transaction.

Bovenkerk, F., & Yesilgoz, Y. (1998). *De maffia van Turkije* [The Turkish mafia]. Amsterdam: Meulenhoff/Kritak.

Chambliss, W. (1975). On the paucity of original research on organized crime: A footnote to Galliher and Cain. *The American Sociologist, 10,* 36-39.

Dunn, G. (1997). Major Mafia gangs in Russia. In P. Williams (Ed.), *Russian organized crime: The new threat?* (pp. 63-87). London: Frank Cass.

Eriksen, T. H. (1993). *Ethnicity and nationalism. Anthropological perspectives.* London: Pluto.

Finckenauer, J., & Waring, E. (1997). Russian émigré crime in the United States: Organized crime or crime that is organized? In P. Williams (Ed.), *Russian organized crime: The new threat?* (pp. 139-155). London: Frank Cass.

Gambetta, D. (1993). *The Sicilian Mafia, the business of private protection.* Cambridge, MA: Harvard University Press.

Gurov, A. (1995). *Krasnaya Mafia* [Red Mafia]. Moscow: Samotzvet Miki Kommerchiskyi Vestnik.

Haller, M. H. (1971). Organized crime in urban society. *Journal of Social History, 5,* 210-234.

Ianni, F.A.J. (1972). *A family business. Kinship and state control in organized crime.* London: Routledge Kegan Paul.

Konstantinov, A., & Dikselius, M. (1997). *Banditskaya Rossiya* [Bandit Russia]. St. Petersburg, Soviet Union: Moskva Olma-Press.

Lyman, M. D., & Potter, G. (1997). *Organized crime.* Upper Saddle River, NJ: Prentice Hall.

Martens, F. T. (1986). Organized crime control: The limits of government intervention. *Journal of Criminal Justice, 14,* 239-247.

Polsky, N. (1971). *Hustlers, beats and others.* New York: Penguin.

Rosner, L. (1995). The sexy Russian Mafia. *Criminal Organizations, 10*(1).

Siegel, D. (1998). *The great immigration. Russian Jews in Israel.* Oxford, UK: Berghahn.

Smith, D. C., Jr. (1990). *The Mafia mystique.* Lanham, MD: University Press.

Sutherland, E., & Cressey, D. (1960). *Principles of criminology* (6th ed.). Philadelphia: J. B. Lippincott.

Williams, P. (1995). The new threat: Transnational criminal organizations and international security. *Criminal Organizations, 9,* 3-19.

Dina Siegel is a cultural anthropologist and an associate professor of criminology at the University of Utrecht. She is the author of Russian Jewish Immigration in Israel *and* The Great Immigration: Russian Jews in Israel. `

Frank Bovenkerk is a cultural anthropologist and a professor of criminology at the University of Utrecht. He has published articles on criminology and organized crime, in particular De Maffia van Turkije *(with Y. Yesilgoz).*

[13]

A COMPARATIVE ASSESSMENT OF CRIMINAL INVOLVEMENT AMONG IMMIGRANTS AND NATIVES ACROSS SEVEN NATIONS

James P. Lynch and Rita J. Simon

This article examines the relationship between immigration policy and crime in seven nations. The countries involved are Australia, Canada, France, Germany, Great Britain, Japan, and the United States. Immigration policy and the criminal involvement of immigrants are compared to determine whether there is a pattern between the two, what that pattern is, and why it exists. The nations examined have very different immigration policies. Some are "immigrant nations," where the volume of immigrants is high, barriers to entry are low, and naturalization is encouraged. Others are "nonimmigrant nations," in which the volume of immigration is relatively low, the barriers to entry are substantial, and permanent settlement and attainment of citizenship are not encouraged. There is a general (but not perfect) pattern in which "immigrant" nations have lower ratios of immigrant to native crime than nations with less liberal policies. It is not clear whether this relationship is due more to the general ability of these nations to integrate foreign populations or to immigration policies per se.

IMMIGRATION STATUTES, POLICIES, AND PRACTICES

Among the nations examined there are substantial differences in immigration policies and practices. Australia, Canada, and the United States appear to conform to the profile of "immigrant nations." In contrast, Germany and Japan have very restrictive immigration policies and fit the profile of "nonimmigrant nations." Great Britain and France have policies that share some of the attributes of immigrant nations and some of the attributes of nonimmigrant nations, while at the same time being quite different from each other.

Admissions

As of 1994, the foreign-born population of the United States comprised 8.7 percent of the total population (U.S. Department of Immigration and Naturalization, 1996). In Australia in 1990, the foreign-born comprised 23 percent of the population (Australian Bureau of Statistics, 1992), and in Canada, as of 1991, 15.6 percent of the population were foreign-born (Citizenship and Immigration, 1994). In Japan, as of 1994, only 1 percent of the population were classified as registered aliens (persons who reside in Japan for more than 90 days) (Macura & Coleman, 1994). As of 1990, approximately 3.1 percent of the British, 8.6 percent of the French (Levy, 1991), and 8.7 percent of the German population were foreign-born (Kurthen, 1995, p. 921). (It must be remembered that the 8.7 percent figure for Germany includes all persons who are not ethnic Germans. So, for example, a Turk whose family has resided in Germany for four generations would still be considered a foreigner. This is substantially different from the concept of "foreign-born" as used in other nations examined here, i.e., persons born in another country. The percentage of foreign-born in Germany, then, is considerably less than 8.7.)

An examination of current immigration policies in the six countries in which immigration of foreign labor has been either an old or a relatively recent phenomenon reveals that all of these countries have adopted some restrictionist statutes. The United States first introduced major across-the-board immigration restrictions with the passage of the Quota Acts in 1921 and 1925. Current immigration policies are a product of the 1990 Immigration Act (Simon & Alexander, 1993), which defines a three-track preference system that grants the greatest number of visas per year to immediate family members—480,000 out of a total of 675,000. Of the remaining 195,000 visas, 140,000 are distributed among those potential immigrants who are likely to make an economic contribution, 27,000 are for those who are highly skilled, and 28,000 visas are available for demonstrably unskilled workers. An additional 55,000 "diversity" visas are available for immigrants from countries that in the past have been well represented in the immigrant pool, especially European countries. As a function of the passage of the Refugee Act of 1980, the president, in consultation with the Congress, can set limits on the number of refugees admitted each year. As of 1990, the limit was set at 125,000.

In Canada and Australia current immigration statutes restrict the number of immigrants and give preference to family reunification. Canada first introduced an immigration point system in 1967 and has revised the allocation of points over the years. In its current form, the 1985 Immigration Act established the following three purposes of immigration: family reunion, economic demands, and humanitarian goals (e.g., refugees and asylum seekers). Of the 200,000 immigrants admitted in 1993, more than half were admitted on the basis of family reunification (Citizenship and Immigration, 1994).

In 1979, Australia established a Numerical Assessment System (NUMAS) for determining the basis on which it would admit immigrants (Hawkins, 1988). NUMAS divided potential immigrant admissions into three categories: family reunification, business, and humanitarian. Of the 80,000 immigrants admitted in 1993, 45,000 gained entry on the basis of family reunification, about 25,000 on the basis of occupational and business skills, and 10,000 were admitted as refugees (Australian Bureau of Statistics, 1994).

In France, immigration is determined and controlled by the Office National de l'Immigration (ONI), which was established in 1945. Beginning in the middle 1970s, preference for immigrants was no longer determined by labor needs except for certain industries (mining, construction, and agriculture), and instead family reunification became first preference for granting visas. By the late 1970s and up through 1981, the ONI had introduced incentives for certain categories of immigrants (e.g., Algerians) to leave the country and not return (Zimmerman, 1995). Families were offered 10,000 francs if they were willing to leave permanently. The ONI set a goal of trying to persuade 35,000 persons to leave each year (Hammar, 1985). By 1988 France was rejecting half of the persons seeking asylum in the country. Beginning in the middle 1980s, on the criterion of family reunification, some 175,000 immigrants have been admitted into France each year (Hammar, 1985).

Long an exporter of emigrants, Great Britain began current British immigration policy with the Immigration Act of 1971, which recognized the right to abode for citizens of the United Kingdom and her colonies and for certain Commonwealth citizens called "patrials" (Hammar, 1985). The only avenue for admission other than qualification in these categories is on grounds of family reunification or work permits. Work permits are only available for persons holding professional qualifications or special skills. In 1993, some 55,000 persons were granted the right of indefinite residence in Great Britain.

Germany has always maintained that "it is not an immigration nation" (Hammar, 1985). The admission of foreigners was always closely tied to labor market needs, and when those needs were met workers were excluded or expelled (Hammar, 1985). During the years immediately preceding and following the Second World War, foreign labor was much in demand. However, even during the period of heavy recruitment of guest workers following the Second World War, these foreign workers were denied legal rights of immigration or residence. The customary length of stay was one year. Specific work permits (which were issued for jobs in a specific firm that no German could fill) and nonspecific work permits (which could be obtained after eight years of residence and five years of uninterrupted work) were issued in the 1970s (Convey & Kupiszewski, 1995). At the present time only the following groups of persons are entitled to a nonspecific work permit: foreigners married to German citizens, citizens of the European Union, and political refugees. In July 1993 asylum seekers were required to demonstrate that they risked political persecution if they returned to their home country; economic persecution was no long sufficient. After the passage of the 1993 Act only 4 percent of asylum seekers were accepted as political refugees (Kurthen, 1995).

The last country included in this study, Japan, can be summarized in a few words. It is virtually impossible for a foreign national to become a Japanese citizen. As of 1994 there were some 1,300,000 aliens living in Japan, more than 80 percent of whom were Koreans who came to Japan initially when Korea was a colony of Japan before the Second World War. Foreigners comprise 1 percent

4   *James P. Lynch and Rita J. Simon*

of the Japanese population. There are fewer than 5,000 refugees in the country and most do not plan to remain (Macura & Coleman, 1994).

The types of restrictions placed on admissions reveal a great deal about a nation's attitude toward immigrants and immigration, but the way in which policies reflect these orientations is not simple. In general, admissions policies are "inviting" when they allow a large number of persons into the country relative to the current population, when they do not subject applicants to extensive screening based upon cultural similarity to the host nation, and when they guarantee, from the beginning, that persons admitted can expect to become permanent citizens if they behave reasonably. Germany and Japan clearly do not satisfy these criteria. Their admissions policies allow for the entry of very few people relative to their population. Those who enter must meet strict criteria that ensure that they will not be a "drain" on the society. The prospect of permanent residence is not assumed and, in some cases, is not even remotely possible (Kurthen, 1995; Taguchi, 1983).

The policies followed in Australia, Canada, and the United States are much more inviting. They allow relatively large numbers of persons in, do not impose excessive screening on those persons, and hold out that those admitted can become permanent residents. The policies in these nations allow for a variety of reasons for admission including family reunification, economic needs of the nation, and refugee status. These reasons for admission strike a balance between the need to integrate current aliens and the admission of new people. Family reunification can be seen as a filter through which candidates for admission must pass. It increases the chances that those who are admitted will not become a burden on society because they have family members who will be responsible for them and will foster their integration into society. It also increases the investment of prior immigrants in the society by allowing them a more complete and normal life. Family reunification is thus both an invitation by the host nation and a protection, a way of filtering out "uncertain" or risky applicants. The various categories of economic reasons for admission allow new people into the society who do not necessarily have family members to help integrate them into the society. These economic immigrants later become the engine for additional family reunification. The mix of approximately 60 percent family and 40 percent economic immigration typical of these immigrant nations virtually ensures a constant flow of immigrants.

The admissions policies followed in France and England are somewhat less inviting. Although France has fairly high rates of admission, they are based almost entirely on family reunification, which can be seen as a way of screening and limiting new entries. Without a substantial number of new admissions, the volume of persons who can be admitted for purposes of family reunification must decline as the number of family members still living in the country of origin declines. Although the disproportionate reliance on family reunification may help to screen and integrate immigrants, it is not a policy that is designed to perpetuate a steady flow of immigrants into the host nation. Britain practices a dual policy by which the entry of patrial and EEC applicants is relatively free and the entry of nonpatrials is largely limited to purposes of family reunification. As in the case of France, this type of admissions policy can be seen as a means of integrating those currently in the country while reducing the flow of new immigrants.

Naturalization

The nature of a country's immigration policy is gauged not only in terms of who and how many people it allows in but also in regard to how completely immigrants are allowed to participate in the life of the nation. Full participation in a country is achieved with citizenship, and the relative ease of naturalization says a great deal about the acceptance of immigrants. Here again the traditional immigrant nations are much more open than nonimmigrant nations, but there is still some unexpected variability in these policies.

Any foreigner who is lawfully admitted to the United States as a permanent resident can apply for citizenship after five years in residence. Spouses and children of resident aliens can apply after three years. Applicants must demonstrate the ability to read and write ordinary English as well as a basic knowledge of United States history and governmental structure. Good moral character is also required; this generally means employment and the absence of serious criminal activity. It is estimated that about 38 percent of an entering cohort of immigrants will ultimately naturalize (U.S. Department of Immigration and Naturalization, 1993).

The naturalization policies in Australia, Canada, Great Britain, and France are open and are very similar to those of the United States. The waiting period for citizenship in Canada was five years until 1977, when it was shortened to three years (Anderson & Lalani, 1994). In Australia, immigrants may become citizens after two years of residence have been completed and a basic knowledge of English has been demonstrated (Thomas & Flynn, 1994). In Great Britain naturalization requires five years of residence and sufficient knowledge of English (Hammar, 1985, p. 106). Citizenship is granted in France after a residency of five years as long as the applicant does not have a record of serious criminal activity (Hammar, 1985). Somewhere between 28 percent and 38 percent of entering cohorts of immigrants in France eventually become naturalized citizens (Ogden, 1991).

In contrast, becoming a naturalized citizen in Germany and Japan is difficult if not impossible. To be considered for naturalization in Germany one must (a) have resided in the country for at least 10 years, (b) hold a secure job, (c) renounce any other citizenship, (d) be fluent in German, and (e) be legally competent and have no police record. There is also a vague standard that allows for considerable agency discretion. It states that an applicant must "support(s) and participate(s) in the national community" or "have developed clear ties with and commitment to the community" (Donle & Kather, 1994). In January 1991 a rule was enacted stating that offspring of labor migrants in Germany could become naturalized if they are between 16 and 23 years of age and have resided in Germany for at least eight years and have at least six years of schooling. They must also give up any other citizenship. Persons over 23 years need 15 years of residence and must provide proof of guaranteed subsistence in Germany. Fewer than 20,000 foreigners a year became naturalized during the 1980s.

In Japan naturalization is even less frequent than in Germany. The law requires that applicants for naturalization must be permanent residents for five years, be self-supporting, and be of good moral character (Shimizu, 1994). Citizenship status, however, is not a right. It is granted at the discretion of the Ministry of Justice and only a very small number of aliens have been naturalized: 140,000 persons in more than 30 years (Taguchi, 1983).

Internal Regulation of Immigrants

France, Germany, and Japan have much more stringent control requirements of aliens than the other nations examined here. In Germany, for example, guest workers must apply for residence and work permits. These permits must be renewed upon change of employment or residence (Hammar, 1985). These episodic checks give immigration authorities the chance to intrude into the lives of immigrants. Although the likelihood of interference may be small, there is the chance that the required permits may not be renewed and the foreign national will be required to leave. This uncertainty reinforces the perception that foreigners are outsiders. The internal controls on foreigners in Germany lessen with the length of residence; recent arrivals must renew their permits at more frequent intervals than persons who have lived in Germany for longer periods of time (Convey & Kupiszewski, 1995). The French and the Japanese have similar control arrangements by which immigration authorities have numerous opportunities to intrude into the lives of immigrants and the discretion to affect a foreigner's ability to remain in the country (Hammar, 1985; Shimizu, 1994). In contrast, persons admitted to the United States, Canada, Australia, and Great Britain have very few obligations that do not also apply to citizens. There are no permits required for employment and housing, for example.

The relative positions of these nations on the various dimensions of immigration policy are summarized in Table 1.

The common perceptions about immigrant and nonimmigrant nations are broadly consistent with immigration policies in the respective nations. Immigrant nations such as the United States, Canada, and Australia have relatively open immigration policies and high proportions of foreign-born persons in the resident population. It is interesting to note that the proportion of foreign-born is higher in both Canada and Australia than it is in the United States, but the immigrant ethos appears to figure much more prominently in the United States than it does in the civic culture of these other societies. Germany, and even more distinctly Japan, are clearly nonimmigrant nations. They have very restrictive (or no) immigration policies, relatively strict policies for the control of resident aliens, very restrictive naturalization policies, and low proportions of foreign-born persons in their populations. France and England have mixed or ambivalent policies. Both the French and the British have very restricted admissions policies based on race and national origin, but naturalization policies are relatively open and pains are taken to ensure equal treatment of residents once they are in the country. The French have stricter internal controls on aliens after they enter the country.

Table 1

Dimensions of Immigrant Policy by Nation

Policy area	Australia	Canada	U.S.	France	England	Germany	Japan
Admit policy	Liberal Open	Liberal Open	Liberal Open	Moderate Open	Restrictive Closed	Restrictive Closed	Restrictive Closed
Admit practice	Liberal Open	Liberal Open	Liberal Open	Liberal Open	Restrictive Closed	Restrictive Closed	Restrictive Closed
Naturalization policy	Liberal	Liberal	Liberal	Liberal	Liberal	Restrictive	Restrictive
Naturalization rate	High	High	High	High	High	Low	Low
Control policy	Minimal	Minimal	Minimal	Substantial	Minimal	Substantial	Substantial
Administrative discretion	Minimal	Minimal	Minimal	Moderate	Minimal	Substantial	Substantial
Public integration efforts	Moderate	Moderate	Low	Moderate	Low	High	Low
Illegal immigration	Low	Low	High	High	Low	Low	Low

8   *James P. Lynch and Rita J. Simon*

CRIMINAL INVOLVEMENT AMONG IMMIGRANTS AND NATIVES ACROSS COUNTRIES

Complexities in the Comparison of Crimes

Before examining the incarceration rates, it is important that we discuss the limitations and complexities involved in making cross-national comparisons of crime and particularly of crime involving immigrants. First of all, it is difficult to assess the volume of crime, in large measure because the concept is so variable across nations. There are minute legal definitions of criminal behavior and these definitions can vary substantially across nations (and in some cases even within nations). In England and Wales, for example, the forcible entry of an "out building" such as a barn or garage (as opposed to a residence) would be burglary whereas in the United States it would not (Mayhew, 1985). These differences in the legal definition of criminal acts will complicate cross-national comparisons. Even when the legal definitions of crime are similar, the procedures used to identify, label, and count criminal behavior can introduce differences across nations (Biderman, 1965; Biderman & Lynch, 1991; Lynch, 1988). Police statistics in a very decentralized police system such as that of the United States will clearly be more variable than in countries with more centralized police systems such as France (Bayley, 1985; Reichel, 1995). Victimization surveys are another common source of data on crime, but they too can employ variable procedures that can affect crime counts cross-nationally (Block, 1993; Lynch, 1993).

Many of these problems in the nonuniformity of cross-national crime statistics are made less damaging if we compare the ratio of the criminal involvement of aliens to the criminal involvement of the native-born population or the criminal involvement of citizens. To the extent that differences in crime statistics are constant across the foreign and native populations within countries, these differences should not affect cross-national comparisons.

It is not clear how tenable this assumption of constancy is. Nations with very restrictive immigration policies and especially those with a great many internal restrictions on aliens may be more likely to detect and record the criminal involvement of aliens as opposed to that of citizens. As our review of immigration policies indicated, nonimmigrant nations have closer supervision of noncitizen residents than countries with less restrictive policies. This could account for higher rates of criminal involvement of aliens relative to citizens in France, Germany, and Japan as compared to the United States, Australia, and Canada. It is important to note, however, that these nations also have many more restrictions on their own citizens than immigrant nations do (e.g., internal passports). This should reduce artificial discrepancies between estimates of the criminal involvement of aliens and those for native populations.

A more serious problem in identifying crimes committed by aliens is the identification of criminals as aliens. In a large proportion of crimes the offender is not known and therefore his or her citizenship cannot be determined. Consequently, we are restricted to comparisons of offenses where the offender is known. Even when the offender is known, his or her citizenship may not be. An even more difficult distinction must be made between foreigners involved in crime and immigrants involved in crime. Immigrants are foreigners who come to the host nation with the intention to stay. Many more foreigners enter host countries for other purposes such as business meetings, conferences, and tourism, with no intention of permanent residence. These "sojourning foreigners" will be recorded in unknown proportions as "aliens" in police and correctional statistics. To the extent that these sojourning foreigners are included in the numerator of crime rates they must also be included in the denominator of those rates. In many countries, it is difficult to assess the number of sojourning foreigners in the country at any given time. Immigration services, for example, may count border crossings but not link those crossings to individual persons. Consequently, one person can account for numerous border crossings. Using crossings or entries would provide a substantial overcount of sojourning foreigners in any given period.

Another problem posed by sojourning foreigners is the fact that nations do not always keep detailed data on how long these visitors stay in the host nation. This is important for the computation of incarceration rates in that persons at risk, e.g., foreigners, should figure in the denominator in proportion to their exposure. Because immigrants and permanent residents are in the country 365 days a year and sojourning foreigners usually have much shorter time in exposure, it would not be appropriate to weight sojourning foreigners and immigrants equally.

Fortunately, the participation of sojourning foreigners in criminal activity is likely to be heavily concentrated in drug crimes rather than other types of common law crimes. A central feature of the drug trade is moving the merchandise across borders. Much of this moving is done by tourists and other sojourning foreigners who are detected at airports or other ports of entry. It is less likely for foreigners to cross borders for the purpose of committing assaults or street robberies. Hence the distortions introduced into crime and incarceration rates by sojourning foreigners would be lessened if drug offenses were not included in rate comparisons.

Finally, there is the problem of citizenship and nativity that confounds many cross-national comparisons of statistical data. Some nations identify offenders or inmates by nation of birth while others distinguish persons according to citizenship. It is possible that definitions of foreigners based upon nativity would include persons who have been in the country for a longer time than groups defined by citizenship status. This could result in lower rates of crime or incarceration for foreigners defined by nativity criteria than for those defined by citizenship.

Although all of these problems complicate cross-national comparisons of crime by immigrants and natives, making these comparisons with the available data is still worthwhile. Only after these comparisons are made can we assess the likelihood that the observed differences are due to noncomparabilities in the data. In some cases, likely errors in the data may be in a direction that could not possibly explain the differences observed. In that event, these flawed data can still be used to inform the issues addressed here.

Comparative Incarceration Rates

The most consistently available cross-national data on criminal involvement of aliens come from incarceration rates. This is the case because there is generally more information available on persons at the time of incarceration than at earlier stages in system processing such as arrest. Consequently, we are better able to determine who is a citizen and who is not at the incarceration stage. The crime data referred to in this article are based on incarceration rates.

In comparing incarceration rates, the pattern that is seen to emerge across the seven nations is that immigrants in the United States, Canada, and Australia, the traditional immigrant receiving countries, have lower overall rates than natives, whereas immigrants in France, Germany, and Japan have higher rates than natives. Great Britain is in between the immigrant nations and the nonimmigrant nations but is closer to the immigrant nations in the ratio of immigrant-to-native rates of incarceration (see Table 2).

Table 2

Incarceration Ratios for Immigrants and Nonimmigrants by Nation and Year

Nation[a]	Year	Ratio
France	1993	6.01
Japan	1993	3.50
Germany	1990	1.90
England	1992	1.29
Australia	1985	0.68
United States	1991	1.13
Canada	1989	0.58

Note. Sources are cited in Appendix A.

[a]This is the ratio of the population-based stock incarceration rate of immigrants to citizens.

Among the three nations for which incarceration rates by types of offense are available (Australia, France, and the United States), there is one category of offense for which immigrants have higher incarceration rates than natives: drug offenses. Table 3 compares the ratios of incarceration rates for immigrants to those for natives across nations for crimes of violence, property, and drug use and trafficking.

Table 3

Incarceration Ratios for Immigrants and Nonimmigrants by Type of Offense, Nation, and Year

Offense	Australia (1985)	United States (1991)	France (1993)
Violence	0.78	0.83	3.35
Property	0.64	0.62	4.83
Drugs	2.29	2.37	NA
Drug trafficking	3.02	1.48	11.06

Note. Sources are cited in Appendix B.

In the United States in 1991, immigrants were 2.37 times as likely as natives to be incarcerated for drug offenses, and in Australia in 1985 immigrants were incarcerated for drug offenses at 2.29 times the rate of natives. In Canada in 1991, among all those imprisoned for drug offenses, 67 percent were natives and 33 percent were immigrants—a much higher percentage than the latter's representation in the population of the country. In England in 1995, 98 percent of all incarcerated immigrants had been convicted of drug offenses (Richards, McWilliams, Cameron, & Cutler, 1995). In France in 1995, 27 percent of incarcerated immigrants had been convicted of drug offenses compared to 22 percent of incarcerated natives. In Germany as of 1991, the rate of immigrants incarcerated for drug offenses was 192 per 100,000 compared to 73 per 100,000 for natives. In Japan, the incarceration rate for drug offenses by immigrants was .6 per 1,000 compared to .1 per 1,000 for natives.

The universal overrepresentation of foreigners in incarceration rates for drug offenses is probably due in some measure to the inclusion of sojourning foreigners rather than immigrants in the numerator of the incarceration rates. Consequently, in comparisons it may be more appropriate to emphasize those crimes where this distortion is less likely. When immigrant and nonimmigrant nations are compared on incarceration rates for violent and property crime only, the patterns are consistent with those observed for overall incarceration rates: Immigrants in immigrant nations have lower incarceration rates relative to natives than immigrants in nonimmigrant nations.

PUBLIC PERCEPTIONS OF THE RELATIONSHIP
BETWEEN IMMIGRANTS AND CRIME RATES

Finally, it is useful to compare these nations in terms of the popular perception of the criminal involvement of immigrants. Cross-national comparisons of public opinion have shown that public opinion toward immigrants is largely negative regardless of the immigration policies of the nation (Simon & Alexander, 1983; Simon & Lynch, in press). It would be interesting to see whether this pattern holds for the perceived criminal involvement of immigrants. Moreover, it would be interesting to see whether perceptions of immigrant criminality are consistent with actual incarceration rates. If perceptions are more negative than the reality, this would suggest anti-immigrant feeling.

Public opinion data from the 1995 International Social Survey do show a relationship between public beliefs about immigrants' propensity to commit crime and the incarceration rates that are described in this article. (Unfortunately, France was not included in that survey.) Responses indicate that the publics in countries with higher immigrant incarceration rates and more restrictive immigration policies are more likely to express strong agreement with the statement "Immigrants increase crime rates." Table 4 provides a more detailed breakdown of the responses.

Table 4

Opinions About Whether Immigrants Increase Crime by Country

Country	% strongly agree	% agree	% neither	% disagree	% strongly disagree	Total
Australia	9.5	21.9	25.6	31.5	11.5	100 (2,390)
Canada	5.0	15.3	24.0	38.4	17.4	100 (989)
Germany[a]	19.3	35.4	21.8	17.4	6.2	100 (1,168)
Great Britain	7.8	18.2	34.9	31.7	7.3	100 (996)
Japan	38.7	26.6	19.8	5.6	9.3	100 (1,223)
United States	7.5	25.9	29.1	30.7	6.8	100 (1,265)

[a]These responses are based on a survey conducted in West Germany. For East Germany the distribution was 28.4, 39.5, 17.7, 11.9, and 2.5. *Note.* Chi-square = 1,313. Degrees of freedom = 20. *p* = .000.

Almost two thirds of the respondents in Japan, the country reporting the highest incarceration rates and the smallest percentage of immigrants, believed that immigrants increase the crime rates in their country. The country that had the second largest percentage of agreement was Germany, which also has the second highest incarceration rate reported in Table 2. Germany, like Japan, has very restrictive immigration policies. The much lower responses among the more traditional immigrant receiving countries (Australia, Canada, and the United States) are also consistent with their lower incarceration rates. The responses of the British public are more closely aligned with the latter group than they are with the German and Japanese responses, and this is consistent with both their incarceration rates and their immigration policy.

CONCLUDING COMMENTS

The pattern revealed in the data suggests that the more restrictive a nation's immigration policy the greater the incarceration rates of foreigners and the greater the public's belief that immigrants increase crime rates in their country. It is not a perfect pattern, however. The disproportionate involvement of foreigners in crime in France (for which, unfortunately, public opinion data are not available) is much greater than that in Germany or Japan, although the latter nations have much more restrictive immigration policies than the former. Nevertheless, the criminal involvement of foreigners is lower than that of the native population in immigrant nations and is substantially and consistently higher than that of the native population in nonimmigrant nations.

It is unlikely that this pattern is due to nonuniformities in the data, such as differences in definitions of immigrants. It is true, for example, that the nations with the lowest ratio of immigrant-to-citizen incarceration rates, i.e., Australia and Canada, are also the nations where "immigrant" is defined as foreign-born as opposed to noncitizen. The "foreign-born" can include a large number of persons who are more integrated into the host society than "noncitizens," e.g., more naturalized citizens or older as opposed to younger persons, and can therefore result in lower incarceration rates. However, there are a number of instances in the data where this relationship between incarceration rates and the definition of immigrant does not hold. France and the United States have similar definitions of immigrant but very different incarceration rates for immigrants and natives. Germany has a much more inclusive definition of immigrant than Australia or Canada but much higher incarceration rates. Although differences in definition may affect the incarceration rates, they do not account for the large and consistent differences observed across nations.

If we can assume that the relationship between immigration policy and the criminal involvement of immigrants observed here is real, we must ask why it occurs. Immigration policy can lead in a very direct way to high levels of incarceration for immigrants, as in the case where an extensive internal control net brings immigrants into contact with the police at higher rates than the native population. Under these conditions, the same underlying rates of criminality for the immigrant and native populations would result in higher incarceration rates for immigrants. The role of immigration policy can be less direct if highly selective admissions policies, either intentionally or unintentionally, choose the more or less crime-prone. Guest worker policies that lure young males (a high offending group) but make it difficult for them to marry or to attain permanent residence could foster higher crime and incarceration rates for immigrants relative to the native-born. The role of immigration policy can be more remote still where it is simply a part of a much larger pattern of institutional arrangements that complicate or facilitate the accommodation of foreigners.

Exclusionary immigration policies could simply reflect the traditions of a nation that relies on cultural homogeneity as a major feature of social control. In such a society immigrants will (and perhaps must) be kept on the margins lest they threaten the value consensus on which social order rests. Even if immigration policies in these nations were to become more inclusive, those who were admitted would find it very difficult to become integrated into the society. This marginality could result in higher rates of criminality among immigrant groups or more intensive official scrutiny of immigrants relative to natives. Both of these conditions could result in the higher incarceration rates that are observed here in nonimmigrant nations. In this case immigration policy is correlated with, but not causal of, differential incarceration rates of immigrants and the native-born.

We do not have the detailed information required to sort these issues out. It is sufficient here to demonstrate that immigration policies and the criminal involvement of immigrants are related. Much more fine-grained and careful work must be done to determine whether this pattern is causal or spurious and, if it is causal, to disentangle the causal process.

REFERENCES

Anderson, S., & Lalani, E. H. (1994). Canada. In D. Campbell & J. Fisher (Eds.), *International immigration and nationality law: Immigration supplement 2* (pp. 11-IX2). Boston, MA: Nihoff.

Australian Bureau of Statistics. (1992). *Australian population trends and prospects, 1990.* Canberra, Australia: Author.

Australian Bureau of Statistics. (1994). *Australian population trends and prospects, 1993.* Canberra, Australia: Author.

Bayley, D. (1985). *Patterns of policing: A comparative international analysis.* New Brunswick, NJ: Rutgers University Press.

Beck, A. J., Gilliard, D., Greenfeld, L., Harlowe, C., Hester, T., Jankowski, L., Snell, T., Stephan, J., & Morton, D. (1993). *Survey of inmates in state prison, 1991.* Washington, DC: Bureau of Justice Statistics.

Biderman, A. D. (1965). Social indicators and goals. In R. Bauer (Ed.), *Social indicators* (pp. 68-153). Cambridge, MA: M.I.T. Press.

Biderman, A. D., & Lynch, J. P. (1991). *Understanding crime incidence statistics: Why the UCR diverges from the NCS.* New York, NY: Springer Verlag.

Block, R. (1993). *Measuring victimization: The effects of methodology, sampling and fielding.* In A. del Frate, U. Zvekic, & J. van Dijk (Eds.), *Understanding crime: Experiences of crime and criminal control* (pp. 163-174). Rome, Italy: United Nations Inter-Regional Crime and Justice Research Institute.

Citizenship and Immigration. (1994). *Facts and figures.* Ottawa, Canada: Minister of Supplies and Services.

Convey, M., & Kupiszewski, M. (1995). Keeping up with Schengen: Migration and policy in the European Union. *International Migration Review, 29*(4), 939-961.

Donle, C., & Kather, P. (1994). Germany. In D. Campbell & J. Fisher (Eds.), *International immigration and nationality law: Immigration supplement 2* (pp. 11-IX2). Boston, MA: Nihoff Publishers.

Hammar, T. (1985). *European immigration policy: A comparative study.* Cambridge, MA: Cambridge University Press.

Hawkins, F. (1988). *Canada and immigration: Public policy and public concern.* Kingston, Ontario: McGill-Queens University Press.

Hazelhurst, K. (1987). *Migration, ethnicity and crime in Australian society.* Canberra, Australia: Australian Institute of Criminology.

Kurthen, H. (1995). Germany at the crossroads: National identity and the challenge of immigration. *International Migration Review, 29*(4), 914-937.

Levy, M. (1991, December). A clarification: Foreigners, immigrants, French citizens of foreign origin. *Newsletter of The National Institute for the Study of Demography*, pp. 24-30.

Lynch, J. P. (1988). A comparison of imprisonment in the United States, Canada, England, and West Germany: A limited test of the punitiveness hypothesis. *Journal of Criminal Law and Criminology, 79*(1), 180-217.

Lynch, J. P. (1993). Secondary analysis of international crime survey data. In A. del Frate, U. Zvekic, & J. van Dijk (Eds.), *Understanding crime: Experiences of crime and criminal control* (pp. 175-192). Rome, Italy: United Nations Inter-Regional Crime and Justice Research Institute.

Macura, M., & Coleman, D. (1994). International migration: Regional processes and responses. *International Migration Review, 29*(4), 914-937.

Mayhew, P. (1985). *Residential burglary: A comparison of the United States, Canada, England, and Wales.* Washington, DC: National Institute of Justice.

Ministry of Justice Japan. (1994). *Summary of the White Paper on Crime.* Tokyo, Japan: Author.

Ogden, P. E. (1991). Immigration to France since 1945: Myth and reality. *Ethnic and Racial Studies, 14*, 294-318.

Reichel, P. (1995). *Comparative criminal justice systems: A topical approach.* Englewood Cliffs, NJ: Prentice-Hall.

Richards, M., McWilliams, B., Cameron, C., & Cutler, J. (1995). Foreign nationals in English prisons: Some policy issues. *The Howard Journal, 34*(3), 195-207.

Shimizu, A. (1994). Japan. In D. Campbell & J. Fisher (Eds.), *International immigration and nationality law: Immigration supplement 2* (pp. 11-IX2). Boston, MA: Nihoff.

Simon, R. J., & Alexander, S. H. (1993). *The ambivalent welcome: Print media, public opinion and immigration.* Westport, CT: Praeger Publishers.

Simon, R. J., & Lynch, J. P. (in press). A comparison of immigration policy and public opinion in seven nations. *International Migration Review.*

Taguchi, S. (1983). A note on current research of immigrant groups in Japan. *International Migration Review, 17*(4), 699-714.

Thomas, D. G., & Flynn, M. J. (1994). Australia. In D. Campbell & J. Fisher (Eds.), *International immigration and nationality law: Immigration supplement 2* (pp. 11-IX7). Boston, MA: Nihoff.

Tomasevski, K. (1994). *Foreigners in prison.* Helsinki, Finland: European Institute for Crime Prevention and Control.

Tournier, P. (1997). La délinquance des étrangers en France—Analyse des statistiques pénale. In S. Palidda (Ed.), *Immigrant delinquency* (pp. 133-162). Brussels, Belgium: European Commission.

U.S. Department of Immigration and Naturalization. (1993). *Statistical yearbook, 1992.* Washington, DC: Government Printing Office.

U.S. Department of Immigration and Naturalization. (1996). *Statistical yearbook, 1995.* Washington, DC: Government Printing Office.

Zimmerman, K. F. (1995). Tackling the European migration problem. *Journal of Economic Perspectives, 9*(2), 45-62.

16   *James P. Lynch and Rita J. Simon*

Appendix A

Sources for Incarceration Rates Found in Table 2

Australia

The denominators for the incarceration rates in Table 2 and Table 3 are taken from Hazelhurst (1987). The Australian-born adult population is taken from Table 39, page 107. The foreign-born population is taken from Table 2. The numerators are from Table 16.

England and Wales

The incarceration rates for citizens and noncitizens in England and Wales are taken from Tomasevski (1994).

France

The incarceration rates for citizens and noncitizens in France are taken from Tomasevski (1994, Table 4, p. 9).

Germany

The incarceration rates for citizens and noncitizens in Germany are taken from Tomasevski (1994, Table 4, p. 9).

Japan

Estimates of the incarceration rates of citizens and noncitizens are taken from imprisonment data in *Summary of the White Paper on Crime* (Ministry of Justice Japan, 1994). Estimates of the total number of persons in prison and the total number of foreigners serving sentence in prison at the end of 1993 are taken from page 24. An estimate of citizen inmates was made by subtracting foreigners from the total prisoner count.

The estimate of the total resident population for Japan in 1993 was 124,764,000. According to the Ministry of Justice (1994, p. 27), 1.1 percent of that population were registered aliens. Multiplying these numbers resulted in an estimate of 1,372,404 registered aliens in 1993. Dividing the number of inmates by the number in the population yielded incarceration rates of .001 for foreigners and .000286 for the native population.

United States

The numerators for the incarceration rates for the United States are taken from the 1991 *Survey of Inmates in State Correctional Facilities, 1991* (Beck et al., 1993) and the corresponding survey for federal institutions. These surveys differentiated between citizens and noncitizens in custody. The denominators for the rates are taken from census estimates of the citizen and resident alien populations.

Appendix B

Sources for Incarceration Rates Found in Table 3

Australia

The denominators for the offense-specific incarceration rates in Table 3 are taken from Hazelhurst (1987). The Australian-born adult population is taken from Table 39, page 107. The foreign-born population is taken from Table 2. The numerators are taken from Table 16 and the offense-specific percentages from Figure 16. Violent offenses include all crimes against persons as well as a joint robbery-extortion classification. Property offenses include all crimes against property, and drug offenses relate to the classification of "drug offenses" used by Hazelhurst.

France

The incarceration rates are computed from data provided in Tournier (1997). Specifically, the numbers of citizens and noncitizens incarcerated for a specific offense are taken from Table 13, page 142. The estimates of the populations of citizens and noncitizens are taken from page 134. Violent crimes include all *crimes* as well as all *vol avec violence* and *coups et blessures volontaire*. This may be a slight overestimate of violent crimes because, according to police statistics, about 30 percent of *crimes* are property offenses. Property offenses include *vol* and *recel*. Drug offenses are *trafic de stupéfiants*.

United States

The numerators for the offense-specific incarceration rates for the United States are taken from the 1991 *Survey of Inmates in State Prison, 1991* (Beck et al., 1993, p. 8) and the corresponding survey for federal institutions. Violent offenses include murder, manslaughter, rape, sexual assault, robbery, and assault. Property offenses include burglary and larceny, and drug offenses refer to drug sale and possession.

[14]

DOES IMMIGRATION INCREASE HOMICIDE?
Negative Evidence From Three Border Cities

Matthew T. Lee
University of Akron

Ramiro Martinez, Jr.
*Florida International University,
National Consortium on Violence Research,
National Institute of Justice Du Bois Fellow*

Richard Rosenfeld
*University of Missouri—St. Louis,
National Consortium on Violence Research*

Understanding the complex relationship between immigration and crime was once a core concern of American sociology. Yet the extensive post-1965 wave of immigration to the United States has done little to rekindle scholarly interest in this topic, even as politicians and other public figures advocate public policies to restrict immigration as a means of preventing crime. Although both popular accounts and sociological theory predict that immigration should increase crime in areas where immigrants settle, this study of Miami, El Paso, and San Diego neighborhoods shows that, controlling for other influences, immigration generally does not increase levels of homicide among Latinos and African Americans. Our results not only challenge stereotypes of the "criminal immigrant" but also the core criminological notion that immigration, as a social process, disorganizes communities and increases crime.

Understanding the social consequences of immigration and urbanization were instrumental concerns of those who created American sociology as a distinct academic discipline (M. Waters 1999). The founders of the Chicago School of sociology were troubled by the urban problems linked to newcomers, and early sociologists wrestled with the connections between immigration and crime. This anxiety produced some of American sociology's most enduring conceptual and empirical work, including classics on social disorganization (Thomas and Znaniecki 1920; Shaw and McKay 1931) and culture conflict (Sutherland 1934; Sellin 1938). Despite the potentially significant effect of immigration on current levels of crime and the high-profile role of this relationship in the history of the discipline, contemporary sociological studies of the link between crime and immigration are scarce.

Direct all correspondence to Matthew T. Lee, Dept. of Sociology, University of Akron, Akron, OH 44325-1905; e-mail: mlee2@uakron.edu

560   THE SOCIOLOGICAL QUARTERLY Vol. 42/No. 4/2001

In this study, we evaluate the effects of recent immigration on the presence of homicide in urban neighborhoods.[1] In addition to its explicit focus on immigration, our study is based on four distinctive analytic approaches. First, the data were purposively drawn from three "border" cities—El Paso, Miami, and San Diego—all of which are major destination points for recent (legal and nonlegal) immigrants and places with some of the longest, most consistently sustained waves of immigration in U.S. history (INS 1987; Martinez and Lee 2000b). The availability of data from three distinct sites allows us to isolate the effects of each city's local context on homicide. These cities exhibit both similarities and differences along key dimensions such as economic deprivation, family structure, the presence of new immigrants, and the level of homicide and can therefore reveal variations in local patterns that are obscured in studies based on aggregated national data sets or on data from a single city. Second, we disaggregate homicide data to the level of the census tract, a meaningful unit of analysis (that roughly approximates neighborhoods) for within-city comparisons, particularly those involving crime (Crutchfield 1989; M. R. Lee 2000).[2]

Third, because the macrosocial factors that influence homicide vary across racial/ethnic groups (Ousey 1999), ethnically disaggregated homicide data were culled directly from each city's homicide investigation unit, which permits the linking of group-specific homicides aggregated to the tract level with census-derived population characteristics. Our goal is to assess the effects of immigration and other population characteristics on the levels of homicide of two historically disadvantaged ethnic groups in the three cities, Latinos and African Americans. Non-Latino whites are only briefly discussed in this investigation because they are less likely than blacks and Latinos to live in communities with elevated levels of deprivation, instability, and criminal violence, that is, the types of communities where recent immigrants tend to concentrate.

Finally, we employ an appropriate estimator to analyze multivariate patterns in homicide: Poisson regression (Long 1997). Ordinary least squares, which dominates previous studies of urban homicide, may not be robust against the highly skewed and truncated distribution of homicide events across areas within cities and therefore may produce biased estimates of the effects of community characteristics on homicide.

SOCIOLOGICAL IMAGES OF IMMIGRANTS AND CRIME

Even though studies of European immigrants in the early twentieth century found that immigrants were generally *less involved* in crime than natives, the stereotype of the criminal immigrant has persisted (Ferracuti 1968; T. Waters 1999; Martinez and Lee 2000b). But with few exceptions (e.g., Hagan and Palloni 1998, 1999), researchers have not investigated the criminal involvement of the post-1965 wave of non-European, largely Latino immigrants. The few available contemporary studies echo the findings from the early research, that immigrants are not particularly crime-prone relative to the native-born, even though they experience deleterious social conditions rivaling or surpassing those of the most disadvantaged native groups (Butcher and Piehl 1998; Hagan and Palloni 1998; Martinez and Lee 2000a). Yet public opinion of recent immigrants remains mixed, at best, and stereotypes endure that provide ideological support for restrictive immigration legislation (Butcher and Piehl 1998; Martinez and Lee 2000b).[3] For example, section 1 of California's controversial Proposition 187 declares that residents "have suffered and are suffering personal injury and damage caused by the criminal conduct of illegal aliens in this state" (quoted in Butcher and Piehl 1998, p. 457).

Ironically, well-established sociological perspectives on crime provide the theoretical underpinnings for the popular image linking immigration to crime. Although few scholars today take seriously the once popular view of immigrants as biologically deficient and therefore inherently criminally disposed, nearly all of the major theories of crime predict that recent immigrants should exhibit high levels of criminal involvement. We briefly sketch the implications for the immigrant-crime link of the three leading perspectives on the social sources of crime and delinquency: opportunity structure, cultural theories, and social disorganization (for more extensive discussions, see Bankston 1998; Martinez and Lee 2000b).

Opportunity Structure

Opportunity structure theories stress the material and social structures that shape the values and activities of different social groups (Bankston 1998). Because legitimate opportunities for wealth and social status are not equally available to all groups, some will "innovate" by taking advantage of available illegitimate opportunities. This type of explanation, in Robert K. Merton's (1938) original formulation, draws attention to the ways in which disadvantaged groups (which often include recent immigrants) may be denied the legitimate means (education, decent jobs) to attain culturally prescribed success and goals (a middle-class lifestyle). Applied to homicide, this perspective suggests that blocked opportunities may result in "instrumental" killings that are fundamentally related to economic motives, such as those committed during the course of robberies, arising out of conflicts over the protection of gang or drug "turf," or as retaliation for thefts, unpaid loans, or gambling debts. Many, if not most, homicides are "expressive" in nature, that is, they are caused by social and emotional, rather than strictly economic and instrumental, reasons. However, Mertonian strain theory can help make sense of these homicides as well, since frustration associated with the means/goals disjunction has been a prominent explanation for violence, which can be understood as an expression of this frustration. In their macro level extension of Merton's theory, Steven F. Messner and Richard Rosenfeld (2001) contend that criminal violence results from an anomic cultural orientation that encourages people to pursue their goals by any means necessary, coupled with a weakening of the external restraints on criminal activity associated with family, educational, political, and other noneconomic institutions.

Scholars have long noted the tendency for new immigrants to settle in urban neighborhoods characterized by poverty, substandard housing, poor schools, and high crime rates (Thomas and Znaniecki 1920; Shaw and McKay 1931; Taylor 1931; Alba, Logan, and Bellair 1994; Hagan and Palloni 1998). Segregated in such neighborhoods, typically composed of earlier arrivals and long-standing residents from the same group, immigrants might be expected to turn to crime as a means to overcome economic opportunities blocked by language barriers, a lack of well-paying jobs in close proximity to home, and possibly overt discrimination. Historical examples abound of immigrants turning to organized crime to gain a foothold in political and economic networks from which they would have otherwise been excluded (Whyte 1943). Other writers have suggested that previously noncriminal immigrant groups may be "contaminated" by the abundance of criminal opportunities provided by natives in the neighborhoods in which immigrants settle (Lambert 1970, p. 284; cf. Sampson and Lauritsen [1997], on the "proximity" hypothesis). According to the opportunity-structure view, immigrant criminality is a function of preexisting structural factors such as poverty (Yeager 1997), a preponderance of young, unattached males (Gurr 1989), or the availability of alcohol (Alaniz, Cartmill, and Parker 1998).

Cultural Perspectives

To this list of structural sources of immigrant criminality, scholars have added cultural influences on criminal involvement and on immigrant crime in particular. The "culture of poverty" thesis—low-income people adapt to their structural conditions in ways that perpetuate their disadvantaged condition—is a prominent example of a cultural explanation for the high levels of crime and violence among disadvantaged groups (Lewis 1965). Thus, engaging in crime as a means of acquiring social status draws children away from schoolwork, which then reduces the probability of future economic advancement. Recent work has stressed the connections between "normative inversions" and changeable structures of inequality, in contrast to viewing criminogenic norms as inherent in the culture of specific racial/ethnic groups (M. R. Lee 2000, p. 193; see also Bruce 2000, p. 181, on the "normative manifestations" of structure). Because immigrants, like ethnic minorities, are generally more likely than native whites to reside in areas where structural conditions have altered the status systems away from idealized middle-class norms and toward a culture of opposition (Anderson 1999), these cultural theories imply that immigrant communities should exhibit high rates of crime (Miller 1958; Wolfgang and Ferracuti 1967).

Another prominent strain of cultural theory that is especially well suited to the immigration-crime relationship developed out of Thorsten Sellin's (1938; see also Sutherland 1934) writings on culture conflict. Sellin (1938, p. 21) recognized that the criminal law reflects the values of the "dominant interest groups" in society and that the values of other social groups, particularly immigrants, were sometimes quite different. In cases in which the cultural codes of subordinate and dominant groups conflict, legal agents label as deviant the behavior of members of the subordinate groups. Nevertheless, the criminal may be acting according to subculturally accepted norms and feel no "mental conflict" when violating the law. Thus, immigrants may violate the law more often than natives due to conflicts at the level of cultural codes and associated problems of acculturation in a new environment characterized by heterogeneous conduct norms (see Y. H. Lee 1998, for a recent study of acculturation and delinquency).

Social Disorganization

The social disorganization perspective, while not denying the effects on crime of cultural influences or the structure of economic opportunities, adds to the other perspectives a concern with the breakdown of community social institutions that results from social change. Robert J. Bursik (1988, p. 521) concisely describes disorganized areas as possessing an "inability to realize the common values of their residents or solve commonly expressed problems." In organized neighborhoods, local institutions (families, schools, churches, businesses, social agencies) work together to realize community goals, protect values, and limit the criminal behavior of community members, especially the young. In addition to making the realization of common values more difficult. a key source of social disorganization is population heterogeneity. which impedes communication and cooperation among distinct cultural groups (Bursik and Grasmick 1993). Carl L. Bankston (1998) notes that immigration may destabilize local institutions by increasing population turnover. The implication is that. when institutions weaken. social control is diminished and crime increases.

William I. Thomas and Florian Znaniecki (1920) set forth one early influential statement of this perspective in their five-volume classic published in 1918–1920, *The Polish Peasant in Europe and America.* They wrote about the many social changes affecting Polish immigrants a century ago, including the disorganizing influences inherent in moving from simple, homogeneous, rural areas of Poland to the complex, heterogeneous, urban areas of the United States. They defined social disorganization as "a decrease of the influence of existing social rules of behavior upon individual members of the group" (Thomas and Znaniecki 1920, p. 2). The effectiveness of social rules, including criminal law, derives from the individual's investment in them in the form of attitudes favorable to conformity. In organized groups, congruence exists between group rules and individual attitudes. Disorganization indicates a gap between rules and attitudes, such that an individual does not feel bound by the rules and is free to disobey them.

Viewed in this light, disorganization was a neutral term emphasizing both the positive and negative consequences of social change. Individual liberation from oppressive community standards, for example, is a positive consequence. However, the concept of disorganization generally has been applied in studies of crime and other social problems. An important contribution of this classic disorganization perspective is the recognition that crime is not only a function of enduring structural (e.g., poverty) or cultural (e.g., "subculture of violence") forces, but it is intimately tied to the fundamental processes of social change. As a major agent of social change, therefore, immigration should inflate levels of crime due to its disorganizing influence on community institutions.

THE COUNTERCLAIM

There are good sociological reasons, then, for anticipating a positive association between levels of immigration and crime. Immigration may be criminogenic through its association with economic disadvantage, conflicting conduct norms, weakened social control, or a combination of economic, cultural, and institutional factors. There are equally good reasons, however, for questioning the standard sociological images of immigration and crime. In fact, current public discourse on the effect of immigration on urban areas is beginning to portray immigration as a positive, stabilizing force. For example, on a recent broadcast of *Talk of the Nation* on National Public Radio (2001, pp. 2, 16), William Frey, a demographer with the University of Michigan, articulated the position that cities with a high proportion of recent immigrants are experiencing a rebirth:

> Immigrant cities and the high-tech cities are the ones that are going to be the shining stars of the future. . . . The ones that are breathing and growing . . . and living are the immigrant cities, the immigrant magnet cities. This is what had made cities to begin with in this country, and I think a lot of these areas are the ones that are really going to breed that diversity and that vitality and that sense of community in ways that many of the other cities don't have.

Far from being a disorganizing and possibly criminogenic force, this view posits immigration as an essential ingredient contributing to the continued viability of urban areas that had experienced population decline and community decay in previous decades.

In this article, we evaluate the counterclaim to the proposition that immigration increases crime. Strong ties to the labor market and family, we argue, offset the potential crime-producing consequences of disadvantage, culture conflict, and community instability and thereby suppress the level of crime in immigrant communities. Specifically, we test the hypothesis that *communities with higher proportions of recent immigrants, other things being equal, will exhibit lower levels of criminal homicide.*

Although several recent studies have called into question the immigration-begets-crime thesis (Butcher and Piehl 1998; Hagan and Palloni 1999; Martinez 2000), and even classic works failed to find a consistent empirical link between immigration and crime (T. Waters 1999; Martinez and Lee 2000b), scholarship that directly investigates the contemporary immigration/crime link is currently in short supply. It is certainly plausible to hypothesize that noncitizen immigrants may be deterred from crime by the potential threat of deportation, thus helping to suppress crime in immigrant neighborhoods.[4] But in addition to this line of reasoning, existing research unrelated to crime offers substantial indirect support of our counterclaim. For example, Alejandro Portes and Alex Stepick (1993) found that, rather than disorganizing communities, immigrants stabilized and revitalized Miami's economic and cultural institutions. The implication is that community social control may actually be strengthened by immigration, an image that is at odds with criminological theory. In fact, sociologists have long argued against the "myth" (Portes 2000, p. 5) that residents of impoverished urban areas are poor (or victimized by criminals) because they are "disorganized" in the sense that they lack common values or strong ties to each other.

Turning to attachments to the labor market, Pidi Zhang and Jimy Sanders (1999) found that immigrants with low-paying jobs may have a greater work incentive than similarly situated natives due to different frames of reference. In effect, the experience of being socialized in a relatively impoverished homeland results in immigrants placing a greater value on jobs than natives who were socialized in the richer host country. Immigrants therefore work longer hours than natives, even coethnic natives (e.g., Mexican immigrants work more hours than American-born Latinos); they also perceive more opportunities for upward mobility, which in turn may lead to high rates of upward mobility vis-à-vis similarly situated native groups (Zhang and Sanders 1999). These perceptions are shaped by the availability of social networks and opportunity structures, with immigrants possibly having greater access to these resources than segregated native-born black populations. For example, some immigrant groups (e.g., Koreans) arrive in the United States better educated than the average native-born American, and therefore more qualified to find jobs in the primary labor market (Alba and Nee 1997). In some cases, immigrants have structural supports that natives lack, such as "transnational networks" or the existence of "ethnic enclaves" that facilitate social and economic stability (Portes 1997; Logan, Alba, Dill, and Zhou 2000). Finally, some immigrant groups are particularly entrepreneurial, such as Cubans in Miami or Koreans in southern California (Logan et al. 2000). All of this implies that immigrants may not display cultural adaptations to structural inequality (i.e., crime) to the extent of disadvantaged native groups, because of immigrants' social capital or differential experiences of relative deprivation.

Another suggestive line of research focuses on perceptions of social justice (NCOVR 2000). The guiding hypothesis of this work is that individuals who believe society is fundamentally unjust will be more likely to break the law than those who believe that society is generally fair. For example, African Americans' experiences of racism and inequality may lead to a sense of social injustice, which in turn plays a mediating role in this group's disproportionate involvement in crime. Immigrants, while also subject to discrimination and deleterious social conditions, may perceive less injustice than African Americans due to different socialization experiences or perhaps to a greater sense of optimism about their prospects for advancement in American society. While immigrant-specific data on this issue are not available, one recent study of southern California found that Latinos were more likely than either whites or African Americans to believe in a just world (Hunt 2000).

These examples are part of a growing body of literature that supports images at odds with standard criminological notions of immigration as a process that facilitates crime. Given the potential for refining theory and informing policy—coupled with the fact that the experiences of recent immigrants (criminal or otherwise) cannot be inferred from those of previous waves (Portes 1997)—an empirical test of our counterclaim is long overdue. We therefore assess the effect of immigration on homicide across three cities that serve as major destinations for immigrants. We focus on Latino and non-Latino black homicide, since these two groups exhibit elevated homicide involvement, high levels of economic disadvantage, and other deleterious structural conditions. Immigrant Latinos also tend to settle in older Latino neighborhoods, many of which are expanding into adjacent non-Latino black communities. Although non-Latino whites are not an explicit concern in this article, we do report results for white models in a note. Our approach allows us to examine differences in the direction and magnitude of the immigration effect for the different ethnic groups and for ethnic differences in the covariates of homicide, such as economic disadvantage and community instability.

In addition, by estimating the effect of immigrant populations, comprised largely of Latinos, on the homicide risk of African Americans, we can assess the *contextual* influence of immigration in urban communities. Immigration may directly influence the crime rates within the immigrant population, but it also may indirectly affect those of other groups by changing the community context in which immigrant and nonimmigrant populations are situated. For example, if high levels of immigration impede communication and consensus on values in a community, social disorganization theory would predict a general increase in crime—and not simply increased criminal involvement of immigrants. The data used in this study, then, enable us to move considerably beyond the narrow focus of prior research on the crime rates of immigrant groups to assess the broader community impacts of immigration.

DATA AND METHODS

In order to assess the effects of immigration and other community characteristics on homicide in the three cities, we gathered data on all criminal homicides (excluding police shootings and excusable homicides) that occurred 1985–1995 directly from the homicide investigation units of the Miami and San Diego police departments and for 1985–1994 in El Paso. We collected all available information on the 3,345 homicides known to police in these three cities during this time period (1,527 in Miami, 412 in

El Paso, and 1,406 in San Diego). Direct access to detailed internal files was essential for distinguishing Latinos from other ethnic groups, which is not fully possible with the FBI's Uniform Crime Reports. The address of the homicide incident is also contained in these files, which enabled us to link each case to data from the 1990 decennial census at the tract level (USBC 1990).[5]

The units of analysis for this study are the 352 census tracts with more than five hundred residents in the three cities: 86 tracts in El Paso, 70 in Miami, and 196 in San Diego.[6] The dependent variables are the black and Latino homicide counts, aggregated to the tract level for the 1985–1995 (1994 in El Paso) period. For reasons explained below, our dependent variable is a "count" rather than a "rate." Thus, we include a measure of the black and Latino populations in our analysis to control for differences in aggregate homicide risk across tracts.

Following the emphasis of social disorganization theory on residential instability as a cause of crime (Bursik and Grasmick 1993), we have constructed an "instability index" that combines measures of vacancy and population turnover. Vacancy rates were computed by dividing the number of vacant housing units by the total number of housing units. The population turnover measure is the number of people who lived in a different housing unit in 1990 than they did five years earlier, divided by the total population. Each of these measures was standardized by subtracting the mean and dividing by the standard deviation; the resulting z-scores were then added to create the index.

We have included the percentage of the population living below the poverty line as a measure of economic deprivation. Since we analyzed tract-level data, we avoided the problem of capturing the spatial clustering of poverty that plagues city-level studies (M. R. Lee 2000). We controlled for the percentage of males between the ages of 18–24 to capture variation in the age group at especially high risk for serious violence. Consistent with past research suggesting that family structure influences homicide (Sampson 1987), we included the percentage of female-headed families with children. Labor market theory (Crutchfield 1989; Crutchfield and Pitchford 1997) suggests that a community's job structure will exert an effect on crime beyond that captured by economic deprivation measures such as the poverty rate. In addition, Latino populations in urban neighborhoods are often characterized as the "working poor." To assess the impact of labor market participation on homicide risk, we included the percentage of jobless males, defined as the number of males not in the labor force divided by the total number of males. Except for the instability index, we employed group-specific measurements for each of these indicators (i.e., black poverty and Latino poverty, family structure, joblessness, and age structure).[7]

Finally, we included a measure of the percentage of "new" immigrants in each tract, defined as those who arrived in the United States in 1980–1990—a period of "explosive" growth in the immigrant population (Logan et al. 2000. p. 99). In line with our previously stated rationale, we controlled for the percentage of foreign-born residents arriving within the past ten years in a given tract. This is not an attempt to measure legality or citizenship— the data do not allow those distinctions—but rather to assess the effects of recent settlement into well-established barrios or enclaves. typical destination points for newcomers.[8]

For reasons stated earlier. although sociological *research* has generally failed to find a link between immigration and crime. sociological *theory* offers ample and rather compelling reasons for supposing that immigration produces crime by increasing disadvantage. weakening community controls. and heightening culture conflict. Moreover. politicians. pundits. and pseudo-academics (Lamm and Imhoff 1985; Tanton and Lutton

1993) have suggested that the newest immigrants are a crime-prone group, a claim seized on by the media with regard to episodes such as illegal border crossings or the 1980 Mariel boatlift in Miami (Martinez 1997). Additional research is necessary, therefore, to assess the adequacy of both the theoretical and popular images of the immigration-crime connection. The current study is the first to examine the impact of recent immigration on homicide risk, independent of other variables known to influence homicide, such as economic disadvantage, residential instability, and age structure, at the neighborhood level across three high-immigration cities.

Estimation Procedures

Homicides are rare events distributed across ecological units such as census tracts in a highly skewed manner. Traditional ordinary least squares regression is not an appropriate estimator for such distributions when transformations of the dependent variable (such as logarithmic transformation) do not induce normality. To accommodate the nonnormal distribution of homicides, we employed a maximum likelihood estimator that is designed to deal with counts. Specifically, homicides are conceptualized as counts of events per unit of time, a description suggesting that use of a Poisson random component (or the related negative binomial specification) is most appropriate (Kohfeld and Sprague 1988; Osgood 2000).[9]

In Poisson regression, parameters are estimated through a maximum likelihood procedure that has a number of desirable properties, including an asymptotic distribution, consistency, and efficiency (Fienberg 1984). Further, the Poisson coefficient divided by its standard error follows a standard t-distribution. Therefore, statistical significance as well as the direction of the effect of each independent variable can be assessed. The general analytic strategy is to assess the independent effect of immigration on the frequency of homicides across census tracts within each of the three cities, controlling for aggregate risk associated with group population size (logged), the structural covariates described above, and spatial autocorrelation in the homicide distributions.

Spatial autocorrelation refers to nonrandom clustering in homicides that is not a function of the explanatory variables in the model. Such clustering may result from diffusion or spillover processes in which high rates of violence in one community result in increases in adjacent or nearby communities (Anselin, Cohen, Cook, Gorr, and Tita 2000). Alternatively, negative spatial autocorrelation, in which high homicide counts in a tract are associated with low counts in nearby tracts, might result from enforcement activity or other conditions that displace crimes across neighborhood boundaries. In other words, because a given tract's homicide level may be influenced by processes external to tract boundaries, researchers must statistically control for these processes or risk incorrectly attributing their effects to internal conditions, such as tract-specific levels of poverty or immigration (see Cliff and Ord [1981] for the classic discussion of spatial autocorrelation models).

While attempts to model external effects represent a relatively recent development in the criminological literature, Kenneth C. Land and Glenn Deane (1992) offer an accepted strategy. In this article, we follow their advice to model spatial autocorrelation in two stages. In the first stage, a "spatially lagged dependent variable" (Land and Deane 1992, p. 237) was created by obtaining the fitted values of the dependent variable (homicide) from a Poisson (or negative binomial) regression on the independent variables. These fitted values were transformed into a spatial lag variable, which was then included with the independent variables in a second-stage regression.[10] The results from the second-stage models are reported here.

For each of the cities we compare models of homicides involving Latino and African American victims. In this way, we can detect the direct influence of immigration in the population groups in which the immigrants are concentrated—Latinos—and the contextual influence of immigration in a nonimmigrant group with an elevated risk for homicide—African Americans. Any differences in these comparisons connected to the larger urban context also can be observed, as well as similarities and differences in the effects on Latino and African American homicide of the neighborhood-level structural covariates.

RESULTS

Table 1 presents descriptive statistics for each of the variables in the analysis. The average number of homicides per tract is higher for Latinos than for blacks in San Diego and El Paso and slightly greater for blacks than Latinos in Miami. These differences reflect, in part, the larger size of the Latino population in the three cities. When converted to

TABLE 1. DESCRIPTIVE STATISTICS

	El Paso Mean (SD)	Miami Mean (SD)	San Diego Mean (SD)
Black homicides	.29 (.59)	9.79 (16.29)	1.95 (4.95)
Annualized rate (per 1,000)	.16	.71	.37
Latino homicides	2.88 (2.84)	8.53 (6.88)	2.78 (6.23)
Annualized rate (per 1,000)	.07	.24	.22
Non-Latino blacks	187 (215)	1259 (1714)	486 (851)
Latinos	4130 (2346)	3179 (2527)	1127 (1399)
Instability Index	−.701 (1.29)	.513 (2.03)	.124 (1.48)
% Poverty			
Black	18.72 (25.73)	38.96 (21.87)	15.80 (19.42)
Latino	29.78 (16.77)	31.95 (16.01)	17.25 (12.89)
% Female-headed families			
Black	19.88 (26.87)	37.01 (30.82)	24.56 (31.11)
Latino	22.54 (9.23)	29.23 (20.71)	19.88 (19.08)
% Male joblessness			
Black	28.98 (28.48)	33.91 (23.89)	18.18 (20.36)
Latino	25.89 (10.43)	29.13 (16.40)	19.08 (13.57)
% Young and male			
Black	8.53 (9.68)	5.27 (5.61)	9.29 (11.00)
Latino	9.14 (2.55)	6.33 (2.86)	10.48 (6.37)
% New immigrants	8.74 (5.80)	26.63 (14.36)	9.62 (8.70)
Spatial lag			
Black	.29 (.06)	9.40 (3.44)	2.13 (.85)
Latino	3.00 (.48)	8.81 (.96)	2.89 (1.12)
Tract N	86	70	196

Note: The homicide values are the tract means for 1985–1995 in Miami and San Diego and for 1985–1994 in El Paso. All other variables (except spatial lags) are from the 1990 census.

average yearly rates per 1.000 tract population. the homicide risk for blacks is considerably higher than for Latinos in each of the cities. a finding that is consistent with previous research (Martinez and Lee 1999). We also observed pronounced differences in risk across the cities for both groups. El Paso has the lowest rates and Miami has the highest. although the difference between San Diego and Miami for Latinos is negligible.

Somewhat less consistent group differences are observed for the poverty, instability. family structure. and joblessness indicators. Poverty rates are higher for Latinos in El Paso. for blacks in Miami, and roughly equal for the two groups in San Diego. Rates of female-headed families are higher for blacks in Miami and San Diego and very similar to those for Latinos in El Paso. Differences between the two groups in joblessness are small in all of the cities, although in El Paso and Miami joblessness is somewhat greater for blacks. We observe no important group differences in the young male fraction of the population.

There are notable differences across the three cities in levels of instability and in the key variable of interest, recent immigration. In both cases, Miami stands out, with instability values several times those for the other two cities and immigration levels almost three times greater. The question to which we now turn is whether recent immigration influences levels of homicide within and across the three cities.

Latino-Specific Models

Consider first the Latino-specific models presented in Table 2. Other than the expected effects for tract population, the only variable with significant effects (at the .01 level) on Latino homicide victimization across all three cities is the poverty rate. Higher levels of poverty are strongly associated with higher levels of homicide. The spatial lag variable is also consistently related to homicide, although only at the .05 level in El Paso and Miami. Specifically, we found that Latino homicide in a given tract is positively related to the characteristics of surrounding tracts, suggesting that a process of diffusion may be at work (Anselin et al. 2000). The instability index is significantly associated with homi-

TABLE 2. POISSON OR NEGATIVE BINOMAL REGRESSION RESULTS FOR LATINO MODELS

	El Paso	Miami[b]	San Diego[b]
Intercept	−9.37** (1.47)	−2.29** (.792)	−5.44** (.953)
(Ln) Population[a]	2.26** (.338)	.762** (.170)	1.32** (.408)
Instability index	.119* (.069)	.002 (.036)	.152* (.085)
% Poverty[a]	.015** (.008)	.032** (.007)	.036** (.011)
% Female-headed families[a]	.010 (.013)	−.012** (.005)	−.015* (.009)
% Male joblessness[a]	.020 (.013)	−.003 (.006)	.005 (.010)
% Young and male[a]	−.003 (.036)	−.040 (.033)	−.008 (.023)
% New immigrants	−.046** (.024)	.000 (.006)	−.007 (.019)
Spatial lag[a]	.483* (.266)	.171* (.095)	.514** (.126)
Log-likelihood (N)	−153.66** (86)	−190.00** (70)	−297.31** (196)

Note: Standard errors are in parentheses.
[a] Group-specific data.
[b] Negative binomial model.
* p < .05; ** p < .01 (one-tailed).

cide in El Paso and San Diego, with less stable neighborhoods exhibiting higher levels of homicide. The percentage of female-headed families is significantly related to homicide in Miami and San Diego; contrary to expectation, the relationship is negative. Communities with a higher fraction of female-headed families have lower levels of homicide. Neither male joblessness nor the young male measure are linked to homicide levels in the three cities. Finally, net of other influences, the percentage of recent immigrants in the neighborhood is significantly associated with Latino homicide levels only in El Paso, where the direction of this effect is negative.

In sum, the results for the Latino models differ somewhat across the three cities. The only substantively important effect that was consistently significant at the .01 level is for poverty. High poverty rates are associated with higher levels of Latino homicide. The lack of a positive relationship between recent immigration and Latino homicide was also uniform; the two were unrelated in two cities and negatively related in El Paso. Other results are less consistent. One possible interpretation is the presence of multicollinearity in the models, which would produce inflated standard errors and instability in the parameter estimates. Inspection of the correlation matrices and diagnostics for the Latino models indicates the presence of collinearity in the El Paso model involving the measure of female-headed families and the poverty rate ($r = .73$) and also between the new immigration variable and poverty ($r = .79$). An examination of the variance inflation factors (VIFs) indicated that the poverty variable was the potential problem (i.e., VIF > 4). We therefore reestimated the El Paso equation with the poverty rate removed. The only difference in results is that the coefficient for the female-headed family measure becomes significant in the model without the poverty rate. There are no indications of multicollinearity in the other models.[11]

The inconsistent results across the cities, therefore, do not appear to be due to instabilities induced by the correlations among the regressors. In any event, we found no inconsistency for the construct of greatest interest, the percentage of recent immigrants. Thus, immigration is not related to higher Latino homicide levels in these three cities.

Black-Specific Models

The results for the black-specific models are displayed in Table 3. Here we found that the population variable is significant in Miami and San Diego. The lack of relationship for this measure of homicide risk in El Paso is due to unique characteristics of the black population in this city, a subject we address below. The instability index is related to black homicide levels in El Paso and San Diego, suggesting that blacks are less likely to be homicide victims in more stable neighborhoods.

Unlike the Latino models, the poverty rate is associated with black homicide in the expected positive direction in only two of the three cities (Miami and San Diego), although male joblessness is consistently related to higher homicide levels. As with the Latino models, the female-headed family measure does not exhibit the positive relationship with black homicide predicted by the literature; it is negative and significant in San Diego and null in Miami and El Paso. The spatial lag term is significant only in San Diego. In other words, controlling for other influences, San Diego neighborhoods where black homicide risk is high tend to be located close to neighborhoods where it is also high. Finally, the immigration measure is negatively related to black homicide levels in Miami, positively related to black homicide in San Diego neighborhoods, and null in El Paso.

TABLE 3. POISSON OR NEGATIVE BINOMAL REGRESSION RESULTS FOR BLACK MODELS

	El Paso	Miami[b]	San Diego
Intercept	−3.83** (1.47)	−2.27** (.647)	−7.03** (.420)
(Ln) Population[a]	.832 (.557)	1.07** (.165)	1.95** (.145)
Instability index.	.291* (.169)	.057 (.049)	.368** (0.65)
% Poverty[a]	−.000 (.011)	.014** (.007)	.013** (.005)
% Female-headed families[a]	.002 (.008)	.001 (.006)	−.006** (.003)
% Male joblessness[a]	.022** (.010)	.009* (.006)	.023** (.004)
% Young and male[a]	−.030 (.030)	.024 (.023)	−.015 (.011)
% New immigrants	−.040 (.052)	−.025** (.007)	.015** (.007)
Spatial lag[a]	2.38 (4.03)	.055 (.046)	.492** (.109)
Log-likelihood (N)	−50.52** (86)	−152.83** (70)	−205.11** (196)

Note: Standard errors are in parentheses.
[a] Group-specific data.
[b] Negative binomial model.
* $p < .05$; ** $p < .01$ (one-tailed).

Inspection of the correlation matrices and regression diagnostics revealed no multicollinearity in the black-specific models.

DISCUSSION AND CONCLUSION

Looking across Tables 2 and 3, we observe a great deal of variation by race and place in the factors that shape group-specific homicide risk within urban communities on the border. However, with only one exception, we found either no relationship or a significant negative relationship between homicide and recent immigration—a trend that also holds for non-Latino white homicide events.[12] The exception is the positive effect of immigration on black homicide in San Diego. One possible interpretation of this result is that homicides in San Diego are more likely to involve intergroup conflicts involving new immigrants and black residents. Another is that new immigrants tend to settle in San Diego communities with preexisting high levels of black-on-black homicide. The latter possibility complements the complex relationships among race/ethnicity, immigration, and crime uncovered by Richard D. Alba, John R. Logan, and Paul E. Bellair (1994) in metropolitan New York. It is plausible that immigrants who settle in predominantly black neighborhoods are not present in sufficient numbers to strengthen local institutions and may in fact be contributing to the disorganization of these areas. Regardless of the explanation, we should point out that San Diego has a low homicide rate relative to cities of a similar size (i.e., over one million people, see Martinez and Lee 2000b).

It is also important not to obscure the general thrust of our results, which in these three border cities does not support either the popular stereotypes of the impact of immigration on crime or the expectations derived from sociological theories.[13] For example, the relationship between immigration and black homicide in Miami provides especially strong support for our counterclaim, both in the statistical results presented here and a separate spatial analysis (M. T. Lee 2000). This research has found that Haitian immigrants in Miami have suppressed homicide levels in the predominantly black areas in which they have settled, while black areas receiving few immigrants continue to have the highest homicide levels in the city. In fact, Haitians in Miami are among the most disadvantaged groups in the country, experiencing both poverty and discrimination, yet they have exceedingly low homicide involvement (Martinez and Lee 2000a). Our knowledge of urban crime would clearly benefit from additional studies of how groups like Haitians maintain low involvement in crime despite adverse social conditions.

Another fairly consistent finding from our research is that indicators of economic deprivation, labor market involvement, and residential instability are related to Latino and black victimization in the three cities. Unlike our result for immigration, these results are entirely in keeping with the expectations of opportunity structure and social disorganization perspectives on the conditions that give rise to crime in urban areas. The poverty rate is the most consistent of the three indicators, exhibiting a significant, positive association with homicide in five of the six models. Instability is significant in four models and joblessness is significant in three. The latter finding is in line with recent research that suggests Latinos are poor but working, while blacks are more likely to be both poor and jobless, since male joblessness was a significant predictor of homicide in all three black models but in none of the Latino models (Wilson and Martin 1982; Logan, Alba, and McNulty 1994; Waldinger 1996). So, although we find some differences across these indicators for the different cities and ethnic groups, together they provide a theoretically coherent picture of the economic and social conditions associated with elevated levels of violent victimization for urban Latinos and African Americans.

The measures of age and family structures (i.e., young males and female-headed families with children) produced findings that are at odds with predictions from the literature. In no case did either of these variables have the expected positive, statistically significant effect. The lack of a positive association between young males and homicide is consistent with other research (M. R. Lee 2000). The female-headed family variable, long thought to contribute to a host of community problems such as crime, depression, and joblessness, among others, did not independently increase homicide in this study—a finding that is in line with recent research that challenges the conventional wisdom on the "pathology of matriarchy" (Biblarz and Raftery 1999, p. 322; see also Mizell 1999). In fact, in two cities we observed a negative relationship between female-headed families and homicide (Latinos in Miami and blacks in San Diego). Of course, the null findings might simply reflect the covariation of the family structure indicator with the poverty rate. If the primary influence of female-headed families on homicide is through their elevated levels of poverty, then controlling for poverty should eliminate their effect on homicide. Regardless of the empirical indications that single-parent families do not inevitably produce crime or other social pathologies, there is little basis in existing criminological theory or prior research for anticipating a *negative* relationship between female-headed family structures and homicide, with poverty and other measures of economic marginalization controlled.

Although our present focus is on immigration, our results suggest that decomposing the relatively crude measure of family structure employed in most studies of homicide (including this one) offers great potential for theoretical advancement. Researchers have devoted substantial efforts to explicating the complex relationship between material resources and family structure (Corcoran 1995), and homicide research must begin to consider these complexities. For example, there are good reasons for economically disadvantaged women to avoid marriage, with many believing that marriage will not contribute additional resources to the family unit. although it may have *negative* conse-quences (e.g., domestic violence, see Edin 2000). In addition, classic research by Carol Stack (1974) suggests that kinship networks may mediate the potentially deleterious effects of female-headed families. By building on the insights of this work, researchers can construct more sophisticated models of the social processes and networks that influence family structure in urban areas. thus contributing to our ability to place crime in its proper social context.

Having explored the similarities and differences across models, we now turn to the special case of black homicide in El Paso, the one example where the idiosyncrasies of race and place superseded many of the expected relationships between homicide and common covariates. Recall that in this model, neither the risk variable (population) nor poverty was significantly related to black homicide. Without an understanding of the social context of the black population of this city, these results would seem counterintu-itive. However, El Paso does not have the problem of concentrated black poverty to the same extent as the deindustrializing cities of the Northeast and Midwest—cities on which so much of our knowledge of homicide has been based. In fact, El Paso has a rela-tively small number of black residents compared to most large cities, and many of them are employed by the military and therefore have stable employment. Although poverty and the number of black residents do not exert independent effects on black homicide, neigh-borhoods with high levels of black male joblessness and residential "instability" (not a race-specific variable) exhibit comparatively high levels of black homicide. The differences in findings across the three cities reinforce the view that policies designed to reduce vio-lence must consider important differences in the local context in which violence is situated.

Some caveats are warranted. First, in order to focus on immigration as a macrological process this study ignored individual-level issues regarding whether either the perpetra-tors or victims of homicide were immigrants. We have directed our attention to the con-ditions of communities that are associated with variation in group levels of criminal violence and made no claims about the individual-level relationships among violence, poverty, immigrant-status, and other factors within communities. Although this approach avoids the ecological fallacy (i.e., the attribution to the individual level of group-level relationships), future work should integrate both individual and community levels of analysis to the extent that data availability will allow. Furthermore, the circumstances under which people immigrate (e.g., political or economic), as well as the segmented assimilation of specific immigrant groups into the core and peripheral economies of urban areas (Logan et al. 2000), likely have important implications for urban crime. The recent immigration of diverse groups of people into large American cities has significantly complicated the relationship between race/ethnicity and violent crime. Yet most studies continue to gloss over this complexity, often dropping high-immigration cities like Miami from their analyses (Parker and McCall 1999). While it was useful to examine the effect of "immigration" on crime, given our current lack of knowledge, future work must attempt to model the effects of specific groups of immigrants, or differ-ent segments within a particular immigrant group (e.g., professionals versus laborers), in order to more fully understand the immigration/crime nexus.

Second, distinguishing legal from illegal immigrants might be a potentially useful strat-egy in crime research and immigration policies (e.g., deportation) that could prevent future violence in many communities. There is however little evidence that "illegal" immi-grants are over involved in violent crime, or at least much more so than "legal" immigrants

574   THE SOCIOLOGICAL QUARTERLY Vol. 42/No. 4/2001

(Hagan and Palloni 1998), even though it is clear that most immigrants live on the economic margins of society. Also, "illegal aliens" cannot be thoroughly separated from legal ones at the local level. It is difficult to single out a community where illegal aliens outnumber legal immigrants, or even a series of street blocks where "illegals" are distinguishable from others. Instead, many are blended into poor Latino families and neighborhoods. Forcibly separating them from their communities through deportation tends to break up families and weaken social bonds and community cohesion, thereby disrupting local conditions. This policy "solution" thereby wreaks more havoc on disadvantaged communities, adding to the consequences of adverse structural conditions. Rather than encouraging a clandestine life, steps to integrate those without "papers" into legal residents would probably prove less harmful in the long run than the traditional use of deportation.

A third concern relates to the cross-sectional nature of our data. A longitudinal analysis is required to advance our understanding of the causal ordering among variables such as immigration, residential instability, poverty, and the ethnic composition of neighborhoods. For example, it is possible that immigration into a given neighborhood may contribute to an increase in residential instability at a later time, which might then shape subsequent homicide levels in that neighborhood or surrounding areas. Future research should therefore employ a longitudinal design in order to disentangle the causal ordering of neighborhood-level social processes that unfold over a period of years and that influence patterns of violent crime.

Notwithstanding these concerns, the major finding of this article—that recent immigration generally does not increase community levels of homicide—has implications for policies that target immigration as a social problem. Our results offer little support for claims that immigration fosters homicide in three large and ethnically diverse border cities. Indeed, native and immigrant groups alike could profit greatly from research into the counterclaim that immigration can be a stabilizing force that suppresses criminal violence.

In the absence of such a research agenda, claims makers will likely continue to link immigrants with crime. The far-ranging consequences of this discourse, which reappears with each successive wave of immigrants, despite its lack of empirical support (Sellin 1938; Hagan and Palloni 1999; Martinez and Lee 2000b), demonstrate the constitutive power of the symbolic order in shaping racial/ethnic identities as well as the social, political, and economic capital of ethnic groups (O. Lee, 1998). For example, Edward J. Escobar's (1999) history of the Los Angeles Police Department's public campaign to connect Mexicans with crime shows clearly the central role this image played in the formation of a crime-prone Mexican public identity—an identity that justified the continued subordination of this group and even ethnically motivated violence (e.g., the Zoot suit riot). Similarly, the symbolic force of the mythology of the "criminal immigrant" contributes to contemporary criminal justice system practices like racial profiling by law enforcement and harsh treatment by the court system, leading to the incarceration of disproportionate numbers of immigrants despite evidence that immigrants as a group are less crime-involved than natives (Hagan and Palloni 1999).

This study offers an empirical assessment of competing claims about immigration and crime that have significant consequences for both immigrants and natives. Our findings suggest that future research along these lines has much to offer sociological theories of crime, popular understandings, and perhaps most importantly, public policies that bear on the complex relationship between immigration and crime. Sociologists have argued that explanations of urban crime require a "somewhat complex story line" (Alba et al.

1994, p. 417). Our study suggests that the transformation of large U.S. cities by the latest wave of immigration has added a theoretically unexpected plot twist that, if replicated, will substantially alter the way this story is told.

ACKNOWLEDGMENTS

An earlier version of this article was presented on August 12, 2000, at the American Sociological Association's annual meeting in Washington, D.C. This article would not have been possible without the generous cooperation of several members of the Miami Police Department (MPD). We thank MPD Police Chief Raul Martinez, former Assistant Chief John Brooks, Lt. Bobbie Meeks, former Lt. John Campbell, Lt. George Cadavid, and past and present detectives in the MPD Homicide Investigations Unit. Thanks also to former San Diego Police Department (SDPD) Chief Jerry Sanders, Lt. Jim Collins, Lt. Glenn A. Breitenstein, and the homicide division detectives for providing access to SDPD data. We also thank S. Fernando Rodriguez for El Paso Police Department homicide data. Our analysis was substantially improved as a result of Robert Baller's unusually insightful and constructive critique. We also appreciate the helpful comments of David F. Greenberg, as well as the *TSQ* editor and anonymous reviewers, on earlier versions of this article. Timothy Bray provided help with creating the spatial lag variable. Funding was provided, in part, to the second author through the National Science Foundation (SBR-9515235), a Ford Foundation Postdoctoral Minority Fellowship, the Harry Frank Guggenheim Foundation and the National Consortium on Violence Research (NCOVR). NCOVR is supported under grant # SBR-9513949 from the National Science Foundation. The conclusions presented in this article are ours alone and should not be taken as the view of any official agency. We are, of course, responsible for any errors, facts, or omissions.

APPENDIX: COMBINED CORRELATION MATRIX FOR THE BLACK AND LATINO MODELS

	1	2	3	4	5	6	7	8	9	
1. Black homicide	—	.44	.07	.45	.15	.20	−.05	.59	.55	1. Latino homicide
2. (Ln) Black population	.46	—	−.17	.34	.09	.19	.05	.47	.29	2. (Ln) Lat population
3. Instability index	.31	.18	—	.26	.17	.09	−.08	.12	.21	3. Instability index
4. Black poverty	.31	.09	.19	—	.47	.38	.01	.43	.39	4. Latino poverty
5. Blk female-headed family	.36	.48	.16	.31	—	.25	−.00	.14	.21	5. Lat fem-head family
6. Black male joblessness	.19	.14	.02	.18	.19	—	.11	.19	.28	6. Lat male joblessness
7. Young black males	−.02	.17	.01	−.11	.09	.13	—	−.05	−.24	7. Young Latino males
8. New immigrants	.10	.04	.12	.37	.22	.19	−.12	—	.70	8. New immigrants
9. Black spatial lag	.59	.32	.30	.39	.31	.16	−.10	.49	—	9. Latino spatial lag

NOTES

1. We chose to focus on homicide for several reasons. First, it is the most reliably recorded crime. Second, the criminological theories we discuss here have been used to explain all types of street crime, including homicide. Finally, public anxiety about urban homicide is high, making our focus especially policy relevant.

2. Census block groups also are valid units for neighborhood level analysis. However, their small size poses difficulties when studying comparatively rare events, such as homicide, partitioned by ethnicity of the victim.

3. The fear that too many crime-prone immigrants are entering the United States is reflected in a national best-selling book promising "common sense about America's immigration disaster," by Peter J. Brimelow (1996, p. 182), a writer at *Forbes* and *National Review* magazines: "Immigration is not the *only* cause of crime. It may not even be the major cause of crime. But it is a *factor*." Such alarmist writings assume a link between immigrants and crime without offering supportive evidence. In fact, Brimelow (1996, p. 182) claims that "there has been no serious academic study of the impact on crime" of the post-1965 wave of immigration.

4. David Greenberg suggested this possibility in a personal communication.

5. We are interested in the *presence* of homicide in a given tract. In order to measure tract-level homicide incidents as accurately as possible, we based our homicide counts on the victim's race for two reasons. First, information on the offender or suspect is missing or possibly unreliable in the substantial number of cases not cleared with an arrest. In addition, Short (1997) points out that findings based on victimization data are also valid for offenders, given the intraracial nature of the vast majority of homicide events.

6. Seven tracts with more than five hundred individuals were excluded in San Diego because they were military bases, airfields, or contained mostly institutionalized populations (e.g., a hospital).

7. We initially included a measure of tract-level ethnic diversity, which was not a significant predictor of homicide, did not change the effect of immigration, and was subsequently dropped in an effort to conserve degrees of freedom.

8. Although there is some overlap between our immigration measure and one of the ten census variables used to construct the instability index (i.e., the number of 1990 Miami city residents living abroad in 1985), the bivariate correlation between recent immigration and the instability index ($r = .12$) in the three cities is quite weak (Appendix). The implication is that the most recent wave of immigration is not a major factor driving neighborhood instability, an issue more fully explored in the multivariate analysis that follows.

9. Due to overdispersed data in three models (Miami blacks and Latinos and San Diego Latinos), we also estimated negative binomial models and present these results in Tables 2 and 3.

10. The procedure we used for creating the spatial lag term was as follows. First, in the program *SpaceStat* (Anselin 1995), we created a distance matrix based on tract centroid coordinates and then merged the file containing this variable with a file containing the fitted values of the dependent variable that we created in *Limdep version 7.0*. Second, we transformed the distance matrix to an inverse distance weights matrix (no limits were imposed so that all tracts received a weight based on their distance). Third, we row standardized the inverse distance weights matrix to adjust each weight so that values across a row summed to one. Finally, we created a spatial lag average using the fitted values of tract-levels of black and Latino homicide and exported this variable back into *Limdep*.

11. The correlation matrices and collinearity diagnostics are available from the authors on request. The Appendix contains a combined matrix for all three cities for the Latino and black models, although the combined relationships vary somewhat from those found in the city-specific matrices.

12. We focused on Latinos and non-Latino blacks because urban homicide and its structural covariates disproportionately affect these groups, and because immigrants in the three cities tend

to settle in Latino or black neighborhoods. However, we also conducted analyses (available from the authors) to test the effect of immigration on non-Latino white homicide levels. We found that recent immigration is a significant, *negative* predictor of white homicide only in San Diego, but not a significant predictor in Miami or El Paso. There is little empirical evidence or theoretical reason to expect that immigration should be positively related to white homicide, given settlement patterns of these groups as well as the generally intraracial nature of homicide.

13. Given the overall lack of relationship between immigration and homicide in this study, we decided to conduct separate analyses (available from the authors) to determine whether immigration was influencing variables commonly associated with neighborhood disorganization: residential instability, female-headed families, and poverty. Using each of these as dependent variables, instead of homicide, we estimated ordinary least squares models for both Latinos and blacks. Immigration was a positive and significant predictor of these dependent variables in only four out of eighteen models: Latino residential instability and poverty in El Paso, Latino poverty in San Diego, and black residential instability in El Paso. In other words, immigration generally is *not* "disorganizing" these communities, with a handful of exceptions. Clearly, these empirical variations are more complicated than extant theories, but it is apparent that sociological explanations of crimes such as homicide must confront the fact that immigration is not the disorganizing influence that many scholars have assumed (see also Portes [2000] on the "myth" of immigration as a disorganizing community process).

REFERENCES

Alaniz, Maria Luisa, Randi S. Cartmill, and Robert Nash Parker. 1998. "Immigrants and Violence: The Importance of Neighborhood Context." *Hispanic Journal of Behavioral Sciences* 20:155–174.

Alba, Richard D., John R. Logan, and Paul E. Bellair. 1994. "Living with Crime: The Implications of Racial/Ethnic Differences in Suburban Location." *Social Forces* 73:395–434.

Alba, Richard D., and Victor Nee. 1997. "Rethinking Assimilation Theory for a New Era of Immigration." *International Migration Review* 31:826–874.

Anderson, Elijah. 1999. *Code of the Street: Decency, Violence, and the Moral Life of the Inner City.* New York: W. W. Norton.

Anselin, Luc. 1995. *SpaceStat: A Software Program for the Analysis of Spatial Data, Version 1.80.* Morgantown, WV: Regional Research Institute, West Virginia University.

Anselin, Luc, Jacqueline Cohen, David Cook, Wilpen Gorr, and George Tita. 2000. "Spatial Analyses of Crime." Pp. 213–262 in *Measurement and Analysis of Crime and Justice,* Vol. 4: *Criminal Justice 2000,* edited by David Dunfee. Washington, DC: National Institute of Justice.

Bankston, Carl L., III. 1998. "Youth Gangs and the New Second Generation: A Review Essay." *Aggression and Violent Behavior* 3:35–45.

Biblarz, Timothy J., and Adrian E. Raftery. 1999. "Family Structure, Educational Attainment, and Socioeconomic Success: Rethinking the 'Pathology of Matriarchy.'" *American Journal of Sociology* 105:321–365.

Brimelow, Peter J. 1996. *Alien Nation: Common Sense about America's Immigration Disaster.* New York: Random House.

Bruce, Marino A. 2000. "Violence among African Americans: A Conceptual Assessment of Potential Explanations." *Journal of Contemporary Criminal Justice* 16:171–193.

Bursik, Robert J., Jr. 1988. "Social Disorganization and Theories of Crime and Delinquency: Problems and Prospects." *Criminology* 26:519–551.

Bursik, Robert J., Jr., and Harold G. Grasmick. 1993. "Economic Deprivation and Neighborhood Crime Rates, 1960–1980." *Law and Society Review* 27:263–283.

Butcher, Kristin F., and Anne Morrison Piehl. 1998. "Cross-City Evidence on the Relationship Between Immigration and Crime." *Journal of Policy Analysis and Management* 17:457–493.

578   THE SOCIOLOGICAL QUARTERLY Vol. 42/No. 4/2001

Cliff, Andrew David. and J. Keith Ord. 1981. *Spatial Processes: Models and Applications.* London: Pion.

Corcoran, M. 1995. "Rags to Rags: Poverty and Mobility in the United States." *Annual Review of Sociology* 21:237–267.

Crutchfield, Robert D. 1989. "Labor Stratification and Violent Crime." *Social Forces* 68:489–512.

Crutchfield, Robert D., and Susan R. Pitchford. 1997. "Work and Crime: The Effects of Labor Stratification." *Social Forces* 76:93–118.

Edin, Kathryn. 2000. "What Do Low-Income Single Mothers Say about Marriage?" *Social Problems* 47:112–133.

Escobar, Edward J. 1999. *Race, Police, and the Making of a Political Identity: Mexican Americans and the Los Angeles Police Department, 1900–1945.* Berkeley: University of California Press.

Ferracuti, Franco. 1968. "European Migration and Crime." Pp. 189–219 in *Crime and Culture: Essays in Honor of Thorsten Sellin*, edited by Marvin E. Wolfgang. New York: John Wiley and Sons.

Fienberg, Stephen E. 1984. *The Analysis of Cross-Classified Categorical Data.* Cambridge, MA: Massachusetts Institute of Technology Press.

Gurr, Ted Robert. 1989. "The History of Violent Crime in America." Pp. 11–20 in *Violence in America*, Vol. 1, edited by Ted Robert Gurr. Newbury Park, CA: Sage.

Hagan, John, and Alberto Palloni. 1998. "Immigration and Crime in the United States." Pp. 367–387 in *The Immigration Debate*, edited by James P. Smith and Barry Edmonston. Washington, DC: National Academy Press.

———. 1999. "Sociological Criminology and the Mythology of Hispanic Immigration and Crime." *Social Problems* 46:617–632.

Hunt, Matthew O. 2000. "Status, Religion, and the 'Belief in a Just World': Comparing African Americans, Latinos, and Whites." *Social Science Quarterly* 81:325–343.

Immigration and Naturalization Service (INS). 1987. *Statistical Yearbook of the Immigration and Naturalization Service, 1986.* Washington, DC: GPO.

Kohfeld, Carol W., and John Sprague. 1988. "Urban Unemployment Drives Urban Crime." *Urban Affairs Quarterly* 24:215–241.

Lambert, John R. 1970. *Crime, Police, and Race Relations: A Study in Birmingham.* London: Oxford University Press.

Lamm, Richard D., and Gary Imhoff. 1985. *The Immigration Time Bomb: The Fragmenting of America.* New York: Truman Talley.

Land, Kenneth C., and Glenn Deane. 1992. "On the Large-Sample Estimation of Regression Models with Spatial- or Network-Effects Terms: A Two-Stage Least Squares Approach." *Sociological Theory* 22:221–248.

Lee, Matthew R. 2000. "Concentrated Poverty, Race, and Homicide." *The Sociological Quarterly* 41:189–206.

Lee, Matthew T. 2000. "Ethnicity, Immigration, and Homicide on the Border: A Comparison of El Paso, Miami, and San Diego (1985–1995)." Ph.D. dissertation, University of Delaware.

Lee, Orville. 1998. "Culture and Democratic Theory: Toward a Theory of Symbolic Democracy." *Constellations* 5:399–455.

Lee, Yoon Ho. 1998. "Acculturation and Delinquent Behavior: The Case of Korean American Youths." *International Journal of Comparative and Applied Criminal Justice* 22:273–292.

Lewis, Oscar. 1965. *La Vida: A Puerto Rican Family in the Culture of Poverty.* New York: Random House.

Logan, John R., Richard D. Alba, Michael Dill, and Min Zhou. 2000. "Ethnic Segmentation in the American Metropolis: Increasing Divergence in Economic Incorporation, 1980–1990." *International Migration Review* 34:98–132.

Logan, John R., Richard D. Alba, and Thomas McNulty. 1994. "Ethnic Economies in Metropolitan Regions: Miami and Beyond." *Social Forces* 72:691–724.

Long. J. Scott. 1997. *Regression Models for Categorical and Limited Dependent Variables.* Thousand Oaks, CA: Sage.

Martinez. Ramiro, Jr. 1997. "Homicide among the 1980 Mariel Refugees in Miami: Victims and Offenders." *Hispanic Journal of Behavioral Sciences* 19:107–122.

———. 2000. "Immigration and Urban Violence: The Link between Immigrant Latinos and Types of Homicide." *Social Science Quarterly* 81:363–374.

Martinez, Ramiro, Jr., and Matthew T. Lee. 1999. "Extending Ethnicity in Homicide Research: The Case of Latinos." Pp. 211–220 in *Homicide: A Sourcebook of Social Research.* edited by M. Dwayne Smith and Margaret Zahn. Newbury Park, CA: Sage.

———. 2000a. "Comparing the Context of Immigrant Homicides in Miami: Haitians, Jamaicans. and Mariels." *International Migration Review* 34:793–811.

———. 2000b. "On Immigration and Crime." Pp. 485–524 in *The Nature of Crime: Continuity and Change*, Vol. 1: *Criminal Justice 2000*, edited by Gary LaFree. Washington, DC: National Institute of Justice.

Merton, Robert K. 1938. "Social Structure and Anomie." *American Sociological Review* 3:672–682.

Messner, Steven F., and Richard Rosenfeld. 2001. *Crime and the American Dream.* 3d ed. Belmont, CA: Wadsworth.

Miller, Walter B. 1958. "Lower Class Culture as a Generating Milieu in Gang Delinquency." *Journal of Social Issues* 14:5–19.

Mizell, C. Andre. 1999. "Life Course Influences on African American Men's Depression: Adolescent Parental Composition. Self-Concept, and Adult Earnings." *Journal of Black Studies* 29:467–490.

National Consortium on Violence Research (NCOVR). 2000. "A Research Program for Better Understanding the Role of Race/Ethnicity in Violence." Unpublished paper.

National Public Radio (NPR). 2001. "Census and the Cities." *Talk of the Nation*, March 28. Transcript available from www.npr.org.

Osgood, D. Wayne. 2000. "Poisson-Based Regression Analysis of Aggregate Crime Rates." *Journal of Quantitative Criminology* 16:21–43.

Ousey, Graham. 1999. "Homicide, Structural Factors, and the Racial Invariance Assumption." *Criminology* 37:405–426.

Parker, Karen F., and Patricia L. McCall. 1999. "Structural Conditions and Racial Homicide Patterns: A Look at the Multiple Disadvantages in Urban Areas." *Criminology* 37:447–477.

Portes, Alejandro. 1997. "Immigration Theory for a New Century: Some Problems and Opportunities." *International Migration Review* 31:799–825.

———. 2000. "The Hidden Abode: Sociology as Analysis of the Unexpected." *American Sociological Review* 65:1–18.

Portes, Alejandro, and Alex Stepick. 1993. *City on the Edge: The Transformation of Miami.* Berkeley: University of California Press.

Sampson, Robert J. 1987. "Urban Black Violence: The Effect of Male Joblessness and Family Disruption." *American Journal of Sociology* 93:348–382.

Sampson, Robert J., and Janet L. Lauritsen. 1997. "Racial and Ethnic Disparities in Crime and Criminal Justice in the United States." Pp. 311–374 in *Ethnicity, Crime, and Immigration*, edited by Michael Tonry. Chicago: University of Chicago Press.

Sellin, Thorsten. 1938. *Culture Conflict and Crime: A Report of the Subcommittee on Delinquency of the Committee on Personality and Culture.* New York: Social Science Research Council.

Shaw, Clifford R., and Henry D. McKay. 1931. *Social Factors in Juvenile Delinquency*: Vol. 2. *Report on the Causes of Crime.* National Commission on Law Observance and Enforcement, report no. 13. Washington, DC: GPO.

Short, James F. 1997. *Poverty, Ethnicity, and Violent Crime.* Boulder, CO: Westview Press.

Stack, Carol. 1974. *All Our Kin: Strategies for Survival in a Black Community.* New York: Harper and Row.

580   THE SOCIOLOGICAL QUARTERLY Vol. 42/No. 4/2001

Sutherland, Edwin H. 1934. *Principles of Criminology.* Chicago: Lippencott.

Tanton, John, and Wayne Lutton. 1993. "Immigration and Criminality in the U.S.A." *Journal of Social, Political, and Economic Studies* 18:217–234.

Taylor, Paul S. 1931."Crime and the Foreign Born: The Problem of the Mexican." Pp. 199–243 in *Report on Crime and the Foreign Born, No. 10,* edited by the National Commission on Law Observance and Enforcement. Washington, DC: GPO.

Thomas, William I., and Florian Znaniecki. 1920. *The Polish Peasant in Europe and America:* Vol. 4: *Disorganization and Reorganization in Poland.* Boston: Gorham Press.

U.S. Bureau of the Census (USBC). 1990. *1990 Census of Population and Housing: Summary Tape File 3A.* Available from http://venus.census.gov/cdrom/lookup.

Waldinger, Roger. 1996. *Still the Promised Land? African-Americans and New Immigrants in Postindustrial New York.* Cambridge, MA: Harvard University Press.

Waters, Mary C. 1999. "Sociology and the Study of Immigration." *American Behavioral Scientist* 42:1264–1267.

Waters, Tony. 1999. *Crime and Immigrant Youth.* Thousand Oaks, CA: Sage.

Whyte, William Foote. 1943. "Social Organization in the Slums." *American Sociological Review* 8:34–39.

Wilson, Kenneth L., and W. Allen Martin. 1982. "Ethnic Enclaves: A Comparison of the Cuban and Black Economies in Miami." *American Journal of Sociology* 86:295–319.

Wolfgang, Marvin E. and Franco Ferracuti. 1967. *The Subculture of Violence: Towards an Integrated Theory in Criminology.* London: Tavistock.

Yeager, Matthew G. 1997. "Immigrants and Criminality: A Review." *Criminal Justice Abstracts* 29:143–171.

Zhang, Pidi, and Jimy Sanders. 1999. "Extended Stratification: Immigrant and Native Differences in Individual and Family Labor." *The Sociological Quarterly* 40:681–704.

[15]

IMMIGRANTS, URBAN POLITICS, AND POLICING IN 1900[*]

M. CRAIG BROWN   BARBARA D. WARNER
State University of New York at Albany   *University of Kentucky*

America's largest cities in 1900 were struggling under the effects of industrialization, urbanization, and immigration. Increasing numbers of immigrants presented political, economic, and cultural threats to the hegemony of native-born middle- and upper-class Americans. As a result, nonimmigrant Americans put pressure on the police to clamp down on urban crime, especially crime related to undesirable aspects of the "foreign" community's lifestyle like the consumption of alcohol. We test conflict theory's threat hypothesis in large American cities in 1900 by relating the percent foreign-born and the arrest rate for drunkenness under numerous controls suggested by criminological research. Because the urban politics of the period revolved around battles between city bosses and reformers, we incorporate political variables into the analysis. The results support a political interpretation of the aggressiveness with which urban police made arrests for drunkenness.

Sociologists in the conflict tradition have long argued that the social control of crime is influenced by many factors besides the rate of illegal behavior. Prominent in this tradition is the threat hypothesis (Blalock 1967; Turk 1969). This hypothesis suggests that in periods of social, political, or economic conflict the power of dominant groups is threatened, resulting in an intensification of social control efforts to maintain the status quo. In the wake of the urban unrest of the 1960s, for example, studies of crime control explored how conditions that threatened the established order affected the scope and performance of city police departments. Although both economic (e.g., poverty, unemployment, income inequality) and racial indicators of threat were examined in these studies, the most consistent finding was a positive relationship between the percent nonwhite in a city and measures of policing like the arrest rate (Liska and Chamlin 1984), the size of the police force (Greenberg, Kessler, and Loftin 1985; Liska, Lawrence, and Benson 1981; Jacobs 1979), and municipal spending on the police (Jackson and Carroll 1981). Moreover, because this relationship was estimated net of the actual level of crime, the racial impact on crime control was not simply a reflection of differing levels of criminal behavior. These findings have

advanced the threat hypothesis as an explanation of the scope and intensity of social control in urban society.

However, there are two general limitations to viewing the link between percent nonwhite and police behavior as unqualified support for conflict theory's threat hypothesis. First, the focus on nonwhites and urban policing in mid-twentieth century makes it unclear whether the relationship is confined to one historical era or whether other "threatening" groups in other turbulent times had a similar impact on policing. Second, the political nature of the threat hypothesis has been neglected, specifically the processes through which community groups and politicians try to influence police behavior. Anchored firmly in the aftermath of the political and racial turbulence of the 1960s, studies of race and policing have been both ahistorical and, ironically, apolitical.[1]

*Direct correspondence to M. Craig Brown, Sociology Department, State University of New York at Albany, Albany, NY 12222. An earlier version of this paper was presented at the 1991 annual meeting of the American Sociological Association in Cincinnati, Ohio. David Duffee and Allen Liska made helpful comments on an earlier draft of the paper.

[1] Wilson and Boland (1978) tested a political variable based on Wilson's (1968) observations about policing styles. They suggested that the aggressiveness of the police in making arrests circa 1975 was a function of a city's "political culture" (Wilson and Banfield 1964). "Reformed" city governments, as measured by the presence of a professional city manager and a nonpartisan city council elected at-large, encouraged the emergence of a professional, i.e., aggressive, style of policing. However, Wilson and Boland's study was a limited exploration of the role of political culture in police behavior in contemporary times. Few of the largest U.S. cities adopted city-manager charters, although they experimented widely with other "progressive" reforms. By focusing on the modern legacies of progressive reforms, however,

We examine police behavior in the 50 largest American cities at the turn of the century to test the threat hypothesis in a different context — the tensions between immigrants and native-born Americans in a rapidly urbanizing and industrializing society. Large variations across cities in the scope of immigration and the pace of social and economic change translate into substantial differences in the economic, political, and cultural threat posed by immigrants and create a promising background for a test of the threat hypothesis.

We test an explicitly political version of the threat hypothesis by examining the extent to which the political structure and culture of a city mediate the immigrant threat and the pressure by the native-born for more aggressive police action. A century ago, urban politics revolved around battles between the classic urban political machines and the forces of moral and political reform. This was the "Age of the Bosses" (Shannon 1969), and as the Progressive Era opened, the tilt of the political struggle between the city bosses, usually acting as agents for the immigrants, and reformers, usually representing the interests of the native middle and upper classes, had profound implications for the aggressiveness of the police in the ethnic enclaves of cities at the turn of the century.

BACKGROUND

Immigrants, Political Machines, and the Politics of Alcohol

Drawn by the economic opportunities created by rapid industrialization and urbanization, immigrants flocked to America's cities in numbers that posed a threat to the hegemony of the native-born population. By 1900, the foreign-born population made up, on average, nearly one-fourth of the total population in the 50 largest cities and ranged as high as 48 percent. The votes of such a relatively large immigrant population, if successfully mobilized, could swing the outcome of city elections. It mattered little that an immigrant population of diverse languages, customs, and interests would

---

Wilson and Boland demonstrated that an examination of the politics of policing in 1900 need not be an antiquarian endeavor — there may well be enduring consequences of these historical developments. Other recent studies that focused on the politics of policing include Chamlin (1990) and Beecher, Linneberry, and Rich (1981).

be difficult to mobilize and control — immigrants and their agents had the *potential* to control city governments, and that potential alone made them a threat to the native-born.

Economic tensions between nonimmigrants and immigrants were also high. The 1890s were years of intense labor conflict and included an economic depression second only to the great depression of the 1930s (Harring 1981, p. 294; Harring 1983, p. 202; Wiebe 1967, p. 124). Widespread failures of banks and businesses meant wage cuts and unemployment, and workers staged mass demonstrations and strikes (Mohl 1985, p. 149). Immigrant workers represented a seemingly infinite supply of cheap labor that attracted the hostility of the native-born (Olzak 1989). Immigrants were also a moral and cultural threat. It is difficult to overestimate the degree to which the native-born population attributed urban decay and disorderliness to the immigrant population: For them, immigrants symbolized the problems of city life (Hofstader 1955, pp. 174–86; Daniels 1990, chap. 10).

No social problem was seen at the root of more urban ills, no social problem was more associated with immigrant social life, and no social problem was more threatening to the middle and upper classes than intemperance (Timberlake 1963). Attempts to control the consumption of alcohol were a response by the native-born to growing cultural, political, and economic pressures from immigrants and were a symbolic attempt to define whose society this was (Gusfield 1963; Harring 1983; Beisel 1990). The long-simmering conflict over alcohol consumption therefore makes the aggressiveness with which police made arrests for public drunkenness an excellent barometer of the response to cultural tension at the turn of the century.

As a symbolic indicator of a formal response to cultural pressures, it may have mattered little who was arrested or whose policy interests were behind the arrests. However, arrests for drunkenness in 1900 were more than symbolic acts. By at least one estimate, arrests for drunkenness involved immigrant workers almost exclusively (Harring 1983, p. 173). Thus, high arrest rates in cities with large immigrant *populations* in all likelihood indicated that foreign-born *individuals* were being arrested. In addition, responding to public drunkenness took initiative, effort, and time, suggesting that a vigorous police response required resources and policy direction. Therefore, the prevalence of arrests for drunkenness should be sensitive to the interests of the groups that controlled the police (Watts 1981, p. 650).

"Moral" issues, including intemperance, increasingly defined urban politics as the new century began (Boyer 1978). On one side were the urban political machines, a byproduct of the massive social and economic changes transforming American cities after the end of the Civil War. Urban political machines were characterized by a political style in which the exchange of jobs and favors for votes was joined to vigorous grassroots organization (Banfield and Wilson 1966; Scott 1969; Wolfinger 1972). According to Weber, the city boss was a "political capitalist entrepreneur" (Gerth and Mills 1958, p. 109) whose main product was the provision of votes, a product manufactured with the reliability of a machine (Scott 1969). In return, the political boss distributed the fruits of power to the organization's workers and the people in the neighborhoods they served.

Because they enjoyed the loyalty of immigrant voters (Merton 1949) and often represented or owned illicit businesses like saloons, gambling halls, and brothels, political bosses, in the view of the native-born community, embodied the political, economic, and cultural threats of the foreign elements of the city. In response, reformers emerged to form the other segment of the urban political dichotomy at the turn of the century.[2]

Reformers pronounced the political bosses culpable for the civic morass. By investigating corruption in the police department and other government agencies, demanding the enforcement of Sunday closing laws for saloons, calling for more aggressive policing of offenses like drunkenness, campaigning to wrest control of city government from the machines, and establishing enduring reform structures like merit systems, reformers sought to tilt the balance of power in their favor. In so doing, the immigrant threat could be curtailed.[3]

Hypotheses

If we translate the threat hypothesis into turn-of-the-century terms, we can derive a set of expectations about the behavior of the police with respect to public drunkenness. First, we expect the relative size of the foreign-born population in a city to positively affect the arrest rate for drunkenness. We also hypothesize that pressures for more aggressive policing in response to the immigrant threat were mediated by the prevailing political environment of the city. Machine politicians, who owed their support to immigrants, should be tolerant toward alcohol consumption and anxious to use their influence to ensure the tolerance of the police. Therefore, we expect the presence of political machines to be associated with low arrest rates for drunkenness. On the other hand, if the changes reformers sought to implement in urban government reflected middle- and upper-class interests, political reform should be associated with high arrest rates for drunkenness. Finally, we expect that introducing these political variables will decrease the impact of the relative size of the foreign-born population on the arrest rate for drunkenness.

DATA AND MEASURES

The Rate of Arrests for Drunkenness

The key dependent variable is the rate of arrests for drunkenness, i.e., the number of arrests per 10,000 population. This rate, which is calculated for the 50 largest U.S. cities in 1900, includes the following offenses: "common drunk," "drunk and disorderly," and "all cases where drunkenness in any form was the primary cause of arrest" (U.S. Department of Labor 1900, p. 919).[4] The class- and ethnic-sensitive nature of arrests for drunk-

---

[2] Historians increasingly question the accuracy and utility of the political machine/reform dichotomy (Dorsett 1972; Thelen 1979; Lotchin 1982; Miller 1982; Teaford 1982), but they have not tested its implications with systematic data.

[3] We do not want to oversimplify the reform movement, which had considerable variety (Mohl 1985, pp. 109–37), including different positions on crime (Haller 1971). Historically, reformers tended to have a political or moral orientation, but the two strains converged by the turn of the century (Boyer·1978, p. 168).

---

[4] The accuracy of crime data has long been a subject for debate. Historians of crime have generally focused on trends in one place over time, easing concerns about the comparability of reporting systems across cities while raising questions about the generalizability of results (Watts 1981; Schneider 1978; Lane 1968; Monkkonen 1981c). Monkkonen (1981b) reported one of the few comparative historical analyses using annual reports of the police departments of 27 cities. His main dependent variable was "order arrests," a combination of offenses that included our drunkenness variable. Although we could not duplicate Monkkonen's variable, a close proxy for 1900 was highly correlated for the 19 cities common to both samples (r = .99).

enness at the turn of the century permits us to link a macro-level rate (the arrest rate for drunkenness) based on a micro-level event (the arrest of an individual for drunkenness) to another macro-level variable (the relative size of the foreign-born population in a city) with confidence.

Immigrants

The size of each city's immigrant population is measured as the percent of the population that is foreign-born (U.S. Census Office 1902a, pp. 103–105). The percent foreign-born is probably the best indicator of the impact of immigration on a city since it is the foreign-born who were the newcomers to American society. This variable also parallels the percent black or percent nonwhite variables used in the urban policing studies of the 1960s.

Urban Politics

Machine politics involve two elements: political mobilization based on patronage, favoritism, or other material inducements; and grassroots political organization in a city's neighborhoods (Scott 1969; Wolfinger 1972; Shefter 1976; Guterbock 1980). Further, two patterns of political machine activity are commonly differentiated: a ward-level pattern in which neighborhood organizations compete with each other and with "regular" political groups for city power; and a citywide pattern in which one machine dominates city politics.

Therefore, we employ a three-category classification of city politics in 1900 based on a review of historical narratives on the politics of specific cities: no organized political machine, ward-level machine(s), and citywide machine. Descriptions of "bosses," ethnic politicians, organizations, constituents, and party activities abound in historical writings about specific cities because political machines were hardworking organizations rather than a shadowy power elite. From these historical descriptions, we ascertained whether political machines were present in each city at the turn of the century.

A code of *no political machine* was assigned if in 1900 the city was described as having no bosses or, if a "boss" was identified, the record clearly indicated the absence of the features used to define machines. The political rhetoric of turn-of-the-century cities was often heated and the "boss" label was liberally applied; occasionally it stuck to an undeserving candidate. Only a handful of cities were classified as having no machine politics. Cities with political machines were then classified by whether or not a political machine exercised citywide control. A city was classified as having a *citywide machine* if 1900 was part of a period in which the machine controlled a majority on the city council and elected their mayoral candidate in successive elections; otherwise cities were classified as having *ward-level machines*. (A brief summary of politics in the 50 cities is available from the first author.)

Although discussions of machine politics and police behavior generally agree that "machine politics" depressed arrest rates for public offenses, predictions about the impact of specific types of machine politics have not always been consistent. Fogelson (1977) suggested that in an era of decentralized policing and urban politics, police behavior was controlled at a neighborhood level by ward politicians. Alternatively, Merton (1949) and the functionalists clearly believed that citywide bosses were the only politicians with enough power to shape the behavior of city agencies like the police.

As an antidote to the influence of political bosses, reformers designed political innovations that changed the face of American urban politics and administration (Rice 1977; Knoke 1982). However, in 1900 progressive reforms were just emerging and some had no impact on the nation's biggest cities or the conduct of their police forces. In contrast, civil service reform, an issue of longstanding and widespread significance in big cities, was in many ways the leading edge of progressive reform. Striking at patronage, which was the heart of the political machine, civil service reforms sought to replace the particularism of machine politics with "merit" considerations — universalistic criteria of appointment and advancement. According to the reform logic, merit systems would ensure that the most qualified people were employed and city government would be freed of politics. This rationalization of employment would, in turn, make government more evenhanded and efficient (Schiesl 1977, pp. 25–45; Maniha 1975).

The institutionalization of merit system reform in each city in 1900 was captured by the number of years (expressed in log terms to compensate for skewness) that the police department had been covered by a merit system.[5] Although the pres-

---

[5] To document the presence of a merit system covering at least the police we began with the records of the chief civil service reform association (Civil Ser-

ence of a longstanding merit system is no guarantee of it's efficacy, we hypothesize that the introduction of merit considerations limited the role of machine politics and increased the influence of the middle and upper classes on the policies of the police toward issues like intemperance. If so, arrest rates for cities "reformed" for a longer period of time should be higher than those for cities that only recently had adopted a merit system or had no merit system.

Control Variables

Six variables served as controls. First, because cities in 1900 varied widely in the number of police officers employed (Harring 1983), the *number of police per 10,000 population* is used as a basic control (U.S. Department of Labor 1900). Thus, our measure of the intensity of social control, the arrest rate, is conditioned on a "prior" measure of social control, the relative size of the urban social control apparatus. This allows us to separate the impact of percent foreign-born from the impact of the size of the police force. It also highlights the aggressiveness of the police by directly netting out the number of police available to make arrests. For a similar approach see Liska and Chamlin (1984).

Second, since no data exist on the actual prevalence of drunkenness in a city, it was necessary to devise a proxy. Otherwise, some cities might have high arrest rates simply because there was more drunkenness. From information on the local brewing industry, the per capita value of malt liquor produced in each city was computed (U.S. Census Office 1902b, pp. 1069–70). This variable is a reasonable proxy for consumption because technical limitations in preservation and distribution at the turn of the century meant that breweries "served a strictly local market" (Tim-

vice Assembly of the United States and Canada 1942). However, comparing dates from the reformers to those in historical accounts of reform in specific cities revealed significant discrepancies. These discrepancies were reconciled by surveying city personnel departments. For our 50 cities, the date used was verified and a copy of either the enabling legislation or the first civil service rules was obtained. Although a logged version of the years (with a constant of one added to each case) since the inception of a merit system covering at least the police was used in the analysis reported here, other forms of the variable — dichotomous (no system vs. system present), trichotomous (no system vs. system present less than 10 years vs. system present more than 10 years), and unlogged number of years — replicated our results.

berlake 1963, p. 103) — few cities were significant exporters of beer (Duis 1983, pp. 43–44).[6] The number of saloons per 10,000 population was also computed for each city (U.S. Department of Labor 1900, pp. 934–35). Because the two variables were highly correlated (r = .501) and only 50 cities were available for analysis, a degree of freedom was saved by standardizing and adding these two indicators to create one proxy for the *level of alcohol consumption.*

Third, a measure of industrialization controls for the possibility that both immigration and the nature of urban politics at the turn of the century were byproducts of the emergence of large-scale manufacturing. From occupational data, *the proportion of the labor force employed in manufacturing pursuits* was calculated (U.S. Census Office 1902a, pp. 124–29). This measure is important for properly specifying the influence of immigration and urban politics, but the impact of industrialization on arrest rates is expected to be marginal.

Fourth, a measure of urbanization — *population density* — (U.S. Department of Labor 1900, pp. 928–33) was used to properly specify estimates of the impact on arrest rates of immigration and urban politics, both of which were associated with the growth of large cities (Teaford 1984). Moreover, high-density cities are associated with classic urban pathologies and can be patrolled more intensively with fewer police, supporting a positive link to arrest rates (Harring 1983, p. 199).

Fifth, because cities varied in the degree to which the foreign-born were segregated in ethnic ghettos, the index of dissimilarity between the foreign-born and the native-born measures the extent of *residential segregation* in each city (U.S. Census Office 1901, pp. 647–84; Massey and Denton 1988). Predictions about the segregation of the foreign-born and arrest rates are mixed. Sociologists studying race and policing argue that residential segregation eases the threat

[6] Unfortunately, we cannot systematically address the question of the exportation and importation of beer. Only a handful of cities were major exporters — Milwaukee, St Louis, and Cincinnati are commonly mentioned. Milwaukee, for example, was a big exporter, especially to Chicago. However, a dummy variable for these three well known exporters did not make a significant contribution to the equations we estimated. At the same time, analyses using just saloons per 10,000 population and another proxy, the mortality rate from alcoholism (U.S. Census Office 1902c), replicated the results reported here.

posed by nonwhites, thereby reducing pressure for police action (Liska and Chamlin 1984). However, historians suggest that separation highlights differences between cultural groups, increases awareness (and fear) of areas and groups at odds with middle-class values, and produces pressure for more police action (Harring 1983; Monkkonen 1988).

The final control variable centered on regional variations. The political environment of post-Civil War southern cities was distinctive (Shefter 1983). Moreover, the pace of social and economic change in the South was slower and the magnitude of immigration much lower than in other regions (Dunlevy 1982), suggesting low arrest rates. On the other hand, historians argue that blacks were the southern equivalent of the foreign-born population in northern cities (Watts 1973; Timberlake 1963, pp. 119–21) and, as a result, some southern cities had high arrest rates for public order offenses despite having small foreign-born populations. Therefore, a *South/non-South* variable was included in the analysis.[7]

RESULTS

Table 1 reports OLS estimates of the impact of percent foreign-born in a city on arrests for drunkenness. Each model incorporates additional control variables. In the first model, percent foreign-born is the only regressor. As expected, the relationship is positive and each increase of one percentage point in percent foreign-born adds about three arrests for drunkenness per 10,000 population.[8]

In Model 2, controls are added for the general level of alcohol consumption and relative size of the police force. The explained variance increases from about 10 percent in Model 1 to about 44 percent in Model 2 ($F = 13.73$; d.f. $= 2,46$; $p < .001$). The coefficient for the foreign-born variable remains positive and of substantial magnitude in the face of additional controls. The percent foreign-born in a city has little zero-order association with either the relative size of the police force ($r = .10$) or the level of alcohol consumption ($r = .03$). (A full correlation matrix, means, and standard deviations are reported in the Appendix.) Therefore, cities in 1900 with large immigrant populations did not generally have a larger social control apparatus, just more aggressive policing. Also, this aggressiveness cannot be explained by higher levels of alcohol consumption. Immigrants may have consumed more alcohol in the public settings (e.g., saloons and beer gardens) favored in the immigrant community and disliked by the middle and upper classes, but, stereotypes aside, cities with a relatively large foreign-born population did not consume alcohol at greater levels than did cities with fewer foreign-born.

The number of police per 10,000 population exerts a powerful positive influence on arrests — the more police the higher the arrest rate for drunkenness. Surprisingly the coefficient for alcohol consumption is significant but negative. Two interpretations are reasonable.[9] First, high levels of alcohol consumption may have overwhelmed the capacity of the police to deal with the problem, a phenomenon termed "system overload" (Geerken

---

[7] The potential role of blacks as a threatening group in southern cities at the turn of the century suggests that "percent black" could be substituted for the regional dummy variable. This variable along with percent foreign-born would capture what are sometimes called the "dangerous classes" (Monkkonen 1981a). This strategy is complicated from a theoretical point of view because blacks in 1900, particularly in the South, were not significantly involved in the political process described here. Nonetheless, we found that the percent black performed in much the same way as the dummy variable for South. Moreover, in the 40 non-South cities, percent black made no meaningful contribution to any of the models, suggesting that the black population was not large enough or politically involved enough at the turn of the century to be much of a "threat" outside the South. Therefore, we retained the dummy variable for South as a more general measure of the region's distinctiveness.

[8] In keeping with theoretical expectations (Blalock 1967) and past research (Jackson and Carroll 1981),

we considered quadratic and cubic transformations of the foreign-born variable. There was some indication that a curvilinear pattern similar to that observed by Jackson and Carroll was appropriate. However, the scatterplot suggested that most curvilinearity resulted from a few extreme cases — excluding one city, Atlanta, rendered the higher order terms not significant. Atlanta had a very high arrest rate for drunkenness but relatively few immigrants. The high arrest rate apparently stemmed from a different "threatening" group — poor blacks (Watts 1973). With only 50 cases, scatterplots and measures of influence were studied very carefully. None of the results reported here are attributable to influential cases.

[9] A less plausible explanation is that vigorous policing of alcohol consumption decreased at least the public forms of consumption most likely to result in arrest. However, the inability or unwillingness of turn-of-the-century urban police to effectively regulate saloons and public drinking undermines this interpretation.

IMMIGRANTS, URBAN POLITICS, AND POLICING IN 1900 299

Table 1. Unstandardized Ordinary Least Squares Coefficients for Regression of Arrest Rate Per 10,000 Population for Drunkenness on Selected Independent Variables: U.S. Cities, 1900

Independent Variable	Model 1	Model 2	Model 3	Model 4	Model 5
Percent foreign-born	3.040*	2.601*	3.132	1.082	1.086
	(1.290)	(1.050)	(1.658)	(1.172)	(1.156)
Alcohol consumption	—	-22.159*	-17.714*	-13.772	-14.072
		(6.699)	(7.447)	(8.044)	(7.609)
Police per 10,000 population	—	10.662*	11.674*	10.078*	10.071*
		(2.379)	(2.705)	(2.342)	(2.312)
Residential segregation	—	—	402.813	—	—
			(282.297)		
Population density	—	—	-2.639	—	—
			(2.432)		
Percent of workforce in manufacturing	—	—	13.100	—	—
			(144.848)		
South	—	—	10.405	—	—
			(41.358)		
Years since adoption of merit system (natural log)	—	—	—	27.255*	26.923*
				(12.091)	(11.668)
Citywide machine	—	—	—	-77.482	-73.314*
				(48.544)	(36.018)
Ward-level machine	—	—	—	-4.228	—
				(32.485)	
Constant	86.377*	-38.335	-97.535	-2.207	-5.445
	(32.791)	(38.093)	(81.468)	(46.438)	(38.711)
R^2	.104	.439	.479	.533	.533
Number of cities	50	50	50	45	45

* $p < .05$

Note: Numbers in parentheses are standard errors.

and Gove 1975, 1977) or "system strain" (Logan 1975). Second, large-scale production and distribution of alcohol created a group of businessmen who were anxious to influence politicians and the police (Duis 1983). The negative sign of the proxy variable for alcohol consumption indicates they may have been successful.

Introducing additional controls for region, industrialization, urbanization, and residential segregation (Model 3) does not add substantially to the explanation of the arrest rate for drunkenness ($F = .81$; d.f. = 4,42; $p > .25$). This conclusion is reinforced using other indicators of each of these variables. In contrast to research on racial segregation in the mid-twentieth century, residential segregation of the foreign-born had no significant impact on arrest rates for drunkenness.

The coefficient for percent foreign-born in Model 3 is similar in magnitude to the estimates in the first two models. However, an increase in the standard error of the estimate for percent foreign-born in Model 3 means that the coefficient

is no longer significant. The increase in the standard error occurs because of the loss of four degrees of freedom due to the additional controls. Also, the increased standard error indicates that some of the added variables are related to percent foreign-born (e.g., for industrialization, $r = .56$). Thus, these variables do not "explain" the impact of the relative size of the immigrant community on the arrest performance of the police.

Models 4 and 5 examine the political dimension of arrests for public intoxication. (Because it was not possible to determine the turn-of-the-century politics of five of the cities, Models 4 and 5 are based on the 45 cities with political data.[10]) Model 4 incorporates three political variables into Model 2. The political variables add

[10] Models 1 through 3 were estimated with all 50 cities to give control variables the best opportunity to make a contribution to the explanation of arrest rates for drunkenness. However, Models 1 through 3 were also estimated for the 45 cities available for Models 4 and 5. The results were replicated.

substantially to the explanation of arrest rates for drunkenness. As expected, the coefficient for the merit system variable is positive and significant, indicating a higher arrest rate for drunkenness when bureaucratic reforms were institutionalized in urban government. The political machine variables, on the other hand, are negative in sign. However, neither political machine variable is significant in Model 4, though the coefficient for the citywide variable is more than one-and-one-half times its standard error. The coefficient of the ward-level variable is of negligible magnitude. Contrary to the expectations of Fogelson (1977), decentralized policing in conjunction with decentralized (i.e., ward-level) machine politics did not result in significantly lower arrest rates for intoxication.[11]

In Model 5, the regression is re-estimated dropping the ward-level variable so that the intercept reflects cities without political machines and those with ward-level machines. The coefficients of both the merit system and citywide political machine variables are now significant: Net of the other variables, police in cities controlled by a citywide political machine made over 70 fewer arrests for drunkenness per 10,000 population than their counterparts in cities without a dominant machine. Turn-of-the-century political machines repaid immigrants and the producers and sellers of alcohol for their support by setting lenient police policies regarding alcohol and public intoxication.

Another important finding in Models 4 and 5 is that the coefficient for the percent foreign-born variable is no longer significant. The relationship between the foreign-born threat and policing was therefore linked through political developments at the turn of the century. However, the pattern of associations behind the regressions shows that the two elements of urban politics were not equally important in the translation of the immigrant threat into higher arrest rates. The presence of a citywide machine in 1900 is uncor-

---

[11] With respect to the arrest rate for drunkenness, cities with ward-level machines were no different from cities without a political machine. One interpretation of this finding is that ward-level machine organizations were omnipresent at the turn of the century, and better case ascertainment would have revealed the existence of machines in cities where historians believe no machines existed. Therefore, the lack of an effect on arrest rates may be due to the fact that these cities weren't *really* different politically. However, this interpretation does not readily extend to cities controlled by a political machine.

related with the percent foreign-born or the years since adoption of a merit system, indicating that machine politics made an independent rather than mediating contribution to the explanation of arrest rates for drunkenness. Although the immigrant community and urban political machines were deeply connected, the presence of a citywide machine was not tied to the relative size of the foreign-born population, i.e., a large foreign-born population may have been necessary but was by no means sufficient for machine control (Shefter 1976). The foreign-born community was not monolithic — different groups had different languages, interests, and political favorites, and the emergence of a citywide political machine was the result of a complicated process of coalition formation. Similarly, the presence of a long-standing merit system may have more to do with the excesses of previous political machines than with consolidated machine control in 1900, although civil service systems were typically justified by the general milieu surrounding patronage politics rather than any specific political machine.

On the other hand, the presence of a long-standing merit system was correlated with the percent foreign-born (r = .48). The political/cultural threat posed by a relatively large immigrant community, whether or not it resulted in machine control, was enough to stimulate merit system reform. Therefore, the structural legacy of reform movements — an emerging government and police bureaucracy — was the primary link between the relative size of the immigrant community and arrest rates for drunkenness.

Finally, alcohol consumption was associated with the presence of a citywide political machine (r = .45), further specifying the negative impact of centralized machine control on arrest rates and explaining why alcohol issues were so inviting to reformers: Control of alcohol struck at two important targets — machine politics and the economic interests sustaining them.

The results provide strong support for a political interpretation of the aggressiveness with which the police made arrests for drunkenness. While immigrants posed a threat to the interests of the native-born population, they presented an opportunity for machine politicians to enhance their influence. Producers and distributors of alcohol were also attractive sources of support for machine politicians. This translated into a liberal outlook by the political machine toward the regulation of a "moral" issue like drinking. The threatened middle and upper classes, on the other hand, sought to retain or regain political influ-

Table 2. Crude and Predicted Arrest Rates for Drunkenness Per 10,000 Population: Seven Cities With Citywide Political Machines, 1900

City	Political Machine (Party)	Arrest Rate for Drunkenness, 1900		
		Crude	Predicted from Model 1[a]	Predicted from Model 2[b]
Philadelphia	Durham (R)	222	159	241
Pittsburgh	Magee-Flinn (R)	145	170	162
Albany	Barnes (R)	94	148	138
Louisville	Whallen-Weaver (D)	72	124	155
Rochester	Aldridge (R)	64	166	127
Milwaukee	Rose (D)	61	183	17
Cincinnati	Cox (R)	61	145	127

[a] Predicted from percent foreign-born (Table 1).

[b] Predicted from percent foreign-born, alcohol consumption, and police per 10,000 population (Table 1).

ence in the face of the immigrant threat by decrying the state of urban government, linking saloons and alcohol to the political situation, pressuring the police for more aggressive efforts at social control, trying to oust machine politicians, and seeking more permanent solutions to the problems of urban government through reforms like merit systems. A closer examination of the histories of cities in which this process occurred most forcefully — cities in which a political machine controlled city government — reveals a clearer picture of some of the variations on this process.

For each of the seven cities with citywide machines in 1900, Table 2 shows the organization and political party in power, the crude arrest rate for drunkenness per 10,000 population, and two predicted arrest rates, one taking into account only the percent foreign-born (Model 1), the other taking into account the percent foreign-born, the police presence, and the level of alcohol consumption (Model 2). Because the analysis demonstrated that citywide political machines had a significant negative effect on arrest rates for drunkenness, the crude arrest rates in Table 2 should be lower than the predicted arrest rates. Nonetheless, these cities varied considerably in the degree to which their arrest rates were lower than the predicted rates. Philadelphia, for example, is a noticeable exception to the tendency for citywide machines to be lenient in their policies toward drunkenness.

Philadelphia had the highest crude arrest rate among these seven cities, (222), exceeding the level predicted by the relative size of its foreign born population (159). The similarity between Philadelphia's crude rate and the rate predicted from percent foreign-born, alcohol consumption, and size of the police force (241) hides the city's uniqueness: Among the 50 cities, Philadelphia was only average in the relative size of its foreign-born community, was well below average in alcohol consumption, *and yet* ranked sixth of 50 in police per 10,000 population. Philadelphia had a big, aggressive police force despite being controlled by a citywide political machine and having a low level of alcohol consumption.

The reason for Philadelphia's uniqueness lies in the composition of the dominant political coalition. Philadelphia was a Republican city largely controlled by native-born Americans (Donagher 1979).[12] With the ascendence of the Republican party, the Democratic ward bosses, who represented "saloon" interests and the old immigrants, were relegated to a minor role (Quay 1969; Silcox 1986). With a relatively small and factionalized ethnic community and a politically impotent Democratic party, little accommodation to immigrant desires was necessary. The Republican organization could handle any "cultural" threat by using a large police force to aggressively implement the policies of the organization. This result amplifies Beisel's (1990) finding that there was little support for anti-vice movements in Philadelphia during this time: The aggressive efforts of the police on behalf of the Republican machine may have made general anti-vice movements unnecessary.

Pittsburgh, also under the control of a Republican machine dominated by business interests (Thrasher 1949), was an exception in that its crude arrest rate was similar to predicted levels. Political coalitions created by the political machines in the remaining cities were much more reliant on immigrant support, especially older, established immigrant groups that were aware of the significance of their numbers and aggressive in the pursuit of their interests. The nature of these governing coalitions illustrates the contribution of immigrant political support to the consolidation of city power and the translation of that power

---

[12] Coming on the heels of a realigning election in 1896 that favored Republicans both nationally and locally (Burnham 1970), the years around the turn of the century were the heyday of Republican machines. However, the nature of the coalition assembled by an organization was more important than the party label when it came to policies regarding alcohol consumption.

into tolerant police policies toward alcohol and low arrest rates for drunkenness.

Cincinnati is a good illustration of how machine organizations forged governing coalitions among significant ethnic groups, protected the economic interests of saloon-keepers and brewers, deflected anti-immigrant hostilities, and resisted pressure for more aggressive policing of alcohol-related offenses. During the 1890s, Republican George B. Cox built a diverse governing coalition following a tumultuous decade of labor unrest, riots, and hostility toward racial minorities and immigrants (Miller 1968; Peacock 1947). Cox drew some support from suburban parts of the city, but the heart of his coalition was built on the voters and ward politicians of Cincinnati's ethnic neighborhoods. Principal among his ethnic supporters were German immigrants who started coming to the city in the 1830s and who built a large, well-established community by the 1890s (Miller 1968, p. 30). Indeed, the Germans were so prominent that by 1870 Cincinnati was virtually bilingual (Hett 1968, p. 2).

Saloons and alcohol issues were important to the Cox machine. Cox himself started out as a saloon-keeper, selected his lieutenants from the ranks of ward politicians and saloon-keepers, and ran his organization out of saloons and gambling joints (Miller 1968, p. 85). There was considerable anti-immigrant sentiment, especially against Germans, in Cincinnati at this time, and much of it was focused on German saloon-keepers (Marcus and Miller 1987). Nonetheless, because of the efforts of the Cox organization, Cincinnati's newly reorganized police accepted the impossibility of regulating the saloons (Miller 1968, p. 97). In addition, the organization was able to deflect much of the considerable pressure to enforce Sunday closing laws, a highly sensitive issue in Cincinnati (Hett 1968, pp. 45–46).

Cincinnati's experience was repeated with local variations in the other cities with citywide political machines. Coalitions were built around prominent, usually longstanding, ethnic groups and important local economic interests. George Aldridge's Rochester, for example, was described as an "open town" (McKelvey 1956, p. 81) with a large, stable immigrant population (Gordon 1927). In Milwaukee, brewers were a critical force behind Mayor Rose's advocacy of a wide-open town, a variety of the "personal liberty" espoused by Rose in his campaigns and endorsed by ethnic voters (Ranney 1981). Indeed, the magnitude of the brewing industry in Milwaukee, which in-

cluded exports to Chicago and beyond, results in an extremely low predicted arrest rate for drunkenness in Table 2.[13] In sum, the history of specific cities strongly supports and expands our interpretation of the regression results. The attitudes of political machines toward offenses like drunkenness depended on local opportunities for assembling a solid coalition, which usually meant seeking out important immigrant groups and economic interests. In turn, machines used their considerable influence with the police to establish priorities consistent with the sources of their strength and resist contrary pressures from reform elements.

CONCLUSION

Perhaps our most striking result is the similarity in the police behavior in American cities in two different contexts. Separated in time by a half-century, focusing on a different "threatening" group, and examining police responses to a different crime, our analysis nonetheless demonstrates a strong and consistent thread in the behavior of the urban police: In both 1900 and the mid-twentieth century, the "threat" represented by a relatively large threatening group results in high arrest rates. Thus, the empirical base of support for the threat hypothesis is broadened considerably.

Moreover, our analysis is more than a replication of studies on race and urban policing. For the first time, we have demonstrated a political link between a threatening group and police behavior. Capitalizing on the machine politics versus reform dichotomy in urban politics at the turn of the century, we showed that control by a political machine typically deflected pressure for arrests for drunkenness, while the presence of a reform institution like the civil service was associated with high arrest rates. Thus, the threat presented by immigrants was mediated by the political culture and structure of the city.

A detailed examination of the historical background of cities controlled by a citywide political machine in 1900 provided further understanding of this process. Urban bosses gained power by exchanging favors to needy groups for votes. If these coalitions were broad enough and durable enough, the political machine could control the political life of a city. In 1900, most political

---

[13] Milwaukee is an influential city in some of the regressions. Again, however, our basic results hold when Milwaukee is excluded from the analysis.

IMMIGRANTS, URBAN POLITICS, AND POLICING IN 1900   303

machines formed working relationships with immigrant groups that were sensitive to attempts to limit the consumption of alcohol. In addition, groups with economic interests in the production or consumption of alcohol vigorously supported the political machines. With their political power, machines resisted attempts to regulate alcohol consumption by influencing the policies and actions of the police.

Political machines were most responsive not to an undifferentiated mass of "immigrants," but to clearly defined groups with standing in the community. Groups that were able to establish themselves in a city and had the numbers and sophistication to advance their interests were taken seriously by machine politicians. In this way, immigrant groups developed a voice in urban politics, a voice used to deflect police pressure on the immigrant community.

M. Craig Brown is an adjunct professor with the Department of Sociology and the School of Criminal Justice at SUNY Albany. He is a research scientist with the New York State Office of Mental Retardation and Developmental Disabilities, where he does research related to policy and planning. In addition to continuing his work with Barbara Warner on ethnicity and crime, his research interests include the emergence of machine politics in U.S. cities, and the social forces explaining the expansion and contraction of public institutions serving the mentally disabled.

Barbara D. Warner is Assistant Professor of Sociology at the University of Kentucky. Her work focuses on macrosociological causes of crime and crime control. Her research examining variations in crime control has attempted to identify mediating variables between community structure and rates of crime control. She is presently examining the level of divergence between police and complainant descriptions of "criminal" events as a potential mediator of neighborhood characteristics and arrest rates in 60 Boston neighborhoods.

Appendix. Means, Standard Deviations, and Correlations for Variables in the Analysis (N = 45)

Variable	(1)	(2)	(3)	(4)	(5)	(6)	(7)	(8)	(9)	(10)	(11)
(1) Arrest rate for drunkenness per 10,00 population	1.00	—	—	—	—	—	—	—	—	—	—
(2) Police per 10,000 population	.50	1.00	—	—	—	—	—	—	—	—	—
(3) Alcohol consumption	-.27	.09	1.00	—	—	—	—	—	—	—	—
(4) Percent foreign-born	.32	.10	.03	1.00	—	—	—	—	—	—	—
(5) Population density	-.07	.32	.29	-.08	1.00	—	—	—	—	—	—
(6) Percent of workforce in manufacturing	.08	-.07	-.00	.56	.18	1.00	—	—	—	—	—
(7) Residential segregation	.05	-.12	-.23	-.33	.05	-.18	1.00	—	—	—	—
(8) Ward-level political machine	.18	-.02	-.08	.11	-.06	-.02	.13	1.00	—	—	—
(9) Citywide political machine	-.24	.15	.45	-.04	.26	.12	-.28	-.08	1.00	—	—
(10) Years since adoption of merit system (natural log)	.42	.22	.01	.48	-.11	.29	-.20	.05	.18	1.00	—
(11) South	-.08	.13	-.12	-.67	.14	-.47	.14	.04	-.08	-.24	1.00
Mean	159.30	12.79	-.11	22.82	12.53	38.90	.15	.67	.16	.78	.22
Standard deviation	103.99	5.11	1.70	11.39	5.88	10.90	.05	.48	.37	1.17	.42

REFERENCES

Banfield, Edward C. and James Q. Wilson. 1966. *City Politics*. New York: Vantage.

Beecher, Janice A., Robert L. Linneberry, and Michael J. Rich. 1981. "The Politics of Police Responses to Urban Crime." Pp. 183–201 in *Reactions To Crime*, vol. 16, edited by D. A. Lewis. Beverly Hills, CA: Sage Criminal Justice System Annuals.

Beisel, Nicola. 1990. "Class, Culture, and Campaigns Against Vice." *American Sociological Review* 55:44–62.

Blalock, Hubert. 1967. *Toward a Theory of Minority-Group Relations*. New York: John Wiley.

Boyer, Paul. 1978. *Urban Masses and Moral Order in America, 1880–1920*. Cambridge: Harvard University Press.

Burnham, Walter Dean. 1970. *Critical Elections and the Mainspring of American Politics*. New York: Norton.

Chamlin, Mitchell B. 1990. "Determinants of Police Expenditures in Chicago, 1904–1958." *Sociologi-*

cal Quarterly 31:485–94.

Civil Service Assembly of the United States and Canada. 1942. *Civil Service Agencies in the United States: A 1940 Census.* Chicago: The Assembly.

Daniels, Roger. 1990. *Coming to America: A History of Immigration and Ethnicity in American Life.* New York: HarperCollins.

Donagher, Richard. 1979. "The Urban Bull Moose: A Case Study of Philadelphia and Pittsburgh." Ph.D. dissertation, Department of History, Fordham University, Bronx, NY.

Dorsett, Lyle W. 1972. "The City Boss and the Reformer: A Reappraisal." *Pacific Northwest Quarterly* 63:150–54.

Dunlevy, James A. 1982. "Regional Preferences and Migrant Settlement: On the Avoidance of the South by Nineteenth-Century Immigrants." Pp. 217–51 in *Research in Economic History,* vol. 8, edited by P. Uselding. Greenwich, CT: JAI.

Duis, Perry. 1983. *The Saloon: Public Drinking in Chicago and Boston, 1880–1920.* Champaign-Urbana: University of Illinois Press.

Fogelson, Robert M. 1977. *Big-City Police.* Cambridge: Harvard University Press.

Geerken, Michael R. and Walter R. Gove. 1975. "Deterrence: Some Theoretical Considerations." *Law and Society Review* 9:497–513.

————. 1977. "Deterrence, Overload, and Incapacitation: An Empirical Evaluation." *Social Forces* 56:424–47.

Gerth, H. H. and C. Wright Mills. 1958. *From Max Weber: Essays in Sociology.* New York: Oxford University Press.

Gordon, Robert M. 1927. "George W. Aldridge: A Study of the Political Career of a Local Boss." M.A. thesis, Department of History, University of Rochester.

Greenberg, David F., Ronald C. Kessler, and Colin Loftin. 1985. "Social Inequality and Crime Control." *Journal of Criminal Law and Criminology* 76:684–704.

Gusfield, Joseph R. 1963. *Symbolic Crusade: Status Politics and the American Temperance Movement.* Urbana: University of Illinois Press.

Guterbock, Thomas M. 1980. *Machine Politics in Transition: Party and Community in Chicago.* Chicago: University of Chicago Press.

Haller, Mark H. 1971. "Civic Reformers and Police Leadership." Pp. 39–56 in *Police in Urban Society,* edited by H. Hahn. Beverly Hills, CA: Sage Publications.

Harring, Sidney L. 1981. "Policing a Class Society: The Expansion of the Urban Police in the Late Nineteenth and Early Twentieth Centuries." Pp. 292–313 in *Crime and Capitalism: Readings in Marxist Criminology,* edited by D. F. Greenberg. Palo Alto, CA: Mayfield.

————. 1983. *Policing a Class Society: The Experience of American Cities, 1865–1915.* New Brunswick, NJ: Rutgers University Press.

Hett, Cristopher B. 1968. "Political Boss of Cincinnati: The Era of George B. Cox." M.A. thesis, Department of History, Xavier University, Cincinnati, OH.

Hofstader, Richard. 1955. *The Age of Reform.* New York: Vintage.

Jackson, Pamela Irving and Leo Carroll. 1981. "Race and the War on Crime: The Sociopolitical Determinants of Municipal Police Expenditures in 90 Non-Southern U.S. Cities." *American Sociological Review* 46:390–405.

Jacobs, David. 1979. "Inequality and Police Strength: Conflict Theory and Coercive Control in Metropolitan Areas." *American Sociological Review* 44:913–25.

Knoke, David. 1982. "The Spread of Municipal Reform: Temporal, Spatial, and Social Dynamics." *American Journal of Sociology* 87:1314–39.

Lane, Roger. 1968. "Crime and Criminal Statistics in Nineteenth-Century Massachusetts." *Journal of Social History* 2:156–63.

Liska, Allen E., and Mitchell B. Chamlin. 1984. "Social Structure and Crime Control Among Macrosocial Units." *American Journal of Sociology* 90:383–95.

Liska, Allen E., Joseph J. Lawrence, and Michael Benson. 1981. "Perspectives on the Legal Order: The Capacity for Social Control." *American Journal of Sociology* 87:413–25.

Logan, Charles H. 1975. "Arrest Rates and Deterrence." *Social Science Quarterly* 56:376–89.

Lotchin, Roger W. 1982. "Power and Policy: American City Politics Between the Two World Wars." Pp. 1–50 in *Ethnics, Machines and the American Urban Future,* edited by S. Greer. Cambridge, MA: Schenkman.

Maniha, John K. 1975. "Universalism and Particularism in Bureaucratizing Organizations." *Administrative Science Quarterly* 20:177–89.

Marcus, Alan I. and Zane L. Miller. 1987. "From Bummer to Boss: Cincinnati's George B. Cox." *Timeline* 4:16–31.

Massey, Douglas S. and Nancy A. Denton. 1988. "The Dimensions of Residential Segregation." *Social Forces* 67:281–315.

McKelvey, Blake. 1956. *Rochester: The Quest for Quality, 1890–1925.* Cambridge: Harvard University Press.

Merton, Robert K. 1949. *Social Theory and Social Structure.* Glencoe, IL: Free Press.

Miller, Zane L. 1968. *Boss Cox's Cincinnati: Urban Politics in the Progressive Era.* New York: Oxford University Press.

————. 1982. "Bosses, Machines, and the Urban Political Process." Pp. 51–84 in *Ethnics, Machines, and the American Urban Future,* edited by S. Greer. Cambridge, MA: Schenkman.

Mohl, Raymond A. 1985. *The New City: Urban America in the Industrial Age, 1860–1920.* Arlington Heights, IL: Harlan Davidson.

Monkkonen, Eric H. 1981a. *Police in Urban America, 1860–1920.* Cambridge, U.K.: Cambridge University Press.

———. 1981b. "A Disorderly People? Urban Order in the Nineteenth and Twentieth Centuries." *Journal of American History* 68:539–59.

———. 1981c. "Toward an Understanding of Urbanization: Drunk Arrests in Los Angeles." *Pacific Historical Review* 50:234–44.

———. 1988. *America Becomes Urban: The Development of U.S. Cities and Towns, 1780–1980.* Berkeley: University of California Press.

Olzak, Susan. 1989. "Labor Unrest, Immigration, and Ethnic Conflict in Urban America, 1880–1914." *American Journal of Sociology* 94:1303–33.

Peacock, Francis G. 1947. "Ohio City Bosses." M.A. thesis, Department of History, Miami University, Oxford, OH.

Quay, William L. 1969. "Philadelphia Democrats: 1880–1910." Ph.D. dissertation, Department of History, Lehigh University, Bethlehem, PA.

Ranney, Joseph A. 1981. "The Political Campaigns of Mayor David S. Rose." *Milwaukee History* 4:2–19.

Rice, Bradley Robert. 1977. *Progressive Cities: The Commission Movement in America, 1901–1920.* Austin: University of Texas.

Schiesl, Martin J. 1977. *The Politics of Efficiency: Municipal Administration and Reform, 1880–1920.* Berkeley: University of California Press.

Schneider, John C. 1978. "Public Order and the Geography of the City: Crime, Violence, and the Police in Detroit, 1845–1875." *Journal of Urban History* 4:183–208.

Scott, James C. 1969. "Corruption, Machine Politics, and Political Change." *American Political Science Review* 63:1142–58.

Shannon, William V. 1969. "The Age of the Bosses." *American Heritage* June: 28–31.

Shefter, Martin. 1976. "The Emergence of the Political Machine: An Alternative View." Pp. 14–44 in *Theoretical Perspectives on Urban Politics,* edited by W. Hawley, et al. Englewood Cliffs, NJ: Prentice-Hall.

———. 1983. "Regional Receptivity to Reform: The Legacy of the Progressive Era." *Political Science Quarterly* 98:459–83.

Silcox, Harry C. 1986. "William McMullen, Nineteenth-Century Political Boss." *Pennsylvania Magazine of History and Biography* 110:389–412.

Teaford, Jon C. 1982. "Finis for Tweed and Steffens: Rewriting the History of Urban Rule." Pp. 133–49

in *The Promise of American History: Progress and Prospects,* edited by S. I. Kutler and S. N. Katz. Baltimore, MD: Johns Hopkins University Press.

———. 1984. *The Unheralded Triumph: City Government in America, 1870–1900.* Baltimore, MD: Johns Hopkins University Press.

Thelen, David P. 1979. "Urban Politics: Beyond Bosses and Reformers." *Reviews in American History* 7:406–12.

Thrasher, Eugene C. 1949. "The Magee-Flinn Political Machine, 1895–1903." M.A. thesis, Department of History, University of Pittsburgh, Pittsburgh, PA.

Timberlake, James H. 1963. *Prohibition and the Progressive Movement, 1900–1920.* Cambridge: Harvard University Press.

Turk, A. 1969. *Criminality and the Legal Order.* Chicago: Rand-McNally.

U.S. Census Office. 1901. *Twelfth Census of the United States.* Vol. 1, Part I. Washington, DC: U.S. Government Printing Office.

———. 1902a. *Abstract of the Twelfth Census of the United States.* Washington, DC: U.S. Government Printing Office.

———. 1902b. *Twelfth Census of the United States.* Manufactures, Part II. Washington, DC: U.S. Government Printing Office.

———. 1902c. *Twelfth Census of the United States.* Vital Statistics, Part II. Washington, DC: U.S. Government Printing Office.

U.S. Department of Labor. 1900. *Statistics of Cities.* Vol. 5. Washington, DC: U.S. Government Printing Office.

Watts, Eugene J. 1973. "The Police in Atlanta, 1890–1905." *Journal of Southern History* 39:165–82.

———. 1981. "Police Priorities in Twentieth Century St. Louis." *Journal of Social History* 14:649–74.

Wiebe, Robert H. 1967. *The Search for Order, 1877–1920.* New York: Hill and Wang.

Wilson, James Q. 1968. *Varieties of Police Behavior.* Cambridge: Harvard University Press.

Wilson, James Q. and Edward C. Banfield. 1964. "Public Regardingness as a Value Premise in Voting Behavior." *American Political Science Review* 58:776–87.

Wilson, James Q. and Barbara Boland. 1978. "The Effect of the Police on Crime." *Law and Society Review* 12:367–90.

Wolfinger, Raymond. 1972. "Why Political Machines Have Not Withered Away and Other Revisionist Thoughts." *Journal of Politics* 34:365–98.

Part III
Transnational Crime and Illegal Immigration

[16]

Trafficking and Human Smuggling:
A European Perspective

John Salt*

ABSTRACT

The article reviews the empirical evidence for trafficking and human smuggling in Europe. It argues that a market for irregular migration services has emerged, in which the mechanisms and forms of organization are still relatively unknown. Irregular migrants using these services are exposed both to unscrupulous service providers and to the immigration and policing authorities, thereby generating a dependence on safeguards provided by the trafficking networks. Thus a symbiosis has developed between trafficker and trafficked.

The enormous interest and concern for trafficking and human smuggling in governmental, inter-governmental and non-governmental organizations, in the media and popular opinion, is running ahead of theoretical understanding and factual evidence. This has implications for policy measures designed to combat trafficking and human smuggling, which may not work and also have unintended side effects.

The article begins with a discussion of the main conceptual and definitional issues confronting researchers and politicians. This is followed by an assessment of the main theoretical approaches that have been developed and an evaluation of current statistical knowledge.

Information on the organizational structure of trafficking organizations is then reviewed, followed by a summary of the characteristics of migrants involved, based on empirical studies that have been carried out. The article concludes by indicating some of the main research priorities.

* Department of Geography, University College London, UK.

INTRODUCTION

Trafficking in migrants has become a global problem which affects a complex matrix of origin, transit and destination countries, their international relations and security and their economies. A number of axioms have emerged which provide a generally accepted framework for the evolution of trafficking, although many details have yet to be empirically verified. The usual starting point is that migrants are driven by a range of home conditions to seek the services of traffickers and that push conditions are dominant. In view of some survey findings that many trafficked migrants are reasonably well off in their home countries, such a generalization should be approached with care.

Trafficking is also assumed to occur because the possibilities for regular migration have declined, as more stringent entry controls force migrants into using illegal channels. A different view is that lax entry controls have made it easier for trafficking to thrive, because anti-trafficking legislation is scarce and its enforcement frequently weak. Whether either (or both) of these views holds, the consequence is the emergence of a market for irregular migration services, in which the mechanisms and forms of organization are still relatively unknown. Irregular migrants using these services are exposed, both to unscrupulous service providers and to the immigration and policing authorities, thereby generating a dependence on the safeguards provided by the trafficking networks. Thus a symbiosis develops between trafficker and trafficked.

Such a schema provides only a starting point, since each step in the analysis presented attracts a number of caveats. Although the existing literature provides broad support for the framework outlined, many of the mechanisms in the trafficking process and empirical knowledge of their effects remain in the realm of (variously informed) speculation.

The purpose of this article is to review the operation of some of these mechanisms and the outcomes in Europe. It is largely derived from a review of the empirical evidence on trafficking and human smuggling carried out for the International Organization for Migration (IOM, 2000). What is revealed is that the enormous interest and concern for trafficking and human smuggling in governmental, inter-governmental and non-governmental organizations, in the media and popular opinion, is running ahead of theoretical understanding and factual evidence. This has implications for policy measures designed to combat trafficking and human smuggling, which may not work and also have unintended side effects.

The article begins with a discussion of the main conceptual and definitional issues confronting researchers and politicians. This leads to an assessment of the main theoretical approaches that have been developed, followed by an evaluation of current statistical knowledge. Information on the organizational structure of trafficking organizations is then reviewed, followed by a summary of the characteristics of the migrants involved, based on the empirical studies that have been carried out. The article concludes by indicating some of the main research priorities.

Inevitably, in such a brief survey some themes concerned with trafficking and human smuggling in Europe today are hardly touched upon. These include methodological and ethical issues, the degree to which those involved are deemed to be criminalized, legislative issues at a range of scales and the relationship between trafficking, smuggling and the asylum regime. Little space is given here to what is a major element in the literature, notably trafficking in women (for example, the number of items dealing specifically with trafficking in women account for almost half of the bibliography of IOM, 2000). Some of these themes are picked up in other papers in this volume.

DEFINITIONS OF THE CONCEPTS OF TRAFFICKING, SMUGGLING AND ORGANIZED CRIME: CONSENSUS AND DISAGREEMENT

The debate over precise definitions for the concepts of "trafficking", "smuggling" and "organized crime" has come to a head only in the second half of the 1990s (IOM, 2000). Contributing to the confusion is the fact that different competent institutions (governments) use a range of descriptive terms: alien smuggling; trafficking of aliens; illegal immigrant smuggling; human trafficking; trade of human beings. Individual research studies have thrown up a few additional terms: "human commodity trafficking" (Williams, 1999); "human trade", "trafficking in human beings" and "trafficking in persons" (Meese et al., 1998). The potential differences of approach to dealing with trafficking depend on how terms are used (Budapest Group, 1996).

In recent years, European states have moved nearer to a consensus on the definition of trafficking. There is growing awareness of a dichotomy between the concepts of smuggling and trafficking. At the global level, the on-going Vienna process is insisting on the differences between the two, and identifying two types of migrant as a result. The main basis for the dichotomy is linked to the purpose of trafficking and the concept of exploitation. This difference has been well expressed in a recent paper by Graycar (1999) who suggests that smuggling is clearly concerned with the manner in which a person enters a country, and with the involvement of third parties who assist him/her to achieve entry. Trafficking is a more complicated concept, in that it requires consideration not only of the manner in which a migrant entered the country but also his/her working conditions and whether he/she consented to the irregular entry and/or these working conditions. Trafficking and more voluntary forms of undocumented migration are best thought of as a continuum, with room for considerable variation between the extremes. It is frequently difficult to establish whether there were elements of deception and/or coercion, and whether these were sufficient to elevate the situation from one of voluntary undocumented migration, to trafficking.

There appears to be a growing acceptance that the main purpose of trafficking is to place persons in situations where their labour can be exploited under conditions which often involve human rights abuses. Trafficking, according to many recent definitions, involves severe forms of labour exploitation. By contrast, the main purpose of smuggling may be simply to facilitate the illegal crossing of a border. However, this is not to say that human rights abuses do not sometimes occur during the course of smuggling operations. Smuggling is a risky activity and migrants often undergo very hazardous journeys which sometimes result in tragedies occurring.

Thus, in effect, trafficking is now associated largely with exploitative work at the destination accompanied by human rights violations. There is an assumption that this work is generally at a location and in a type of employment chosen by the traffickers, although there is evidence too that migrants are often at least partially aware of the circumstances in which they are placing themselves. However, trafficking may sometimes involve an element of what has come to be defined as smuggling, particularly when it uses the same routes, forged documentation and organizational networks as the smugglers. Further, those who are being smuggled frequently have little idea of the degree and nature of exploitation that awaits them. In consequence, it may in certain circumstances be more appropriate to use the term "trafficking" generically to include "smuggling", leaving "abusive exploitation" to describe those employment conditions that contravene human rights and are usually illegal.

The failure to agree on precise definitions is not surprising in what may still be described as a novel migration issue, still under-researched, and where no comprehensive typological studies have been carried out. Thus, for example, the particular human rights issues and special needs of trafficked women have led some researchers to call for a separate definition of this aspect of illegal migration. A clear analysis and agreed statement of the different types of trafficking and trafficked migrants has become essential. The current uncertainties about concepts and definitions will hinder reaching a consensus on legislative and judicial frameworks to combat trafficking at national and international levels.

THEORETICAL DEVELOPMENTS

These conceptual and definitional uncertainties present analytical difficulties to researchers accustomed to existing migration theories. Traditionally, international migration has been conceived of as a relationship between, on the one hand, an individual or household moving for purposes of permanent settlement or work and, on the other, a government acting as gatekeeper for entry into a country and acquisition of its citizenship. Most explanatory theoretical frameworks are based on this notion. Trafficking and smuggling challenge traditional migration theories in a number of ways. They blur the boundaries between forced and voluntary movements and between legality and illegality; they question the degree of choice able to be exercised by the migrant (notably whether and where to move and work) and by the state (how to manage entry and conditions of employment) and they affect (and may determine) the geographical pattern of flows. They require a theoretical approach which encompasses the system of institutionalized networks, consisting of organizations, agents and individuals, which are part and parcel of modern trafficking and human smuggling. Each of these stands to gain some form of remuneration from irregular movement and consequently has a vested interest in promoting migration.

There are two overlapping theoretical approaches towards trafficking currently in vogue. One approaches the subject from an economic perspective, emphasizing trafficking as a business; the other regards it as essentially a criminal activity and takes a legalistic view. Other perceptions do exist, for example, viewing trafficking as a response to humanitarian requirements (Morrison, 2000), but coherent theoretical constructions are absent.

The main theoretical developments have emphasized trafficking/smuggling as an economic activity. Such an approach places trafficking and smuggling within the broader concept of migration as a business in which institutions (which may include all or part of trafficking organizations) seek to make profit. Salt and Stein (1997) have produced a hypothetical model of trafficking as a business which presents it as an intermediary system in the global migration business facilitating movement between origin and destination countries. Trafficking networks are presented as business organizations. The IOM studies on Poland, Hungary and Ukraine (Okólski, 1999; Juhász, 1999; Klinchenko et al., 1999) successfully applied the model.[1]

An extension of the business approach is proposed by Kyle and Liang (1998) who suggest that trafficking should be viewed as a consequence of the commodification of migration, from which organizations are able to make profits from peoples' mobility. They propose that such commodification, upon which there is a distinct lack of theoretical and empirical research, is a feature of global transnational migration in which there are roles for diverse institutions, of which traffickers comprise one set.

The relationship between the economic and the criminal is frequently referred to in the literature on trafficking and human smuggling, attention being paid especially to the nature of the work in which trafficked migrants often find themselves. Flexibilization of employment in the service sector across Europe has provided many opportunities for illegal working. This, combined with the marginalization of certain groups in society as a result of rising unemployment in parts of the Central and Eastern European (CEE) region, has led to the suggestion that a "re-feudalization" of the service sector is occurring, in which traffickers can play an active role (Omelaniuk, 1998).

A similar idea has been explored by Ruggiero (1997) who compares modern trafficking with the historical concept of slavery. He analyses trafficking in humans today against a background characterized by the growth of hidden sectors within European economies – sectors which include a variety of legal, semi-legal and illegal activities. Thus he places trafficking in migrants in the realms of both business and criminal activities. His conclusion is that there is a link between conventional organized crime and a range of activities which have an entrepreneurial character being carried out in the market economy. When trafficking is geared to the provision of jobs, the beneficiaries are found to be those within the hidden economies which commission the smuggling operations and employ the smugglers. The businesses involved range from the quasi-legal to the overtly criminal and may overlap. The trafficking process may also be seen as one which satisfies a set of labour demands, some of which may be for illegal employment through a supply controlled by organized crime (Savona, 1996).

The emergence of international criminal organizations has been linked to changes in global politics and economies, leading to interdependence between nations, ease of travel and communications and economic globalization (Williams, 1994, quoted in Heikkinen and Lohrmann, 1998). Transnational criminal organizations are defined as "mobile, well organized, internationally adaptable and can be involved in multiple activities in several countries" (Heikkinen and Lohrmann, 1998: 3). However, the degree to which trafficking as a whole is part of or synonymous with large-scale organized crime is debated (Finckenauer, 1998; Ruggiero, 1997). A crime like trafficking can be organized and complex, operating over long periods of time and requiring sophisticated arrangements. However, once the criminal activity is carried out the organizational structure that supports it may be dissolved. In contrast, international criminal organizations continue to exist after the criminal activity and may be involved in multiple criminal activities at the same time (Finckenauer, 1998).

Neither of these theoretical approaches is fully inclusive, particularly from the standpoint of their treatment of human rights issues. Juhász (1999) draws attention to the importance of non-economic push factors, in that different migrants (like asylum seekers and economic migrants) should not be regarded as interchangeable homogeneous commodities. Others argue that placing trafficking firmly within the bounds of criminality, and thus illegality, makes it difficult to apprehend those elements of migration that are associated with trafficking but which have a quasi-legal status and those cases where the status of the migrant drifts in and out of legality during the process as a whole (IOM, 2000). What we can say is that theoretical developments in the field of trafficking and human smuggling still require much attention.

STATISTICAL DATA

To the theoretical gaps must be added those in basic information. It is almost axiomatic for papers reviewing trafficking/smuggling to lament the statistical void and to call for research to fill the many *lacunae*. Often the statistics produced by countries experiencing trafficking are held by numerous services and organizations there, collected in different ways at different times, use diverse terminologies and so are not comparable within the country let alone from one country to another. The absence of statistics transcends the whole field of trafficking/smuggling.

The conceptual and definitional problems referred to earlier in this paper are linked to the availability – or rather lack – of statistical data on trafficking and human smuggling. How can we define what we are not sure how to measure and vice versa? Not only is it unclear what data might be collected but under whose auspices. One review of the statistics on trafficking collected by governments produced a list of reasons for their current inadequacy (IOM, 1998).

First, unlike other migrations, trafficking is a covert activity and most data are for operational purposes within the criminal system. However, trafficking crimes are not specifically defined in many countries and so they have no readily available database. Some countries reported no trafficking legislation, while in others institutions responding to the questionnaire gave divergent opinions. Thus it would appear that trafficking is a new problem and national legislative (and therefore data) systems have not caught up. Second, the lack of trafficking legislation means that cases may be dealt with under associated legislation and so trafficking cases are not defined as such. Third, methods of data collection in individual countries are ad hoc rather than systematic. Individual authorities collect statistics using their own definitions and for their own purposes. Fourth, in most countries no single agency acts as a focal point for collection, collation or harmonization of statistics on trafficking. Finally, sharing of information between states is on an ad hoc basis, particularly with respect to countries of origin of trafficked migrants.

General problems associated with statistical data on trafficking

Despite a steady improvement in the availability of statistics on international migration in Europe during the last decade, there are still enormous gaps.

Numerous researchers and organizations have pointed particularly to the situation in Central and Eastern Europe and the former Soviet Union where inadequate methods of data collection and the absence of appropriate legislation mean that official statistics on legal migrations are only slowly becoming available (see, for example, OECD, Annual; Salt, 1999; UNESCO, 1998). Statistics on illegal migration which have any degree of reliability are especially hard to come by even in those countries with good statistical sources and systems (Delaunay and Tapinos, 1998). They are normally based on border apprehension data or court records and it is unclear how far revealed trends are a reflection of changing detection systems and methods of recording rather than of real flows of illegal migrants. Attempts to calculate true levels of illegal migration normally use some estimate, usually based on the views of officials, of the proportion of illegal migrants who are apprehended. Linking these to trafficking is even more difficult and attempts to do so usually require heroic leaps of faith.

At the heart of the data issue is a matter of concept. Intuitively we might seek data on numbers of traffickers but that presupposes that it is possible to establish the organizational and spatial parameters within which they work. Do we wish to know the number of trafficking businesses or their numbers of employees? Operating within individual countries or across several? Whether migrants are trafficked, individually or in groups? What their characteristics and motivations are? A major difficulty is to distinguish between illegal migration and trafficking. Often the two terms are used interchangeably instead of one being regarded as a subset of the other.

Discussions about data availability – or rather the lack of it – mostly focus on the scale of trafficking/smuggling as measured by the number of migrants involved. Statistical data on the characteristics of those trafficked are in even shorter supply and almost without exception are derived from surveys. The most detailed information comes from the succession of IOM surveys during the 1990s (see, IOM, 2000), most notably those in Poland, Hungary and Ukraine (Okólski, 1999; Juhász, 1999; Klinchenko et al., 1999). The lack of hard data, combined with the fact that many commentators on trafficking repeat estimates derived from interviews with officials, means that many of the statistics quoted are in (often large) round numbers, are uncheckable and are frequently rehearsed.

While most countries in Western Europe can provide some statistics on illegal border crossings, we as yet have little information in any detail on trafficking and smuggling in individual countries in the region. No in-depth, survey-based studies, similar to those in Hungary, Poland and Ukraine have been carried out in any Western European country. There is some irony in the fact that for trafficking and human smuggling our main empirical knowledge comes from that part of the continent – the CEE countries – where statistics on legal migration are still relatively weak.

Estimates of the scale of trafficking

Most statistical data on numbers trafficked are at best crude estimates. Sometimes assumptions are made based on estimates of illegal migration which are themselves usually highly flawed. The only official data come from apprehensions, court records and deportations, but these are partial and in any case refer to migrants who have been picked up and not necessarily to those trafficked or to the traffickers themselves.

Most data used in the trafficking and human smuggling literature refer to illegal migrants, with built-in assumptions that the estimated numbers are a surrogate for trafficked or smuggled migrants. In consequence, there are very few studies which actively link illegal migrants and trafficking. A notable exception is that of Lederer (1997).

The most widely accepted and quoted figure for the scale of trafficking in Europe was produced in 1994 by Jonas Widgren. He estimated that in 1993 there were 250-350,000 illegal migrant entries into Western Europe. The figure was calculated on the basis of extrapolations of how many illegal migrants reached their goal as a reflection of the known numbers of migrants apprehended when seeking to transit through the green borders of intermediate countries on their way to their final goal. Analysis of border control data showed 60,000 apprehensions. Widgren then estimated, based on discussions with border control authorities, that at least 4-6 times that number got through undetected. In addition to illegal migrants there were, at the time, 690,000 asylum seekers in Western Europe of whom he suggested about half were not in need of protection. He further suggested that 15-30 per cent of illegals "could be estimated" to have used the services of traffickers during some part of their journey, although again there is a speculative element in the proportion. Between 20 and 40 per cent of asylum claims were estimated to be unfounded, about 300,000. Thus, 40-100,000 illegal migrants and 60-120,000 asylum seekers were estimated to have used traffickers in 1993, a total ranging from 100,000 to 220,000.

Sometimes estimates are presented from confidential, usually operational, sources. For example, a US government report in 1995, based on a nine-month study by officials of the State and Justice Departments, Immigration and Naturalization Service, CIA, FBI and Coast Guard, came up with a figure of 500,000 illegal aliens entering Western Europe each year, with a similar number waiting in Central and Eastern Europe and the former Soviet Union (Branigin, 1995). Moscow was estimated to have 200,000 illegal aliens temporarily resident

40   *Salt*

at any one time. However, it is not clear how many of these people went through the hands of traffickers.

A more recent attempt to estimate numbers trafficked between the CEE countries and Western Europe was also based on border apprehensions and the assumption that at most one in three migrants who attempt to cross CEE borders illegally is ever caught (IOM/TCC and ICMPD, 1999: 42). It proposed a figure of 100-300,000 migrants entering Western Europe illegally from CEE countries, of whom perhaps 25-75,000 were estimated to have been smuggled by traffickers.

The principal assumption in such estimates is that of the proportion of total illegal, trafficked or smuggled migrants who are apprehended. Appropriate figures are normally derived from interviews with officials and border guards. What is not known is how accurate these are. Interviews with border guards and officials in Hungary by Juhász (1999) revealed that estimates of the proportion of cases discovered were many and varied even within the organization most qualified to make them, the border guard service itself. At senior levels there was a high degree of optimism and a belief that the majority of those illegally crossing the border were caught. However, from the central bodies down to the operative units this optimism decreased dramatically, while those actually patrolling the border judged their own effectiveness to be only ten per cent. Differences of opinion regarding the proportions caught were also evident from interviewees in the Ukraine study (Klinchenko et al., 1999). The officials and border controllers said that less than one per cent of those trying to cross the country's western border illegally succeeded, but migrants themselves put the proportion between a third and a half. Similar problems beset attempts to calculate the scale of illegal migration. In Ukraine, the Ministry of Internal Affairs estimated there were 20-30,000 illegal foreigners, whereas some of the experts interviewed suggested that half- to one million was more realistic, a calculation based on border guard statistics of numbers entering and leaving. For Poland, too, estimates need to be treated with caution. Individual border guards gave wildly different figures, ranging from 20 to 90 per cent, of the proportions of apprehended migrants who were trafficked (Okólski, 1999).

A further problem is what is actually to be measured. Juhász's study (1999) used an "illegal crossing event" as the unit of measurement in creating a database of illegal migration to and from Hungary. Such an event occurs each time an individual is arrested. Creating a statistical record to fit the variety of potential situations soon makes the complexity apparent. Multiple events can occur for a single person who is arrested, sent back, tries again and is recaught. Someone simply turned back at the border or arriving in a refugee camp is not recorded in the database, whereas someone caught by the border guard of a neighbouring country and sent back to Hungary is recorded. Additional complications arise because crossings may be in or out and both should be included.

Estimating how many illegal crossings are trafficked or smuggled presents additional difficulties. Almost certainly, incidences of trafficking are severely underestimated in illegal border crossing data since the involvement of a smuggler is registered only if the immigrant admits to this being the case upon being caught or if the smuggler is caught. One illustration provided by Juhász (1999) of the under-estimation of smuggling was that only one-third of the apprehended migrants from Asian countries was recorded as having received any kind of assistance, despite the unlikelihood that they would have had sufficient local knowledge to cross the borders of the many countries on their route on their own.

The number of illegal migrants and smugglers recorded depends not only on how many attempt a crossing but also on the effectiveness of the border guards, which can affect comparisons of data pertaining both to periods of time and sections of the border. Official estimates may sometimes be used to justify more resources. For example, in 1997 the 30,000 plus illegal migrants caught in the vicinity of the Czech-Slovak border were estimated by the Interior Ministry of the Czech Republic to be only 10 per cent of those crossing illegally. To conform to EU requirements, the Interior Ministry reckoned that another 1,000 border police were needed at a cost of US$ 26 million (Jakl, 1998).

THE ORGANIZATION OF TRAFFICKING

Types of trafficking organizations

As trafficking has risen up the political agenda and knowledge of its operations has spread, so the initial, rather simplistic, views have metamorphosed into an appreciation of something more complex. Two common assumptions are that trafficking and smuggling are growing and becoming more organized (Europol, 1999). Growth is assumed because the "raw materials", in the form of potential illegal migrants, are regarded as almost unlimited, the business is already big with a high turnover and is also one of low risk, since the threat from law enforcement agencies is low, especially as most trafficking organizations seem to be based outside Western Europe. There is also an assumption that trafficking is growing because it is becoming more organized, though the evidence for this trend is not clear.

The degree of organization might reasonably be reflected in the size of the groups smuggled. In recent years, "event-related" information has provided a wealth of facts about individual situations, normally based on official reports relating to cross-border apprehensions. There is a lack of systematic analysis of such information, increasingly available through official sources but as yet not brought together. Where such information has been examined it does not always tell the same story. Austrian data, for example, suggest that a trafficking organization typically consists of a group of 20-30 individuals and that at present around 25 such groups are running illegal immigration operations in Austria (Europol, 1999). However, the Hungary study by Juhász (1999) indicates that the majority interviewed (60 per cent) crossed into Hungary alone or with no more than two other persons. Not all of these were trafficked/ smuggled. Forty per cent of those entering Hungary and 30 per cent who were continuing West and who were assisted by traffickers were in groups of 20 or more. Juhász relates these differences to whether migrants were assisted by "smugglers" or "helpers". The former were paid, the latter provided their assistance seemingly upon humanitarian grounds, with no financial benefit proved. Those who were "helped" typically moved in smaller groups. However, there is no clear distinction, since group sizes were found to be flexible, changing according to route and time.

Organizational structures

Only recently has systematic empirical information on the structure of trafficking organizations become available. The organizational model produced by Salt and Stein (1997) divided the trafficking process into three consecutive stages: first, the process of mobilization by which migrants are recruited in origin countries; second, the requirements en route as migrants are transported from origin to destination countries; and third, the processes by which migrants are inserted and integrated into destination countries. Each of these is characterized by a set of trafficker roles and there are varying degrees of centralization. The model was based on reported events rather than the study of specific trafficking organizations.

Recent evidence is providing a sounder empirical basis for determining how trafficking and smuggling operations are organized. Quoting Hungarian intelligence, Juhász (1999: 36) describes the majority of smuggling organizations operating in Hungary as "well-organized, linked together across many countries, professionally structured and highly disciplined". They typically have a cellular and hierarchical structure where executive units are left in the dark about a higher level control that is well organized and difficult to penetrate. They began when a set of initially isolated individuals involved in trafficking began to cooperate and eventually developed into international businesses no longer coordinated from Hungary.

The structure is flexible. The trafficking organization as a whole is more likely to consist of several loosely interconnected and competitive networks where the market is continuously being re-shared than to be a single core. As any one network grows it may incorporate others and recruit more international staff with different ethnic origins, allowing it to specialize. Thus, according to the Hungarian border guards, foreign and not Hungarian networks run the trafficking market in Hungary.

The evidence from Poland confirms many of the findings from Hungary, but at the same time significant differences emerge in how trafficking is organized (see the paper by Okólski in this volume for details of organizational structures in Poland). Interviewees in Poland confirmed that the trafficking business there is conducted with a high degree of informality, adaptability and flexibility. The organizational structure is again hierarchical. At the top is a "brain", a leadership that is thought to look after the entire route and its security. At the next level are found internationally linked "Mafia" bosses in each country through which a route runs. Only those in the top two strata have direct international connections. Next down are bilingual teams organizing trafficking in specific border areas, a similar situation to that found in Hungary, then local collaborators with specific tasks. The bottom level is occupied by, often freelance, individuals who occasionally perform specific tasks like letting a car or driving. However, for many organizations, trafficking is a supplementary or marginal area of business. Many of those supervising trafficking routes (at the second level) are foreign-born persons with Polish citizenship or a permanent residence permit in Poland. Many belong to an ethnic group, live in large cities and have extensive underworld connections.

Quite how trafficking organizations are reacting to changes in their business environment is an important issue. There is an underlying assumption that recent integration and transition processes in Europe present new market opportunities (ICMPD, 1999) though the empirical evidence is either lacking or scattered. The business development literature suggests that what can reasonably be expected is that groups will merge or takeover, with small, non-powerful organizations being absorbed or pushed aside by bigger ones. The latter will then divide up the market, perhaps on the basis of cultural, historical or ethnic considerations. Already there is some evidence of this, with references to "turf wars" between rival organizations. For example, rivalry between ethnic Albanian and Roma traffickers has resulted in them shooting each other in Varnsdorf in the Czech Republic, a town on the German border which is a focal point for illegal migration and a major transit centre (Jakl, 1998).

Organized crime and organized criminal activity

A common view is that trafficking and organized crime are closely related, although good information is scarce. Europol (1999) believes that there is evidence to substantiate a link based on the following indications: different nationalities are smuggled on the same transport; travel over great distances needs organization on a considerable scale; travel in groups needs organization; large amounts of money change hands; routes are changed quickly and easily when necessary which implies a high level of organization; immediate legal assistance is available when things go wrong; there is swift reaction to counter measures taken by the authorities. However, the report goes on to note that despite these indications there is no clear proof that illegal immigration is organized by internationally acting criminal groups. In a subsequent report, Europol (1999) states that there are links between migrant trafficking and other forms of crime even though there are no reliable data to support this. It distinguishes between criminal groups and organized crime. The latter is structured with a strict internal division of tasks, but there is a "grey zone" when attempting clear-cut definitions.

Adding to the debate, ICMPD (1999) questions whether organized crime is actually expanding its activities into human trafficking, pointing out that criminal groups rely on expertise, skills and means acquired in the old activities. When expanding to new criminal areas (like trafficking), the new activity is often incorporated into the old pattern. It goes on to argue that the linkages between organized crime and trafficking may be described as horizontal or vertical: horizontal because of the chains of individuals involved in different forms of activity, and vertical because of the sequence of crimes.

The "multi-crime" nature of these organizations has attracted considerable attention. Ruggiero (1997) suggests that there is a link between organized crime and a wide range of activities of an entrepreneurial character which are being carried out in market economies. The same point is made by Savona (1997) who argues that in organized crime "businesses" range from quasi-legal to overtly criminal in nature and may also overlap, and that criminal organizations seek business opportunities in those contexts where law enforcement is weaker or less effective. For example, money laundering may be effected where banking officials are open to corruption and offshore systems may be used where anonymity is the rule. At their Moscow conference in 1997, the Global Survival Network and the International League for Human Rights identified "multi-product" criminal organizations which deal in a range of goods and activities, namely, drugs, stolen vehicles, transport of illegal aliens, organized prostitution and gambling, together with legitimate enterprises (GSN/ILHR, 1997).

Who are the traffickers?

Information on the characteristics of traffickers and smugglers is sketchy and derived from scattered and often case/country specific sources. A key issue is the degree to which trafficking is in the hands of nationals of destination or origin countries. Europol (1999) notes that members of the criminal organizations engaged in sexual exploitation are often of the same nationality as the women they control. Statistics from Poland and Germany show that 60-70 per cent of organized crime as a whole is in the hands of foreigners, although no indication is available from this source specifically for trafficking. However, it is suggested that people smuggling operations are overwhelmingly in the hands of foreigners, with citizens of Balkan countries, the former Soviet Union and

China being highly represented in the smuggler population (North Atlantic Assembly, 1996).

Statistics compiled in the Netherlands by the Stichting gegen Vrouwenhandel (STV) over a two-year period 1994-1996 showed that in 1996 23.1 per cent of those apprehended for trafficking came from East European countries. About one-third were of Polish origin and almost half came from the former Soviet Union. These percentages correspond to the percentages of trafficked migrants from these regions, which confirms the suspicion that trafficking organizations require the cooperation of nationals in the victims' countries of origin. Overall, about 30-40 per cent of traffickers apprehended in the Netherlands originated from there. In Germany, the equivalent proportion was 40 per cent (Meese et al., 1998). In Poland, Siron and Van Baeveghem (1999) also found that traffickers are mostly Polish by birth: in 1995, 72 per cent of traffickers apprehended were of Polish origin; by 1997 this had risen to 79 per cent. Some of the operators in Poland, however, were conducting their activities from Ukraine, Belarus and Russia, with each stage of the route managed by the nationals concerned. In Hungary, Juhász (1999) noted that the nationality of traffickers had evolved. Before 1995 only 12 per cent were Hungarian, but in 1997-98 the figure had increased to over two-thirds. In contrast, proportions of Romanians and Slovakians had declined. However, echoing the Polish experience, Hungarian border guards reckoned that the trafficking market in Hungary was ruled by foreign-based organizations. As a general rule, it seems that as the networks grow they become composed increasingly of ethnically diverse personnel.

Some information is emerging on the age and sex of traffickers. Bruinsma and Meershoek (1999) record that of those traffickers arrested in the Netherlands, 90 per cent were male of average age 34 and with a history of criminal activity in their home countries. In Poland, traffickers were mostly male aged between 15 and 55 and trafficking for the sex trade was mostly undertaken by younger men in the 20-25 age group (Siron and Van Baeveghem, 1999).

CHARACTERISTICS OF TRAFFICKED AND SMUGGLED MIGRANTS

Lack of empirical studies means that there is a paucity of information in the literature concerning the characteristics of trafficked migrants. For the most part, the studies that have been carried out have been with small and unrepresentative samples (IOM, 2000). They provide snapshots rather than a comprehensive picture and thus far no study has tried systematically to bring the various findings together. The emphasis tends to be on age and gender and there is very little on their socio-economic status and other aspects of their lives in their home countries. Much of the information relates to women in the sex industry and is often derived from the casebooks of concerned NGOs.

Nationality

Information on nationality is limited, though a common thread during the 1990s seems to have been a widening of the field away from Central and Eastern Europe to encompass origins in Asia, Africa and the Middle East (IOM, 2000). All studies indicate a wide range of origin nationalities. In the Ukrainian survey of Klinchenko et al. (1999), the 108 trafficked migrants interviewed were from twenty-three different nationalities. The nationalities apprehended frequently reflect geographical location. The most significant nationalities among migrants trafficked to the Baltic States have been Kurds, Afghans, Somalis, Chinese, Iranians, Iraqis, Ethiopians and Sri Lankans (Ulrich, 1995). The nationalities of migrants trafficked into Europe generally had further expanded to include parts of Eastern Europe (former Yugoslavia, Romania, Bulgaria) and most of the former Soviet Union (Salt and Stein, 1997). Other examples are Tamils being trafficked into Russia to camp around Moscow (Morrison, 1998) and Kurds leaving Turkey for Sarajevo (Kuci, 1998). In most of these studies the numbers of the individual nationalities involved and their significance in migrant flows overall are not represented. Generally, information from NGOs, other support agencies and detention centres in Belgium, the Netherlands and Germany shows a steady increase in trafficked migrants from the CEE countries since 1993 (Meese et al., 1998).

Europol (1999) has drawn up some very general observations on the nationalities of women being trafficked into some of the states of the European Union. In France, the numbers of foreign prostitutes (presumed trafficked) are rising and nationalities include those of the Maghreb, Sub-Saharan Africa, Eastern and Western Europe (mainly the Iberian peninsula), Latin America and East Asia. Germany reported that the trend in trafficked women has swung from South America, Africa and the Far East in the 1970s to CEE countries since the end of the 1980s. Women trafficked into Italy came mainly from the CEE region and Africa. The Netherlands reported an increase in women from Hungary, the former Yugoslavia and the Baltic States. In Spain, prostitutes were brought in from the Dominican Republic and Africa. In Sweden the women came in from the Baltic States and the CEE countries. The Metropolitan Police in the UK reported rising numbers of women from Central and Eastern Europe and large-scale trafficking from Latin America, particularly Brazil.

Within the sex trade in Western Europe, the literature suggests there has been a shift in migrant origins away from the developing countries in Africa and Asia towards new sources in Central and Eastern Europe, although no detailed breakdowns are available (Shannon, 1999; IOM/TCC and ICMPD, 1999; Beare, 1999; Siron and Van Baeveghem, 1999). There is a trend for young women and girls to be trafficked from countries where socio-economic conditions are difficult and from post-conflict areas. Recently, Kosovars and females from other parts of the former Yugoslavia and Albania have been especially at risk (OSCE, 1999).

Demographic characteristics

Information on the demographic characteristics of trafficked and smuggled migrants comes from a diverse series of observations and studies. Migrants interviewed in the three IOM studies in Eastern Europe were predominantly male, around 90 per cent (see the paper in this volume by Okólski). Between half and two-thirds are in their twenties and a few are over 40 (Okólski, 1999; Juhász, 1999; Klinchenko et al., 1999). Proportions married varied, depending upon origin. A different gender balance has been shown for Western Europe. More women than men are being trafficked into Belgium, the Netherlands and Germany from Poland and Hungary. The women are generally in their early twenties (Meese et al., 1998).

Economic skills and education

Details of the levels of education and what skills trafficked migrants possess are beginning to emerge from surveys. Illegal transit migrants through Lithuania were generally well educated. Only a small minority were illiterate with over 60 per cent having received secondary education and 25 per cent college or university education. Over 50 per cent possessed language skills, with just over 16 per cent being able to speak two or more foreign languages (IOM, 1997). Many migrants entering Ukraine had enjoyed high social status at home. Of the sample interviewed by Klinchenko et al., (1999), one-third had run their own businesses, 11 per cent had had stable jobs, 9 per cent had been temporarily employed and only 11 per cent had been unemployed. Migrants trafficked into Poland tended to polarize into two categories of attainment: 23 per cent had achieved post-secondary education and 29 per cent had received vocational training (Okólski, 1999). According to Siron and Van Baeveghem (1999), women trafficked into Poland from Ukraine, Belarus and Russia are more likely than others to be highly educated, often with university degrees.

Motivation

A range of motives for migrants to place themselves in the hands of traffickers and smugglers has emerged from the literature. Partial as these findings are, they indicate the complexity of these forms of illegal migration and the futility of addressing them with a narrow range of policy solutions. Motivations vary according to demographic characteristics, nationality and country of origin, geographic location and personal circumstances.

Studies carried out for the Ludwig Boltzmann Institute of Human Rights in Vienna have explored female trafficking and forced prostitution in the Czech Republic, Slovakia and the Ukraine. They conclude that the post-communism economic vacuum before stable market economies could be established has hit female socio-economic conditions hardest so that women and girls of working age have every incentive to seek to improve their lot by migrating further west (Hybnerová and Scheu, 1999; Knaus and Reiter, 1999). Women trafficked into Austria (IOM, 1996) were motivated without exception by economic reasons. Austria was reported by friends and acquaintances as a very prosperous country where good money could be earned quickly. The same motivation was found among Czech women who had naive ideas of easy earnings abroad (Hybnerová and Scheu, 1999). Similarly, in Ukraine adverse economic conditions and the exclusion of women from the formal and regulated labour market combined to form a strong push factor (Klinchenko et al., 1999).

Of those migrants trafficked or smuggled into Ukraine, a third named armed conflict as the major reason for migrating; 27 per cent cited political reasons; 21.3 per cent gave economic reasons. An additional incentive was found to be relatives abroad (40 per cent). Younger women often embarked on the journey to the West with the permission of their husbands and parents (Klinchenko et al., 1999). Amongst the sample interviewed in Hungary by Juhász (1999), the primary reason for emigrating was war, notably from Kosovo, Afghanistan, Sierra Leone and Liberia. Most migrants left their homeland for good because their lives were directly threatened or because living conditions (economic and cultural) had become intolerable. Long-term ideas of employment or asylum were unclear since their immediate (short-term) goal was survival. Among the Algerians, there was fear and a feeling of insecurity on the streets of the towns they came from. Embassy officials regarded them as economic migrants and this was in part true. Migrants from Eastern Europe, Romania particularly, were often motivated by a thirst for adventure and the pursuit of irrational aims. These states had been cut off from the West for so long that a distorted picture, fed by banned western radio, had fed the dream of the "legendary Western welcome". Many others were urged on by the impossibility of maintaining a decent standard of living in some states of the former Soviet Union. Apart from women travelling with their husbands and children, most females were trafficked for the sex trade.

WHERE DO WE GO FROM HERE?

There is much that we still do not know about trafficking and human smuggling as they affect Europe. This is, perhaps, not surprising in view of the covert nature of the phenomena. However, given their high profile on the political agendas of both the European Union and individual states, the lack of basic knowledge is sobering at the least. The research agenda set out here should be seen as only the beginning. It is presented for debate and not for prescription.

Business and market development

Most commentators agree that trafficking and human smuggling are best analysed in business terms. There are some fundamental aspects of the business organization of trafficking that require investigation. First, further research is needed into how the trafficking industry is evolving. It is reasonable to assume that it will share many features with legitimate businesses although it is unclear how far this analogy should be taken. It is probable, for example, that there are differences between legitimate and illegitimate management structures, particularly given the need for tight security within trafficking organizations. At present, trafficking consists of both large and small businesses but there is as yet no information on how these interact and how far rationalization is likely through franchises, take-overs and cooperation. As new niche businesses develop we need to know whether they are independent or part of larger operations. It is also possible that new and distinctive trafficker roles may develop.

The nature of the markets being developed and served by traffickers and illegal migrants need to be investigated to determine whether new ones are emerging within Europe and how their potential is being tapped. For example, niche markets, such as prostitution, trafficking into manufacturing sweatshops and ethnic economic enclaves need to be identified and analysed in business terms.

The relationship with organized crime

The concept of organized crime needs to be more sharply defined and a closer look taken at how far it is involved in trafficking. Okólski's paper in this volume, for example, indicates strongly that the relationship is anything but straightforward. Trafficking may be only one of a series of nefarious business interests within the portfolios of organized groups and there may be competition between these interests. We have little idea how far trafficking in people is the dominant business for such organizations. Furthermore, information communication and technology (ICT) is clearly being used by these organizations but it is not yet known how and to what extent the World Wide Web is being used for recruitment, communication and management.

Implications for migration policy

Trafficking and illegal migration may generally interact significantly with broader migration policy and research needs to be undertaken to determine whether this interaction itself initiates change in national immigration policies and, if so, in what direction. As part of this process we need to ascertain more clearly how far the priority to ensure national security (the state controlling its borders and citizenship) conflicts with the promotion of the security of the individual (ensuring basic human rights) and with the achievement of successful integration of all migrants and their host societies.

At the inter-state level, it is by no means clear how migration relations between European states are affected by trafficking and human smuggling, whether they are actually harmed or if constructive dialogue occurs and whether there is a spillover into other areas of relations. International agreements are urging the need for exchange of information, but it is as yet unknown how freely states engage in this and how inter-state cooperation compares in efficiency with cooperation within and between trafficking organizations. It could be that states are at a disadvantage because they operate mainly as discrete units with collaborative (and slow) response structures.

Migrant outcomes

Most of the research on trafficking focuses on how migrants get to their destinations. With the exception of those working illegally in the sex trade, there is a dearth of information on the outcomes for most of the migrants involved. Little is currently known about how most trafficked migrants earn a livelihood, how the migration cycle ends for the trafficked/smuggled migrant, both in and out of debt bondage and what the relationship is between the apprehended individual and the criminal system at the destination.

In order to obtain answers to these questions, the old academic chestnut "we need more research" applies *a fortiori*. In particular, comprehensive surveys are urgently needed for Western European countries similar to those carried out further east and using the same methodology. In that way, the experiences of individual countries, geographically located in different parts of Europe's trafficking/smuggling system, can be used as lenses to allow us to see more clearly what is going on.

NOTE

1. These three studies are due to be published by IOM in the summer of 2000 in a book entitled *Migrant Trafficking and Human Smuggling in Europe*.

Trafficking and human smuggling: a European perspective 51

REFERENCES

Beare, M.E.
 1999 "Illegal migration: personal tragedies, social problems, or national security threats?", in P. Williams (Ed.), *Illegal Immigration and Commercial Sex: The New Slave Trade*, Frank Cass, London: 11-41.

Branigin, W.
 1995 "U.S. targets world traffic in migrants", *International Herald Tribune*, Friday, 29 December: 3.

Bruinsma, G.J.N., and G. Meershoek
 1999 "Organised crime and trafficking in women from Eastern Europe in the Netherlands", in P. Williams (Ed.), *Illegal Immigration and Commercial Sex: The New Slave Trade*, Frank Cass, London: 105-118.

Budapest Group
 1996 *Anti-Trafficking Model Legislation*, report of the Budapest Group prepared by Belgium and Poland with the support of IGC for the meeting of the Expert Group of the Budapest Group, Ljubljana, 13-14 June: 14.

Delauney, D., and G. Tapinos
 1998 *La mesure de la migration clandestine en Europe, vol. I and II*, Eurostat, Luxembourg, working papers 3/1998/E/No.7.

Europol
 1999 *General Situation Report 1996-97: Illegal Immigration*, The Hague, file no. 2562-52: 30.

Finckenauer, J.O.
 1998 "Migration and organised crime", in *Migration and Organised Crime: Proceedings of the International Conference on "Migration and Crime: Global and Regional Problems and Responses"*, Courmayeur Mont Blanc, Italy, 5-6 October, ISPAC: 155-169.

Graycar, A.
 1999 "Trafficking in human beings", paper presented at the International Conference on Migration, Culture and Crime, Israel, 7 July.

GSN/ILHR (Global Survival Network/International League for Human Rights)
 1997 *The Trafficking of NIS Women Abroad: An International Conference, November 3-5*, Conference Report, Moscow: 61.

Heikkinen, H., and R. Lohrmann
 1998 *The Involvement of Organized Crime in the Trafficking in Migrants*, IOM unpublished paper, 10.

Hybnerová, S., and H. Scheu
 1999 *Legal Study on the Combat of Trafficking in Women and Forced Prostitution in the Czech Republic*, Ludwig Boltzmann Institute, Vienna: 22.

ICMPD (International Centre for Migration Policy Development)
 1999 *The Relationship Between Organised Crime and Trafficking Aliens*, study prepared by the Secretariat of the Budapest Group, Vienna: 33, BG 1/99.

IOM (International Organization for Migration)
 1996 *Trafficking in Women to Austria for Sexual Exploitation*, IOM Migration Information Programme, Budapest: 37.
 1997 *The Baltic Route: The Trafficking of Migrants through Lithuania*, IOM Migration Information Programme, Budapest: 46.

IOM (International Organization for Migration)
1998   *Analysis of Data and Statistical Resources Available in the EU Member States on Trafficking in Humans, Particularly in Women and Children for Purposes of Sexual Exploitation,* A Project of the International Organization for Migration (IOM) for the European Commission's STOP Programme, Final Report, IOM, Geneva: 44.
2000   *Migrant Trafficking and Human Smuggling in Europe,* Geneva.
IOM/TCC/ICMPD (International Organization for Migration/Technical Cooperation Centre for Europe and Central Asia/International Centre for Migration Policy and Development)
1999   *Migration in Central and Eastern Europe: 1999 Review,* IOM, Geneva: 150.
Jakl, R.
1998   "Shootout in Varnsdorf", *Transitions,* December: 35-39.
Juhász, J.
1999   *Human Smuggling and the Trafficking of Migrants in Hungary,* IOM, Geneva: 108.
Klinchenko, T., O. Malinovska, I. Mingazutdinov, O. Shamshur
1999   *Country Studies on Migrant Smuggling and Trafficking: The Case of Ukraine,* IOM Technical Cooperation Centre for Europe and Central Asia, Vienna: 104.
Knaus, K., and G. Reiter
1999   *Combat of Trafficking in Women and Forced Prostitution: International Standards,* Ludwig Boltzmann Institute of Human Rights, Vienna: 33.
Kuci, A.
1998   "Stuck in Sarajevo", *Transitions,* December: 52-53.
Kyle, D.J., and Z. Liang
1998   "The development and organisation of trans-national migrant trafficking from China and Ecuador", a paper presented to the Conference on Managing Migration in the Twenty-first Century, 21-23 June, Hamburg, Germany: 26.
Lederer, H.W.
1997   "Illegale Ausländerbeschäftigung in der Bundesrepublik Deutschland", a paper prepared for the Friedrich-Ebert-Stiftung and Presented at the FES Conference Zuwanderung und illegale Beschäftigung, Bonn, 27 May, Bonn: 51.
Meese, J., K. Van Impe, and S. Vanheste
1998   *Multidisciplinary Research on the Phenomenon of Trafficking in Human Beings from an International and National Perspective: A Pilot Study with Poland and Hungary,* University of Ghent Research Group Drug Policy, Criminal Policy, International Crime, Ghent: 168.
Morrison, J.
1998   *The Cost of Survival: The Trafficking of Refugees to the UK,* The Refugee Council, London: 97.
2000   *The Trafficking and Smuggling of Refugees. The End Game in European Asylum Policy?* United Nations High Commissioner for Refugees (UNHCR), Geneva: 94, (draft only).
North Atlantic Assembly. SubCommittee on Civilian Security and Cooperation
1996   *Organised Crime and Illegal Immigration: Findings and Conclusions from a Seven-Country Inquiry,* Draft Special Report, 10.

OECD (Organisation for Economic Cooperation and Development)
    Annual SOPEMI Country Reports, Paris.
Okólski, M.
    1998   *Combating Migrant Trafficking in Poland: Results of a Recent Study with Interviews of Relevant National Actors, IOM Regional Seminar on Migrant Trafficking through the Baltic States and Neighbouring Countries,* 17-18 September, Vilnius, Lithuania: 16.
    1999   *Migrant Trafficking in Poland: Actors, Mechanisms and Combating,* preliminary results of the IOM/ISS 1998 study. Final report presented to International Organization for Migration, Technical Cooperation Centre (ICMPD), Vienna: 104.
Omelaniuk, I.
    1998   *Measures to Combat Human Trafficking in Central and Eastern Europe, IOM Regional Seminar on Migrant Trafficking through the Baltic States and Neighbouring Countries, September 17-18 1998,* Vilnius, Lithuania, International Organization for Migration (IOM), Geneva: 12.
OSCE (Organization for Security and Cooperation in Europe)
    1999   "Trafficking in human beings: implications for the OSCE", Background Paper 1999/3, Review Conference, September 1999, ODIHR (Office for Democratic Institutions and Human Rights), Warsaw, Poland: 74.
Ruggiero, V.
    1997   "Trafficking in human beings: slaves in contemporary Europe", *International Journal of the Sociology of Law,* (25): 231-244.
Salt, J.
    1999   *Current Trends in International Migration in Europe,* Council of Europe, Strasbourg.
Salt, J., and J. Stein
    1997   "Migration as a business: the case of trafficking", *International Migration,* 35(4): 467-494.
Savona, E.U.
    1996   "Dynamics of migration and crime in Europe: new patterns of an old nexus", paper prepared for the ISPAC International Conference on Migration and Crime: Global and Regional Problems and Responses, Courmayeuer, 5-8 October, Transcrime Working Paper no. 8.
    1997   "Globalisation of crime: the organisational variable", paper prepared for the 15th International Symposium on Economic Crime, Jesus College Cambridge, UK, 14-20 September, Transcrime Working Paper, 15: 26.
Shannon, S.
    1999   "Prostitution and the Mafia: the involvement of organised crime in the global sex trade", in P. Williams (Ed.), *Illegal Immigration and Commercial Sex: The New Slave Trade,* Frank Cass, London: 119-144.
Siron, N., and P. Van Baeveghem
    1999   *Trafficking in Migrants through Poland: Multidisciplinary Research into the Phenomenon of Transit Migration in the Candidate Member States of the EU, with a View to the Combat of Traffic in Persons,* University of Ghent Research Group [in] Drug Policy, Criminal Policy, International Crime, Antwerp/Apeldoorn, Maklu, (10): 326.

54   *Salt*

Ulrich, C.J.
   1995   *Alien-Smuggling and Uncontrolled Migration in Northern Europe and the Baltic Region*, HEUNI (European Institute for Crime Prevention and Control), Helsinki, HEUNI Papers, 7: 22.

UNESCO (United Nations Educational, Scientific and Cultural Organization)
   1998   *International Migration in Central and Eastern Europe at the Threshold of the XXI Century: New Trends and Emerging Issues,* Meeting of Experts, Moscow (Russia), 8-10 September.

Widgren, J.
   1994   "Multilateral cooperation to combat trafficking in migrants and the role of international organizations", discussion paper submitted [to the] 11th International Organization for Migration Seminar on Migration, 26-28 October 1994, Geneva: International Response to Trafficking in Migrants and the Safeguarding of Migrant Rights, paper no. 6, Seminar Secretariat, International Organization for Migration (IOM), Geneva: 11.

Williams, P.
   1999   "Trafficking in women and children: a market perspective", in P. Williams (Ed.), *Illegal Immigration and Commercial Sex: The New Slave Trade*, HEUNI Papers, Frank Cass, London: 145-170.

TRAITE ET INTRODUCTION CLANDESTINE D'ETRES HUMAINS: UNE PERSPECTIVE EUROPÉENNE

Cet article examine l'évidence empirique de la traite et de l'introduction clandestine d'êtres humains en Europe. Il affirme qu'un marché est apparu pour des services de migration illégale, dont on ne connaît pas encore très bien les mécanismes, ni les formes d'organisation. Les migrants illégaux ayant recours à de tels services s'exposent autant aux prestataires peu scrupuleux des services en question qu'aux services de police et d'immigration des pays concernés, ce qui engendre une dépendance à l'égard des protections offertes par les réseaux de trafiquants. Il en résulte une symbiose entre le trafiquant et celui qui en est victime.

L'intérêt et l'inquiétude considérables que suscitent ces questions de traite et d'introduction clandestine d'êtres humains dans des enceintes gouvernementales, intergouvernementales et non gouvernementales, comme dans l'opinion publique et les médias, ont une bonne longueur d'avance sur l'appréhension du phénomène et sur les témoignages concrets qui devraient le documenter. Cela se répercute sur les mesures politiques destinées à lutter contre ce phénomène, qui de ce fait risquent d'être non productives d'effets et qui peuvent aussi avoir des effets secondaires non souhaitables.

L'article commence par un débat sur les principales questions conceptuelles et théoriques auxquelles sont confrontés les chercheurs et les hommes politiques. Viennent ensuite une évaluation des grandes approches théoriques qui ont été adoptées, ainsi qu'une appréciation des connaissances statistiques actuellement disponibles.

L'auteur passe ensuite en revue l'information existante sur la structure organisationnelle des filières de trafic, puis dresse un tableau récapitulatif des caractéristiques des migrants concernés, sur la base des études empiriques qui ont été faites sur le sujet. L'article se termine par la présentation de quelques-unes des principales priorités en matière de recherche.

TRÁFICO Y CRUCE CLANDESTINO DE PERSONAS: UNA PERSPECTIVA EUROPEA

Este artículo examina la prueba empírica del tráfico y del cruce clandestino de personas en Europa. Sostiene que ha surgido un mercado de servicios de migración irregular con mecanismos y formas de organización pocos conocidos. Los migrantes irregulares que recurren a estos servicios se exponen a proveedores de servicios inescrupulosos y a las autoridades de inmigración y policía, por lo cual dependen en gran medida de la salvaguardia que ofrecen las redes de traficantes. Por tanto, se desarrolla una relación de simbiosis entre el traficante y la persona objeto de tráfico.

El enorme interés y preocupación a que dan lugar el tráfico y el cruce clandestino de personas en organizaciones gubernamentales, intergubernamentales y no gubernamentales, en los medios de comunicación y en la opinión pública, va más allá de la comprensión teórica y de la evidencia factual. Ello tiene repercusiones en las medidas políticas destinadas a luchar contra el tráfico y el cruce clandestino de personas, que probablemente no funcionan y que también tienen efectos secundarios imprevistos.

Este artículo inicia el debate sobre las principales cuestiones conceptuales y de definición con que se enfrentan estudiosos y políticos. Luego analiza las principales perspectivas teóricas que han sido desarrolladas y evalúa los conocimientos sobre las estadísticas actuales.

También examina la información sobre la estructura orgánica de las organizaciones de tráfico de personas y ofrece un resumen sobre las características de los migrantes concernidos, basado en estudios empíricos realizados. Este artículo concluye enumerando algunas de las principales prioridades en materia de investigación.

[17]

Illegal Chinese Immigration Into the United States: A Preliminary Factor Analysis

John Z. Wang

Abstract: *Since August 1991, a new type of international criminal activity, using oceangoing ships, has appeared. Illegal Chinese immigrants are entering various countries throughout the world, including the United States. This new wave of illegal global migration has promoted several social problems in the countries and areas affected: unauthorized employment, substandard housing, political asylum schemes, and related crimes such as murder, kidnapping, ganging, and prostitution. This article will analyze some of the causal factors that lead to the situation. Furthermore, a theoretical explanation of the "demand and supply/pull and push" model will be discussed. Finally, some countermeasures are offered as policy recommendations to combat or curtail this worldwide smuggling operation. Based on a content analysis and personal interviews with illegal Chinese immigrants, the current article suggests that this new crime phenomenon involves transnational criminal groups. It results from the demand for cheap labor in Chinatowns in the United States, the abundant labor supply in China's coastal regions, and the huge profit from such smuggling activities.*

On January 12, 2000, a dozen illegal Chinese immigrants were detected in a soft-top container on a cargo ship near the Port of Seattle, Washington. Three dead bodies were also found inside the container (Murphy, 2000). This incident highlights a growing problem: illegal Chinese immigrants being smuggled into the United States by cargo ships or fishing vessels. Obviously, this new modus operandi of illegal alien smuggling has raised some serious questions for law enforcement agencies as well as policy makers: What characteristics does this new illegal Chinese immigration have? What are the causal factors and theoretical explanations for this new crime phenomenon? What are the countermeasures that can be taken to combat or curtail the oceangoing smuggling operation?

Whereas the smuggling routes by air were briefly discussed in an earlier article (Wang, 1993), an attempt is made in this article to focus on (a) the reasons behind the involvement of Taiwanese oceangoing vessels, (b) the causal factors and theoretical perspectives for the new crime phenomenon, and (c) policy recommendations for countermeasures.

Due to the difficulty and sensitivity involved in obtaining the data regarding the topic, the majority of the information provided in this article comes from five sources: (a) a content analysis of some major English and Chinese newspapers in the United States, (b) personal interviews with illegal Chinese immigrants working in Chinese restaurants and sweatshops both in the Houston and Los Angeles areas, (c) personal interviews with social workers working with illegal Chinese immigrants who were detained in Immigration and Naturalization Service (INS) detention centers, (d) personal interviews with INS agents investigating illegal Chinese immigration, and (e) personal interviews with Chinese law enforcement personnel during a trip to China in June of 2000.

BACKGROUND

Illegal alien smuggling and related criminal activities have been confronted by U.S. law enforcement agencies for many years. However, this current surge of illegal Chinese immigration bears two new features. First, Taiwanese fishing ships are used for transportation. Second, the vast majority of the illegal Chinese are coming from one area: Fujian (Fukieu) Province of China.

Although many illegal Chinese immigrants were still coming by air beginning in August 1991 (Mydans, 1992), a new type of smuggling operation began to take shape: Taiwanese oceangoing ships were now being used to smuggle illegal Chinese immigrants to the United States. It is suggested that the occurrence of this new type of operation is explained by the reduced overhead, increased profit, and simple logistics involved (no passports and minimal bribery required). Furthermore, this new criminal operation is different from the air smuggling operation in terms of techniques involved, networking used, the number of persons smuggled (about 150 persons per ship), and the amount of money charged (about $30,000 per head).

In brief, the use of oceangoing ships to smuggle illegal Chinese immigrants seems to be an alternative to smuggling by air, which appeared to have been put into operation in 1991. Nevertheless, the oceangoing smuggling is attributable to more complex causal factors.

FACTOR ANALYSIS

Since August 1991, thousands of Chinese illegal immigrants have made their way to the United States after several months of voyage, enduring tremendous hardship and financial risk. Such an international illegal migration cannot occur without both macro- and micro-causal factors. The former cover historical, economic, and social aspects, whereas the latter include some situational factors that resulted from the political asylum policy of the INS, the Chinese Student Protection Act, and the discontinuation of the use of Taiwanese fishing vessels as described below.

HISTORICAL FACTORS

Historically, Chinese overseas migration dates back several centuries. Most immigrants were from the Guangdong (Canton) Province and a small portion from Fujian Province. Many of the early immigrants sailed for Malaysia, Thailand, Indonesia, Philippines, Singapore, and other Southeast Asian countries. Many others came to the United States during the California gold rush and the grand railway construction. During those days, immigrants' passage was purchased by their employers who then used their labor to repay the debt. This kind of migration was not considered illegal in the sense that there were no specific regulations to prohibit such labor practices in either the United States or China.

Today the geographical feature of immigration (legal or illegal) has reversed. The majority of the illegal immigrants come from Fujian Province and only a few from the Guangdong Province. Almost 99% of those illegal immigrants from Fujian Province come from Changle, Lianjiang, and Minhou counties, a hilly coastal region opposite Taiwan. The people in the region are well known for their hard work and adventures in seeking better fortune.

As a historical tradition in the region, a family feels very proud and is respected if one of the sons can send back from overseas a large sum of money to help build a new house and/or sponsor a village banquet. Thus, for the past two centuries, an individual who migrates (legally or illegally) carries with him or her an entire family's hope for a better future. Such a hope still exists in the area, especially in the three counties in Fujian Province mentioned above. In other words, Fujian Province has been richer than many other parts of China, yet it is commonly believed by the local people that those who migrate do better than do those who stay behind.

Another factor is the term *immigration chain*, where one "seed" individual settles down in the United States and induces other family members or relatives to join him or her. Unfortunately, the quickest method still remains the path of illegal immigration. Thus, it is this immigration chain that promotes the international migration (legal or illegal), which has remained a historical phenomenon in the region.

ECONOMIC FACTORS

Many of the illegal immigrants are young farmers and fishermen from mountainous villages along the southern coast of the Fujian Province. Cultivated land is so scarce that most families have only a fraction of an acre to farm. The per capita income for farmers in China is only about $125 per year (Kristof, 1993). At the same time, China's economy is growing at an astounding 14% per year, along with inflation, arbitrary levies, and corruption. The booming economy stimulated by the economic reform in the area provides many opportunities for those young educated people who have job skills and consequent earning power. On the other hand, young farmers or fishermen who have less education or job skills or no money from abroad frequently find themselves at a disadvantage to compete. Therefore, the legitimate means to obtain legitimate goals is perceived to be blocked or at least limited. As result, many of those who feel disadvantaged in competition and angry at inflation, arbitrary levies, and corruption attempt illegal means to realize their legitimate goals. Though some want more political or religious freedom, most of those who come to the United States or other countries do so in search of economic opportunities that do not exist at home as a consequence of the economic liberalization in China (Fritsch, 1993).

SOCIAL FACTORS

As the economic reform in China deepens, especially along the coastal regions, it unavoidably undermines the regulatory and integrative functions of certain social institutions (police and village government). As these institutions become less functional, people may suddenly find themselves in a situation in which many new opportunities exist because of the loosening of social controls formerly exercised by these social institutions. First, local governments do not now have the type of tight control over the population that they had formerly. No one has to report if a farmer or fisherman disappears from his village or a worker resigns from his factory job. Second, border controls have been loosened to a great extent due to the more liberal policies toward Hong Kong, Macau, and Taiwan. Regular police and armed police have redirected their efforts to a thriving business—smuggling of cigarettes, drugs, weapons, pornography, and cultural antiques. Individual trips both in and out have become easier, requiring less official permission. Third, the economic boom promotes privatization. Private boats that used to be rare are now owned by many farmers or fishermen, presenting a greater chance of mobility at some off-coast islands that have been heavily used as transit points for smuggling. Finally, the economic reform, unfortunately, has also resulted in growing corruption among local police and government officials. Passports and exit documents can be bought at a price. The new situation has also led to an emergence of Mafia-style criminal syndicates that have contacts in Taiwan, Hong Kong, and Chinatowns in the United States (Booth, 1991, p. 157).

SITUATIONAL FACTORS

Some situational factors have also played a role in the new surge of illegal Chinese immigration. Situational factors mean that some social events act as catalysts, triggering the overall condition to change in the context of the micro factors.

The first situational factor has stemmed from the INS asylum policy. Under the policy, any alien can apply for asylum if his or her life or freedom would be threatened on account of race, religion, nationality, membership in a particular social group, or political opinion (Asylum, 1990). According to the policy, Chinese citizens who arrive in the United States, legally or illegally, can apply for political asylum merely by stating their opposition to the family planning policy that started in China in 1979 which allows only one child per family. The INS has accepted this as a legitimate political reason and granted political asylum to illegal Chinese immigrants accordingly. Therefore, more and more Chinese follow this path, claiming that they would face persecution if they were deported. This policy has resulted in a sudden growth of political asylum seeking. From April to May of 1993, at the immigration service's Newark office only, 2,853 Chinese applied for political asylum, more than the total number of Chinese applicants in all of 1992 (Fritsch, 1993). About 80% of Chinese applicants were granted political asylum, compared to about 35% overall in the previous year. Those who were denied asylum could still appeal, winning a few months' grace period. In addition, 30% of the aliens claiming to be seeking asylum in the New York area failed to appear for their court dates (Fritsch, 1993). They simply disappeared.

Although applicants asking for political asylum still have to wait for their turn on the INS's long waiting list, the Chinese Students Protection Act of 1992 provided an across-the-board approach that smuggling groups were quick to abuse. The Act, first issued as an Executive Order on April 11, 1991, and then passed by the U.S. Congress on October 9, 1992, permits any Chinese national who arrived on or before April 16, 1990, to apply for permanent residence status (a green card) due to the Tiananmen Square incident. The implementation of the Act started on July 1, 1992, and ended 1 year later. Usually, a permanent residence status can only be obtained after several years of waiting, plus several thousands of dollars of legal fees. Given this golden opportunity, many illegal immigrants, so long as they were in the United States, could simply make a false claim and provide false documents, stating that they arrived before April 11, 1991. This situational factor explains the sudden increase of illegal Chinese immigrants coming to the United States from 1992 to 1993.

The boom in the illegal Chinese immigration was also fueled when Taiwan prohibited fishing with drift nets in 1992. Without providing any alternative, this policy change drove several hundred owners of such ships out of business and created a new business—smuggling groups purchased these ships and refitted them for carrying illegal immigrants. The majority of the vessels used for smuggling are converted Taiwanese drift net fishing vessels. Some have been converted to general cargo vessels, whereas others have kept their rigging for fishing. These vessels carry flags from a variety of countries, such as Panama, the Dominican Republic, or Honduras.

In brief, the flow of illegal immigration from China to the United States is due neither to a one-time nor a single cause action. Instead, the flow can be characterized by several waves of migration impacted by the historical, economic, social/political, and situational factors in both China and the United States.

THEORETICAL PERSPECTIVE

It is still premature to offer a comprehensive theoretical perspective to explain the new wave of illegal Chinese immigration to the United States. Even so, it can be theorized that the supply-demand or pull-or-push hypothesis largely accounts for the new crime phenomenon.

Since the 1920s the economic mainstay of American Chinatowns has been largely dependent on two types of industrial subsections—the tourist industry and the manufacturing industry. The main units in the tourist industry consist of restaurants, meat and fish markets, groceries, laundry shops, curio stores, import bazaars, and sidewalk stalls, which line the main thoroughfares of American Chinatowns. The manufacturing industry, on the other hand, basically refers to garment factories or sweatshops. Since the 1990s, competition for the tourist dollar both within and outside Chinatowns has become very keen. Therefore, to survive, owners of these retail businesses have no other choice but to find job seekers willing to work longer hours under inferior working conditions and at lower wages. As a result, there has been an increasing demand for such cheap labor among the small businesses in major Chinatowns in the United States. Such employment, however, cannot be readily found in the general labor market.

Illegal Chinese immigrants are ideal candidates for such jobs for several reasons. First, they have no work permits so they cannot bargain over wages. Second, they speak the same dialects (Fujianese or Cantonese) as their employers and are thus easy to control. Third, as new arrivals, they know little about their work rights, such as minimum wage and medical insurance. Finally, they cannot report any exploitation to the authorities owing to their illegal status.

In China, on the other hand, the abundant supply of those seeking a better life constitutes the other driving force in the current alien smuggling business. In other words, whereas the need for cheap labor among small businesses in Chinatowns in the United States serve as potential labor market (the demand or the pull), many young fishermen and farmers in the Fujian Province who want to come to the United States looking for a "fortune" provide a rich source for the growing demand in the United States (the supply or the push). However, the two cannot be connected without the linking component—smuggling groups.

The huge profit generated by smuggling illegal immigrants has attracted many crime groups. As a matter of fact, *snakeheads* (smuggling leaders) in smuggling groups are also encouraged by the low risk of penalties, even if smugglers are caught (*Committee Hearing of INS Testimony,* 1991, p. 27). On average, snakeheads charge from $30,000 to $60,000 per person depending on the method (e.g., air, oceangoing ships, or container ships), routes, and number of people in the group. Those illegal immigrants have to pay from 5% to 10% as down payment, which they borrowed from relatives or criminal groups.

In summary, the demand-supply hypothesis suggests that as long as there exists a demand for cheap labor, an abundant supply of such cheap labor, and a profitable smuggling in-between that can take advantage of various social oppor-

SUPPLY OF CHEAP LABOR ←——→ PROFIT BY SMUGGLING ←——→ DEMAND OF CHEAP LABOR

Illegal Chinese Immigration

HISTORICAL FACTORS ←——→ ECONOMIC FACTORS ←——→ SOCIAL FACTORS ←——→ SITUATIONAL FACTORS

Figure 1

tunities, a surge of illegal immigration will likely continue to occur. Simply stated, the rise of the new transnational criminal activity can be better understood in terms of new economic opportunities combined with the absence of countervailing constraints that could prevent or inhibit such opportunities (Williams, 1995). Figure 1 shows the summary for a theoretical framework proposed by this inductive study.

It is also proposed here that the above theoretical framework calls for further quantitative data for testing and modification. It is hoped that the theoretical attempt can promote a better understanding of the new crime phenomenon under discussion.

POLICY IMPLICATIONS

The smuggling organizations have earned hundreds of millions of dollars in profit and have grown in size, complicity, and sophistication. Even more disturbing is a documented trend toward a transnational criminal cooperation among triads and gangs from the United States, China, Taiwan, and Hong Kong (*Committee Hearing on Statement*, 1991, p. 4). Their purpose is to perpetuate the criminal operation. This in turn presents alarming implications for the law enforcement community. Equally disturbing is the latest development that illegal Chinese immigrants are being smuggled into U.S. western coastal areas in containers of cargo ships (Young, 2000) and into British Columbia, Canada (Brooke, 1999).

Because illegal Chinese immigration has become a transnational crime, some comprehensive countermeasures to address this new crime phenomenon are required to further strengthen the current federal strategies. First, the INS should conduct more routine inspections of work sites suspected of hiring undocumented workers in Chinatowns. In other words, an effort should be made to cut demand in job markets for illegal immigrants. If the number of undocumented workers can be reduced, many new jobs will be open for those citizens and aliens who are legally entitled to them. At a minimum, frequent checks of employers who realize the INS may come knocking at the door unannounced should be a way to discourage the practice of hiring illegal immigrants. In a word, frequent inspections by the INS, if done properly and without abuse, are necessary tools in cutting down job markets for illegal immigrants. This internal sanctioning system works well because it punishes employers who hire illegal immigrant workers largely for economic reasons (Snowden, 1998).

Second, the INS might increase the fine for employers who knowingly employ undocumented workers. As illustrated earlier, by hiring illegal immigrants who are desperate for work, these small business owners are able to pay subminimum wages with few, if any, benefits. The lack of opportunity for unskilled illegal Chinese immigrants makes them easy prey for exploitation (Pennsylvania Crime Commission, 1990). In view of such ruthlessness, the rationale for tougher policies is necessary to deal with employers to avoid creation of an underground community of second-class residents compelled to live on the fringe of society (substandard housing) and who are consequently likely to resort to criminal activities to survive (Chen, 1988).

Along the same line, a new supplementary sanction is needed for the INS, permitting it to fine any person who provides assistance to smuggling of illegal immigrants, ranging from lending money to providing housing or shelter. The purpose of this measure would be to deter illegal immigrants from obtaining any assistance from their relatives in the United States, thus making the illegal immigration chain more difficult to sustain. Third, the INS should reevaluate its current screening practice for political asylum in terms of the one-child policy and the Falun Gong policy. The latter refers to the recent situation in which the Chinese government has declared the Falun Gong an illegal cult in China. Falun Gong is a powerful mind/body cultivation practice based on some religious belief. In many reports, however, applicants or attorneys present fake information to have asylum granted due to the two above sociopolitical situations in China about which INS officials lack understanding.

Next, the INS should implement joint efforts with law enforcement agencies in China to produce a series of TV programs. The purpose of the TV campaign would be to let people know the actual life that illegal immigrants have experienced in the United States. This effort would make it more difficult for recruiters of smuggling groups to attract and cheat potential illegal immigrants.

Fifth, given the number of illegal immigrants, the current detention capacity of the INS is inadequate. Even when illegal immigrants are caught, they often are released pending further hearings, due to the lack of detention holdings. As a consequence, a large percentage simply disappear and fail to appear in court. Some of them are even coerced into an underworld of forced labor, drug dealing, prostitution, and gang-related activities. For these reasons, extradition treaties with countries and areas concerned (including China) are essential to facilitate deportation proceedings. Obviously, rapid deportation would send a clear message to prospective illegal immigrants, serving as another deterrent factor.

Finally, illegal immigration is a transnational crime. It is therefore important to seek international cooperation among law enforcement agencies. It is necessary to establish liaison offices in the countries and areas concerned to quickly exchange intelligence information. This effort could help combat smuggling operations at their source. However, U.S. law enforcement is at a distinct disadvantage in terms of investigation because few agents can speak northern Fujianese. In this sense, law enforcement agencies at both federal and local levels should purposely strive to recruit personnel who can speak the dialect of northern Fujian. In addition, it is suggested that the citizenship requirement for a sworn officer position be exempted for a language specialist. Alternatively, an individual with the language skill may be initially hired under a civilian status if she or he has a permanent residency status.

Further precautions are in order due to some new trends. First, the Canadian west coast route is being explored by smuggling groups. As the U.S. Coast Guard has tightened interception in American territorial waters around Guam during 1998 and 1999, smuggling groups have shifted their targets toward the Canadian west coast, namely the Vancouver area. On July 20, 1999, the first Chinese ship was intercepted in the Vancouver area. The Canadian authorities in Vancouver released 74 illegal immigrants, pending resolution of their petitions for refugee status. Within a month, 51 had disappeared, presumably for the United States. The release of illegal immigrants promoted a series of landing attempts in the area in the following months. In the summer of 1999, four trawlers were intercepted by the Canadian Navy off British Columbia and 600 undocumented Chinese were detained. The selection of the Canadian west coast route was an extension of past targets along the west Pacific Rim after the Los Angeles, San Francisco, and Seattle areas.

The Vancouver area is being used as a transit point for illegal immigrants to go to the United States for the following reason: Vancouver has a large Chinese population. It has been estimated that 20% are ethnic Chinese. Therefore, it is much easier for illegal Chinese immigrants to find shelter, legal service, and employment in this area.

In addition, since 1999, other countries (e.g., Russia, Great Britain, Germany, Holland, Yugoslavia, Croatia, Italy, Japan, Australia, and some Latin American countries) have begun to see an increase of illegal Chinese immigrants. Some of these countries (Croatia and Italy) are being used simply as transit points on the way to the western European countries or the United States.

There is some evidence that new illegal immigrants are being recruited from other provinces in China, such as Wenzhou in Zhejian Province. Also, smuggling groups are targeting women and minors because they will receive lower penalties in the United States if apprehended and also be in greater demand for prostitution.

Since off-loading points on the west and east coasts and land-crossing points along the American-Mexican border have been used by smuggling groups, alternative landing points will likely appear around the four U.S. territories, namely,

American Samoa, Puerto Rico, Virgin Islands, and Guam. As a matter of fact, Guam was utilized as a transit point during 1998 and 1999.

Finally, smuggling groups have begun to smuggle people first to the Caribbean countries, such as Jamaica, the Dominican Republic, or Haiti, and then fly the illegal immigrants to Miami, using either fake or genuine Japanese tourist passports because there is a treaty on visa exemption between the United States and Japan. Actually, smuggling groups can even use these passports repeatedly because of an identification problem: Americans have difficulty differentiating people of Asian descent. (To Americans, all Asians look alike.)

CONCLUSION

The smuggling by oceangoing ships represents a major expansion of the small groups of Chinese laborers coming to the United States by air through Canada and Central America. It is believed that those intercepted are only the tip of the iceberg. Some American officials think that 100,000 Chinese are now being smuggled into the United States each year. Even if the conducive situational factors no longer exist, it is impossible to predict whether this wave will come to an end soon. On the contrary, several cargo ships with illegal Chinese immigrants have been intercepted near Long Beach, Los Angeles, and Seattle since May of 1999 (Verhovek, 2000). Moreover, it has been suggested that other crime syndicates may follow the same route, such as those in India and Pakistan (*Testimony From Kenneth Yates*, 1992, p. 17).

The recent tide of illegal Chinese immigration has begun to attract international attention. The operation is transnational in that smugglers have to hire recruiters, sailors, corrupt officials, drivers, document forgers, employment agents, and gangs in mainland China, Hong Kong, Taiwan, the United States, and other involved countries. The smuggling of illegal Chinese immigrants by sea has gone beyond just an immigration issue. Obviously, the illegal Chinese immigration is a manifestation of Asian organized crime groups that are committing transnational crime.

ACKNOWLEDGMENTS

The author would like to thank those anonymous reviewers from the INS, the Coast Guard, and other federal law enforcement agencies for their helpful comments and valuable information on earlier drafts of this article. Also, the author is grateful for the valuable corrections on the final draft from anonymous reviewer(s) from the Journal. Finally, the comments from my colleagues, Dr. Sam Torres and Dr. Bruce Berg, are also well appreciated.

REFERENCES

Asylum, 8 U.C.S.A. § 1158 (West 1990).

Booth, M. (1991). *The triads: The growing global threat for the Chinese criminal societies.* New York: St. Martin's.

Brooke, J. (1999, September 30). Canada taking harder line with illegal Chinese migrants. *New York Times,* p. A14.

Chen, A. (1988). The development of immigration law and policy: The Hong Kong experience. *McGill Law Journal, 33,* 631-675.

Chinese Students Protection Act of 1992, Pub. L. No. 102-404, 2 Stat. 1969 (1992).

Committee hearing of INS testimony: Hearing before the U.S. Senate Committee on Governmental Affairs, 101st Cong. (1991).

Committee hearing on statement of Mr. Wong: Hearing before the U.S. Senate Committee on Governmental Affairs, 101st Cong. (1991).

Fritsch, J. (1993, June 7). One failed voyage illustrates flow of Chinese immigration. *New York Times,* pp. A1, B5.

Kristof, N. (1993, June 7). High hopes, and stakes, for China's boat people. *New York Times,* p. B5.

Murphy, K. (2000, January 12). Smuggling of Chinese ends in a box of death, squalor. *Los Angles Times,* pp. A1, A16.

Mydans, S. (1992, March 21). Chinese smugglers' lucrative cargo: Humans. *New York Times,* pp. A1, A7.

Pennsylvania Crime Commission. (1990). *Organized crime in Pennsylvania: A decade of change, 1990 report.* Conshohocken, PA: Printing House of the Commonwealth of Pennsylvania.

Snowden, L. (1998). Can we control illegal immigration? Evaluating methods of immigration law enforcement. *Security Journal, 11,* 171-177.

Testimony from Kennete Yates: Hearing before the U.S. Senate Committee on Governmental Affairs, 102nd Cong. (1992)

Verhovek, S. (2000, January 12). Deadly choice of stowaways: ship containers. *New York Times,* pp. A1, A20.

Wang, Z. (1993). Some new crime trends in China: Their impact on the United States. *Police Studies, 16,* 11-19.

Williams, P. (1995). The new threat: Transnational criminal organizations and international security. *Criminal Organizations, 9,* 13-24.

Young, P. (2000, January 3). 18 more Chinese entrants are held. *Press-Telegram,* pp. A1, A5.

John Z. Wang, Ph.D.
Associate Professor
Department of Criminal Justice
California State University–Long Beach
Long Beach, CA 90840
USA

[18]

THE SANCTUARY MOVEMENT AND THE SMUGGLING OF UNDOCUMENTED CENTRAL AMERICANS INTO THE UNITED STATES: CRIME, DEVIANCE, OR DEFIANCE?

GREGORY L. WILTFANG
Department of Sociology
Western State College
Gunnison, Colorado

JOHN K. COCHRAN
Center for the Study of Crime, Delinquency and Social Control
Department of Sociology
University of Oklahoma
Norman, Oklahoma

We introduce the concept of defiant behavior: actions that, although often defined politically as crime, are defined by their actors as necessary, legitimate, and morally appropriate. We then link this concept to two distinct substantive subfields of sociology: (1) criminology and the sociology of deviance and social control, and (2) political sociology and the sociology of social movements. A review of the literature on organized defiance suggests a clear theoretical confluence between the microstructural concept of biographic availability, drawn from the resource mobilization and political process perspectives within the sociology of social movements, and social control theories of crime and deviance. Likewise, there is a similar confluence between the socialization effects of prior activism, also from the resource mobilization perspective, and differential association/social learning theory in criminology. Finally, we present results from a study of the defiant activities of some members of the sanctuary movement. The form of defiance examined here, the smuggling of undocumented Central Americans across the United States-Mexico border, provides a unique test of the scope and power of both social

Received 19 April 1993; accepted 7 September 1993.

Both authors contributed equally to this paper. We want to acknowledge and thank Ronald L. Akers, Harold G. Grasmick, Robert J. Bursik, Jr., Mitchell B. Chamlin, and Leonard Beeghley for their helpful comments on an earlier draft of this manuscript.

A version of this paper was presented at the 41st annual meeting of the American Society of Criminology, November 8–12, 1989, Reno, Nevada.

Address correspondence to Gregory L. Wiltfang, Department of Sociology, Western State College, Gunnison, CO 81231.

102   G. L. WILTFANG AND J. K. COCHRAN

*control and social learning theories. Based on self-report survey data
collected from a sample of 141 participants in the Tuscon, Arizona,
sanctuary movement, our findings provide strong support for social learning theory but fail to support social control theory. In fact, the observed
effects of the control theory variables are generally in a direction opposite
to that predicted by the theory. Implications of the study for the theoretical development of criminology and deviance and for the sociological
study of social movements are discussed.*

Sociologists have long recognized the links between social
problems, social movements, and deviant behavior (Blumer 1955;
Gusfield 1955; Becker 1963; Horowitz and Liebowitz 1968; Merton and Nisbet 1971; Mauss 1975; Spector and Kitsuse 1977; Best
1989). As argued in these and other works, social movements tend
to coalesce and organize around social problems in an attempt to
alleviate them. Often the actions of movement participants oppose
the interests of other parties and organizations. When these oppo-
sitional groups are more powerful than the social movement organization, attempts at social control may occur, often with the
actions of the movement participants defined as deviant and occasionally as criminal.

Such is the case of the actions of the sanctuary movement and
its conflict with the U.S. federal government's Immigration and
Naturalization Service (INS). Organized to come to the aid of undocumented Central Americans, members of the sanctuary movement have had some of their activities defined as felonies by the
INS and the federal courts. Because violations of U.S. immigration
laws are crimes, traditional theories of crime and deviance should
have the power and scope to provide reasonable explanations for
such actions.

Traditional theories of deviance and juvenile delinquency are
often claimed to be useful explanations of adult criminality. Yet,
empirical tests of these theories with data on adult criminality are
rare. The question we pose here is whether these theories can
explain the unique form of adult criminality of social movement
activists. The task we set for several of these theories is to predict
involvement in the defiant activities of the North American sanctuary movement.

Our paper's purpose is threefold. First, we discuss those social
movement activities we refer to as "defiant actions" and how they
have been commonly treated in the crime and deviance literature.

Next, we attempt to bridge disciplinary boundaries between works in the sociology of crime and deviance and the sociology of social movements by highlighting their theoretical overlap. We argue that the social learning and social control theories of criminology are reflected in the theories of social movement activism. Finally, we test social control theory and social learning theory as rival explanations with self-reported survey data on defiant acts collected from a sample of sanctuary movement activists.

SOCIAL MOVEMENT ACTIVISM: CRIME, DEVIANCE, OR DEFIANCE?

Civilization always has a ready supply of discontents. The fit between sociocultural arrangements and our wishes, desires, and ideals is rarely perfect. History provides a continuing chronicle of moments when people have banded together set on changing their society (or at least parts of it) to better fit their ideals. Examples abound: efforts to organize labor against capital; abolitionists helping slaves to freedom on the underground railroad; the temperance movement to control alcohol consumption; women's suffrage; sit-ins to desegregate lunch counters; young men burning their draft cards to protest conscription; efforts to gain access to military bases where nuclear weapons are housed to protest their existence or to dismantle or disable them; the bombing of or blocking access to medical clinics to protest abortion; peasants demanding land reforms; students and workers in communist countries demanding democratic freedoms; the declaration of public sanctuaries for Central Americans to protest foreign policy and immigration policies and practices.

The challenges made and actions taken by social movement activists (on their own behalf or on the behalf of others) are collective attempts to contest the prevailing structures of power and definitions of reality in order to realize the movement's visions. Movement members, motivated by such visions, may peacefully "nudge," "bump," or violently try to "shove aside" the barriers standing between them and the realization of their visions. Often legitimate institutional avenues (where they exist) are explored, tried, and exhausted by movement members before they turn to more extraordinary measures. Requests or petitions may turn into demands if officials are indifferent. Such indifference may exacer-

104   G. L. WILTFANG AND J. K. COCHRAN

bate discontent, often leading to outbursts of defiance in the form of riot, rebellion, or revolution. The reactions provoked by these movements will vary according to the perceived threat they pose to the status quo and the powers that be.

Whether a movement's actions are defined either as heroic or despicable rests on the values of the observer, and perhaps more important, on the values held by the target of the movement's protests and demands. The actions may be defined by the target (quite often the state) as "criminal," "acts of aggression," "acts of terrorism," or "a threat to national security."

It is surprising that the acts of social movement participants are rarely examined in the mainstream deviance literature (for an exception see Hagan and Simpson 1974). This omission, however, has been noted in several classic critiques of the sociology of deviance (e.g., Lemert 1951; Liazos 1972; Thio 1973). For instance, Liazos (1972, p. 119) argued that too much attention is paid to "the popular and dramatic forms of deviance;" what he calls the study of "nuts, sluts, and perverts." He even suggested that "we should banish the concept of 'deviance' and speak of oppression, conflict, persecution, and suffering." He argued further that we continue to "neglect conditions of inequality, powerlessness, institutional violence, and so on, which lie at the bases of our tortured society."

When the actions of social movement activists are studied, they are often described as "political crimes" or "political deviance." Simon and Eitzen (1986) and Timmer and Eitzen (1989), for example, specifically mention the sanctuary movement in their discussions of political crime. But the study of political crime has been a low priority topic among sociologists who study deviance (e.g., Schur 1980; Greenberg 1981). Moreover, political crime is often narrowly defined as an offense against the state, such as espionage, treason, assassination, terrorism, or sedition (Kircheimer 1961; Clinard and Quinney 1967).

Chambliss (1988, p. 81), however, defines political crime as "crimes committed by people in order to maintain or change existing political power relations." This definition directs attention to the importance of the intent or motivation of the political criminal. Political criminals are typically seen as "committed nonconformists" rather than immoral and aberrant deviants (Merton and Nisbet 1971). In contrast to conventional street criminals, political criminals announce their intentions publicly, challenge the very legitimacy of laws or their application in specific situations, aim to change the norms they are denying, do not have personal gain as a goal, and appeal to a higher morality by pointing out the void between professed beliefs and actual practices (Merton and Nisbet, 1971, pp. 829–832).

We feel these conceptions of political crime are flawed, for they entail an implicit, often unquestioned acceptance of the legitimacy of the normative stance of the state. This is especially pertinent to the types of acts considered here: social activism. We suggest that the more neutral and descriptive term *defiant behavior* be used to describe acts of groups involved in political and economic conflict. This term avoids the implicit normative baggage associated with "political crime" or "political deviance."

As we use the term, defiant behavior refers to actions consciously taken by groups of individuals to explicitly challenge policies and/or practices of a sociocultural system. The term *defiant behavior* avoids prejudging the "nature" of such acts, and it highlights the fact that definitions of these acts as moral or immoral, just or unjust, criminal or deviant, generally emerge from struggles for power. Central to such power struggles is the ability and the authority to define reality. Groups engaged in struggles for power, justice, and peace often call into question the legitimacy of the status quo and its agents. For sociologists to conceptualize such actions as examples of "deviance" or "criminality" is to adopt implicitly the normative frame of reference of those who are able to control the definition of the situation. As labeling theorists have often noted, acts considered to be deviant or criminal are relative and are often the result of the actions of the powerful against those struggling for a share of that power.

Our use of the term *defiant behavior* links issues of deviance with issues of power and politics. Defiant acts are committed by individuals representing groups struggling against other groups for the power to name, label, or define reality, or at least some significant aspect of it; defiant acts are struggles over the power to control meaning and the opportunities to act on the basis of this meaning. Rather than use the terms *crime* or *deviance* to characterize the acts of sanctuary activists in their struggles with the U.S. government, we define their work with undocumented Central Americans as *defiant* acts. To better capture the reality and the conflictive nature of these acts, we feel the use of the term *defiance* is warranted, justifiable, and appropriate.

106   G. L. WILTFANG AND J. K. COCHRAN

THE SANCTUARY MOVEMENT[1]

The clash between sanctuary movement activists and agents of the United States Immigration and Naturalization Service (INS) had its beginnings in the early 1980s and continues to the present day. It centers on differing definitions and interpretations of current political and economic conditions in Central America and the growing number of Central Americans, especially from El Salvador and Guatemala, who have emigrated to the United States since the early 1980s. Because of the government's view of current socio-political conditions in the region, many Central Americans are denied refugee status and political asylum in the United States.

The government's position is that the vast majority of Central Americans coming to the United States are "economic migrants," not political refugees. While admitting that human rights violations were widespread in both El Salvador and Guatemala during the early 1980s, the State Department maintains that human rights violations in these countries have greatly decreased in recent years and that most Central Americans leave their countries out of a desire to escape dire economic circumstances for better paying jobs in the United States, not out of a personal fear of persecution by right-wing death squads or left-wing guerrillas.

Sanctuary activists challenge this view. They argue that widespread human rights violations still continue. Drawing on the personal testimonies of many Salvadorans and Guatemalans, activists argue that these persons meet both international and domestic criteria for refugee status: they are fleeing conflicts and the ravages of civil wars in their home countries and have a right to political asylum in the United States under the provisions of the 1980 Refugee Act. While those who were fleeing communist countries were frequently granted asylum, the chances of Central Americans receiving political asylum in the United States are slim (Crittenden 1988; Quamman 1986). They are more likely to be deported if apprehended. Deportees risk murder, rape, and torture upon return to their homelands (see ACLU—Political Activism Project cited in Quammen 1986).

[1]While there are several journalistic accounts of the sanctuary movement (e.g., Quamman 1989; Crittenden 1988; Davidson 1988; Golden and McConnell 1986; MacEoin 1985; MacEoin and Riley 1982; Quammen 1986), until fairly recently, there has been surprisingly little study of the movement by social scientists (cf. Ferrell and Wiltfang 1988; Hildreth 1989; Kowalewski 1990; Wiltfang and McAdam 1991).

Activists argue that the primary reason the government refuses to recognize these Central Americans as refugees is its fear that embarrassing questions may be raised about U.S. foreign policy in that region, a policy that contributes to the continuing flood of Central-American refugees by providing economic and military assistance to governments that frequently engage in the wholesale torture and slaughter of their citizenry.

Moreover, sanctuary activists contend that the continuing mistreatment and deportation of thousands of undocumented Central Americans by the INS constitute severe human rights violations. They see INS policies and practices regarding Central Americans as contrary to both international and domestic law. Such gross human rights violations demand that people of conscience take the actions necessary to publicly oppose and work to correct the government's mistreatment of Central Americans.

Sanctuary is a grassroots, religiously based social movement. Its members have actively defied the federal government by declaring public sanctuaries for Central American refugees. A primary goal of the movement is to bring the refugee crisis to center stage by educating the general public about U.S. foreign policy in Central America and by showing the public the human costs of such policies through the presence of refugees and their stories (Ferrell and Wiltfang 1988).

Not all sanctuary movement actions are seen by the government as crimes. For example, the movement has worked within established INS procedures to bond out Central Americans from detention centers and to provide them with legal assistance. Sanctuary also helps undocumented Central Americans by providing them with various social services such as educational services, medical services, and assistance finding clothing, housing, and jobs. While these services are technically illegal, the INS has not, to date, taken action against the movement for these actions. It is the "evasion services" provided by sanctuary activists that the INS sees as federal crimes. These evasion services involve helping refugees avoid capture and deportation by border officials by means of an underground railroad that helps the refugees find a safe haven.

Sanctuary activists, however, define their work with Central Americans as "civil initiative," not criminal acts of civil disobedience to unjust laws. For activists, it is the U.S. government that is guilty of failing to enforce its own immigration and refugee laws equally. Activists see their own defiant actions as consistent with U.S. immigration law, international law, humanitarian principles, and a number of historical precedents based on Judeo-Christian ethics.

Because of this, the actions of those in the sanctuary movement are especially well suited to our purposes. Some persons in the movement are involved in defiant acts defined by the government as federal crimes, especially those involving the smuggling of undocumented Central Americans on the underground railroad. Sanctuary workers have been indicted in Arizona, New Mexico, and Texas. The perceived seriousness of sanctuary activism was dramatized by the highly publicized 1985–1986 trial of the "Tucson 11" on 71 federal charges (*United States v. Maria de Socorro Pardo de Aguilar et al.* 1989).

The U.S. government's long and extensive 1984 investigation of the movement in Arizona, "Operation Sojourner"; its infiltration of the movement using undercover operatives; the seriousness of the criminal charges brought against the defendants, both North and Central American; the naming of a number of unindicted coconspirators; and the time and expense of 6 months of trial (from October 22, 1985 to May 1, 1986) all graphically illustrate the seriousness of the conflict between the U.S. government and the sanctuary activists.

EXPLAINING DEFIANT BEHAVIOR

To our knowledge, no one has made explicit use of existing theories of crime and deviance to explain the etiology of defiant acts. Given the current disciplinary segregation of sociology (Collins 1986), we are not surprised. Our reading of the literature in both social movement activism and in deviance and criminology suggests an interesting theoretical confluence between these two divergent substantive areas. The theories commonly used in the study of social movement activism and in the study of crime and deviance are quite similar in both their underlying assumptions and general concepts. As we show below, theories of social movement activism employ concepts similar to those found in traditional theories of deviance. However, specialists in crime and deviance have largely ignored the acts of social movement participants, and specific reference to the large literature in criminology and deviance is seldom, if ever, made by social movement scholars. We see this as unfortunate and unnecessary. We take a step toward remedying this state of affairs through a theoretical "cross-fertilization."

Theories of Social Movement Activism[2]

Two theoretical strategies are used to account for why people participate in social movement activities: (1) individual, motivational explanations and (2) microstructural explanations. The former looks for factors within the individual to account for activism. "Internal" factors are assumed to make individuals more susceptible to movement appeals or to compel the individual to participate. While intuitively attractive, empirical support has been less than convincing. The second strategy posits microstructural factors external to the individual to explain activism. Individuals are seen as structurally available rather than psychologically or attitudinally compelled to act. Attention centers on whether the individual's structural location facilitates or constrains activism.

The dominant microstructure perspective in the study of social movements is derived from resource mobilization (RM) theory. An early exposition of this approach suggests that social change and conflict be viewed as "mobilizing, converting, and transferring resources from one group and one arena of action to other groups and actions . . ." (Oberschall 1973, p. 27). Resources "can be anything from material resources—jobs, income, savings, and the right to material goods and services—to nonmaterial resources—authority, moral commitment, trust, friendship, skills, habits of industry, and so on. . . . Mobilization refers to the processes by which a discontented group assembles and invests resources for the pursuit of group goals. Social control refers to the same processes, but from the point of view of the incumbents or the group that is being challenged" (Oberschall 1973, p. 28).

RM theorists assume grievances are widespread and the motivation to participate in social activism is constant. Rather than focusing on motivation, the central focus of RM theorists is on the differential ability of groups to organize around these grievances. Microstructural explanations do not focus on the question "Why do individuals participate?" Rather, they provide answers to the question "Why do so many others fail to participate?"

[2]The reader is referred to the review of the social movement literature by McAdam, McCarthy, and Zald (1988); we draw heavily from their review.

110   G. L. WILTFANG AND J. K. COCHRAN

RM analysts downplay the role of beliefs, attitudes, and ideology and focus on microstructural factors to account for social
movement recruitment and participation. At least two microstructural factors are consistently found to predict activism: a history of
prior activism and biographical availability.

Biographical availability is defined as "the absence of personal constraints that might increase the costs and risks of movement participation." Examples include lack of full-time employment and limited or no family responsibilities (McAdam 1986,
p. 70). This explanation focuses on the biographical context in
which contact between the would-be participant and the movement is accomplished. A negative relationship is predicted between biographical availability and activism: social constraints decrease the likelihood of activism.

McCarthy and Zald (1973) note that the unusually high numbers of students and autonomous professionals active in movements reflect the way biography constrains activism. Snow and
Rochford (1983, p. 3) found that "a substantial majority of [Hare]
Krishna recruits had few countervailing ties which might have
served to constrain their participation in the movement." The influence of biographical availability has also been demonstrated in
a number of other studies (e.g., Rochford 1985; McAdam 1986).

The other factor, a history of prior activism, highlights the
importance of socialization. Socialization is defined as "processes
by which individuals selectively acquire skills, knowledge, attitudes, values, and motives current in the groups of which they are
or will become members" (Sewell 1963). Traditional contexts of
socialization include: family, church, school, and peer group (Gecas 1981). But as Snow and Machalek (1982), Snow et al. (1986),
and McAdam (1986) remind us, socialization also takes place in
the context of social movements. Activists do not generally "join"
social movements as full-fledged activists. Instead, they are gradually socialized into the behavioral requirements and ideological
proscriptions peculiar to the movement and expected of the activists. A history of prior activism is thus positively linked to movement participation through its socializing effect.

Three explanations are used to account for the positive relationship between prior and subsequent activism. The first is that
prior experience with activism increases one's skills. Familiarity
with a particular form of social behavior increases the likelihood of
subsequent involvement. Familiarity may come from sources other

than direct experience, but experience is by far the most important. Individuals who have engaged in collective action in the past can be expected to be more likely to possess the knowledge required to do so in the future.

A second explanation centers on role theory and the process by which individuals learn any new social role (McAdam 1986). The point is that "activist" is as much a social role as "college student" or "sociologist." In the course of movement activities, new recruits are gradually socialized into this role (Lofland 1977). The longer they stay in the movement, the greater the importance recruits are likely to attach to the role of "activist" and the more salient that identity becomes for them. As one accords any role greater importance, the desire to act out the role increases, so that subsequent activism becomes a means of confirming or reinforcing an important part of one's identity.

A third explanation rests on the "opportunity costs" expended in any longstanding line of action. One can be thought to invest time, energy, and relationships, as well as more tangible resources, in pursuing activism. The costs of exit from such a line of action are thus substantial and thereby encourage continued adherence to the role.

Theories of Crime and Delinquency

Differential association/social learning theory (Sutherland and Cressey 1966; Burgess and Akers 1966; Akers et al. 1979; Akers 1985) and social control theory (Hirschi 1969) continue to serve as leading explanations of social deviance, especially adolescent deviance. Tests of these theories, empirically comparing the scope and power of two or more of them, and various attempts to integrate these theories form a large research literature. Yet, it should be noted that these theories have been tested primarily with survey data on adolescent deviance, not adult deviance. Moreover, these theories have not been tested with data on the defiant acts of social movement activists.

Differential Association/Social Learning Theory

Sutherland's differential association theory is probably the most influential of the sociological theories of deviant socialization. He and others in that tradition have directed their attention to articulating the social psychological processes involved in deviant socialization (Liska 1987). The theory states that deviant behavior

112   G. L. WILTFANG AND J. K. COCHRAN

is an expression of attitudes (definitions) favorable to deviant behavior learned in association with others in intimate social relations.

Burgess and Akers (1966) integrated differential association
theory with behavioral reinforcement theory to produce a theory of
deviant behavior that has come to be referred to as social learning
theory (Akers 1985). They assume that behavior is a response to
rewards and punishments. As the balance of rewards and punishments that follow behavior increase, the frequency of the behavior
increases. This formulation argues that deviant behavior is no different from any other behavior; it can be understood as a response
to rewards and punishments.

Thus, defiant behavior is expected when there is exposure to
models exhibiting defiant behavior (imitation), when there is more
association with defiants and their norms than with conformists
(differential association), when defiance is differentially reinforced
(that is, a greater balance of rewards to costs; differential reinforcement), and where there are more positive or neutralizing attitudes
than negative attitudes (definitions) toward defiance.

Social Control Theory

While there are a number of different social control theories
(Kornhauser 1978; Liska 1987), they all share the same premise: a
weakening of conventional social controls leads to deviance. Control theories differ from differential association/social learning theories on the role of deviant motivation in deviant behavior. Social
learning theorists assume that deviants differ from conformists in
terms of deviant motivation. They focus on how some people, but
not others, come to acquire these motives. The theory predicts that
as a consequence of interaction in primary social relations, some
people learn attitudes and values that motivate or "push" them
into norm violations.

Social control theorists, on the other hand, assume that norm
violations are generally so attractive, exciting, and profitable that
most people are naturally inclined or motivated to violate or challenge norms. For example, Hirschi (1969, p. 31) argues that it is not
necessary to explain the motivation for delinquency since "we are
all animals and thus all naturally capable of committing criminal
acts." Rather than assuming a high level of conformist motivation
and asking why some people violate norms, control theorists assume a high level of deviant motivation and ask why most people

conform. Social control theorists assume that people conform because of inner and outer social controls. The theory predicts the highest level of deviance from those for whom such controls are weak, broken, or nonexistent.

A leading version of control theory is Hirschi's (1969) social bonding theory, which focuses on a combination of controls or bonds to society. The theory proposes four "elements" that serve to bind or integrate the individual to society: attachment to others, commitment to conventional lines of activity, involvement in conventional activities, and belief in general conventional norms. If these elements are strong, conformity is expected; when they are weakened or fail to develop, then individuals are free to pursue their inclination toward deviance. Thus, control theory predicts that defiant behavior is more likely when attachment to others is low, when commitment to and involvement in conventional activities is low, and when there is low belief in general conventional norms.

A Theoretical Confluence Between the Dominant Theoretical Explanations

It can be said from the outset that both sets of theories (i.e., microstructural theories of social movement activism and theories of deviance) are versions of both socialization theory and control theory. They vary in their degree of clarity and in the explicitness of their concepts and propositions. Moreover, a concern with testing competing theories and with theoretical integration is far more developed in criminology than in the study of social movement activism (cf., Wiltfang 1993).

It should be clear that microstructural accounts of movement activism and control theories are based on similar assumptions: the motivation to participate, whether in delinquency or social movement activism, is held to be fairly constant. The microstructural accounts are, in essence, control theories. While less explicit than Hirschi's bonding theory, we believe a case can be made that focuses on the absence of personal constraints that decrease the costs and risks of defiant activism. For adults, these constraints would involve full-time employment, marriage and family responsibilities, attendance at religious services, and other attachments, commitments, and involvements. Both biographical availability and social control theory predict a constraining effect of these factors on defiant behavior.

114   G. L. WILTFANG AND J. K. COCHRAN

Likewise, defiant behavior is predicted by the socialization theories of both substantive areas to be positively associated with the influence of other activists, the amount of time devoted to social movement activities, and previous experiences with social activism. Our task is to assess the relative efficacy of social learning and social control theories in predicting the defiant behavior of sanctuary activists.

DATA AND METHODS

The study is limited to the defiant acts of sanctuary activists in Tucson, Arizona. The choice is a logical one. First, the lead author lived in Tucson for several years, making it possible to study the movement. Second, his active participation in local sanctuary activities afforded an entree to local activists not available elsewhere. Third, while other areas of the country are active in sanctuary activities, Tucson is seen by many people as the birthplace of the movement. However, the single most important consideration in our decision was Tucson's close proximity—roughly 90 miles—to the United States-Mexico border.

Tucson's location near the United States-Mexico border significantly affects the *form* of sanctuary activities take there. Tucson is located in one of three corridors (the other two being California and Texas) through which people from Mexico and Central America enter the United States. Consequently, a considerable amount of volunteer effort is expended in helping refugees to cross the border safely and to avoid contact with U.S. border officials. Also, because of Tucson's location, many refugees find their own way to sanctuary churches in Tucson to seek help. As a result, the ranks of Tucson sanctuary activists include many who are involved in what objectively are the most defiant of movement activities. This fact assured us of an identifiable population of sanctuary activists and sufficient variation in our dependent variable, defiant behavior.

The lead author's status as an "insider" allowed him to distribute questionnaires to the movement's rank-and-file membership. Questionnaires were distributed at several meetings of movement activists. In addition, questionnaires were given to several activists who agreed to distribute them to participants engaged in perhaps the most defiant and dangerous form of sanctuary activism, the pickup and transporting of the refugees. These data-gathering efforts resulted in a total of 51 completed questionnaires.

To insure that persons with more marginal activist involvement were also included in the sample (for example, those who only contributed money or clothing or attended fund-raising events), questionnaires were mailed to 180 individuals on a list of persons who had made financial contributions to the movement. Ninety of the 180 questionnaires were returned. Thus, a final sample of 141 persons was drawn.

Measurement of Variables

Dependent Variables

Sanctuary workers who have direct contact with undocumented Central Americans face legal risks and costs. Each refugee contact can carry a prison sentence of up to 5 years and/or fines up to $2,000. In addition, workers who are stopped by the border patrol during a run from the border may have the vehicles used in transporting Central Americans seized and auctioned by the government, whether or not formal charges are brought against the sanctuary workers.

We capture some of the risks associated with this defiant behavior through three measures. First, an additive index of involvement in defiant sanctuary activities was constructed from respondents' reports of their participation in six sanctuary activities that involve direct contact with undocumented Central Americans: transporting refugees across the border, around town, and out of town; providing educational services for them; and finding housing and jobs for them. Respondents were asked to indicate whether or not they had ever participated in any of these activities. Slightly more than a third of our sample (38%) reported having participated in at least one activity. In addition to this index, two measures of the frequency of participation in specific high-risk defiant activities are included in the analysis. Respondents were asked to indicate how many times they have transported refugees both from the border as well as around town.

Independent Variables

Six indicators of concepts central to social learning theory are used to predict these four indicators of defiant behavior. First, a trichotomous measure of differential association (DA1) was constructed from the responses given to two items: "Did you know anyone who was active in sanctuary before you got involved?"

116   G. L. WILTFANG AND J. K. COCHRAN

and "Did they influence you to become involved?". Possible responses were (1) Didn't know anyone before involvement; (2) Knew someone, but wasn't influenced by them; and (3) Knew someone and was influenced by them. This variable captures the "significant other" component of differential association theory. We expect the variable to be positively associated with involvement in the high-risk defiant activities of sanctuary participation.

Our second social learning variable measures the respondent's estimation of the number of hours per week, on average, that he or she is involved in a large and varied array of both mundane and defiant sanctuary activities (SANCHRS). This variable serves as a measure of the participant's frequency of exposure to prodefiant patterns. It too is expected to be positively related to the dependent variables.

Evidence shows that prior experience in other forms of social activism paves the way for future involvements (McAdam et al. 1988). Respondents were asked to report on their prior participation in other, nonsanctuary social movement actions. Three variables measure this experience and represent exposure to prodefiant learning environments. The first (OTHACT) is an additive index of affirmative responses to a four-item inventory of prior activist experiences. Respondents were asked whether they had ever taken part in a labor strike, a civil rights demonstration, an antiwar demonstration, or school-related demonstrations. We predict that higher scores on this prior activism index will be associated with higher scores on the dependent variables.

Respondents were also asked about their prior social movement involvements. They were asked to indicate whether or not they are or have been involved in 15 social movements. Affirmative responses were summed into an additive index of social movement involvement (SOCMINV). Again, high scores on this index represent exposure to prodefiant learning environments and are hypothesized to be positively associated with the high-risk defiant activities of sanctuary activists.

A third measure of prior experience describes the level of activism of the respondent's family. Subjects were asked to indicate whether or not, while they were growing up, their family environment included "a tradition of radical activism." Affirmative answers indicate an early learning environment through which models of activism could be imitated. This measure is also consistent with Sutherland's concept of "priority." We expect that a history of family activism will be positively related to our defiant behavior variables.

The sixth and final social learning variable indirectly taps a level of social reinforcement for sanctuary participation. Respondents were asked to think of persons important to them and to estimate how many of these persons they would lose contact with if they did not participate in sanctuary activities (SANCFRND). We assume that the threat of losing these significant relationships, at least in part, may serve to maintain (reinforce) sanctuary involvement. Moreover, we suggest that this variable can also serve as a proxy measure of Sutherland's concept of "intensity." Whether used as a measure of social reinforcement (Akers 1985) or as a measure of intensity of associations (Sutherland and Cressey 1966), we expect a positive relationship between this variable and our dependent variables.

Thus, the survey instrument provides us with a set of six indicators that are reasonably consistent with the operational definitions of several key social learning concepts. These variables have been coded such that support for the theory will be indicated by positive correlations between them and the three measures of defiant behavior.

According to control theorists, the greater one's attachment and commitment to conventionality, the greater one is bonded to and integrated in society and the lower the probability of participation in defiant behavior. We assess the influences of six measures of the respondent's attachment or commitment to conventional statuses/roles and activities on our measures of defiant behavior.

First, respondents were asked whether they were employed full-time (WORKSTAT), whether they were married (MARSTAT), and whether they had any children living at home (KIDSHOME). They were also asked to report their level of educational attainment (NUMEDYRS), the number of voluntary organizations to which they belong (NUMORG), and how often they attend religious services (ATTEND). Each of these six items are surrogate measures of control theory concepts of adult-level attachment and commitment to conventionality; they are proxies for ties that bind. Following social control theory, we expect that respondents who work full-time, are married, and have children living at home are less likely to participate in the high-risk defiant activity of the sanctuary movement. In addition, we expect that those who have

118   G. L. WILTFANG AND J. K. COCHRAN

attained higher levels of education, who are active members in voluntary organizations, and who attend religious services regularly are less likely to participate in high-risk defiance. Support for social control theory will be indicated by negative correlations observed between these six variables and the four measures of defiant behavior.

Method of Analysis

Ordinary least squares (OLS) multiple regression techniques were used in our analysis. Separate regression equations for the variables of social learning theory and social control theory are constructed first. Then, all 12 exogenous variables are placed in a single regression equation. Our concern is with both the relative and cumulative effects of the variables from these two rival theories. The standard level of statistical significance ($p < .05$) is used; however, because the sample was purposive, these significance levels are included for heuristic purposes only. Our aim is to predict relationships between theoretically meaningful variables in this sample, not to make predictions about some larger population.

FINDINGS

Tables 1 through 3 present the results of the OLS regression analyses testing the relative effects of variables from the two theories on the three measures of defiant acts. The results of our analyses provide considerable support for social learning theory, but clearly fail to support social control theory. In fact, the few significant parameter estimates of social control effects are, by and large, in the direction opposite to that predicted by the theory. That is, social control effects are positively associated with these forms of defiant behavior, not negatively associated as predicted from the theory.

In Table 1, the additive index of involvement in defiant sanctuary activities is regressed upon the various independent variables in three separate models: Model 1 presents the findings for the effects of the social learning theory indicators, Model 2 presents the findings of the social control model, and Model 3 presents the findings of a combined social learning-social control model. Three variables in the social learning model (Model 1) are significantly and positively related to the defiant behavior index; these are: average hours per week devoted to sanctuary activities (B = .24),

TABLE 1. Prevalence of participation in defiant activities

| | Prevalence of Participation in Defiant Activities[a] | | | | | |
| | 1 | | 2 | | 3 | |
Variable	b	B	b	B	b	B
DA1	.079	.048			.033	.020
	(.118)				(.119)	
SANCHRS	.033	.243*			.029	.218*
	(.010)				(.010)	
OTHACT	.299	.235*			.258	.203*
	(.107)				(.108)	
SANCFRND	.856	.391*			.910	.415*
	(.167)				(.171)	
SOCMINV	−.022	−.109			−.025	−.126
	(.017)				(.017)	
FAMACT	−.164	−.031			−.094	−.018
	(.390)				(.392)	
WORKSTAT			.479	.154*	.374	.120
			(.276)		(.241)	
MARSTAT			−.209	−.066	.081	.026
			(.294)		(.250)	
KIDSHOME			.625	.184*	.482	.142*
			(.325)		(.283)	
NUMEDYRS			.026	.043	.020	.033
			(.052)		(.044)	
NUMORG			.001	.002	−.036	−.063
			(.052)		(.047)	
ATTEND			.121	.155*	.063	.080
			(.068)		(.059)	
constant	.078		−.211		−.586	
R^2	.343*		.096*		.401*	
F	11.68		2.38		7.14	
	$p < .0001$		$p = .0324$		$p < .0001$	

*Indicates significance at the .05 level.
[a]Unstandardized and standardized regression coefficients with standard errors in parentheses.

prior activism (B = .24), and friendships established through sanctuary involvement (B = .39). Overall, this model accounts for 34.3% of the variance in the defiant behavior index. Thus, these data support social learning theory.

The social control model (Model 2), on the other hand, fails to receive support from these data; for instance, the model ac-

120   G. L. WILTFANG AND J. K. COCHRAN

counts for only 9.6% of the variance in the dependent variable. Moreover, while three indicators of social control attain statistically significant effects, none of the effects are in the theoretically expected, inverse direction. Instead, they are positively related to the defiant behavior index and suggest that those who have developed and maintained a bond to conventional society are in fact more likely to engage in the defiant behaviors associated with sanctuary.

The findings in the combined model (Model 3) replicate those of the separate models (Models 1 and 2). Social learning theory variables are significantly and positively related to defiant behavior, while indicators of social control theory are neither significantly nor inversely correlated with defiance. Furthermore, when the social learning variables are first entered into the model as a block, they account for 34% of the variance in the dependent variable, and the inclusion of the social control variables adds only another 5.8% to the variance explained. If the ordering of these blocks of variables is reversed, such that the social control variables are entered first, then the difference in the power of these two rival models is still observed. When entered first as a block, the social control measures account for only about 10% of the variance in the defiant behavior index, and the social learning variables account for an additional 30% of the variance. Thus, these data provide clear and consistent support for social learning theory and provide little support for social control theory.

Similar results are observed in Table 2. Here, the same models described in Table 1 are used to explain variation in the reported frequency of transporting refugees from the border. Again, only social learning theory finds support. In the social learning model (Model 1), two measures are significantly related to transporting refugees: friendships established through sanctuary involvement ($B = .38$) and prior activism within the family of orientation ($B = .14$). This model accounts for 17% of the variance in the dependent variable.

The social control model (Model 2) accounts for only 5% of the variance in the dependent variable and does not attain statistical significance ($F = 1.28$, $p = .2960$). Two of the model's measures are significant, but only one, having children at home, is related to the dependent variable in the predicted, negative direction ($B = -.19$). When indicators of both theories are combined into a single model (Model 3), the same general pattern of findings in

TABLE 2. Frequency of transporting refugees across border

	Frequency of Transporting Refugees Across Border[a]					
	1		2		3	
Variable	b	B	b	B	b	B
DA1	.168	.016			.172	.016
	(.835)				(.848)	
SANCHRS	.079	.093			.083	.098
	(.071)				(.073)	
OTHACT	−.324	−.040			−.452	−.056
	(.758)				(.775)	
SANCFRND	5.199	.377*			5.591	.405*
	(1.180)				(1.222)	
SOCMINV	−.149	−.120			−.141	−.113
	(.119)				(.124)	
FAMACT	4.875	.145*			3.951	.117
	(2.755)				(2.801)	
WORKSTAT			3.744	.192*	3.865	.198*
			(1.777)		(1.720)	
MARSTAT			.356	.018	1.219	.061
			(1.898)		(1.789)	
KIDSHOME			−4.093	−.192*	−3.545	−.166*
			(2.097)		(2.021)	
NUMEDYRS			−.383	−.102	−.359	−.095
			(.338)		(.317)	
NUMORG			−.006	−.002	−.071	−.020
			(.333)		(.335)	
ATTEND			−.123	−.025	−.595	−.121
			(.438)		(.423)	
constant	.572		8.317		7.704	
R^2	.173*		.052		.229*	
F	4.67		1.23		3.17	
	$p < .0002$		$p = .2960$		$p < .0006$	

*Indicates significance at the .05 level.

[a]Unstandardized and standardized regression coefficients with standard errors in parentheses.

Models 1 and 2 is observed. Again, the power of social learning theory is clearly evident. Social learning variables account for 17.3% of the variance in the dependent variable when entered first and 18% when entered last. Bonding variables, on the other hand, account for only 5.2% when entered first and 5.6% when entered last.

TABLE 3. Frequency of transporting refugees around town

	Frequency of Transporting Refugees Around Town[a]					
	1		**2**		**3**	
Variable	**b**	**B**	**b**	**B**	**b**	**B**
DA1	−1.775	−.092			−2.542	−.131
	(1.530)				(1.545)	
SANCHRS	.419	.266*			.443	.282*
	(.130)				(.133)	
OTHACT	.206	.014			−.188	−.013
	(1.387)				(1.412)	
SANCFRND	6.576	.258*			6.859	.269*
	(2.160)				(2.227)	
SOCMINV	−.004	−.002			.016	.007
	(.218)				(.226)	
FAMACT	4.936	.079			5.072	.082
	(5.045)				(5.105)	
WORKSTAT			3.880	.107	3.545	.098
			(3.286)		(3.134)	
MARSTAT			1.362	.037	4.367	.118
			(3.511)		(3.261)	
KIDSHOME			2.324	.059	.827	.021
			(3.878)		(3.683)	
NUMEDYRS			.748	.107	.950	.136
			(.623)		(.577)	
NUMORG			−.476	−.071	−.855	−.128
			(.615)		(.610)	
ATTEND			1.044	.115	.632	.069
			(.810)		(.772)	
constant	3.076		−10.978		−15.872	
R^2	.189*		.052		.251*	
F	5.22		1.22		3.58	
	$p = .0001$		$p = .2979$		$p = .0001$	

*Indicates significance at the .05 level.
[a]Unstandardized and standardized regression coefficients with standard errors in parentheses.

Table 3 presents the findings from tests of the two theories on the frequency of transporting refugees around town. As in the previous two tables, the data provide some support for social learning theory and little support for social control theory. For instance, the social learning model (Model 1) significantly accounts for 18.9% of the variance in the dependent variable, while in Model 2, the social control model, only 5.2% is explained. Moreover, the social control model fails to attain statistical significance ($F = 1.22$, $p = .2979$). Two of the six social learning variables are significantly and positively related to this form of defiant behavior: SANCHRS ($B = .27$) and SANCFRND ($B = .26$). However, none of the effects of the social control measures attain statistical significance.

The combined social learning-social control model (Model 3) produces identical results to those observed in Models 1 and 2 and in the previous tables. That is, the social learning variables clearly outperform the social control variables in explaining adult defiant behavior.

Social Control Theory: A Caveat

What can we conclude from our analyses? On the one hand, these data provide consistent support for social learning theory and fail to support social control theory. These findings hold for each of the three measures of defiant behavior associated with sanctuary work and suggest that both the scope and power of social learning theory is superior to that of its rival. Moreover, this conclusion concerning the superiority of social learning theory is consistent with the majority of studies that have examined the relative strengths of social learning theory and social control theories on more ordinary forms of deviant behavior such as delinquency and drug use (see, for instance, Elliott et al. 1985 or Akers and Cochran 1985). On the other hand, our data were never originally intended to measure social control variables; all of our measures are surrogates or proxies of social control concepts and we are limited by the secondary nature of this analysis. Hence, we are guarded against any statements that would bring premature closure to this issue. Had other measures been available, perhaps social control theory would have performed better at accounting for the defiant behavior we examined.

Moreover, some of our measures of social control, such as attendance at religious services, employment status, and the presence of children at home, produced positive rather than the expected negative effects on defiant behavior. We initially interpreted these findings as contradictory to social control predictions. However, upon closer examination, these findings are not so surprising. For instance, given that sanctuary is a religiously based social movement, it seems reasonable that its participants are themselves religious, as indicated by their reported attendance at religious services. Hence, the positive effect for this item should have been anticipated. Likewise, the lead author, a participant in the movement, observed during his activities that many of the employed participants held jobs in which they enjoyed great autonomy or that sanctuary activities (e.g., social services, teaching, etc.) fit nicely into the normal routines and responsibilities of their job (see Wiltfang and McAdam 1991 for an extended discussion of this finding). Many were clergy, teachers, university faculty, and other autonomous professionals. These occupations provided them with numerous opportunities to participate in sanctuary without adversely affecting their work status. Hence, the positive effect of employment status on defiant behavior observed here. Finally, while we predicted that having young children at home would constrain persons from participating in some of the more defiant aspects of the movement, we observed that this constraining effect was not only absent, but that participants with children were actually more involved in these activities. Interviews with these participants revealed that the movement worked out informal child care arrangements for members with children and that children present during a border run were used consciously for impression management purposes to give an image of conventionality (Wiltfang and McAdam 1991). In sum, the secondary nature of our data and the surrogate nature of some of our measures preclude us from dismissing social control theory entirely as a potential explanation for defiant activism. However, we are confident of social learning theory's ability to accurately predict these defiant sanctuary behaviors.

CONCLUSION

In this paper we introduce the concept of *defiant behavior,* actions which, although often defined as crimes by agents of social control, are defined by their actors as necessary, legitimate, and morally appropriate. Examples of such defiant actions are numerous and include, as discussed here, actions by members of the sanctuary movement to assist undocumented Central Americans with their attempts to gain entrance into the United States. Because defiant behaviors are typically organized actions of social activism, they are a highly salient topic of study for scholars of social movement participation. However, works within this area of study have been largely descriptive and often atheoretical. In fact, a concern for testing and integrating theories is underdeveloped within the sociology of social movements. Because movement actions are often defined as crimes, defiant actions should be an important area for criminologists to examine. Yet, criminology has generally ignored this issue and has made little use of existing theories to explain this type of defiance. We feel this is an unfortunate and unnecessary state of affairs; both of these areas of sociological study, as we have shown, can be greatly enhanced through disciplinary desegregation and cross-fertilization.

Our study is unique in that we addressed this problem by establishing the theoretical confluence between two of the leading theories of crime and deviance (i.e., social control theory and social learning theory) and microstructural factors associated with social activism from resource mobilization theory. Our aim was to test the scope of these overlapping theories with self-report survey data on the defiant actions of members of the sanctuary movement. We believe because of their shared substantive interest, scholars working in criminology and in social movements might mutually benefit from a theoretical and empirical project such as ours. For instance, the knowledge base and literature in the study of social movements can benefit from using well-developed theories in crime and deviance and adapting them to the special interests of the field. Likewise, theoretical and empirical interests in criminology and the sociology of deviance can be similarly promoted by using data and concepts from the social movement literature. As we see it, perhaps the most productive direction for this convergence is the type of behavior that is defiant, nonconformist, and associated with an organized social movement (e.g., efforts by members of the Plowshares to gain access to military bases where nuclear weapons are housed to protest their existence and to dismantle or disable them or the bombing of or blocking access to medical clinics by members of Operation Rescue to protest and prevent abortions).

We urge scholars working in these and other substantive areas to follow our lead. While most of us share at least an attachment to the idea that social factors are important in addressing questions about the human condition, we must also admit that we tend to live in quite different neighborhoods in our pursuit of this important idea. Communication between neighborhoods occasionally happens, but not often enough. The view of sociology as a united community of scholars working together on a common set

126   G. L. WILTFANG AND J. K. COCHRAN

of problems does not fit the reality of our current activities. This is a condition which, as we have shown here, can be rectified.

REFERENCES

Akers, Ronald L. 1985. *Deviant Behavior: A Social Learning Approach.* 3rd ed. Belmont, CA: Wadsworth.

Akers, Ronald L. and John K. Cochran. 1985. "Adolescent Marijuana Use: A Test of Three Theories of Deviant Behavior." *Deviant Behavior* 6:323–346.

Akers, Ronald L., Marvin D. Krohn, Lonn Lanza-Kaduce, and Marcia J. Radosevich. 1979. "Social Learning and Deviant Behavior: A Specific Test of a General Theory." *American Sociological Review* 44: 635–655.

Becker, Howard S. 1963. *Outsiders.* New York: Free Press.

Best, Joel (ed.). 1989. *Images of Issues: Typifying Contemporary Social Problems.* New York: Aldine de Gruyter.

Blumer, Herbert E. 1955. "Social Movements." Pp. 99–220 in *Principles of Sociology,* edited by A. M. Lee. New York: Barnes and Noble.

Burgess, Robert L. and Ronald L. Akers. 1966. "A Differential Association-Reinforcement Theory of Criminal Behavior." *Social Problems* 14:128–147.

Chambliss, William J. 1988. *Exploring Criminology.* New York: MacMillan.

Clinard, Marshall B. and Richard Quinney. 1967. *Criminal Behavior Systems: A Typology.* New York: Holt Rinehart and Winston.

Collins, Randall. 1986. "Is 1980s Sociology in the Doldrums?" *American Journal of Sociology* 91:1336–1355.

Crittenden, Ann. 1988. *Sanctuary.* New York: Weidenfeld and Nicolson.

Davidson, Miriam. 1988. *Convictions of the Heart: Jim Corbett and the Sanctuary Movement.* Tucson: University of Arizona Press.

Elliott, Delbert S., David Huizinga, and Suzanne S. Ageton. 1985. *Explaining Delinquency and Drug Use.* Beverly Hills, CA: Sage.

Ferrell, Jack F. and Gregory L. Wiltfang. 1988. "The Sanctuary Movement on Stage: The Politics and Morality of a Central and North American Drama." *Review of Latin American Studies* 1:11–20.

Gecas, Viktor. 1981. "Contexts of Socialization." Pp. 165–199 in *Social Psychology: Sociological Perspectives,* edited by Morris Rosenberg and Ralph Turner. New York: Basic Books.

Golden, Renny, and Michael McConnell. 1986. *Sanctuary: The New Underground Railroad.* Mary Knoll, NY: Orbis Books.

Greenberg, David F. (ed.). 1981. *Crime and Capitalism.* Palo Alto, CA: Mayfield.

Gusfield, Joseph R. 1955. "Social Structure and Moral Reform: A Study of the Women's Christian Temperance Union." *American Journal of Sociology* 61:221–232.

Hagan, John and John H. Simpson. 1974. "Ties that Bind: Conformity and the Social Control of Student Discontent." *Sociology and Social Research* 61:521–538.

Hildreth, Anne Marie. 1989. "Collective Action, Individual Incentives, and Political Intent: The Sanctuary Movement." Dissertation: University of Iowa.

Hirschi, Travis. 1969. *Causes of Delinquency.* Berkeley, CA: University of California Press.

Horowitz, Irving Louis and Martin Liebowitz. 1968. "Social Deviance and Political Marginality: Toward a Redefinition of the Relation between Sociology and Politics." *Social Problems* 15:280–296.

Kircheimer, Otto. 1961. *Political Justice: The Use of Legal Procedure for Political Ends.* Princeton, NJ: Princeton University Press.

Kornhauser, Ruth. 1978. *Social Sources of Delinquency.* Chicago: University of Chicago Press.

Kowalewski, David. 1990. "The Historical Structuring of a Dissident Movement: The Sanctuary Case. *Research in Social Movements, Conflict and Change.* 12:89–110.

Lemert, Edwin M. 1951. *Social Pathology.* New York: McGraw-Hill.

Liazos, Alexander. 1972. "The Poverty of the Sociology of Deviance: Nuts, Sluts, and Perverts." *Social Problems* 20:103–120.

Liska, Allen E. 1987. *Perspectives on Deviance.* 2nd ed. Englewood Cliffs, NJ: Prentice-Hall.

Lofland, John. 1977. *Doomsday Cult.* New York: Irvington.

MacEoin, Gary. 1985. *Sanctuary: A Resource Guide for Understanding and Participating in the Central American Refugees' Struggle.* San Francisco: Harper and Row.

MacEoin, Gary, and Nivita Riley. 1982. *No Promised Land: American Refugee Policy and the Rule of Law.* Boston: Oxfam America.

Mauss, Armand L. 1975. *Social Problems as Social Movements.* Philadelphia: Lippincott.

McAdam, Doug. 1986. "Recruitment to High-Risk Activism: The Case of Freedom Summer." *American Journal of Sociology* 92:64–90.

McAdam, Doug, John D. McCarthy, and Meyer N. Zald. 1988. "Social Movements." Pp. 695–737 in *Handbook of Sociology,* edited by Neil Smelser. Newbury Park, CA: Sage.

McCarthy, John D. and Mayer N. Zald. 1973. *The Trend of Social Movements in America: Professionalization and Resource Mobilization.* Morristown, NJ: General Learning Press.

Merton, Robert K. and Robert A. Nisbet (eds.). 1971. *Contemporary Social Problems* 3rd ed. New York: Harcourt, Brace, Jovanovich.

Oberschall, Anthony. 1973. *Social Conflict and Social Movements.* Englewood Cliffs, NJ: Prentice-Hall.

Quammen, David. 1986. "Seeking Refuge in a Desert: The Sanctuary Movement." *Harper's* 273:58–64.

Rochford, E. Burke. 1985. *Hare Krishna in America.* New Brunswick, NJ: Rutgers University Press.

Schur, Edwin M. 1980. *The Politics of Deviance.* Englewood Cliffs, NJ: Prentice-Hall.

Sewell, William H. 1963. "Some Recent Developments in Socialization Theory and Research." *The Annals of the American Academy of Political and Social Sciences* 349:163–181.

Simon, David R. and D. Stanley Eitzen. 1986. *Elite Deviance.* 2nd ed. Boston: Allyn and Bacon.

Snow, David A. and Richard Machalek. 1982. "On the Presumed Fragility of Unconventional Beliefs." *Journal for the Scientific Study of Religion* 21:15–26.

Snow, David A. and E. Burke Rochford, Jr. 1983, August. "Structural Availability, the Alignment Process and Movement Recruitment." Paper presented at the annual meeting of the American Sociological Association, Detroit, MI.

Snow, David A., Louis A. Zurcher, and Sheldon Ekland-Olson. 1986. "Social Networks and Social Movements: A Microstructural Approach to Differential Recruitment." *American Sociological Review* 45:787–801.

Spector, Malcolm and John I. Kitsuse. 1977. *Constructing Social Problems.* Menlo Park, CA: Cummings.

Sutherland, Edwin H. and Donald R. Cressey. 1966. *Criminology.* 7th ed. Philadelphia: Lippincott.

Thio, Alex. 1973. "Class Bias in the Sociology of Deviance." *The American Sociologist* 8:1–12.

Timmer, Doug A. and D. Stanley Eitzen (eds.). 1989. *Crime in the Streets and Crime in the Suites: Perspectives on Crime and Criminal Justice.* Boston: Allyn and Bacon.

United States v. Maria de Socorro Pardo de Aguilar et al. 871 F.2d 1436 (9th Cir. 1989).

Wiltfang, Gregory L. 1993. "Identity and Activism." Unpublished manuscript.

Wiltfang, Gregory L. and Doug McAdam. 1991. "The Costs and Risks of Social Activism: A Study of Sanctuary Movement Activism." *Social Forces* 69:987–1010.

Part IV
Immigrants as Victims

[19]

IMMIGRANTS AS VICTIMS OF CRIME

PETER L. MARTENS

National Council for Crime Prevention, P.O. Box 1386, SE-111 93 Stockholm, Sweden

ABSTRACT

The present paper is a review of the empirical research done on crime victimisation and anxieties about crime among immigrants and native Swedes. Immigrants more often than native Swedes have been a victim of personal crimes, whereas no differences worth mentioning are found regarding victimisation through property crimes. Immigrants more often than native Swedes are afraid of being victimised in various social contexts. Thereby, immigrants with a non-European appearance are more often a victim of personal crimes than are other immigrants. They also feel less safe in various everyday contexts. The relative impact of social background factors on crime victimisation and fear of crime is discussed. Swedish victim surveys are few in number and the present knowledge of crime victimisation and fear of crime in different ethnic groups is superficial. It is pointed out that more systematic research is needed.

INTRODUCTION

The Swedish research on immigrants' involvement in crime and the criminal justice system has to a great extent focused on immigrants as offenders (Ahlberg, 1996; von Hofer, Sarnecki and Tham, 1997; Martens, 1997a; Sveri, 1973, 1980, 1987; von Hofer, 1994). These studies have unanimously arrived at the conclusion that immigrants have higher crime participation rates than native Swedes. This is particularly the case for crimes of violence and theft crimes. Furthermore, the crime rates between various immigrant groups vary significantly (see Ahlberg, 1996; Martens, 1997a). Victim surveys are few in Sweden. Although victim studies have found that immigrants tend to be over-represented as victims of crime, this aspect has not been called to attention in the public debate on the immigrants' offending. Nor have the research findings from the victim studies left any very deep impression on the Swedish debate on criminal policy. The purpose of the present paper is to bring together the research results from the available victim studies and further illuminate in what ways immigrants and native Swedes differ regarding their exposure to crime and worries about being victimised.

Before presenting the surveys done so far to estimate the prevalence of victimisation of crime and fear of crime among immigrants and Swedes, it is necessary to give a short descriptive overview of the current immigrant population in Sweden and immigration to Sweden during the last 50 years.

200

IMMIGRANTS IN SWEDEN

The number of immigrants

At the end of 1994 the population of Sweden was approximately 8.8 million. Of this figure, about 922,000 persons were born abroad (first generation immigrants). This means that almost 10.5 percent of the Swedish population consists of first generation immigrants. About 537,500 persons were foreign nationals, i.e. slightly more than 6 percent of the population of the country. Slightly more than half the first generation immigrants had become Swedish citizens by the end of 1994.

There were about 676,500 second generation immigrants (persons born in Sweden, who had at least one parent born abroad) at the end of 1994, i.e. 8.5 percent of the population. These second generation immigrants were mostly Swedish citizens (85 percent).

To sum up, there were about 1.6 million people in Sweden who, at the end of 1994, were immigrants or had an immigrant background, i.e. slightly more than 18 percent of the Swedish population. Most of them, 72 percent, were Swedish citizens and 28 percent were foreign nationals.

Ethnic composition

The statistics of the immigrants' country of birth reveal that at the end of 1994 (Table 1), first generation immigrants were to a considerable extent persons born in a European country. A third of first generation immigrants were from a Scandinavian country and a third from another European country (Turkey not included). The Finns were by far the largest single group, comprising almost 23 percent of the total group. Persons born in the former Yugoslavia came next (12 percent of first generation immigrants) followed by Iran and Norway (5 percent each), Denmark, Poland and Germany (4 percent each), and finally Turkey and Chile (3 percent each).

Second generation immigrants are clearly dominated by persons with a Nordic background. Over half had parents from a Nordic country. By far the largest group are those with a Finnish background (a third of the total group of second generation immigrants). Persons whose parents came from Norway, Denmark and (West)Germany are also relatively common with percentages ranging from 7 to 10 percent. The composition of the national background of second generation immigrants is influenced to a substantial extent by immigrants who came to work in Sweden and then settled down in the 1970s and earlier.

TABLE 1
Persons with Immigrant Backgrounds, December 31, 1994

| Country of Birth | Born Aborad – First Generation | | Born in Sweden – Second Generation | | TOTAL |
	Swedish Nationals	Foreign Nationals	Swedish Nationals	Foreign Nationals	
Nordic Countries	*173 023*	*125 821*	*305 283*	*43 857*	*647 984*
Denmark	21 765	19 142	45 787	6 956	93 650
Finland	129 618	78 178	206 759	28 283	442 838
Iceland	380	3 905	1 152	921	6 358
Norway	21 260	24 591	54 787	7 697	108 340
Other European Countries	*151 921*	*154 582*	*161 358*	*21 638*	*489 499*
Greece	8 890	3 551	10 078	1 153	23 671
Yugoslavia	28 642	83 678	28 289	8 396	149 005
Poland	24 461	14 548	21 838	1 686	62 533
Romania	6 258	4 627	2 781	355	14 021
Gr. Britain	3 733	8 836	10 362	1 657	24 588
Germany	26 153	10 347	47 272	3 122	86 894
Hungary	11 783	3 016	12 524	323	27 646
Africa	*18 037*	*26 924*	*19 544*	*3 196*	*67 501*
Ethiopia	4 449	6 935	3 189	867	17 440
North-America	*7 245*	*8 353*	*15 872*	*1 498*	*32 968*
USA	6 362	7 384	14 239	1 347	29 332
Latin-America	*29 396*	*24 075*	*20 462*	*800*	*74 733*
Chile	13 241	13 954	10 350	184	37 729
Asia	*97 555*	*102 767*	*59 414*	*14 737*	*274 473*
India	8 299	1 654	3 513	141	13 607
Iraq	6 712	16 677	4 349	1 716	29 454
Iran	19 146	29 547	7 617	2 936	59 246
Rep Korea	7 981	466	1 421	27	9 895
Lebanon	10 414	11 179	8 591	1 064	31 248
Soc Rep Vietnam	5 872	3 347	2 964	443	12 626
Syria	5 157	3 915	5 538	435	15 045
Thailand	3 206	4 116	2 429	319	10 070
Turkey	13 450	15 792	14 237	6 706	50 185
Oceania	638	1 594	1 101	142	3 475
Unknown	44	80	389	7 377	7 890
TOTAL	477 859	444 196	583 223*	93 245	1 598 523

Note. 'Swedish Nationals' includes about 10,000 children of Swedes living abroad. Foreign born 'Swedish Nationals' includes former foreign nationals.
* The grand total 583,223 is the number of people with Swedish citizenship who have at least one parent born in another country. The subtotals show the number who have at least one parent from the indicated region. A person with one parent born in one region and the other parent born in another will be counted twice in the subtotals but only once in the total.
Source: Swedish Immigration Board (1995) p. 15.

202

Geographic differences

The proportion of persons born abroad is largest in the big cities. At the end of
1992, the proportion of persons born abroad was 16 percent in Greater Stockholm, just over 13 percent in Greater Malmö and just over 12 percent in Greater
Gothenburg. The proportions of persons with foreign nationality in these cities
were 10.2 percent, 8.0 percent and 7.8 percent respectively. There are large
variations within the big cities with a certain tendency for immigrant density to
be greatest in neighbourhoods with social poblems (low-status neighbourhoods)
and least in high-status neighbourhoods (neighbourhoods with private housing)
(Statistics Sweden and The National Board of Immigration, 1993: 30–31).

Immigration to Sweden

The ethnic composition of the immigrants in Sweden of today is a consequence
of the immigration that has taken place during the last 50 years. Sweden became
an immigrant country after World War II. During the war, Sweden accepted
around 130,000 refugees from the occupied neighbouring Nordic countries and
30,000 refugees from the Baltic States. When the war was over, Sweden adopted
a generous policy on refugees and immigrants and immigration exceeded emigration. Since then immigration has changed in character and may be described
as having two main phases: an influx of *immigrant labour* up to the end of the
1960s and an influx of *refugees* as from the beginning of the 1970s.

Swedish industry expanded rapidly after the war and there was a shortage of
indigenous labour. Labour had to be recruited in other countries. From the
post-war years up to the beginning of the 1970s, immigration consisted mainly
of an influx of immigrant labour. Most of these immigrants came from the Nordic
countries. During the 1950s, there was also an influx of labour from Germany,
Austria and Italy and in the 1960s from Yugoslavia and Greece. Throughout these
years immigration was relatively unrestricted.

However, at the end of the 1960s, the rules controlling immigrant labour from
non-Nordic countries were tightened up so that recruitment was brought into line
with labour market requirements. In 1972 recruitment of foreign labour ceased
entirely. Persons from the other Nordic countries were exempted from these rules
as the Nordic countries have had an open labour market since 1954. Since the
mid-1970s, the Nordic labour pool has also dwindled owing to a reduced demand
for labour.

Since the beginning of the 1970s immigration of refugees has gradually
increased. These refugees are mainly from eastern Europe and the Third World.
Another category of immigrants that has grown is family immigrants: this means
relatives of former labour immigrants (mainly Yugoslavs and Greeks) but above
all members of the families of refugees. Refugee immigration has resulted in a
radical change in the composition of the immigrant population. Increasingly

immigrants have come from non-European countries such as Chile, Iran and Turkey.

Up to the beginning of the 1970s roughly ten percent of immigrants came from a non-European country. Since then this percentage has gradually increased. From the mid-1980s up to the early 1990s, around half the immigrants came from a country outside Europe. Immigration from non-European countries has, with few exceptions, been immigration of refugees and has been strongly linked with political developments in the countries concerned, such as the military coup in Chile in 1973, the civil war in Eritrea (1985–1991) and the civil wars in the Middle East (Iran, Iraq, Lebanon, etc.). In recent years there has been an increase in migration from eastern Europe as a consequence of the fall of communism and, above all, the war in the former Yugoslavia.

VICTIM SURVEYS

Victim surveys in Sweden are few in number. Sweden participated in the International Crime Survey (Alvazzi del Frate, Zvekic and van Dijk, 1993), but this study did not collect any information about the respondents' immigrant background.

Statistics Sweden has carried out continuous surveys on the living conditions of the population since 1974 (Statistics Sweden, 1995). The purpose of these surveys is to study various welfare indicators such as health, economy, employment, education, housing, social life, etc. The degrees to which people are exposed to crime and show fear of crime in their neighbourhood are seen as important indicators of social welfare. The questions about exposure to crime have focused on crimes of violence and property crimes. In these surveys the respondents' ethnic background was categorised in broad terms such as respondent 'born in Sweden', 'born abroad' or respondent's 'parents born abroad'.

In the 1990s some smaller local crime and victim surveys were carried out and included both adults and schoolchildren. The Stockholm Project is an example (Wikström, 1990a). This project focused on eight neighbourhood areas in Stockholm. In the adult survey of 1990 about 1,600 persons living in the areas were sampled and interviewed by telephone, and asked *inter alia*, if they had been victims of violence and theft. The survey was replicated in 1992. The study of young people was of ninth-grade pupils in the schools located in the eight neighbourhood areas, carried out in class. A questionnaire was administered containing, *inter alia*, questions on victimisation. The study was carried out in 1990 and then replicated with a few changes to the questionnaire in 1992.

In 1993 the Swedish Center for Immigration Research (CEIFO) at Stockholm University carried out an extensive survey of attitudes towards immigrants in the Swedish population (Lange and Westin, 1993; Westin and Lange, 1993; Lange, 1995a, 1995b). A special survey of attitudes of immigrants from Finland, Poland, Chile and Iran towards Swedes was also carried out. In cooperation with the

204

Swedish National Council for Crime Prevention, some questions on fear of crime and being a victim of violence and theft were included. The results have been presented and discussed in greater detail in Martens (1997b).

Furthermore, Wikström (1985 and forthcoming) has made special studies of police recorded violent crimes and deadly violence, recording, among other background variables, the suspected persons' and their victims' country of birth.

VICTIMS OF CRIMES OF VIOLENCE

Three aspects of being a victim of violent crime will be considered here, namely violence causing death, violence causing physical injuries and threats of serious violence. Gaining an insight into lethal violence requires access to the reports of the police investigation and a systematic recording of relevant information from these reports. Information on exposure to violence causing injuries and exposure to threats of serious violence is best obtained by asking relevant questions in the kind of crime surveys mentioned above. However, one has to be aware that some respondents might perceive questions about their exposure to violent acts as a private matter and therefore be unwilling to give honest answers.

Violence causing death

The ethnicity of victims of lethal violence in Stockholm from 1951 to 1991 has, according to Wikström (forthcoming), changed over the four decades. In the 1950s, 4 percent of the male victims were born in a foreign country whilst in the 1980s the percentage was 28 percent. For female victims the increase was from 5 percent in the 1950s to 24 percent in the 1980s. The risk of becoming a victim of lethal violence during the period of 1980–1991 was most pronounced for immigrants with a Finnish background (9.4 per 100,000), followed by those with an African and a Latin–American background (5.4 and 2.7 per 100,000, respectively). For the Swedes the victimisation risk was 1.6 per 100,000 and for the foreign born, in total, 4.7 per 100,000.

Serious violence

The Swedish victimisation studies have shown that being a victim of violence with physical injuries is quite rare. The surveys of Statistics Sweden show that 2 percent of the native Swedes have been a victim of violence with visible marks within a period of one year. The corresponding rates are 2.2 percent for naturalized Swedish citizens, 3.2 percent for foreign citizens, 4.4 percent for Finnish citizens and 1.8 percent for citizens of a South-European country (Statistics Sweden, 1995 p. 75).

The surveys of Statistics Sweden found, furthermore, that serious violence is more than twice as common among second-generation immigrants than among native Swedes (4.4 percent versus 2 percent). However, the children of foreign born immigrants are quite young and, if age is controlled, the difference between second generation immigrants and native Swedes becomes less pronounced.

The adult interviews in the Stockholm Project in 1990 also showed some differences in exposure to violence between persons born in Sweden and persons born abroad. In 1989, 3.7 percent of persons born abroad experienced violence requiring medical attention at least once during a one-year period, compared to 0.6 percent of the indigenous Swedes (Wikström, 1991).

The CEIFO survey confirms that being a victim of violence causing physical injuries is rare among the different ethnic groups in the study. About two percent of the respondents in each group reported that they had been a victim, the difference between the groups not being statistically significant (Martens, 1997b).

Separate logistic regression analyses for immigrants and native Swedes in the CEIFO survey, where demographic variables were entered as regressors and victimization of serious violence was the dependent variable, resulted in slightly different patterns of correlation for the two groups (Martens, 1997b). Renting a flat in a publicly owned house (i.e. flats owned by non-profit organisations) was a significant factor for both the immigrants and the Swedes. All respondents who rented a flat in a publicly owned house were at greater risk of being a victim of serious violence than respondents living in a tenant-owned flat (condominium) or a single family house. Among immigrants, single persons were at greater risk than cohabiting persons. Among native Swedes male respondents were at greater risk than female respondents. Furthermore, young Swedish respondents (under 26 years of age) were at greater risk than their older counterparts of becoming a victim of serious violence.

The analyses of the CEIFO survey data also reveal that the respondents' lifestyle has an independent relationship with victimization by serious violence among indigenous Swedes but not among immigrants (Martens, 1997b). Swedes who often go out in the evening to enjoy themselves are at greater risk of being a victim of serious violence than Swedes who seldom or never go out in the evening. Among the immigrants there is no marked difference between persons with different lifestyles regarding their risk of victimisation.

Threats of violence

The surveys of Statistics Sweden reveal that persons with an immigrant background are more often exposed to some form of violence and threats of violence than are native Swedes (Statistics Sweden, 1995 Table 2.6). Among the native Swedes the prevalence of being as victim of threats is 3.6 percent compared to 5.2 percent asmong foreign citizens living in Sweden. The corresponding pre-

206

valences of being a victim of violence or threat of violence are almost 6 percent
and 8.6 percent respectively. Above all it is second generation immigrants who
are most exposed to violence. Only 6 percent of indigenous Swedes had been
victims of violence or threat of violence over a 12 month period, compared with
11 percent of second generation immigrants, though when age is controlled, the
difference turns out to be less apparent. Young people (16–24 years) are generally
those who are most exposed to these crimes. Throughout the population, 16
percent had been exposed to violence and threats of violence during 1992–1993,
whilst among second generation immigrants of similar age, the proportion was
19 percent. In the other age categories there is no difference worth mentioning
(Statistics Sweden, 1995, p. 76).

The CEIFO survey produces higher prevalence rates for threats of violence
than the surveys of Statistics Sweden. In the CEIFO survey slightly less than 14
percent of the native Swedes reported that they had been exposed to threats of
violence during 1992, which is a higher rate than for Finnish and Polish immigrants (see Table 2), but a lower rate than for the two non-European immigrant
groups.

TABLE 2
Prevalence of victimisation of serious threats during 1992 by country of birth and sex

Threats of violence	Country of birth				
	Iran	Chile	Poland	Finland	Sweden
Total	16.1	19.5	8.8	10.3	13.8***
Men	14.7	19.0	7.6	9.6	16.3
Women	19.3	20.0	9.4	10.8	11.0**

*** p<0.001
** p<0.01

Among the Polish and Finnish immigrants, female respondents, more often
than male respondents, report that they have experienced threats of violence.
Among native Swedes the relationship is the reverse.

Separate logistic regression analyses for the immigrants and the native Swedes
in the CEIFO survey (Martens, 1997b), where demographic variables were
entered into the model to explain the respondents' experiences of threats of
violence, reveal that being under the age of 26 and being single are two common
independent factors correlating with victimisation. Young respondents and single
respondents were at greater risk of being victims of threats of violence than older
and cohabiting respondents. Among immigrants, being not employed was an
additional significant risk factor. Among native Swedes the respondents' sex,
yearly income and type of tenure were additional significant independent factors.
For the Swedes being male, living in a household with a low income and renting

a flat in a publicly owned house (owned by a non-profit organisation) were conditions associated with having been exposed to threats of violence.

Furthermore, the respondents' lifestyle has an independent effect on their experience of threats (Martens, 1997b). Those who often went out to enjoy themselves in the evening were more often exposed to threats than those who seldom or never went out in the evening. Separate analyses for the different immigrant groups reveal that this relationship holds good among the Swedes and the other two European immigrant groups. There is no relationship between lifestyle and experience of threats worth mentioning among the two non-European groups.

By whom were the victimized respondents threatened when it happened the last time?

The results of the CEIFO survey show that it is considerably more common that the threatening person is unknown to the victim (the respondent) than that the person is acquainted with or is closely related to the victim (Martens, 1997b). The commonest context of exposure to threat is in the context of leisure activities in a public place, with the threat being from a stranger. This might occur, for example, when the victim is visiting a pub, a restaurant or some other place of entertainment. This form of threat is more prevalent among males than among females in all ethnic groups.

Serious threats from a person with whom the victim is cohabiting or had cohabited, i.e. threats related to family conflicts, are more common among immigrant groups than among native Swedes (Martens, 1997b). In all ethnic groups women are more often exposed to family related threats than are men.

Males from a non-European country (Iran and Chile) were more likely than females to report that they had been subjected to threats by a stranger when at work. The relationship is the reverse among European groups, especially among native Swedes. Here females more often than males report that they have been subjected to threats by a stranger when at work (Martens, 1997b). The difference can probably be explained by the different kinds of jobs done by different immigrant groups and by the extent to which men and women from the different groups are in the workforce.

It is furthermore more common among immigrants of non-European origin (from Iran and Chile) than among their European counterparts that they have been seriously threatened because of their appearance, their foreign accent or their ethnic background. This is the case for both males and females.

208

VICTIMS OF PROPERTY CRIMES

The surveys of Statistics Sweden have demonstrated that households with an immigrant background are more often than native Swedes exposed to property crimes in the form of theft or damage. About a third of the persons with foreign citizenship reported that they themselves, or somebody in their household, had been a victim of a property crime at least once during a one-year period. Among naturalized Swedish citizens the prevalence rate was 28 percent and among children of immigrants (second generation immigrants) 33 percent. This has to be compared to 24 percent in the total population (Statistics Sweden, 1995 p. 139). However, the differences between native Swedes and respondents with different ethnic backgrounds disappear when demographic variables such as sex, age, phase in the family cycle, region of residence and type of housing are controlled for.

A weakness of the surveys of Statistics Sweden is that victimisation through theft or damage were not treated as separate phenomena. The CEIFO survey, on the other hand, asked separate questions about the respondents' experiences as a victim of theft and a victim of property damage (Martens, 1997b).

Theft

In the CEIFO survey about a quarter of the respondents reported that somebody in their household had been subjected to theft during 1992 (Martens, 1997b). The variation between the different ethnic groups was small and not statistically significant. The most common types of theft were theft of a bicycle, motorcycle or parts of these vehicles, theft of an object in or from a car and theft of an object stored in a cellar, loft or other storage space. The differences between ethnic groups were small and not statistically significant, with the exception of theft of property from a storage space, for which Polish and Chilean households were more likely to report that they had been a victim.

Separate logistic regression analyses for immigrants and native Swedes were performed, where demographic variables were entered as regressors into the model and the households' experience of theft of property was the dependent variable. The analyses revealed (Martens, 1997b) that the respondents' age was a significant independent factor. Young respondents (under the age of 26), whether a native Swede or an immigrant, were more likely to report that they themselves or somebody in their household had had their property stolen at least once during a one-year period. Among native Swedes, living in a big city county was an additional risk factor and among immigrants having a higher education was a factor associated with victimisation.

Damage to property

Between 10 and 15 percent of the respondents in the different ethnic groups in the CEIFO survey said that they or somebody in their household had had their property damaged at least once during 1992 (Martens, 1997b). The difference between the groups was not statistically significant. The commonest form of damage was that done to a car, followed by damage done to something on a car or in a car and damage done to property in the victim's dwelling. There was no significant difference between ethnic groups.

Marked differences between ethnic groups were, however, found for damage done to a motorcycle or a bicycle and to property stored in a cellar, loft, garage etc. Households with an Iranian background were less likely to be exposed to damage done to a motorcycle or bicycle. Immigrants from Chile and Poland were more likely to have their property damaged when stored in a cellar, loft or garage (see Martens, 1997b).

Separate logistic regression analyses for immigrants and native Swedes were carried out, whereby background variables were entered into the regression model as independent variables and the households' exposure to property damage as the dependent variable. The analyses revealed (Martens, 1997b) that living in a big city county is the only independent factor associated with a household being a victim of property damage. This was the case both for immigrants and for native Swedes.

FEAR OF CRIME

Being afraid of becoming a victim of crime in various everyday contexts can circumscribe a person's social life. This fear of crime can result in a person tending to avoid different social and cultural events in which he or she might otherwise have participated. To put it in Hale's words

> "People who are afraid of being criminally victimised change their habits ... If they do go out they tend to constrain their behaviour to safe places at safe times. They tend to avoid activities they perceive as dangerous, such as walking down some streets, getting close to particular 'types of people', travelling on public transport, or going to certain forms of public entertainment." (Hale, 1996; p. 82).

The surveys of Statistics Sweden have shown that immigrants are more likely than native Swedes to feel uneasy about going out in the evening, even in their own neighbourhood. There is a tendency for immigrants from a non-Nordic country to feel less comfortable than immigrants from Nordic countries. About 17 percent of native Swedes had refrained at least once from going out in the evening because they feel unsafe. The corresponding percentage for naturalized

210

immigrants was 27 percent, for foreign citizens 26 percent and for citizens of non-Nordic countries 32 percent. Almost 9 percent of native Swedes have often refrained from going out in the evening, compared to 18 percent of naturalized immigrants, 14 percent of foreign citizens and almost 18 percent of non-Nordic citizens (Statistics Sweden, 1995 p. 271).

The adult survey of the Stockholm Project in 1990 showed that respondents born in a foreign country were more likely than those born in Sweden to feel unsafe when going out in the evening in their own neighbourhood. However, when other background factors were controlled for, the relationship between foreign background and feeling unsafe in one's neighbourhood almost disappeared (Wikström, 1991 p. 53).

In the CEIFO survey 'fear of crime' was indexed by a composite measure consisting of items reflecting whether the respondents feel uncomfortable or not in five different social contexts, namely (a) going to the movies or to the theatre; (b) going to a restaurant, a disco or a bar; (c) going to a sports event (such as a soccer or an ice hockey game); (d) going to a club meeting or an evening class; and (e) going by bus or tram (i.e. using public transport). Those who avoided at least one of these situations were defined as being afraid of being criminally victimised (see Martens, 1997b).

The prevalence of fear of crime varied significantly between the ethnic groups surveyed in the CEIFO study (see Table 3). Fear of crime was most prevalent among the non-European immigrants (Iranians and Chileans) and least prevalent among native Swedes and Finnish immigrants. Among the non-European immigrants in the survey, about 22 percent worried about crime in at least one of the social contexts. Among the Swedes and Finns the prevalance rate was about 10 percent.

TABLE 3
Percentage of respondents who worry about becoming a victim of crime in five different social contexts by country of birth

Fear of crime	Country of birth				
	Iran	Chile	Poland	Finland	Sweden
Percentage worrying	22.3	21.8	16.2	10.6	9.3***

*** p<0.001

Separate logistic regression analyses for the immigrants and the native Swedes in the CEIFO survey were performed with the social background factors as regressors and the index of fear of crime as the dependent variable. The analyses revealed (see Martens, 1997b) that living in a big city county is a common independent factor correlated with fear of crime. No matter whether the respondent was an immigrant or a native Swede, those who live in a big city county were more likely to feel so insecure that they avoided various day-to-day situations. In addition, low household income was a significant factor among immigrants and being a female was an important factor among Swedes in explaining respondents' fear of crime.

When exposure to serious violence or threats of serious violence (here as a composite variable) and exposure to property crimes (both theft and damage of property) are entered as two regressors, in addition to the social background factors, into the regression model to explain fear of crime, it appeared (see Martens, 1997b) that experience as a victim of crime is part of the explanation of respondents' fear of crime. Among native Swedes it is mainly exposure to violence or threat of violence that has an independent relationship with fear of crime. Among immigrants, both experience as a victim of violence or threats of violence and experience as a victim of property crime influence feelings of insecurity in various day-to-day contexts.

In a logistic regression analysis based on all ethnic groups in the CEIFO survey (i.e. all the respondents in the survey for whom the index of fear of crime was relevant) and where the respondents' country of birth was entered as a separate regressor into the model to explain fear of crime in addition to the other social background factors, it appeared (see Martens, 1997b) that being a female respondent, living in a household with a low income and living in a big city county were all factors associated with feelings of insecurity. Furthermore, coming from a country outside Europe (i.e. Iran or Chile) was significantly related to fear of crime. When the regression model was performed separately for male and female respondents, fear of crime was associated with having a non-European origin only for males. For females, living in a big city county was the only significant independent background factor correlated with fear of crime.

SUMMARY AND CONCLUSIONS

The results from the Swedish victim studies presented above can be summarized along two axes, focusing first on the different types of crime and then on the independent correlates of the different social background factors with victimisation, including fear of crime.

Victimisation and fear of crime

Violence leading to death is very rare in Sweden. Foreign born persons have a higher risk of becoming a victim of deadly violence than native Swedes. Immigrants with a Finnish background have the highest victimisation risk, followed by immigrants from a country in Africa.

There is generally only a small risk of becoming a victim of violence causing physical injuries. The victim studies suggest that immigrants more often than

212

Swedes have been a victim of serious violence. One of the studies found that Finnish citizens are at a relatively higher risk of becoming a victim of serious violence than other foreign citizens.

Persons renting a flat in a publicly owned house (i.e. flats owned by non-profit organisations) are in general at a greater risk than persons living in a tenant-owned flat (condominium) or a single-family house etc. Among Swedes lower age and being a male is related to the risk of becoming a victim. Among immigrants being single is a risk factor, whereas age and sex do not seem to be of significant importance as risk factors. Swedes who often go out to enjoy themselves in the evening are more often at risk than those with a more home-oriented lifestyle. Lifestyle seems not to be related as much to immigrants' risk of becoming a victim of serious violence.

Immigrants are slightly more likely than native Swedes to be a victim of threats of violence. Non-European immigrants (from Iran and Chile) are probably at a greater risk than other immigrant groups in relation to threats, in particular females.

The threats experienced by the non-European immigrant groups can be related to their different (non-Nordic) appearance, their foreign accent or their ethnic origin. Among immigrants, females more often than males have been a victim of threats, whereas males are at greater risk than females among Swedes. Threats related to a conflict with a spouse or ex-spouse are more common among immigrants than among Swedes. Females more often than males refer to threats related to family conflicts. Young persons and single persons are at special risk of becoming a victim of serious threats, irrespective of their ethnic background. Among immigrants, being out of the workforce is a significant risk factor for becoming a victim, whereas the background variables of sex, yearly income and type of housing have an influence among immigrants.

There is no difference worth mentioning between immigrants and native Swedes regarding their experiences of having their property stolen.

Being young seems to be a risk factor for becoming a victim of theft irrespective of immigrant status. Swedes living in a big city county are at greater risk of having their property stolen than their counterparts living in other counties. Immigrants with a higher educational status more often report that they have had their property stolen.

There are no differences between immigrants and Swedes regarding the risk of having their property damaged. Only one social background variable was independently associated with the experience of damage to one's property, namely whether respondents lived in a big city county. This holds true for both immigrants and Swedes.

Immigrants more often than Swedes hesitate to participate in various everyday events and situations because they are afraid of being victimised. Immigrants from non-European countries (Iran and Chile) more often report such worries about being a victim of crime than immigrants from European countries. This relationship is valid for males in particular.

Living in a big city county is a common factor among immigrants and Swedes related to fear of crime. Among immigrants low income is related to fear of crime and among the Swedes female respondents more often than male respondents worry about crime.

The Influence of social background factors

Irrespective of whether a person is an immigrant or an indigenous Swede:

- *low age* is associated with being exposed to serious violence, threats of serious violence and thefts of property.
- *being single* is associated with being a victim of serious violence and threats of serious violence.
- *living in a big city county* is associated with feeling unsafe in various day-to-day contexts and with being exposed to property crimes.
- *renting a flat in a publicly owned house* (non-profit housing) is associated with the experience of serious violence and threats of serious violence.

Significant sex differences have been found for Swedes, but not for immigrants, in relation to experiencing serious violence, threats of serious violence and fear of crime. Swedish males are to a greater extent than Swedish females exposed to serious violence and threats of violence. Swedish females, on the other hand, are more likely to worry about crime in various social contexts.

There are some social background factors which are significantly related to victimisation, but which are difficult to interpret in general terms. Among immigrants, higher education is associated with the household's experience of thefts, being out of the labour market is associated with threats of violence, and low household income is associated with fear of crime. Among Swedes, low income of the household is associated with having been subjected to threats of violence.

Non-European immigrants

The CEIFO survey showed that immigrants from Iran and Chile are particularly exposed to *threats of serious violence*. These threats have to a considerable extent to do with their non-Nordic appearance and their foreign accent. Sometimes the threats may have been related to ethnic background and political affiliation of these immigrant groups (i.e. conflicts within groups).

The CEIFO survey also found that the immigrants from Iran and Chile more often than other ethnic groups *worry about crime* in various social contexts. Their fear of crime might, of course, be a consequence of their relatively high exposure to threats of violence while in Sweden. But being afraid of becoming a victim of

214

crime in these immigrant groups might also be a consequence of having been persecuted in their own country and having had traumatic experiences before or during the flight to Sweden (cf. Martens, 1995).

Research needs

Victim studies are relatively few in number in Sweden but there has been an increased interest in these studies in recent years. Recently a series of surveys in different regions of Sweden has been carried out with the purpose of estimating the risks of victimisation and the extent to which people feel unsafe. Results from these surveys will soon be published (see Wikström, Torstensson and Dolmén, 1997). At the Swedish National Council for Crime Prevention, yearly victim surveys are planned. One purpose of these projected surveys is to collect information that is useful for illuminating changes in crime trends as reflected in the official crime statistics.

An important aim of victim surveys is to obtain an idea of how risks of victimisation are distributed across different sections of the population. In order to obtain more information about the victimisation risks among immigrants, specially designed studies that systematically focus on specific immigrant groups are needed. The immigrant groups in the survey should be chosen strategically. There is a certain link between offending and victimisation (Baron, 1997). When choosing the immigrant groups for a victim study, it would be convenient to make use of what is known about the offending patterns among different immigrant groups (see, for example, Ahlberg, 1996). One can also expect that ethnic differences in vulnerability to victimisation and in worries about crime are associated with public attitudes to foreigners or, rather, people's ethnic prejudices. A victim study of different immigrant groups should therefore take advantage of the research on ethnic discrimination developed at the Swedish Center for Immigration Research at Stockholm University (c.f. Lange, 1995a, 1995b).

To sum up, it seems that immigrants have higher risks of becoming a victim of personal crimes, whereas there is no noteworthy difference between them and native Swedes regarding the risks of property crime victimisation. Furthermore, immigrants more often than native Swedes are afraid of being victimised in various social contexts. Thereby, immigrants with a non-European appearance are probably more often a victim of personal crimes than are other immigrants. They also feel less safe in various everyday contexts. Even if there are some differences between immigrants and Swedes regarding crime victimisation and fear of crime, one cannot take for granted that the explanatory factors behind the victimisation risks and anxieties differ that much between the two groups. On the contrary, the CEIFO survey suggests that several social background factors explaining victimisation are common for immigrants and native Swedes.

A relatively high proportion of immigrants live in the big cities. Also a high proportion rent a flat in a publicly owned house located in a neighbourhood area with a high density of persons with economic and social problems. This description is particularly valid for immigrants who came to Sweden during the last decade or so. Thus, different housing conditions might be one important explanation for differences in vulnerability to victimisation between immigrants, or some groups of immigrants, and native Swedes.

Another important factor that might contribute to the observed differences between immigrants and native Swedes is people's attitudes to foreigners and their ethnic prejudices. Public attitudes to foreigners probably undergo changes as the general social conditions in the society change. During the last few years Sweden has experienced an economic recession with an increase in unemployment rates. The increased unemployment has particularly affected immigrants. The most recently arrived immigrants have problems in earning their living and therefore remain dependent on social assistance and supplementary benefits. In a trying economic situation there is a risk that people in general no longer perceive immigrants as a resource for the country but rather as a burden. Hostile attitudes towards immigrants develop gradually and are spread out in the whole population. In public debate arguments reflecting hostility towards immigrants have obtained a foothold. Even the politicians now plead for a more restricted immigration policy. This development has contributed to allowing hostile attitudes towards immigrants to become more openly expressed. It may also have contributed to an increase in provocative acts against immigrants. Immigrants with a non-Nordic appearance are likely to be the targets closest at hand for hostile attacks.

REFERENCES

Ahlberg, Jan. (1996). *Criminality among Immigrants and Their Children.* A Statistical Analysis (in Swedish). BRÅ-report. Fritzes; Stockholm.

Alvazzi del Frate, Anna, Ugljesa Zvekic and van Dijk, Jan J.M. (Editors) (1993). *Understanding Crime. Experiences of Crime and Crime Control.* Acts of the International Conference Rome, 18–20 November 1992. United Nations Interregional Crime and Justice Research Institute, Ministry of Justice the Netherlands and Ministry of the Interior Italy. Publication No. 49. Rome: United Nations Interregional Crime and Justice Research Institute.

Baron, S. (1997). Risky lifestyles and the link between offending and victimisation. *Studies on Crime and Crime Prevention*, **6** (1), 71–89.

Hale, C. (1996). Fear of crime: A review of the literature. *International Review of Victimology*, **4**, 79–150.

Hanns, Hofer von (1994). *Foreign Citizens in the Criminal Statistics 1993* (in Swedish). Statistics Sweden Promemoria 1994:1. Statistics Sweden; Stockholm.

Hanns, Hofer von, Sarencki, Jerzy and Tham, Henrik (1997). Ethnic Minorities and Crime: An international perspective – Sweden. In *Ethnic Minorities and Crime: An international perspective*. (Ineke Haen Marshall, ed.). Sage Publications; Beverly Hills.

216

Lange, Anders. (1995a). *Immigrants about Discrimination: A Study on Ethnic Discrimination Based on a Questionnaire and Personal Interviews* (in Swedish). University of Stockholm, Swedish Center for Immigration Research CEIFO and Statistics Sweden; Stockholm.

Lange, Anders. (1995b). *Immigrants about Discrimination II: A Study on Ethnic Discrimination Based on a Questionnaire and Personal Interviews* (in Swedish). University of Stockholm, Swedish Center for Immigration Research CEIFO. CEIFO-Report Series, no. 70; Stockholm.

Lange, Anders and Charles Westin. (1993). *Youth about the Immigration II.* Ways of Relating to Immigration and Immigrants 1993 (in Swedish). The Swedish Center for Immigration Research CEIFO. Stockholm University; Stockholm.

Martens, Peter L. (1995). Immigrants and Crime Prevention. In *Integrating Crime Prevention Strategies: Propensity and Opportunity* (Per-Olof H. Wikström, Ron V. Clarke and Joan McCord, eds). Fritzes; Stockholm.

Martens, Peter L. (1997a). Immigrants, crime, and criminal justice in Sweden. *Crime and Justice. A Review of Research.* **21**, pp. 183–255.

Martens, Peter L. (1997b). Offending and Victimisation among Swedes and some Immigrant Groups. Some Results from an Interview Study (in Swedish). *Unpublished manuscript.* National Council for Crime Prevention.

Statistics Sweden. (1995). *Victims of Violence and Property Crimes 1978–1993* (in Swedish). Statistics Sweden Report No 88. Statistics Sweden; Stockholm.

Statistics Sweden and Swedish Immigration Board. (1993). *Statistical Notes about Immigrants* (in Swedish). Booklet from Statistics Sweden and Swedish Immigration Board; Stockholm.

Sveri, Britt. (1973). Criminality Among Foreigners. A Comparison between Swedish and Foreign Citizens based on the Criminal Statistics (in Swedish). *Svensk Juristtidning*, **58**, 279–310.

Sveri, Britt. (1980). *Criminality Among Foreigners. A Comparison between Persons Convicted for More Serious Crimes in 1967 and 1977* (in Swedish). Stockholm University; Stockholm.

Sveri, Britt. (1987). *Recidivism in Crime among Foreign Citizens* (in Swedish). Stockholm University; Stockholm.

Swedish Immigration Board (1995). Statistics 1994 (in Swedish). Swedish Immigration Board (Statens invandrarverk, SIV); Norrköping.

Westin, Charles and Lange, Anders (1993). *The Ambiguous Tolerance.* Ways of Relating to Immigration and Immigrants 1993. The Swedish Center for Immigration Research CEIFO (in Swedish). University of Stockholm; Stockholm.

Wikström, Per-Olof H. (1985). *Everyday Violence in Contemporary Sweden. Ecological and Situational Aspects.* BRÅ-report 1985:15. Liber/Allmänna Förlaget; Stockholm.

Wikström, Per-Olof H. (1990). The Stockholm Project: An Introduction. In *Crime and Measures Against Crime in the City* (Per-Olof H Wikström, ed.). BRÅ-report 1990:5. Allmänna Förlaget; Stockholm.

Wikström, Per-Olof H. (1990b). Age and Crime in a Stockholm Cohort. *Journal of Quantitative Criminology*, **6**, 61–84.

Wikström, Per-Olof H. (1991). *Social problems, victimisation and fear of crime* (in Swedish). BRÅ-rapport 1991:5. Allmänna förlaget; Stockholm.

Wikström, Per-Olof H. Forthcoming. *Deadly Violence –Social Contexts and Trends* (in Swedish). Research report from the Swedish Police College; Stockholm.

Wikström, Per-Olof H., Marie Torstensson, and Lars R. Dolmén. (1997). *Local Area Problems, Victimisation, and Fear of Crime in Stockholm County* (in Swedish). Report 1997:4, Research unit of the Swedish Police College. Swedish Police College (Polishögskolan); Stockholm.

[20]

Aggressive Youth Cultures and Hate Crime

Skinheads and Xenophobic Youth in Germany

MEREDITH W. WATTS

University of Wisconsin–Milwaukee

Contemporary bias crime in Germany increased dramatically after unification and remained at a relatively high, though fluctuating, level for the decade. Right-wing skinheads and neo-Nazis played a significant role in the violence, but at least one third of the violent incidents came from informal groups of young males who were not affiliated. This represents a shift in anti-Semitic and antiforeigner violence from the 1980s and earlier, when the perpetrators were likely to be older and affiliated with identifiable ideological groups. Contemporary xenophobia is not only linked to aggressive elements of youth culture but appears to be increasingly connected to local and international ideological networks. Electronic media such as the Internet have given both the political and commercial entities of skinhead and right-wing culture a means of support and growth.

Xenophobic aggression in postunification Germany is not identical with what is called hate crime or hate violence in the United States, nor are the official data kept by the Federal Office for the Protection of the Constitution to monitor bias-inspired crimes directly comparable with U.S. definitions. The law in the Federal Republic of Germany reflects a reaction against the Nazi past and aims to forbid "Nazi" speech and propaganda. The law also provided for the monitoring of acts motivated by right-wing extremism, anti-Semitism, and antiforeigner bias. This produces several special categories of crime that may seem unusual to citizens of the United States, such as (a) disturbing or defaming the dead (the charges invoked to sanction desecration of Jewish grave sites and memorials), (b) "public incitement" and "instigation of racial hatred" (charges used to suppress racist public speech), and (c) distribution of Nazi propaganda or "literature liable to corrupt the young."

Other aspects of German law forbid the promotion of a Nazi-like political party, denial of the Holocaust, and use of the symbols associated with officially banned groups. The latter provision criminalizes the display of Nazi-era symbols (e.g., the swastika, the "Hitler greeting") but has been steadily expanded to forbid a wide variety of flags, emblems, and other symbols that were employed by groups banned by the Federal Constitutional Court.

What these laws do not do (compared to bias crime legislation in the United States) is define hate crime or hate violence as such, nor do they include any special recognition of gender, disability, or sexual orientation. On the other hand, they go much further than laws in many other contemporary democracies in limiting certain types of biased or racist speech, particularly when it is directed at groups victimized in the Holocaust.

Although the German law obviously reflects a special set of historical and legal circumstances, it results in an exemplary national data effort in certain categories of bias crime. The law requires national reporting of incidents by all police agencies. This ensures data gathering that is more intensive and more complete than is currently the case in most other nations (particularly in comparison with the United States where hate crime reporting is still voluntary and highly variable). As a result, German data provide a better basis than that of most nations for examining trends and developments in certain categories of hate-motivated violence. This feature of the law makes it possible to analyze trends in right-wing and xenophobic[1] violence in Germany, developments that reflect a particular national situation but that also show international characteristics that may help us understand hate violence in other societies as well.

THE COURSE OF RIGHT-WING VIOLENCE

Perhaps the first question concerns the basic historical development of right-wing violence in Germany. Table 1 and Figure 1 place the era of "modern" xenophobia in Germany in perspective. In 1989 and 1990, immediately prior to unification, there were fewer than 200 violent incidents per year. That figure more than quadrupled by 1992 and reached its contemporary peak in the following year. Shock of the German public (expressed dramatically by candlelight processions in sympathy with the victims), consolidation of the criminal justice agencies in the new federal states in the east, and stepped-up enforcement activities by security agencies all played a part in the decline. Since then, there have been oscillations between 600 and 800 violent incidents per year—a decline from the peak but still high compared to the preunification period (for a more extended discussion, see Watts, 1997, chap. 2).

A second question concerns the targets of violence. Unlike federal (and some state) hate crime statutes in the United States, German law does not provide for special reporting of violence based on sexual orientation, gender, or disability. However, it is quite specific about crimes that can be attributed to anti-Semitic, antiforeigner, or right-wing motivation. Since unification (beginning officially in 1990), the targets of attack have remained relatively constant. As Table 2 shows, about 60% of the violent incidents have been directed against foreigners. Anti-Semitic attacks, including desecration of graves and memorial sites, have

TABLE 1:   The Course of Right-Wing Violence in Germany, 1989-1998

Year	Number of Violent Acts[a]
1989	173
1990	178
1991	849
1992	1,485
1993	1,322
1994	784
1995	612
1996	624
1997	790
1998	708

SOURCE: Bundesamt für Verfassungsschutz [Federal Office for Protection of the Constitution] (1997, 1998d). See also Watts (1997, chap. 2).
a. The official term refers to violent acts "with demonstrated or assumed right-wing motivation."

accounted for about 2% of all violent incidents. Foreigners are a significant presence in Germany (with a population of more than 7 million) and account for the vast majority (60%) of attacks against persons. By contrast, the number of Jews in Germany is probably not much more than one hundredth that of foreigners, even allowing for a doubling of the Jewish population over the decade (due primarily to immigration from the former Soviet Union). Thus, whereas only 2% of the total offenses involve Jewish persons or institutions, the per capita rate is high.

Political opponents such as "autonomous" leftist groups and rival youth cultures accounted for another 14% of the total. The last category ("other") contained 24% of the incidents; it refers to offenses where the perpetrators were identifiably right wing but the victims were not foreigners, Jews, or political enemies (examples might be damage to property during a demonstration or assaults against police or bystanders).

WHO ARE THE PERPETRATORS?

But who are these "rightists?" Increasingly, the perpetrators of hate violence of the past decade have tended overwhelmingly to be young males, usually acting in groups. But how young? And in what kind of groups—skinheads, neo-Nazis, or informal groups of young men looking for excitement?[2] As Table 3 shows, modern xenophobia indeed has a youthful face. Data from 1996 show that 30% of the perpetrators were ages 16 to 17 and that more than two thirds of all perpetrators were 20 years of age or younger.

This aggressive activism on the part of teenaged and young adult males represents a historical "modernization" of xenophobic violence. Prior to 1980, those

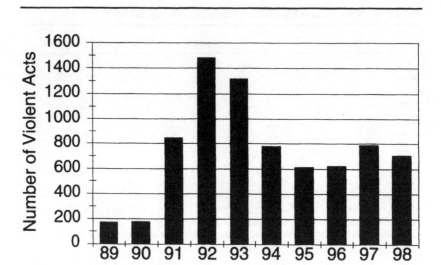

Figure 1: Right-Wing Violence
SOURCE: Verfassungsschutzbericht (1997, 1998).

TABLE 2:   Targets of Right-Wing Violence in Germany, 1995-1998

Type	Number of Offenses[a]	Percentage of Total
Antiforeigner	1,269	60
Anti-Semitic	38	2
Against political opponents	303	14
Other[b]	512	24
Total	2,122	100

SOURCE: Bundesamt für Verfassungsschutz [Federal Office for Protection of the Constitution] (1997, 1998d).
a. The official term refers to violent acts "with demonstrated or assumed right-wing motivation."
b. "Other" includes acts of violence where the perpetrators are identified as "rightists" but where the incident or target does not involve the previous three categories. Examples might be a march in which store windows are broken or a confrontation with citizens or bystanders.

younger than 20 years of age accounted for only 40% of the incidents (see Watts, 1997, p. 269). The earlier form of rightist activism involved somewhat older perpetrators who were more likely to be associated with neo-Nazi groups (and, presumably, had more developed right-wing ideological positions than today's younger activists). In comparison with this earlier period, today's typical activist is much younger[3] and less likely to be a member of a neo-Nazi organization.

Accompanying this shift toward youthful activism has been a trend away from classic, membership-based organizational forms. The young perpetrators

TABLE 3:   Age of Perpetrators (1996)

Age	Percentage	Cumulative Percentage
16-17	30	30
18-20	37	67
21-30	27	94
31-40	3	97
Older than 40	3	100

SOURCE: Bundesamt für Verfassungsschutz [Federal Office for Protection of the Constitution] (1996). (For earlier years, see Watts, 1997, p. 269.)

are less likely than their predecessors to be ideologically sophisticated and organizationally connected. This does not mean they are isolated; on the contrary, they are part of a xenophobic culture that includes both the older organizational forms and a heterogeneous (and often highly spontaneous) youth culture. This last point is not an obvious one, but we can make sense of it looking at recent skinhead history and at the data on the organization connections of actual perpetrators. Here, we have two questions: How have developments in the skinhead scene contributed to the subculture of racism? and How much have skinheads contributed to the rise in violence?

TRENDS IN EXTREMISM AND
AGGRESSIVE SUBCULTURES

Historically, only a portion of the skinhead style has been explicitly racist or neo-Nazi. Most histories of the movement point to its British working-class origins and to its multiracialism in membership and music tastes. But, those accounts also point to the split of the skinheads into "left" and "right" factions in the 1980s. Somewhere in between these politicized factions are the apolitical skins (who probably make up the majority). The actual numbers in each group are difficult to identify because the boundaries are fluid, and stylistic variations are not always recognizable to the outsider. To make things more difficult, it is not unusual for German skins to refer to themselves as "more or less left" when they actually mean that they are not right. For young Germans in the east, to be truly left was largely discredited with the fall of the East German regime. This was particularly the case for skinheads, who were likely to see being right as the logical place for rebellion to take place in a socialist society.

The right-wing scene has been notorious for its fluidity and unpredictable actionism, a frustration both for the more orthodox rightists who would like to organize them and for the security agencies who would like to monitor them. However, there is a countervailing tendency that seems to have been accelerating throughout the decade—there are signs that such international groups as the Blood and Honour (British) and the Hammerskins (United States) have added discipline, ideology, and an international network to the right-wing skinhead culture. Not only do both movements have global pretensions, but the latter group refers to itself, ominously, as the Hammerskin Nation.

All this points to a rightist milieu that contains a diverse mix of elements—informal groups of xenophobic youth; "subcultures" with a recognizable, aggressive style (such as skinheads); and ideological groups that are disciplined and organized. Those who identify themselves as rightist skinheads are a dramatic presence among perpetrators (Anti-Defamation League, 1995; Hamm, 1993), but available data suggest that they are only one part of a much broader class of aggressive xenophobes.

In his study of perpetrators in the early 1990s, Willems found that 38% of those arrested for antiforeigner violence in the early 1990s were identified as skinheads (Willems, 1995). Heitmeyer and Müller (1995) found that 46% of their interviewees who were involved in antiforeigner violence thought of themselves as skinheads. Prior to 1990, however, the term *skinhead* hardly surfaced with respect to anti-Semitic or antiforeigner violence—not only was there a smaller amount of violence, but some 90% of the perpetrators in that earlier period were identified with neo-Nazi or other classic right-wing extremist groups (Kalinowsky, 1990). In other words, the 1990s were characterized by a surge in xenophobic violence that was carried by aggressive subcultures that were different from the traditional ideological groups on the right.

In comparison to Germany, information on the role of skinheads in the United States is somewhat less systematic and therefore less conclusive. Levin and McDevitt (1993) estimated that the most ideological perpetrators of hate crimes are probably no more than 1% of the total perpetrators. The authors suggested that skinheads are part of this group of violent perpetrators who attack out of an ideological "mission" to drive out the target group. However, data from Germany and elsewhere suggest that skinheads and other aggressive subcultures may not act primarily from racial or ideological motivations but are motivated by "thrill-seeking" and other opportunistic or criminal motives. Thus, it is difficult to estimate the contributions of skinheads in the perpetration of hate crimes or bias-motivated attacks and just as difficult, at the moment, to compare accurately the various types of perpetrators from one nation to another.

Direct comparison across nations is also made difficult because of the nature of the data (compared to Germany, police reports in the United States are less systematic in establishing the political motivation or membership of the perpetrators). As a result, figures from the United States are not comparable (either in relative accuracy or in estimated magnitude) with that of Germany; however, it is clear that racist skinheads are involved in a number of dramatically violent incidents nationally and internationally (Anti-Defamation League, 1995; Southern Poverty Law Center, 1998).

Thus, to reiterate an obvious point: Only some skinheads are racists, and most racists are not skinheads. Yet, skinheads have played a growing role in xenophobic violence. But, what do we know of the "skinhead" contribution to the broader culture of aggressive xenophobia? To put the numbers in perspective, Willems (1995) found that in addition to the 38% who were identifiable with skinhead culture in some way, about 25% of the perpetrators were associated with right-wing extremist groups. Another 19% were members of informal groups or cliques with no specific ideological identification (most of the remaining perpetrators not accounted for in the above categories had prior records and were classified as "criminal," though this category no doubt overlaps the others). Heitmeyer and Müller (1995) found that roughly 27% of the rightist youth they interviewed were associated with neo-Nazi (rather than skinhead) groups. Taken together, these studies indicate that skinheads make up the largest single category of perpetrators in Germany, with members of neo-Nazi organizations a distant second. By either account, at least one third of the attacks are committed by youth who are not associated with these easily identifiable groups.

Skinheads have represented a major portion of the problem, but they were still only one part of a much broader pattern of violence. According to the German Federal Office for the Protection of the Constitution, the total estimate of "right-wing extremist potential" in Germany grew steadily in the last half of the 1990s. A closer look at the various groups (see Table 4) shows that the largest single numerical change has occurred in the estimated strength of right-extremist political parties (these are parties that are "on watch" by the agency but are not classified/banned as "neo-Nazi"). The number of hard-core ideologues represented by the neo-Nazis has remained relatively constant; other growth areas have been among those classified as "violence-prone rightists" and "other groups" (see Figure 2). The latter category contains a diverse cluster of Kameradschaften, discussion groups, and informal cliques that seem to have proliferated (but whose numbers are notoriously hard to estimate due to their informal organizational forms).

Also hard to estimate is the exact number of persons in the violence-prone category; yet, it is on this diffuse group that the federal office has focused much of its concern over the decade. This category contains the heart of the perpetrator category—potentially violent young people (mostly males); its numbers are largely a matter of estimate (because there are no "organizations" to infiltrate or membership records to confiscate). It is this category that contains the skinheads, the group with the most identifiable style and appearance among the violence prone. Obviously, the German government views this category as a growing source of danger. The rise in the number estimated to be violence prone thus reflects an increase in aggressive youth. It is also likely that the increase in their estimated numbers results from a heightened perception on the part of monitoring agencies that the danger from unorganized, aggressive youth is growing. If the numbers are truly on the rise, then it is an increase in the potential—rather

TABLE 4:   Estimated Right-Wing Extremist Potential, 1995-1998

Extremist Group	Year			
	1995	*1996*	*1997*	*1998*
Violence-prone rightists	6,200	6,400	7,600	8,200
Neo-Nazis	1,980	2,420	2,400	2,400
Political parties	35,900	33,500	34,800	39,000
Other groups	2,660	3,700	4,300	4,500
Total	46,740	46,020	49,100	54,100
Total minus multiple memberships	44,610	45,300	48,400	53,600

SOURCE: Bundesamt für Verfassungsschutz [Federal Office for Protection of the Constitution] (1997, 1998d).

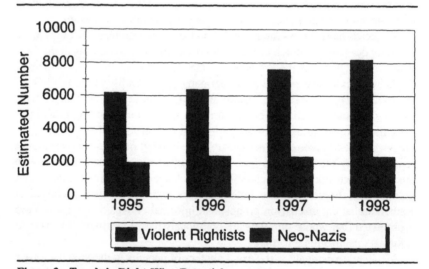

Figure 2:   Trends in Right-Wing Potential

than the actual—rate of perpetration. In recent years, the number of violent offenses has declined somewhat (see Table 1).

EVOLUTION AND CHANGE
IN SKINHEAD CULTURE

The skinhead scene actually consists of many scenes with elements borrowed from other subcultures. For this reason, it is impossible to speak of skinheads as if they all shared an identical culture, ideology, or organizational structure; there are also evolution and change in the scene. Three types of development are worth noting: The first is adaptation of the skinhead style to fit the local political culture. The second is in the increased networking of skinhead groups; this includes organization diffusion above the local level and reflects the internationalization of skinhead style. The third is in the commercialization and commodification of skinhead culture.

In the first development, the international skinhead style (much like other subcultural styles) can be "downloaded" from international media and adapted to fit local conditions. This produces variation not only in the groups themselves but in their local "partners." As local variations include cultural elements that respond to the particular culture and community, the network of potential supporters varies from one place to another. For example, in the United States, racist skinhead groups may be allied locally with neo-Nazi groups, with traditional organizations such as the Ku Klux Klan, or with such groups as Aryan Nations or the World Church of the Creator. In Germany, rightist skinheads may find political partners with neo-Nazi groups or with Kameradschaften and political "discussion groups." White supremacist groups (often imported from the United States) also have some appeal because they offer a racist model that is not associated with the Nazi era (thereby avoiding both the stigma of association with the Nazi period and reducing the likelihood of being banned or prosecuted).

This ideological and associational variation has counterparts in the United States, as in the example of the Nazi Low Riders of Antelope Valley, California. Although the name conjures up images of Los Angeles Latino subculture, this group combined elements of skinhead culture, Nazi ideology, racism, and a business sideline in the methamphetamine trade (Finnegan, 1997). Local variations such as these show that such subcultures are dynamic and difficult to capture in a simple ideological or political definition. Local scenes show a kind of cultural entrepreneurship that combines national and international models with the political culture of the local community.

There also appears to be a growing network of rightist culture on both the local and international levels. Though their impact is difficult to estimate, there is evidence from a number of sources that the right-wing elements of the skinhead scene have become more structured and that they have increased their capacity to cooperate with other groups. Those partner groups often provide the organizational structure, capacity for logistics, and tactical planning (e.g., for demonstrations) that skinheads have traditionally lacked. Most of all, those groups may provide ideological structure and tutelage.

The hard street-fighting style of many skins has long been used by other rightist groups for its intimidation value. According to former neo-Nazi Ingo Hasselbach (1996), "The skins were our storm troopers—the idiots who cleared the streets for us and intimidated our enemies—and enjoyed a bit of violence anytime" (p. 171). However, there is evidence that by the end of the decade skins had expanded beyond this role of "useful idiots" (Hasselbach's term) and that they had done it beyond national boundaries. In early 1999, skinheads from

Croatia, Slovenia, and Germany joined neo-Nazis from Hungary and elsewhere for a demonstration in Budapest. Rightist skins were a common sight at Aryan Nation meetings in the United States, the White Aryan Resistance actively recruited violent skinheads in the early 1990s, and a well-known watchdog organization argues that the skinhead scene is moving "from chaos to conspiracy" (Southern Poverty Law Center, 1998, p. 23). In Germany, connections have developed between the skins and various neo-Nazi groups and, more recently, to rightist political parties; in particular, the National Democratic Party and its youth organization, the Young National Democrats, have actively sought contact and cooperation with right-wing skins (Bundesamt für Verfassungsschutz, 1998a, 1998b, 1998c).

If the actual extent of political networking is a bit difficult to estimate, the evidence for the international commercialization of skinhead culture seems more easily quantifiable. In Germany, data on this trend come from the fact that police and government agencies monitor both "hate speech" and material that is considered "harmful to youth." For example, music and public speech can be targeted for official repression if they are placed by authorities under either of these categories. Thus, in a 1993 operation that would seem unusual to citizens in the United States, German national and provincial agencies prosecuted rightist and "White power" skinhead bands and took legal action against commercial distributors of their music.

In a similar action in 1997, police and security agencies in 10 federal states searched the homes and places of business of 24 individual and corporate distributors of music judged to be racist. Confiscated in the action were several thousand CDs and various Nazi memorabilia and propaganda material. Also captured were computers, business files, and, in one case, an automatic weapon with ammunition (Landesamt für Verfassungsschutz, 1998).

Despite these periodic waves of concerted suppression and interdiction by authorities, the number of concerts and distributors of skinhead materials (and literature) increased steadily through the late 1990s (see Figure 3). The number of bands also increased, showing a 20% surge in 1 year alone (from fewer than 80 in 1997 to roughly 100 in 1998). Repression efforts run up against two major obstacles. The first is the increase in commercialization and commodification, in which skinhead and racist culture is turned into products (e.g., music, clothes) and marketed for economic gain. This produces an economic incentive for the continuation and exploitation of skinhead and racist culture.

The second, interrelated, trend is the internationalization of that commercial culture that allows concerts and distributors to operate effectively from other countries. To escape German sanctions, bands, literature, and concerts are likely to appear in Denmark or Sweden (in fact, it was from Denmark that American neo-Nazi Gary Lauck was extradited to Germany in 1995). Of course, the United States is the prime international center for the distribution of skinhead, White power, and extremist material. The development of electronic networks such as the World Wide Web has promoted this globalization, increased the

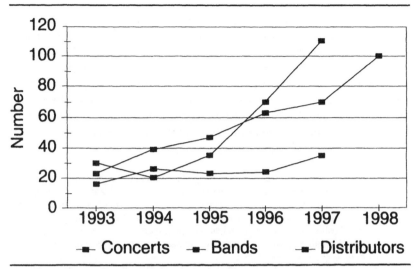

Figure 3: Trends in Skinhead Culture

commercial availability of rightist materials, and undermined German attempts
to suppress skinhead culture. Ideological/commercial Web sites (usually based
in the United States but reachable from virtually anywhere) have expanded; Web
sites suppressed in Canada, Germany, and elsewhere reappear in the freer
cyberspace of the United States where they exist alongside entrepreneurial
American extremists.

DISCUSSION

Germans are not alone in the surge of xenophobia and hate crime. There are
signs that similar developments are occurring throughout industrial societies
undergoing modernization and structural change, stress in employment markets, and a significant influx of people perceived as foreign. Though these structural and social problems all affect Germany, they are common throughout contemporary democracies. So, too, is xenophobic violence and bias crime.

The preceding analysis dealt with rightist potential (and the role of skinheads
within it) in one country. The German data are more complete than information
available in other nations, but they are not identical with what would be categorized as hate- or bias-crime in the United States. Notably, offenses based on gender and sexual orientation are not included (as indeed they are not in a number of
American states). These differences in emphasis make it difficult to compare
trends across nations with accuracy. Even so, the data are helpful in pointing out
some of the major trends in xenophobic culture in Germany and elsewhere.

Some of our concerns go beyond what the data can clearly tell us. However, we can make some reasonably well-grounded speculations about the role of aggressive youth cultures in contemporary bias crime. I would like to suggest some propositions that seem sensible based in part on the analysis presented here. Each is supported to a greater or lesser extent by current information, but to have more certainty, more comparable data from other nations will be needed. Indeed, we will need far more systematic data for the many jurisdictions of the United States because, unlike Germany, reporting under U.S. hate crime legislation is voluntary and still far from being complete.

- First of all, youth cultures are often not just passing fads. The decline of the skin-heads has long been predicted, but it has changed, expanded, and internationalized in the two or more decades since it first appeared. As a style, it has some ephemeral characteristics that will undoubtedly change further and even disappear. But, like rock and roll music (whose death has been predicted for four decades), there is no reason to doubt that this or a similar youth culture will continue to express some form of aggressive xenophobia.
- The early skinhead style originally emerged from British working-class culture as an expression of a strong, working-class masculinity. Segments of it later split into politicized left and right, with the racist segment emerging as an amalgam of aggressive masculinity and explicit xenophobia. This racist tendency was augmented by a sporadic, but growing, connection with ideological elements of the extreme and racist right. What resulted was a three-part poison of aggression, xenophobia, and ideology that has been much more self-sustaining than any of the individual components alone. Where younger persons, particularly males, are confronted with economic modernization and dislocation for which they are ill prepared, and where scapegoats in the form of various cultural "outsiders" are perceived as threats, this three-part poison will continue to produce aggressive sub-cultures (of which skinheads are only one contemporary variant).
- The skin/fascho scene has developed elements of a subculture that includes music, fanzines (fan magazines), concerts, and other more or less organized symbolic and cultural events. This helps provide an integration of the scene as well as a sense of identity—of being part of something much larger, more powerful, and even some-what "dangerous." This provides the basis for a self-sustaining scene—it falls short of being a "movement," but it provides a network through which movement-like connections can develop.
- The skinhead scene has broken out of its parochial/provincial boundaries to establish important links to ideological groups—groups that provide the "intellectual" part of the fascho program, offer a "standing organization," and maintain a durable political opportunity structure. The skins might not be interested in organizing, say, a Rudolf Hess Memorial day (a German neo-Nazi tribute day, substituted for Hitler's birthday, which cannot be celebrated publicly); the neo-Nazis do that. But, the skins can show up, act badly, and lend a show of force and aggressive power. They typically horrify the orthodox rightists, but both groups gain from the odd alliance. Moreover, skinheads have graduated from being what Hasselbach (1996) called "useful idiots"; some have crossed the ideological line and become part of the organizational neo-Nazi right. They maintain links to the skin scene and provide a bridge from the rowdy skinhead style to the more disciplined structures on the right.

- The scene of youthful xenophobic aggression has broken out of its provincialism to establish links to international groups. There are many reports of contacts to a variegated international network, particularly in the United States, United Kingdom, Scandinavia, the Netherlands, and to a lesser degree Spain (relations with the Czechs, Poles, Hungarians, and other central Europeans are somewhat more strained, but they exist). Explicitly racist groups such as Blood and Honour and the Hammerskin Nation provide an international style that is easily downloaded and adapted from the World Wide Web, music, and literature. In Germany, the government estimates that there are more than 200 skinhead or racist Web sites (in the United States, there are far more, of course); many of them are in English to broaden their impact (or because they use North American Internet providers to avoid German censorship).
- Concerts of White power bands are typically discouraged, even prosecuted, in Germany. Bands are raided, CDs confiscated, concerts broken up or forbidden, and leaders prosecuted under German hate speech laws that forbid glorification of Nazis, racist speech, or defamation of victims of the Holocaust. It is even illegal to deny that the Holocaust existed or to slander Jews in public speech. This suppression is undermined by global electronic networks and by support for the scene from abroad.
- The example of skinheads provides some insight into the dynamics of international commercialization—a phenomenon that appears to help stabilize the scene, allow it to expand, and give it a longer life than might have been expected. The same is true, but more so, for right-wing extremist groups and sentiment. This commercial dimension includes cultural artifacts, memorabilia, music, and literature that provide an economic incentive for widening and deepening the scene.
- The structural conditions that produced skinhead groups all over the world are still present. Where they are not solved, skinheads or some other subcultural phenomenon is likely to persist. Status anxiety, identity problems in declining working-class culture, and the compensatory needs of underemployed or threatened young people, particularly males, are continuing problems. These problems, and the youth cultures they produced, extend well beyond the boundaries of the less advantaged. Although the expression of such xenophobia may have significant origins in threatened segments of the housing and labor markets, that xenophobia has been transported politically and culturally to a much broader segment of the population (e.g., middle-class youth, young women, and a variety of nations that have developed "copy-cat" scenes).[4]
- The psychological need for an identity and sense of meaning remains. Not all youth can answer that need with conventional achievement in work, education, and family, but some find it easier or more exciting to use physical and symbolic aggression against out-groups. This form of identity can be extremely unrealistic and dysfunctional (especially when based on a mythopoetic White race, or the like, which either does not exist or, if it does, hardly appoints these youth as its "sword and shield"). This is not a productive identity search, but it will continue to have power where other sources of positive identity are not available.
- Last, although racist skinheads and other aggressive cliques may seem atavistic, they may actually be on the cutting edge of modern xenophobia. Their spontaneous and unpredictable style was traditionally seen as a disadvantage, but a trend in the far right throughout the decade comes to favor this seemingly primitive form of action. Increased repression of extremist groups by various national governments has led to organizational innovations. In the United States, the concept of leaderless resistance sprang up on the far right to promote action that is not controlled by a specific organizational center. The concept was developed among

American extremists to replace the standard organizational model that proved vulnerable to government infiltration and prosecution. But, small groups of aggressive youth had long been the source of spontaneous, "unorganized" violence. Skinheads and other aggressive subcultures are part of a fluid milieu that is held together by symbols, idea fragments, cultural events, and electronic media—but often without any classic organizational structure. This relatively unorganized base then provides a place from which the more ideological of them are likely to find their way into parties, movements, and discussion circles. Thus, the language and symbols may often sound like the "same old thing," but underlying the familiar slogans is a significant change—the right has modernized and adapted, and it has taken on a more youthful face than was the case a generation ago.

NOTES

1. The term *xenophobia* can refer to a generalized antipathy toward out-groups in general or toward a specific target group such as foreigners, Jews, homosexuals, and others. In German usage, the term *Fremdenfeindlichkeit* refers to antipathy against foreigners, although *Xenophobie* is increasingly used. I have tried elsewhere to make these distinctions somewhat more carefully. In this discussion, I try (without complete success) to use *xenophobia* when referring to the more inclusive concept. The terms *antiforeigner* and *anti-Semitic* not only denote the more specific antipathies, they also correspond to the primary categories in the official Germany agency reports.

2. This is not the place for an analysis of the causes and appeals of youthful xenophobia, but some useful starting points are Bergmann (1998); Boehnke, Hagan, and Hefler (1998); Hagan, Merkens, and Boehnke (1995); Oesterreich (1998); Watts (1997, 1999); Watts and Zinnecker (1998); and Willems (1995). For a closer look at the role of young females on the right, see Mushaben (1996).

3. Other discussions of aggressive German youth cultures in the early 1990s can be found in Watts, 1997 (particularly in chaps. 1, 6, 7, and 9). For a more detailed analysis of the shift in public opinion and violence during the 1980s and 1990s, see Watts, 1997 (particularly chap. 2). A detailed chronology of postunification xenophobia is provided by Rainer Erb (cited in Kurthen, Bergmann, & Erb, 1997, pp. 263-285).

4. This conclusion obviously refers to the spread of aggressive youth culture, the primary topic of this discussion. I do not mean it to be a global proposition about the origins of xenophobia or to imply that youth are the source of xenophobia. What I have argued from the German data, though, is that xenophobic youth have been the primary source of rightist violence in the past decade.

REFERENCES

NOTE: Sources are provided in English wherever possible, though in many cases the data reported are available only in German. In those cases, I have provided a translation of the original title and institutional name (when a governmental agency is the data source). Readers interested in the extensive German literature on the subject might start with the bibliographies in Watts (1997) and in Kurthen, Bergmann, and Erb (1997).

Anti-Defamation League. (1995). *The skinhead international: A worldwide survey of neo-Nazi skinheads*. New York: Author.
Bergmann, W. (1998). Violence as social control: Right-wing youth in Germany. In M. W. Watts (Ed.), *Cross-cultural perspectives on youth and violence* (pp. 99-115). New York: JAI.
Boehnke, K., Hagan, J., & Hefler, G. (1998). On the development of xenophobia in Germany: The adolescent years. *Journal of Social Issues, 3*, 585-602.

Bundesamt für Verfassungsschutz [Federal Office for Protection of the Constitution]. (1996). *Verfassungsschutzbericht* [Online]. Retrieved August 15, 1998, from: http://www.bundesregierung.de/02/0201/innen

Bundesamt für Verfassungsschutz [Federal Office for Protection of the Constitution]. (1997). *Verfassungsschutzbericht* [Online]. Retrieved August 15, 1998, from: http://www.bundesregierung.de/02/0201/innen

Bundesamt für Verfassungsschutz [Federal Office for Protection of the Constitution]. (1998a, March). *Rechtsextremistische Skinheads. Entwicklung, Musik-Szene, Fanzines* [Right-wing extremist skinheads: Development, music scenes, fanzines] [Online]. Retrieved November 1, 1998, from: http://www.verfassungsschutz.de

Bundesamt für Verfassungsschutz [Federal Office for Protection of the Constitution]. (1998b, July). *Right-wing extremism in the Federal Republic of Germany: Situation report* [Online]. Retrieved November 1, 1998, from: http//www.verfassungsschutz.de

Bundesamt für Verfassungsschutz [Federal Office for Protection of the Constitution]. (1998c, March). *Right-wing extremist activities in INTERNET* [Online]. Retrieved November 1, 1998. from: http://www.verfassungsschutz.de

Bundesamt für Verfassungsschutz [Federal Office for Protection of the Constitution]. (1998d). *Verfassungsschutzbericht* [Online]. Retrieved August 15, 1998, from: http://www.bundesregierung.de/02/0201/innen

Finnegan, W. (1997, December 1). The unwanted. *The New Yorker*, 61-78.

Hagan, J., Merkens, H., & Boehnke, K. (1995). Delinquency and disdain: Social capital and the control of right-wing extremism among East and West Berlin youth. *American Journal of Sociology, 100*, 1028-1052.

Hamm, M. (1993). *American skinheads: The criminology and control of hate crime*. Westport, CT: Praeger.

Hasselbach, I. (with Reiss, T.). (1996). *Führer-ex: Memoirs of a former neo-Nazi*. New York: Random House. (Portions excerpted in Hasselbach, I. [with Reiss, T.] (1996, January 6). How Nazis are made. *The New Yorker*, 36-57.

Heitmeyer, W., & Müller, J. (1995). *Fremdenfeindliche Gewalt junger Menschen. Biographische Hintergründe, soziale Situationskontexte und die Bedeutung strafrechtlicher Sanktionen* [Antiforeigner violence of young people: Biographical background, social context and the significance of legal sanctions]. (1995). Bad Godesberg, Germany: Forum.

Kalinowsky, H. H. (1990). *Rechtsextremismus und Strafrechtspflege. Eine Analyse von Strafverfahren wegen mutmaßlicher rechtsextremististischer Aktivitäten und Erscheinungen* [Right-wing extremism and the law: An analysis of legal proceedings of suspected right-extremist activities] (3rd ed.). Bonn, Germany: Bundesministerium der Justiz.

Kurthen, H., Bergmann, W., & Erb, R. (Eds.). (1997). *Antisemitism and xenophobia in Germany after unification*. New York: Oxford University Press.

Landesamt für Verfassungsschutz. (1998). *Landesverfassungsschutzbericht* (Report of the Provincial Office for Protection of the Constitution, Hamburg) [Online]. Retrieved March 29, 1999, from: http://www.hamburg.de/Behoerden/LfV/v-bericht

Levin, J., & McDevitt, J. (1993). *Hate crimes: The rising tide of bigotry and bloodshed*. New York: Plenum.

Mushaben, J. M. (1996). The rise of femi-Nazis? Female participation in right-extremist movements in unified Germany. *German Politics, 5*, 240-261.

Oesterreich, D. (1998). Authoritarianism and aggression: German youth and right-wing extremism. In M. W. Watts (Ed.), *Cross-cultural perspectives on youth and violence* (pp. 39-51). New York: JAI.

Southern Poverty Law Center. (1998, Fall). Chaos to conspiracy: Racist skinhead violence growing more organized. *Intelligence Report*, pp. 23-24.

Watts, M. W. (1997). *Xenophobia in united Germany: Generations, modernization, and ideology*. New York: St. Martin's.

Watts, M. W. (1999). Xenophobia among young Germans in the nineties. In S. Hübner-Funk & M. du Bois-Reymond (Eds.), *Intercultural reconstruction: Trends and challenges* (pp. 117-139). Berlin, Germany: Walter de Gruyter.

Watts, M. W., & Zinnecker, J. (1998). Varieties of violence-proneness among male youth. In M. W. Watts (Ed.), *Cross-cultural perspectives on youth and violence* (pp. 117-145). New York: JAI.

Willems, H. (1995). Development, patterns and causes of violence against foreigners in Germany: Social and biographical characteristics of perpetrators and the process of escalation. *Terrorism and Political Violence, 7,* 162-181.

[21]

FEAR OF CRIME AMONG AN IMMIGRANT POPULATION IN THE WASHINGTON, DC METROPOLITAN AREA

YAW ACKAH

Delaware State University

Between 1989 and 1991, the District of Columbia (or DC) recorded the highest per capita homicide rate in the country, making it "the murder capital" (Office of Criminal Justice Plans and Analysis [OCJPA], 1992). In fact, DC and Dallas set new records for homicides in 1991 (Criminal Violence, 1993). That fear pervades life in the capital was well illustrated in a study by Harriston, Thomas, York, and Warden (1991), who reported that 60% of the residents there had modified their routine social activities because of fear of crime. Their finding is supportive of others that have reported that the fear of crime has caused 60% of Americans to limit the places they go by themselves (see, e.g., Bucuvalas, 1991; Research and Forecasts, 1983; Warr & Stafford, 1983).

The present study is timely given that, like other parts of the country, the immigrant population in the District and its environs (Maryland and Virginia) is rapidly increasing (Bigman, 1990). In addition to the more than 250 robberies committed against immigrant cab drivers, several other immigrants were slain on the job in a 5-week period in 1992 (Escobar, 1992; OCJPA, 1992). The Centers for Disease Control and Prevention now regard murder as an epidemic. There is little doubt that today's most dangerous and fear-invoking places are urban centers, and DC is a quintessential example (Lee, 1985; Perry, Hsieh, & Pugh, 1994; Taylor & Hale, 1986; Yin, 1985).

The key questions to ask, then, are twofold: Do immigrants in DC fear crime as do the other residents, and can the variables that explain fear in nonimmigrant samples also explain fear in immigrant populations? These questions are poignant given that the sample's race is disproportionately represented in the statistics on crime victims and those who have fear of crime in the United States (Belyea & Zingraff, 1988; Coston, 1994; Gorden & Riger, 1989; Lewis, 1989).

The primary purpose of this study is to explore the correlates of fear of crime among a sample of Ghanaian immigrants in the Washington, DC metropolitan area. To date, no study has examined fear among immigrant populations in DC. However, we can sharpen our measurement tools through cross-cultural studies of other groups (Sundeen, 1984). This strategy allows us to key in on immigrant-specific variables, while simultaneously maintaining a continuity with extant research on fear of crime. In addition, it minimizes the problems of specification in the models we construct to guide our investigations.

In a study of fear of crime among foreign students, Sundeen (1984) argued that their exotic cultures, coupled with the relatively lower crime rate in their countries, affect their perceptions of, and responses to, criminal victimizations. Sundeen reported that the variables that best explained fear of crime among American samples were their perceptions of neighborhood dangerousness, perceived local police protection, victimization experiences, and gender. Among the immigrant students, on the other hand, he found that high levels of participation in their cultural activities and prior knowledge of crime in the United States increased their fear. The student's original home country showed a weak relationship with the immigrant's fear of crime. Length of stay in the United States, however, was inversely related to fear of crime. Length of stay and participation in cultural activities are related to the issue of acculturation as we are proposing in this study, although Sundeen (1984) did not directly discuss them as such. Sundeen's (1984) study suggests that we can improve our understanding of the fear of crime among immigrant populations by including hitherto unexplored variables in our models.

Such a cross-cultural approach makes possible an examination of crucial issues such as the relationships between acculturation and the immigrant's fear of crime. Although earlier studies have linked more acculturation to high levels of distress (Berry & Kim, 1988), recent research (Vega et al., 1994) has found an inverse relationship between them. In this study, acculturation is explored as it relates to the immigrant's fear of crime, rather than to the individual's distress.

FEAR OF CRIME

Since the 1960s, fear of crime has been recognized as a social fact that is equally as important as crime itself (see Perry et al., 1994; Lawrence & Sanchirico, 1982; Lewis & Salem, 1986; Liska, 1982; Sundeen, 1984). Studies on fear of crime generally have focused on organismic and environmental characteristics, as well as causal variables. For example, the literature indicates that among American samples, age is positively related to fear of crime (Donnelly, 1988; Ward, LaGory, & Sherman, 1986). Income is, however, inversely related to fear of crime even when race, age, and gender are held constant (Sundeen & Mathieu, 1976), probably because high-income earners live in presumably safe neighborhoods (Skogan & Maxfield, 1981; Yin, 1985). Males also report less fear than females due to the greater female vulnerability to gender-specific crimes such as rape (Donnelly, 1988; LaGrange & Ferraro, 1989). Other studies have found positive relationships between both violent personal and vicarious victimizations, and fear of crime (Coston, 1988; Kranich, Berry, & Greider, 1989; Smith & Hill, 1991; Yin, 1985). Gerbner and Gross's (1987) cultivation hypothesis posits a direct link between violence on television to fear of crime. Researchers have also reported more fear of crime in urban, rather than in rural, residents (Kennedy & Krahn, 1984; Merry, 1980). These relationships are embodied in Yin's (1985) framework of fear of crime, which provides the perspective upon which the reasoning in this study is grounded.

Yin's (1985) conceptual framework is summarized in the equation $F = f(P, E)$, and interpreted as fear is a function of the person and the environment. The personal or organismic factors include age, gender, criminal victimization experiences, prior information about crime, and perception of neighborhood dangerousness, whereas some environmental factors are the ethnic composition of one's neighborhood, the local police protection from criminal victimization, participation in social activities, and signs of incivility in one's neighborhood (Ito, 1993; Yin, 1985). Fear of crime results from an interplay of these coexisting and interacting organismic and environmental forces (Coston, 1994; Skogan & Maxfield, 1981; Sundeen, 1984; Yin, 1985).

The personal factors occupy a central place in the theory because fear of crime is basically fear for oneself (Yin, 1985). The fear results from a personal assessment or perception of one's vulnerability to criminal victimization, which is made in the context of one's neighborhood. Such a perception of vulnerability is predicated on a stocktaking of the individual's personal characteristics that suggest a weakness to the individual. It is this subjective perception of one's vulnerability that is critical to the presence or absence of fear of crime, and not what others may objectively perceive to be the true state of affairs. It is a social psychological fact that what people perceive as real is real in the consequence. Hence, a female immigrant may correctly or wrongly perceive herself as especially vulnerable because of gender or insufficient assimilation into the American culture (Coston, 1994). This subjective perception can induce fear irrespective of its objective irrationality (Jaycox, 1979). The environmental factors entail those features that signify environmental peril or crime, and are therefore associated with fear. Both the personal and environmental factors may affect fear of crime independently. Hence, the same criminogenic situation may produce different, bi-polaric fear reactions in two individuals (e.g., a citizen and an immigrant) who are exposed to it simultaneously.

The crucial question that the fear of crime model addressed was what factors determine the probability that a Ghanaian immigrant in the Washington, DC metropolitan area will have fear of crime. An appendage to this question was whether these factors differ from those that determine fear among other populations. Given the above analysis, it was hypothesized that fear of crime among Ghanaian immigrants in the Washington, DC metropolitan area will differ from other populations because of the presence of variables such as length of stay in the United States, participation in social activities, perception of neighborhood dangerousness, prior knowledge of crime, and work schedule.

The relationships in the model are best explicated within the context of the immigrant's sociocultural background (Sundeen, 1984). Hence, to make the subsequent discussions meaningful, aspects of the Ghanaian culture are presented to the extent that they relate to criminal victimization and the fear of crime among Ghanaian immigrants.

ASPECTS OF THE GHANAIAN CULTURE

Ghana is located on the west coast of Africa south of the Sahara. Ghanaians may be categorized into five broad ethnic groups with the Akans (45%) comprising the largest group (Ghana Bureau of Statistics, 1993; Nortey, 1983). Although aspects of the Ghanaian culture described here through the ethnographic present are characteristic of the Akans who form the bulk of the sample in this study, they also apply to the other ethnic groups in several respects.

According to Sarpong (1973), important Ghanaian cultural values include respect for authority, old age, and spiritual and sacred objects. The Ghanaian culture also emphasizes trust and compassion for strangers as reflected in their adage, "The stranger does not sleep in the streets." It thus seems antithetical that the President's Commission on Law Enforcement and Administration of Justice (1967) reported that fear of crime is basically a fear of strangers. Future studies may examine how this cultural value of trust for strangers affects the Ghanaian's fear of crime. Family and community ties are also stressed, hence Ghanaians are loyal to their kinsmen (Sarpong, 1974). The practice of this cultural norm can be observed at Ghanaian funerals, child-naming events, and weddings; or when a kinsman gets into some trouble with the law.

Common taboos include suicide; theft; incest; certain kinds of assault such as striking a woman or one's parents, for whatever reason; and a sexual relationship with a prepubertal girl. It is believed that breaking a serious taboo can result in adverse mystical and physical consequences for the society. For example, fornicating with a prepubertal girl can cause either a famine in the community or the death of the adult fornicator (Sarpong, 1974). However, God does not punish those who commit wrongs inadvertently.

Murder is probably the most serious taboo because spilling blood on the sacred earth can precipitate a disaster for the whole society. It is also believed to be shameful and a double tragedy to die intestate (Sarpong, 1974). An assessment of the reaction of a Ghanaian immigrant to criminal victimization (i.e., fear of crime) can best be made within the context of his or her sociocultural milieu.

METHODOLOGY

SURVEY DESIGN

The community-based data to assess fear were collected through a simple random sampling of 300 Ghanaian immigrants (sample frame, $N = 450$) who lived in the Washington, DC metropolitan area. The instrument was an adaptation of those developed by Sundeen (1984), Lee (1982), and Warr and Stafford (1983). The questionnaires were self-administered because all the respondents were literate in the English language. To increase the response rate, two reminders were sent to those who had not returned their completed questionnaires. Out of the 300 questionnaires distributed, 197 were returned, giving a response rate of 65.6%. In a study containing sensitive variables such as the immigrant's length of stay in the United States (which to the immigrant is a probe into one's immigration status), a response rate of 50% is adequate for analysis and reporting (Kish, 1965).

DEMOGRAPHIC CHARACTERISTICS OF THE SAMPLE

The sample consisted of 53% males and 47% females, with 93% younger than 45 years of age, and a mean age of 34.8 years. Most of them (68%) were residents of urban centers in Ghana that had populations in excess of 26,000 people. The majority (63.4%) were married, whereas the rest were single (28.6%), separated (1%), or divorced (5%). Also, nearly three quarters of the respondents (70%) earned an average annual family income of less than $30,000, whereas 30% received more than $30,000 at the time of the survey. Their employment status showed that the overwhelming majority (97.5%) were employed, and only 2.5% were temporarily unemployed. Their places of employment were distributed as follows: DC (37%), Maryland (41%), and Virginia (21%).

MEASURES

Although some variables were measured at the nominal and ordinal levels, the combination of a large number of categories in the ordinal level variables and the very high predictive power of path analysis is enough to offset serious distortions in the analysis (Asher, 1983; Bohrnstedt & Carter, 1971). The nominal variables were analyzed as dummy variables.

Fear of crime was conceptualized as the "psychological [and social] reactions to possible crime victimization" (Yin, 1985). To obtain the most valid and reliable indicators of fear of crime, it is best to specify the type of crime to the respondent (Ferraro & LaGrange, 1987; Warr & Stafford, 1983). Hence, based on the 13 most frequently reported crimes in the DC area (OCJPA, 1989) (see the appendix), fear of crime was measured as a composite of a respondent's perception of risk of victimization, perception of crime seriousness, and a respondent's fear of these 13 specific crimes. Responses were graduated on an 11-point scale ranging from 0 to 10. To assess perceived risk, responses ranged from 0 = *certain it will not happen to me* to 10 = *certain it will happen to me*. Responses to the perceived seriousness question ranged from 0 = *least serious* to 10 = *most serious*, whereas those for the fear of crime question ranged from 0 = *not afraid at all* to 10 = *very afraid*.

Eleven independent variables were included in the model (see Table 1 and Figure 1). The first group consists of the variables that extant studies have related to fear of crime among Americans: income, gender, victimization experience, the mass media, and population size of place of residence. Because these variables have already been identified in several studies, they were categorized as the old variables.

Income was measured on a 4-point Likert-type scale ranging from 1 = *less than $10,000* to 4 = *more than $30,000*. Gender was measured as a dummy variable with 0 = *male* and 1 = *female*. Victimization experience refers to whether the respondent had ever been a victim of any of the 13 specific crimes since his or her arrival in the United States. Responses were dichotomized as 0 = *no* and 1 = *yes*. Media was assessed by the frequency of exposure to crime news. The responses, measured on a 5-point Likert-type scale, ranged from 1 = *rarely or never* to 4 = *very frequently*. Population size examined whether the respondent lived in an urban or rural center in Ghana. Because only Accra has a population of 1 million (Ghana Bureau of Statistics, 1993), responses consisted of four categories ranging from 1 = *10,000* to 4 = *more than 40,000*.

The new variables were prior knowledge of crime, length of stay in the United States, perception of relative dangerousness, participation in social activities, and work schedule. These were referred to as new because they had not been examined among Ghanaian immigrants.

Prior knowledge of crime. Prior knowledge of crime entails a respondent's prior knowledge of the crime rate in the United States antecedent to arrival here. The specific question was the following: "Prior to your arrival in the U.S., how did you rate crime in the USA?" Responses ranged from 1 = *very low* to 5 = *very high*. The follow-up question was "How would you rate crime in the USA

TABLE 1
Pearson's Correlation Matrix for Variables in the Fear of Crime Model

	INC	GED	LOC	VIC	MED	STY	PPS	WOS	PRR	DAG	SOC	FOC
INC	1	-.41	.08	.34	.13	-.03	.48	.43	-.18	.32	-.06	-.27
GED		1	-.19	-.11	-.06	.10	-.18	-.13	.19	.01	.12	.17
LOC			1	.10	.12	-.16	.13	.19	-.13	.08	-.05	.03
VIC				1	.15	-.09	.28	.27	-.10	.37	-.01	-.08
MED					1	.07	.22	.06	.01	.28	-.05	.18
STY						1	.07	-.03	-.12	-.06	.04	-.05
PPS							1	.28	-.20	.23	.05	-.22
WOS								1	-.23	.11	-.01	.01
PRR									1	.04	.02	.02
DAG										1	.06	-.13
SOC											1	.13
FOC												1

NOTE: INC = income; PPS = population size; GED = gender; SOC = social activities; LOC = locus of control; WOS = work schedule; VIC = victimization; PRR = prior information; MED = mass media; DAG = perception of danger; STY = length of stay; FOC = fear of crime.

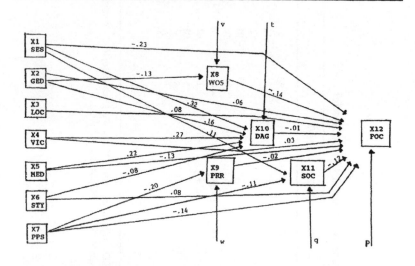

Figure 1: Modified Model of Fear of Crime
NOTE: SES = socioeconomic status; GED = gender; LOC = locus of control; VIC = victimization; MED = mass media; STY = length of stay; PPS = population; WOS = work schedule;
PRR = prior information; DAG = perception of danger; SOC = social activities; FOC = fear
of crime.

now compared with when you first arrived in the country?"
Responses to this question ranged from 1 = *much lower* to 5 = *much
higher.*

Perception of relative dangerousness. Perception of relative
dangerousness refers to the perceived relative dangerousness of a
respondent's current neighborhood in the United States compared
with others in the DC area, and these current neighborhoods in the
United States compared with the respondents' former neighborhoods in Ghana. The responses comprised an index of two 5-point
item scales, ranging from 1 = *less dangerous* to 5 = *more
dangerous.*

Length of stay in the United States. Length of stay in the United
States was measured with two questions on the duration of residence (in years) in both the immigrant's current, and if applicable,
former addresses here in the United States. It was hypothesized that
the longer the length of stay, the more the acculturation, and hence
the less the fear of crime.

Participation in social activities. It was hypothesized that participation increases the feelings of fear because more participation indicates less acculturation into the American society (Berry & Kim, 1988). Additionally, participation increases the respondent's access to crime stories through the grapevine that can cause vicarious fear (Sundeen, 1984). This variable entails 5-point scale items on participation in Ghanaian social activities. The specific questions asked how frequently respondents participated in Ghanaian social activities, if there had been any change in participation, and if so the reason for this change in participation. Responses to the first question ranged from 1 = *do not attend any* to 5 = *attend all.* Responses to the second question were 1 = *less frequently* and 2 = *more frequently.* The third was an open-ended question on the reasons for the change in the frequency of participation.

Locus of control. Locus of control measured whether one believed that one or outside forces controlled what happened in one's life. The responses were dichotomized as 0 = *no* and 1 = *yes.* The follow-up was an open-ended question to enable the externalists to indicate what actually controls their lives.

Work schedule. Although Sundeen (1984) did not examine the work schedule in his study, given the great current interest in work-related victimizations in the country (e.g., of immigrants in the DC area) (Escobar, 1992; Harriston et al., 1993), it was considered relevant enough to be incorporated into the revised model. Responses ranged from 0 = *mornings* to 2 = *nights.* In addition, because most criminal victimizations in the DC area occur at night between the hours of 9 p.m. and 3 a.m. (OCJPA, 1992), it was hypothesized that respondents who worked the night schedule would report more fear of crime than those who worked the day schedule.

DATA ANALYSIS

The results are introduced with a univariate analysis, followed by an examination of the relationships among the variables using a simple bivariate analysis (Pearson's *r*) to determine significant patterns of response to key variables. The ordinary least squares path analysis is used to determine the strength of the causal relations among the variables specified in the fear of crime model.

RESULTS

UNIVARIATE RELATIONSHIPS

The analyses revealed that almost all the respondents (90%) had lived in the United States for an average of 6 years. Nearly 70% received an annual family income of less than $30,000, hence most of them (71.4%) were blue-collar workers. The majority of the respondents (74.5%) perceived their current neighborhoods in the United States as more dangerous than those in Ghana. However, only 11.8% indicated that their current neighborhoods were more dangerous than other neighborhoods in the metropolitan area. Predictably, virtually all the respondents (91%) indicated that they attend Ghanaian cultural activities, a few or many times. On the whole, there were fewer personal than vicarious victimizations. For example, important instances of personal victimizations were burglary (12%), forcible robbery (12%), weapon threat (26%), car theft (9%), and conned out of money (24%). As is consistent with the literature, the percentages for vicarious victimizations were much higher: burglary (42%), forcible robbery (64%), weapon threat (67%), car theft (62%), and conned out of money (78%). Prior to their arrival in the United States, 61.5% thought that the crime rate here was very high, and since their arrival most (73%) of them think that it is higher than they thought prior to their arrival. More important, virtually all of them (99%) still consider crime to be a very serious problem. Predictably, many of them expressed fear of possible criminal victimization generally (68%), and specifically fear of robbery (68%), burglary (67%), and of getting killed (81%). That only a quarter (25%) worked the night schedule may be related to this fear. In reference to locus of control, 56% of the internalists reported that they believed they controlled what happened in their lives. The externalists, however, attributed their life events to destiny (12%), luck (27%), evil forces (6%), or to other external forces (50%). An interesting finding was that almost all the respondents (95%) reported that they were wary of strangers, which given the presentation of the Ghanaian culture above is an anomaly. A plausible explanation is that this is reflective of the impact of acculturation and may play an important part in explicating the Ghanaian immigrant's fear of crime.

BIVARIATE RELATIONSHIPS

The bivariate correlations among the variables in the model are shown in Table 1. As the table indicates, crime victims saw their neighborhoods as dangerous places ($r = .37, p < .000$). It was not unexpected that those who frequently heard crime news also perceived their neighborhoods as dangerous places ($r = .28, p < .000$). The table also shows that urban residents ($r = .28, p < .001$) and those who worked the night schedule ($r = .27, p < .001$) often bore the brunt of criminal victimizations. Contrary to findings reported in the literature, high-income earners reported that they saw their neighborhoods as dangerous places ($r = .32, p < .000$). It was not surprising, however, that those who were urban residents in Ghana before their arrival here were more prepared to work the night schedule than their rural counterparts ($r = .28, p < .000$). It is probable that urban residents are more familiar with working night schedules than their rural counterparts. It also emerged that respondents who had prior knowledge about the crime rate in the United States preferred to work a day schedule, ($r = -.23, p < .004$) possibly because of the impact of vicarious victimization—that is, assuming that this relationship has a substantive validity. The data also revealed that respondents who perceived their current neighborhoods as more dangerous than their previous neighborhoods in Ghana ($r = .13$) and who frequently participated in Ghanaian social activities ($r = .13$) reported increased fear of crime. Although these relationships were not statistically significant, they do have important substantive significance. It emerged that the internalists reported less fear of crime ($r = .03$) than the externalists ($r = -.05$), and attended Ghanaian social activities more than the latter. A possible explanation is that the externalists, who indicated more fear of

crime than the internalists, avoided these social activities that usually took place at night as a precautionary measure. It will be
recalled that the OCJPA (1989) had reported that most crimes in the
district take place at night. Prior information ($r = .02$) and work
schedule ($r = .01$) were minimally correlated with the fear of crime.
The old variables, which had important relationships with fear of
crime, were income ($r = -.27$, $p < .001$), gender ($r = .17$, $p < .05$),
and media ($r = -.18$, $p < .05$).

MULTIVARIATE RELATIONSHIPS

Although both the standardized (B) and the unstandardized (β)
beta coefficients are presented in Table 2 and Figure 1, the discussion is based on the standardized beta (B) because this sample is
generally a homogeneous group, for example, in terms of age,
marital status, employment status, income, and ethnicity.

In Equation 1, work schedule was regressed on gender, which
showed that the male respondents worked the night schedule more
often than their female counterparts ($B = -0.13$). This could be a
function of the large number of males in the sample and their preferred type of work, or to the reluctance of the female respondents
to work the night schedule. Gender explained only 2% of the variance in the work schedule model.

The regression of prior knowledge on population size in Equation 2 revealed that prior to their arrival here, urban respondents
knew less about the crime rate than urban residents ($B = -0.20$, $p <
.01$). Although the beta weight was statistically significant at the
.01 level, this relationship clearly lacks substantive significance
because urban residents in Ghana generally have greater access to
both national and international news. Population size explained 4%
of the variance in the prior information model.

Next, the perception of neighborhood dangerousness was
regressed on the following five exogenous variables: income, gender, victimization, mass media, and length of stay. The analysis
showed that high-income earners were more concerned about the
safety of their neighborhoods than the low-income earners ($B =
0.28$, $p < .001$). It needs to be pointed out that a concern about crime

is not synonymous with fear of crime (Furtensburg, 1971). Other variables that showed notable impact on the resident's perceptions were victimization experiences ($B = 0.26, p < .001$), mass media ($B = 0.22, p < .001$), and gender ($B = 0.17$). These beta weights suggest that a female respondent who had been a victim and who frequently heard crime news would have a negative perception of her neighborhood. In addition, new residents were more likely to perceive their neighborhoods as dangerous places ($B = -0.07$) than old residents. Jointly, the five variables explained more than a quarter (28%) of the variance in the perception of neighborhood dangerousness model.

Given that high levels of acculturation and psychological distress have been related to population size and income (Vega et al., 1994), social activities was regressed on population size and income. Urban residents ($B = 0.11$) and low-income groups ($B = -0.11$) attended Ghanaian social functions more often than their counterparts. Population size and income explained only 2% of the variance in the social activities model.

Finally, to determine the strength of the relationships of the predictor (or independent) variables (both direct and indirect) with the outcome variable, fear of crime, it was regressed on all the variables in the main model. The analyses show that those who worked a night schedule had more fear of crime than the day schedule workers ($B = 0.14, p < 01$). Similarly, but contrary to Sundeen's (1984) findings, respondents who knew about the crime rate prior to their arrival here reported less fear of crime ($B = -0.02$). The prior knowledge presumably prepared them for the adjustment into their new environment. This probably explains why those who perceived their current neighborhoods as more dangerous than others in the DC area and their neighborhoods in Ghana reported less fear of crime ($B = -0.02$). This either suggests that with time living in the more dangerous neighborhood becomes associated with lower fear, or that persons with less fear were more willing to live in the dangerous neighborhoods. It is, therefore, perplexing that Ghanaian immigrants who had lived in their neighborhoods for some time reported more fear of crime than newly arrived immigrants ($B = -0.08$). This contrasts Sundeen's (1984) finding that as immigrants

TABLE 2
Reduced and Structural Equation for Fear of Crime

Dependent Variable	INC x1	GED x2	LOC x3	VIC x4	MED x5	STY x6	PPS x7	SOC x8	WOS x9	PRR x10	DAG x11	R²
WOS												
B		-0.13										0.02
β		-4.89										
SE		0.08										
PRR												
B							-0.20**					0.04
β							-0.30					
SE							0.08					
DAG												
B	0.28***	0.17		0.26***	0.22***	-0.07						0.25***
β	0.25	0.57		0.14	0.14	-0.01						
SE	0.08	0.08		0.07	0.07	0.07						
SOC												
B	0.11						0.11					0.01
β	-0.17						0.29					
SE	0.09						0.09					
FOC												
B	-0.23***	0.06*	0.08	0.03	-0.13**	-0.08	0.14**	0.12	0.14**	-0.02	-0.02	0.15**
β	-7.25	7.25	1.50	0.64	-3.01	0.23	-8.12	0.08	0.47	-0.94	-0.69	
SE	0.11	0.09	0.08	0.09	0.08	0.08	0.09	2.72	0.09	0.08	0.09	

NOTE: INC = income; GED = gender; LOC = locus of control; VIC = victimization; MED = mass media; STY = length of stay; PPS = population size; SOC = social activities; WOS = work schedule; PRR = prior information; DAG = perception of danger; FOC = fear of crime.
*p < .05. **p < .01. ***p < .001.

568

adjust to their environment they acquire a sense of security. This finding ceases to appear anomalous when we consider that the respondents belong to a minority group who usually report high fear of crime in the United States. We may assume that the newly arrived has not yet been socialized into the pervasive sense of fear in the district. Yet, frequent participation in social and cultural activities also increased fear of crime ($B = 0.12$). Because more participation in only the individual's social activities has been linked to less acculturation, this pattern appears to lend credence to the hypothesis that acculturation reduces the immigrant's apprehensions, suspicions, and feelings of fear. A similar relationship was reported by Sundeen (1984). These conflicting findings deserve a closer look before we can make conclusive statements on the relationships between and among the variables.

Similar to findings among American samples, it emerged that low-income earners had more fear of crime than high-income groups ($B = -0.23$, $p < .001$). In addition, respondents who were urban residents in Ghana reported less fear of crime than rural residents ($B = -0.14$, $p < .01$). This could be indicative of a familiarity with the higher crime in the urban centers of Ghana. Contrary with the literature, frequent exposure to crime news reduced fear of crime ($B = -0.13$, $p < .05$). That females ($B = 0.06$, $p < .05$) and former crime victims ($B = 0.03$) reported fear of crime was supportive of findings in the literature.

The total direct effects of the five old variables ($B = -0.41$) emerged as slightly more important predictors of fear of crime than the total direct effects of the six new variables ($B = 0.38$). This suggests the relevance of both the new and the old variables in the explanation of fear of crime. Such a conclusion is buttressed by the fact that the combined direct impact of all the variables on fear of crime ($B = -0.27$) was more important than their combined indirect impact ($B = -0.03$). On the downside, the model explained only 15% of the variance in the fear of crime model. This, however, provides a rationale for its further examination particularly with respect to specification.

570   JOURNAL OF BLACK STUDIES / MARCH 2000

DISCUSSION

This study attempted to explore the fear of crime among a sample of Ghanaian immigrants in the Washington, DC metropolitan area. The significance of the survey is that it was administered in a metropolitan area that has one of the highest crime rates in the country. This study provides the first report on the fear of crime among immigrants in the DC metropolitan area. This study also provides theoretical validity for the consideration of variables such as work schedule, participation in social activities, the duration of residence, locus of control, and knowledge of the crime rate prior to arrival in the United States as critical in the explanation of fear of crime among Ghanaian immigrants.

The analysis of the data shows that the majority of the Ghanaian immigrants in this study experience fear of crime. However, those who were urban residents in Ghana reported less fear than rural residents probably because they were more familiar with the higher crime rates in the urban centers of Ghana. A perplexing finding that emerged was that a prolonged stay in the United States did not reduce an immigrant's fear of crime or fear of strangers. It will be recalled that the univariate analysis showed that almost all the respondents experienced fear of strangers. An explanation of this consistent finding in this study is that the immigrant is affected by the media sensationalization of crime news and its related vicarious victimization. Paradoxically, those who were familiar with the crime rate in the United States prior to arrival reported less fear. This underscores the need for the American embassies abroad as well as the Ghanaian and American media to provide accurate information on the crime situation in the United States to potential visitors.

Other areas of further research could be the assessment of the impact of the dynamic relationships between people's perceptions of the crime situation and their victimization experiences on fear of crime. Given that working a night schedule and having a negative perception of one's neighborhood are related to fear of crime, it would be a wise policy strategy to embody the physical and social improvements of neighborhoods in fear and/or crime reduction interventions. After all, extant research clearly demonstrates that fear of crime does not manifest in a vacuum but is initiated by conventional crime.

It emerged that the more the participation in cultural/social activities, and therefore the lower the level of acculturation into the American society (irrespective of the duration of residence), the greater the fear. An explanation of this finding is that although participation in Ghanaian social activities strengthens ethnic bonds and social support, it also limits the immigrant's social outlook to the specific subgroup. Hence, although Ghanaian immigrants need to maintain their sociocultural ties, it is equally essential that they widen their social interactions to include people from different ethnic groups. Programs such as Africa Day and others that bring immigrants into contact with people of different racial and ethnic backgrounds are in the right direction. Such social interactions reduce suspicions, stereotyping, and fear of crime, which as the literature suggests is basically fear of strangers.

To the extent that the impact of the new variables on fear of crime was less than anticipated, we would be wary to extrapolate our findings beyond the sample in this study. However, at a minimum, this limitation remains a fertile ground for future research that should incorporate the new variables that have been identified in this study. Comparative studies of American and other ethnic groups would also sharpen our measurement of fear of crime. Absent of purposeful research efforts into the immigrant's fear of crime, and in light of the findings in this study, one should hesitate to conclude that other variables are irrelevant to improving our intuitive understanding of the fear of crime among Ghanaians, as well as other immigrants, in the Washington, D.C. metropolitan area.

572   JOURNAL OF BLACK STUDIES / MARCH 2000

APPENDIX: FEAR OF CRIME

Respondents were asked to indicate their levels of fear of 13 specific and most frequently reported crimes in the Washington, D.C. metropolitan area. The responses were graduated on an 11-point scale ranging from 0 = *not afraid at all* to 10 = *very afraid.*

1. Having someone break into your home while you are away.
2. Having someone break into your home while you are present.
3. Being sexually attacked.
4. Being hit by a drunken driver while you are in your car.
5. Having something taken from you by force.
6. Having strangers loiter near your home late at night.
7. Being threatened with a club, a knife, or a gun.
8. Being beaten up by a stranger.
9. Being beaten up by someone you know.
10. Having your car stolen.
11. Being cheated or conned out of your money.
12. Being murdered by a stranger.
13. Being murdered by someone you know.

REFERENCES

Asher, H. (1983). *Causal modeling* (2nd ed.). Beverly Hills, CA: Sage.

Bigman, L. (1990). *Connections.* Washington, DC: The Africans in Washington Project.

Bohrnstedt, G. W., & Carter, T. M. (1971). Robustness in regression analysis. In H. L. Costner (Ed.), *Sociological quarterly.* San Francisco: Jossey-Bass.

Brillon, Y. (1987). *Victimization and fear of crime among the elderly.* Toronto, Canada: Butterworths.

Coston, C.T.M. (1988). *An explanation of the fear of crime among shopping-bag ladies in New York.* Unpublished doctoral dissertation, The State University of New Jersey.

Donnelly, P. G. (1988). Individual and neighborhood influences on fear of crime. *Sociological Focus, 22*(1), 69-85.

Escobar, G. (1990, November 21). Man arrested in I-295 slaying. *The Washington Post,* p. 1.

Ferraro, K. F., & LaGrange, R. L. (1987). The measurement of fear of crime. *Sociological Inquiry, 57*(1), 70-101.

Gerbner, G., & Gross, L. (1976). Living with television: The violence profile. *Journal of Communications, 26,* 173-199.

Ghana Bureau of Statistics. (1991). *Economic survey.* Accra, Ghana: Central Bureau of Statistics.

Harriston, K., Thomas, P., York, M., & Warden, S. (1991, July 28). In the line of fire: Deadly force in the D.C. area. *The Washington Post.*

Ito, K. (1993). Research on the fear of crime: Perceptions and realities of crime in Japan. *Crime & Delinquency, 39,* 385-392.

Kennedy, L., & Krahn, H. (1984). Rural-urban origin and fear of crime: The case for rural baggage. *Rural Sociology, 49,* 247-260.

Kish, L. (1965). *Survey sampling.* New York: John Wiley.

Krannich, R. S., Greider, T., & Little, R. L. (1985). Rapid growth and fear of crime: A four-community comparison. *Rural Sociology, 50,* 193-209.

LaGrange, R. L., & Ferraro, K. (1989). Assessing age and gender differences in perceived risk and fear of crime. *Criminology, 27,* 697-719.

Lee, Y. H. (1985). *Fear of crime among a foreign group in a university setting (Korean, Women, Married).* Unpublished master's thesis, Michigan State University.

Merry, S. E. (1981). *Urban danger: Life in a neighborhood of strangers.* Philadelphia, PA: Temple University Press.

Moore, M. H., & Trojanowicz, R. C. (1988). *Policing and the fear of crime.* Washington, DC: Department of Justice.

Nortey, D.N.A. (1983). Ghana. In E. H. Johnson (Ed.), *International handbook of contemporary development in criminology: Europe, Africa, the Middle East, and Asia* (pp. 273-288). Westport, CT: Greenwood Press.

Office of Criminal Justice Plans and Analysis (OCJPA). (1991). *Crime and justice report.* Washington, DC: Author.

President's Commission on Law Enforcement and Administration of Justice. (1967). *The challenge of crime in a free society.* Washington, DC: Government Printing Office.

Sarpong, P. (1973). *Ghana in restrospect: Some aspects of Ghanaian culture.* Accra, Ghana: Ghana Publishing.

Skogan, W. G., & Maxfield, M. G. (1980). *Coping with crime: Victimization, fear and reactions to crime in three American cities.* Beverly Hills, CA: Sage.

Smith, L., & Hill, G. (1991). Perceptions of crime seriousness and fear of crime. *Sociological Focus, 24,* 315-327.

Sundeen, R. A. (1984). Explaining the fear of crime among international students from developing countries: A revised model. *Criminal Justice Review, 2,* 7-13.

Ward, R., LaGory, M., & Sherman, S. (1986). Fear of crime among the elderly as person/environment interaction. *The Sociological Quarterly, 27,* 327-341.

Warr, M., & Stafford, M. (1983). Fear of victimization: A look at the proximate causes. *Social Forces, 61,* 1033-1043.

Yin, P. (1985). *Victimization of the aged.* Springfield, IL: Charles C Thomas.

[22]

Willingness to Report Crimes:
The Role of Ethnic Group
Membership and Community Efficacy

Robert C. Davis
Nicole J. Henderson

Law enforcement experts and observers of immigrant communities have suggested that immigrants are reluctant to report crimes to the police. Various reasons have been advanced to support this idea, ranging from distrust of authorities to fear of retaliation or deportation to lack of confidence in the police. This study examined willingness to report crimes among residents of six ethnic communities in New York City. In spite of the pessimism expressed in the literature, the authors found that large majorities of respondents said that they would report break-ins, muggings, family violence, and (to a lesser extent) drug selling. Persons who said that their ethnic community was likely to work together to solve local problems and those who believed that their community wielded political power were more likely than those whose communities were disenfranchised to say that they would report crimes.

Keywords: *crime reporting; immigrants; policing; victimization; ethnic*

Two notorious allegations of police misconduct in New York City threw a national spotlight on police dealings with immigrants as well as with established ethnic minorities. In the 1997 Abner Louima case, police in Queens were accused of brutalizing a Haitian immigrant held at a Brooklyn precinct house. Louima, a bank security guard and married father, was taken into custody when police came to break up a fight between two women at a Brooklyn music club. Two officers were convicted of sodomizing him with a plunger after strip searching him in a bathroom of the precinct.

In the 1999 case of Amadou Diallo, four special unit police officers faced grand jury charges of second degree murder in the shooting of an unarmed West African immigrant. Diallo was confronted by officers—again all White—from the NYPD's Street Crimes Unit in the doorway of his Bronx apartment building. The officers, who apparently had mistaken Diallo for a suspected

---

ROBERT C. DAVIS: Vera Institute of Justice. **NICOLE J. HENDERSON**: Vera Institute of Justice.

serial rapist and who may have believed that he was reaching for a gun, shot the street peddler 41 times.

The two incidents tapped into deep-seated frustrations that immigrants and established ethnic minorities have harbored concerning their treatment at the hands of the police. A recent Harris poll ("Changing Attitudes Toward the Police," April 7, 1999) highlighted serious concerns about relations between police and ethnic minorities, for example:

- Most Americans (55%) believe that local police are guilty of brutality against African Americans or Hispanics at least occasionally. Among African Americans, this figure rises to 79%.
- Although only 16% of Whites say that they are sometimes afraid that the police will stop and arrest them even when they are completely innocent, fully 43% of African Americans express this fear.

These poll numbers concur with ample literature that shows serious problems in relations between police and minority communities. Although research has shown that people generally hold favorable views of the police (e.g., Mastrofski, Parks, Reiss, & Worden, 1998, 1999), it has also consistently demonstrated that members of minority communities are more hostile toward and fearful of the police than Whites. Recent studies (e.g., Reisig & Parks, 2000; Weitzer & Tuch, 1999) as well as those dating back as far as the 1960s concur that African Americans evaluate the police more negatively than White citizens (Browning, Cullen, Cao, Kopache, & Stevenson, 1994; Campbell & Schuman, 1972; Hahn, 1969; Jacob, 1971; McCord & Howard, 1968; Scaglion & Condon, 1980; Skogan, 1978; Webb & Marshall, 1995). Moreover, such negative attitudes toward the police are not confined only to African Americans. Hadar and Snortum (1975) reported that Mexican Americans as well as African Americans gave the police lower ratings than Whites.

Although the literature has made clear that there are special problems policing racial minorities, problems are likely to be exacerbated when communities contain large numbers of foreign-born minorities. This is true because immigrants may come to this country with a strong distrust of authority and without an understanding about the role of police in a democratic society. In an earlier study (Davis & Erez, 1996), police and prosecution officials interviewed believed that immigrants are more reluctant to report crimes than native-born Americans. Other observers have expressed this belief as well, although solid empirical data are lacking (Junger, 1990; Meeker & Dombrink, 1988; Pogrebin & Poole, 1990a, 1990b; Sorenson & Telles, 1991).

Greater reluctance by immigrants to report criminal incidents to authorities would not necessarily be expected based on empirical studies of crime reporting. Much of this literature examines how situational factors, such as type of crime, monetary losses, seriousness of injuries, and influence of bystanders, affect people's willingness to report crimes (e.g., Bachman, 1993; Finkelhor & Ormrod, 2001; M. S. Greenberg, Ruback, & Westcott, 1982; M. S. Greenberg, Wilson, Ruback, & Mills, 1979; Kury, Teske, & Wurger, 1999; Laub, 1981). Attempts to assess individual differences in willingness to report crimes have found little variation in reporting rates according to demographic characteristics (e.g., Bachman, 1998; Harlow, 1985; Skogan, 1984) or attitudes toward the police (Fishman, 1979; Skogan, 1984).

However, few empirical studies have probed the decision calculus of persons in a position to report crimes in a way that could potentially differentiate immigrants from nonimmigrants. Kidd and Chayet (1984) proposed a model of crime reporting that represents one of the only attempts to develop a theoretical understanding of the processes that govern how people decide whether or not to report crimes. Kidd and Chayet argued that the decision to report crimes is a function of fear of retaliation by the offender, feelings of helplessness or powerlessness, confidence in the ability of the police to apprehend the offender, and mistrust of authorities.

Several of these factors would tend to operate in a way that would discourage crime reporting within communities composed largely of immigrants. For example, police in many underdeveloped countries are ineffective against crime because they are poorly paid and suffer from low morale and a lack of professionalism. In fact, it is not uncommon for police to supplement their income by looking the other way when crimes are committed or by participating in criminal activity themselves (Neild, 1999). Immigrants who have experienced the police in their country of origin as ineffective or dishonest are unlikely to have confidence in the effectiveness of the police when they migrate to the United States. Misimpressions may be prolonged by a language barrier that prevents immigrants from receiving information about policing from mass media or officers themselves to nearly the same extent as English speakers (Pogrebin & Poole, 1990c). Conaway and Lohr (1994) demonstrated empirically that crime reporting is directly related to prior experiences with the police.

Distrust of law enforcement officials is also a factor in Kidd and Chayet's (1984) model that would tend to depress crime reporting by immigrants. Many immigrants come here carrying the baggage of bad experiences with authorities in their country of origin (Pogrebin & Poole, 1990b). When they do have contact with police here, the contact may be negative because of misunderstandings arising from cultural or language differences. Immigrants' mistrust imported from the country of origin may be exacerbated out of concern about their immigration status (e.g., Meeker & Dombrink, 1988). Law

enforcement officers interviewed in a midwestern city expressed concern
that immigrants do not report because they associate the police with Immigration and Naturalization Services (Herbst & Walker, 2001). Distrust of
authorities may be exacerbated by community norms against seeking help
from outsiders (Yoshioka, DiNoia, & Ullah, 2001).

Fear of retaliation mentioned in Kidd and Chayet's (1984) model is especially salient for immigrants victimized by members of their own nationality.
Many immigrants are victimized by organized rings involved in prostitution,
extortion, and fraud (Horowitz, 2001). These criminals are likely to know the
victim and where he or she lives and are often ruthless in retaliating against
victims who seek redress through the criminal justice system.

Finally, many immigrants tend to settle in ethnically heterogeneous, high-
crime urban neighborhoods—exactly the kinds of communities likely to promote apathy, a low sense of collective efficacy, and a lack of social cohesion
(S. W. Greenberg, Rohe, & Williams, 1982). Such neighborhoods are
thought to promote violence and other antisocial behaviors (e.g., Sampson,
Raudenbush, & Earls, 1997). According to Kidd and Chayet (1984), residents of such neighborhoods may be less likely to report crime because they
feel a sense of helplessness and powerlessness.

Gaining the cooperation of immigrants in crime reporting and police
activities is important because their numbers are large and growing. For
example, in 1980, just more than 14 million foreign-born individuals were
living in the United States (U.S. Bureau of the Census, 1980), and by 1990,
the number of foreign-born people had nearly risen to 20 million (U.S.
Bureau of the Census, 1990).

THE CURRENT STUDY

This article examines crime reporting behavior among immigrant communities and the factors that shape willingness to report, including contacts
with the police, attitudes toward the police, and membership in their local
ethnic community. The current work complements earlier work in which we
examined barriers to participation in the criminal justice system for victims
who are recent immigrants (Davis, Erez, & Avitabile, 1998, 2001). We found
that, although immigrants did face some special problems, overall their experience in the criminal justice system was not unlike that of native-born victims. That is, most immigrant victims were satisfied with their treatment by
criminal justice officials, and when they did have complaints, the complaints
were similar in nature to those of native-born victims. However, criminal justice officials we interviewed believed that many immigrant victims never

used the criminal justice system because they were reluctant to report crimes to the police. Field work in two multiethnic neighborhoods (Jackson Heights, New York, and Logan, Philadelphia) suggested that underreporting was especially acute in ethnic communities that were poorly organized and disenfranchised from the local power structure.

Although other authors have suggested that underreporting among immigrants is commonplace, there has been heretofore little empirical data to support or negate this belief. In the study reported here, we asked immigrants directly whether they had been victims of a recent crime and whether they reported it. We also asked whether they would be willing to report various crimes if they were to witness them. Using this information, we develop a statistical model of crime reporting behavior based loosely on the conceptual framework developed by Kidd and Chayet (1984). Our work tests the extent to which people's failure to report crimes is rooted in factors related to Kidd and Chayet's model, including (a) a sense that their ethnic community is not politically powerful or efficacious, (b) confidence in police abilities, and (c) perceptions of police misconduct. In addition, we also relate crime reporting to experience with the police and to demographic factors such as gender, age, and home ownership.

METHOD & RESEARCH DESIGN

Selection of Site and Ethnic Communities

With 53% of its 128,000 residents foreign-born, Jackson Heights has been called the "United Nations of New York." Its diverse immigrant communities include large numbers of persons of Asian descent (Chinese, Indian, and Korean), Hispanic descent (Dominicans, Colombians, and Ecuadorians), European descent (Italians, Irish, and German), and African descent. In our previous work (Hillenbrand & Davis, 1993), interviews with police and leaders of ethnic communities suggested that there are substantial differences between the various immigrant communities in perceptions of the police and willingness to become involved in the U.S. justice system. For these reasons— and because our previous work familiarized us with the neighborhood, its organizations, and its leaders—we determined to use the 115th precinct in Jackson Heights as the sampling frame for the proposed research.

We targeted six ethnic groups for the survey, including four communities composed largely of immigrants (Colombians, Dominicans, Indians, and Ecuadorians). The other two ethnic groups, Italians and African Americans, were well-established communities. These communities included few immigrants and were included as comparisons to the four newcomer groups. Each of the six communities was healthy and viable, with active grassroots organizations. However, according to police and community leaders, these six communities differed in such important areas as proportion of undocumented immigrants, degree of community organization, and confidence in the police.

Sampling Frame

Using a 1990 census database made available by the New York City Planning Department, a sampling plan was developed.[1] The objective of the plan was to yield a representative sample of 200 residents from each of the six targeted ethnic communities. To achieve this objective, we employed a cluster sampling methodology that sampled block groups with high concentrations of the six ethnic groups. For each block group selected, we set a quota for one or more ethnic groups based on the prevalence of those groups in the 1990 census. Then we sampled every nth house to fill the quota. For example, if our quota was 25 and there were 100 households in the block group, we would sample every fourth household. If the first sampling failed to yield enough completed interviews to fill the quota, we sampled additional households from the same block group until the quota was met.

For each of the six subsamples, a sufficient number of block groups was sampled to yield approximately 400 households. If the initial sample of 400 households proved insufficient, we sampled additional blocks in the same manner.

The sample size projected was designed to yield a 7% to 8% margin of error in estimates, given the 130,000 population from which we were drawing. That meant that we would be able to reliably detect differences of 15% and greater in dependent measures between ethnic groups. That seemed appropriate because we were interested in policy questions (e.g., Are there substantial differences between ethnic groups in experience with the police?), rather than questions involving theory.

Interviewing Procedures

To increase the trust of residents, we began a publicity effort prior to beginning interviews. We contacted ethnic and local newspapers and radio stations. Our overtures were greeted with interest, and stories about our work appeared in three papers and two radio stations. We also were able to enlist the help of several local churches in publicizing our work from the pulpit or in bulletins. It was our hope that this publicity would help to decrease suspicion of our work by potential respondents, particularly recent immigrants with high levels of suspicion of authorities.

Once publicity efforts had been completed, we sent out interviewers to do a listing or enumeration of the addresses of all residential structures on sampled streets. We used a reverse telephone directory to match phone numbers to the listing of addresses. For the bulk of residences for which phone numbers were available, interview attempts were made by phone. When residences did not have a phone or had an unlisted number, we dispatched interviewers to conduct in-person interviews.

When contact was made, interviewers attempted to determine whether any member of the household fell into one of the study's six targeted ethnic groups. The individual answering the phone was asked the following screening question: Does anyone in this household identify themselves with any of the following ethnic groups: Ecuadorian, Indian, Colombian, Dominican, African American, or Italian? If a positive response was given, the interviewer began the process of identifying which household member was to be interviewed.

Once it had been established that the household had passed the ethnicity screen, the interviewer decided whom to interview on the basis of residents' dates of birth. We selected from among residents at home at the time of our call the person older than 18 years of age who had the most recent birthday. However, this decision process proved challenging for some respondents, so we soon changed the procedure to select the person whose first name began with the letter closest to the beginning of the English alphabet.

Interviewer Selection and Training

Three full-time interviewers were bilingual in English and Spanish. Several part-time interviewers were proficient in Italian and Hindi. One of the full-time and all of the part-time interviewers were recruited locally within Jackson Heights with the assistance of ethnic community organizations.

Initially, interviewers received a 1-day training session, which included instruction in sampling protocols and practice administering survey instruments. Following orientation, interviewer trainees were assigned to work with senior project staff for several days to master interviewing skills.

Response Rate

Among 4,168 households contacted for the study, 1,622 did not have a member of the six targeted ethnic groups. Seventy-five were disqualified due to physical impairment or recency of moving to the neighborhood. Among the 2,471 remaining eligible households contacted, interviews were completed with 1,123, or 45%.

Measurement

All potential respondents were asked questions to establish their ethnic group membership. Those eligible for the survey based on those answers were asked questions in the following domains.

Willingness to Report Crimes

We used an approach to measuring this construct that proved successful in our earlier research on citizen reporting of drug crimes (Hillenbrand & Davis, 1993). We first asked respondents whether they believed that people in their ethnic community were likely to report various criminal situations to the police, adapted from the list used by Hillenbrand and Davis (1993). Respondents' beliefs were then ranked on a 5-point scale.

Following the questions on beliefs about reporting in their community, we asked respondents whether they had witnessed the same list of criminal acts, whether they called the police, and, if not, why not. We also asked the respondents whether they hypothetically would report various criminal situations to the police.

Community Empowerment

We asked two questions that assessed the extent to which respondents perceived their ethnic communities to be integrated into the local political power structure. The first asked whether they felt that their ethnic group was well-represented in local politics. The other asked whether local politicians were responsive to the needs of their ethnic community.

Community Efficacy

We adapted a scale developed by Chavis and Wandersman (1990) for research on block associations and used in our previous work on community anti-drug organizations (Davis, Smith, Lurigio, & Skogan, 1991). For example, the following question was used: If there was a problem in receiving some service from the city, do you think that persons in your ethnic community could get the problem solved?

Perceptions of Police Misconduct

This scale measures the extent to which people are fearful and distrustful of the police. To measure this concept, we used a modified version of Jefferson and Walker's (1993) Distrust of Police Measure. Jefferson and Walker's scale measures the extent to which people thought the police took part in various forms of misconduct, including using threats when questioning people, using unnecessary violence, maintaining inaccurate records, and making up evidence (i.e., Do you fear that the police will use violence against you?).

Perceptions of Police Competence

This scale measures the extent to which respondents feel that the police are doing a good job. Our measure was based on the 10-item Chicago Attitudes Toward Community Policing Scale (Johnson, 1993), designed to assess citizen evaluations of police in their neighborhoods. The items asked about police responsiveness to neighborhood concerns and whether citizens believe the police are doing a good job in their neighborhood.

Experience With the Police

We adapted a scale used by the Chicago Community Policing Evaluation Consortium (Johnson, 1993). The 11-item Chicago Experiences with Police Scale (Johnson, 1993) counts the number of different reasons why a person has had contact with the police during the past year. The scale has both citizen-initiated and police-initiated components. The citizen-initiated items include calls to report crimes, emergencies, suspicious persons, odd noises, and other events. Items also include questions on whether citizens contact the police in order to receive or give information about community concerns or other noncrime experiences. The police-initiated items include questions about whether the police have stopped the individual on the street while he or she was out walking or pulled him or her over while driving.

Respondent Characteristics

Previous studies on perceptions of the police have indicated the importance of respondent characteristics, including socioeconomic status (i.e., education, employment, household income, and income source), age, gender, and history of victimization (see Webb & Marshall, 1995 for a recent review). We included these variables as well as length of time that respondents have been in the United States, time in the neighborhood, immigration status, and number of members of household.

Subjects

The study included 201 Colombians, 200 Ecuadorians, 200 Dominicans, 176 African Americans, 176 Indians, and 170 Italians. Twenty-seven percent of the sample was born in the United States and 73% in other countries. Respondents had been in the United States for an average of 16 years and had been in their present neighborhood for an average of 11 years.[2] An overwhelming majority (94%) claimed to be legal residents of the United States.

Fifty-six percent of respondents were women and 44% men. The median age of the sample was 37 years.[3] Most respondents (77%) lived in family units of two to four persons. But 17% lived alone and 6% lived in households of five or more persons. Fifty-eight percent of households had children living in them.

Sample participants were primarily lower middle class. Seven in 10 respondents in the sample had graduated secondary school. About one third (31%) owned their own homes.[4] Most were in the work force: Forty-seven percent had worked full-time during the previous week and another 12% had worked part-time. The sample also included housekeepers (18%) and those who had retired (10%) or were in school (4%). Respondents who worked did so for an average of 45 weeks during the previous year. Household income was less than $20,000 for 42% of the sample and was higher than $20,000 for 58%.

RESULTS

Reporting in Hypothetical Situations

We found major differences between the six ethnic communities in willingness to report four criminal activities, including muggings, break-ins, drug sales, and domestic violence. The highest rates of reporting were for break-ins: Eighty-three percent of respondents said that they would be very likely to report a break-in to someone's home. Thirteen percent said that they would be somewhat likely to report, and just 4% said that they would not be likely to report a break-in that they witnessed. African Americans had the greatest percentage who said that they would be very likely to report a break-in at 93% (see Table 1). Ecuadorians and Indians were at the low end, with 76% and 77%, respectively, saying that they would very likely report a break-

TABLE 1:   Percentage of Respondents "Very Likely" to Report Specific Crimes According to Ethnic Groups

Type of Crime	African Americans	Ecuadorians	Colombians	
Break-ins	93%	76%	87%	
Muggings	88%	70%	78%	
Family violence	66%	70%	80%	
Drug sales	59%	46%	49%	
Type of Crime	Dominicans	Indians	Italians	Prob.
Break-ins	81%	77%	85%	.000
Muggings	78%	67%	83%	.000
Family violence	80%	65%	61%	.000
Drug sales	44%	55%	73%	.000

in. Although the differences by ethnicity were not substantial, they did attain statistical significance.

Muggings were the next most likely crimes to be reported, with 77% of respondents saying that they would be very likely to report a mugging, 18% saying that they would be somewhat likely, and 5% saying that they would be unlikely to report a mugging to authorities. Once again, African Americans had the highest proportion (88%) that said that they would be very likely to report a mugging. Indians and Ecuadorians had the lowest percentages at 67% and 70%, respectively. Again, these differences attained statistical significance.

Our data contradict the often-expressed idea that immigrants are unlikely to report family violence. Overall, 71% of respondents said that they would be very likely to report family violence incidents, 21% said that they would be somewhat likely, and 8% said they were not likely. Colombians and Dominicans had the most respondents who said that they would be very likely to report family violence, each with 80%.

All four of the other ethnic groups had between 60 and 70% of respondents who said that they would be very likely to report family violence. These differences were statistically significant as well.

Drug selling was the crime least likely to be reported to authorities. Only 54% of respondents said that they would be very likely to report it, 24% said that they would be somewhat likely, and 22% said they were not likely. Italians had the highest proportion that said that they would be very likely to report it (73%). The three Latino communities had the lowest proportions,

with 44% of Dominicans, 47% of Ecuadorians, and 49% of Colombians saying that they would be very likely to report drug selling to the authorities.
These results were also highly reliable.

We combined the individual items to create a composite scale of willingness to report crimes. The reliability (alpha) for this four-item scale was 0.69.
There was a significant difference between the six ethnic communities on the
composite measure.[5] Italians and African Americans, the longest-established
communities, had the highest composite scores (2.71 and 2.70, respectively).
Ecuadorians and Indians had the lowest composite scores (2.52 and 2.53,
respectively).

A multivariate analysis conducted with this scale showed no significant
differences in willingness to report among the six ethnic groups once other
factors were introduced into the model (see Table 2). The best predictors of
willingness to report were measures of community efficacy: Respondents
who perceived their communities as better able to solve problems and more
politically empowered expressed greater willingness to report crimes than
other respondents. Experience with the police also played a significant role in
willingness to report: Those persons who had had voluntary contacts with the
police expressed greater willingness to report crimes and those who had had
involuntary contacts expressed less willingness. Finally, respondents who
had been victims during the past year tended to express less willingness to
report crimes than those who had not been victims.

Reporting Actual Crimes

In addition to asking respondents hypothetical questions about reporting
crimes, we also asked those who were victimized whether they had reported
crimes they experienced to authorities, including robbery, assault, burglary,
domestic violence, and ethnic hate crimes. About 2 in 3 (63%) had reported
the crime to police.

Because numbers of particular crimes are small—only 40 persons said
they were victims of family violence and 21 claimed to be victims of bias
crimes[6]—we did not try to break this figure down according to type of victimization. We did, however, break down reporting of actual crimes by ethnicity.
Consistent with the questions on hypothetical reporting, African Americans
were somewhat more likely than other groups to report actual crimes. Nearly
three quarters of African Americans who were victimized reported it to the
police compared to about 60% of the five other ethnic groups (see Table 3).
Because of the small numbers, however, this difference did not approach statistical significance.

TABLE 2:   Multivariate Analysis of Willingness to Report Crimes

Variable	Coefficient	Wald Statistic[a]	Significance
Ethnicity[b]		1.57	.905
African American	−.12	0.29	.589
Ecuadorian	.21	1.26	.263
Colombian	.05	0.07	.795
Dominican	−.08	0.22	.640
Italian	−0.8	0.16	.686
Age	−.01	1.33	.248
Education	.06	0.84	.360
Own/rent home	−.26	1.82	.178
U.S. born	.05	0.05	.832
Gender	−.17	1.10	.293
Community efficacy	.63	21.45	.000
Comm. empowerment	.44	9.65	.002
Victim past year	−.31	6.20	.013
Stopped by police	−.33	4.51	.034
Contacted police	.16	10.25	.001
Police misconduct	.21	2.96	.085
Police effectiveness	.09	0.75	.386

a. Wald statistics are an indication of the effect of each independent variable, controlling for the effects of the other predictors. The larger the Wald statistic, the more explanatory power that a variable has.
b. Coefficients for ethnicity indicator variables are deviations from overall mean. One category (Indian) was omitted to avoid overdetermination of the model.

TABLE 3:   Proportion of Respondents Who Reported Actual Crimes Among Six Ethnic Communities

	African Americans	Ecuadorians	Colombians	Dominicans	Indians	Italians
%	74	˙61	65	61	60	61
n	(31)	(67)	(57)	(59)	(45)	(33)

CONCLUSIONS

In spite of pessimism expressed in the literature about the reluctance of immigrants to report crimes to the police, we found that large majorities of respondents said that they would report break-ins, muggings, and family violence. Respondents were less enthusiastic about reporting drug selling but, even here, a majority said that they would inform authorities.

Surprisingly, willingness to report crimes was not strongly linked to perceptions of police effectiveness or police misconduct. But it was linked to experience: Respondents who had had involuntary contacts with the police were less likely to say that they would report a crime, whereas those who had had voluntary contacts were more willing to report. The best predictors of crime reporting, however, were the measures of community empowerment: Persons who said that their ethnic community was likely to work together to solve local problems and those who believed that their community wielded political power were more likely than those whose communities were disenfranchised to say that they would report crimes.

Others have found that community efficacy is an important predictor of crime rates. For example, Sampson et al. (1997) found that *collective efficacy* (defined as a combination of neighborhood cohesion and informal social control) was inversely related to neighborhood violence and homicide rates. Bursik and Grasmick (1999) argued that the ability of a neighborhood to solicit resources from external sources is important for effective regulation of crime and delinquency. Our measures of community efficacy share some characteristics of the Sampson et al. and Bursik and Grasmick conceptualizations. We speculate that one way in which community efficacy leads to lower crime rates is by an increased willingness of residents to report crimes and suspicious incidents to authorities.

Our findings also lend support to the community justice view that criminal justice planning must consider a community's social networks and institutional capacity. The comprehensive community initiatives that have come out of that tradition are designed to address multiple neighborhood problems simultaneously through coordination and collaboration of efforts (Clear & Karp, 1998). Our findings suggest that, to increase citizens' willingness to report crimes, it may not be sufficient to conduct civic responsibility advertising campaigns or even to attempt to increase confidence in the police. It may be necessary to promote a community's sense of empowerment and integration into the local political structure.

Having noted the importance of a comprehensive approach, it is still important for the police specifically to find ways to reach out to immigrant communities and find ways to build trust. Respondents in our study have suggested some ways that this might be done. They believed that the most effective ways to bridge the gap between the police and ethnic communities was to increase the number of foot patrol officers and to sponsor meetings with the community. The fact that many departments across the country are adopting these approaches is a positive sign in the development of greater confidence in the police in immigrant communities.

We caution that our findings are based on immigrant communities in New York City. New York is unique and may attract people who possess unique or special skills or backgrounds.[7] The experiences of the immigrant communities we studied may not parallel those of Chinese, Mexican, Russian, or the many other immigrant groups that have come to the United States in large numbers in recent years. Still, we believe that the theme of empowerment that emerged from our research is likely to be important to immigrant groups regardless of where they come from and where they settle.

NOTES

1. The plan was developed with assistance from experts from the University of Baltimore's Schaffer Center for Public Policy.

2. Median time in the United States for foreign-born respondents was 11 years; 1 in 4 immigrants had been in the United States for 6 years or less.

3. These sample gender and age distributions are relatively similar to census data for Jackson Heights, where 51% of residents are females and the average age is 35 years (Department of City Planning, 1992).

4. The sample proportion of homeowners is comparable to the 34% figure for Jackson Heights (Department of City Planning, 1992).

5. $F(5, 1071) = 5.32, p < .0001$.

6. Persons who responded affirmatively to the question, "During the past year, has anyone assaulted you or damaged your property because you are [ethnic identity]?"

7. We are indebted to an anonymous reviewer for this observation.

REFERENCES

Bachman, R. (1993). Predicting the reporting of rape victimizations: Have rape reforms made a difference? *Criminal Justice and Behavior, 20*(3), 254-270.

Bachman, R. (1998). The factors related to rape reporting behavior and arrest: New evidence from the National Crime Victimization Survey. *Criminal Justice and Behavior, 25*(1), 8-30.

Browning, S., Cullen, F. T., Cao, L., Kopache, R., & Stevenson, T. (1994). Race and getting hassled by the police: A research note. *Police Studies, 15,* 3-22.

Bursik, R. J., Jr., & Grasmick, H. G. (1999). Economic deprivation and neighborhood crime rates, 1960-1980. In F. R. Scarpitti & A. L. Nielsen (Eds.), *Crime and criminals: Contemporary and classic readings* (pp. 298-308). Los Angeles: Roxbury.

Campbell, A., & Schuman, H. (1972). A comparison of Black and White experiences in the city. In C. M. Haar (Ed.), *The end of innocence: A suburban reader.* Glenview, IL: Scott Foresman.

Chavis, D. M., & Wandersman, A. (1990). Sense of community in the urban environment: A catalyst for participation and community. *American Journal of Community Psychology, 18,* 55-82.

Clear, T. R., & Karp, D. R. (1998). The community justice movement. In D. R. Karp (Ed.), *Community justice: an emerging field.* Lanham, MD: Rowman & Littlefield.

Conaway, M. R., & Lohr, S. L. (1994). Longitudinal analysis of factors associated with reporting crime. *Journal of Quantitative Criminology, 10*(1), 23-39.

Davis, R. C., Erez, E., & Avitabile, N. (1998). Immigrants and the criminal justice system: An exploratory study. *Violence and Victims, 13*, 21-30.

Davis, R. C., Erez, E., & Avitabile, N. (2001). Access to justice for immigrants who are victimized: The perspectives of police and prosecutors. *Criminal Justice Policy Review, 12*, 183-196.

Davis, R. C., Smith, B. E., Lurigio, A. L., & Skogan, W. G. (1991). *Community response to crack: Grassroots anti-drug programs*. Final report of Victim Services (New York) to the National Institute of Justice.

Department of City Planning. (1992). *Demographic profiles: A portrait of New York City's community districts from the 1980 and 1990 censuses of population and housing*. New York: Author.

Finkelhor, D., & Ormrod, R. (2001). Factors in underreporting of crimes against juveniles. *Child Maltreatment, 6*(3), 219-229.

Fishman, G. (1979). Patterns of victimisation and notification. *British Journal of Criminology, 19*(2), 146-157.

Greenberg, M. S., Ruback, R. B., & Westcott, D. R. (1982). Decision making by crime victims: A multimethod approach. *Law & Society Review, 17*, 47-84.

Greenberg, M. S., Wilson, C. E., Ruback, R. B., & Mills, M. K. (1979). Social and emotional determinants of victim crime reporting. *Social Psychology Quarterly, 42*(4), 364-372.

Greenberg, S. W., Rohe, W., & Williams, J. (1982). *Safe and secure neighborhoods: Physical characteristics and informal territorial control in high and low crime neighborhoods*. Washington, DC: National Institute of Justice, U.S. Department of Justice.

Hadar, I., & Snortum, J. R. (1975). The eye of the beholder: Differential perceptions of police by the police and the public. *Criminal Justice and Behavior, 2*, 37-54.

Hahn, H. (1969). Violence: The view from the ghetto. *Mental Hygiene, 53*, 509-512.

Harlow, C. W. (1985). *Reporting crimes to the police*. Washington, DC: U.S. Department of Justice, Bureau of Justice Statistics.

Herbst, L., & Walker, S. (2001) Language barriers in the delivery of police services: A study of police and Hispanic interactions in a midwestern city. *Journal of Criminal Justice, 29*(4), 329-340.

Hillenbrand, S., & Davis, R. C. (1993). Residents' perceptions of drug activity, crime, and neighborhood satisfaction. In R. Davis, A. Lurigio, & D. Rosenbaum (Eds.), *Drugs and the community* (pp. 5-18). Springfield, IL: Charles C Thomas.

Horowitz, C. (2001). *An examination of U.S. immigration policy and serious crime*. Washington, DC: Center for Immigration Studies.

Jacob, H. (1971). Black and White perceptions of justice in the city. *Law and Society Review, 5*, 69-89.

Jefferson, T., & Walker, M. A. (1993). Attitudes to the police of ethnic minorities in a provincial city. *British Journal of Criminology, 33*(2), 251-266.

Johnson, T. A. (1993). *The public and the police in the city of Chicago*. Chicago: Centers for Urban Affairs and Policy Research, Northwestern University.

Junger, M. (1989). Discrepancies between police and self-report data for Dutch racial minorities. *British Journal of Criminology, 29*(3), 273-284.

Kidd, R. F., & Chayet, E. (1984). Why do victims fail to report? The psychology of criminal victimization. *Journal of Social Issues, 40*, 39-50.

Kury, H., Teske, R. H. C., & Wurger, M. (1999). Reporting of crime to the police in the federal republic of Germany: A comparison of the old and the new lands. *Justice Quarterly, 16*(1), 121-151.

Laub, J. H. (1981). Ecological considerations in victim reporting to the police. *Journal of Criminal Justice, 9,* 419-430.

Mastrofski, S. D., Parks, R. B., Reiss, A. J., & Worden, R. E. (1998, July). Policing neighborhoods: A report from Indianapolis. *National Institute of Justice Research in Brief.*

Mastrofski, S. D., Parks, R. B., Reiss, A. J., & Worden, R. E. (1999, July). Policing neighborhoods: A report from St. Petersburg. *National Institute of Justice Research in Brief.*

McCord, W., & Howard, J. (1968). Negro opinions in three riot cities. *American Behavioral Scientist, 11,* 24-27.

Meeker, J. W., & Dombrink, J. (1988). The undocumented and their legal needs. *Humboldt Journal of Social Relations, 15*(2), 105-132.

Neild, R. (1999). *Confronting a culture of impunity: The promise and pitfalls of civilian review of police in Latin America.* Washington, DC: Washington Office on Latin America.

Pogrebin, M. A., & Poole, E. D. (1990a). Culture conflict and crime in the Korean American community. *Criminal Justice Policy Review, 4*(1), 69-78.

Pogrebin, M. A., & Poole, E. D. (1990b). Crime and law enforcement policy in the Korean American community. *Police Studies, 13*(2), 57-66.

Pogrebin, M. A., & Poole, E. D. (1990c). South Korean immigrants and crime: A case study. *Journal of Ethnic Studies, 17*(3), 47-80.

Reisig, M. D., & Parks, R. B. (2000). Experience, quality of life, and neighborhood context: A hierarchical analysis of satisfaction with the police. *Justice Quarterly, 17,* 607-629.

Sampson, R. J., Raudenbush, S., & Earls, F. (1997). Neighborhoods and violent crime: A multilevel study of collective efficacy. *Science, 277,* 918-924.

Scaglion, R., & Condon, R. (1980). Determinants of attitudes toward city police. *Criminology, 17,* 485-494.

Skogan, W. G. (1978). Citizens' satisfaction with police services: Individual and contextual effects. *Policy Studies Journal, 6,* 469-479.

Skogan, W. G. (1984). Reporting crime to the police: The status of world research. *Journal of Research in Crime and Delinquency, 21*(2), 113-137.

Sorenson, S. A., & Telles, C. A. (1991). Self-reports of spousal violence in a Mexican-American and non-Hispanic White population. *Violence and Victims, 6*(1), 3-15.

U.S. Bureau of the Census. (1980). *Census of population and housing.* Washington, DC: Author.

U.S. Bureau of the Census. (1990). *Census of population and housing.* Washington, DC: Author.

Webb, V. J., & Marshall, C. F. (1995). The relative importance of race and ethnicity on citizen attitudes toward the police. *American Journal of Police, 14*(2), 45-46.

Weitzer, R., & Tuch, S. A. (1999). Race, class, and perceptions of discrimination by the police. *Crime and Delinquency, 45,* 494-507.

Yoshioka, M. R., DiNoia, J., & Ullah, K. (2001). Attitudes toward marital violence: An examination of four Asian communities. *Violence Against Women, 7*(8), 900-926.

[23]

Risk, fear, harm: Immigrant women's perceptions of the "policing solution" to woman abuse

SANDRA WACHHOLZ[1] & BAUKJE MIEDEMA[2]

[1]*Criminology Department, University of Southern Maine, Portland, Maine;* [1]*Research Associate Family Medicine, Dalhousie University, Dr Everett Chalmers Hospital, Fredericton, New Brunswick*

Abstract. Over the last two decades in Canada, police intervention in woman abuse cases has become one of the primary responses to this form of violence against women. As a review of the literature reveals, however, very few studies have sought to examine women's perceptions of the "policing solution" to woman, and only a handful have explored the views of immigrant women. This is an unfortunate hiatus as studies indicate that criminal justice intervention in woman abuse cases can often bring in tow a multitude of harms to women who are socially and economically marginalized. As a step towards addressing this hiatus, this article reports on the perceptions held by forty-eight immigrant women about the "policing solution" to woman. The data were generated from focus group interviews that occurred in New Brunswick in the spring of 1997. Many of the women indicated that they held a number of fears about police intervention in woman abuse cases and they identified a myriad of forms of harm that could and often does occur pursuant to police involvement in such situations given immigrant women's socio-economic vulnerability. The concerns and feelings that the women expressed about police intervention mirror, at some level, many of the emotional responses and dynamics that arise for women when they experience woman abuse.

Introduction

Over the last two decades in Canada there has been a growing interest in developing a more aggressive criminal justice response to woman abuse. Fueled by a desire to emphasize the criminal nature and seriousness of woman abuse, various jurisdictions have adopted a variety of new police programs and policies to address woman abuse, with mandatory charging policies resting as the cornerstone of many of these initiatives.[1] As such, police intervention in woman abuse cases has become one of the primary responses to this deeply structural social problem.

Although the notion and practice of increased police intervention in woman abuse cases has received wide support among various state officials and women advocates, it is identified by many as a limited and inherently problematic approach that can do little to deter such violence or alter the socio-economic conditions that sustain woman abuse (Currie and MacLean,

1992; DeKeseredy and MacLoed, 1997). Clearly, police intervention in these cases does send important messages about the serious criminal nature of woman abuse and it does provide victims with some level of immediate protection. However, increasing numbers of studies provide evidence of the limited role that initiatives such as mandatory arrest policies can play in reducing woman abuse. Few arrests are ever prosecuted, and there is evidence to suggest that in some instances certain individuals are more frequently violent if they are arrested (Martin and Mosher, 1995; Sherman, 1992a; Sherman and Smith, 1992). Concomitantly, various studies report a trend in "dual arrest" where the female victims of abuse are also arrested by the police – a practice which some suggest points to the over enforcement of mandatory arrest policies (Martin, 1997).

While there is a growing body of critique of the current police practices designed to address woman abuse, a review of the literature reveals that very few studies in Canada have sought to directly examine women's perceptions of and willingness to invoke police intervention. This is an unfortunate hiatus for as Martin and Mosher (1995: 3) argue, criminal justice intervention in woman abuse cases can often bring a multitude of harms to women, "particularly those who are socially and economically marginalized."

One group that is thought to be especially resistant to police intervention given the multiple levels of oppression that many endure is immigrant women. To date, however, much of the information about their perceptions of police intervention in woman abuse cases has been biographical, anecdotal, or "second hand" in nature and has generally focused on the views of immigrant women who reside in large, urban areas (MacLeod et al., 1993). This has left many important questions unanswered. For example, given the added level of isolation that many immigrant women who reside in rural areas endure, do they fear that police intervention in cases of woman abuse will generate even greater isolation for them? Recognizing the need for research in this area, the authors of this article conducted focus group interviews with forty-eight immigrant women who reside in New Brunswick, a predominately rural province, in an effort to explore their perceptions of police intervention in woman abuse cases; approximately one-third of the participants indicated that they had been abused by a partner or husband while residing in Canada. The research was part of a larger project that was designed to examine the reasons why abused immigrant women are reluctant to access the criminal justice system and justice related services.

Like the unfolding layers of an onion, many of the women indicated that they held a number of fears about police intervention in woman abuse cases and they identified a myriad of forms of harm that could and often does occur pursuant to police involvement in such situations given immigrant women's socio-economic vulnerability. The concerns and feelings that the women expressed about police intervention mirror, at some level, many of the emotional responses and dynamics that arise for women when they experience woman abuse. For example, a significant number of the women stated that calling the police could isolate them from their friends and community, foster feelings of disempowerment, and place them in a position where they are forced to interact with someone who they may not trust, but who has power over them. Such findings reflect a pattern, as DeKeseredy and MacLeod (1997: 4) would argue, where "well-intentioned responses to woman abuse can actually add to the experiences of uncertainly, isolation, unequal power dynamics, unfairness and low self-esteem that . . . women suffer at the hands of their abusers."

This article reviews these findings and, as such, highlights some of the many reasons why the "policing solution" to woman abuse can do little to address the needs of this population. Joining a growing body of literature, the authors argue that police intervention needs to be "de-centered" as the eminent response to woman abuse. The article begins with a succinct discussion of the development of and support for the "policing solution" to woman abuse and then turns to a discussion of the participants perceptions of police intervention in immigrant woman abuse cases.

Support for the policing solution to woman abuse

As Loader (1997: 11) notes, "those who seek to mobilize more or 'tougher' policing as a response to crime find themselves swimming with the emotional tide." Clearly over the last two decades in Canada the emotional tide has been flowing toward greater and more aggressive police intervention in woman abuse cases. Government reports, the media, and academic journals are replete with arguments advocating for such action (Martin and Mosher, 1995). Victim and women's advocate groups have played an important role in ushering in state-based reforms against violent men. Frustrated by the police's selective inattention historically to woman abuse, these advocates have worked on a number of fronts to secure more decisive police action in cases of woman abuse (Davis and Smith, 1995; Martin and Mosher, 1995). The culmination of support for a more aggressive criminal justice response to woman abuse has produced such legal initiatives as mandatory arrest and no-drop prosecutorial policies.

It is important to note that while there is significant support for the law and order, police solution to crime in general, and to woman abuse in particular, a burgeoning collection of research has been generated which points to the rather limited role the police can play in reducing crime. For example, numerous studies now suggest that increasing the number of police officers and shortening police response times to crime scenes have made little difference to crime rates (Bayley, 1994; Loader, 1997). In turn, as noted earlier, the mandatory arrest policies that have arisen across Canada have done little to reduce woman abuse (Morley and Mullender, 1992). However, even against the weight of this evidence, general public sentiment continues to be ". . . marked by high 'fantasy content' regarding what the police can and should do" (Elias, 1987; cited in Loader, 1997: 3).

The increased emphasis and faith in police involvement in woman abuse cases is, in part, thought to be driven by liberal, legal ideology. The promotion of aggressive police intervention is premised on the belief that by treating woman abuse like other assaults, female victims will be afforded more equality of opportunity to justice and will be provided with greater equal rights. Justice demands, according to liberal philosophy, ". . .that those who are similarly situated receive similar treatment" (Martin and Mosher, 1995: 15). However, the "policing solution" not only resonates well with the tenets of liberal, legal philosophy, but it is also congruent with current neo-conservative, law and order ideologies regarding crime control. Within this belief system, the police are thought to be a viable and critical means to reduce crime.

Loader (1997) notes, however, that such social divisions as class, race, gender and ethnicity structure the faith granted to the police. The axes of such social divisions can foster different types of relationships between the police and certain groups in society. Marginalized groups may be less willing to grant respect and authority to the police pursuant to certain experiences that they have had with them. In this regard, many immigrant women may be quite resistant to police intervention in situations of woman abuse given their experiences with the police in Canada and in their countries of origin. The harm that police intervention may foster based on immigrant women's socio-economic vulnerability may also function as a disincentive to calling the police.

As noted earlier, however, very little research has been undertaken to explore immigrant women's perceptions of police intervention in woman abuse cases. Most documents that address the issue of abused immigrant women's perceptions of the police are based on anecdotal information or on a few select case studies. Studies based on predominantly non-immigrant populations have found that many abused women do not believe that arrest and incarceration can effectively address woman abuse. As a case in point, Chalmers and Smith (1988) indicated that only six percent of the 106 battered women in their study viewed police involvement as the best means to end woman abuse. The sample consisted of individuals who had resided in a battered women's shelter in Saskatchewan. The overwhelming majority of these women considered the provision of shelters and public education to be more desirable than police intervention.

In one of the few Canadian studies designed to examine abused immigrant women's perception of police intervention in woman abuse cases, Martin and Mosher (1995) found that the eleven women in their study held strong reservations about the police and about their ability to deal effectively with male violence against women. The eleven participants were women from Latin America who were residing in Toronto and members of "Women of Courage", an organization established to support survivors of wife abuse. As revealed through in-depth interviews, the women were united by their experiences of abuse and by their shared fear of police intervention.

Their concerns about invoking police involvement are summarized in the following passage:

> When questioned about the factors which they considered in deciding whether or not to call the police three of the women expressed fear of deportation or other negative immigration consequences ... The other factors which women considered in deciding whether to contact the police were as follows: feelings of shame and betrayal if police were involved (three); fear of ruination of the family (two); fear that police involvement would make things worse (five); fear of children's aid involvement (two); fear of the financial consequences should her husband be incarcerated (three); concern for her husband (two); that it would be useless to contact the police (three); concern about language barriers (two) and; fear of the police (one)   (Martin and Mosher, 1995: 21).

Even in the wake of such fear, six of the women contacted the police. The participants did not, however, lend their full support to the mandatory arrest, no-drop prosecutorial policy adopted by the police and courts in Toronto.[2] Seven of the eleven women felt that the abuser should always be charged, but only one woman indicated that she liked the policy of mandatory arrest in combination with a no-drop prosecutorial policy. The overwhelming majority of the women felt the victims of woman abuse should have the right to dismiss charges against their abusers.

Various documents produced by organizations and government bodies also suggest that abused immigrant women are often afraid to invoke police intervention (Currie, 1995; MacLeod and Shin, 1990). As a case in point, Godin (1994) notes that some abused immigrant women may be reluctant to call the police given that they have immigrated from a country where the police were seen as part of an oppressive state. This account is not, however, based on an empirical study.

306   SANDRA WACHHOLZ AND BAUKJE MIEDEMA

As this review has attempted to demonstrate, then, little empirical research has been undertaken to examine immigrant women's perceptions of the "policing solution" to woman abuse even though immigrant women are a significant and important percentage of the Canadian population, accounting for approximately 16% of the female population in 1991 (Statistics of Canada, 1996). As a step toward addressing this problem, this article provides data that has been generated from the direct participation and insight of immigrant women and, in particular, abused immigrant women.

Methodology

Data collection method

Given that focus groups involve a group effort that often produces a wide range of information, ideas, and insights (Festervand, 1985), this method was identified as a useful technique through which to explore immigrant women's perceptions of police intervention in woman abuse cases. Another reason for selecting this method was that focus groups have been known to foster friendships and networking among research participants who share similar interests, concerns, and problems. It was the hope of the researchers that the focus group meetings would serve as a catalyst for this process.

Six focus groups were held in different locations ranging from small towns to larger cities across New Brunswick in the early spring of 1997. The focus groups were co-facilitated by the researchers and took place in a diverse range of locales: offices of volunteer organizations, church basements, and living rooms. Each focus group began with the presentation of two case vignettes (See Appendix A for a review of the vignettes). The first vignette described a situation where a woman was being abused and the participants were asked to imagine that she was a native born citizen residing in their country of origin. They were then encouraged to describe how women in their country of origin generally deal with woman abuse. The second vignette described a situation that was similar to the first, but in this instance the abused woman was an immigrant who had lived in Canada for five years. The participants were again asked to describe how the woman might deal with the situation, assuming that she was from their country of origin. The case vignettes inevitably led to discussion about the utility and effectiveness of police intervention in woman abuse cases. Throughout the course of the focus group discussions, contingency questions were asked about the police. It is important to note that the case vignettes allowed the women to talk about their abuse in the third person, if they wished to do so.

PERCEPTIONS OF THE "POLICING SOLUTION" TO WOMAN ABUSE   307

Profile of the participants

Forty-eight immigrant women, who had been recruited from various immigrant organizations, participated in the focus groups. To generate this group of women, the researchers contacted the chairpersons of immigrant women organizations who, upon learning about the objectives and ethical considerations of the study, approached potential participants. In a few of the research sites, the chairpersons provided a list of potential participant to the researchers and who then made contact with the women. Of the forty-eight participants in the study, forty-two agreed to provide demographic information about themselves and their families.

The women immigrated to Canada from a broad array of areas of the world: Africa, South East Asia, the Middle East, Latin America, and Europe. Almost all of the women had accompanied their husband to New Brunswick where, in most instances, the husbands had secured a job. In a few cases the women came to marry a Canadian citizen or they came to work, generally as nannies. In fact, the majority of women could be characterized as "reluctant immigrants". They were immigrants or refugees who came solely because their husbands wanted to move to Canada.

The majority of the women worked within their homes and had spouses with professional jobs. While the range of their family income was broad, from under $20,000 to over $100,00, the average was $54,000 with a mode of $20,000. Four of the women indicated that they had less than a tenth grade education; however, almost half (N=19) reported that they had some level of university education. Most of the women could not speak French upon arrival in Canada, but reported that their command of the English language was fairly adequate at their point of entry into the country. As noted earlier, approximately one-third of the participants indicated that they had been abused by a partner or husband while residing in Canada; the abuse included one or more of the following injurious behaviors: physical abuse; sexual abuse, psychological abuse; emotional abuse; financial abuse; and spiritual abuse. None of the women stated that they had contacted the police.

Research results: Holding a mirror to the dynamics that surround woman abuse

As DeKeseredy and MacLeod (1997) have noted, a significant number of governmental policies that have been established to address woman abuse have had the unanticipated consequence of limiting women's choices and increasing their fear. Reflecting this pattern, virtually all of the immigrant women who participated in the focus groups expressed a variety of concerns and fears about the "policing solution" to woman abuse. They indicated that in many instances police intervention could actually create or add to the dynamics that are part of abusive relationships – e.g. social isolation, unequal power dynamics, and male control. Thus, police intervention was generally viewed by the participants as an action that could foster harm and suffering which, as they emphasized, was often compounded by their socio-economic vulnerability as immigrant women and by their status as residents of a predominantly rural province where the immigrant population is small.

The discussion of the data, which is presented below, is divided into four sections which correspond to dynamics that surround woman abuse: social isolation, unequal power dynamics, control and surveillance, and uncertainly and insecurity. Each section begins with a succinct discussion of a given dynamic and then turns to an overview of the interface between the dynamic and data from the focus groups. It is important to note that while each dynamic is presented separately, they are not mutually exclusive.

Social isolation

Social isolation is one of the dynamics that often surrounds the lives of women who experience woman abuse. In some instances a woman may be forced by a controlling partner or husband to separate herself from potential sources of support and friendship, while in other situations such factors as embarrassment and fear may compel a victim of woman abuse to withdraw from her family, friends, and community (Kirkwood, 1993). Thus, for a variety of complex reasons, "violence encourages isolation" (Thorn-Finch, 1992: 3).

The experience of social isolation was, in fact, part of the lives of a significant number of the participants in the focus groups. Over half of the women stated that they were reluctant to contact the police as doing so meant that they might face even greater levels of loneliness. Most of the women who expressed this concern (N=17) stated that invoking police intervention could bring dishonor and shame to an immigrant woman's husband, family and ethnic community, and thus could sever their relationships with those who could assist and support them. Reflecting this concern one woman stated, "My husband is a very proud man. If I called the police I would hurt his pride and my family's honor."

Almost all of the participants indicated they felt that woman abuse was a personal matter that should be handled privately within the family through mediation. As one woman stated, "You can't go around to the police or courts with a family matter or even a quarrel between friends." As such, sustaining loyalties to one's husband, family, and community was often cited as a taking precedent over calling the police, and it was identified as a means to avoid isolation.

As seven women noted, the prospect of contacting the police was particularly frightening given that they already felt a great deal of social, cultural, and linguistic isolation as residents of New Brunswick, a province where the immigrant population is relatively small. In 1991, only three percent of the residents of New Brunswick were immigrants while in Ontario, in that same year, twenty-four percent of the population was born outside of Canada (Statistics Canada, 1996). To complicate matters even further for immigrant women in New Brunswick, there are virtually no culturally specific programs or services for those who experience woman abuse. The few programs that do exist in Canada for abused immigrant women are generally located in large urban cities such as Victoria, Montreal and Toronto. Thus, given the scarcity of programs and the small immigrant population in New Brunswick, police assistance was seen by a number of the participants as an action that would only compound their social isolation and leave them feeling even more alone and forgotten.

Unequal power dynamics

Woman abuse is an expression and mechanism of the structural oppression of women (Kirkwood, 1993; Barnett and LaViolette, 1993). At the core of this problem is male domination over women that occurs across the institutional structures of society and within women's daily lives (Thorne-Finch, 1992). For a number of the participants, the prospect of calling the police appeared to hold, at some level, the potential to create or recreate the unequal power dynamics that surround woman abuse. One-third of the women said that they would not seek police assistance in cases of woman abuse as such action meant that they would have to interact with someone who they feared and did not trust, but who held power over them. Their fear of the police appeared to be based, in part, on their perceptions of and experiences with police practices in their country of origin. As Currie (1995: 36) has explained:

> In some cases, the experiences of ethnocultural minority community members with the police may result in a view of the police as repressive and discriminatory. Police may have been experienced in the past as corrupt, undisciplined and discriminatory. In the cases of refugees or immigrants from authoritarian states, the police may have been direct agents of oppression – taking part in torture, disappearance and murder.

In this regard, ten of the women stated that in their country of origin the police often oppress and assault citizens. These women were reluctant to use the police in Canada out of fear that an officer would use his or her authority to engage in physical force with either the victim or offender in woman abuse cases. The following statements made by various women reflect this fear: "If

310   SANDRA WACHHOLZ AND BAUKJE MIEDEMA

you call the police they may beat up your husband"; "If you call the police you may be in even more trouble as the police officer may be a batterer himself."

Reflecting yet another concern about the power differential between themselves and the police, approximately one-third of the participants said that they would not invoke police intervention as they feared the police would ridicule and discredit their claim of abuse – a fear shared by non-immigrant women as well (Home, 1994). This feeling of distrust appeared to by tied, in part, to their status as women. Lamenting about the fact that most police officers are male, one woman stated, "If I called the police they would laugh at me and ask, 'Why did you marry him?' " This was a particularly pronounced concern for several of the women who were married to non-immigrant men. They feared that the police would be more inclined to believe their husbands because they were born in Canada.

Finally, one-fifth of the women said that their fear of encountering racist treatment by Canadian police was another factor that would inhibit them from reporting woman abuse. In such instances, the police were seen as in a position to use their power over immigrant women to carry out racist practices. One woman felt, for example, that the Canadian police operate on ". . . some very stereotypical ideas [about immigrant women]." This woman went on to state that most police assume that immigrant women are abuse victims who are capable of enduring victimization, a practice which may offer immigrant women less protection.

For a variety of reasons, then, many of the participants in the study felt that invoking police assistance would place them in a position where they would have to deal with someone who wielded power over them, but whom they did not trust. Thus, as one woman stated, ". . . that would be the last thing you would do, go to the police."

Control and surveillance

As Kirkwood (1993: 63) notes, "Control by one over another exists when one person has greater influence over the other's behavior or perspectives than does that person herself." In situations where abuse is occurring between a couple, male control over the female victim is a central aspect of the relationship. The needs, wants, and behavior of the female partner are often profoundly influenced by the demands of an abusive male (DeKeseredy and MacLeod, 1997; Kirkwood, 1993).

A number of the participants spoke openly about the controlling behavior of their partners. In this regard one woman stated, "You have to follow him no matter what." As another woman said, "I just followed my husband . . . like a dog" Thus, for many of these women, seeking police intervention was an action that could expand rather than reduce the level of social control that was already part of their lives. Calling the police meant that they might encounter individuals who would attempt to assert control over their needs, wants, and destiny.

In particular, one-fourth of the participants stated that they feared calling the police as such action might ultimately bring them into contact with immigration authorities who could deport them and their families. As one woman stated simply, "[if I called the police] ... I would be deported." It is important to note that a woman who is a landed immigrant is protected from deportation if her sponsorship breaks down pursuant to woman abuse; however, many of the women in the study did not know this. To complicate matters, several women indicated that some abusive spouses threatened to withdraw sponsorship if they reported the abuse. Such threats, as Jang et al. (1990: 2) have argued, are a means to keep women silent and are a "way to maintain power and control over them."

Child protection officials were cited by five of the women as another state authority that they feared and thought might intervene in their lives if they contacted the police. These women feared that their children might be removed from their home under the assumption that they could not provide a safe environment for them, a finding that has appeared in other studies of immigrant women (Martin and Mosher, 1995). Reflecting this fear, one woman lamented, "The [abused] woman is already so vulnerable ... and then they take her children away, they say that you are a misfit parent for the children." For this woman and others, police assistance in woman abuse cases was seen as holding the potential to invoke various forms of state surveillance and control over themselves and their families.

Fear of losing control over the decision about how to deal with the behavior of an abusive male surfaced as another reason why several of the women would not contact the police in situations of abuse. Six of the participants indicated that they would not call for law enforcement assistance given the expanded police power to arrest in domestic abuse cases which has been in place in New Brunswick since 1987. The women who expressed resistance to New Brunswick's mandatory arrest policy generally felt that it was far too inflexible, reduced their control over a situation, and could do little to end the violence. Lamenting about the loss of control over a situation that could occur for a woman pursuant to the mandatory arrest policy in New Brunswick, one woman stated, "Everyone has the right to tell you when you are abused and send you to whatever service exists ... everyone has the right to tell you, you know, your husband is abusing [and then make an arrest]." As this woman's words indicate, useful police intervention was not equated with mandatory arrest.

312   SANDRA WACHHOLZ AND BAUKJE MIEDEMA

Insecurity and uncertainty

Women who are the victims of abuse often experience a number of challenges
to their physical, emotional, social, and financial well-being as a result of their
partners' violent and controlling behavior. As such, battered women's lives
are often surrounded by a host of insecurities. For many of the participants,
calling the police was perceived as an action that could only compound the
insecurities and uncertainties that are part of the lives of abused immigrant
women. In this regard, over half (N=25) of the women indicated that they
would not seek police intervention in situations of woman abuse as such
assistance would only create or exacerbate their socio-economic vulnerability
and insecurity.

In particular, thirteen of the participants feared they would incur long-term
financial insecurity if they called the police given their economic dependency
on their partners. Invoking law enforcement assistance meant that their partners could be arrested and might subsequently lose their jobs. If this would
happen, as one woman said, you would have to become a welfare recipient
"... and eventually you [would] decide you are better off with him."

Clearly, fear of encountering financial problems at the outset of leaving
an abusive partner is a concern shared by non-immigrant women as well.
However, the risk of incurring economic insecurity is generally greater for
immigrant women given the multiple levels of oppression that many experience. Across Canada, immigrant women are over represented in low skill,
low paying jobs (Status of Women Canada, 1997). They often face, as Martin
and Mosher (1995: 25) have underscored, "... a discriminatory workplace
which siphons them into job ghettoes characterized by low pay and lack
of job security." These factors, in combination with the Canadian government's unwillingness to accredit various foreign diplomas, credentials and
degrees, foster economic marginalization for immigrant women (Miedema
and Nason-Clark, 1989).

With respect to the employment status of the participants, the majority
(N=22) worked within the home in unpaid labor. Of those who were employed, seventy percent worked in part-time, low wage service industry jobs.
Many of the women stated that they would have difficulty supporting themselves financially if they separated from their partners. The concerns that
they raised about their ability to achieve financial independence were tied,
in large part, to their circumstances as immigrant women. It is important to
note, however, that many of the women's situations were compounded by the
fact that they were residing in small, rural communities with relatively high
unemployment rates.

In summary, then, there are many reasons why immigrant women are
reluctant to invoke police assistance in cases of woman abuse. While the

"policing solution" to woman abuse has won the support of police departments and various other groups across Canada, virtually all of the participants felt that it could do little to address the needs of abused immigrant women. In light of this fact, as one woman stated, you simply ". . . don't go outside to the police or to the law."

De-centering the policing solution to woman abuse

As the data revealed, most of the participants viewed police intervention as a form of assistance that could only add to the harm and suffering that immigrant women experience pursuant to woman abuse. The "policing solution" rests, however, at the center of the state's response to the deeply structural problem of woman abuse (Currie, 1990; Currie and MacLean, 1992; Rottenberg, 1994). The focus of this solution is on detecting and addressing individual fault. In the process, it functions to individualize and depoliticize woman abuse. As Currie and MacLean (1992: 25) state, "Wife beating has been transformed from a critique of patriarchal power to demands for protection from male power. While the latter is a documented real need, the problem is that its satisfaction has been equated with justice for women."

In light of these concerns, a growing number of critics have argued that the "policing solution" needs to be de-centered from its position as the eminent solution to woman abuse. The notion of "de-centering" refers to a process, as Carol Smart (1989: 5) explains, where an emphasis is placed on thinking about nonlegal strategies to address social problems and on discouraging ". . . a resort to law as if it holds the key to unlock women's oppression." De-centering the "policing solution" is thought to hold the promise of creating an environment where greater emphasis would be placed on thinking about ways to address the forms of structural oppression that work to condone and sustain woman abuse, which would thus signal a movement back toward the transformative demands of the battered women's movement.

The process of de-centering the "policing solution" was, in fact, strongly endorsed by the immigrant women who participated in the focus groups. As one woman said, "This help from the government or whatever, it is not really solving your problems, it's just splitting [up families]." Thus, rather than suggesting there should be more "law and order" state controlled responses to woman abuse, the women called for the introduction of various forms of structural reform and community based initiatives to address the abuse that immigrant women experience.

With respect to structural reform, several of the women called for the development or enhancement of social policies that would function to reduce immigrant women's socio-economic inequality. Their suggestions included,

314   SANDRA WACHHOLZ AND BAUKJE MIEDEMA

for example, access to job training programs that would meet the specific eth-
nocultural needs of immigrant women; governmental accreditation of foreign
credentials; free, accessible, and long-term language training programs; and
universal social welfare programs that would provide affordable housing and
adequate living allowances. Reflecting on these needs one woman stated:

> In a lot of cases, the [immigrant] woman has to stay in an abusive rela-
> tionship because they don't have employment and welfare doesn't give
> her enough earnings to support the family and to pay the rent and to
> live on her own ... An immigrant woman needs a lot ... there's a lot of
> things that have to be done and need to be done.

This woman, like others, went on to suggest that if progress was going to
be made in addressing immigrant woman abuse, it was critical to change the
social, economic, and political conditions that nourish such violence.

In terms of community-based initiatives, the participants proposed various prevention and intervention strategies that were designed to address the
particular needs of immigrant women. Notably, none of the strategies that
they proposed emphasized increased apprehension and punishment of male
abusers. Instead, they generally focused on community partnership initiatives to deal with abuse. For example, several of the women stated that every
immigrant and refugee organization that deals with immigrant men and women should have on-going education and information sessions about woman
abuse. In particular, several of the women called for increased collaboration
between immigrant and refugee agencies and woman abuse projects and shelters. In discussing this collaborative effort, some of the women noted that it
would be very useful if women from battered women shelters would provide
presentations in settlement and language programs. The use of videos, as
an important visual aid for those struggling with French and English, was
identified as a valuable way to discuss woman abuse.

With respect to intervention strategies, conflict resolution mechanisms
such as family or community mediation were cited as the preferred means
to deal with woman abuse, and many of the women spoke of the historical
and cultural use of such techniques in their country of origin. Reflecting an
interest in mediation one woman stated, "I feel the government should first of
all try to make sure that they don't approach [the couple] to break up ...
instead maybe they should try and give counseling to both ... give them
six months or four months." Many of the participants shared this view and
thus called for the creation of more culturally specific counseling and support
services for both abusive immigrant men and the victims of abuse – women
and children.

As this succinct review of some of the strategies proposed by the participants suggests, police intervention does not rest as solution to woman abuse for this population. Rather than mobilizing the police, social policies to address immigrant women's socio-economic oppression, mediation, and community education partnerships were identified by virtually all of the participants as the most desirable way to deal with immigrant woman abuse.

Conclusion

As Loader (1997: 11) has argued, "The overarching consequence of an affective attachment to the 'policing solution' is to engender quite a limited set of ways of thinking, speaking, and acting vis-a-vis crime and social order." Clearly, attachment to this solution does run strong and deep across a significant percentage of the population in Canada, and a great deal of public dialogue, energy and funding has been directed toward using it as a means to address woman abuse. In the process, the transformative demands of the battered women's movement have been overshadowed by this state "law and order" crime control response (Currie and MacLean, 1992; Martin and Mosher, 1995).

As the participants in this study indicated, however, it is a solution that they believe can do little to address the needs of abused immigrant women. Given the socio-economic oppression that many immigrant women endure, the participants felt that police intervention could only enhance the pain and suffering of abused immigrant women. It was deemed to be a response that could actually replicate, at some level, the conditions and experiences that surround abuse: isolation, inequality, control, and unequal power dynamics. Many of these conditions, as the participants suggested, are even more complex and problematic for immigrant women who reside in a predominantly rural province such as New Brunswick where there are few culturally specific services and the immigrant communities are small.

Clearly, the voices of the participants shed light on how a well-intentioned state response such as the "policing solution" can function to perpetuate rather than reduce harm. What is needed, as these women and others have argued, are social policies and program initiatives that would "... explore new ways of living, relating, helping and supporting [immigrant women]" (DeKeseredy and MacLeod, 1997: 168).

316   SANDRA WACHHOLZ AND BAUKJE MIEDEMA

Notes

1. For purposes of this study, woman abuse is defined as consisting of the following injurious behaviors perpetrated against a woman by man who is either her husband or common law partner: physical abuse, sexual abuse, psychological abuse, emotional abuse, financial abuse, and spiritual abuse.
2. No-drop prosecutorial policies prohibit the victims of woman from being able to take action that would lead to the withdrawal of criminal charges once they have been filed against an abusive male.

Appendix A

Vignette One:
   A thirty-five year old woman, married for 10 years and with two children, is experiencing physical abuse at the hands of her husband.
This woman was born in your country of origin and is currently residing there.
   1. How would she deal with the abuse?

Vignette Two:
   A thirty-five-year-old immigrant woman who has been residing in Canada for five years is currently experiencing abuse at the hands of her husband. She has been married for ten years and has two children. She lives in a small village in New Brunswick.
   1. Assuming that this woman is from your country of origin, how would she deal with the abuse?
   2. Are there any reasons why she would not contact the criminal justice system for assistance?

References

Barnett, Ola W. and Alyce D. LaViolette, *It Could Happen to Anyone: Why Battered Women Stay,* (London: Sage Publications, 1993).

Bayley, D., *Police for the Future,* (Oxford: Oxford University Press, 1994).

Chalmers, Lee and Pamela Smith, "Wife Battering: Psychological, Social, and Physical Isolation and Counteracting Strategies," in Tigar McLaren (ed.), *Gender and Society: Creating a Canadian Women's Sociology,* (Toronto: Copp Clark Pittman Ltd., 1988).

Currie, Dawn H. and Brian D. MacLean, "Women, Men and Police: Losing the Fight against Wife Battery in Canada," in Dawn H. Currie and Brian D. MacLean (eds.), *Rethinking the Administration of Justice,* (Halifax, Nova Scotia: Fernwood Press, 1992).

Currie, Dawn H., "Battered Women and the State: From the Failure of Theory to a Theory of Failure," *The Journal of Human Justice* 1995, 1: 77–96.

Davis, Robert and Barbara Smith, "Domestic Violence Reforms: Empty Promises or Fulfilled Expectations," *Crime and Delinquency* 1995, 41: 541–552.

DeKeseredy, Walter S. and Linda MacLeod, *Woman Abuse: A Sociological Story,* (Toronto: Harcourt Brace, 1997).

PERCEPTIONS OF THE "POLICING SOLUTION" TO WOMAN ABUSE 317

Elias, N., *Involvement and Detachment,* (Oxford: Oxford University Press, 1987).

Festervand, T., "An Introduction and Application of Focus Group Research on the Health Care Industry," *Health Marketing Quarterly* 1985, 2: 199–209.

Godin, Joanne, *More than a Crime: A Report on the Lack of Public Legal Information Materials for Immigrant Women Who are Subject to Wife Assault,* (Ottawa: Department of Justice Canada, 1994).

Home, Alice, "Attributing Responsibility and Assessing Gravity in Wife Abuse Situations: A Comparative Study of Police and Social Workers," *Journal of Social Service Research* 1994, 19: 67–84.

Jang, D., D. Lee and R. Merolle-Frosch, "Domestic Violence in the Immigrant Community and Refugee Community: Responding to the Needs of Immigrant Women," *Response to the Victimization of Women and Children* 1990, 13: 2–7.

Kirkwood, Catherine, *Leaving Abusive Partners,* (London: Sage Publications, 1993).

Loader, Ian, "Policing and the Social: Questions of Symbolic Power," *British Journal of Criminology* 1997, 48: 1–18.

MacLeod, Linda and Maria Shin, *Isolated, Afraid and Forgotten: The Service Delivery Needs and Realities of Immigrant and Refugee Women Who are Battered,* (Ottawa: Health and Welfare Canada, 1990).

MacLeod, Linda, Maria Shin, Queenie Hun, Jagrup Samra-Jawanda, Shalen Rai and Eva Wasilewska, *Like a Wingless Bird: A Tribute to the Survival and Courage of Women Who are Abused and Speak neither English nor French,* (Ottawa: Department of Canadian Heritage, 1993).

Martin, Dianne L. and Janet E. Mosher, "UnKept Promises: Experiences of Immigrant Women With the Neo-Criminalization of Wife Abuse," *Canadian Journal of Women and the Law* 1995, 8: 3–44.

Miedema, Baukje and Nancy Nason-Clark, "Second Class Status: An Analysis of the Lived Experiences of Immigrant Women in Fredericton," *Canadian Ethnic Studies* 1989, 21: 63–73.

Morley, Rebecca and Audrey Mullender, "Hype or Hope? The Importation of Pro-Arrest Policies and Batterers' Programmes from North America to Britain as Key Measures for Preventing Violence Against Women in the Home," *International Journal of Law and the Family* 1992, 6: 265–288.

Smart, Carol, *Feminism and the Power of Law,* (London: Routledge, 1989).

Sherman, Sherman, "The Influence of Criminology and Criminal Law: Evaluating Arrests for Misdemeanor Domestic Violence," *Journal of Criminal Law and Criminology* 1992a, 83: 1–45.

Sherman, Sherman and Douglas Smith, "Crime, Punishment, and Stake in Conformity: Legal and Informal Control of Domestic Violence," *American Sociological Review* 1992b, 57: 680–690.

Statistics Canada, *Profiles: Total Immigrant Population,* (Ottawa: Minister of Supply and Services Canada, 1995).

Status of Women Canada, *Gender and Immigration: Some Key Issues,* (Ottawa: Policy Directorate, 1997).

Thorne-Finch, Ron, *Ending the Silence: The Origins and Treatment of Male Violence Against Women,* (Toronto: University of Toronto Press, 1992).

Name Index